Programming Languages

Programming Languages
Principles and Paradigms

Allen B. Tucker
Bowdoin College

Robert E. Noonan
College of William and Mary

 **Higher Education**

Boston   Burr Ridge, IL   Dubuque, IA   Madison, WI   New York   San Francisco   St. Louis
Bangkok   Bogotá   Caracas   Kuala Lumpur   Lisbon   London   Madrid   Mexico City
Milan   Montreal   New Delhi   Santiago   Seoul   Singapore   Sydney   Taipei   Toronto

The McGraw·Hill Companies

Higher Education

PROGRAMMING LANGUAGES: PRINCIPLES AND PARADIGMS, SECOND EDITION

1 2 3 4 5 6 7 8 9 0 DOC/DOC 0 9 8 7 6

ISBN-13 978–0–07–286609–4
ISBN-10 0–07–286609–8

Publisher: *Alan R. Apt*
Developmental Editor: *Rebecca Olson*
Executive Marketing Manager: *Michael Weitz*
Project Coordinator: *Tracy L. Konrardy*
Senior Production Supervisor: *Kara Kudronowicz*
Associate Media Producer: *Christina Nelson*
Senior Coordinator of Freelance Design: *Michelle D. Whitaker*
Cover Designer: *Rokusek Design*
(USE) Cover Image: *Rokusek Design*
Compositor: *Lachina Publishing Services*
Typeface: *10/12 Times Roman*
Printer: *R. R. Donnelley Crawfordsville, IN*

6822137

Library of Congress Cataloging-in-Publication Data

Tucker, Allen B.
  Programming languages : principles and paradigms / Allen Tucker, Robert Noonan. — 2nd ed.
    p.   cm.
  Includes index.
  ISBN 978–0–07–286609–4 — ISBN 0–07–286609–8 (hard copy : alk. paper)
  1. Programming languages (Electronic computers). I. Noonan, Robert. II. Title.

QA76.7.T83   2007
005.13—dc22   2006014822
                                                                   CIP

www.mhhe.com

To Maida.

Allen Tucker

To Debbie and Paul.

Robert Noonan

The study of programming languages has evolved rapidly since we began developing the first edition of this book in 1999. For instance, Java has become the dominant language in computer science curricula, beginning with CS1. Agile programming has emerged as a coherent approach to software design, and its language preferences are different from those of traditional programming. The use of formal methods in software design has begun to creep into the mainstream, and its importance is now significant.

In response to these and other recent events, this edition hopes to capture the excitement and new challenges that accompany the design of today's and tomorrow's programming languages. For instance, this edition has a broader and deeper coverage of all four programming paradigms and the languages that accompany them.

	Language Coverage	
Paradigm	First Edition	This Edition
Imperative (Chapter 12)		C Ada Perl
Object-Oriented (Chapter 13)	Java	Java Smalltalk Python
Functional (Chapter 14)	Scheme Haskell	Scheme Haskell
Logic (Chapter 15)	Prolog	Prolog

The second major change in this edition is that the discussion of language design principles in the early chapters (2–11) has been greatly expanded. We have added new examples from contemporary languages (like Python and Perl), using an informal style of presentation. Moreover, we have eliminated most coverage of older languages that are no longer in widespread use (such as Pascal and Modula).

The core principles of programming languages—syntax, names, types, semantics, and functions—are the subjects of Chapters 2, 4, 5, 7, and 9, respectively. These chapters provide a hands-on study of those principles using a broader and deeper selection of languages and examples than the first edition.

Readers who prefer an implementation-based treatment of syntax, type systems, semantics, functions, and memory management will find this material in the companion Chapters 3, 6, 8, 10, and 11. These chapters can be used selectively to enrich the core principles with which they are related. For example, the study of syntax in Chapter 2 can be enriched by studying the lexical and syntactic phases of a compiler in Chapter 3. *We emphasize that any or all of these companion chapters may be skipped, especially in a first course on programming languages.*

π

Three companion chapters include optional sections with more formal mathematical treatments. These optional sections are marked with the same marginal graphic as this paragraph to indicate that they are optional. Appendix B provides a review of the key discrete mathematics topics and notations underlying these sections for students who need a quick refresher.

Finally, the special topics chapters (16, 17, and 18) provide detailed introductions to the study of event-handling, concurrency, and program correctness. The first edition had covered two of these (event-handling and concurrency), but the chapter on correctness is new to this edition.

Overall, this new edition contains a broad and deep coverage of the principles, paradigms, and special topics in programming languages. The book now has 18 chapters. Since individual instructors have different views on what should be emphasized in a programming languages course, this book provides a variety of options.

EMPHASIS

This text emphasizes a thorough, hands-on treatment of the key issues in programming language design. It provides instructors and students with a mixture of explanatory-based and implementation-based experiences. The implementation-based experiences includes hands-on experimentation with the design and implementation of a modest subset of C, called *Clite,* which is fully defined in Appendix A for easy reference.

As noted above, this edition has an expanded treatment of the major programming paradigms. We believe that to master a paradigm, students must actively use that paradigm to solve a programming problem. If, for example, your students have no experience with functional programming, we recommend that they learn enough Scheme or Haskell to complete a reasonable programming project. To paraphrase one reviewer's comments:

To understand a paradigm you must become the paradigm.

If, on the other hand, your introductory, discrete mathematics, or AI course already includes functional programming, you might choose to skip this chapter and emphasize another paradigm or special topic instead.

COURSE ORGANIZATION

Figure 1 shows how the text divides into three major sections:

- Principles
- Paradigms
- Special Topics

In the first section, Chapters 2, 4, 5, 7, and 9 cover five core *principles*—Syntax, Names, Types, Semantics, and Functions. Parts of the remaining chapters (3, 6, 8, 10, and 11) in this section can be added to provide a deeper level of topic coverage. On

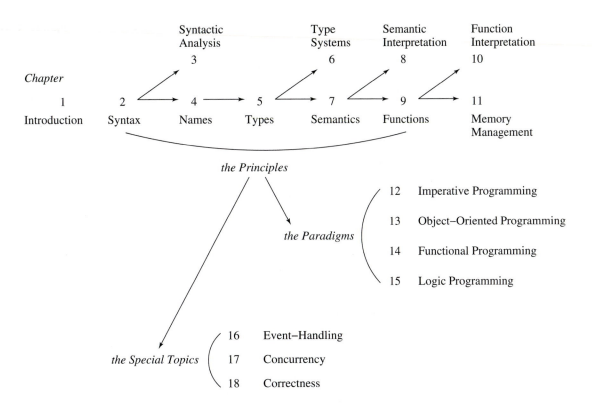

| Figure 1   Content dependencies among the chapters.

the other hand, advanced or graduate courses may include several of these topics, while de-emphasizing material in the later chapters.

The second section of the text covers the four major programming *paradigms:*

- Imperative programming
- Object-oriented programming
- Functional programming
- Logic programming

These chapters are relatively independent of each other and can be studied in any order. However, a one-semester course will normally include one or two of these chapters, in addition to the principles. The choice of paradigms, of course, may vary with the preferences of the instructor and the content of other courses in the curriculum. For instance, if the curriculum regularly offers a course in object-oriented design, Chapter 13 can be skipped.

Chapter 12 is completely new to this edition; it demonstrates the key features of imperative programming in each of three different languages: C, Ada, and Perl. C was chosen because it illustrates the problems caused by weak typing. In contrast, Ada is strongly typed, thus providing an interesting comparison with C. Finally, Perl was chosen because it illustrates a dynamically typed scripting language. For instructors who include Chapter 12, we recommend that at least one language unfamiliar to students be covered in enough depth to assign an interesting programming project.

Chapter 13 has undergone a major rewrite from the first edition. Now, the features of an object-oriented language are explored using Java, Smalltalk, and Python. Smalltalk is included because of its simplicity, Java because of its dominance, and Python because of its agility in scripting applications. Students who have had an introductory sequence in Java, but no course in object-oriented design and programming, may benefit from learning one of the other two languages. The object-oriented paradigm will continue to be important in the future.

The functional and logic programming paradigms (Chapters 14 and 15) continue to be distinctive in their applications and respective programming styles. Our treatment of functional programming includes parallel Scheme and Haskell discussions, so that students can master the ideas of functional programming by studying either language and omitting the other.

The third section of the text covers three *special topics:*

- Event-handling
- Concurrency
- Correctness

An undergraduate programming languages course will normally not have time to cover more than one of these topics. The fact that some of these topics appear elsewhere in the curriculum can help instructors decide which one(s) to include in the programming languages course.

Chapters 16 and 17, *Event-Handling* and *Concurrency,* represent unusual control issues that can be well-treated in a study of programming languages. Both are seeing increasing visibility in programming applications, especially in scientific computing and embedded systems. Key topics that students need to cover in these areas include communication, deadlocks, message passing, nondeterminism, event-handling, interprocess communication, and a sampling of the many and varied applications (e.g., operating systems, GUI interactions, and home alarm systems) in which these topics regularly appear.

Finally, we are excited about the new Chapter 18 on *Correctness,* which discusses recent developments in programming language support for formal methods. For example, the developers of Spark Ada report 100 times fewer bugs with 3-5 times higher productivity rates using a technique called *correctness by construction* [Barnes, 2003]. Because we believe that the support for more formal approaches to software design will be increasingly important to programming languages in the future (much like object-oriented programming is very important now), we hope that instructors will consider including this chapter in their programming languages courses.

Chapter 18 begins with a review of axiomatic semantics [Hoare, 1969] and its use in the verification of imperative programs. It expands this theory by covering the concept of *design by contract* [Meyer, 1988] in object-oriented languages, and its application using the Java Modeling Language (JML). This chapter also covers the concept of structural induction and its use to prove the correctness of functional programs.

It can be argued that some of the topics in the latter chapters belong in other courses, rather than in a study of programming languages and paradigms. For example, the study of concurrency, event-driven programming, and program correctness can each be viewed as a separate course. Moreover, much of the material in Chapters 3, 6, 8, 10, and 11 can be viewed as the basis for a separate compiler course. Because many undergraduate programs do not offer such separate courses in these topics, this text provides an opportunity to introduce them in the setting of a programming languages course.

PREREQUISITES AND OTHER GUIDANCE

Students entering this course should have completed at least an introductory course and a data structures course. In the data structures course, students should have become familiar with linked lists, stacks, flexible arrays, and hash tables.

Moreover, knowledge of Java is a prerequisite if the course includes any of the following implementation-oriented chapters: 3, 6, 8, 16, and 17. Without knowledge of Java, students should have experience with C, C++, or C# from their data structures course.

We recommend that students also have access to a good Java tutorial, reference manual, and programming environment. Such tutorials and references are readily available on the Web (see, for example, http://java.sun.com/docs/books/tutorial/). Some of our discussions depend strictly on features that have been introduced in Java 1.4 and 1.5. These features are clearly noted in the text.

We also hope that students will have some modest mathematical skills, as would be found in an elementary discrete mathematics or discrete structures course. While this is not a strict prerequisite, it is essential for students who engage the mathematically oriented sections in some of the chapters (3, 6, 8, 10, and 18). A review of the basic ideas of functions, sets, logic, and proof is provided in Appendix B.

This text is consistent with the recommendations of *Computing Curricula 2001* [CC2001, 2001]. It also covers all the topics in the Programming Languages course described in the *Liberal Arts Model Curriculum* [Walker and Schneider, 1996], and its newer 2005 draft version (*www.lacs.edu*).

With regard to *Computing Curricula 2001,* the material in this text covers all of the topics (PL1 through PL11) in the Programming Languages section of the core body of knowledge. It also covers other topics in that core body of knowledge, such as event-driven and concurrent programming (PF6), memory management (OS5), functional and logic programming (IS), and software engineering (SE). This text treats each topic in greater depth than that suggested by *Computing Curricula 2001.*

LANGUAGE RESOURCES AND WEBSITE

The software for this text can be used with any implementation of Java 1.5 or higher. We have implemented the Java software for this book using Sun's Java 1.5. Here is a list of Web-based sources that we recommend for tutorial and other information on the major languages covered in this book.

Language	Web Source
Ada	gnu.org
C, C++	gnu.org
Haskell	haskell.org
Java 1.5	java.sun.com
Perl	perl.com
Prolog	swi-prolog.org
Python	python.org
Scheme	drscheme.org
Smalltalk	squeak.org

A suite of software and other support to accompany this text is available at the website **www.mhhe.com/tucker.** It contains the following materials:

- A complete Java implementation of the syntax, type system, and semantics of Clite.
- A downloadable set of all the runnable programs discussed in this text.
- A set of PowerPoint slides to support course lectures.
- Answers to the exercises (available to instructors via a secure password).

Acknowledgments

Many persons have helped guide us in the development of this text. James Lu was a key collaborator in the early conceptualization of the first edition. Bill Bynum at the College of William and Mary and Laurie King at the College of the Holy Cross contributed to Chapters 4 and 8, respectively. David Coppit at William and Mary introduced us to the use of proof trees, which appear in Chapter 18. Students at Bowdoin and William and Mary contributed to the first edition and early versions of this edition. Notably, Doug Vail developed solutions to some of the more challenging problems. Wyatt Dumas helped rewrite the software for the second edition and made significant contributions to the content of two chapters. We thank all of our reviewers:

Phil Ventura	*University of Buffalo, SUNY*
Aaron Keen	*California Polytechnic State University, San Luis Obispo*
John Donald	*San Diego State University*
Tia Watts	*Sonoma State University*
Ron Olsson	*University of California, Davis*
Thomas D. Rethard	*University of Texas, Arlington*
Alex Thornton	*University of California, Irvine*
Gerald Baumgartner	*Ohio State University*
Ken Slonneger	*University of Iowa*
David R. Falconer	*California State University, Fullerton*
Tae W. Ryu	*California State University, Fullerton*

Qi Cheng	*University of Oklahoma*
Rainey Little	*Mississippi State University*
Jay-Evan J. Tevis	*Auburn University*
John Hannan	*Pennsylvania State University*
Neelam Soundarajan	*Ohio State University*
Robert van Engelen	*Florida State University*
Shannon Tauro	*University of California, Irvine*
Gloria Melara	*California State University, Northridge*
Amer Diwan	*University of Colorado, Boulder*
Susan Gauch	*University of Kansas*
Henri Casanova	*University of California, San Diego*
Cristina V. Lopes	*University of California, Irvine*
Salih Yurttas	*Texas A&M University*
Roman W. Swiniarksi	*San Diego State University*
Amar Raheja	*California State Polytechnic University, Pomona*
Franck Xia	*University of Missouri, Rolla*
Rajendra K. Raj	*Rochester Institute of Technology*
Randall D. Beer	*Case Western Reserve University*
Robert M. Cubert	*University of Florida*
Liang Cheng	*Lehigh University*
David Hemmendinger	*Union College*

for their careful reading and constructive comments throughout the development of the first and second editions of this text, which are greatly improved by their collective insight. The authors offer a special thanks to David Hemmendinger of Union College for his careful editing and extensive suggestions, most of which have been incorporated into this edition.

Finally, we would like to thank our editors, Rebecca Olson and Alan Apt, for their vision, guidance, and support. They have guided the development of the second edition with extraordinary skill.

Allen B. Tucker   **Robert E. Noonan**
Bowdoin College   *College of William and Mary*

Brief Contents

Contents

About the Principal Authors

Allen B. Tucker is the Anne T. and Robert M. Bass Research Professor of Natural Sciences in the Department of Computer Science at Bowdoin College. He earned a BA in mathematics from Wesleyan University and an MS and PhD in computer science from Northwestern University.

Professor Tucker has publications in the areas of programming languages, software design, natural language processing, and curriculum design. He has been a Fulbright Lecturer at the Ternopil Academy of National Economy in Ukraine, a visiting Erskine Lecturer at the University of Canterbury in New Zealand, and a visiting lecturer at Esigelec in France. He is a Fellow of the ACM.

Robert E. Noonan is a Professor of Computer Science at the College of William and Mary, where he has taught for 30 years. He earned an AB in mathematics from Providence College and an MS and PhD in computer science from Purdue University.

He has published in the areas of programming languages, compiler construction, and software engineering. He is a member of the ACM, SIGPLAN, SIGCSE, and the Liberal Arts Computer Science (LACS) Consortium.

Overview

"A good programming language is a conceptual universe
for thinking about programming."
Alan Perlis

CHAPTER OUTLINE

Like our natural languages, programming languages facilitate the expression and communication of ideas between people. However, programming languages differ from natural languages in two important ways. First, programming languages also enable the communication of ideas between people and computing machines. Second, programming languages have a narrower expressive domain than our natural languages. That is, they facilitate only the communication of *computational* ideas. Thus, a programming language must meet different requirements than a natural language. This text explores these requirements and the language design alternatives that they evoke.

In this study, we identify the many similarities between programming languages and natural languages. We also examine the fundamental differences that are imposed by the computational setting in which a program must function. We examine the features of programming languages both abstractly and actively. That is, we combine a conceptually rich treatment of programming language design together with a hands-on laboratory-based study of how these concepts impact language designers and programmers in a wide range of application domains.

This study is important because today's computer science students will be the designers and users of tomorrow's programming languages. To become an informed language designer and user, you will need to understand languages broadly—their features, strengths, and weaknesses across a wide range of programming styles and applications. Knowing one language and application domain does not provide such breadth of understanding. This book will help you to obtain that breadth.

1.1 PRINCIPLES

Language designers have a basic vocabulary about language structure, meaning, and pragmatic concerns that helps them understand how languages work. Their vocabulary falls into three major categories that we call the *principles* of language design.

- Syntax
- Names and types
- Semantics

Many of the concepts in these categories are borrowed from linguistics and mathematics, as we shall learn below. Together, these categories provide an organizational focus for the core Chapters 2, 4, 5, 7, and 9 respectively. Additional depth of study in each category is provided in the companion chapters (3, 6, 8, 10, and 11) as explained below.

Syntax The *syntax* of a language describes what constitutes a structurally correct program. Syntax answers many questions. What is the grammar for writing programs in the language? What is the basic set of words and symbols that programmers use to write structurally correct programs?

We shall see that most of the syntactic structure of modern programming languages is defined using a linguistic formalism called the *context-free grammar*. Other elements of syntax are outside the realm of context-free grammars, and are defined by other means. A careful treatment of programming language syntax appears in Chapter 2.

A study of language syntax raises many questions. How does a compiler analyze the syntax of a program? How are syntax errors detected? How does a context-free grammar facilitate the development of a syntactic analyzer? These deeper questions about syntax are addressed in Chapter 3.

Names and Types The vocabulary of a programming language includes a carefully designed set of rules for naming entities—variables, functions, classes, parameters, and so forth. Names of entities also have other properties during the life of a program, such as their scope, visibility, and binding. The study of names in programming languages and their impact on the syntax and semantics of a program is the subject of Chapter 4.

A language's *types* denote the kinds of values that programs can manipulate: simple types, structured types, and more complex types. Among the simple types are integers, decimal numbers, characters, and boolean values. Structured types include character strings, lists, trees, and hash tables. More complex types include functions and classes. Types are more fully discussed in Chapter 5.

A type system enables the programmer to understand and properly implement operations on values of various types. A carefully specified type system allows the compiler to perform rigorous type checking on a program before run time, thus heading off run-time errors that may occur because of inappropriately typed operands. The full specification and implementation of a type system is the focus of a deeper study in Chapter 6.

Semantics   The meaning of a program is defined by its *semantics*. That is, when a program is run, the effect of each statement on the values of the variables in the program is given by the semantics of the language. Thus, when we write a program, we must understand such basic ideas as the exact effect that an assignment has on the program's variables. If we have a semantic model that is independent of any particular platform, we can apply that model to a variety of machines on which that language may be implemented. We study semantics in Chapter 7.

The implementation of run-time semantics is also of interest in a deeper study of semantics. How does an interpreter work, and what is the connection between an interpreter and the specification of a language's semantics? These deeper questions are studied in Chapter 8.

Functions represent the key element of procedural abstraction in any language. An understanding of the semantics of function definition and call is central to any study of programming languages. The implementation of functions also requires an understanding of the static and dynamic elements of memory, including the *run-time stack*. The stack also helps us understand other ideas like the scope of a name and the lifetime of an object. These topics are treated in Chapter 9.

The stack implementation of function call and return is a central topic deserving deeper study. Moreover, strategies for the management of another memory area called the *heap*, are important to the understanding of dynamic objects like arrays. Heap management techniques called "garbage collection" are strongly related to the implementation of these dynamic objects. The stack and the heap are studied in detail in Chapters 10 and 11 respectively.

1.2   PARADIGMS

In general, we think of a "paradigm" as a pattern of thought that guides a collection of related activities. A programming paradigm is a pattern of problem solving thought that underlies a particular genre of programs and languages. Four distinct and fundamental programming paradigms have evolved over the last three decades:

- Imperative programming
- Object-oriented programming
- Functional programming
- Logic programming

Some programming languages are intentionally designed to support more than one paradigm. For instance, C++ is a hybrid imperative and object-oriented language, while

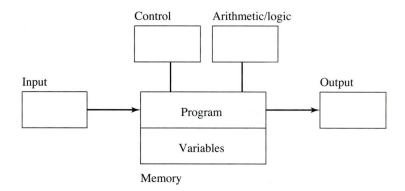

| **Figure 1.1**   **The von Neumann-Eckert Computer Model**

the experimental language Leda [Budd, 1995] is designed to support the imperative, object-oriented, functional, and logic programming paradigms. These languages are reminiscent of earlier efforts (notably, PL/I, Algol 68, and Ada) to design a single language that was more general-purpose than other programming languages of its day. With the exception of C++, these efforts have failed to attract sustained interest.

Imperative Programming   *Imperative programming* is the oldest paradigm, as it is grounded in the classic "von Neumann-Eckert" model of computation (see Figure 1.1). In this model, both the program and its variables are stored together, and the program contains a series of commands that perform calculations, assign values to variables, retrieve input, produce output, or redirect control elsewhere in the series.

Procedural abstraction is an essential building block for imperative programming, as are assignments, loops, sequences, conditional statements, and exception handling. The predominant imperative programming languages include Cobol, Fortran, C, Ada, and Perl. The imperative programming paradigm is the subject of Chapter 12.

Object-Oriented Programming   *Object-oriented (OO) programming* provides a model in which the program is a collection of objects that interact with each other by passing messages that transform their state. In this sense, message passing allows the data objects to become active rather than passive. This characteristic helps to further distinguish OO programming from imperative programming. Object classification, inheritance, and message passing are fundamental building blocks for OO programming. Major object-oriented languages are Smalltalk, C++, Java, and C#. OO programming is studied in Chapter 13.

Functional Programming   *Functional programming* models a computational problem as a collection of mathematical functions, each with an input (domain) and a result (range) spaces. This sets functional programming apart from languages with an assignment statement. For instance, the assignment statement

```
x = x + 1
```

makes no sense either in functional programming or in mathematics.

Functions interact and combine with each other using functional composition, conditionals, and recursion. Major functional programming languages are Lisp, Scheme, Haskell, and ML. Functional programming is discussed and illustrated in Chapter 14.

Logic Programming   *Logic (declarative) programming* allows a program to model a problem by declaring what outcome the program should accomplish, rather than how it should be accomplished. Sometimes these languages are called *rule-based* languages, since the program's declarations look more like a set of rules, or constraints on the problem, rather than a sequence of commands to be carried out.

Interpreting a logic program's declarations creates a set of all possible solutions to the problem that it specifies. Logic programming also provides a natural vehicle for expressing nondeterminism, which is appropriate for problems whose specifications are incomplete. The major logic programming language is Prolog, and the logic programming paradigm is covered in Chapter 15.

1.3   SPECIAL TOPICS

Beyond these four paradigms, several key topics in programming language design deserve extensive coverage in a text such as this one. These topics tend to be pervasive, in the sense that they appear in two or more of the above paradigms, rather than just one. Each of the following is briefly introduced below.

- Event-handling
- Concurrency
- Correctness

Event-Handling   *Event-handling* occurs with programs that respond to events that are generated in an unpredictable order. In one sense, an event-driven program is just a program whose behavior is fully determined by event-handling concerns. Event-handling is often coupled with the object-oriented paradigm (e.g., Java applets), although it occurs within the imperative paradigm as well (e.g., Tcl/Tk). Events originate from user actions on the screen (mouse clicks or keystrokes, for example), or else from other sources (like readings from sensors on a robot). Major languages that support event-handling include Visual Basic, Java and Tcl/Tk. This topic is treated in Chapter 16.

Concurrency   *Concurrent programming* can occur within the imperative, object-oriented, functional, or logic paradigm. Concurrency occurs when the program has a collection of asynchronous elements, which may share information or synchronize with each other from time to time. Concurrency can also occur within an individual process, such as the parallel execution of the different iterations of a loop. Concurrent programming languages include SR [Andrews and Olsson, 1993], Linda [Carriero and Gelenter, 1989], and High Performance Fortran [Adams and others, 1997]. Concurrent programming is treated in Chapter 17.

Correctness   *Program correctness* is a subject that, until recently, has had only academic interest. However, newer languages and language features are evolving that support the design of provably correct programs in a variety of application domains. A program is *correct* if it satisfies its formal specification for all its possible inputs.

Proof of correctness is a complex subject, but language tools for formal treatment of correctness by programmers are now becoming available. For instance, the Spark/Ada system [Barnes, 2003] and the Java Modeling Language [Leavens *et al.*, 1998] provide good examples. We introduce the topic of program corrrectness in Chapter 18.

1.4 A BRIEF HISTORY

The first programming languages were the machine and assembly languages of the earliest computers, beginning in the 1940s. Hundreds of programming languages and dialects have been developed since that time. Most have had a limited life span and utility, while a few have enjoyed widespread success in one or more application domains. Many have played an important role in influencing the design of future languages.

A snapshot of the historical development of several influential programming languages appears in Figure 1.2. While it is surely not complete, Figure 1.2 identifies some of the most influential events and trends. Each arrow in Figure 1.2 indicates a significant design influence from an older language to a successor.

The 1950s marked the beginning of the age of "higher-order languages" (HOLs for short). A HOL distinguishes itself from a machine or assembly language because its programming style is independent of any particular machine architecture. The first higher-order languages were Fortran, Cobol, Algol, and Lisp. Both Fortran and Cobol have survived and evolved greatly since their emergence in the late 1950s. These languages built a large following and carry with them an enormous body of legacy code that today's programmers maintain. On the other hand, Lisp has substantially declined in use and Algol has disappeared altogether.

However, the innovative designs of these early languages have had powerful influence on their successors. For example, Fortran's demonstration that algebraic notation could be translated to efficient code is now taken for granted, as are Cobol's introduction of the record structure, Pascal's design for one-pass compiling, and Algol's demonstration that a linguistic grammar could formally define its syntax.

Perhaps the greatest motivator for the development of programming languages over the last several decades is the rapidly evolving demand for computing power and new applications by large and diverse communities of users. The following user communities can claim a major stake in the programming language landscape:

- Artificial intelligence
- Education
- Science and engineering
- Information systems
- Systems and networks
- World Wide Web

The computational problem domains of these communities are all different, and so are the major programming languages that developed around them. Below we sketch the major computational goals and language designs that have served each of these communities.

Artificial Intelligence The artificial intelligence programming community has been active since the early 1960s. This community is concerned about developing

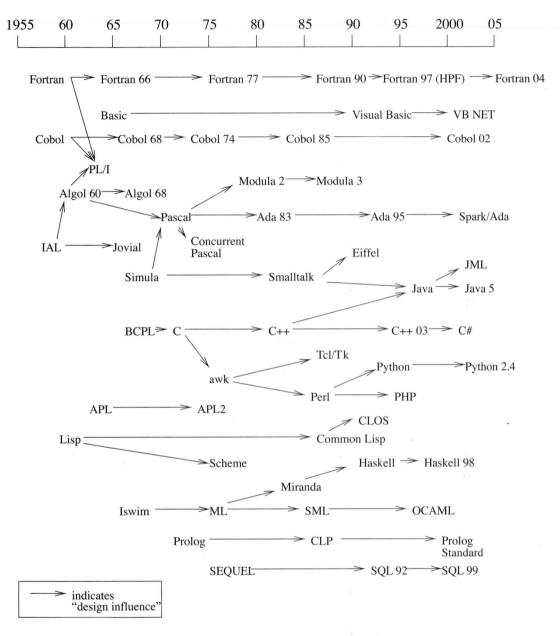

| Figure 1.2   **A Snapshot of Programming Language History**

programs that model human intelligent behavior, logical deduction, and cognition. Symbol manipulation, functional expressions, and the design of logical proof systems have been central goals in this ongoing effort.

The paradigms of *functional programming* and *logic programming* have evolved largely through the efforts of artificial intelligence programmers. Prominent functional programming languages over the years include Lisp, Scheme, ML, and Haskell. The prominent logic programming languages include Prolog and CLP.

The first AI language, Lisp (an acronym for "*List* Processor"), was designed by John McCarthy in 1960. Figure 1.2 suggests that Lisp was dominant in early years and has become less dominant in recent years. However, Lisp's core features have motivated the development of more recent languages such as Scheme, ML, and Haskell. The strong relationship between Lisp and the *lambda calculus* (a formalism for modeling the nature of mathematical functions) provides a firm mathematical basis for the later evolution of these successors. The lambda calculus and its relationship with functional languages are explained more fully in Chapter 14.

In the logic programming area, only one language, Prolog, has been the major player, and Prolog has had little influence on the design of languages in other application areas.

Education In the 1960s and 1970s, several key languages were designed with a primary goal of teaching students about programming. For example, Basic was designed in the 1960s by John Kemeny to facilitate the learning of programming through *time sharing*, an architecture in which a single computer is directly connected to several terminals at one time. Each terminal user shares time on the computer by receiving a small "time slice" of computational power on a regular basis. Basic has enjoyed great popularity over the years, especially as a teaching language in secondary schools and college-level science programs.

The language Pascal, a derivative of Algol, was designed in the 1970s for the purpose of teaching programming. Pascal served for several years as the main teaching language in college-level computer science curricula.

During the last decade, these languages have been largely replaced in educational programs by such "industrial strength" languages as C, C++, and Java. This change has both benefits and liabilities. On the one hand, learning an industrial strength language provides graduates with a programming tool that they can use immediately when they enter the computing profession. On the other hand, such a language is inherently more complex and cumbersome to learn as a first language in undergraduate coursework.

The recent emergence of Python may provide a vehicle through which introductory computer science courses can return to simplicity and concentrate again on teaching first principles. For example, Python has a more transparent syntax and semantics, which makes it more amenable to mastery by a novice than any of its industrial strength alternatives. Moreover, introductory courses using Python seem to introduce a richer variety of computer science topics courses using C, C++, or Java.

Science and Engineering The scientific and engineering programming community played a major role in the early history of computing, and it continues to play a major role today. The first programs were written in the 1940s to predict the trajectories of ballistics during World War II, using the well-worn physics formulae that characterize bodies in motion. These programs were first written in machine and assembly language by specially trained mathematicians.

A major driving force behind scientific and engineering applications throughout their history is the need to obtain as much processing power as possible. The processing power of today's supercomputers is measured in *teraflops* (trillions of floating point operations per second), and the current leader runs at a speed of 280 teraflops under the standard performance benchmark called LINPAK (see **www.top500.org** for more information). Many of today's scientific and engineering applications are models of complex natural systems in fields like bioinformatics and the earth and atmospheric sciences.

The first scientific programming language, Fortran I, was designed by John Backus at IBM in 1954 [Backus and *et al.*, 1954]. The acronym "Fortran" is an abbreviation for "*For*mula *Tran*slator." Fortran is probably the most widely used scientific programming language today.

Early versions of Fortran had many problems, however. The most difficult problem was that of consistency—the same Fortran program ran differently on different machines, or else would not run at all. These problems gave rise to several new efforts. One such effort produced the language Algol, short for "*Algo*rithmic *L*anguage," which was designed by an international committee in 1959. Algol's principal design goal was to provide a better-defined language than Fortran for both the computation and the publication of scientific and mathematical algorithms.

Algol was originally named the "*I*nternational *A*lgebraic *L*anguage" (IAL). The language Jovial was designed by Jules Schwartz in the 1960s to refine and augment the features of IAL. This acronym stands for "*J*ules' *O*wn *V*ersion of the *I*nternational *A*lgebraic *L*anguage." *Jovial* was widely used in US Department of Defense applications.

Another interesting language called APL (short for "*A P*rogramming *L*anguage") [Iverson, 1962] was designed by Kenneth Iverson in the 1960s to facilitate the rapid programming of matrix algebraic and other mathematical computations. APL had an extended character set that included single-symbol matrix operators that could replace the tedium of writing `for` loops in most cases. The proliferation of such special symbols required the design of a specialized keyboard to facilitate the typing of APL programs. APL programs were known for their brevity; a matrix computation that required an explicit `for` loop in a conventional language needed only a single symbol in APL. APL's brevity was also its curse in many people's eyes. That is, most APL programs were so terse that they defied understanding by anyone but the most skilled technicians. The cost of supporting a specialized character set and stylized keyboard also contributed to APL's demise.

To this day, scientific computing remains a central activity in the history of programming and programming languages. Its problem domain is primarily concerned with performing complex calculations very fast and very accurately. The calculations are defined by mathematical models that represent scientific phenomena. They are primarily implemented using the *imperative programming* paradigm. Modern programming languages that are widely used in the scientific programming arena include Fortran 90 [Chamberland, 1995], C [Kernighan and Ritchie, 1988], C++ [Stroustrup, 1997], and High Performance Fortran [Adams and others, 1997].

The more complex the scientific phenomena become, the greater the need for sophisticated, highly parallel computers and programming languages. Thus, *concurrent programming* is strongly motivated by the needs of such scientific applications as modeling weather systems and ocean flow. Some languages, like High Performance Fortran, support concurrent programming by adding features to a widely used base language (e.g., Fortran). Others, like SR and Occam, are designed specifically to support concurrent programming. General purpose languages, like Java, support concurrency as just one of their many design goals.

Information Systems Programs designed for use by institutions to manage their information systems are probably the most prolific in the world. Corporations realized in the 1950s that the use of computers could greatly reduce their record-keeping tedium and improve the accuracy and reliability of what they could accomplish. Information systems found in corporations include the payroll system, the accounting system, the online sales and marketing systems, the inventory and manufacturing systems, and so forth. Such systems are characterized by the need to process large amounts of data (often organized into so-called databases), but require relatively simple transformations on the data as it is being processed.

Traditionally, information systems have been developed in programming languages like Cobol and SQL. Cobol was first designed in the late 1950s by a group of industry representatives who wanted to develop a language that would be portable across a variety of different machine architectures. Cobol stands for "*Common Business Oriented Language*," uses English as the basis for its syntax, and supports an *imperative* programming style.

Cobol programs are constructed out of clauses, sentences, and paragraphs, and generally tend to be more wordy than comparable programs in other languages. The aim here was to define a language that would be easy for programmers to assimilate. Whether or not that aim was ever reached is still open for discussion. Nevertheless, Cobol quickly became, and still remains the most widely used programming language for information systems applications.

By contrast, SQL [Pratt, 1990] emerged in the 1980s as a *declarative* programming tool for database specification, report generation, and information retrieval. SQL stands for "*Structured Query Language*" and is the predominant language used for specifying and retrieving information from relational databases. The relational database model is widely used, in part because of its strong mathematical underpinnings in relational algebra.

More recently, businesses have developed a wide range of electronic commerce applications. These applications often use a "client-server" model for program design, where the program interacts with users at remote sites and provides simultaneous access to a shared database. A good example of this model is an online book ordering system, in which the database reflects the company's inventory of books and the interaction helps the user through the database search, book selection, and ordering process. *Event-driven programming* is essential in these applications, and programmers combine languages like Java, Perl, Python and SQL to implement them.

Systems and Networks Systems programmers design and maintain the basic software that runs systems—operating system components, network software, programming language compilers and debuggers, virtual machines and interpreters, and real time and embedded systems (in cell phones, ATMs, aircraft, etc.). These types of software are closely tied with the architectures of specific machines, like the Intel/AMD x86 and the Apple/Motorola/IBM PowerPC.

Most of these programs are written in C, which allows programmers to get very close to the machine language level. Systems programming is typically done using the *imperative* design paradigm. However, systems programmers must also deal with *concurrent* and *event-driven* programming, and they also have special concerns for program *correctness* as well.

Thus, the primary example of a systems programming language is C, designed in the early 1970s in part to support the coding of the Unix operating system. In fact, about 95 percent of the code of the Unix system is written in C. C++ was designed by Bjarne Stroustrup in the 1980s as an extension of C to provide new features that would support object-oriented programming.

The programming language Ada is named after Ada Lovelace, who is believed to have been the first computer programmer. In the early 1800s, she worked with the computer inventor Charles Babbage. The development of Ada was funded by the US Department of Defense, whose original goal was to have a single language that would support all DoD applications, especially command and control and embedded systems applications. While Ada never achieved this particular goal, its design has some notable features. Today, Ada provides a robust host upon which the Spark compiler provides tools to support program correctness.

Scripting languages are widely used today for a variety of systems tasks. For example, an awk program can be designed quickly to check a password file in a Unix machine for consistency. Some of the primary scripting languages are awk [Kernighan and Pike, 1984], Perl [Wall *et al.*, 1996b], Tcl/Tk [Ousterhout, 1994], and Python [Lutz, 2001]. We treat scripting languages in Chapter 12, where Perl programming is explored in some detail.

World Wide Web   The most dynamic area for new programming applications is the Internet, which is the enabling vehicle for electronic commerce and a wide range of applications in academia, government, and industry. The notion of Web-centric computing, and hence Web-centric programming, is motivated by an interactive model, in which a program remains continuously active waiting for the next event to occur, responding to that event, and returning to its continuously active state.

Programming languages that support Web-centric computing use *event-driven* programming, which encourages system-user interaction. Web-centric computing also uses the *object-oriented* paradigm, since various entities that appear on the user's screen are most naturally modeled as objects that send and receive messages. Programming languages that support Web-centric computing include Perl, PHP [Hughes, 2001], Visual Basic, Java, and Python.

1.5   ON LANGUAGE DESIGN

Programming language design is an enormous challenge. Language designers are the people who create a language medium that enables programmers to solve complex problems. To achieve this goal, designers must work within several practical constraints and adopt specific goals which combine to provide focus to this challenge. This section provides an overview of these design constraints and goals.

1.5.1 Design Constraints

The following elements of computational settings provide major constraints for language designers.

- Architecture
- Technical setting
- Standards
- Legacy systems

Architecture   Programming languages are designed for computers. This fact is both a blessing and a curse to language designers. It is a blessing because a well-designed and implemented language can greatly enhance the utility of the computer in an application domain. It is a curse because most computer designs over the past several decades have been bound by the architecture ideas of the classic von Neumann-Eckert model discussed above. Many languages, like Fortran, Cobol and C, are well-matched with that architecture, while others, like Lisp, are not.

For a few years, it became attractive to consider the idea of computer architecture as a by-product of language design, rather than as a precursor. In the 1960s, Burroughs designed the B5500, which had a stack architecture particularly suited to running Algol programs. Another effort produced the genre of Lisp machines that emerged in the early 1980s. These machines were configured so that Lisp programs would run efficiently on them, and they enjoyed a degree of success for a few years. However, Lisp machine architectures were eclipsed in the late 1980s by the advent of Reduced Instruction Set Computer (RISC) architectures, on which Lisp programs could be implemented efficiently.

So as we consider the virtues of various language design choices, we are always constrained by the need to implement the language efficiently and effectively within the constraints imposed by today's variations of the classical von Neumann model. The notion that a good language design can lead to a radically new and commercially viable computer architecture is probably not in the cards.

Technical Setting   Not only are language designs constrained by the limits of computer architectures, they must also satisfy other constraints imposed by the technical setting in which they are used: the application area, the operating system, Integrated Development Environment (IDE), the network, and the other preferences of a particular programming community. For example, Fortran is implemented on certain platforms by different compilers to suit the needs of scientific programmers. These programmers work in various professions that use their own software design styles, tools, and (above all) their own natural languages for communication among themselves. This larger picture of the complex setting for language design is summarized in Figure 1.3.

Some languages are intentionally more *general-purpose* in their design, aiming to serve the interests of a wide range of applications. For instance, Ada [The Department of Defense, 1983] was designed to be useful for all applications supported by the Defense Department, while Cobol [Brown, 1977] was designed to support all business-oriented applications. While Cobol was moderately successful in its goal, Ada has been far less successful.

Other languages are designed to be more *special-purpose* in nature. For instance, Prolog [Clocksin and Mellish, 1997] was designed to serve the narrow interests of natural language processing, theorem proving, and expert systems. C was designed primarily to support the interests of systems programming, although it has since been adopted by a broader range of applications. And Spark/Ada and JML were designed, respectively, to support the formal proof of correctness of Ada and Java programs.

Standards   When a programming language receives wide enough usage among programmers, the process of *standardization* usually begins. That is, an effort is made to define a machine-independent standard definition of the language to which all of its

Figure 1.3   Levels of Abstraction in Computing

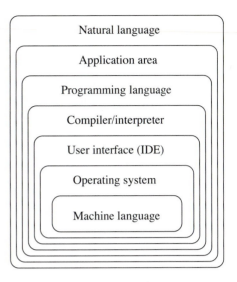

implementors must adhere. Language standardization generally stabilizes the language across different platforms and programming groups, making program portability feasible.

The two major organizations that oversee and maintain standards for programming languages are the American National Standards Institute (ANSI) and the International Standards Organization (ISO). Several languages have been standardized over the years since the language standardization process began. Some of these, along with their most recent dates of standardization, are:

ANSI/ISO Cobol (2002)

ISO Fortran (2004)

ISO Haskell (1998)

ISO Prolog (2000)

ANSI/ISO C (1999)

ANSI/ISO C++ (2003)

ANSI/ISO Ada (2005)

ANSI Smalltalk (2002)

ISO Pascal (1990)

The language standardization process is complex and time-consuming, with a long period of community involvement and usually a voluminous definition of the standard language as its outcome.

Standardization of programming languages has been accompanied by the standardization of character sets (e.g., the ASCII and UNICODE sets) and libraries (e.g., the C++ Standard Template Library) that directly support programming activities.

The value of standardization to the community is that software and hardware designers play a role in the process and commit their implementations of compilers and interpreters to conform to the standard. Such conformity is essential to maintain portability of programs across different compilers and hardware platforms.

Some have argued language standardization is a negative influence because it inhibits innovation in language design. That is, standard versions of languages tend to last for long periods of time, thus perpetuating the life of the poor features alongside that of the most valuable features. However, ISO and ANSI standards are reviewed every five years, which provides a modest buffer against prolonged obsolescence.

More information about specific language standards and the standardization process itself can be found at the websites **www.ansi.org** and **www.iso.org**.

Legacy Systems   It is well-known that the great majority of a programmer's time is spent maintaining *legacy systems*. Such systems are those software artifacts that were designed and implemented by former programming staff, but are maintained and updated by current staff. The largest body of code for legacy systems is probably written in Cobol, the most dominant programming language for information systems during the last four decades.

In order to support the maintenance of legacy code, updated and improved versions of old languages must be *backward compatible* with their predecessors. That is, old programs must continue to compile and run when new compilers are developed for the updated version. Thus, all syntactic and semantic features, even the ones that are less desirable from an aesthetic point of view, cannot be thrown out without disrupting the integrity of legacy code.

For this reason, older programming languages have become overburdened with features as new versions emerge; languages rarely become more compact as they evolve. This is especially true for Fortran, Cobol, and C++, which was designed as a true extension of C in order to maintain backward compatibility with legacy code.

The design of Java, although a lot of its features are reminiscent of C++, departed from this tradition. As a central theme, Java designers wanted to free their new language from having to support the less desirable features of C++, so they simply cut them out. The result was a more streamlined language, at least temporarily. That is, recent versions of Java have added many new features without removing a comparably large set of obsolete features. Perhaps it is inevitable that, as any language matures, it naturally becomes more feature-burdened in order to address the increasing demands of its application domain.

1.5.2 Outcomes and Goals

In light of these requirements, we are led to ask two important questions:

1   How does a programming language emerge and become successful?
2   What key characteristics make an ideal programming language?

Looking briefly at the past, we first observe that some successful programming languages were designed by individuals, others were designed by industry-wide committees, and still others were the product of strong advocacy by their corporate sponsors. For instance, Lisp and C++ were designed primarily by individuals (John McCarthy and Bjarne Stroustrup, respectively), while the languages Algol, Cobol, and Ada were designed by committees.[1] PL/I, Java, and C# are the products of their corporate sponsors (IBM, Sun, and Microsoft, respectively). So it's not clear that the design process—individual, committee, or corporate sponsorship—has much overarching influence on the success of a language design.

Since this study aims to prepare readers to evaluate and compare programming languages in general, it is important to have a small set of key characteristics by which you can do this. We shall call these *design goals*, since they have served as effective measures of successful language designs over the years:

- Simplicity and readability
- Clarity about binding
- Reliability
- Support
- Abstraction
- Orthogonality
- Efficient implementation

Simplicity and Readability   Programs should be easy to write. They should also be intelligible and easy to read by the average programmer. An ideal programming language should thus support writability and readability. Moreover, it should be easy to learn and to teach.

Some languages, like Basic, Algol, and Pascal, were intentionally designed to facilitate clarity of expression. Basic, for instance, had a very small instruction set. Algol 60 had a "publication language" which provided a standard format for typesetting programs that appeared in published journal articles. Pascal was explicitly designed as a teaching language, with features that facilitated the use of structured programming principles.

Other languages were designed to minimize either the total number of keystrokes needed to express an algorithm or the amount of storage that the compiler would require. Surely, the designers of APL and C valued these economies.

Clarity About Binding   A language element is *bound* to a property at the time that property is defined for it. A good language design should be very clear about when the principal binding time for each element to its properties occurs. Here are the major binding times.

- Language definition time: When the language is defined, basic data types are bound to special tags, called *reserved words*, that represent them. For example, integers are bound to the identifier `int`, and real numbers are bound to `float` in the language C.
- Language implementation time: When the compiler or interpreter for the language is written, values are bound to machine representations. For example, the size of an `int` value in C is determined at language implementation time.

---

1. In the case of Ada, the design process also had an element of competition—several competing designs were evaluated, and Ada emerged as the most suitable language to meet the Defense Department's needs.

- Program writing time: When programs are written in some languages, variable names are bound to types, which remain associated with those names throughout the run of the program. For instance, a variable can be bound to its type at the time it is declared, as in the declaration

```
int x;
```

which binds the variable x to the type int.

- Compile time: When programs are compiled, program statements and expressions are bound to equivalent machine language instruction sequences.
- Program load time: When the machine code is loaded, the static variables are assigned to fixed memory addresses, the run-time stack is allocated to a block of memory, and so is the machine code itself.
- Program run time: When programs are running, variables are bound to values, as in the execution of the assignment x = 3.

Sometimes, an element can be bound to a property at any one of a number of alternative times in this continuum. For example, the association of a value with a constant may be done either at program compile/load time or at the beginning of run time. When such choices are possible, the notion of *early binding* means simply that an element is bound to a property as early as possible (rather than later) in this time continuum. *Late binding* means to delay binding until the last possible opportunity.

As we shall see in Chapter 4, early binding leads to better error detection and is usually less costly. However, late binding leads to greater programming flexibility (as illustrated in Chapter 14). In general, a language design must take all these alternatives into account, and decisions about binding are ultimately made by the language designer.

Reliability   Does the program behave the same way every time it is run with the same input data? Does it behave the same way when it is run on different platforms? Can its behavior be independently specified in a way that would encourage its formal (or informal) verification?

Especially pertinent to these questions is the need to design appropriate exception handling mechanisms into the language. Moreover, languages that restrict aliasing and memory leaks, support strong typing, have well-defined syntax and semantics, and support program verification and validation would have an edge in this category.

Support   A good programming language should be easily accessible by someone who wants to learn it and install it on his/her own computer. Ideally, its compilers should be in the public domain, rather than being the property of a corporation and costly to obtain. The language should be implemented on multiple platforms. Courses, textbooks, tutorials, and a wide base of people familiar with the language are all assets that help preserve and extend the vitality of a language.

Questions related to cost may be of more concern to individual programmers and students, rather than to corporate or government employees whose software costs are generally covered by their jobs. The history of programming languages has seen success on both sides. For instance, C, C++, and Java are nonproprietary languages, available in the public domain for a wide variety of platforms. On the other hand, C# and Eiffel are vendor-supported languages whose use is constrained by their cost and the platforms/ IDEs on which they are implemented.

Abstraction   Abstraction is a fundamental aspect of the program design process. Programmers spend a lot of time building abstractions, both data abstractions and procedural abstractions, to exploit the reuse of code and avoid reinventing it. A good programming language supports data and procedural abstraction so well that it is a preferred design tool in most applications.

Libraries that accompany modern programming languages attest to the accumulated experience of programmers in building abstractions. For example, Java's class libraries contain implementations of basic data structures (e.g., vectors and stacks) that, in earlier languages, had to be explicitly designed by programmers themselves. How often have we reinvented a sorting algorithm or a linked list data structure that has probably been implemented thousands of times before?

Orthogonality   A language is said to be *orthogonal* if its statements and features are built upon a small, mutually independent set of primitive operations. The more orthogonal a language, the fewer exceptional rules are needed for writing correct programs. Thus, programs in an orthogonal language often tend to be simpler and clearer than those in a non-orthogonal language.

As an example of orthogonality, consider the passing of arguments in a function call. A fully orthogonal language allows any type of object, including a function definition, to be passed as an argument. We shall see examples of this in our discussion of functional programming in Chapter 14.

Other languages restrict the types of objects that can be passed in a call. For example, most imperative languages do not allow function definitions to be passed as arguments, and therefore are not orthogonal in this regard.

Orthogonality tends to correlate with conceptual simplicity, since the programmer doesn't need to keep a lot of exceptional rules in her head. Alan Perlis put it this way:

> It is better to have 100 functions operate on one data structure than 10 functions on 10 data structures.

On the other hand, non-orthogonality often correlates with efficiency because its exceptional rules eliminate programming options that would be time- or space-consuming.

Efficient Implementation   A language's features and constructs should permit a practical and efficient implementation on contemporary platforms.

For a counterexample, Algol 68 was an elegant language design, but its specifications were so complex that it was (nearly) impossible to implement effectively. Early versions of Ada were criticized for their inefficient run-time characteristics since Ada was designed in part to support programs that run in "real time." Programs embedded in systems like airplanes had to respond immediately to a sudden change in input values, like wind speed. Ada programs stood at the intersection of the sensors that provided the readings and the mechanisms that were to respond to them. Early implementations of Ada fell far short of these ambitious performance goals. The harshest critics of Ada's performance were known to utter, "Well, there's 'real time' and then there's 'Ada time'!"

Initial implementations of Java had been criticized on this same basis, although recent refinements to Sun's Java compiling system have improved its run-time performance.

1.6 COMPILERS AND VIRTUAL MACHINES

An implementation of a programming language requires that programs in the language be analyzed, and then translated into a form that can be either:

1 Run by a computer (i.e., a "real machine"), or
2 Run by an interpreter (i.e., a piece of software that simulates a "virtual machine" and runs on a real machine).

Translation of the first kind is often called *compiling*, while translation of the second is called *interpreting*.

Compilers The *compiling* process translates a source program into the language of a computer. Later, the resulting *machine code* can be run on that computer. This process is pictured in Figure 1.4. For example, Fortran, Cobol, C, and C++ are typical compiled languages.

The five stages of the compiling process itself are lexical analysis, syntactical analysis, type checking, code optimization, and code generation. The first three stages are concerned with finding and reporting errors to the programmer. The last two stages are concerned with generating efficient machine code to run on the target computer.

A compiled program's machine code combines with its input to run in a separate step that follows compilation. Run-time errors are generally traceable to the source program through the use of a debugger.

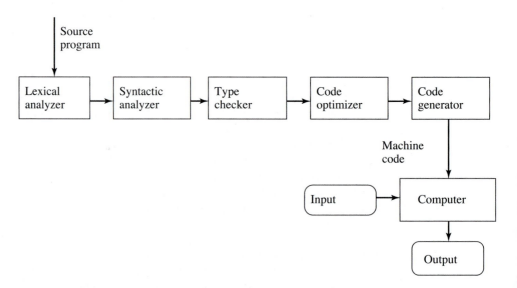

| **Figure 1.4**   **The Compile-and-Run Process**

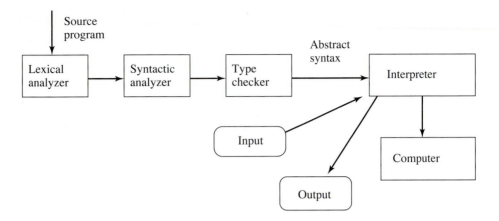

| **Figure 1.5** **Virtual Machines and Interpreters**

We shall have some opportunities to explore the first three stages of compiling in Chapters 3 and 6. However, the subjects of code generation and optimization are typically covered in a compiler course and will not be addressed in this text.

Virtual Machines and Interpreters Other languages are implemented using an *interpretive* process, as shown in Figure 1.5. Here, the source program is translated to an intermediary abstract form, which is then interpretively executed. Lisp and Prolog, for instance, are often implemented using interpreters (although compilers for these languages also exist).

As Figure 1.5 suggests, the first three stages of a compiler also occur in an interpreter. However, the abstract representation of the program that comes out of these three stages becomes the subject of execution by an interpreter. The interpreter itself is a program that executes the steps of the abstract program while running on a real machine. The interpreter is usually written in a language distinct from the language being interpreted.

Sometimes a language is designed so that the compiler is written only once, targeting the code for an abstract *virtual machine*, and then that virtual machine is implemented by an interpreter on each of the different real machines of the day. This is the case for Java, whose abstract machine was called the Java Virtual Machine (JVM) [Lindholm and Yellin, 1997]. When making this choice, the Java language designers gave up a bit of efficiency (since interpreted code generally requires more resources than machine code) in favor of flexibility and portability. That is, any change in the Java language specification can be implemented by altering a single compiler rather than a family of compilers.

A major advantage of compiling over interpreting is that the run-time performance of a compiled program is usually more efficient (in time and space) than its interpreted performance. On the other hand, the quality of interaction with the system that the programmer enjoys can be better with an interpreter than with a compiler. Since program development is interactive, individual program segments (functions) can be tested as they are designed, rather than waiting for the entire program in which they are to be embedded to be complete.[2]

Later versions of Java have gained back some of this efficiency loss by embedding a just-in-time (JIT) compiler into the JVM. This feature enables the JVM byte code to be translated on-the-fly into the native machine code of the host machine before it is executed.

The virtual machine concept is valuable for other reasons that can offset its inherent loss of efficiency. For example, it is expedient to implement a language and its interpreter using an existing virtual machine for the purpose of design or experimentation with the language itself. Similarly, it is useful to study language design foundations and paradigms by using an available *interpreter* that facilitates experimentation and evaluation of programs in that language.

The virtual machine concept has an immediate practical value in this study. That is, you will have access to an interpreter for a small C subset called *Clite*. The use of *Clite* facilitates much of our work because it eliminates machine-specific details that can often hide the principles and other ideas being taught. For instance, in the study of language syntax, you can exercise the *Clite* interpreter to explore the syntactic structure of different language elements, like arithmetic expressions and loops.

1.7 SUMMARY

The study of programming languages includes principles, paradigms, and special topics. The principles are studied both conceptually and in a hands-on way, via the Clite interpreter.

Mastery of one or more new paradigms—imperative, object-oriented, functional, or logic programming—is also important to this study. This activity helps us to appreciate a broader range of computing applications and discover approaches to problem solving with which we are not yet familiar.

Investigation of one or more special topics—event-handling, concurrency, or correctness—allows us to look carefully at three particular language design features and the programming challenges that surround their effective utilization.

In all, we hope that this study will help broaden your view and your technical skills across the wide landscape of programming languages. In particular, you should expect to acquire:

- An appreciation for the use of hands-on tools to examine the principles of language design.
- An appreciation for the value of different programming paradigms that are particularly powerful in specific application domains.
- Laboratory experiences with new languages and design tools, both for testing the principles and for mastering new problem solving techniques.

To support this study, you may occasionally visit the book's website. All the programs that appear in the book can be downloaded from that website, along with other pedagogical and learning aids.

---

2. However, the development of modern debuggers and IDEs for compiled languages have substantially neutralized this advantage in recent years.

EXERCISES

1.1   An online Web search on "programming languages" will yield links to major information sources for all the major programming languages, past and present. For each of the following languages, use the Web to learn something about it. Write, in your own words, a brief (one paragraph) summary of its distinguishing features, as well as its historical relationship with other languages that preceded or followed it.

(a)   Eiffel

(b)   Perl

(c)   Python

1.2   Give an example statement in C, C++, or Java that is particularly unreadable. Rewrite that statement in a more readable style. For instance, have you ever seen the expression A[i++] in a C/C++ program?

1.3   Unreadable code is not the exclusive province of C, C++, and Java. Consider the following strongly held opinions about the weaknesses of particular languages over the last four or more decades:

> It is practically impossible to teach good programming to students that have had a prior exposure to BASIC; as potential programmers they are mentally mutilated beyond hope of regeneration. E. Dijkstra

> The use of COBOL cripples the mind; its teaching should, therefore, be regarded as a criminal offence. E. Dijkstra

> APL is a mistake, carried through to perfection. It is the language of the future for the programming techniques of the past: it creates a new generation of coding bums. E. Dijkstra

> There does not now, nor will there ever exist, a programming language in which it is the least bit hard to write bad programs. L. Flon

(a)   Dijkstra seems not to have much regard for Basic, Cobol, or APL. However, he *did* have a high regard for Algol and its successors. Do enough reading on the Web to determine what general features Algol possessed that would make it superior to languages like Basic, Cobol, and APL.

(b)   What does Flon mean by this last statement? Are programming languages inherently flawed? Or is he suggesting that programmers are inherently inept? Or is there a middle-ground interpretation? Explain.

1.4   Give a feature of C, C++, or Java that illustrates orthogonality. Give a feature different from the one discussed in the text that illustrates non-orthogonality.

1.5   Two different implementations of a language are *incompatible* if there are programs that run differently (give different results) under one implementation than under the other. After reading on the Web and in other sources about early versions of Fortran, can you determine whether or not Fortran had incompatible versions? In what specific form (statement type, data type, etc.) did this incompatibility appear? What can be done to eliminate incompatibilities between two different implementations of a language?

1.6   The standardization effort for the language C began in 1982 with an ANSI working group, and the first C standard was completed in 1989. This work was later accepted as an ISO standard in 1990 and has continued until the present day. Read enough on the Web to determine what significant changes have been made to the C standard since 1990.

1.7 Find the C++ standard on the Web. What is meant by *nonconformant* when the standard discusses a language feature supported by a particular compiler? For the C++ compiler on your computer, are there nonconformant features?

1.8 After learning what you can from the Java website **java.sun.com** and other sources, what can you say about the status of the Java standardization effort by ANSI and ISO at this time?

1.9 Find the Python 2.4 version on the Web. What new features does this version add to Python 2.3? What old features of Python are eliminated by the newer version, if any?

1.10 Compare two languages that you know using the goals for language design outlined in Section 1.5.2. For each goal, determine which of the two languages meets the goal better and justify your conclusion with an example. For instance, in comparing C and Java you could conclude that C has more efficient implementations because it compiles to native code rather than an interpreter.

Syntax

2

"...a language that is simple to parse for the compiler, is also simple to parse for the human programmer."

Niklaus Wirth [1974]

CHAPTER OUTLINE

When we think of a program, we distinguish its form (how it is written) from its meaning (what happens when we run it). Generally speaking, the form of a program is called its *syntax*, while the meaning of a program is called its *semantics*. Compilers detect syntax errors in our programs, as well as type and declaration errors, while run-time errors like division by zero are semantic in nature. More precisely, we can define syntax as follows:

> **Definition**: The *syntax* of a programming language is a precise description of all its grammatically correct programs.

Syntax can be described by a set of rules, just as it is for natural languages. For instance, the rule that a sentence must end with a proper terminator (a period, a question mark, or an exclamation mark) is part of the syntax of the English language. For a programming language, a clear and precise description of its syntax is particularly important; without such a specification, compiler writers and programmers would not function well.

Formal methods for defining syntax have been used since the emergence of Algol in the early 1960s [Naur (ed.), 1963], and have been used for defining the syntax of most languages ever since. In this chapter, we explore the use of both formal and informal methods for defining the syntax of a programming language, at the lexical, concrete, and abstract syntax levels.

> **Definition**: A language's *lexical syntax* defines the rules for basic symbols including identifiers, literals (e.g., integer and floating point), operators, and punctuation.

> **Definition**: A language's *concrete syntax* refers to the actual representation of its programs using lexical symbols as its alphabet.

> **Definition**: A language's *abstract syntax* carries only the essential program information, without concern for syntactic idiosyncrasies like punctuation or parentheses.

Abstract syntax is a very useful tool for linking the syntactic expressions in a language with their semantics, as we shall see in later chapters.

To help illustrate our study, we introduce the simple imperative mini-language Clite, which will be a useful tool for examining the syntactic and semantic properties of programming languages. Clite has the following characteristics:

- It is a subset of C/C++, so programs written in Clite will compile and run using a standard C/C++ compiler, needing only a few standard `#include`'s.
- Unlike C and C++, Clite has a concise syntactic specification, which facilitates discussing fundamental concepts in syntax.
- The simplicity of Clite facilitates implementation of an interpreter for it, providing a hands-on supplement to learning.

2.1 GRAMMARS

The syntax of a language can be largely specified using a formalism called a *grammar*. A grammar is written in a language-description-language, or *metalanguage*, and its purpose is to define all the legal strings of characters that can form a syntactically valid program. Grammars are a metalanguage based on a formal theory developed by the linguist Noam Chomsky [1957], which defined four levels of grammar, known as *regular*, *context-free*, *context-sensitive*, and *unrestricted*. The Chomsky hierarchy is discussed further in Section 3.1.

Definition: A *context-free grammar* has a set of productions *P*, a set of terminal symbols *T*, and a set of nonterminal symbols *N*, one of which, *S*, is distinguished as the *start symbol*.

Definition: A grammar *production* has the form $A \rightarrow \omega$ where *A* is a nonterminal symbol and ω is a string of nonterminal and terminal symbols.

One form of context-free grammar, called Backus-Naur Form (BNF for short) has been widely used to define the syntax of programming languages.

2.1.1 Backus-Naur Form (BNF) Grammars

In 1960, BNF was adapted from Chomsky's theory by John Backus and Peter Naur to express a formal syntactic definition for the programming language Algol [Naur (ed.), 1963]. Like many texts, we use the term *BNF grammar* as a synonym for context-free grammar. For a more complete discussion of the differences between the two, see Observation (p. 26).

A production is a rule for rewriting that can be applied to a string of symbols called a *sentential form*. A production is interpreted as follows: the nonterminal *A* can be replaced by ω in a sentential form. The symbol *A* is often called the *left-hand side*, while the string ω is called the *right-hand side* of the production. In BNF grammars, the sets of terminal and nonterminal symbols are disjoint.

When a BNF grammar is used for defining programming language syntax, the *nonterminals N* identify the language's grammatical categories like *Identifier*, *Integer*, *Expression*, *Statement*, and *Program*. The start symbol *S* identifies the principal grammatical category being defined by the grammar (typically *Program*), and is usually defined in the first production. The *terminal symbols T* form the basic alphabet from which programs are constructed.

To illustrate these ideas, here is a pair of productions that defines the syntax of the grammatical category *binaryDigit*:

$binaryDigit \rightarrow 0$

$binaryDigit \rightarrow 1$

This pair defines a *binaryDigit* as either 0 or 1, but nothing else. The nonterminal symbols are all the symbols that appear on the left-hand side of at least one production. For the above grammar, *binaryDigit* is the only nonterminal. The terminal symbols are all the other symbols that appear in the productions; for the above grammar, 0 and 1 are the terminal symbols.

When a series of productions all have the same nonterminal symbol on their left-hand sides, they may be combined into a single production. For example, the above two productions can be abbreviated by:

$binaryDigit \rightarrow 0 \mid 1$

In this case, the alternatives are separated by a vertical bar (|), which literally means "or," so the interpretation remains the same as the original pair of productions. In this example, both the right arrow and vertical bar are *metasymbols*, which are symbols that are part of the metalanguage and are not part of the language being defined.

Observation

Backus-Naur form

BNF began as a specific metalanguage used to define the syntax of Algol 60. Nonterminals consisted of names which were written in angle brackets, which also appeared on the left-hand side of at least one production. All other symbols except the metasymbols ::= and | were interpreted as terminal symbols.

Thus, the grammar for an *Integer* would appear in BNF as:

```
<integer> ::= <digit> | <integer> | <digit>
<digit> ::= 0 | 1 | 2 | 3 | 4 | 5 | 6 | 7 | 8 | 9
```

Later, an ISO standard (ISO 14977 [1996]) was developed for BNF grammars, but has been largely ignored.

The original BNF notation tried to incorporate the character set limitations of the input mechanisms of the day. As computer technology made it possible to use the standard computer input devices to create more expressive notations, the more limited notations were abandoned. We see an instance of that in this text, in which having the authors typeset the mathematics was unimaginable 40 years ago.

In honor of the pioneering work of Backus and Naur in developing BNF and using it to define the syntax of Algol, we use the term *BNF grammar* as a synonym for the term *context-free grammar* used by Chomsky.

The right-hand side of a BNF production can be any sequence of terminal and nonterminal symbols, allowing a variety of interesting constructs to be concisely defined. Consider the following BNF grammar $G_{integer}$, which defines the grammatical category *Integer* as a sequence of decimal *Digit*s.

$$Integer \rightarrow Digit \mid Integer\ Digit$$
$$Digit \rightarrow 0 \mid 1 \mid 2 \mid 3 \mid 4 \mid 5 \mid 6 \mid 7 \mid 8 \mid 9$$

Here, the second production defines the usual decimal digits. The first production allows an *Integer* to be either a *Digit* alone or an *Integer* followed by a *Digit*. Its second alternative illustrates the use of recursion to define an arbitrarily long sequence of symbols. This production thus defines an *Integer* as a sequence of one or more digits.

2.1.2 Derivations

To determine whether a particular string of symbols belongs to a grammatical category, the production rules for that category can be used to derive the string. For example, suppose we want to determine if 352 is an *Integer*. To do this, we can develop a *derivation* for this string using the production rules of the grammar.

1. First, write down the start symbol *Integer*.
2. Replace the *Integer* with the string *Integer Digit*, which is allowed by the second alternative on the right-hand side of the first production rule.
3. Substitute *Integer Digit* for *Integer* in this string, again using the same rule, producing the string *Integer Digit Digit*.

4 Substitute *Digit* for *Integer* in this string, this time using the first alternative in the first production rule, gaining *Digit Digit Digit*.

5 Substitute 3 as a particular kind of *Digit* using the second production rule, achieving the string 3 *Digit Digit*.

6 Substitute 5 for the next *Digit* in this string, achieving the string 3 5 *Digit*.

7 Finally, substitute 2 for *Digit* in this string, deriving the string 352.

Technically, a *derivation* is a sequence of strings separated by the symbol ⇒ in which at each step a nonterminal is replaced by the right-hand side of one of its productions. The first string in the series is the desired grammatical category and the last is the string to be derived. The above sequence of steps, therefore, is properly written as follows:

$$Integer \Rightarrow Integer\ Digit$$
$$\Rightarrow Integer\ Digit\ Digit$$
$$\Rightarrow Digit\ Digit\ Digit$$
$$\Rightarrow 3\ Digit\ Digit$$
$$\Rightarrow 35\ Digit$$
$$\Rightarrow 352$$

Here, each instance of ⇒ denotes the application of a single production rule to transform a string one step closer to the string to be derived. Each string in such a derivation is called a *sentential form*, which can contain both terminal and nonterminal symbols. For instance, the sentential form 3 *Digit Digit* occurs in the fourth step of this derivation.

Thus, we have just derived the string 352 as an instance of the grammatical category *Integer* according to the grammar $G_{integer}$. Our derivation is a proof by construction that

$$Integer \Rightarrow^* 352$$

That is, the string 352 can be derived from the grammatical category *Integer* in zero or more derivation steps. The symbol ⇒* is an instance of the Kleene star notation, in which the star * is used to denote zero or more occurrences of the symbol to its left, in this case, the *derives symbol* (⇒).

We can now define precisely the meaning of the term *language* from a purely syntactic point of view:

Definition: The *language* L defined by a BNF grammar G is the set of all terminal strings that can be derived from the start symbol.

For example, the language defined by the grammar $G_{integer}$ is the set of all strings that are finite sequences of decimal digits, thus forming the syntactic category *Integer*. The string 352 is a particular member of this language, since we can derive it using the productions of $G_{integer}$. The derivation given above is called a *leftmost derivation* because, at each step, we replaced the leftmost nonterminal in the sentential form by one of its alternatives. Many other derivation sequences are possible. For example, we could replace the rightmost nonterminal at each step, in which case we would have a *rightmost derivation*. That is:

$Integer \Rightarrow Integer\ Digit$
$\Rightarrow Integer\ 2$
$\Rightarrow Integer\ Digit\ 2$
$\Rightarrow Integer\ 5\ 2$
$\Rightarrow Digit\ 5\ 2$
$\Rightarrow 352$

2.1.3 Parse Trees

Another way to demonstrate that a particular string is a member of the language defined by a BNF grammar is to describe the derivation in graphical form. This form is called a *parse tree*, in which each derivation step corresponds to a new subtree. For example, the derivation step:

$Integer \Rightarrow Integer\ Digit$

can be written as the subtree:

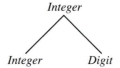

The root of each subtree in a parse tree is the node corresponding to the nonterminal for which the substitution is being made in a derivation, and the immediate children in left-to-right order correspond to the right-hand side of the production used in that substitution.

A complete parse tree for the derivation of the string 352 is shown in Figure 2.1. Note that once the parse tree is drawn, the order of the derivation steps is lost; both the leftmost and rightmost derivations result in the same tree.

Figure 2.1 Parse Tree for 352 as an *Integer*

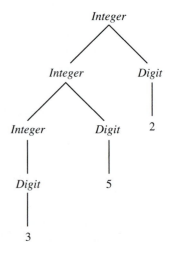

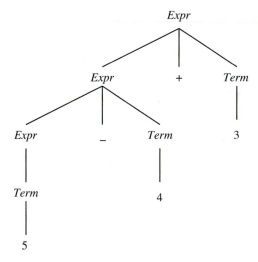

| **Figure 2.2** **Parse of the String** $5 - 4 + 3$

The parse tree has several other notable features. First, the root node of the parse tree always contains the start symbol of the grammar (*Integer* in this example). Second, every internal node contains a nonterminal (in this case, *Integer* or *Digit*). In fact, there are always the same number of internal nodes in the parse tree as there are steps ($\Rightarrow$) in the derivation (6 in this example). Third, each internal node has as its direct descendants the elements that appear on the right-hand side of a grammar rule, in order from left to right. Finally, the leaves of the parse tree are always terminal symbols of the grammar. Reading the leaves from left to right reconstructs the string being parsed (352 in this example).

In summary, a derivation is a simple linear representation of a parse tree, and is often more helpful when the string being derived does not possess an interesting grammatical structure. A parse tree is preferred when the grammatical structure is more complex, as we shall see in several examples below.

Consider the grammar G_0, which defines the language of arithmetic expressions having the operators $+$ and $-$ and one-digit integer operands.[1]

$$Expr \rightarrow Expr + Term \mid Expr - Term \mid Term$$
$$Term \rightarrow 0 \mid \ldots \mid 9 \mid (\,Expr\,)$$

A parse tree for the string $5 - 4 + 3$ for grammar G_0 is given in Figure 2.2.

The structure of this parse tree is somewhat more interesting than for grammar $G_{integer}$. A left-to-right interpretation of the leaves in this tree suggests that the expression is evaluated as though it had been written $(5 - 4) + 3$. This interpretation yields a different numerical result than if we calculate $5 - (4 + 3)$. This reflects the fact that the left operand of the operator $+$ is an *Expr*, which subsequently derives the string $5 - 4$.

---

1. In grammars intended for human consumption, long sequences of alternatives are often elided. Thus, $0 \mid \ldots \mid 9$ stands for $0 \mid 1 \mid 2 \mid 3 \mid 4 \mid 5 \mid 6 \mid 7 \mid 8 \mid 9$ in the second rule of G_0.

Similarly, the string 3, which is derived from the *Term* to the right of the operator $+$, is its right operand.

2.1.4 Associativity and Precedence

The example of Section 2.1.3 shows that the structure of a parse tree can be used to help interpret the meaning of a derived string. Here we explore how the structure of a grammar can be used to define the associativity and precedence of operators in expressions.

> **Definition**: An operator has higher *precedence* than another operator if the former should be evaluated sooner in all parenthesis-free expressions involving only the two operators.

Using ordinary mathematics, in the expressions $5 + 4 \times 3$ and $5 \times 4 + 3$, the multiplication is always evaluated before the addition, and thus has the higher precedence. So these expressions are equivalent to $5 + (4 \times 3)$ and $(5 \times 4) + 3$, respectively.

> **Definition**: *Associativity* specifies whether operators of equal precedence should be performed in left-to-right or right-to-left order.

Using ordinary mathematics, the binary minus operator has left associativity, so the expression $5 - 4 - 3$ is equivalent to $(5 - 4) - 3$.

Consider again the parse tree for the string $5 - 4 + 3$ given in Figure 2.2. In a very real sense the occurrence of the specific operators $+$ and $-$ is irrelevant in determining the structure of the parse tree. For the string $5 + 4 - 3$ we get the same tree structure, except the operators $+$ and $-$ are interchanged. Indeed the same tree structure occurs for the strings $5 + 4 + 3$ and $5 - 4 - 3$. From this observation, we can conclude that the operators $+$ and $-$ have the same precedence in this grammar. This occurs because each of the operators $+$ and $-$ occurs as an alternative in the definition of *Expr*.

Furthermore, the use of left recursion in the production rules for *Expr* in grammar G_0 makes these operators left associative. Had right recursion been used in the grammar, the operators would have been right associative.

With these insights, we can define a slightly more interesting grammar G_1 for the binary operators $+$, $-$, $*$, $/$, $\%$ (remainder), and $**$ (exponentiation).[2] In normal mathematical usage, the first four operators are left-associative, while the exponentiation operator is right-associative (that is, 2^{3^4} means 2^{81} rather than 8^4).

$$Expr \rightarrow Expr + Term \mid Expr - Term \mid Term$$
$$Term \rightarrow Term * Factor \mid Term \mathbin{/} Factor \mid$$
$$Term \mathbin{\%} Factor \mid Factor$$
$$Factor \rightarrow Primary ** Factor \mid Primary$$
$$Primary \rightarrow 0 \mid \ldots \mid 9 \mid (\,Expr\,)$$

Precedence is determined by the length of the shortest derivation from the start symbol to the operator and left- or right-associativity is determined by the use of left or right recursion, respectively. These properties are summarized for grammar G_1 in Table 2.1.

---

2. C-style languages including C++ and Java lack an exponentiation operator. While the caret would be a natural choice, it is already used for *bitwise exclusive or* in these languages. So we adopt Fortran's exponentiation operator (**) instead.

Table 2.1

Associativity and Precedence
for Grammar G_1

Precedence	Associativity	Operators
3	right	**
2	left	* / %
1	left	+ -

Consider the parse tree in Figure 2.3 for 4 ** 2 ** 3 + 5 * 6 + 7 which uses grammar G_1. This parse tree interprets the expression as though it had been written

((4 ** (2 ** 3)) + (5 * 6)) + 7.

The parse tree clearly demonstrates that exponentiation associates from right to left. Although not shown in this example, grammar G_1 enables the multiplication and addition operators to associate from left to right. This tree also shows the precedence of exponentiation versus addition and addition versus the multiplication operators. For grammar G_1, readers should convince themselves that this is the only parse tree that can be derived from the string 4 ** 2 ** 3 + 5 * 6 + 7. This can be proved by trying different strategies and showing that no other tree with the root *Expr* and leaves 4 ** 2 ** 3 + 5 * 6 + 7 can be derived using G_1.

Understanding the relationship between the structure of the grammar and the associativity and precedence of its operators is important for language designers. It is not the case that all languages follow the same principles in this regard. For instance, all of Smalltalk's [Goldberg and Robson, 1989] arithmetic operators associate strictly from left to right without any precedence, while the APL [Iverson, 1962] operators associate from right to left without any precedence.

2.1.5 Ambiguous Grammars

When designing a grammar, it is important to avoid making ambiguous specifications — specifications that can be interpreted two or more different ways.

> **Definition**: A grammar is *ambiguous* if its language contains at least one string with two or more distinct parse trees.

Normally, an unambiguous grammar is preferred because there should be only one valid interpretation for each string in its language. However, ambiguity may be tolerable in some instances, especially when its introduction significantly reduces the number of rules in the grammar. That is, there is a tradeoff between the size of the grammar and the information it is trying to convey.

Consider grammar G_2, which is an ambiguous version of G_1:

Expr → *Expr Op Expr* | (*Expr*) | *Integer*
Op → + | - | * | / | % | **

This grammar can be disambiguated using Table 2.1.

Note that such a grammar grows only by one new alternative as each new operator is added. For languages like C, C++, and Java the number of precedence levels and operators makes their grammars quite large. An alternative to building precedence into the grammar is to use an ambiguous grammar and then specify the precedence and associativity separately, for instance in a table (e.g., see Table 2.1). The number of

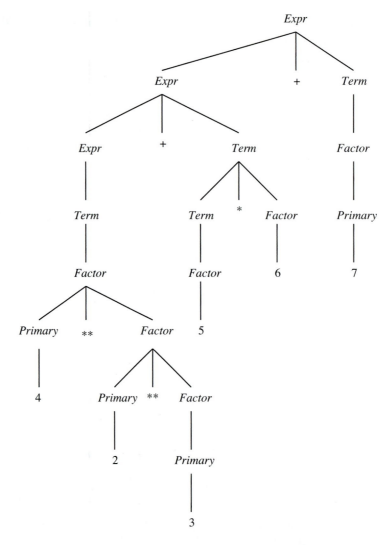

| **Figure 2.3**   **Parse of 4 ** 2 ** 3 + 5 * 6 + 7 for Grammar G_1**

rules in the grammar is slightly larger for languages like C++ because they contain unary prefix and postfix operators and several different types of operands. However, a full unambiguous grammar for C++ expressions would have a distinct nonterminal for each precedence level, thus vastly increasing its size and complexity.

To show that G_2 by itself is ambiguous, we need only find some string that has two distinct parse trees. Observing that the language of grammar G_0 is a subset of the language of G_2, we use the example $5 - 4 + 3$ in Figure 2.4 to show two distinct parse trees. Using the natural interpretation of each, the left tree evaluates to 4, while the right tree evaluates to -2.

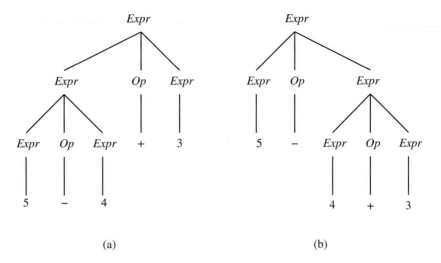

(a)   (b)

| **Figure 2.4**   **Ambiguous Parse of** $5 - 4 + 3$

Another example of syntactic ambiguity is known as the *dangling else* problem. Consider the following grammar fragment G_{if}:

$$\textit{IfStatement} \rightarrow \texttt{if} \; (\textit{Expression}) \; \textit{Statement} \; |$$
$$\texttt{if} \; (\textit{Expression}) \; \textit{Statement} \; \texttt{else} \; \textit{Statement}$$
$$\textit{Statement} \rightarrow \textit{Assignment} \; | \; \textit{IfStatement} \; | \; \textit{Block}$$
$$\textit{Block} \rightarrow \{ \; \textit{Statements} \; \}$$
$$\textit{Statements} \rightarrow \textit{Statements} \; \textit{Statement} \; | \; \textit{Statement}$$

It is not difficult to see that these particular rules produce the dangling else, since they allow two different attachments of an else clause to a nested if. Consider the following example:

```
if (x<0)
    if (y<0) y = y - 1;
    else y = 0;
```

Grammar G_{if} permits the else clause to be attached to either if. These alternative parse trees are sketched in Figure 2.5, where the broken line represents an elided subtree.

The issue here is deciding to which if the else should be attached. If the parse attaches the else clause to the second if statement, y will become 0 whenever x<0 and y>=0. However, if the parse attaches the else clause to the first if statement, y will become 0 whenever x>=0.

Some language specifications, such as C and C++ [Stroustrup, 1997], resolve this ambiguity by giving an informal English-language description of how the attachment should be made. For instance, such a description would state that every else clause is associated with the textually closest preceding unmatched if statement. If a different attachment is desired, the programmer must insert braces { }. For example, to force

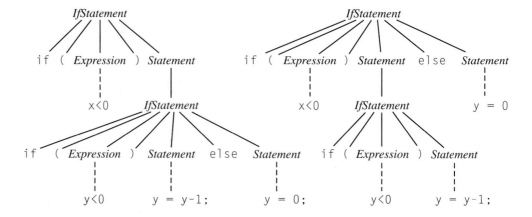

| **Figure 2.5**   The *Dangling Else* Ambiguity

the attachment of else clause to the first (outer) if statement in the above example, the programmer would insert braces in the following way:

```
if (x<0)
    { if (y<0) y = y - 1; }
else y = 0;
```

Now the second line identifies a *Block*, which is specified in grammar G_{if} as a list of one or more statements enclosed in braces. Of course, an *IfStatement* is a perfectly good statement to enclose in braces.[3]

Java solves the dangling else problem by expanding the BNF grammar for an *IfStatement* in an interesting way. The Java specification [Gosling *et al.*, 1996] separates the definition into two different syntactic categories, *IfThenStatement* and *IfThenElse-Statement*, each of which is a subcategory of the general category *Statement*:

$$If ThenStatement \rightarrow \text{if } (Expression) \ Statement$$

$$If ThenElseStatement \rightarrow \text{if } (Expression) \ StatementNoShortIf$$

$$else \ Statement$$

Notice that the second of these rules requires a *StatementNoShortIf* before its else part. *StatementNoShortIf* includes all statements that are not *IfThenStatements,* but it may include other *IfThenElseStatements*. This stipulation rules out an *IfThenStatement* as the first alternative before an else clause, thus eliminating any ambiguity about how to associate the else clause when it occurs in a program. If there is another if statement nested inside this *IfThenElseStatement*, it must itself have an explicit else clause.[4]

---

3. This syntactic design of the if statement originated with Algol-60 [Naur (ed.), 1963], which used the reserved words begin for left brace and end for right brace. Pascal also follows this convention. C-style languages, beginning with C, use the left brace for begin and right brace for end.

4. This strategy can be considerably more complicated than the above summary would suggest. For example, each looping statement derivable from *StatementNoShortIf* must have a special nonterminal that restricts a loop body to a *StatementNoShortIf.*

A third approach to the dangling else problem originated with Algol-68 [van Wijngaarden (ed.) *et al.*, 1969], in which naturally nested constructs such as ifs, loops, and functions/procedures each terminate with a unique keyword. The convention in Algol-68 was that the closing keyword was the opening keyword spelled backwards. Thus, the dangling else problem was solved because every if statement, with or without an else clause, had to be terminated with the keyword fi. For example, the ambiguity shown in Figure 2.5 would be resolved by the Algol-68 programmer in either of the following two ways, respectively:

```
if (x<0)
    if (y<0)
        y := y-1;
    else y := 0;
    fi
fi
if (x<0)
    if (y<0)
        y := y-1;
    fi
else y := 0;
fi
```

Some recent languages have adopted some form of this convention, including the Bourne shell [Kernighan and Pike, 1984], Modula [Wirth, 1982], SR [Andrews and Olsson, 1993] and Ada [Cohen, 1996].

2.2 EXTENDED BNF

Since Algol 60, some form of BNF has been a workhorse for describing the syntax of programming languages. Several minor variations have been introduced, but they have not affected the basic expressive power of BNF. These variations have been introduced mainly to improve the clarity and brevity of syntax descriptions.

Extended BNF (EBNF for short) simplifies writing a grammar by introducing metasymbols for iteration, option, and choice. Consider the BNF grammar G_0 from Section 2.1.3, for instance:

$Expr \rightarrow Expr + Term \mid Expr - Term \mid Term$
$Term \rightarrow 0 \mid \ldots \mid 9 \mid (Expr)$

The first of these rules defines an *Expression* as a series (or list) of one or more *Terms* separated by + or − signs. EBNF permits the elimination of left recursion in this rule as follows:

$Expr \rightarrow Term \{ (+ \mid -) Term \}$

In this rule both the braces and the parentheses are metasymbols. The braces {} denote zero or more occurrences of the symbols that are enclosed within the braces. The parentheses ( ) enclose a series of alternatives from which one must be chosen. Brackets [ ], when used as EBNF metasymbols, enclose an optional sequence of symbols (brackets are not used in this example).

One added complication with EBNF is distinguishing the use of braces, parentheses, and brackets as metasymbols from their use as ordinary terminal symbols. Wirth [1977] proposed enclosing all terminal symbols in quotes (" "). A more modern convention is that all terminal symbols are written in a special font. Here we use the convention that they appear in a `fixed width` font (for example, the `(`, `)`, `+` and `-` symbols in the above grammar) and that the metasymbols (other than right arrow) appear in a bold font.

An example of the use of brackets as metasymbols occurs in the EBNF version of grammar G_{if} of Section 2.1.5:

IfStatement → `if` (*Expression*) *Statement* **[** `else` *Statement* **]**

This rule should be read as an *IfStatement* is defined to be a terminal `if`, followed by an *Expression* in parentheses, followed by a *Statement*, followed by an optional `else` part consisting of the terminal `else` followed by a *Statement*. Like its counterpart in Section 2.1.5, this grammar is ambiguous.

We prefer the EBNF notation, which is often called *Wirth-style EBNF*, for describing and illustrating language syntax in the remainder of this book. This preference is guided by the fact that definitions of language syntax in EBNF tend to be slightly clearer and briefer than BNF definitions. In particular, EBNF eliminates the unnecessary use of recursive definitions to describe lists, which are fundamental in the syntax of programming languages. There are declaration lists, statement lists, parameter lists, and so on.

A variant of EBNF, which we term *C-style EBNF*, is used by Kernighan and Ritchie [1988] in the definition of ANSI C, by Stroustrup [1997] in the definition of C++ and by Gosling *et al.* [1996] in the definition of Java. A description of this notation is provided by Stroustrup [1991, p. 478]:

> In the syntax used in this manual, syntactic categories are indicated by *italic* type, and literal words and characters in `constant width` type. Alternatives are listed on separate lines except in a few cases where a long set of alternatives is presented on one line, marked by the phrase "one of." An optional terminal or nonterminal is indicated by the subscript "opt" . . . .

The subscript "opt" corresponds to our metabrackets but without the ability to group an optional sequence of several terminal and nonterminal symbols together. Thus, the grammar G_{if} would be written in this notation as follows:

ifstatement :

        `if` (*expression*) *statement* *elsepart*$_{opt}$

    elsepart :

        `else` *statement*

Another EBNF variation is the *syntax diagram*, which was popularized by its use in the syntactic definition of the Pascal language [Jensen and Wirth, 1975]. Syntax diagrams can help to clarify the syntax of various language constructs when they are being taught to beginning programmers. They were widely used in Pascal textbooks

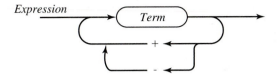

Expression

Term

+

-

| **Figure 2.6**   **Syntax Diagram for *Expressions* with Addition and Subtraction**

written for the introductory programming course; see, for example, [Cooper and Clancy, 1985]. Figure 2.6 gives an example syntax diagram for the idea of an *Expression* with any number of addition operators.

The meaning of this syntax diagram is self-explanatory from its form. We read the diagram from left to right, and all the paths that lead to the right-hand arrowhead define legal *Expressions*. That is, an *Expression* consists of a *Term* followed by a sequence of zero or more occurrences of a + together with a *Term*. In other words, an *Expression* is a sequence or list of one or more *Terms* separated by + symbols.

Neither EBNF nor the syntax diagram is any more powerful than BNF for formally describing language syntax. We can demonstrate this easily for Wirth-style EBNF in the following way. Let A be a nonterminal and x, y, z be arbitrary sequences of terminals and nonterminals. Any EBNF rule having metabraces:

$$A \rightarrow x \, \{ \, y \, \} \, z$$

can be equivalently rewritten without metabraces as follows:

$$A \rightarrow x \, A' \, z$$
$$A' \rightarrow \epsilon \mid y \, A'$$

where A' is a unique new nonterminal. Note that the first alternative in the rule for A' is an empty string ϵ, meaning A' can be replaced by nothing. Strategies for the elimination of metabrackets (option) and metaparentheses (alternative group) from EBNF rules are similar and left as an exercise.

Thus, the EBNF alternative is often used in describing the syntax of a language because it yields simpler rules than BNF. We demonstrate this in Section 2.3 by describing the syntax of a simple language that is a subset of C/C++.

2.3   SYNTAX OF A SMALL LANGUAGE: CLITE

The ideas discussed in this chapter provide a basis for describing the syntax of a complete programming language. However, so as not to be overwhelmed by the details, we have chosen to define a subset of C, a language that we call *Clite*. This language should be familiar to anyone who has written a program in C, C++, or Java.

A complete grammar for Clite, called G_{Clite}, is shown in Figure 2.7. This grammar is much smaller than the grammars for various real languages, as shown in Table 2.2.

In this discussion, we will not mimic the style commonly used to define a language (e.g., [Jensen and Wirth, 1975]) where each major construct is introduced by first presenting its syntax, then its compile-time semantics, and finally its run-time semantics.

$$Program \rightarrow \texttt{int main ( ) \{ } Declarations \ Statements \texttt{ \}}$$

$$Declarations \rightarrow \texttt{\{ } Declaration \texttt{ \}}$$

$$Declaration \rightarrow Type \ Identifier \texttt{ [[} Integer \texttt{]] \{ , } Identifier \texttt{ [[} Integer \texttt{]] \} ;}$$

$$Type \rightarrow \texttt{int | bool | float | char}$$

$$Statements \rightarrow \texttt{\{ } Statement \texttt{ \}}$$

$$Statement \rightarrow \texttt{; | } Block \ | \ Assignment \ | \ IfStatement \ | \ WhileStatement$$

$$Block \rightarrow \texttt{\{ } Statements \texttt{\}}$$

$$Assignment \rightarrow Identifier \texttt{ [[} Expression \texttt{]] = } Expression \texttt{ ;}$$

$$IfStatement \rightarrow \texttt{if (} Expression \texttt{) } Statement \texttt{ [else } Statement \texttt{]}$$

$$WhileStatement \rightarrow \texttt{while (} Expression \texttt{) } Statement$$

$$Expression \rightarrow Conjunction \texttt{ \{ || } Conjunction \texttt{ \}}$$

$$Conjunction \rightarrow Equality \texttt{ \{ \&\& } Equality \texttt{ \}}$$

$$Equality \rightarrow Relation \texttt{ [} EquOp \ Relation \texttt{]}$$

$$EquOp \rightarrow \texttt{ == | != }$$

$$Relation \rightarrow Addition \texttt{ [} RelOp \ Addition \texttt{]}$$

$$RelOp \rightarrow \texttt{ < | <= | > | >= }$$

$$Addition \rightarrow Term \texttt{ \{ } AddOp \ Term \texttt{ \}}$$

$$AddOp \rightarrow \texttt{ + | - }$$

$$Term \rightarrow Factor \texttt{ \{ } MulOp \ Factor \texttt{ \}}$$

$$MulOp \rightarrow \texttt{ * | / | \% }$$

$$Factor \rightarrow \texttt{ [} UnaryOp \texttt{] } Primary$$

$$UnaryOp \rightarrow \texttt{ - | ! }$$

$$Primary \rightarrow Identifier \texttt{ [[} Expression \texttt{]] | } Literal \ | \ \texttt{(} Expression \texttt{)}$$
$$| \ Type \ \texttt{(} Expression \texttt{)}$$

$$Identifier \rightarrow Letter \texttt{ \{ } Letter \ | \ Digit \texttt{ \}}$$

$$Letter \rightarrow \texttt{a | b | ... | z | A | B | ... | Z}$$

$$Digit \rightarrow \texttt{0 | 1 | ... | 9}$$

$$Literal \rightarrow Integer \ | \ Boolean \ | \ Float \ | \ Char$$

$$Integer \rightarrow Digit \texttt{ \{ } Digit \texttt{ \}}$$

$$Boolean \rightarrow \texttt{true | false}$$

$$Float \rightarrow Integer \ \texttt{.} \ Integer$$

$$Char \rightarrow \texttt{' } ASCIIChar \texttt{ '}$$

| **Figure 2.7** **Syntax of Clite**

| **Table 2.2** Grammar Sizes for Various Languages

Language	Approximate Pages	Reference
Pascal	5	[Jensen and Wirth, 1975]
C	6	[Kernighan and Ritchie, 1988]
C++	22	[Stroustrup, 1997]
Java	14	[Gosling *et al.*, 1996]

Instead, our purpose here is to take a deeper look at syntax, leaving the discussion of semantics and other design issues to later chapters.

Although the grammar G_{Clite} does a good job of presenting the syntax of various constructs, a number of related syntactic issues are not addressed:

1 Comments.
2 The role of whitespace.
3 Distinguishing between symbols such as the single symbol <= from the two symbols < and =.
4 Distinguishing identifiers from keywords like if.

The remainder of this section will address these and other syntactic issues.

The grammar G_{Clite} has two levels: the lexical level and the syntactic level. As we shall see in Section 2.4, these levels correspond to distinct parts of a compiler. All of the issues listed above are lexical issues.

2.3.1 Lexical Syntax

The last eight grammar rules in Figure 2.7, starting with the definition of an *Identifier*, address lexical issues. They define the syntax of an *Identifer* and various forms of *Literal*. In addition, all the keywords and other terminal symbols in the first 23 production rules of G_{Clite} are also part of the lexical level.

The input alphabet for the lexical syntax is the set of printable ASCII characters, which excludes the NUL character (ASCII code 0), the control characters (ASCII codes 1–26) excepting the tab character (9), the DEL character (127), and all characters whose codes exceed 127. The ASCII character set is described in detail in Section 5.3. The terminal strings that are derivable in the lexical syntax are called *tokens*, and they are classified into the following groups:

- *Identifier*s
- *Literal*s, including *Integer*s, true and false, *Float*s, and *Char*s
- Keywords: bool char else false float if int main true while
- Operators: = || && == != < <= > >= + - * / % ! [ ]
- Punctuation: ; , { } ( )

Typically, tokens may not contain embedded whitespace characters. The definition of *whitespace* commonly includes the space and tab characters, the end of line character or characters, and comments. For example, when >= is typed without an embedded space, it is treated as one token, but the text > = constitutes two tokens. Similarly, consider the following Pascal program fragment:

```
while a < b do
```

Here, whitespace is required between the keyword while and the identifier a, and also between b and do. Whitespace is not required to separate a from < or < from b.

Tokens are analyzed by compilers using a greedy algorithm that looks for the longest sequence of characters that constitute a valid token independent of its context. In the above example, without whitespace after the while, the characters whilea would form a valid *Identifier* token, even though no such identifier may have been declared and whilea < does not form a prefix of a valid statement. Conversely, the character sequence a< does not form a valid token, while both the character sequences a and < do form valid tokens. Hence, whitespace between these two characters is unnecessary.

Note that the grammar G_{Clite} does not define the syntax of a comment, leaving it to be defined outside the grammar, as is the case in the definitions of both Pascal [Jensen and Wirth, 1975] and C [Kernighan and Ritchie, 1988]. Clite uses the // comment convention of C++.

An *Identifier* is made up of letters (A–Z, a–z) and digits (0–9), and starts with a letter. So, by this definition, the string if is both an *Identifier* and a *Keyword* (see the definition of *IfStatement*). How, then, are identifiers distinguished from keywords? In most languages all keywords are so-called *reserved words*, in the sense that no identifier may have the same spelling as a reserved word. Clite follows this convention, and its reserved words are:

```
bool   else   float   int    true
char   false  if      main   while
```

Note that main is not reserved in either C or C++. Instead, it is a special identifier that names the function where program execution begins.

The Clite grammar in Figure 2.7 defines four kinds of literals. *Integer* literals are conventional, consisting of a sequence of one or more decimal digits. Some languages provide for expressing integer literals in bases other than base 10, using a variety of conventions.

A floating point literal has a sequence of digits with an embedded decimal point. At least one digit is required before and after the decimal point. This convention was adopted by the authors many years ago, when learning that the number 5. was legal in Fortran, but the number .5 was illegal. The opposite convention was true in Algol. However, the numbers 5.0 and 0.5 are legal in both languages. Most languages provide floating point numbers, both in scientific notation and in single and double precision.

The Clite grammar also does not bind the range of valid values for either integers or floating point numbers. Nor does it say how they are stored. These are type and semantic issues, which we discuss more fully in Chapters 5–8.

The Clite *Boolean* literals are the reserved words true and false. *Character* literals are composed of single, printable ASCII characters (see Section 5.1) enclosed in single quotes ('), such as 'a' and 'b'.

2.3.2 Concrete Syntax

The syntactic structure of a complete program is a tree derived from the program's sequence of tokens and its grammar. The *concrete syntax* of a program is the tree that represents a parse of its sequence of tokens, beginning with the start symbol in its grammar. For instance, the root of any Clite program's parse tree is the syntactic category *Program*, having direct descendants a series of tokens including `main`, a subtree of *Declarations*, and a subtree of *Statements*.

C style languages use the semicolon ; as a declaration and statement terminator, rather than as a statement separator as in Algol and Pascal. Only the *Block* statement does not terminate with a semicolon, which terminates with a right brace.

A *Declaration* in Clite consists of a type followed by a list of identifiers, separated by commas. The built-in types are: `int`, `float`, `bool`, and `char`. Note that this declaration style is the opposite of the convention in Pascal, Ada, and UML, in which the list of identifiers precedes the type. Here are two examples:

```
int i, j;
float x;
```

Statements in Clite include *Assignment* using = as an assignment operator, *Block* (a series of statements enclosed in braces { }), *IfStatement*, and *WhileStatement*. Note that the rule for *IfStatement* makes the grammar ambiguous, suffering from the dangling else problem. This is resolved in the usual way [Stroustrup, 1991]:

> The else ambiguity is resolved by connecting an `else` with the last encountered `else`–less if.

This is the only ambiguity in the Clite grammar in Figure 2.7.

The concrete syntax of Clite permits expressions over various operators. The use of metabraces { } at various precedence levels, as in the rule for *Addition*, is meant to imply left associativity. Note that the use of metabrackets (implying optional) is used to define both *Equality* and *Relation*, making the *EquOp* and *RelOp* operators non-associative. Metaparentheses are not used in the Clite grammar of Figure 2.7.

Note that the middle section of the grammar in Figure 2.7 is devoted to defining unambiguously the seven precedence levels, their associated operators, and associativity. For full C++, four pages of [Stroustrup, 1997] are devoted to defining the concrete syntax of expressions. This results from the large number of operators and precedence levels. In contrast, the definition of C [Kernighan and Ritchie, 1988] uses an ambiguous expression grammar, leaving the precedence and associativity of the operators to be specified outside the grammar.

Even when the expression subgrammar is unambiguous, understanding is improved by specifying the precedence and associativity of expression operators in a table, which for Clite from highest precedence to lowest is given in Table 2.3.

This specification differs from C/C++ in two important ways. First, Clite has many fewer operators and resulting precedence levels. For a comparison of C, C++, and Java, see Table 2.4. In the table precedence levels are shown from highest to lowest, separated from the next level by a horizontal line.

Table 2.3

Operator Precedence
and Associativity in Clite

Operators	Associativity
Unary - !	none
* / %	left
+ -	left
< <= > >=	none
== !=	none
&&	left
||	left

Second, neither the equality operators nor the relational operators are associative, which is an idea borrowed from Ada [The Department of Defense, 1983]. In C/C++ you can write expressions such as:

```
if (a < x < b)
```

which is presumably attempting to test whether x has a value strictly between a and b. However, as long as b > 1, the expression will evaluate to true. This results from the fact that a < x evaluates to either 0 or 1. So making these operators associative is a questionable design decision.

Nothing in the Clite grammar specifies the types of operands required by each operator or the type of result returned. These are type and semantic issues not addressed by the concrete syntax, and are discussed more fully in Chapters 5–8.

2.4 COMPILERS AND INTERPRETERS

The logical structure of a compiler is given in Figure 2.8. Each box in the figure represents a *phase*, which is a logically cohesive operation that transforms the source program from one representation to another, as explained below. In contrast is the notion of a *pass*, which is a complete reading of the current representation of the source program. Many one pass compilers have been written; in contrast, many PL/I compilers used multiple passes in the semantics phase. Optimizing compilers are usually multipass.

A source program begins as a stream of characters. The job of the *lexical analyzer* (or *lexer* for short) is to scan the program and transform it into a stream of tokens. As part of this transformation, all whitespace, including comments, is discarded. Similarly, all character sequences that do not form valid tokens are discarded, after an error message is generated.

Since both the lexical and syntactic analysis phases are based on a grammar, the reasons for having a separate lexical analysis phase need to be explained. Historically, these reasons are:

1   The design of the lexical analyzer is based on a much simpler and faster machine model than the context-free model used for syntactic analysis.
2   For a non-optimizing compiler, approximately 75 percent of the total compile time is often consumed in lexical analysis. Any improvement that makes this phase run faster has a comparable impact on total compile time.

| **Table 2.4**   Precedence and Operators in C, C++, and Java

Operation (decreasing precedence)	Associativity	C	C++	Java
Scope resolution	left		::	
Member selection	left	.	.	.
Pointer member selection	left	->	->	
Subscripting	left	[]	[]	[]
Function call	left	()	()	()
Value construction	left	()	()	()
Post-increment	left	++	++	++
Post-decrement	left	--	--	--
Size of object	right	sizeof	sizeof	
Size of type	right	sizeof	sizeof	
Pre-increment	right	++	++	++
Pre-decrement	right	--	--	--
Complement	right	~	~	~
Unary minus	right	-	-	-
Unary plus	right	+	+	+
Address of	right	&	&	
Dereference	right	*	*	
Allocate	right		new	new
Deallocate	right		delete	
Deallocate array	right		delete[]	
Cast	right	()	()	()
Member selection	left	.*	.*	
Pointer member selection	left	->*	->*	
Multiply	left	*	*	*
Divide	left	/	/	/
Modulo	left	%	%	%
Add	left	+	+	+
Subtract	left	-	-	-
Shift left	left	<<	<<	<<
Shift right	left	>>	>>	>>
Less than	left	<	<	<
Less than or equal	left	<=	<=	<=
Greater than	left	>	>	>
Greater than or equal	left	>=	>=	>=

| Table 2.4   Precedence and Operators in C, C++, and Java (*Continued*)

Operation (decreasing precedence)	Associativity	C	C++	Java
Equal	left	==	==	==
Not equal	left	!=	!=	!=
Bitwise and	left	&	&	&
Bitwise exclusive or	left	^	^	^
Bitwise inclusive or	left	|	|	|
Logical and	left	&&	&&	&&
Logical inclusive or	left	||	||	||
Conditional assignment	left	? :	? :	? :
Assignment	right	=	=	=
Assignment with multiply	right	*=	*=	*=
Assignment with divide	right	/=	/=	/=
Assignment with modulo	right	%=	%=	%=
Assignment with add	right	+=	+=	+=
Assignment with subtract	right	-=	-=	-=
Assignment with shift left	right	<<=	<<=	<<=
Assignment with shift right	right	>>=	>>=	>>=
Assignment with and	right	&=	&=	&=
Assignment with inclusive or	right	|=	|=	|=
Assignment with exclusive or	right	^=	^=	^=
Throw exception	left		throw	throw
Comma sequencing	left	,	,	,

3 Prior to the creation of ASCII, each computer had its own idiosyncratic character set. Hiding this character set in the lexer made porting a compiler to a new machine easier. Even today vestiges of this problem still exist, with the ASCII, Unicode, and EBCDIC character sets being used.

4 The end-of-line convention also varies from one operating system to another. For example, the Apple Macintosh (prior to Mac OS/X) uses a carriage return (ASCII 13) as an end of line character, Linux/Unix uses a newline (or linefeed) character (ASCII 10), and Microsoft Windows uses a carriage return/new line combination. For many modern languages, but not all, this problem is handled by the language's runtime support library. In earlier days it was not, so this operating system dependency was hidden inside the lexical analyzer.

The second phase of a compiler is the *parser*, or *syntactic analysis* phase. The *syntactic analyzer* reads a stream of tokens and constructs a parse tree, according to

Figure 2.8   Major Stages in the Compiling Process

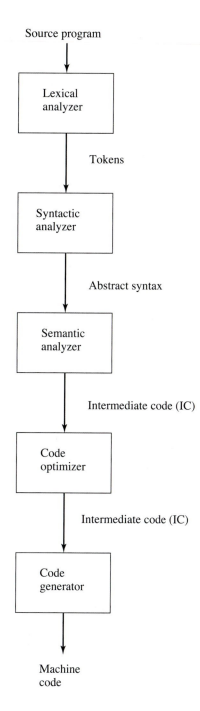

Source program

Lexical analyzer

Tokens

Syntactic analyzer

Abstract syntax

Semantic analyzer

Intermediate code (IC)

Code optimizer

Intermediate code (IC)

Code generator

Machine code

the rules of the grammar. A complete parser is developed for Clite in Section 3.3. The output of a parser can be a parse tree, as shown in Figure 2.9. Alternatively, the output can be an abstract syntax tree, whose advantages will be discussed more fully in Section 2.5.

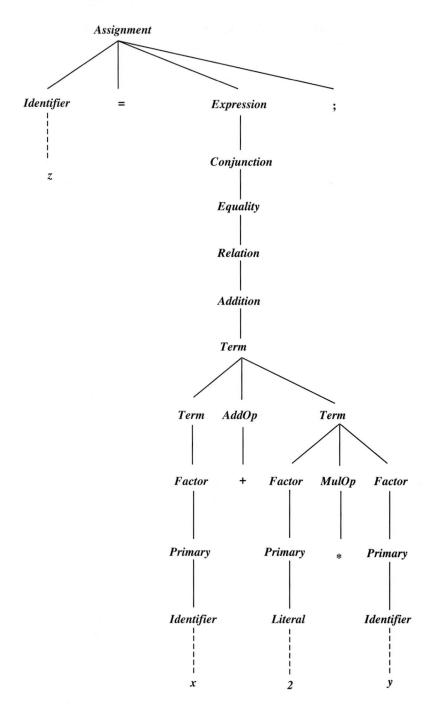

| **Figure 2.9** Parse Tree for z = x + 2 * y ;

As an example of parsing, consider parsing the input $z = x + 2 * y;$, with the aim of obtaining a parse tree with the *Assignment* using the grammar G_{Clite}. The *Assignment* grammar rule requires an *Identifier* followed by =, an *Expression*, and ;. For this particular string to parse successfully, z must be an instance of the grammatical category *Identifier* and $x + 2 * y$ must be an instance of the category *Expression*. Thus, the subtree rooted at *Expression* in Figure 2.9 must be developed as a separate task, using different grammar rules. That is, additional rules for *Term*, *Factor*, and *Primary* come into play as these subtrees are developed.

The third phase of the compiler is the *semantic analysis* phase or *type checker*. This phase is responsible for ensuring that the compile-time semantic rules of the language are enforced, such as:

- All identifiers referenced in the program are declared.
- The operands for each operator have an appropriate type.
- Implied conversion operations, for example, integer to float, are inserted where needed.

In the event that any of the compile-time semantic rules are violated, an appropriate error message is generated. The output of this phase is an intermediate code (IC) tree, which is basically a transformed abstract syntax tree at a lower level of abstraction. For example, in Clite the token + is used to indicate both integer and floating point addition. In the IC tree there might be separate operators for each type of addition. The broad issues of type checking, as well as a type checker for Clite, are discussed more fully in a later chapter.

The purpose of the *code optimization* phase of a compiler is to improve the intermediate code based on the target machine architecture. Common improvements include finding constant expressions and evaluating them at compile-time, reordering code to improve cache performance, finding common subexpressions and replacing them with a reference to a temporary, and so on. A good code optimizer can greatly improve a program's runtime execution speed.

The final phase of the compiler is the *code generation* phase, in which target machine code is constructed. This phase is responsible for deciding which machine instructions to use, how to allocate registers, and other machine dependent details.

In contrast to a compiler, an *interpreter* is a form of translator in which the last two compiler phases are replaced by a program that directly executes (or interprets) the intermediate code. There are two general kinds of interpreters: pure and mixed. In a *pure interpreter* each statement is tokenized, parsed, semantically checked, and interpreted each time it is executed. Most Basic translators and virtually all shell command interpreters, for example, Bourne shell, are pure interpreters. In contrast, most scripting languages, for example, Perl, are translated using *mixed interpreters*, which first translate the entire script (or program) once per execution into intermediate code and then repeatedly interpret the intermediate code without further translation.

Sun's Java JDK is an unusual example of a mixed interpreter system in that the Java compiler `javac` *compiles* Java source code into an external form of intermediate code known as a *byte code* file that is interpreted using a virtual machine called the "Java Virtual Machine" (JVM for short). The Java byte code interpreter is named `java`, and it simulates the behavior of the JVM. Further complicating the situation, in recent years

Sun has added an "on the fly" code generator to the interpreter that translates frequently executed portions of the program to native machine code.

Later chapters use Clite as a basis for discussing type systems and semantics, as well as for representing expressions in a recurring example on symbolic differentiation. This chapter continues the discussion of syntax by examining the transition from syntax to semantics.

2.5 LINKING SYNTAX AND SEMANTICS

So far, we have explored tools for defining the lexical and syntactic levels of a language, including an overview of the lexical and syntactic analysis phases of a compiler. It would seem that the output of the parser (syntactic analysis phase) should be a parse tree. In this section we consider the idea of an alternative to the parse tree for representing the structure and content of a program.

The need for such an alternative is manifold. Take another look at the parse tree given in Figure 2.9. Since many of the nonterminals in that tree convey no information, it would be useful to get rid of them. Suppose we perform the following transformations on this parse tree:

1 Discard all the separator (or punctuation) terminal symbols, such as semicolons.
2 Discard all nonterminals which are trivial roots, that is, ones with only a single subtree. An example is the symbol *Term* which is the leftmost interior tree node derivable from *Expression*.
3 Finally, replace the remaining nonterminals with the operators which are a leaf of one of their immediate subtrees. An example is replacing the symbol *Assignment* with the operator =.

What results is a tree like the one given in Figure 2.10, which is called an *abstract syntax* tree. It is helpful to contrast this tree with the original parse tree in Figure 2.9. The abstract syntax tree contains fewer intermediate nodes and subtrees, while it has the same essential structure as the original expression. Thus, this tree contains all the important information of the original parse tree, but is much smaller. These gains would be far more dramatic when parsing a complete program that uses the entire grammar for Clite.

A second argument for using abstract syntax is that it can reveal the essential syntactic elements in a program without over-specifying the details of how they are written by the programmer. Consider, for example, the following Pascal and C/C++ looping statements:

Pascal	*C/C++*
| ```
while i<n do begin
      i := i + 1
end
``` | ```
while (i<n) {
      i = i + 1;
}
``` |

These two loops obviously accomplish the same result; their syntactic differences are not essential to the fundamental looping process that they represent.

When thinking about a loop abstractly, we discover that the only essential elements are a *test* expression (i<n in this case) for continuing the loop and a statement which is

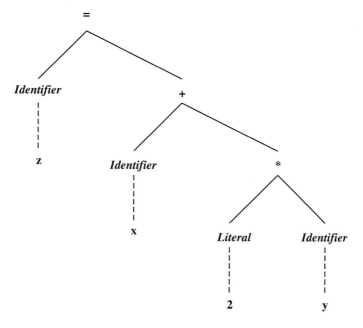

| Figure 2.10   Abstract Syntax Tree for z = x + 2 * y ;

the *body* of the loop to be repeated (incrementing the variable i in this case). All the other elements that appear in these two looping statements constitute nonessential *syntactic sugar*.

2.5.1 Abstract Syntax

Thus, it is valuable to define the structure of a programming language on a more functional level than that which is offered by its EBNF syntax. *Abstract syntax* is a notation that allows the parser to strip away the syntactic sugar and generate a tree that contains only the essential elements of the computation.

The abstract syntax of a programming language can be defined using a set of rules of the following form:

$$Lhs = Rhs$$

where *Lhs* is the name of an abstract syntactic class and *Rhs* defines the class as:

1   A list of one or more alternatives. For instance, in the concrete syntax of the Clite grammar in Figure 2.7, there are really only four kinds of *Expression*: identifiers, literals or values, ones with a unary operator, and ones with a binary operator.

2   A list of essential components that define a member of that class, separated by semicolons (;). Each such component has the form of an ordinary declaration, identifying an abstract syntax class and a list of one or more field names, separated by commas (,).

$$Assignment = Variable \texttt{ target; } Expression \texttt{ source}$$
$$Expression = Variable \mid Value \mid Binary \mid Unary$$
$$Binary = Operator \texttt{ op; } Expression \texttt{ term1, term2}$$
$$Unary = Operator \texttt{ op; } Expression \texttt{ term}$$
$$Variable = String \texttt{ id}$$
$$Value = Integer \texttt{ value}$$
$$Operator = \texttt{ + } \mid \texttt{ - } \mid \texttt{ * } \mid \texttt{ / } \mid \texttt{ !}$$

| **Figure 2.11**   **Partial Abstract Syntax for the Grammar of Figure 2.7**

An abstract syntax class in either alternative may correspond to a well-known mathematical domain, such as *Integer*, *String*, or *Boolean*. The purpose of the field names permits semantic processing to reference abstract components by name.

Consider, for example, the concrete syntactic rules for *Assignment* and *Expression* that appear in Figure 2.7; an abstract syntax for this grammar is given in Figure 2.11. The rule for *Expression* is an instance of the first type of abstract syntax rule, while *Assignment* is an instance of the second type of rule. The definition of a *Binary* expression indicates the potential usefulness of having field names since it contains two *Expressions*. Not surprisingly, since the concrete grammar is recursive, so too is the abstract syntax definition.

For example, consider the abstract syntax of a *Binary* expression. The definition in Figure 2.11 defines the abstract syntax class *Expression* as having three components: op, which is a member of the abstract syntax class *Operator*; and term1 and term2, which are members of the abstract syntax class *Expression*.

One immediate by-product of using abstract syntax is that it provides a basis for defining the abstract structure of a language as a set of Java classes. Below, for instance, is a prototype Java class definition for the abstract syntax of *Expression*:

```
class Binary extends Expression {
    Operator op;
    Expression term1, term2;
}
```

While this prototype definition ignores many implementation issues (visibility, constructors, accessor methods, and so on), it does contain all the instance variables that characterize the class *Binary*. That is, a Binary is a kind of Expression and has an op which is an Operator and a term1 and term2, which are members of the class Expression.[5]

In Figure 2.11, the abstract syntax class *Expression* represents a group consisting of multiple abstract syntax classes, including variables, integer values (literals), and expressions involving binary and unary operators and the appropriate number of operands.

---

5. The notion of class hierarchy that is built into object-oriented languages like Java makes this particular specification straightforward to implement. Another feature of Java objects that emerges by this approach to abstract syntax is the ability to query an object to determine its class. We shall exploit these features of Java as we discuss the type systems and runtime semantics of languages in later chapters.

In terms of a Java implementation, groups such as an *Expression* would be implemented as an abstract class, since no object could be created as a `new Expression()`.

```
abstract class Expression { }
```

Hopefully, we have now made a case for separating abstract syntax from concrete syntax. While the two are, in a sense, redundant, in another sense they are not. That is, the concrete syntax tells the programmer concretely what to write in order to have a valid program in language X. However, the abstract syntax allows valid programs in language X and language Y to share common abstract representations. Ideally, an interpreter or run-time system for a program worries less about how certain ideas, like loops, are expressed concretely and more about what specific computational requirements are to be conveyed out of the expression and into the run-time environment for the program.

That is the role of the abstract syntax: to provide a link between syntax and semantics, between form and function. We explore the usage of that link in later chapters.

2.5.2 Abstract Syntax Trees

Consider the rules in Figure 2.11 that define the abstract syntactic class *Expression* and its subclasses *Binary* and *Unary*. These rules name the essential elements of an *Expression* without regard to how it is formed concretely by the parser. That is, the concrete syntax provides the definition of the form of an expression, while the abstract syntax provides the definition of its essential elements.

An abstract syntax tree provides a concise vehicle for describing the individual elements of an *Expression,* throwing away the intermediate nodes and subtrees that do not contain essential information. To build an abstract syntax tree, each abstract syntactic category—like *Binary*—has an associated node with as many fields as there are distinct elements on the right-hand side of its rule. For instance, the node associated with a *Binary* has three fields, and looks like Figure 2.12.

In contrast, the abstract syntax category *Expression* has no information fields; it serves merely as a grouping mechanism. Hence, an *Expression* need not be implemented as a node; as already noted, a Java implementation would typically implement an *Expression* as an abstract class. As an example, Figure 2.13 shows a Java implementation of the abstract syntax tree for the assignment statement `z = x + 2 * y;`.

2.5.3 Abstract Syntax of Clite

Abstract syntax, as discussed in Section 2.5, forms a basis for linking the syntax and semantic analysis phases of a compiler. As we have seen, it allows a considerably more compact parse tree than the concrete syntax, and yet it conveys all the required information for semantic processing. That is, abstract syntax is adequate for determining the meaning of a program.

In the next few chapters, Clite will be used as a vehicle for discussing many technical aspects of modern imperative and object-oriented programming languages. Because it is a subset of C/C++, Clite will be familiar to readers who have written some programs

| Figure 2.12   **Structure of a Binary Node**

op	term1	term2

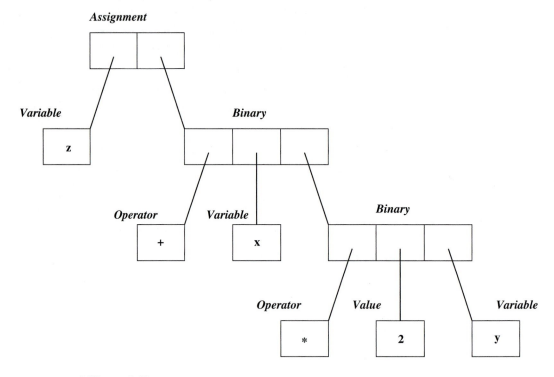

| **Figure 2.13**   **Abstract Syntax Tree for the** *Assignment* z = x + 2 * y ;

in C, C++, Ada, or Java. In later chapters, the abstract syntax of Clite will serve as a starting point for discussing important features of type systems, runtime semantics, and memory management. This section introduces the abstract syntax of Clite.

The abstract syntax of Clite extends the basic ideas presented in this previous section. An informal summary of the categories and their meanings is given below:

Program: having *Declarations* and a *Compound*.

Declarations: a sequence of individual *Declarations*.

Declaration: an individual variable, its type and size (if an array).

Type: a member of the set {int, bool, float, char}.

Statement: having subclasses *Compound, Skip, Assignment, Conditional,* and *Loop*.

Compound: a sequence of individual *Statements* that are executed in the order they appear. Each one appears at the same level in an abstract syntax tree.

Skip: the empty statement.

Assignment: a statement that assigns the value of an *Expression* to a variable.

Conditional: having an *Expression* (the test) and two *Statements* (the thenbranch and the elsebranch), one of which is executed and the other is skipped. In the case of an if-then statement, the elsebranch is instantiated as a *Skip* statement.

$$Program = Declarations\ \texttt{decpart};\quad Statements\ \texttt{body};$$
$$Declarations = Declaration^*$$
$$Declaration = VariableDecl\ |\ ArrayDecl$$
$$VariableDecl = Variable\ \texttt{v};\ Type\ \texttt{t}$$
$$ArrayDecl = Variable\ \texttt{v};\ Type\ \texttt{t};\ Integer\ \texttt{size}$$
$$Type = \texttt{int}\ |\ \texttt{bool}\ |\ \texttt{float}\ |\ \texttt{char}$$
$$Statements = Statement^*$$
$$Statement = Skip\ |\ Block\ |\ Assignment\ |\ Conditional\ |\ Loop$$
$$Skip =$$
$$Block = Statements$$
$$Conditional = Expression\ \texttt{test};\ Statement\ \texttt{thenbranch, elsebranch}$$
$$Loop = Expression\ \texttt{test};\ Statement\ \texttt{body}$$
$$Assignment = VariableRef\ \texttt{target};\ Expression\ \texttt{source}$$
$$Expression = VariableRef\ |\ Value\ |\ Binary\ |\ Unary$$
$$VariableRef = Variable\ |\ ArrayRef$$
$$Binary = Operator\ \texttt{op};\ Expression\ \texttt{term1, term2}$$
$$Unary = UnaryOp\ \texttt{op};\ Expression\ \texttt{term}$$
$$Operator = BooleanOp\ |\ RelationalOp\ |\ ArithmeticOp$$
$$BooleanOp = \texttt{\&\&}\ |\ \texttt{||}$$
$$RelationalOp = \texttt{=}\ |\ \texttt{!=}\ |\ \texttt{<}\ |\ \texttt{<=}\ |\ \texttt{>}\ |\ \texttt{>=}$$
$$ArithmeticOp = \texttt{+}\ |\ \texttt{-}\ |\ \texttt{*}\ |\ \texttt{/}$$
$$UnaryOp = \texttt{!}\ |\ \texttt{-}$$
$$Variable = String\ \texttt{id}$$
$$ArrayRef = String\ \texttt{id};\ Expression\ \texttt{index}$$
$$Value = IntValue\ |\ BoolValue\ |\ FloatValue\ |\ CharValue$$
$$IntValue = Integer\ \texttt{intValue}$$
$$FloatValue = Float\ \texttt{floatValue}$$
$$BoolValue = Boolean\ \texttt{boolValue}$$
$$CharValue = Character\ \texttt{charValue}$$

| **Figure 2.14**   **Abstract Syntax of Clite**

Loop: having an *Expression* (the test) and a *Statement* (the body of the loop) that is repeated as long as the test remains *true*.

Expression: having subclasses *Variable, Value, Binary,* and *Unary.*

Binary: having an *Operator* and two *Expressions.*

Unary: having an *Operator* and a single *Expression.*

Operator: &&, ||, !, <, <=, ==, ! =, >, >=, +, −, ∗, and /, representing:

> The boolean operators: `and`, `or`, `not`;
>
> The relational operators: `less than`, `less or equal`, `equal`, `not equal`, `greater than`, `greater`, `or equal`; and
>
> The arithmetic operators: `plus`, `minus`, `times`, `divide`.

Value: having subclasses *IntValue*, *FloatValue*, *BoolValue*, and *CharValue*.

IntValue: having an integer value.

FloatValue: having a floating point value, representing a computer approximation to a non-integer value.

BoolValue: having a Boolean value, that is, either `true` or `false`.

CharValue: having a single character value.

A formal description of the abstract syntax of Clite is given in Figure 2.14. This description provides an adequate foundation from which an abstract syntax tree for an entire program can be described.

A complete parser for Clite that can produce abstract syntax trees for Clite programs (like the fragment shown in Figure 2.13) is available at the book website. This is a useful tool for readers who want to work with the hands-on aspects of syntax that appear in many exercises at the end of the next few chapters.

2.6 SUMMARY

This chapter has introduced the basic idea of syntax and its importance to the design of contemporary programming languages. *Syntax* refers to the structure of a program's text, while *semantics* refers to its meaning, or runtime behavior. Programmers benefit from having a language whose syntax is easily learned and clearly understood.

Ambiguity in syntactic description occurs when a program fragment has two or more different interpretations. Syntactic ambiguity can be generally avoided, especially when a formal metalanguage like EBNF is used. Many language features, like *associativity* and *precedence* of operators, can be clearly and concisely defined by such a syntax description.

The syntax of a language is conveniently described at two levels—the *lexical* level and the *concrete* level. Lexical syntax helps define several fundamental classes of *tokens* in a language, like identifiers and constants.

A compiler has several stages, the first two being lexical and syntactic analysis. The remaining stages of a compiler—semantic analysis, code optimization, and code generation—depend upon successful completion of the first two stages. The notion of *abstract syntax* provides a means by which the essential elements of a program can be passed to these later stages for efficient analysis.

A small minilanguage called Clite is introduced in this chapter to help clarify various issues in syntax. We shall return to this language in later chapters as we explore language design issues beyond syntax—types, names, functions, and semantics.

EXERCISES

2.1   Using the grammar $G_{integer}$, develop a leftmost derivation for the integer 4520. How many steps are required for this derivation? In general, how many steps are required to derive an integer with an arbitrary number, say d, of *Digits*?

2.2   Using the grammar $G_{integer}$, develop a rightmost derivation for the integer 4520.

2.3   Develop a leftmost derivation for the *Identifier* value *a2i*, using the BNF syntax given in Figure 2.7.

2.4   Develop a rightmost derivation for the *Identifier* value *a2i*, using the BNF syntax given in Figure 2.7.

2.5   Using the grammar of Figure 2.7, draw parse trees for each of the following:
(a) x = x + a - 1;
(b) a = b * c / d;
(c) i = i + j * k - 3;

2.6   Using the following grammar:

> *Expr* → *Expr* + *Term* | *Expr* * *Term* | *Term*
> *Term* → 0 | ... | 9 | (*Expr*)

draw a parse tree for each of the following:
(a) 5 + 4 * 3
(b) 5 * 4 + 3

2.7   Using the following grammar:

> *Expr* → *Term* + *Expr* | *Term* * *Expr* | *Term*
> *Term* → 0 | ... | 9 | (*Expr*)

draw a parse tree for each of the following:
(a) 5 + 4 * 3
(b) 5 * 4 + 3

2.8   Using the following grammar:

> *Expr* → *Expr* + *Term* | *Term*
> *Term* → *Term* + *Factor* | *Factor*
> *Factor* → 0 | ... | 9 | (*Expr*)

draw a parse tree for each of the following:
(a) 5 + 4 * 3
(b) 5 * 4 + 3

2.9   Using the following grammar:

> *Expr* → *Expr* + *Expr* | *Expr* * *Expr* |
>   0 | ... | 9 | (*Expr*)

draw a parse tree for each of the following:
(a) 5 + 4 * 3
(b) 5 * 4 + 3

2.10 Using the following grammar:

$$Expr \rightarrow + Expr\ Expr\ |\ * Expr\ Expr\ |$$
$$0\ |\ \ldots\ |\ 9$$

draw a parse tree for each of the following:
(a) + 5 * 4 3
(b) + * 5 4 3

2.11 Argue convincingly that the parse tree given in Figure 2.2 for the expression $5 - 4 + 3$ is the only possible parse tree. Hint: enumerate the other possibilities and show that they do not work.

2.12 Show how the Java subgrammar for *IfThenStatement* eliminates any ambiguity in the if statement. That is, sketch the parse tree using the Java BNF rules, and then argue that no other parse trees can be found using these rules.

2.13 Consider the grammar rules for *IfStatement* and *Statement* given in Section 2.1.5. Show how they can be altered to eliminate their ambiguity illustrated in the text. That is, show how the grammar can be changed so that the programmer can explicitly distinguish the two alternative attachments of the "dangling else," as shown below:

```
if (x<0) if (x==0) y = y - 1; else y = 0; fi
if (x<0) if (x==0) y = y - 1; fi else y = 0; fi
```

Here, the new keyword fi is used to end any statement that begins with the keyword if. (It functions like a right brace, where the if is the left brace.)

2.14 Give a grammar and an example if statement for each of the following languages: (a) Perl, (b) Python, (c) Ada.

2.15 Give translation rules for the EBNF alternatives involving metabrackets and metaparentheses to standard BNF.

2.16 Rewrite grammar G_2 as a set of syntax diagrams.

2.17 Pick one of the following languages: Perl, Python, Ada, C, C++, Java, or another instructor-approved language. Consult an authoritative source and write a report that summarizes the definition of the language with respect to size and type of its grammar, the appearance of ambiguity in the grammar, its number of reserved words, the precedence and associativity of operators, and so on. Cite your sources.

2.18 Research the number of reserved words in each of the following languages: (a) Perl, (b) Python, (c) Ada, (d) C, (e) C++, (f) Java.

2.19 Give a set of grammar rules that define the syntax of a variable declaration in Perl. Give an example.

2.20 Draw an abstract syntax tree for each of the parse trees that you defined for Exercise 2.5, using the abstract syntax for *Assignment* given in Figure 2.11.

Lexical and Syntactic Analysis

"Syntactic sugar causes cancer of the semicolon."

Alan Perlis

CHAPTER OUTLINE

The purpose of this chapter is to provide an overview of the implementation of a lexer (lexical analyzer) and a parser (syntactic analyzer). Because the lexer is based on a simpler model than a context-free grammar, the chapter begins with a brief look at the Chomsky grammar hierarchy.

In Section 3.2 we examine alternative specifications of tokens of Clite, including regular sets and deterministic finite state automata. The latter provides a model that is easily implemented, as we demonstrate by showing a partial implementation for the lexical portion of the Clite grammar.

Next we develop a recursive descent parser for a small portion of the concrete syntax of Clite. In order to do so, we develop a number of auxiliary algorithms. We then show how to convert an EBNF grammar to a recursive descent parser.

This chapter is not intended to replace a course on compiler construction. However, it is useful for those schools that do not offer such a course and for those students who do not take such a course. Also, knowing how to construct a recursive descent parser is a very useful algorithm to have in one's repertoire, particularly for "little languages." For example, some of the solutions to exercises in this text use the technique of describing data using a simple grammar and then constructing an internal representation for the data using a simple recursive descent parser (see Exercise 3.21).

3.1 CHOMSKY HIERARCHY

Chomsky [1957] defined four classes of grammars, each of which corresponds to a unique class of language and theoretical machine. In order from the simplest to the most complex, these types of grammars are:

- Regular grammars.
- Context-free grammars (equivalent to BNF grammars).
- Context-sensitive grammars.
- Unrestricted grammars.

Only the first two categories are used in programming languages; the last two categories are included only for completeness. Context-free grammars were discussed in Section 2.1.

Recall from Section 2.1 that a grammar consists of a set of productions, a set of nonterminal symbols N, a set of terminal symbols T, and a start symbol S that must be a nonterminal. Terminal symbols are the alphabet of the language being defined, whereas nonterminal symbols represent language concepts. Using the concrete syntax of Clite as an example, terminal symbols include the reserved words (e.g., while, if), literals (e.g., 542, 1.5, true), operators, etcetera. Nonterminals represent Clite concepts such as a *Statement*, an *Expression*, etcetera.

In the Chomsky hierarchy, only the form of a production changes from one type of grammar to another. The concept of terminals, nonterminals, and the start symbol remains the same.

Regular grammars are the simplest class, and are equivalent to so-called *regular expressions* and *finite-state automata* (both discussed in Section 3.2) in their expressive power. A *right regular grammar* (or right linear grammar) may only have productions of the following form:

$$A \rightarrow \omega \, B$$
$$A \rightarrow \omega$$

where $\omega \in T^*$ (a string of zero or more terminals[1]) and $B \in N$ (a single nonterminal). In other words each alternative of a production can have at most one nonterminal and, if present, it must be the rightmost symbol. Nonterminal B may be the same nonterminal as A; that is, direct recursion is permitted. Rewriting the production for *Integer* of Figure 2.7 (Clite) as a right regular grammar we get:

$$Integer \rightarrow 0 \; Integer \; | \; \ldots \; | \; 9 \; Integer \; |$$
$$0 \; | \; \ldots \; | \; 9$$

---

1. T^* is another example of the use of the Kleene star notation.

or equivalently in EBNF:

$Integer \rightarrow (0 \mid \ldots \mid 9) \, Integer \mid$
$\qquad 0 \mid \ldots \mid 9$

An alternative defines *left regular grammars* (or left linear grammars) equivalently except that the single nonterminal in an alternative, if present, must be the leftmost symbol. Rewriting the production for *Integer* of Figure 2.7 (Clite) as a left regular grammar we get:

$Integer \rightarrow Integer \, 0 \mid \ldots \mid Integer \, 9 \mid$
$\qquad 0 \mid \ldots \mid 9$

or equivalently in EBNF:

$Integer \rightarrow Integer \, (0 \mid \ldots \mid 9) \mid$
$\qquad 0 \mid \ldots \mid 9$

Regular grammars, and their equivalent forms of regular expressions and finite state automata, are used in the construction of tokenizers for converting streams of characters to tokens (or basic symbols). This is discussed in detail in Section 3.2.

Regular grammars are considerably less powerful than context-free or BNF grammars. For example, a well known theorem is that the language

$$\{a^n b^n \mid n \geq 1\}$$

is not a regular language; that is, the language cannot be generated by a regular grammar. In a programming language grammar such as Clite, some terminal symbols do come in matching pairs: parentheses in expressions, braces in statement lists, etcetera. Regular languages cannot handle the simplest case of balancing parentheses, where all the left parentheses precede all the right parentheses. Therefore, regular grammars are inadequate to properly describe the syntax of a programming language.

Context-free grammars, in the form of BNF grammars, have already been discussed in some detail. An advantage of context-free grammars is that for a wide class of unambiguous grammars, there are table-driven parsers (see Observation on page 81). Context-free grammars correspond to push-down automata, which are discussed in Section 3.3.

Context-sensitive grammars have productions defined as follows [Hopcroft and Ullman, 1979]:

$$\alpha \rightarrow \beta$$

such that $|\alpha| \leq |\beta|$, where $\alpha, \beta \in (N \cup T)^*$. That is, unlike context-free grammars, the left-hand side symbol is not restricted to being a single nonterminal, but instead can consist of a string containing both terminal and nonterminal symbols. The restriction on context-sensitive grammars is that the length of the right-hand side of an alternative cannot be smaller than the size of the left-hand side, except that the start symbol may derive the empty string. In a derivation the sentential form cannot shrink in size from one derivation step to the next. Context-sensitive grammars can ensure that program identifiers are declared and have the type appropriate for the context.

From the point of view of defining the syntax and semantics of a programming language, context-sensitive languages (i.e., languages defined by a context-sensitive grammar G) have many undesirable properties; for example:

- Given a terminal string ω and grammar G, it is undecidable whether or not $\omega \in L(G)$, that is, whether ω is derivable from G. In our terms, it is undecidable whether a program is valid according to G.

- Given a terminal string ω and grammar G, it is undecidable whether L(G) has any valid strings. In other words, it is undecidable whether a context-sensitive grammar for Clite defines any valid Clite programs.

For our purposes, the term *undecidable* means that you cannot write a computer program that is guaranteed to halt for all its inputs and decide the question. For such reasons, context-sensitive grammars are not used in the treatment of programming language syntax.[2]

Unrestricted grammars drop the length restriction on the size of a right-hand side. Unrestricted grammars are equivalent to Turing machines, or, equivalently, full C/C++. Unrestricted grammars can compute any computable function [Hopcroft and Ullman, 1979]. From the viewpoint of defining the syntax of a programming language, unrestricted grammars suffer from the same undesirable properties as context-sensitive grammars.

3.2 LEXICAL ANALYSIS

As already noted in Section 2.4, the purpose of the lexical analysis phase of a compiler is to transform the source program from a sequence of characters to a sequence of tokens. In the process, whitespace and comments are discarded. In this section, we show how a lexer is designed and implemented for the lexical portion of the Clite grammar of Figure 2.7, augmented by the definitions of whitespace and comments.

> **Definition**: A *token* is a logically cohesive sequence of characters representing a single symbol.

Examples include an identifier, a reserved word (e.g., `while`), a literal (e.g. `3.1416`), an operator (e.g., `!=`), and punctuation (e.g., `;`).

As discussed in Section 2.4, historically the lexer has been a separate phase for the following reasons:

1 The design of the lexical analyzer is based on a much simpler and faster machine model than the context-free model used for syntactic analysis.

2 For a non-optimizing compiler, approximately 75 percent of the total compile time is often consumed in lexical analysis. Any improvement that makes this phase run faster has a comparable impact on total compile time.

3 Prior to the creation of ASCII, each computer had its own idiosyncratic character set. Hiding this character set in the lexer made porting a compiler to a new machine

---

2. Context-sensitive issues such as name resolution and type-checking can be handled by an attribute grammar. An alternative explored in Chapter 8 is denotational semantics.

easier. Even today vestiges of this problem still exist, with the ASCII, Unicode, and EBCDIC character sets being used.

4 The end-of-line convention also varies from one operating system to another. For example, the Apple Macintosh uses a carriage return (ASCII code 13) as an end-of-line character, Linux/Unix uses a newline (or linefeed) character (ASCII code 10), and Microsoft Windows uses a carriage return/newline combination. For many modern languages, but not all, this problem is handled by the language's runtime support library. In earlier days it was not, so this operating system dependency was hidden inside the lexical analyzer.

The lexicon of Clite is the set of tokens that are defined by the grammar, plus the following grammatical categories:

- Identifiers, for example: `token`
- Integer literals, for example: `80`
- Floating point literals, for example: `3.1415`
- Character literals, for example: `'a'`

That is, for example, when the parser is expecting an identifier, it does not care which specific identifier is seen, just that it is an identifier. This is very different than a reserved word such as a `while`, which when seen at the beginning of a statement determines the type of statement and its structure. Boolean literals are left out of the list above because the only such literals are reserved words.

We need to add to the above list whitespace, comments, an end-of-line indicator (needed for `//` comments), and an end-of-file indicator. These added items, except the last, are discarded by the lexer, since the parser does not need to know about them. Thus, the complete list of sequences of characters to be recognized is:

- *Identifiers*: a letter followed by a sequence of zero or more letters and digits
- *Literals*, including:
  - Integer literals: a sequence of one or more digits
  - Floating point literals: a sequence of one or more digits followed by a period followed by a sequence of one or more digits
  - Character literals: ' a single printable character '
- Keywords: `bool char else false float if int main true while`
- Operators: `= || && == != < <= > >= + - * / ! [ ]`
- Punctuation: `; , { } ( )`
- Whitespace: space or tab characters
- Comments:
  - Single line: `//` any-characters end-of-line
- End-of-line
- End-of-file

Any other character is illegal.

In Section 3.2.1, an alternative way of specifying the lexicon of a programming language is presented.

3.2.1 Regular Expressions

An alternative to regular grammars for formally specifying a language at the lexical level is the *regular expression*. The language of regular expressions is summarized below, using syntax adapted from the Lex family [Mason *et al.*, 1992] of lexical generators:

Regular Expression	Meaning
x	A character x (stands for itself)
\x	An escaped character, e.g., \n
{ name }	A reference to a name
M | N	M or N
M N	M followed by N (concatenation)
M*	Zero or more occurrences of M
M+	One or more occurrences of M
M?	Zero or one occurrence of M
[aeiou]	The set of vowels: a, e, i, o, u
[0-9]	The set of digits, 0 through 9
.	Any single character

Note that Lex uses \ to escape characters that would otherwise be interpreted as metacharacters (such as braces, \{ and \}), whereas here we use the fixed width font for all nonmetacharacters.

With these conventions, we now redefine Clite's various lexical syntactic classes in Figure 3.1. Note that parentheses can be used to group elements of a regular expression. Each line consists of the category being defined and its definition as a regular expression.

The first six definitions are ancillary ones. The first definition defines the set of printable characters in ASCII as consisting of all the characters from the space character

Category	Definition
anyChar	[-~]
letter	[a-zA-Z]
digit	[0-9]
whitespace	[\t]
eol	\n
eof	\004
keyword	bool | char | else | false | float | if | int | main | true | while
identifier	{ letter }({ letter } | { digit })+
integerLit	{ digit }+
floatLit	{ digit }+\.{ digit }+
charLit	'{ anyChar }'
operator	= | || | && | == | != | < | <= | > | >= | + | - | * | / | ! | [|]
separator	; | , | { | } | (|)
comment	//({ anyChar } | { whitespace })*{eol}

| **Figure 3.1** **Regular Expressions for Clite Lexical Syntax**

(ASCII code 27) through the tilde character (ASCII code 126). The second line defines the set of letters, including both upper and lower case, while the third line defines the set of digits. Next the whitespace characters, excluding end-of-line, are defined. The final two ancillary definitions define the end-of-line and end-of-file characters using conventions adapted from Linux/Unix.

The remaining lines, except the last, define the various tokens: identifiers; keywords; integer, floating point, and character literals; operators; and separators (or punctuation). The last definition specifies a // comment, which can include printable characters and whitespace, terminating with the end of a line (represented by a newline or linefeed character).

Regular expressions are a popular tool in language design because they readily support the automatic generation of lexical analyzers. That is, rather than manually designing and writing code for a lexical analyzer, one can submit the regular expressions directly to a lexical-analyzer generator. Two commonly used generators are the Lex family (Lex, Flex, etc.) for generating C/C++ code and JLex for generating Java code. More information about this can be found in various texts on compiler design [Aho *et al.*, 1986; Appel, 1998].

Given the above definition of the input space, how do we design a program to recognize these sequences? We explore this question next.

3.2.2 Finite State Automata

As already noted, there are several equivalent ways of specifying the input space of a lexer: natural language (such as given above), a regular grammar (preferably right regular), or regular expressions. Translators for the latter two convert them first to a *deterministic finite state automaton* (DFSA) and then extract a lexer from the DFSA.

Once having acquired the understanding of how a DFSA to recognize tokens and other sequences of characters (such as comments) is constructed and converted to code, for simple character sequences one rarely has to go through the exercise again. However, in an attempt to avoid this discussion of DFSAs, the first edition of this text presented an ad hoc design. The solutions to Exercises 3.14 and 3.15 present types of problems in which the material in this section should always be used; the authors have encountered compilers in which these problems were incorrect.

> **Definition**: A *finite state automaton* has:
> 1   A set of states, represented by nodes in a graph.
> 2   An input alphabet, augmented by a unique symbol representing end of input.
> 3   A state transition function, represented by directed edges from one node to another, labeled by one or more alphabet symbols.
> 4   A unique start state.
> 5   A set of one or more *final states* (states with no exiting edges).

A finite state automaton is *deterministic* if for each state and input symbol there is at most one outgoing arc from the state labeled with that input symbol.

For example, a finite state automaton that recognizes identifiers is given in Figure 3.2, where S is the start state and F is the final state. The symbol l represents the set of letters, while the symbol d represents the set of digits; $\$$ is the end of input marker. The automaton in Figure 3.2 is deterministic.

Figure 3.2   A Finite State Automaton for Identifiers

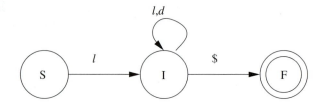

A *configuration* of a finite state automaton consists of a state and the remaining input, terminated by the special end of input symbol. A *move* consists of traversing the arc exiting the state that corresponds to the leftmost input symbol, thereby consuming it; if no move is defined for the state-input symbol pair, the automaton halts in error, rejecting the input. An input is *accepted* if, starting with the start state, the automaton consumes all its symbols and halts in a final state.

Using the automaton of Figure 3.2, the following steps are taken to accept the input a2i$ starting in state S:

1   Move to state I with input 2i$.
2   Move to state I with input i$.
3   Move to state I with input $.
4   Move to state F with no remaining input.

Since state F is a final state, a2i is thus accepted as a valid identifier. Formally, this sequence of steps is written as follows:

$$
\begin{aligned}
(S, a2i\$) &\vdash (I, 2i\$) \\
&\vdash (I, i\$) \\
&\vdash (I, \$) \\
&\vdash (F,)
\end{aligned}
$$

where $\vdash$ denotes a *move*. Thus, we have shown:

$$(S, a2i\$) \vdash^* (F,)$$

that is, the DFSA accepts the string $a2i\$$ in zero or more moves, terminating in a final state. Note that $\vdash^*$ is another use of the Kleene-star notation.

To facilitate the design of a DFSA for recognizing the lexical syntax of Clite, the following conventions will be used:

- An explicit terminator symbol appears only for the Clite source program as a whole, rather than for each lexical category.

- The symbol l represents an arbitrary letter and d an arbitrary digit. The symbols *eoln* and *eof* represent end-of-line and end-of-file respectively. All other symbols represent themselves.

- An unlabeled directed arc represents any other valid input symbol; that is, the set of all valid input symbols minus the arc labels for the other arcs exiting from the same state.

- Recognition of tokens ends in a final state (one with no exiting arcs).
- Recognition of nontokens have arcs back to the start state.
- Recognition of end of file, representing the end of the source program.

Finally, the automaton must be deterministic. To ensure this, we drop the recognition of keywords from the DFSA, since they form a subset of the identifiers. We also consider together all token classes that have a common prefix. For example, both `int` and `float` literals begin with a sequence of digits. For another example, the division symbol and the comment both begin with a /, so they are considered together.

The required DFSA for Clite is sketched in Figure 3.3. To fit the diagram onto one page many of the cases for simple punctuation and operators are omitted (one of each type is presented). For example, the case for character + appears but the cases for the other other one-character tokens (-, *, and so on) are omitted. Similarly, the case for distinguishing the assignment operator (=) from the equality operator (==) is given, but not less than (<) vs. less or equal (<=), and so on. Note that occurrences of whitespace *ws*, including *eoln*, and comments transition back to the start state *S*. The subdiagrams for identifier and integer and floating point literal are similar to Figure 3.2.

It should also be noted that this design ignores reserved words, which greatly simplifies the DFSA. Instead, once having recognized an identifier, the code implementing the DFSA does a simple table lookup to distinguish reserved words from identifiers.

The lexical analyzer (lexer) implements this DFSA. In that implementation, the lexer assumes that parser calls it each time another token is needed. Thus, the lexer needs to remember where it left off consuming input source characters each time it is called.

Moreover, the presence of loops in the DFSA will cause the lexer to advance one character too far in the input. For example, consider the following source input:

```
if (a<b)
```

In the absence of whitespace after the a, the DFSA will recognize a as an *Identifier* only after advancing to the < symbol. The next call on the lexer will immediately advance to the next character, namely b. There are several possible solutions to this problem:

1   Use a peek (look-ahead) function to allow examination of the next character without consuming it. From an execution time perspective, this is the least efficient design.

2   Use a push-back function so that a character can be returned to the input when needed. The push-back would be used in recognizing identifiers and digit strings, for example, yet remains quite efficient.

3   Adopt the convention that moving out of the start state does **not** consume a character. From an execution time perspective, this is the most efficient design, since each character is examined exactly once.

Our DFSA design for Clite uses the third alternative. This necessitates introducing an extra transition to advance the input in several places. For example, in the case where a plus character (+) is seen exiting the start state, an unlabeled transition to a new state is added in order to remain one character ahead.

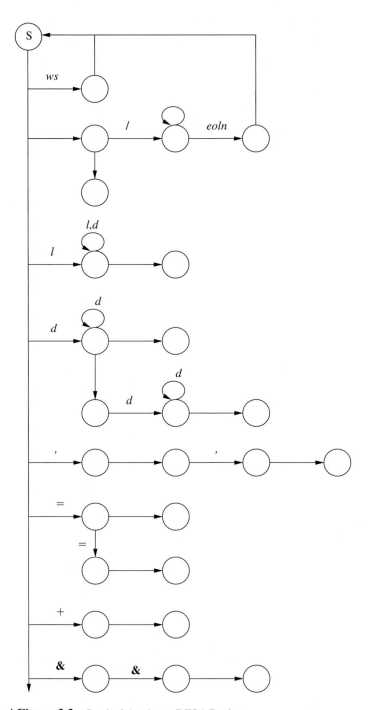

Figure 3.3 Lexical Analyzer DFSA Design

Here *ws* represents whitespace characters, *d* digits, *l* letters, *eoln* end-of-line, *eof* end-of-file, and all other characters themselves. An unlabeled arc represents all other characters.

Observation

Pushback function variant

An interesting variant of using a pushback function to perform a lookahead occurred in several of ETH's Pascal compilers. Pascal allowed subranges of the form x..y, where both x and y had to be either integer constants or integer literals. Consider the subrange 5..12 in the absence of whitespace. To distinguish it from the floating point literal 5.12, the compiler had to advance to the second period. Lacking a pushback feature, the lexer replaced the second period with a colon :. Testing confirmed that the compiler would accept 5:12 as a valid range, even though it was illegal Pascal lexical syntax.

3.2.3 From Design to Code

With these considerations in mind, we can now implement a DFSA for Clite.[3] Since the cases for both whitespace and comments loop back to the start state, at the outermost level, the function to get the next token should be a do-while loop containing a large switch statement, as shown in Figure 3.4.

The loop repeats until something other than whitespace or a comment is found, at which point the loop can be exited via a return statement. The variable ch containing the current input character must be global since its value must be remembered from one invocation of the method next to the next invocation; the variable ch is initialized to a space character.

To complete the DFSA to lexer code translation process, the following rules should be followed:

1 The code corresponding to traversing an arc from node *A* to node *B* must get the next character, unless *A* is the start state.
   (a) If the arc label *x* is a single character, there should be a test ch == x.
   (b) If the arc label x is a set, there should be a test that effectively implements *ch* ∈ *x*, that is, a test for *ch* in the desired set.

```
private char ch = ' ';
public Token next( ) {
      do {
            switch (ch) {

                  ...

            }
      } while (true);
}
```

| **Figure 3.4**   **Outline of Next Token Routine**

---

3. Strictly speaking, this step could be accomplished mechanically, as has been done in many parser generators. That is, we could generate tables representing the DFSA and use a table-driven algorithm as the lexer; early versions of Lex used this approach. The problem with this approach is that the resulting lexer performs up to 10 times slower than when the DFSA is hand-translated to code.

(c) If the arc is unlabeled, there should be a test to ensure that `ch` is not one of the labels on any of the other arcs. (If this is the only arc exiting the state, no test is needed.)

2 A node having an arc to itself corresponds to a `do-while` loop, where the condition corresponds to the arc's label.

3 Otherwise the move is translated to a `switch` (or `if`) statement, with each arc being a separate case. If one of the arcs is unlabeled, it becomes the default case. Otherwise, the default case is an error case.

4 A sequence of transitions becomes a sequence of translated statements.

5 A complex subdiagram is translated by boxing its components so that each box is effectively one node, and then translating each box using an outside-in strategy.

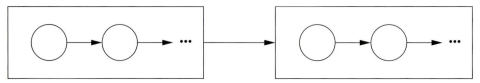

Applying these rules to the DFSA design in Figure 3.3 results in the code given in Figure 3.5, again with similar cases elided. To simplify this code, the auxiliary routine `nextChar` translates an end-of-line to the newline character and an end of file to a Control-D character, using common Linux/Unix conventions. These assumptions work for Clite because the source program is restricted to printable (noncontrol) characters (excepting only the tab character).

This skeleton uses several auxiliary methods to accomplish its task. Some are implementations of the auxiliary regular expression definitions, such as `isLetter`:

```
private boolean isLetter(char c) {
    return (c>='a' && c<='z' || c>='A' && c<='Z');
}
```

Others are methods representing common code. For example, the basic logic to process the characters of an identifier is repeated for processing a whole number and a decimal fraction:

```
private String concat(String set) {
    StringBuffer r = new StringBuffer("");
    do {
        r.append(ch);
        ch = nextChar();
    } while (set.indexOf(ch) >= 0);
    return r.toString( );
}
```

```
public Token next( ) { // Return next token
    do {
        if (isLetter(ch)) { // ident or keyword
            String spelling = concat(letters + digits);
            return Token.keyword(spelling);
        } else if (isDigit(ch)) { // int or float literal
            String number = concat(digits);
            if (ch != '.') // int Literal
                return Token.mkIntLiteral(number);
            number += concat(digits);
            return Token.mkFloatLiteral(number);
        } else switch (ch) {
        case ' ': case '\t': case '\r': case eolnCh:
            ch = nextChar();
            break;

        case '/': // divide or comment
            ch = nextChar();
            if (ch != '/') return Token.divideTok;
            // comment
            do {
                ch = nextChar();
            } while (ch != eolnCh);
            ch = nextChar();
            break;

        case '\': // char literal
            char ch1 = nextChar();
            nextChar(); // get '
            ch = nextChar();
            return Token.mkCharLiteral("" + ch1);

        case eofCh: return Token.eofTok;

        case '+': ch = nextChar();
            return Token.plusTok;
        ...
        case '&': check('&'); return Token.andTok;
        case '|': check('|'); return Token.orTok;

        case '=':
            return chkOpt('=', Token.assignTok,
                               Token.eqeqTok);
        ...
        } // switch
    } while (true);
}
```

| **Figure 3.5**   **Clite Lexer Tokenizer Method**

Two other auxiliary methods are `check` and `chkOpt`. The first of these, `check`, is used to process two character tokens in which the first character by itself is not a valid token; an example is the conjunction operator &&. The second, `chkOpt`, processes two character tokens in which the first character, by itself, is also a valid token. If its character argument is absent, it returns the first token argument; if present, it returns the second token argument. It also advances the source character stream as needed. In this case, an example is the assign operator = versus the equality operator ==.

A complete implementation of the `Lexer` and `Token` classes for the lexical syntax given in Figure 2.7 can be downloaded from the book website. Although this implementation is done in Java, it can easily be translated to C, C++, or Ada.

To illustrate the operation of the `Lexer`, consider the following example Clite program:

```
// a first program with
// two comment lines
int main() {
    char c;
    int i;
    c = 'h';
    i = c + 3;
} // main
```

For this program, the lexer produces the list of tokens given in Figure 3.6, excluding the end of file token. In the list, most tokens appear as themselves. Four token types (*Identifier*, *IntLiteral*, *FloatLiteral*, and *CharLiteral*) appear with their token type and their associated value.

3.3 SYNTACTIC ANALYSIS

Definition: The purpose of the *syntactic analyzer*, or *parser*, is to construct a parse tree using as input the stream of tokens provided by the lexer.

The output of the parser is usually an abstract syntax tree. The motivation for using an abstract syntax tree, rather than a parse tree, was discussed in Section 2.5.1.

```
int
main
(
)
{
char
Identifier c
;
int
Identifier i
;
```

```
Identifier c
=
CharLiteral h
;
Identifier i
=
Identifier c
+
IntLiteral 3
;
}
```

| **Figure 3.6**   **List of Tokens from Sample Program**

Definition: A *recursive descent* parser is one in which each nonterminal in the grammar is converted to a function which recognizes input derivable from that nonterminal.

For a language with a large grammar like C/C++, Java, or Ada, a parser generator would be used to generate a table-driven parser (see Observation on page 81). However, for languages with small grammars a recursive descent parser is preferred. Examples of such languages include configuration files, expressions in spreadsheets, and "little languages" like the one in Exercise 3.21.

As we saw in Section 2.1, the grammar of a programming language defines the structure of all the different parts of a program, such as arithmetic expressions (e.g., x+2*y), assignment statements (e.g., z=2*x+y;), loop statements (e.g., for (i=0; i<n; i++) a[i]=a[i] + 1;), function definitions, declarations of variables (e.g., int n;), and even complete programs. A language's EBNF syntax provides a precise definition upon which the generation of a parse tree from a stream of tokens can be based.

Consider the syntactic categories *Assignment* and *Expression*, which include all sequences of *Tokens* that describe arithmetic calculations and assignment of the result to a variable. A simple EBNF grammar for these categories, abbreviated out of the Clite grammar in Section 2.3, is shown in Figure 3.7. This grammar will serve as the example grammar for constructing a parser. In the grammar the terminal symbol *Literal* denotes only an integer literal, that is, an unsigned whole number.

3.3.1 Preliminary Definitions

In preparation for constructing a parser for this expression grammar, we need to define four preliminary concepts: *augmented grammars*, *First*, *nullable*, and *left dependency graph*.

Algorithms that construct parsers sometimes require the grammar to be in *augmented form*. In this form, a new start symbol S' is introduced with a single rule, namely:

$$S' \rightarrow S\,\$$$

where S is the original symbol and $\$$ is a new terminal symbol representing the end of information. For example, in Section 3.2 this terminal was the end-of-file token.

Another key concept used in the construction of parsers is the *First* set, which contains all terminals that are leftmost symbols derivable from a given symbol. That is:

$$First(X) = \{a \in T \mid X \Rightarrow^* aw, \; w \in (N \cup T)^*\}$$

Figure 3.7
Concrete Syntax for Assignments and Expressions

Assignment → *Identifier* = *Expression* ;

Expression → *Term* { *AddOp Term* }

AddOp → + | −

Term → *Factor* { *MulOp Factor* }

MulOp → * | /

Factor → [*UnaryOp*] *Primary*

UnaryOp → − | !

Primary → *Identifier* | *Literal* | (*Expression*)

First(X) can be read as the set of all terminal symbols that can occur as the leftmost symbol in a derivation starting from X. When X is a terminal symbol, it follows that:

$$First(a) = \{a\}$$

That is, the set *First(a)* contains only a itself.

When ω is an arbitrary string of terminals and nonterminals $X_1 \ldots X_n U \ldots$, the set *First(ω)* is defined as follows:

$$First(X_1 \ldots X_n U \ldots) = First(X_1) \cup \ldots First(X_n) \cup First(U)$$

$$\text{where } X_1, \ldots, X_n \text{ are nullable}$$

$$\text{and } U \text{ is not nullable.}$$

A nonterminal is *nullable* if it derives the empty string, that is:

$$A \Rightarrow^*$$

Since terminals do not derive anything but themselves, terminals are not nullable.

A first glance at the EBNF grammar of Figure 3.7 suggests that none of the nonterminals are nullable, since none of the alternatives for any nonterminal is empty. However, this is not the case. To find the set of nullable nonterminals, we can use the following algorithm [Knuth, 1971]:

```
int oldSize;
Set nullable = new Set();
do {
    oldSize = nullable.size();
    for (Production p : grammar.productions()) {
        boolean allNull = true;
        for (Symbol t : p.rule())
            if (! nullable.contains(t))
                allNull = false;
        if (allNull)
            nullable.add(p.nonterminal());
    }
} while (nullable.size() > oldSize); // nullable grew
```

Basically, the algorithm iterates over all the production rules in the grammar. For each such production p, if either p is an empty rule or all the symbols in the rule are nullable, then the nonterminal on the left-hand side of the production is added to the set of nullable symbols. This algorithm is guaranteed to halt; otherwise, each iteration of the do while would make the set nullable grow by at least one nonterminal symbol. However, the set of nonterminals in a grammar is always finite.

Before applying the algorithm to the grammar of Figure 3.7, let us rewrite the grammar, applying the following transformations:

1. Put the grammar into augmented form using $ to designate end of input.
2. Rename all the nonterminals using one and two character abbreviations, to facilitate drawing the needed graphs.

3 Abbreviate the token *Identifier* as i, and *Literal* as l.

4 Replace each metaconstruct with a named nonterminal as outlined at the end of Section 2.2. Recall that if A is a nonterminal and x, y, z are arbitrary sequences of terminals and nonterminals, then any EBNF rule having metabraces:

$$A \rightarrow x \{ y \} z$$

can be equivalently rewritten without metabraces as follows:

$$A \rightarrow x\, A'\, z$$
$$A' \rightarrow |\, y\, A'$$

where A' is a unique new nonterminal.

For example, applying these transformations to the grammar in Figure 3.7 we obtain the grammar in Figure 3.8. In this new grammar the nonterminals E' and T' represent the iteration in the original *Expression* and *Term* productions, while F' represents the optional *UnaryOp* in the original *Factor* production.

Now if we apply the nullable algorithm to this new grammar in Figure 3.8, we obtain the following sets of nullable nonterminals:

Pass	Nullable
1	$E'\ T'\ F'$
2	$E'\ T'\ F'$

The algorithm discovers all the nullable nonterminals on the first pass, but requires a second pass to discover that there are no additional ones.

Next, we define the *left dependency* graph of a grammar G. Each terminal or non-terminal symbol is a node in this graph. For each production of the form:

$$A \rightarrow U_1 \ldots U_n X w$$

Figure 3.8
Rewritten
Expression Grammar

$$S \rightarrow A\ \$$$
$$A \rightarrow i\ =\ E\ ;$$
$$E \rightarrow T\ E'$$
$$E' \rightarrow |\ AO\ T\ E'$$
$$AO \rightarrow +\ |\ -$$
$$T \rightarrow F\ T'$$
$$T' \rightarrow |\ MO\ F\ T'$$
$$MO \rightarrow *\ |\ /$$
$$F \rightarrow F'\ P$$
$$F' \rightarrow |\ UO$$
$$UO \rightarrow -\ |\ !$$
$$P \rightarrow i\ |\ l\ |\ (E)$$

Table 3.1

First Set for Expression Grammar

Nonterminal	First
A	i
E	! – i l (
E′	+ –
AO	+ –
T	! - i l (
T′	* /
MO	* /
F	! - i l (
F′	! –
UO	! –
P	i l (

we draw an arc from A to X if either $n = 0$ or $U_1, \ldots, U_n$ are nullable; that is, if either there is nothing to the left of X or all symbols to the left of X are nullable. Applying this rule to Figure 3.8 results in the left dependency graph of Figure 3.9.

Computing *First(A)* from the left dependency graph is now straightfoward. *First(A)* consists of all the terminal symbols in the left dependency graph which are reachable from A. Applying this method visually to the graph results in the column labeled **First** in Table 3.1.

An algorithm for computing all the nodes which are reachable from a given node can be sketched as follows:

```
Set reachable(Node start) {
    Set set = new Set( );
    set.add(start);
    int oldSize;
    do {
        oldSize = set.size();
        for (Node a : set)
            set.add(a.to( ));
    } while (set.size() > oldSize);
    return set;
}
```

3.3.2 Recursive Descent Parsing

With these initial concepts defined, we are now ready to construct a parser from an EBNF grammar. There are several different algorithms for parsing, and each has its advantages and disadvantages (see Observation on page 81). The particular parsing algorithm we present here is called a *recursive descent parser.*[4]

---

4. Formally, recursive descent parsing is a variant of LL(1) parsing, which moves from left to right in the input stream and needs to look ahead only one token to make any parsing decision. This feature is guaranteed by the particular grammar under consideration. Most modern languages, such as Java, have grammars that permit efficient parsing.

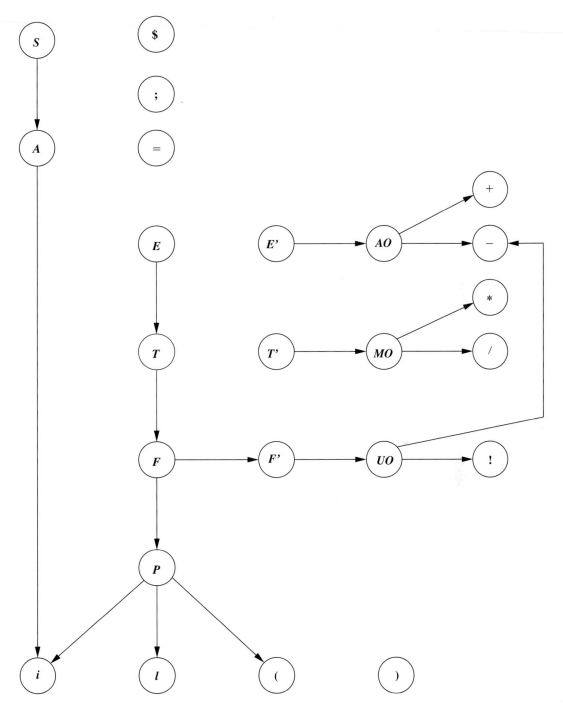

| **Figure 3.9   Left Dependency Graph for Expression Grammar**

The goal of any parser is to build a parse tree from the stream of tokens produced by the lexer. Recursive descent parsers have a method corresponding to each nonterminal in the grammar. The job of each such method is twofold:

1 To recognize the longest sequence of tokens derivable from it in the input stream, and
2 To build an abstract syntax subtree and return an object in the abstract class which is the root of that subtree.

Thus, we need an algorithm for converting production rules to code. If the parser cannot recognize the input, that is, implicitly build a parse tree, it will halt with an error message identifying the first error found.

Each method of the recursive descent parser corresponds to a nonterminal symbol A in the grammar. That method is constructed directly from the EBNF grammar rule(s) of the form $A \rightarrow \omega$, and the method's name is A. Thus, using the grammar of Figure 3.7 as an example, there will be methods named assignment, expression, addOp, term, mulOp, factor, unaryOp, and primary. Assuming A has a corresponding abstract syntax category, the method will have a return type.

As an example, let us construct a Java method that parses input of the concrete syntactic class *Assignment*, and generates an abstract syntax tree defined by the grammar in Figure 2.11. The concrete syntax rule that governs the design of this method (see Figure 3.7) is:

Assignment → *Identifier* = *Expression* ;

First, we construct an appropriate skeleton method:

```
private Assignment assignment ( ) {
    ...
    return new Assignment(...);
}
```

Guided by the right-hand side of this production rule, this method must contain code that recognizes an *Identifier,* the operator =, an *Expression,* and the separator ;, in that order.

Two auxiliary methods are generally helpful in this process: match and error. The call match(t) either retrieves the next token or displays a syntax error, depending on whether or not the current token matches the expected token t:

```
private String match (TokenType t) {
    String value = token.value();
    if (token.type().equals(t))
        token = lexer.next();
    else
        error(t);
    return value;
}
```

The call `error(t)` displays an error message to the screen and terminates the parsing process:

```
private void error(TokenType tok) {
    System.err.println("Syntax error: expecting: " + tok
                        + "; saw: " + token);
    System.exit(1);
}
```

In our implementation, a token consists of two parts: a type and a value. The former determines the lexical class of the token (e.g., *Identifier*, *Literal*), and the value is its string value (e.g., ch, 1). For most tokens, knowing its type is sufficient.[5]

Using these auxiliary methods, the translation of the rule for *Assignment* into a method continues as follows.

1 Each symbol in the right-hand side of the rule is translated in sequence, resulting in a sequence of four more statements.

2 The first symbol to be translated is a terminal, so the translation is to call method `match`, passing it an *Identifier*. Moreover, the concrete category *Identifier* corresponds to the abstract category *Variable* in this context, so a new local variable `target` is declared and initialized with the value returned by `match`.

3 A similar translation is applied to the terminal symbol =, but since this terminal has no role in the abstract syntax (it is "syntactic sugar"), no new local variable is needed.

4 The nonterminal *Expression* is translated to a call to method `expression`, and the result is assigned to a new local variable `source` corresponding to the abstract category *Expression*.

5 Finally, the terminal symbol ; is punctuation, so it is matched as in step 3 above.

The resulting method looks like this:

```
private Assignment assignment ( ) {
    // Assignment --> Identifier = Expression ;
    Variable target = new Variable(match(Token.Identifier));
    match(Token.Assign);
    Expression source = expression();
    match(Token.Semicolon);
    return new Assignment(target, source);
}
```

Critically, this method relies on a method `expression`, which takes the current token (the one that follows the operator =) and parses the ensuing stream of tokens to derive and return an abstract parse tree for *Expression*. Given the rule

Expression → *Term* { *AddOp Term* }

---

5. However, for the token *Identifier* and the literals integer, float, and character, a value is associated with the token, giving the spelling of the identifier, the digits which make up the integer literal, etc. In the lexer, there is a constant token for all but the identifier and literal tokens; the latter must be dynamically created for each occurrence. This design is easily translatable to Ada, C, or C++.

we may construct the required method as follows.

1 The return type is established as *Expression* and a return statement is inserted.
2 The nonterminal *Term* is translated to a method call with an *Expression* return type.
3 The iteration is translated to a `while` loop with the test ensuring that the current token is in First(*AddOp*), namely, is either a plus (+) or a minus (-). We use an auxiliary method *isAddOp* to perform the test.
4 The body of the loop is the translation of the symbols *AddOp Term*. Strictly speaking, the translation of the symbol *AddOp* should result in a call on a method that uses a switch to determine if the current token is a plus or a minus. Since the `while` loop test already ensures this, we manually optimize the code to be a call to get the next token.
5 The nonterminal *Term* is again translated to a method call with an *Expression* return type.

Because of the iteration in the production, we have the same lookahead problem as we did in Section 3.2.3. The solutions, except applied to tokens instead of characters, are also the same: a peek function, a push back function, or stay one token ahead. Since we prefer the latter, our translation of productions to code assumes that, when method `expression` is called, `token` already has the value of the first token to be recognized, and upon exit `token` will be left with the value of the next token following the fully-parsed production rule. This convention is followed for every parsing method except the augmentation rule.

The resulting method is shown in Figure 3.10. This method reflects the fact that an *Expression* has at least one *Term,* and if the next token is a plus or minus, then it must be followed by another *Term*. Since there can be any number of occurrences of an *AddOp* and a *Term,* the EBNF iteration is translated to a loop. Ultimately, method `expression` recognizes the longest sequence of *Term*s separated by pluses and minuses.

This method also relies on the existence of a method `term`, whose construction is similar to that of `expression`. The methods for the remaining syntactic categories *Term*, *Factor*, and *Primary* for this grammar also appear in Figure 3.10.

Consider parsing the input z=x+2*y; as an *Assignment* and generating the abstract syntax tree shown in Figure 2.13. First, the method `assignment` is called while scanning the *Identifier* z. This corresponds to constructing the root of an abstract parse tree *Assignment*. The first statement matches an *Identifier*, which corresponds to constructing the leftmost subtree of *Assignment* in Figure 2.13. Next, the operator = is matched, and it is not retained in the abstract tree because it is no longer needed. The third statement calls method `expression`, which creates the other abstract subtree *Expression* for *Assignment*. The method `expression` is looking at an *Identifier* token; so it calls `term`, which calls `factor`, which calls `primary`, which matches the token. All of this corresponds to drawing the left subtree of *Expression*. Unwinding the call stack of `primary`, `factor`, and `term` effectively finishes creating the remaining subtrees shown in Figure 2.13.

Figure 3.11 summarizes an algorithm named algorithm T, for translating a production into code. Because each iteration in a production rule is translated into a while loop, the parser will loop until it has gone one token too far. This problem is identical to the looping problem in the DFSA of Section 3.2.2 and admits to the same solutions. Algorithm T

```
private Expression expression () {
    // Expression --> Term { AddOp Term }
    Expression e = term();
    while (isAddOp()) {
        Operator op = new Operator(match(token.type()));
        Expression term2 = term();
        e = new Binary(op, e, term2);
    }
    return e;
}

private Expression term () {
    // Term --> Factor { MultiplyOp Factor }
    Expression e = factor();
    while (isMultiplyOp()) {
        Operator op = new Operator(match(token.type()));
        Expression term2 = factor();
        e = new Binary(op, e, term2);
    }
    return e;
}

private Expression factor() {
    // Factor --> [ UnaryOp ] Primary
    if (isUnaryOp()) {
        Operator op = new Operator(match(token.type()));
        Expression term = primary();
        return new Unary(op, term);
    }
    else return primary();
}

private Expression primary () {
    // Primary --> Identifier | Literal | ( Expression )
    Expression e = null;
    if (token.type().equals(TokenType.Identifier)) {
        e = new Variable(match(TokenType.Identifier));
    } else if (isLiteral()) {
        e = literal();
    } else if (token.type().equals(TokenType.LeftParen)) {
        token = lexer.next();
        e = expression();
        match(TokenType.RightParen);
    } else error("Identifier | Literal | (");
    return e;
}
```

| **Figure 3.10   Recursive Descent Parser for Expressions**

1   Name the method A. If A has a corresponding abstract syntactic category A', make the method's return type A', and add a `return new A'` statement in a way that ensures that all of A's fields are properly initialized.

2   If ω is the terminal y, check that the current token t is an instance of a y, and then get the next token. Otherwise, issue an error message and halt (the token is in error). If y corresponds to a field in the abstract syntax definition of A', assign its value to that field.

3   If ω is the nonterminal B, call the method B and assign the value returned by B to a `new` variable in the abstract syntactic category B'.

4   If ω is an iteration using metabraces $\{\omega'\}$, translate it to a while loop. The body of the while loop is T applied recursively to the contents of the iteration ω'. If t is the current token, the loop test is $t \in First(\omega')$; as in Section 3.2, there are a number of ways to implement such tests.

5   If ω is a set of alternatives $\omega_1 \mid \ldots \mid \omega_n$, with or without metaparentheses, translate it to a switch (or sequence of if/else–if's) on the current token t. Recursively apply T to each ω_i, where the case tests correspond to $t \in First(\omega_i)$. If none of the alternatives is empty, then the default case should be that the token is in error; otherwise, the default case is empty.

6   If ω is an optional choice using metabrackets $[\omega']$, it can be rewritten as $(\omega' \mid)$ and translated using the previous rule.

7   If ω is of the form $X_1 \ldots X_n$, apply T recursively to each X_i, resulting in the sequence of statements: $T(X_1); \ldots ; T(X_n)$.

| **Figure 3.11**   **Algorithm T for Encoding the Rule $A \rightarrow \omega$ into Method A**

assumes that in recognizing a nonterminal A, method A begins by finding the first token that is derivable from A and ends by finding the first token that does not match a string derivable from A. The method A thus matches the longest string derivable from the nonterminal A.

Algorithm T is applied to all productions except the augmentation production. The latter is responsible for:

1   Getting the first token.

2   Calling the method corresponding to the original start symbol of the grammar.

3   Checking that all the information has been consumed, but **not** fetching a token after end of file (see Section 3.2.3).

Recursive descent parsing requires that the grammar not be left recursive; that is, there cannot exist a nonterminal A such that $A \Rightarrow^+ A \ldots$.[6] Otherwise the parser can go into an infinite recursive loop, because under some input condition the method A can call itself without consuming any input; having done this once, it will continue to do so indefinitely. This is another reason why EBNF grammars are preferred, since direct left recursion is always replaceable by iteration.[7]

---

6. The nonterminal A derives itself as its leftmost symbol using one or more derivations. In Kleene-star notation, a plus means one or more of the symbol to its left.

7. Fortunately, there is a simple check for left recursion, namely, the presence of a cycle in the left dependency graph. It turns out that all of the nonterminals in the cycle are left recursive. For our example grammar, no cycles are present in Figure 3.9.

Observation

Table-driven parsers

For implementing a compiler or translator for a programming language such as C, C++, Java, or Ada, normally a parser generator such as yacc/bison or JavaCC is used, although some C compilers [Waite and Carter, 1993] use recursive descent. Most parser generator systems generate table-driven parsers.

LL(1) is a top-down parser that is basically a table-driven version of recursive descent, where the 1 indicates the amount of lookahead, namely, 1 token. Table-driven parsers are preferred for large grammars because the algorithm is fixed and only the table size grows as a function of the grammar. The first "L" in *LL(1)* indicates that the input is read and processed left-to-right, while the second "L" indicates that the parse tree is constructed using a leftmost derivation.

Using the grammar of Figure 3.8 and numbering each alternative production starting at zero, we get the following LL(1) parse table:

N	id	lit	+	-	*	/	!	(	)	;
A	1									
E	2	2						2		
E'			4	4					3	3
AO			5	6						
T	7	7						7		
T'			8	8	9	9			8	8
MO					10	11				
F	12	12						12		
F'	13	13		14			14	13		
UO				15			16			
P	17	18						19		

The LL(1) parsing algorithm initially pushes the right-hand side of the augmentation rule (e.g., $A\$$) onto the stack so that the A is on the top. Then repeat the steps below, where X is the current top of the stack and a is the current input token.

1 If X and a are both the end symbol $, halt and accept the input.
2 If X is a terminal symbol: if X equals a, pop X off the stack and get the next token; otherwise halt in error.
3 If X is a nonterminal: if table[X, a] is empty, halt in error. Otherwise, it must contain a production number p; push the symbols of the production onto the stack in right to left order so that the leftmost symbol is on top.

The more widely used parsing algorithm is LR(1), which builds the parse tree bottom up, instead of top down as is the case for LL(1). Because of this, an LR(1) parser is able to handle left recursive grammars such as grammar G_1 of Section 2.1.4. Furthermore, it is a theorem that every LL(1) grammar is also LR(1). For more information on LR(1) parsers, see a compiler text such as [Aho *et al.*, 1986].

3.4 SUMMARY

This chapter presented a brief look at the Chomsky hierarchy of formal languages, in order to present regular grammars as a basis for constructing a lexical analyzer.

Next, an in-depth look at the design and implementation of a lexical analyzer for Clite was presented. First, the concept of a token and the other tasks of a lexical analyzer were discussed. Regular expressions were used as an alternate way of specifying tokens. For manually designing a lexer, deterministic finite state automata (DFSA) were presented. Finally, the translation of a DFSA to code was given.

In the last section of this chapter, the construction of a recursive descent parser was given. Several ancillary definitions and algorithms were presented, including augmenting a grammar, computing the set of nullable nonterminals, and computing the set of leftmost terminals derivable from each nonterminal A (termed First(A)). Finally, a method of translating each production of the form $A \rightarrow \omega$ into a method A for parsing ω was given.

EXERCISES

3.1   Rewrite the productions for each of the following nonterminals as right regular grammars: *Identifier*, *Float*.

3.2   Rewrite the productions for each of the following nonterminals as left regular grammars: *Identifier*, *Float*.

3.3   Draw a DFSA for identifiers that contain only letters and digits, where the identifier must have at least one letter, but it need not be the first character. Hint: everything to the left of the leftmost letter must be a digit.

3.4   Try to define the language $\{a^n b^n\}$ using a regular grammar. Discuss why this might not be possible.

3.5   Try to define the language $\{a^n b^n\}$ using a DFSA. Discuss why this might not be possible.

3.6   Determine why older languages such as Fortran and Cobol are case insensitive.

3.7   What parts of the language PHP are case sensitive? What parts are case insensitive? Can you find a rationale for the separation?

3.8   Develop a thorough test suite for `Lexer`. Explain the purpose of each test case.

3.9   Show the moves made using the DFSA for identifiers given in Section 3.2.2 in accepting the following: (a) a, (b) a2, (c) a2i, (d) abc.

3.10   For floating point numbers in scientific notation, give: (a) a right regular grammar; (b) a regular expression; (c) a DFSA. Give examples of numbers that are legal and illegal.

3.11   Extend the lexer to include floating point numbers in scientific notation using your design from the previous exercise.

3.12 For numbers in bases of the form `base # number #` (without embedded whitespace) give: (a) a right regular grammar; (b) a regular expression; (c) a DFSA. The `base` should be expressed in decimal; the number should use upper or lowercase letters to represent digits greater than 9. Does your definition ensure consistency of the number with respect to the base, for example, 8#99# is illegal?

3.13 For C-style `/*  ...  */` comments, give: (a) a right regular grammar; (b) a regular expression; (c) a DFSA.

3.14 Implement in the lexer your design of C-style `/*  ...  */` comments.

3.15 Design and implement a portion of a lexer which handles arbitrary sequences of the following: (a) integers of the form: d^+ (where d is a digit); (b) floating point numbers of the form: $d^+.d^+$; (c) subrange operator (...). Thus, the following consists of three tokens: 10.81, namely, an integer 10, the subrange operator, and another integer 81.

3.16 Consider the following grammar:

$$S \rightarrow \ |\ a\ |\ (T)$$
$$T \rightarrow T, S\ |\ S$$

After augmenting the grammar:
(a) Draw the left dependency graph.
(b) Compute *First* for each nonterminal.

3.17 Add semantics to the recursive descent parser that computes the value of each expression and prints the value. For implementing variables, restrict them to single lowercase letters and use an array with the variable used as an index; initialize the array to zero.

3.18 Enhance the Clite parser found at the book website by adding a method:

```
private boolean matches(int[] tok)
```

that returns true if `token.type()` matches one of the `tok[]`, and false otherwise. The method should not advance the token. Use this method to eliminate `isAddOp()`, `isMulOp`, etcetera.

3.19 Can a language have no reserved words? That is, suppose every reserved word (such as `if` and `for`) were merely a predefined identifier, which the programmer is free to redefine. Can such a language exist? Explain.

3.20 Add a `display` method to each of the abstract syntax classes in Figure 2.11 so that an abstract syntax tree for *Assignment* can be displayed in an indented notation. For instance, the abstract syntax tree for the *Assignment* $z = x + 2*y$; should be displayed as follows:

```
=
    z
    +
        x
        *
            2
            y
```

3.21 Design an abstract syntax and implement a recursive descent parser for expressions to be symbolically differentiated. The grammar is a Polish-prefix grammar:

$$Expr \rightarrow Op\ Expr\ Expr\ |\ Primary$$
$$Op \rightarrow +\ |-|*\ |\ /$$
$$Primary \rightarrow Integer\ |\ Letter$$

where an *Integer* is an arbitrary sequence of digits and a *Letter* is a single lowercase letter representing a mathematical variable. To simplify the assignment, you may assume that the *Expr* is error-free and that the *Expr* appears on one line with tokens separated by one or more spaces or tabs. The program should display the abstract syntax tree.

Names

4

"The first step toward wisdom is calling things by their right names."
Anonymous Chinese Proverb

The effective naming of variables, functions, types, classes, and other entities is an important programming skill. Understanding the various uses and implications of referencing a name in different contexts is often not a simple task.

Recall from Chapter 1 that the term *binding* is an association between an entity (such as a variable) and a property (such as its value).

Definition: A binding is *static* if the association occurs before run-time.

Definition: A binding is *dynamic* if the association occurs at run-time.

The time at which a binding occurs for a name plays a fundamental role. For example, static scoping, whereby a name is bound to a specific declaration before run time, should be familiar to most programmers since it is the mechanism used by all the major languages to resolve references. But some languages delay name resolution until run time. In order to understand both static and dynamic scoping, we examine the notion of a symbol table and its use at compile/run time to implement static/dynamic scoping, respectively.

Besides name resolution, we also consider the visibility of a name. In some languages the redeclaration within a scope of a name may hide other instances of the same name. Overloading permits different instances of the same function or operator name to be resolved based on the number or types of its arguments.

The lifetime of a variable name refers to the time interval during which the variable is allocated memory, which can occur statically or dynamically. In the latter case a variable's lifetime is bound to the execution of statements in its scope. Some languages provide mechanisms for extending the lifetime of such variables.

Beginning in this chapter we use the term *C-like* language to include all versions of C, C++, and Java and Pascal-like language to include both Pascal and Ada.

4.1 SYNTACTIC ISSUES

Names are used in programs to denote many different entities: variables, types, functions, etcetera. In this section, we consider the basic syntax of names. Another term for name is *Identifier*.

Strict lexical rules determine how a name can be constructed. For instance, we saw in Chapter 2 that a Clite *Identifier* must be a series of letters and digits, beginning with a letter. This is a common theme for creating names in most programming languages.

Early languages were uppercase only and placed strict limits on the length of an identifier (see Observation). Later languages, such as Pascal and Ada, continued the tradition of case insensitivity, so that any one of `alpha`, `Alpha`, or `alPha` names the same entity. In contrast, in C-like languages names are *case sensitive*, so that, for example, `alpha` and `Alpha` do not name the same entity. The web scripting language PHP is partly case sensitive and partly case insensitive, which is also a questionable design decision.

Many languages allow the use of one or more special characters in identifiers, but some restrict their usage; for example, Cobol allows the hyphen character, but an identifier cannot begin or end with a hyphen. Others, such as C-like languages, not only allow a special character (the underscore _), but do not restrict its use.

Definition: Most languages have a predefined collection of names called *reserved words* or *keywords* that carry special meaning and cannot be used as identifiers.

Reserved words include names that are useful in parsing a program because they identify major constructs. In C-like languages these keywords include `int`, `if`, and `while`.

Observation

Naming in Fortran

Fortran, the first high-level programming language, was originally uppercase only because the primary input device (the keypunch machine) and the line printers were uppercase only. Fortran was designed and implemented for the IBM 709/704 computers, which had a 6-bit character (termed BCD) and a 36-bit word. So the designers of Fortran limited the size of an identifier to a maximum of 6 characters, stored left justified with trailing space characters, since the 709/704 lacked the ability to address individual characters.

These conventions were standardized in Fortran 66 and 77 and kept unchanged until Fortran 90. However, by then computers had largely migrated to ASCII (or, in the case of IBM mainframe computers, EBCDIC), which permitted lowercase characters. The simplest convention seemed to be, in the case of Fortran, not to distinguish upper from lowercase in names. Otherwise, all reserved words would have to be entered in uppercase, to maintain backward compatiblity. Fortran 90 standardized this decision.

In some languages (e.g., Pascal and Scheme), in addition to reserved words, there are *predefined identifiers* that have a special meaning; unlike reserved words, the programmer is free to redefine them. Library function names generally fit into this category. Such a feature can be either a blessing or a curse. On the one hand, it helps to minimize the number of reserved words in a language. On the other hand, it can lead to confusing programs. For example, consider the following (legal) Pascal program fragment, which redefines the meaning of the predefined identifier true:

```
program confusing;
const true = false;
begin
  ...
  if (a < b) = true then
      f(a)
  else
      g(b);
  ...
end.
```

In this case, procedure f is called if a >= b, the opposite of what the code seems to say. Allowing the redefinition of an important *Identifier* like true is thus a poor language design decision.

A language designer has to decide between making predefined identifiers reserved versus allowing the programmer the ability to redefine such identifiers. Cobol took the former approach, with the result that there are hundreds of reserved words. Most modern languages take some form of the latter approach, thereby minimizing the number of reserved words. Pascal-like languages allow the basic type names like *integer* to be redefined, while C-like languages make them reserved.

4.2 VARIABLES

An important use of naming is the naming of variables, which are fundamental in imperative and object-oriented programming. In such languages a variable is a name for a memory location (or block of locations).

> **Definition**: A *variable* is a binding of a name to a memory address. In addition, a variable has a type, a value, and a lifetime.

Any of these bindings plus others can be either static or dynamic, creating interesting variations among languages. These features of variables also bear upon how a language is implemented. For instance, if a language requires that all variable names be declared before they are referenced in a program, then the semantic analysis phase of a compiler must include a list of declared names and their associated data types; this list is often called a *symbol table*, which is covered in Section 4.4.

Programmers use variables to name individual and aggregated memory locations; for the remainder of this chapter, we will treat the two as equivalent. A program variable has four basic bindings:

- Name.
- Address (which is an implementation issue).
- Type.
- Value.

These items can be either statically or dynamically bound. The various types of values that can be assigned to variables are discussed in Chapter 5. The address of a variable uniquely identifies the actual memory location where a variable's value is stored. Addressing a variable's value is also introduced in Chapter 5, where the strong association between a pointer and an address is established.

Algol 68 [van Wijngaarden, 1969] was the first language to clearly distinguish between the use of a variable's name to denote its address, the variable's *l-value*, versus the use of its name to denote the value itself, the variable's *r-value*. Consider the assignment statement:

```
x = y + 1;
```

Such a statement should be read: assign to the memory address denoted by the variable x the value of the expression which is the sum of the value of the variable y and one. Note that when used as a left-hand side value (l-value), the variable identifier x denotes an address, while when used as a right-hand side value (r-value), the variable identifier y denotes the value stored at the address.

Algol 68 allowed the program to explicitly distinguish the address of a variable from its value. A variable of type `int` was denoted as a `ref int`, that is, a reference to an integer. What C++ calls a `const` (a constant) was denoted as an `int` in Algol 68, conceptually the same as the `int` 1.

ML [Ullman, 1998] also supports such *explicit dereferencing* of a variable in a program. For example, the ML expression:

```
x := !y + 1;
```

uses the operator ! to convert the reference y to a value. Most languages do not require explicit dereferencing for ordinary variables in assignment statements. However, many compilers use an abstract syntax representation approximating the above ML statement with explicit dereferencing operators inserted.

However, for pointer variables, explicit dereferencing is often useful. C/C++ use the unary star * to dereference a pointer variable. For example, in the code fragment:

```
int x, y;
int *p;
x = *p;
*p = y;
```

the third statement assigns to the l-value of x the value of the memory address referenced by p, that is, the r-value of the r-value of p. The last line assigns to the memory location referenced by p, the r-value of y. Note that the value of p itself, a memory location, remains unchanged.

4.3 SCOPE

Early computers had very limited memories by today's standards from a few kilobytes (thousands of bytes) to a few hundred kilobytes. As programs have grown in size, name collision has become an increasingly important issue. To enable programmers to reuse the same identifier within a program, the concept of the *scope* of a name is used.

> **Definition**: The *scope* of a name is the collection of statements which can access that name binding.

As with most issues, the binding of a name to a scope can be either static or dynamic, with the latter examined in Section 4.6.

> **Definition**: In *static scoping*, a name is bound to a collection of statements in accordance with its position in the source program.

Thus, static scoping can be performed at compile time and is independent of the execution history of the program. Because the name binding can be determined by a simple scan of the program, static scoping improves program readability and supports a better level of compile-time checking.

Most modern languages, including C/C++, Java, Python, and Ada, use static scoping. Because static scoping is based on the grammatical structure of a program, it is sometimes called *lexical scoping*. Which grammatical structures constitute a scope varies by language; before examining this question, we first define some terminology.

In most languages scopes can be nested. Two different scopes are either *disjoint* or *nested*. When two scopes are disjoint, the same name can be bound to different entities without any interference at all.

The simplest case of what constitutes a scope consists of the early versions of Fortran, in which a compilation unit constituted a single scope, which could not be nested. A Fortran compilation unit consisted of either the main program or a single function or procedure, and so all scopes were nonoverlapping; none could be nested.

However, in some sense this is a naive view. All languages support an outer scope in which certain methods or libraries exist and can be accessed; what is in this scope

Table 4.1

What Constitutes a Scope

	Algol	C	Java	Ada
Package	n/a	n/a	yes	yes
Class	n/a	n/a	nested	yes
Function	nested	yes	yes	nested
Block	nested	nested	nested	nested
For Loop	no	no	yes	automatic

and how entities can be accessed varies by language. Fortran and C export functions and procedures to this outer scope.

Departing from Fortran, an Algol 60 compilation unit constituted a scope within which functions and procedures introduced new scopes and could be nested. In addition a compound statement, bracketed by the reserved words begin and end, constitutes a scope, and these could be nested as well. A compound statement with declarations is called a *block* in Algol, and such declarations can include variable or function declarations. In an Algol 60 scope, however, all declarations must precede all other statements.

More recent languages have incorporated some of Algol 60's scoping conventions. For example, C-like languages follow the Algol tradition of allowing a compound statement (like a block, except enclosed with braces rather than begin and end) to contain new declarations, and hence to introduce a new scope. But C/C++ do not allow nested functions.

An attempt to summarize the question of what constitutes a scope for several major languages is given in Table 4.1. In the table, the compilation unit is left out, since it always constitutes a scope. Also, the table is not meant to be definitive in the sense that not all grammatical entities which constitute a scope for a given language appear in the table. Instead the table should be viewed as an attempt to present "the big picture."

Consider the column for the language C; it supports neither packages nor classes, so the question is not applicable (n/a). Functions constitute a scope, but cannot be nested. Blocks (statement lists enclosed in braces) do constitute a scope and can be nested. Finally, a for loop variable cannot be declared as part of the for statement; in contrast, the for loop variable is automatically declared in Ada and its scope extends only to the for header and loop body.

Definition: The scope in which a name is defined or declared is called its *defining scope*.

Definition: A reference to a name is *nonlocal* if it occurs in a nested scope of the defining scope; otherwise the reference is *local*.

Consider the simple C sort function given in Figure 4.1. The scope of the temporary variable t includes lines 6–9, which is also its defining scope. Since there are no nested blocks within lines 6–9, all references to t are local. Thus, t can only be referenced by the statements enclosed by the braces on lines 5 and 10. This use of a compound statement to declare a variable improves the readability of the program, since the scope of the variable is limited.

C further specifies that all declarations must precede all other types of statements in a block; thus, a reference can occur only after the name is declared. That is, the code may not contain a forward reference to a declared name. C++ and Java allow a

```
1    void sort (float a[ ], int size) {
2         int i, j;
3         for (i = 0; i < size; i++)
4             for (j = i + 1; j < size; j++)
5                 if (a[j] < a[i]) {
6                     float t;
7                     t = a[i];
8                     a[i] = a[j];
9                     a[j] = t;
10                }
11   }
```

| **Figure 4.1**   **Example Scopes in C**

declaration to appear anywhere within a block provided the *no forward reference* rule is not violated. A *forward reference* is a reference to a name that occurs before the name has been declared.

Continuing with the example in Figure 4.1, the scope for a and size is lines 2–10, that is, everything between the braces on lines 1 and 11. Similarly, the scope for i and j is the same block, but references to either name must occur after the declaration on line 2. The references to i on lines 3–5 and to j on lines 4–5 are also local. But the references to these names on lines 7–9 are nonlocal, since lines 6–10 is a nested scope within the defining scope for i and j. This important issue is addressed more thoroughly in Section 4.5.

An interesting kind of scope is the for statement, as in a C++/Java, where a new control variable may be declared. In this case, the scope of that variable is limited to the body of the loop:

```
for (int i = 0; i < 10; i++) {
    System.out.println(i);
    ...
}
... i ... // invalid reference to i
```

Here, the reference to i following the for loop body is invalid, since the scope of the variable i is limited to the loop body. Ada also supports this capability; however, in Ada the for loop control variable is implicitly and automatically declared.

The Java class scope is interesting because it is an exception to the *no forward reference* rule. In declaring a class, the instance variables and methods can be declared in any convenient order. While most Java texts declare all the instance variables before any of the methods (following the Algol/Pascal tradition), a few texts follow the opposite convention. More importantly, methods can appear in any order, independent of which methods refer to other methods; this greatly improves writability.

So far, we have avoided the issue of resolving references to names where there are multiple declarations of the same name. In order to address that issue properly, we first look at the role and implementation of the symbol table of a compiler.

4.4 SYMBOL TABLE

One of the tasks of the semantic analysis phase of a translator (see Section 2.4) is to construct a *symbol table* of all declared names and their bindings.

> **Definition**: A *symbol table* is a data structure kept by a translator that allows it to keep track of each declared name and its bindings.

For the remainder of this section, we assume that each declared name is unique within its local scope. That is, the only other declarations of the same name occur in either a disjoint scope or a nested scope. This important assumption will be relaxed in Section 4.8.

The data structure used for a local scope can be any implementation of a dictionary or set, where the name is the key. Given a name, we query the dictionary for the binding associated with the name. It returns a binding only if the name was declared in the current scope; otherwise, it returns a special value indicating that no such name-binding declaration occurred in the local scope.[1]

All we need now is an algorithm for handling valid nonlocal references. The fact that such references occur in a scope that is nested within the defining scope suggests using a stack of scopes, as follows:

1. Each time a scope is entered, push a new dictionary onto the stack.
2. Each time a scope is exited, pop a dictionary off the top of the stack.
3. For each name declared, generate an appropriate binding and enter the name-binding pair into the dictionary on the top of the stack.
4. Given a name reference, search the dictionary on top of the stack for the name.
   (a) If found, return the binding.
   (b) Otherwise, repeat the process on the next dictionary down in the stack until the name is found.
   (c) If the name is not found in any dictionary in the stack, report an error.

For the C program in Figure 4.1, the stack of dictionaries at line 7 would look as follows (top to bottom):

<t, 6>
<j, 4>, <i, 3>, <size, 1>, <a, 1>
<sort, 1>

where the name-binding pair is shown as an ordered pair and the binding is shown only as the line number where declared, for simplicity. Note that the name sort is in the outer scope from the parameters and the function body. From this vantage point, the reference to t on line 7 is a local reference, while the references to a and i are nonlocal.

In contrast, the symbol table at line 4 and again at the start of line 11 would appear as follows (top to bottom):

<j, 4>, <i, 3>, <size, 1>, <a, 1>
<sort, 1>

The scope containing t has not been encountered yet at line 4 and is exited at the end of line 10.

---

1. The observant reader will have noted here the reliance on the *no forward reference* rule.

For languages which use static scoping, the symbol table is constructed during the semantic analysis phase of compilation (see Section 2.4) and lasts through the remainder of the compilation process. Section 4.5 considers the case where there are multiple instances of definitions of the same name.

4.5   RESOLVING REFERENCES

The referencing environment is important because it defines the collection of statements in which a name can be validly referenced.

> **Definition**: For static scoping, the *referencing environment* for a name is its defining scope and all nested subscopes.

We use this definition and the knowledge of how a symbol table works to consider disjoint scopes and nested scopes which redefine a name within its referencing environment.

Figure 4.2 presents an example of both nested and disjoint scopes in which there are three declarations of the name i, two of j, and one of all of the others. The individual symbol tables for each scope are as follows:

1   The outer scope consists of the two variables declared on line 1 plus the three functions: <h, 1>, <i, 1>, <B, 2>, <A, 8>, <main, 14>.

2   Function B's scope contains the parameter plus the two variables on line 3: <w, 2>, <j, 3>, <k, 3>.

3   Function A's scope consists of the two parameters on line 8 plus the declaration on line 9: <x, 8>, <y, 8>, <i, 9>, <j, 9>.

```
1   int h, i;
2   void B(int w) {
3        int j, k;
4        i = 2*w;
5        w = w+1;
6        ...
7   }
8   void A (int x, int y) {
9        float i, j:
10       B(h);
11       i = 3;
12       ...
13  }
14  void main() {
15       int a, b;
16       h = 5; a = 3; b = 2;
17       A(a, b);
18       B(h);
19       ...
20  }
```

| **Figure 4.2   References in Disjoint and Nested Scopes**

4 Function `main`'s scope consists of the two variables declared on line 15: <a, 15>, <b, 15>.

When these functions are compiled, the stack of symbol tables for each function looks as follows:

Function	Stack of Symbol Tables
B	<w, 2>, <j, 3>, <k, 3>
	<h, 1>, <i, 1>, <B, 2>, <A, 8>, <main, 14>
A	<x, 8>, <y, 8>, <i, 9>, <j, 9>
	<h, 1>, <i, 1>, <B, 2>, <A, 8>, <main, 14>
main	<a, 15>, <b, 15>
	<h, 1>, <i, 1>, <B, 2>, <A, 8>, <main, 14>

With this information we can easily resolve the nonlocal and multiply defined references:

Line	Reference	Declaration
4	i	1
10	h	1
11	i	9
16, 18	h	1

4.6 DYNAMIC SCOPING

In terms of symbol tables, the dictionary for each scope can be built at compile time, but managing the stack of scopes is done at run time. As a scope is entered at run time, its dictionary is pushed onto the top of the symbol table and popped when exited. Name resolution is performed at run time rather than compile time, but otherwise is the same.

Definition: In *dynamic scoping*, a name is bound to its most recent declaration based on the program's execution history.

Again using Figure 4.2 as our example and assuming dynamic scoping, let's examine resolution of the reference to i on line 4. Assume a call history of: main (line 17) → A (line 10) → B. The run-time symbol table looks like:

Function	Dictionary
B	<w, 2>, <j, 3>, <k, 3>
A	<x, 8>, <y, 8>, <i, 9>, <j, 9>
main	<a, 15>, <b, 15>
	<h, 1>, <i, 1>, <B, 2>, <A, 8>, <main, 14>

The reference to i on line 4 resolves to the one declared in A on line 9, since that is the first i encountered.

If, instead, we consider the call history: main (line 18) → B, the run-time symbol table looks like:

Function	Dictionary
B	<w, 2>, <j, 3>, <k, 3>
main	<a, 15>, <b, 15>
	<h, 1>, <i, 1>, <B, 2>, <A, 8>, <main, 14>

The reference to i now resolves to the one declared globally on line 1.

The purpose of the examples is to make clear that name resolution of nonlocal references using dynamic scoping requires a knowledge of the run-time history of the program. In particular, different run-time histories can result in different name resolutions for the same reference.

Although dynamic scoping is used in early versions of Lisp (before Common Lisp), APL, Snobol, and Perl, it has proved to be particularly error prone and has largely been abandoned. Dynamic scoping is no longer a common feature of modern languages, except Common Lisp and Perl which also support static scoping.

There are several reasons for prefering static scoping. First, dynamic scoping compromises the ability to statically type check references to nonlocal variables, since not all the nonlocals for a statement inside a called function can be statically identified. Second, all variables in a function that calls other functions are visible to those called functions (and hence can be altered), which tends to reduce the reliability of a program in general. Finally, access to a nonlocal variable by following a chain of dynamic links tends to be more time consuming than access to a nonlocal in a statically scoped environment. For these reasons, dynamic scoping tends not to be a feature of modern programming languages.

The next section returns to static scoping in order to consider the issue of visibility.

4.7   VISIBILITY

As shown in Figure 4.2 on page 93, a name redeclared in a nested scope effectively *hides* the outer declaration. This results because a reference defaults to the inner declaration.

> **Definition**: A name is *visible* to a reference if its referencing includes that reference and the name is not redeclared in an inner scope.

A name is thus visible throughout its referencing environment provided it is not hidden by a redeclaration in some nested subscope. Some languages provide a mechanism for referencing a hidden name. In Java, for example, a hidden class instance variable, say x, can be referenced as this.x, where this refers to the current object. Consider the following program fragment:

```
1   public class Student {
2      private String name;
3      public Student (String name, ...) {
4         this.name = name;
5         ...
6      }
7   }
```

```
procedure Main is
    x : Integer;
    procedure p1 is
        x : Float;
        procedure p2 is
        begin
            ... x ...
        end p2;
    begin
        ... x ...
    end p1;
    procedure p3 is
    begin
        ... x ...
    end p3;
begin
    ... x ...
end main;
```

| **Figure 4.3** **Ada Program with Multiple Declarants of a Name**

The parameter name on line 3 hides the variable declared on line 2; so line 4 uses the notation this.name to reference the hidden variable.

Ada permits a name to be explicitly qualified, thereby allowing both a local and a global variable with the same name to be referenced within the same block. Consider the skeletal Ada program shown in Figure 4.3. Here, we see two variables declared with the name x, one an Integer and the other a Float. The references to x in p3 and main access the Integer variable, while the references to x in p1 and p2 access the Float variable. However, either of the references in p1 or p2 can be changed to main.x in order to access the Integer variable instead. This feature in Ada extends to blocks as well, since any Ada block can be named.

4.8 OVERLOADING

Until now, we have assumed that, in each defining scope, there is no more than one declaration of a given name. The ability to use the same name for related entities can improve both the readability and the writability of a language by reducing name clutter. For example, being able to print a variable of any type, as in Java, is much simpler than remembering to use WriteInt( ) for integers, WriteReal( ) for floating point values, and so on, as in Modula.

Definition: *Overloading* uses the number or type of arguments to distinguish among identical function names or operators.

An example is the age-old practice of overloading a language's built-in arithmetic operators and functions. Most languages overload the operators +, -, *, / to denote either integer or floating point arithmetic, depending on the types of the operands. In more modern languages this overloading has been extended to cover all the variants of integer and floating point values (e.g., single and double precision). Java also overloads the operator + to denote string concatenation whenever at least one of the operands is of type String. Overloading also extends to built-in functions. In Fortran, the input/output statements read and write accept any of the language-defined types.

Historically, none of the major early languages extended overloading to user-defined functions and operators. This led to the anomaly in Modula that different names for input/output functions were used for distinct types. For instance, the name Read( ) is used only for characters, ReadInt( ) for integers, ReadString( ) for strings, and ReadReal( ) for floating point numbers. This departure from Pascal occurred because the input/output functions were built-in in Pascal, but were ordinary external library routines in Modula.

Ada was the first widely used language to extend the overloading of operators to programmer-defined types and functions.[2] It seemed natural to the designers of Ada that, if one were to define a new type to implement mathematical vectors, the operator + should be extendible to denote vector addition. Ada also allows overloading based on the return type, unlike other languages supporting overloading.

C++ also allows both arithmetic operators and methods to be overloaded, while Java restricts overloading to methods. Java allows method names within the same class to be overloaded, as long as the actual method invoked can be determined by either the number or the types of the parameters. An example occurs in the PrintStream class, where the methods print and println are heavily overloaded:

```
public class PrintStream extends FilterOutputStream {
    . . .
    public  void  print(boolean b);
    public  void  print(char c);
    public  void  print(int i);
    public  void  print(long l);
    public  void  print(float f);
    public  void  print(double d);
    public  void  print(char[ ] s);
    public  void  print(String s);
    public  void  print(Object obj);
}
```

Java allows both an instance variable and a method to have the same name, since all references to the method are suffixed by parentheses ( ):

```
public class Student {
    private String name;
    . . .
    public String name ( ) { return name; }
```

---

2. At the time, this was a great leap of faith. The only known algorithms for performing name resolution on programmer-defined overloaded operators and functions were exponential in their time complexity!

Note that the method `name( )` contains a reference to the instance variable `name`, and there is no ambiguity here. In fact, a common idiom in Java programming is to define an accessor method in a class that returns the value of the instance variable of the same name, as this example illustrates.

4.9 LIFETIME

The earliest imperative languages, namely, Fortran and Cobol, used static allocation for both variables and functions; that is, the memory to be used was assigned at compile time. In the case of functions, there was only a single memory area for both the arguments and the return address; because of this, recursive functions were not supported. See Chapters 9 and 10 for a more complete discussion.

In the case of variables, the burden of managing memory was totally the responsibility of the programmer in the event that the required program memory exceeded the amount available. Since this was a common occurrence given the limited physical memories of the time, a great deal of the effort in writing a program was spent in managing memory.

With the development of Algol came the notion that memory for variables, including function parameters and return address, should be allocated at run time when a scope was entered and deallocated when the scope was exited. At the time this was a radical idea, since no one knew how to implement such a memory management scheme at the time.

Basic memory management used by all modern languages today is based on this concept. The remainder of this section explores the implication of this fundamental notion and how various languages allow the lifetime of a variable or object to be extended. Chapter 10 presents a more implementation-oriented view of this issue. In the discussion here we ignore the issue of dynamic space allocation via a `new` or `malloc` command (and its deallocation), a subject explored in Chapter 11.

> **Definition**: The *lifetime* of a variable is the time interval during which the variable has been allocated a block of memory.

The major difference in program semantics between the static memory allocation of Fortran and the scope-based allocation of Algol is that in the former case, a variable never forgets its value. Consider the variable t of Figure 4.1 on page 91. On each iteration of the loop for j whatever memory may be allocated for t is also deallocated. For this particular example, the deallocation is not a problem since t does not need to remember its value.

However, consider the problem of writing a function that counts the number of times it has been called.

```
double Func( ) {
    int count = 0;
    ...
}
```

From a use viewpoint, only the function needs to access the count. However, if the count variable is declared within the function, the value of the count is lost each time the function is exited under the Algol memory allocation policy. The alternative is to increase the scope of the count variable for the sole purpose of increasing its lifetime.

The remainder of this section considers language mechanisms which break in some way the "scope equals lifetime" rule, while keeping it as the default case.

For example, a Pascal program consists of a single compilation unit. The variables declared at the compilation unit level are effectively statically allocated, no matter how they are implemented. Thus, such variables keep their values over the life of the program.

C allows multiple compilation units. The variables declared at the compilation unit level (e.g., h in Figure 4.2 on page 93) are all effectively statically allocated. Such variables retain their memory and thus, their values, even as a program's execution enters and exits their compilation unit.

The other feature added by C is the ability to declare a variable static. When used with a variable declared inside a function, the variable is statically allocated. If used with a variable declared at the compilation unit level, it has no effect on the variable's memory allocation, since such variables already use static allocation.

Java also allows variables declared at the class level to use the static modifier. Such variables or objects have their memory statically allocated.

4.10 SUMMARY

This chapter covers the key concepts of names and their bindings in contemporary programming languages. The binding of a name to a variable and its type play a key role in the development of a type system for a language.

EXERCISES

4.1 Pick one of the following languages: Python, Modula, Ada, C#, or Perl. After consulting an authoritative reference, discuss each of the following requirements for that language:
(a) Declaration before use.
(b) Overloading of operators for programmer-defined types.
(c) Binding time of array size.
(d) What constitutes a scope.
(e) Location of a declaration within a scope.

4.2 After consulting an authoritative reference on the requirements for using global variables in C, answer the following questions.
(a) How can they be accessed in other compilation units?
(b) How can global variables be hidden from other compilation units?
(c) Why would you want to hide global variables?

4.3 C and C++ distinguish between declarations and definitions. What is the distinction? Give an example of each each.

4.4 Explain the use of header files in C and C++. Why doesn't Java use header files?

4.5 Most programming languages prohibit redeclaring the same variable name within the same scope.
(a) Explain why types alone cannot be used to distinguish such a duplication.
(b) What is the difference between this restriction and the absence of such a restriction for overloaded functions?

4.6 For the language C, give three examples of r-values that cannot be l-values. Give three more examples of l-values? Are there l-values that cannot be r-values? Explain.

Types

5

"Types are the leaven of computer programming; they make it digestible."
Robin Milner

CHAPTER OUTLINE

The types available to a programmer are many and varied. There is a common core of basic types that all languages support (integers, reals, booleans, and characters), as well as several nonbasic types (pointers, arrays, structures, and functions). This chapter summarizes these ideas and their uses in several contemporary languages.

> **Definition**: A *type* is a collection of values and a collection of operations on those values.

For example, the familiar integer type has values $\dots, -2, -1, 0, 1, 2, \dots$, and operations $+, -, *, /, <, \dots$ on those values. The type `boolean` has values `true` and `false` and operations $\wedge, \vee$, and $\neg$ (*and, or,* and *not,* respectively) on those values.

Usually, a computer type has a finite number of values, due to the fixed memory size allocated to store them. This is particularly problematic for numeric types. There are exceptions, however. For instance, Smalltalk uses unbounded fractional numbers by default and the Haskell type `Integer` represents unbounded integers, which allows arithmetic to simulate more accurately the full range of mathematical operations. Java has a similar feature, which is embodied in its class `BigInteger`. But these represent the exceptions.

In general, however, the use of a fixed memory size to store integers can result in an arithmetic operation that generates a value outside the valid range. Try computing 20! (factorial) using a fixed memory size integer; the value exceeds the limits of a 64-bit integer.

Even more problematic is the use of fixed memory size floating point numbers to approximate mathematical rational numbers. For example, using binary floating point, the number 0.2 is not exact in binary; so computing 5×0.2 is not exactly 1. Computational floating point is inconsistent with its corresponding mathematical counterpart.

In the early high-level languages, Fortran, Algol, and Cobol, all of the types in the language were built in. Over time the inadequacy of this became obvious. Suppose, for example, the programmer needed a type `color` to represent colors that you could display on a monitor. Typically, an integer of some size was used with some portion of the bits representing the colors red, green, and blue (RGB). Surely, multiplying two colors together makes no sense, but using an integer representation allows just such a meaningless operation. The purpose of types in programming languages is to provide programmers ways of conveniently and effectively defining new types in order to build programs that better model a solution.

5.1   TYPE ERRORS

By default, the machine representation of data carries no explicit type-related information. That is, machine data is just a sequence of bits, making it essentially *typeless*. These bits are subject to different interpretations.

For example, consider the following 32-bit string:

0100 0000 0101 1000 0000 0000 0000 0000

where we have added the spaces for readability. These 32 bits could represent any one of the following:

1   The floating point number 3.375.
2   The 32-bit integer 1,079,508,992.

3   Two 16-bit integers 16472 and 0.

4   Four ASCII characters @ X NUL NUL.

Without more information, there is no way to know which interpretation is correct.

One of the many difficulties of programming in a machine-level (assembly) language is that the burden of keeping track of the data types of variables falls entirely on the programmer. For instance, incorrectly fetching a 32-bit quantity that represents an integer and performing a machine-level floating point addition on it essentially creates garbage as a result.

> **Definition**: A *type error* is any error that arises because an operation is attempted on a data type for which it is undefined.

Type errors are a common problem in assembly language programming. Programming in a higher-level language usually reduces type errors, since compilers and run-time systems are designed to identify them.

Thus, the proper definition and implementation of data types in programming language design is enormously important. A so-called *type system* can provide a basis for early detection (at compile time) of incorrect usage of data by a program.

> **Definition**: A *type system* is a precise definition of the bindings between the type of a variable, its values, and the possible operations on those values.

The idea of a type system has changed dramatically since the emergence of programming from the machine level and its evolution through the last three decades. For example, consider the history of the C programming language, which was developed in the late 1960s to permit porting the Unix operating system among different machine architectures. C was originally based on the typeless language BCPL. But as C developed through the 1970s and 1980s to Kernighan and Ritchie C to ANSI C to C++, it acquired better and stronger typing features. However, adding new typing rules to a language is not as simple as it seems [Stroustrup, 1994, p. 20]:

> During writing and debugging, I acquired a great respect for the expressiveness of Simula's type system and its compiler's ability to catch type errors. I observed that type errors almost invariably reflected either a silly programming error or a conceptual flaw in the design. ... In contrast, I had found Pascal's type system to

Observation

The cost of a bug

One of the axioms of modern software engineering practice is that an undetected error in a development phase costs, on average, an order of magnitude more to fix in the next phase. For example, suppose a type error caught during the implementation phase costs $1 to fix. If such an error were not caught until the testing phase, it would cost an average of $10 to fix. Moreover, catching the same error after the testing phase would cost about $100 to fix. For example, a bug in the floating point multiplication algorithm in early models of the Intel 386 chip cost $472 millon to fix, since the bug was not caught before the chip went to market.

be worse than useless—a straightjacket that caused more problems than it solved by forcing me to warp my designs to suit an implementation-oriented artifact.

5.2 STATIC AND DYNAMIC TYPING

A type system imposes specific constraints, such as the requirement that values used in an arithmetic operation must be numeric. Such constraints cannot be expressed syntactically in EBNF. For some languages (e.g., C) type checking is performed at compile time, while for other languages (e.g., Perl) type checking is performed at run time. In either case the type system is part of the language's semantics, compile-time semantics in the former case, and run-time semantics in the latter.[1] In Java, for example, most type checking occurs at compile time, but casting of objects is checked at run time.

Some languages, like C and Ada, require that a single type be bound to a variable when the variable is declared, remaining bound throughout its life at run time. This allows the type of the value of an expression to be determined at compile time.

> **Definition**: A language is *statically typed*, if the types of all variables are fixed when they are declared at compile time.

Other languages, like Perl, Python and Scheme, allow the type of a variable to be redefined each time a new value is assigned to it at run time.[2] To implement this feature, a type indicator is stored at the run time with each value.

> **Definition**: A language is *dynamically typed* if the type of a variable can vary at run time depending on the value assigned.

Recall that a *type error* is any error that occurs when an operation is attempted on a type of value for which it is not well defined. For example, consider the C expression x+u.p, where u is defined as the union {int a; float p;}:

```
u.a = 1;
...
x = x + u.p;
```

This code snippet is an instance of a type error enabled by the fact that both int and float values of u share the same memory word, which is initialized with an int value. If x is a float, the expression x+u.p causes an int value to be involved in a floating point addition without being converted to a floating point representation, generating a garbage result.[3]

> **Definition**: A programming language is *strongly typed* if its type system allows all type errors in a program to be detected either at compile time or at run time.

---

1. Some texts refer to any error detected at compile time as a syntax error. However, the usage of types is part of the meaning (or semantics) of a program.

2. Some authors refer to such languages as *untyped* or *typeless* in the sense that the type of the variable is not specified in the program source. We believe that this usage is misleading, preferring to reserve these terms to describe languages, such as assembly/machine languages, in which neither variables nor values are typed.

3. In some C compilers the situation is worsened by the fact that an int occupies 16 bits, while a float is 32 bits. This error cannot, in general, be detected at either compile time or run time.

Whether a language is statically or dynamically typed does not prevent it from being strongly typed. For example, Ada and Java are strongly typed languages, while C and C++ are not. Dynamically typed languages such as Scheme and Perl are strongly typed since the typing of values themselves and the run time checking of those values by the interpreter prevent undetected type errors. The example given above exposes one of several problems in the type system of C. Strong typing generally promotes more reliable programs and is viewed as a virtue in programming language design.

The next two sections examine built-in types. *Basic types* denote data values that are atomic, or indivisible from the programmer's viewpoint. In contrast, *nonbasic types* correspond to data that is composed from other data. For example, various kinds of lists, arrays, and sets are nonbasic types.

5.3   BASIC TYPES

A programming language's basic types usually correspond to the data types that are available on contemporary machines. Table 5.1 summarizes the basic types that are available in C,[4] Ada, and Java.

Assuming a modern 32-bit computer, memory requirements for these types are usually measured using the following delineations of memory units:

- *Nibble:* four contiguous bits of memory; a half-byte
- *Byte:* 8 contiguous bits of memory
- *Half-word:* 16 contiguous bits $= 2$ bytes
- *Word:* 32 contiguous bits of memory $= 4$ bytes
- *Double word:* 64 contiguous bits $= 8$ bytes
- *Quad word:* 128 contiguous bits $= 16$ bytes

Historically, the word size has varied; some word sizes used have included 8, 12, 16, 18, 24, 32, 36, 48, and 60 bits. As 64-bit machines replace 32-bit machines, a word should become associated with 64 bits.

As an example, in Java the notion of a byte is defined as an explicit type, and a Java `byte` accommodates $2^8 = 256$ distinct binary values. A Java `short` value occupies a half-word, an `int` value occupies a word, and a `long` value occupies a double word. Java is unusual in that the language prescribes the above sizes of the integral types. Most

| **Table 5.1**   Basic Types in C, Ada, and Java

Type	C	Ada	Java
Byte			byte
Integer	short, int, long	integer	short, int, long
Real number	float, double	float, decimal	float, double
Character	char	character	char
Boolean		boolean	boolean

---

4. C99 supports a Boolean type, but at this time few compilers appear to support it.

languages, including C, C++, and Pascal, leave to the compiler implementor the task of binding types to memory sizes; in many cases the standards specify minimum sizes for each type. Ada allows the programmer to specify the required range for each variable, but the range may trigger a compile error if it exceeds what the compiler supports.

Because each of these numeric types is finite in size, an arithmetic operation can produce a value that is outside its defined range. For example, consider the addition 2,147,483,647 + 1 using 32-bit two's complement arithmetic; the addition generates a value outside the allowable range. Some machines (e.g., MIPS) generate an interrupt when such an error occurs; however, many, including the Java Virtual Machine, do not [Arnold and Gosling, 1998, p. 358]:

> If overflow occurs, then the sign of the result is not the same as the sign of the mathematical sum of the two operand values.

Failure to generate an interrupt or exception when overflow occurs is a design mistake that unnecessarily complicates the programmer's life.[5]

In C-like languages (using C-style syntax), the following `int` operations are functions that take two `int` arguments and return an `int` value as a result:

```
+, -, *, /, %
==, !=, <, <=, >, >=
```

The % denotes the *modulo* function that returns the integer remainder. The rest of these have conventional behaviors except for division, which in mathematics would normally produce a real number as a result.

Note that C-like languages, except Java, are unusual in that the equality and relational operators produce an `int` result. To enable a consistent interpretation, the value zero is interpreted as `false` and all other values are interpreted as `true`. Perl also uses this convention.

In most programming languages, a real number is a nonintegral value stored in floating point format in either single- (e.g., C `float`) or double-precision format (e.g., C `double`), depending on the precision and range of values needed. For current 32-bit machines, a `float` value requires a 32-bit memory word, while a `double` value requires a 64-bit word.

Floating point values in IEEE format are represented using *scientific notation*, in which a value is represented as a product of a binary number with a single nonzero digit to the left of the decimal point and an appropriate power of 2. For example, the decimal number 123.45 is represented in decimal scientific notation as 1.2345×10^2. Computers use binary rather than decimal to represent numbers, but otherwise follow the same principle. Computationally, a real value is stored as a product of a binary real value with a single 1 to the left of the binary point and an appropriate power of 2. Older machines do not follow the IEEE format but use some form of scientific notation.

Consider representing the decimal real number 3.375 in binary scientific notation. Conversion to binary is done by splitting the number into its integer and fractional parts

5. The bit pattern 100...0 in two's complement arithmetic could be interpreted as the value *undefined*, instead of as a negative number with no positive counterpart. Such a design would simplify the semantics of many debugging situations (for example, the identification of uninitialized variables).

Single precision:

s	e	m

bit 0   1–8   9–31

s = sign
e = exponent
m = mantissa

Double precision:

s	e'	m'

bit 0   1–11   12–63

| **Figure 5.1   IEEE 754 Floating Point Number Representation**

and converting each part separately to binary. The integer part of 3.375 is 3, which in binary is 11_2. The fractional part 0.375 is 0.011_2, since $0.375 = 0.25 + 0.125 = 2^{-2} + 2^{-3} = 0.011_2$. Thus, the scientific notation for 3.375 in binary is:

$$3.375_{10} = 11.011_2 = 1.1011_2 \times 2^1$$

Modern computers invented after 1980 use the IEEE 754 standard for representing floating point values [Goldberg, 1991]. This standard is summarized in Figure 5.1. A single-precision normalized floating point number has:

- A sign bit s with 0 denoting $+$ and 1 denoting $-$,

- An 8-bit exponent e denoting a power of 2 and encoded as the true exponent $+127$ (all one bits). The number 127 is termed the *bias* and the encoding is called *excess 127 notation*, and

- A 32-bit mantissa m denoting a binary fraction in the range 0 through 1 and interpreted as the number $1.m$. The "1." in the fraction is commonly referred to as the *hidden bit*.

Altogether, this represents the number:

$$(-1)^s \times 1.m \times 2^{e-127}$$

Note that the number 0.0 is represented using the all zero-bit pattern. The double-precision version allows more bits for the exponent and binary fraction, thus adding to the range of values that can be represented, as well as the number of significant digits.

Single precision allows a range of approximately $\pm 10^{38}$ to 10^{-38}, while double precision allows a range of $\pm 10^{308}$ to 10^{-308}. Single precision numbers have about 7 significant decimal digits in the mantissa, while double precision number precision have 16 significant decimal digits.

The IEEE 754 standard also provides unique representations for unusual numbers, like *infinity* (all 1s in the exponent and all 0s in the mantissa) and *not a number* (NaN) (all 1s in the exponent and not all 0s in the mantissa). Denormalized floating point numbers are also defined to provide a representation for numbers that are smaller than the smallest normalized value (all 0s in the exponent and any nonzero mantissa).

To continue our example, consider the decimal number 3.375. It has a sign bit of 0, since the number is positive. Since the true exponent is 1, the machine exponent is $127 + 1 = 128$ in decimal or 1000 0000 in binary, since the machine exponent is stored in excess 127 notation. Finally, the mantissa is the value after the binary point: 101 1000 0000 0000 0000 0000 in single precision binary. Putting together the sign, exponent, and mantissa, we get:

0 1000 0000 101 1000 0000 0000 0000 0000

Most exact decimal numbers like 0.2 do not have exact representations in binary floating point. Thus, when we perform certain arithmetic operations on them, like 5×0.2, we obtain a result that is not quite the same as the mathematical result ($5 \times 0.2 \neq 1.0$ in this case). These and other problems associated with floating point arithmetic are discussed in some detail in [Hennessy and Patterson, 1998, Chapter 4] and in [Goldberg, 1991].

In C/C++, the following operations take two `float` operands.

```
+, -, *, /
==, !=, <, <=, >, >=
```

Each operation in the first group returns a `float` result, while each operation in the second group returns an `int` which, as explained above, is usually interpreted as a boolean.

Two issues are raised by this capability. First, most of the same symbols listed here are identical with those used for integer operations. For instance, the addition of two integers is denoted by + and computes an `int` result, while the addition of two floating point numbers also uses + but delivers a `float` result. This is an instance of the more general notion of operator overloading.

> **Definition**: An operator or function is said to be *overloaded* when its meaning varies depending on the types of its operands or arguments or result.

The overloading of built-in operators and functions (e.g., I/O functions) has been in use since the earliest days of Fortran. More interesting examples of overloading are discussed in Chapter 4.

The second issue raised here is that the above floating point operator definitions are incomplete. That is, they do not include the cases where one or the other operand is `int` rather than `float`. This is called "mixed mode" arithmetic in Fortran, and its instances for the above operations are summarized as follows:

```
float (+, -, *, /) int
int (+, -, *, /) float
float (==, !=, <, <=, >, >=) int
int (==, !=, <, <=, >, >=) float
```

The first two produce a `float` result, while the last two produce an `int` result.

For example, consider the sum $2.5 + 1$ involving a `float` and an `int`. The most appropriate result for this sum is 3.5, which cannot be represented as `int`; it must be `float` or `double`. To achieve this result, the `int` value 1 must be converted to its `float` equivalent before the sum is computed, since there are no mixed mode operations at the machine level.

Table 5.2

The Value 2 in
Various Data
Representations

Type	Bits
char	0000 0000 0011 0010
short	0000 0000 0000 0010
int	0000 0000 0000 0000 0000 0000 0000 0010
float	0100 0000 0000 0000 0000 0000 0000 0000

Type Conversion   At the machine level, arithmetic operations require that both operands be the same type (int, float, or double). To simulate a mixed mode operation, one of the operands must have its value converted to the type of the other. Such a conversion is termed a *type conversion*, since it creates a different bit pattern to represent the value in a different type.

As an example, consider the various representations of the Java value 2 given in Table 5.2. Interpreting the Unicode character '2' as a 16-bit integer would give the integer value 50 (see Table 5.3). The 16-bit and 32-bit integer representations are identical, except for the 16 extra leading zeros in the 32-bit version. Interpreting the floating point number 2.0 as an integer would give the integer value 2^{30}, a very large number. So a type conversion is often needed to guarantee the proper interpretation of a value in preparation for performing an arithmetic operation on that value.

A type conversion is called a *narrowing* conversion if the resulting value permits fewer bits than the original value (thus potentially losing information). For example, in converting a float to an int, the fractional part after the decimal point will be lost. For instance, converting 2.4 to an int results in the value 2, with the loss of the fraction 0.4.

A type conversion is called a *widening* conversion if the resulting value requires no fewer bits than the original value (usually without loss of information). Thus, converting 2 to a float results in the value 2.0, which is mathematically equivalent. We use the term *usually* because there are exceptions. For instance, converting a sufficiently large 32-bit integer to a 32-bit floating point number results in the loss of the lower order 8 bits of the integer value; thus, the two values are only approximately equal.

Languages should support *implicit* type conversions only if they are widening conversions. Thus, for example, the expression 2.5 + 1 is allowed because it is interpreted as 2.5 + float(1), where the conversion function float() is considered a widening conversion.

Historically, both numeric and string data types have had problems because of implicit narrowing conversions. Problems with strings have resulted primarily from the use of fixed size strings.

In general, defining the various kinds of implicit type conversions permitted in a programing language must be done with care. Consider the algorithm in Figure 5.2 that defines arithmetic type conversions in ANSI C [Kernighan and Ritchie, 1988, p. 198]. These are messy rules! Often they are not well understood by programmers, and sometimes they give surprising results. For instance, the effect of some of these rules is to remove the sign from a signed value.

Narrowing conversions should require the program to explicitly invoke a type conversion function. In any set of implicit conversions, there is the danger that the result

If ...	then convert ...
either operand is `long double`	the other to `long double`
either operand is `double`	the other to `double`
either operand is `float`	the other to `float`
either operand is `unsigned long int`	the other to `unsigned long int`
the operands are `long int` and `unsigned int`	
and `long int` can represent `unsigned int`	the `unsigned int` to `long int`
and `long int` cannot represent `unsigned int`	both operands to `unsigned long int`
one operand is `long int`	the other to `long int`
one operand is `unsigned int`	the other to `unsigned int`

| **Figure 5.2**   **ANSI C Implicit Type Conversion Rules**

will be unexpected, sometimes even to the language designer. A classic example from the language PL/I is:

```
declare (a) char(3);
...
a = '123';
a = a + 1;
```

in which the final value of a is three space characters, not '124' as expected. The danger here is that although the type conversion rules may be reasonable in isolation, the ways in which they interact are not always well-understood.

The term *type coercion* is used to denote an implicit change of a value from one type to another that may or may not involve a type conversion. In the latter case the value remains unchanged, only its type has changed. An example from Java would be:

```
String s = "abc";
...
Object obj = s;
```

In this case the string s is coerced to an *Object*, but the value remains the same, namely, a string object.

Character Sets   Older languages, such as C, use the ASCII character set, which has a 7-bit encoding. On modern machines each such code is stored in an 8-bit byte, with the character codes above 127 unspecified; most modern operating systems use the so-called *Latin-1* encoding, which does specify the codes above 127.

The ASCII character set and their character codes in base 8 (octal)[6] are given in Table 5.3. The character codes 000–037 and 177 octal (0–31, 127 decimal) are not printable. All of the codes 001–037 can be generated via control key combinations; for example, nl can be generated via Ctrl-J and is the familiar linefeed or newline

---

6. Showing the character codes using hexadecimal might have been better, but would not fit horizontally on the page.

| Table 5.3   ASCII Character Set

Octal	0	1	2	3	4	5	6	7
00x	null	soh	stx	etx	eot	enq	ack	bell
01x	bs	ht	nl	vt	np	cr	so	si
02x	dle	dc1	dc2	dc3	dc4	nak	syn	etb
03x	can	em	sub	esc	fs	gs	rs	us
04x	␣	!	"	#	$	%	&	'
05x	(	)	*	+	,	−	.	/
06x	0	1	2	3	4	5	6	7
07x	8	9	:	;	<	=	>	?
10x	@	A	B	C	D	E	F	G
11x	H	I	J	K	L	M	N	O
12x	P	Q	R	S	T	U	V	W
13x	X	Y	Z	[	\	]	^	_
14x	'	a	b	c	d	e	f	g
15x	h	i	j	k	l	m	n	o
16x	p	q	r	s	t	u	v	w
17x	x	y	z	{	|	}	~	del

character \n. Many of the names for the codes 001–037 are abbreviated; for example, bs for backspace, ht for horizontal tab, nl for newline, cr for carriage return, etcetera. From this table we see that the character 2 has octal code 062 (decimal 50).

A Java char value uses the Unicode [Unicode Consortium, 2000] UTF-16 character set, which is a 16-bit standard for character encoding, instead of the more conventional ASCII[7] 7-bit standard. The Unicode standard defines three character sets, an 8-bit UTF-8, a 16-bit UTF-16, and a 32-bit UTF-32; UTF-8 includes ASCII and is a proper subset of UTF-16, which, in turn, is a proper subset of UTF-32. The Unicode UTF-16 character set provides a rich assortment of characters that allow Java programs to embody a more international vocabulary than its predecessors. A sampling of the Unicode UTF-16 character set's coverage of the world's languages and other character sets is given in Table 5.4.

As the table suggests, the Unicode standard includes codes for character sets that span the world's major written languages. It also includes punctuation marks, diacritics, mathematical symbols, and a wide array of other technical symbols. It provides codes for modifying characters, such as the tilde (~), and codes that are used to encode accented letters (ñ). The Unicode standard is constantly being updated (see **www.unicode.org** for more detailed information). Its current version defines codes for 49,194 characters from the world's alphabets and other symbol sets.

---

7. ASCII is the *American Standard Code for Information Interchange*, which is a subset of the ISO standard 8859-1 8-bit code known as the Latin-1 character set, which is properly embedded within the Unicode set, as shown in Table 5.4.

| **Table 5.4** Sampling of the Unicode UTF-16 Character Set

Unicode Value (hex)	Characters	Unicode Value (hex)	Characters
\u0000-\u007F	ASCII set	\u0F00-\u0FBF	Tibetan
\u0100-\u024F	Latin extended	\u10A0-\u10FF	Georgian
\u0300-\u036F	diacritics	\u2000-\u206FF	punctuation
\u0300-\u036F	Greek	\u20A0-\u20CF	currency
\u0400-\u04FF	Cyrillic	\u2190-\u21FF	arrows
\u0530-\u058F	Armenian	\u2200-\u22FF	mathematics
\u0590-\u05FF	Hebrew	\u2300-\u23FF	technical
\u0600-\u06FF	Arabic	\u2440-\u245F	OCR
\u0B80-\u0BFF	Tamil	\u25A0-\u25FF	geometrics
\u0C00-\u0C7F	Telugu	\u2700-\u27BF	Dingbats
\u0C80-\u0CFF	Kannada	\u30A0-\u30FF	Katakana
\u0E00-\u0E7F	Thai	\u3200-\u32FF	CJK letters
\u0E80-\u0EFF	Lao	\uAC00-\uD7A3	Hangul

5.4 NONBASIC TYPES

In the next few sections, we discuss data types that are constructed from the basic ones. The primary constructed data types include enumerations, pointers, character strings, arrays, records, and unions (or case-variant records).

5.4.1 Enumerations

Another type that is strongly related to the integer type is the *enumeration*. Supported by many languages, enumerations provide a way to assign names to a series of integral values. This allows the names to be used in programs in place of their associated integral values, enhancing readability of the program text itself.

C, C++, Java and Ada support enumerations in similar ways. For example, the following C/C++ declaration:

```
enum day {monday, tuesday, wednesday, thursday,
    friday, saturday, sunday};
enum day myDay = wednesday;
```

defines an integral type `day` and a variable `myDay` initialized to the value `wednesday`. In C/C++ the values of this type are treated as if they were the integers 0, ... , 6 respectively, so that the variable `myDay` can be treated as if it were an ordinary `int` variable.

A Java 1.5 enumeration type is more powerful than its counterpart in C, C++, or Ada. Consider the Java code fragment in Figure 5.3. This code defines `Day` as an `enum` type, which is a subclass of the Java class `Enum`. The values `Monday, Tuesday, ..., Sunday` are implicitly ordered by the order of their appearance in the definition, as is also true in C/C++ and Ada. Every Java `enum` type is `Comparable` and `Serializable`, and it inherits the methods of Java class `Object`, like `toString`, which is needed in the last line of Figure 5.3. (See Chapter 13 for a fuller discussion of classes.)

```
import java.io.*;
...
enum Day {Monday, Tuesday, Wednesday, Thursday, Friday,
         Saturday, Sunday};
...
for (Day d : Day.values()) {
    System.out.println(d);
}
```

| **Figure 5.3**   **Java 1.5** enum **Example**

The advantage of enumeration types in general is that they allow the code to become more readable. If enumerations are not available (or not used), a type like day must be simulated by associating its values with the integers 0–6 and using integer operators and assignments. In the Java version, the use of enum renders the code even more reliable, since all of Java's extensive type checking is naturally applied to all enum objects at compile time.

5.4.2 Pointers

A *pointer* is a value that represents a memory address or reference. It provides a level of indirection in referencing memory that other data types do not. Pointers are commonly used in C, C++, Ada, and Perl.

C provides two pointer operations: the *address of* operator (unary &) takes a variable argument and returns the address of the variable, and the *dereferencing* operator (unary *) takes a reference and produces the value of the reference.

To illustrate the use of pointers, consider the linked list defined by a Node in C/C++:

```
struct Node {
    int key;
    struct Node* next;
};
struct Node* head;
```

Here, a Node is a pair of values, an integer key and a pointer next. Thus, Node is a recursive data structure. The pointer head refers to the first Node in the list. An example linked list is depicted in Figure 5.4.

Pointers are often considered the bane of reliable software development, since programs which use pointers tend to have more errors. In particular, some languages (e.g., C) require the programmer to explicitly manage pointers to both allocate and deallocate dynamic data structures. However, this type of *dynamic memory management* is so complex that most programmers don't do it well. This topic is further explored in Chapter 11.

Pointers are particularly troublesome in C because array references and pointers are considered equivalent. For example, the two functions given in Figure 5.5 are semantically identical. In particular, the use of a pointer in the increment statement inside the for loop of the function on the right is more cryptic than its counterpart on the left.

| **Figure 5.4**   **A Simple Linked List in C**

Nevertheless, the code on the right illustrates the relationship between an array index and a pointer. That is, if a is an array, then the reference a is the same as the address of a[0]. This leads to the rule that if **either** E1 or E2 is a pointer type (i.e., its value is an address), then:

$$E1[E2] = *((E1) + (E2))$$

where unary $*$ is the dereferencing operator. For example, using Figure 5.5 if a is of type float[ ] and i is an int, then:

```
a[i] = *(a + i) = i[a]
```

Thus, C makes no effective distinction between the array index i and a pointer referencing the ith element of a. For program clarity, array indexing should be preferred since it is less error prone than pointer arithmetic.

A classic C example of the use of pointers for array indexing is the implementation of the strcpy function given in Figure 5.6. Deciphering this code relies on knowing that strings p and q are arrays of characters ending in a NUL character, which is interpreted as false. In this process, the code does not prevent the array p from being overrun, which will occur if the storage block allocated to p is shorter than the length of string q.

While C/C++ and Ada have not found a way to remove pointers from their vocabulary, other languages, including functional and logic languages and some object-oriented languages such as Java, have done so. Java, functional languages such as Scheme and Haskell, and the logic language Prolog all make heavy use of pointers, even though pointers are not part of the vocabulary of these languages. Removing explicit pointers from a language does not eliminate the ability to do dynamic memory allocation and deallocation of complex structures, as we shall see in Chapter 14. We study dynamic memory management in Chapter 11.

```
float sum(float a[ ], int n)          float sum(float *a, int n)
{                                     {
    int i;                                int i;
    float s = 0.0;                        float s = 0.0;
    for (i = 0; i < n; i++)               for (i = 0; i < n; i++)
        s += a[i];                            s += *a++;
}                                     }
```

| **Figure 5.5**   **Equivalence of Arrays and Pointers in C/C++**

```
void strcpy (char* p, char* q) {
   while (*p++ = *q++) ;
}
```

| **Figure 5.6**   The `strcpy` **Function**

5.4.3 Arrays and Lists

Arrays are indexed sequences of values; in a statically typed language, all the values in an array must have the same type. Here is the syntax of some example array declarations in C:

```
int A[10];
float C[4][3];
char S[40];
```

The variable A is a one-dimensional array of `int`s, while the variable C is a two-dimensional array of `float`s, composed of four 3-entry rows. Although some early languages (e.g., Fortran) restricted the maximum number of dimensions in an array, most current languages do not.

Technically, C-like languages restrict arrays to be one dimensional, which is suggested by the above declaration of C. However, any one-dimensional array declaration may be expanded to produce an "array of arrays." For instance, the array C declared above is technically an array of three 4-element arrays. Note the odd syntax for declaring the number of rows and columns in C; this oddity is retained in C++ and Java as well. An advantage to this design is that it is possible to create a nonrectangular two dimensional, that is, a two-dimensional array in which each row has a different number of columns.

All the above arrays have statically bound sizes in each dimension. Many languages permit the creation of arrays whose size in each dimension can be determined at run time. For example, in Java all arrays are dynamically sized at run time, but once they are created their sizes are fixed.

The basic array operator is the indexing operator, which references a single entry in an array by naming its index. Examples include `a[3]` and `c[i+1][j-1]`, using the arrays declared above. In C-style languages the index set for any dimension is $\{0, \ldots, n-1\}$, where n is the size of that dimension. In contrast, Fortran uses $\{1, \ldots, n\}$, while Pascal and Ada allow for the explicit declaration of lower and upper bounds of each dimension. For example, the above declarations in Ada might appear as:

```
a : array(-4..5) of INTEGER;
c : array(1..4, 0..2) of FLOAT;
s : array(1..40) of CHARACTER;
```

Pascal's arrays are statically sized, with static bounds for each dimension. In such languages the static array bounds are part of the array type, which [Stroustrup, 1994] referred to as a straightjacket.

Ada's arrays are also statically sized, but with a bit more flexibility in declaring the size. This feature is called "unconstrained," which means that the range of index values for a declared array is determined implicitly by the number of elements in its initial value. For example:

```
a : array(INTEGER range <>) of INTEGER :=
    (1 | 10 => 12, 2 .. 8 => 0, 9 => 33);
```

initializes array a to the index range $1 \ldots 10$ and initial values $12, 0, 0, \ldots, 0, 33, 12$.

Pascal-like languages permit indices to be any of the integral types, including ints (of all sizes), chars, and enums. The type char, when viewed through its encoding, can be treated as just another integral type.

The languages Ada and Java check the value of each array index to ensure that it is in range, although in Ada compilers checking may require invoking a compile time option. Neither C nor C++ mandate index checking at run time and almost no C/C++ compilers implement index checking, even as an option. Because of the equivalence of arrays and pointers, it is unclear how index checking could be implemented in these languages (see Section 5.4.2 for examples).

Implementation Issues   The semantic phase of a compiler constructs a block of information for each array including (depending on the language): array element type, array element size, index type for each dimension, index range or size for each dimension. In particular, this information is needed to calculate memory addresses for indexed expressions like A[i] and to perform index range checking at run time, if required. This information is termed a *dope vector*, and may exist only at compile time or partially at run time, depending on the language.

As an example, consider the Java array declaration:

```
int[ ] A = new int(n);
```

At run time, every reference of the form a[i] must have an index value i between 0 and $n - 1$, and every value assigned to a[i] must have type int. Since the value of i or n cannot be determined before run time, the run-time portion of the dope vector must contain the size of the array. In fact, Java makes this information available as a.length.

In contrast, C and C++ do not require run-time index checking for arrays. Indexing overruns in C/C++ arrays are a widespread source of run-time errors in large software systems; often these errors appear as "memory protection faults." Buffer overflows are a type of indexing overrun that is exploited by hackers to break into systems. Thus, strongly typed languages like Java and Ada that provide index range checking have advantages over C/C++ for software reliability.

In Java a dope vector might contain the element size e, the element type, the number of elements n, and the address of the array's first element to facilitate index calculations. For example, the dope vector and the layout of array A when n = 10 are shown in Figure 5.7, assuming an int occupies 4 bytes.

The memory address of the first element *addr(a[0])* can be used to compute the address of any other element *addr(a[i])* with element size e using the following formula:

$$addr(a[i]) = addr(a[0]) + e \cdot i$$

Static Area

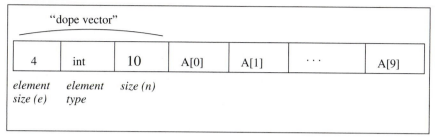

| **Figure 5.7** Memory Allocation for the One-Dimensional Array A

For example, the memory address of a[2], assuming the size of an int is 4 bytes, is calculated as:

$$addr(a[2]) = addr(a[0]) + 4 \cdot 2 = addr(a[0]) + 8$$

This calculation generalizes to two- and higher-dimensional arrays by extending the dope vector with sufficient information to enable the calculation of the address of an individual element. For example, a static memory allocation for the two-dimensional array C declared above is illustrated in Figure 5.8.

Here, we note that C has 4 rows and 3 columns, individual elements are stored in contiguous memory locations, one row at a time, and the two-dimensional array is rectangular (guaranteed by the static allocation size). This is called *row-major order*. Calculation of the address of C[i][j], given values for indexes i and j, can be defined in the following general way, again taking into account the number of addressable units (bytes) an individual element requires.

$$addr(C[i][j]) = addr(C[0][0]) + e \cdot (ni + j)$$

For example, the address of C[2][1] is computed by:

$$addr(C[2][1]) = addr(C[0][0]) + 2 \cdot (3 \times 2 + 1)$$
$$= addr(C[0][0]) + 14$$

For historical reasons, Fortran stores the elements of its two-dimensional arrays in *column-major* order. That is, all the elements of the first column are stored in contiguous

Static Area

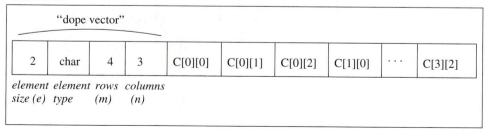

| **Figure 5.8** Memory Allocation for Array C in Row-Major Order

Static Area

| Figure 5.9   Memory Allocation for Array C in Column-Major Order

memory locations, then all the elements of the second column, and so forth. For example, if our example array C were declared in a Fortran program, its elements would be allocated to memory as shown in Figure 5.9.

With this change, the calculation of the address of C[i][j] now becomes:

$$addr(C[i][j]) = addr(C[0][0]) + e \cdot (mj + i)$$

For example, the address of C[2][1] changes to:

$$addr(C[2][1]) = addr(C[0][0]) + 2 \cdot (4 \times 1 + 2)$$
$$= addr(C[0][0]) + 12$$

In strongly typed languages, range checking for array references cannot, in general, occur until run time, since the values of indexes i and j vary during program execution. For languages with 0-origin indexing, the following range checking code must be executed for the arrays a and c declared above:

- For each reference A[i], check that $0 \leq i < n$.

- For each reference C[i][j], check that $0 \leq i < m$ and $0 \leq j < n$.

In some situations it is possible to guarantee at compile time that an invalid index cannot occur. Consider the following loop in Java:

```
double sum = 0.0;
for (int i = 0; i < A.length; i++)
    sum += A[i];
```

The range of values of index i is $0, \ldots, A.length - 1$, which is precisely the range of valid legal subscripts for array A.

In languages like Ada, which allow nonzero origin indexing, the dope vector must contain additional information to enable effective address calculation and run-time range checking for references like A[i] and C[i][j]. This information includes the (nonzero) lower bound for the index in each array dimension, as well as either the size of that dimension or the upper bound of its index. As with Java, Ada makes this information available for inspection at run time.

In some languages, all the elements of an array are automatically preinitialized at the time they are declared; in others they are not. For instance, Java follows the convention that arrays of numbers (int, float, short, long, and double) have all their elements preinitialized to 0, arrays of char are preinitialized to '\u0000', arrays of references to objects are preinitialized to null, and arrays of booleans are preinitialized to false.

In some languages, the programmer can initialize an array's elements at the time the array is declared. The following Java declaration initializes all six integers in the 2x3 array T to the integer value 1:

```
int[][] T = {{1, 1, 1},{1, 1, 1}};
```

Lists and Slices It is often desirable in programming to look at an entire section of an array at once, such as a contiguous portion of a row or an entire column of a two-dimensional array. For instance, consider the following Python declaration:

```
b = [33, 55, 'hello', 'R2D2']
```

Here the array b (known as a *list* in Python) is *heterogeneous*, since the values of different entries can have different types. Python lists are indexed beginning at 0, so that the reference b[0] returns the value 33.

A *slice* of a Python list is a contiguous series of entries, specified by its beginning index and length. For example, the slice b[0:3] refers to the sublist [33, 55, 'hello']. Ada also supports array slicing.

A rich collection of operations using list slices is available in Python. For example, the operators + and = designate list concatenation and assignment, respectively. So the following Python dialog[8] gives some interesting results:

```
>>> b
[33, 55, 'hello', 'R2D2']
>>> b[2:2] + 2*['C3PO', 'Luke']
['hello', 'R2D2', 'C3PO', 'Luke', 'C3PO', 'Luke']
>>> b[:0] = b
[33, 55, 'hello', 'R2D2', 33, 55, 'hello', 'R2D2']
```

The first operation builds a list by concatenating two lists, the second containing two copies of the list ['C3PO', 'Luke']. The second operation inserts a new copy of list b at the beginning of list b, effectively doubling its length.

Many opportunities for using dynamic lists and their operations occur in functional programming. We shall revisit this topic in great detail in Chapter 14 on functional programming, where lists are used extensively to solve various programming problems.

5.4.4 Strings

Strings are so fundamental to programming that they are now directly supported by most programming languages. Historically, neither Fortran nor Algol 60 had any support for strings; Cobol had statically sized strings, with only a limited set of operations. C, as a relatively modern language, is unusual, since it does not explicitly support character strings as a distinct data type.

---

8. Here, the carets >>> indicate a prompt from the Python interpreter.

Instead, C strings are encoded as arrays of ASCII characters, one character per byte, with an additional NUL character (all bits zero) appended at the end. For example, to declare the string variable `greeting` and assign it the value "hello," the C programmer would write:

```
char greeting[] = "hello";
```

but the string "hello" requires 6 bytes, one for each of the 5 characters plus one for the NUL character, which marks the end of the string. Beyond the declared length of the character string array, all characters following the ASCII character NUL in memory will have unknown or undefined values. Transformations on this value are performed one character at a time.

Thus, the design of strings in C is error prone because:

1 The programmer must remember to allocate at least 1 extra byte for the trailing NUL character.
2 The string assignment `a = b` where `a` and `b` are strings is erroneous; instead you must use the library function `strcpy`. It is the programmer's responsibility to ensure that the storage allocated for `a` is capable of holding all the characters in `b`, up to and including the trailing NUL.

Ada provides for fixed size strings, which, like C, are arrays of characters. However, unlike C, an Ada string of size 6, for example, always holds exactly 6 characters. Thus, the assignment of the string "hello" can only be made to a string variable of declared size 5 without incurring a run-time error.

In contrast, a *String* behaves as a built-in type in Java, Perl, and Python, capable of holding an unbounded number of characters. In these languages, a *String* variable is not declared with a size, as it is in C and Ada, nor does the programmer know (or care) how strings are stored at run time. Here is the above declaration rewritten in Java:

```
String greeting = "hello";
```

Java, Perl, and Python all provide vast libraries of string operations and functions, including concatenation, case conversion, pattern matching, and substring. Java and Python provide many operations through class libraries.

5.4.5 Structures

A *structure* or *record* is a collection of elements of potentially differing types. So structures are like Python lists in the sense that the types of their elements can vary. However, they are unlike arrays and lists because their elements have distinct names and are accessed by name rather than by index. The individual elements of a structure are often called *fields*.

Structures first appeared in Cobol and PL/I, after being omitted from both Fortran and Algol 60. The current abstract form of a structure originated in both Pascal-style languages and C-style languages, even though their concrete syntax differs. Java omits structures entirely, having effectively subsumed them within the more general notion of a class. C++ has both structures and classes, retaining structures in order to maintain backward compatibility with C.

As an example, consider the following C structure and variable declaration that models an individual employee in an organization:

```
struct employeeType {
    int id;
    char name[26];
    int age;
    float salary;
    char dept;
};
struct employeeType employee;
```

Every field within a structure may have a different data type. In this example, we see that the types are `int`, `char[]`, `int`, `float`, and `char`. However, every field name within a structure must be unique.

Individual fields within a structure are usually allocated in a contiguous block. The number of bytes actually allocated and the order of the fields allocated is machine and compiler dependent. For example, some compilers allocate the fields in the reverse order of declaration. Also, some machines require, for example, that a 32-bit `int` or `float` be allocated at an address that is a multiple of 4. So while the minimum allocation for `employeeType` is 39 bytes, under the assumptions just cited, the allocation requires 44 bytes. Programs that make assumptions about storage order and size will encounter portability problems.

The only significant operation, besides assignment, on structures is the structure reference (field selection) operator, denoted by a dot. The structure reference operator associates from left to right; its first operand is an expression that identifies the structure, and its second operand is an identifer *id* that identifies a field within the structure. As an example, the reference `employee.age` selects the `age` field of the structure variable `employee`. Thus, an assignment statement like:

```
employee.age = 45;
```

is legal because `employee` is a `struct` containing the `int` field `age`.

In object-oriented languages, a class can be viewed as an extension of a structure because it encapsulates functions together with instance variables (see Chapter 13). A class's instance variables themselves are comparable to the fields of a structure, ignoring for the moment that some object-oriented languages may limit their accessibility.

5.4.6 Variant Records and Unions

Years ago, memory was scarce. Programmers had to be very economical with the way they defined array and record structures so that a minimum amount of storage was wasted. Part of this economy could be realized by using *variant records*, in which two or more different fields share the same block of memory.

Fortran was the first language to support the concept of variant records, in the form of its `EQUIVALENCE` statement. This turned out to be a very unsafe feature, since programmers had to keep the processing of the two variables separate throughout the run-time life of the program. For instance, if A and B are defined to share the same memory block purely for the sake of saving memory, all the code that accesses A must be nonoverlapping in time with all the code that accesses B.

Later languages, including Pascal and Ada, defined variant records in a more constrained way, one that led to a more disciplined style of programming while still supporting the memory economies afforded by the EQUIVALENCE statement.

While variant records provide a certain level of clarity in type definitions, as illustrated above, they seem to be less widely used in modern applications. One reason may be that memory is not nearly as scarce as it had been in the 1960s, when Fortran and Cobol were the predominant imperative languages.

In C-like languages, a *union* type realizes the goal of a variant record since it permits two or more different ways of viewing the same storage location. Consider the following type declaration in C/C++:

```
union myUnion {
        int i;
        float r;
};
union myUnion u;
```

Any variable of type myUnion, like u, permits two ways of accessing the same storage locations. Under the u.i variant, the location is viewed as an integer, whereas under the u.r variant, the location is viewed as a floating point value. In systems programming tasks (including the writing of compilers, portions of operating systems, utilities such as grep) activities such as bit-level access to floating point numbers is often desirable.

However, the union or variant record type creates a weakness in a language's type system. Any language with such a construct is not strongly typed, unless other restrictions are imposed. Using the example above, the same bit pattern can be treated as either an int or a float value, which creates precisely the problem discussed in Section 5.1. Languages that have this flaw in their type systems include C, Pascal, C++ (because of its backward compatibility with C), and Modula.

Pascal-like languages also have a *tagged discriminant* union in which a tag field is declared. The tag in Ada is used by the compiler to keep track of the type of variant currently active, thus closing the above-mentioned hole in the type system. Consider the following Ada version of the above example, in which the tag field b has been added to the union record type:

```
type union(b : boolean) is
    record
        case b is
            when true =>
                i : integer;
            when false =>
                r : float;
        end case;
    end record;
```

```
tagged : union;
begin
    tagged := (b => false, r => 3.375);
    put(tagged.i);
```

Ada syntax requires both the variant and the tag to be assigned in one statement; any attempt to assign to either the variant or the tag separately results in a compile time error. The first statement after the `type` declaration sets the tag and assigns the r variant a value consistent with this tag setting.

Thus, Ada can check each reference to a variant at run time to ensure that the reference is consistent with the current setting of the tag. Note that the last line above violates the type system by accessing the i variant field of the record without checking to ensure that its use is consistent with the current tag setting. Thus, the reference `tagged.i` generates a run-time error, since the tag indicates the current value is a floating point number, not an integer. Replacing the reference to i in the `put` statement with r eliminates the type error.

Programmers today seem to be unaware of the union type and rarely use the construct in programs. However, simulating a union type by using an ordinary struct as a basis for several concrete realizations is a popular practice. Consider the following C++ example that defines a struct `Value` which holds one of an int, float, char, or bool:

```
struct Value {
// Value = int intValue | boolean boolValue |
//         float floatValue | char charValue
    enum Type type;
    int intValue; boolean boolValue;
    float floatValue; char charValue;
}
```

This `struct` mimics the Java abstract class `Value` that appears in the abstract syntax of Clite (see Section 2.5.3). The `enum type` can take on one of five values indicating which kind of value is stored or *undefined*, indicating that no valid value is stored.

5.5 RECURSIVE DATA TYPES

In Section 5.4.2, we saw how the elements of a linked list could be recursively defined in C using the structure `Node` as a basis. Recursion is a natural tool for situations like that because the number of `Nodes` in a linked list varies at run time, but the nature of each `Node` does not.

Beyond structures, some programming languages support the recursive definition of data types in a more general way.[9] To illustrate, consider the following Haskell type definitions related to the abstract syntax of Clite that was introduced in Chapter 2.

---

9. In this section, we introduce recursive data types using Haskell; we will explore their usefulness more fully in Chapter 14.

```
data Value = IntValue Integer | FloatValue Float |
            BoolValue Bool | CharValue Char
            deriving (Eq, Ord, Show)
data Expression = Var Variable | Lit Value |
              Binary Op Expression Expression |
              Unary Op Expression
              deriving (Eq, Ord, Show)
type Variable = String
type Op = String
type State = [(Variable, Value)]
```

The first line in this definition is an example of a Haskell *algebraic type* definition, where the new type Value is defined as either an Integer, a Float, a Bool, or a Char value (these are basic types in Haskell, as they are in most other languages).[10]

The second line in this definition is similar; it recursively defines the data type Expression as having any one of four alternative forms. Expression is recursively defined, since any number of Clite Expressions may be nested.

The next two lines define the types Variable and Op as particular kinds of the basic type String. The last line defines the type State as a list of pairs, each having a Variable and a Value.

With these definitions, various functions that analyze or interpret abstract Expressions in Clite can be written as transformations on that recursively defined data type. This particular example will be more fully exploited in Chapter 8 which examines the semantic interpretation of programming languages and Section 14.3.8 which examines the implementation of Clite in Haskell.

5.6 FUNCTIONS AS TYPES

In languages like Fortran, C/C++, Ada, and Java, there are many kinds of entities that are not "first-class citizens" of the language. One obvious example is a control structure such as an *if* or *while* statement, in that an instance of such a statement cannot be assigned as a value to a variable nor passed as an argument. In many languages, functions are not "first-class citizens."

The need to pass functions as arguments appeared early in the history of Fortran. An example included plotting routines which drew graphs of functions such as $y = f(x)$. Another common example includes root solvers for $y = f(x)$. Fortran allowed functions as parameters, but Fortran did not allow programmer-defined types of any kind including functions. Thus, Fortran compilers were unable to check at compile time that an appropriate function was being passed.

Pascal, on the other hand, did allow function types. So a general root solver (such as Newton's method) could declare the type of argument it required:

```
function Newton(a, b: real; function f: real): real;
```

_____

10. The clause deriving (Eq, Ord, Show) asserts that this new type inherits the equality, ordering, and display characteristics of its component types, thus allowing us to use equality (==), ordering (<), and display (show) functions on any of its values.

The arguments `a` and `b` are x values on either side of the root. We are also given that function `f` returns a real number, but the number of arguments of `f` is unspecified. This feature was largely omitted from most Pascal compilers.

One use of an interface class in Java solves precisely this problem (a more complete discussion of interface classes occurs in Section 13.2.8). Such an interface definition is as follows:

```
public interface RootSolvable {
    double valueAt(double x);
}
```

Any class that `implements` this interface could then be passed as an argument to our Newton root finder, whose signature would be:

```
public double Newton(double a, double b, RootSolvable f);
```

Despite this capability, functions are still not first-class citizens even in Java. For example, a Java function cannot construct a new function and return it as a value. Instead it is limited to returning only functions that already exist.

The key message here is that a function should be a type. The generality that this feature brings to programming is significant, as we shall see in Chapter 14.

5.7   TYPE EQUIVALENCE

Sometimes, we need to know when two types are equivalent. For instance, in the description of Pascal [Jensen and Wirth, 1975, p. 149], we read:

> The assignment statement serves to replace the current value of a variable with a new value specified as an expression. ... The variable (or the function) and the expression must be of identical type ....

However, the Pascal Report fails to define the term *identical type*. In fact, two early ETH Pascal compilers implemented this check using different definitions. It is important to define this term clearly, both for the proper implementation of the assignment and for the proper implementation of parameter passing for nonbasic types.[11]

For instance, consider the following C example:

```
struct complex {
    float re, im;
};
struct polar {
    float x, y;
};
```

---

11. Fortunately, the ANSI/ISO Pascal standard later corrected this oversight by defining the notion of the "same type."

```
struct {
      float re, im;
} a, b;
struct complex c, d;
struct polar e;
int f[5], g[10];
```

The question is which of the above variables have the same type?

Under *name equivalence* two types are the same if they have the same name. In the example above, the variables c and d are thus the same type because they share the type name struct complex. However, a and c are not the same type, since they have different type names; in fact, a is an anonymous struct. For the same reason, d and e are not the same type either.

The other form of type equivalence is *structural equivalence* in which two types are the same if they have the same structure. For record types, having the same structure includes the number and order of the fields, as well as the name and type of each field. Under structural equivalence all of a, b, c, and d would have the same type. The variables d and e would have different types, since the two field names are different (even though both have two floating point fields).[12]

Consider the question of type equivalence from the perspective of a compiler, where types are implemented as references to a tagged case-variant record. If the type has a name, the name and the type (pointer) are entered into a symbol table so the type can be retrieved by name. Similarly, a variable and a pointer to its type (but not a type name) are entered into a symbol table. So, under name equivalence two types are the same if the pointers reference the same entry in the symbol table. In the above example, a and b are the same type under name equivalence.

Ada uses name equivalence for types, which extends to arrays and pointers. In fact, Ada syntactically forbids most instances of anonymous types. C uses name equivalence for structs and unions and structural equivalence for other constructed types, including arrays and pointers. Thus, in the above C example, f and g are the same type, since both are one dimensional int arrays; the size does not matter.

Like Ada, Java requires that both classes and interfaces have names. So Java uses name equivalence to determine whether two classes are the same. When using an object where a specific interface is required, Java requires that the declared class of the object implement the interface; this is a specific syntactic and semantic requirement.

5.8 SUBTYPES

A *subtype* can be viewed as a type that has certain constraints placed on its values or operations.

---

12. In the real world the types complex number and polar coordinates are, in fact, distinct in their behaviors, which gives credence to this conclusion.

In Ada, subtypes can be directly specified for variables, arrays, and other data structures. For instance, consider the following Ada declarations:

```
subtype one_to_ten is Integer range 1 .. 10;
type Day is (Monday, Tuesday, Wednesday, Thursday,
             Friday, Saturday, Sunday);
subtype Weekend is Day range Saturday .. Sunday;
type Salary is delta 0.01 digits 9
             range 0.00 .. 9_999_999.99;
subtype Author_Salary is Salary digits 5
             range 0.0 .. 999.99;
```

Here, the subtype one_to_ten constrains the type Integer, the subtype Weekend constrains the range of values of its supertype Day, and the subtype Author_Salary constrains the range of values for its supertype Salary. Variables can be declared for any of these types or subtypes, with full compile-time type checking enforced for their respective constraints.

In Java, subtypes are realized through the class hierarchy. That is, an object s of class S can be assigned to an object t of class T, $t = s$, provided either S and T are the same class or S is a subclass of T. Executing such an assignment does not change the run-time type of the object assigned to t. However, the compiler treats t as though it is of class T, in the sense that only the methods of class T may be invoked. Thus, such an assignment is a kind of widening conversion because no information is lost.

Consider the Java class Number and its subclass Integer defined in java.lang, along with their usage in the following Java fragment:

```
1   Integer i = new Integer(3);
2   ...
3   Number v = i;
4   ...
5   Integer x = (Integer) v;
```

The assignment in line 3 is allowed because an Integer is a subclass of the Number class.[13] The opposite assignment in line 5 requires a cast to avoid a compile time type error. The cast is checked at run time to determine if the object stored in v is of class Integer or one of its subclasses. If Integer were not a subclass of Number, the failure of the cast would be detectable at compile time and reported as a type error.

5.9 POLYMORPHISM AND GENERICS

According to the dictionary, the term *polymorphic* comes from Greek and means "having many forms." In programming, polymorphism is somewhat different from the idea of overloading.

> **Definition**: A function or operation is *polymorphic* if it can be applied to any one of several related types and achieve the same result.

---

13. Such an assignment is dangerous in C++ because information can be discarded.

An advantage of polymorphism is that it enables code reuse. For example, the logic of sorting an array should not necessarily vary with the type of the data elements being sorted. Consider the following simple sort routine in Ada:

```
procedure sort (in out a : list) is
begin
    for i in a'first .. a'last-1 loop
      for j in i+1 .. a'last loop
        if a(i) > a(j) then
          begin t : integer := a(i);
            a(i) := a(j);
            a(j) := t;
          end if;
        end loop;
      end loop;
end sort;
```

The only operations which are type-dependent are the assignment operator and the greater-than comparison. Assignment is type-dependent only in knowing the size of an object. Even for basic data types (see Section 5.3), comparisons are clearly type-dependent.

Recognizing the need to avoid redundancy and support polymorphism, Ada introduced the concept of *generics* or *templates*. A *generic function* or procedure is a template that can be instantiated at compile time with concrete types and operators. In Ada one or more such routines can be collected into a package and parameterized by both the element type and the comparison operator, as shown in Figure 5.10. Generic procedures like this one are examples of *parametric polymorphism*.

In this case, the binding of the argument to a type is deferred from programming time to compile time:

```
package integer_sort is new generic_sort( Integer, ">" );
```

Such a delay in binding creates flexibility, since the sort procedure needs to be written only once, but it can be reused to sort different types of data. With this feature, no loss of static type checking occurs; it only adds to the complexity of language implementation.

Consider a slightly more complicated example, namely, implementing a stack as a linked list of records. In this case, the only type dependent operation is assignment, which only depends on the size of the object being stored in the stack. Here we show only the push operation, again in Ada:

```
package stack_pck is
    type stack is private;
    procedure push (i : integer; in out s : stack);
    ...
```

```
private
    type stack is access node;
   type node is record
       val : integer;
       next : stack;
   end record;
end stack_pck;

package body stack_pck is
procedure push (i : integer; in out s : stack) is
begin
    node n = new node;
    n.val = i;
    n.next = s;
    s = n;
end push;
...
end stack_pck;
```

The stack contains only integer data. However, as with any collection data structure, other than the assignment operator, the stack code does not depend on the type of data stored in the stack.

As with `sort`, Ada permits parameterization of the element type in the `stack`, as shown in Figure 5.11. The only parameter for this template is the type of data being stored.

Ada, C++, and Java 1.5 all provide generics or templates for this purpose.[14] The basic implementation mechanism in C++ can be thought of as macro expansion, much like the `#define` facility of the C preprocessor. First, the actual parameters are textually substituted for the generic parameters, and the resulting text is then compiled.

Object-oriented languages also support generic collections (such as a stack) through *inheritance*, in which a new class can be a subclass of another class. In particular, in Java every class is a subclass of the `Object` class. So all collection classes in Java store `Object`s or a subclass of `Object`. Further simplifying this approach is the fact that every object variable stores a reference or pointer to the object, rather than the object itself. Since all pointers are the same size, independent of the class of an object, implementation of a collection class does not require the use of generics. A simple implementation of a stack class is:

---

14. Java 1.5 templates are implemented differently from Ada or C++ generics. An adequate comparison requires a deeper knowledge of object-oriented programming, and so we defer this until Chapter 13.

```
public class Stack {
   private class Node {
      Object val;
      Node next;
      Node(Object v, Node n) {
        val = v; next = n;
      }
   }
   private Node stack = null;

   ...

   public void push(Object v) { stack = new Node(v, stack); }
}
```

```
generic
   type element is private;
   type list is array(natural range <>) of element;
   with function ">"(a, b : element) return boolean;

package sort_pck is
   procedure sort (in out a : list);
end sort_pck;

package sort_pck is
procedure sort (in out a : list) is
begin
   for i in a'first .. a'last - 1 loop
     for j in i+1 .. a'last loop
       if a(i) > a(j) then
          declare t : element;
          begin
            t := a(i);
            a(i) := a(j);
            a(j) := t;
          end;
       end if;
     end loop;
   end loop;
end sort;
end sort_pck;
```

| **Figure 5.10   Generic Sort in Ada**

```
generic
   type element is private;

package stack_pck is
   type stack is private;
   procedure push (i : element; in out s : stack);
   ...

private
   type stack is access node;
   type node is record
      val : element;
      next : stack;
   end record;
end stack_pck;

package body stack_pck is
procedure push (i : element; in out s : stack) is
begin
   node n = new node;
   n.val = i;
   n.next = s;
   s = n;
end push;
...
end stack_pck;
```

| **Figure 5.11**   **A Generic Stack in Ada**

Note the use of the inner Node class, which is really just a record with a constructor. A more complete discussion of inheritance is given in Chapter 13.

We have already seen in Section 5.4.6 an example of the use of inheritance in a subclass to override a method in a parent class to provide the appropriate functionality for the subclass. Such examples of *pure polymorphism* are common in Java; a common example is providing a toString( ) method in a class, thereby overriding the one in the Object class.

Another approach, again from Java, uses an interface to create a generic function. Although an interface can be subclassed, we can for the moment envision it as just a collection of method signatures. A class which implements an interface is required to provide implementations of all the functions in the interface.

Consider a generic sort function in Java:

```
public static void sort (Comparable[ ] a) {
    for (int i = 0; i < a.length; i++)
        for (int j = i+1; j < a.length; j++)
            if (a[i].compareTo(a[j]) > 0) {
                Comparable t = a[i];
                a[i] = a[j];
                a[j] = t;
            }
}
```

The logic mimics that of the earlier Ada program. There are two major differences. First, the type of the formal parameter a is Comparable, which is the interface:

```
public interface Comparable {
    public abstract int compareTo(Object o);
}
```

Second, the greater than operator is replaced by a call to the compareTo() method.

Thus, an array of objects of any class which implements the compareTo() method can be used in our generic sort. The method compareTo() must return a negative number if the receiver of the message is less than the argument, zero if equal, and a positive number if greater.

5.10   PROGRAMMER–DEFINED TYPES

Recall the definition of a type given at the beginning of the chapter: a type is a set of values and a set of operations on those values. Structures (discussed in Section 5.4.5) allow us to define a representation for a new type. But, historically, they had two problems:

1   The representation is not hidden.
2   No operations on the new type can be defined.

An attempt to solve this problem was the development of abstract data types, which allowed the representation to be hidden. It also allowed the type provider the ability to define operations on the new type. Abstract data types are discussed in Section 13.1.

Object-oriented programming (OOP) provides a powerful means for programmers to define new types. Because OOP is a distinct paradigm, we discuss its type definition features extensively in Chapter 13.

5.11 SUMMARY

This chapter has covered the types that are supported in several programming languages. These types include numbers, logical values, pointers, character strings, arrays, structures, and functions. The relationship between a type and its machine representation has also been discussed.

Several unusual features of types have also been presented, including array slicing, the use of pointers as array indexes, the concept of variant records, and the difference between static and dynamic allocation of arrays and structures. Recursive data types, which are particularly important in functional programming, are also introduced here.

This chapter thus provides groundwork for the next two chapters, which look more carefully at the relationship between variables, their types, and their appearance in expressions and functions that transform their values. These relationships are crucial to an understanding of the type checking features and run-time behavior of programming languages.

EXERCISES

5.1 For your favorite language and compiler (other than Java), list all the basic types supported and their sizes in bytes.

5.2 For your favorite language that supports a boolean type answer the following questions. Is it ordered? Is it convertible to an integer? Argue based on principles as to why this is useful or not.

5.3 Java does not allow nonboolean values for logical tests, unlike other C-like languages. Argue based on principles as to why this is useful or not.

5.4 Write a program to read in a 32-bit floating point value, then print the value and its bit representation. Hint: use a `union` type.

5.5 What is the 32-bit floating point bit representation for 0.2? 0.5? 0.3? 1.0?

5.6 What is the 32-bit floating point bit representation for 0.1?

5.7 Write a program to read in a 32-bit integer value, then print the value and its bit representation. Hint: use a `union` type.

5.8 What is the 32-bit integer representation for 0? 1? −1? 2? −2? 3? −3?

5.9 What is the difference between a *big-endian* and a *little-endian* machine? Cite at least one computer architecture of each kind. How do these architectures affect the values given in Table 5.2?

5.10 Ada provides two remainder operators. What is the difference between them? For your favorite language and machine, which remainder operator do they implement?

5.11 Pick one of the following languages: Pascal, Modula, Ada, C, C++, C#, Java, or other instructor-approved language. Consult an *authoritative* source. Write a report that researches the definition of the language with respect to implicit unsafe type conversions in both assignment statements and expressions.

5.12 In your favorite language, use 32-bit integers to compute N factorial for 2, 3, ... For what value of N do you get an error? How does the error manifest itself?

5.13 Compare enums in Java 1.5 to those in C/C++. Write a demo program for each language. What is the fundamental difference linguistically between the two?

5.14 Consider the C fragment:

```
char a[20];
char b[20];
```

The assignment statement a = b generates a compile error. Give at least two possible interpretations of the assignment, and for each one fix either the declarations or assignment as needed to match the interpretation.

5.15 Like Python, Ada also supports the operation of array slicing.
(a) Compare this operation with its Python counterpart discussed in this chapter.
(b) Give three realistic examples of the use of array slicing, either in Ada or in Python.

5.16 Perl and Python support dynamic arrays. Discuss the implementation of dynamic arrays in your favorite language.

5.17 Perl and Python both support *hash arrays* or *associative arrays*. What are they? Give one realistic example of their use. How would you simulate an associative array in your favorite language?

5.18 Consider the languages ML, Scheme, and Python. Write a brief report that compares and illustrates how the notion of *type equivalence* is used in each of these languages.

5.19 Define an EBNF and abstract syntax for adding record structures to Clite. The EBNF for a structure reference should use the "dot" notation discussed in this chapter. The concrete and abstract syntax of *Declaration*, *Expression*, and *Assignment* should be modified.

5.20 Using your definitions in the previous exercise, design an algorithm that determines whether two records are structurally equivalent.

5.21 Explore the definition of recursive data types in ML. Rewrite the Haskell example shown in this chapter using ML.

5.22 After consulting an authoritative source, write a brief report that discusses the treatment of *type equivalence* in C, Perl, or Python.

5.23 Extend the EBNF and abstract syntax of Clite to include structures or records. Implement an algorithm that determines whether two records are structurally equivalent.

6

Type Systems

"I was eventually persuaded of the need to design programming notations so as to maximize the number of errors which cannot be made, or if made, can be reliably detected at compile time."

C. A. R. Hoare

CHAPTER OUTLINE

Concern for improved program reliability and early detection of errors has forced designers to strengthen the type checking capabilities of languages. A good type system allows the types of values that occur in every expression in a program to be determined before that expression is executed (either at compile time or dynamically, during program interpretation), thus greatly reducing the chance of a type-related error. This chapter explores the elements of type systems and illustrates how one can be designed for the small language Clite.

Definition: The detection of type errors, either at compile time or at run time, is called *type checking*.

A programming language's *type system* provides a means of defining new types and determining when a type is used properly. A type system can be defined either informally or formally. In this chapter we develop an informal type system for Clite, and then show how a static type checker can be implemented using the Clite abstract syntax introduced in Chapter 2.

We also discuss an abstract syntax tree transformer for Clite, which converts over-loaded operators such as + into type specific operators. It inserts explicit type conversions as needed to ensure that both operands conform in their type to that required by the operator.

Recall from Chapter 2 that Clite has four basic types: int, float, bool, and char. It has array declarations and references, but no type constructors no struct, no union, and no pointer type. With this simplicity, we can define a rigorous type system for Clite and show how its abstract syntax enables a straightforward implementation.

Clite is a simple language. A Clite program has a single function named main, whose body has a single scope; there are no nested scopes and no global declarations. Including array declarations and references,[1] Clite is statically bound, so that all type errors can be detected at compile time. Moreover, all implicit type conversions are also detectable at compile time.

The semantic phase of the compiler (see Figure 2.8) must also check that:

1   Each declared variable's *Identifier* must be unique, and it must not be a keyword.
2   Each variable referenced within any expression in the program must have been declared.

Strictly speaking, neither of these is part of a type system. However, we will include them here as though they were.

In passing, we might ask why these two added constraints are not somehow defined in the EBNF syntax of Clite. Unfortunately, the limited nature of EBNF prevents such context-sensitive constraints from being expressed. That is, EBNF is not powerful enough to express syntactic ideas that depend on the context in which a syntactic category (like *Identifier*) occurs.[2] Instead, we must look to the abstract syntax of a program and ask what sort of algorithm can be designed to ensure that these constraints are not violated.

One way to implement a language's type system is to write a set of boolean-valued functions that mathematically define rules such as the two above. This approach characterizes the formal modeling of a type system, and such a model for Clite is presented in Section 6.3.

Another way to implement a language's type system is to state the rules in a highly stylized English, alongside an algorithm that implements those statements. To illustrate this approach, consider the simple Clite program in Figure 6.1 which computes the factorial of 8.

In this program, the variables named n, i, and result declared in the program (line 3) must each be unique. The variable n referenced in lines 4 and 7 must be declared; similarly the variable i in lines 5, 7, 8, and 9 and the variable result in lines 6 and 9

---

1. See Chapter 11 for more discussion of dynamic allocation of arrays.

2. This limitation of BNF grammars is usually exposed in a study of formal (Chomsky-type) languages, and would occur in a course on the theory of computation or compilers.

```
1 // compute the factorial of integer n
2 void main ( ) {
3      int n, i, result;
4      n = 8;
5      i = 1;
6      result = 1;
7      while (i < n) {
8          i = i + 1;
9          result = result * i;
10     }
11 }
```

| **Figure 6.1**   **A Small Clite Program**

must be declared. So informally, we can see that the Clite program in Figure 6.1 is valid
with respect to these two added rules.[3]

6.1   TYPE SYSTEM FOR CLITE

How do we model and implement validity checks for Clite programs? Such a model
requires a collection of validity functions, which represent rules like "all declared variables have unique names." Each validity function *V* may return a boolean value indicating
whether or not that part of the program's abstract syntax tree is type valid, and it is called
whenever its respective rule needs to be checked. That is:

$$V : AbstractSyntaxClass \rightarrow \mathbf{B}$$

A type checking system also relies on a *type map* which is a function that binds
each declared variable name to its type. The type map can be extracted from the abstract
Declarations for the Clite program in the following way:

```
public static TypeMap typing (Declarations d) {
    TypeMap map = new TypeMap();
    for (Declaration di : d)
        map.put (di.v, di.t);
    return map;
}
```

Recall that the abstract syntax for a Clite *Declaration* is:

$$Declaration = VariableDecl \mid ArrayDecl$$
$$VariableDecl = Variable \text{ v}; \; Type \text{ t}$$
$$ArrayDecl = Variable \text{ v}; \; Type \text{ t}; \; Integer \text{ size}$$

---

3. Again we note that the added constraints on identifiers are not strictly part of a type system.

Observation

Security in C/C++/Java

Clite is more secure than C/C++, since the latter permits implicit narrowing conversions in an assignment statement [Kernighan and Ritchie, 1988, p. 208]:

> The type of an assignment statement is the type of its left operand ... In the simple assignment with =, the value of the expression replaces that of the object referred to by the lvalue. ... Both operands have arithmetic type, in which case the right operand is converted to the type of the left by the assignment.

There are no restrictions on this assignment even if it is a narrowing conversion. This weaknesses in the type system allows information to be lost without warning.

Assignment conversion in Java for numeric or char operands, follows a somewhat more restrictive set of rules.

- If the expression on the right has type byte, short, char, int, long, or float, its value may be widened to an equivalent double value.
- If it is byte, short, char, int, or long, it may be widened to a float value.
- If it is byte, short, char, or int, it may be widened to a long value.
- If it is byte, short, or char, it may be widened to int.
- If it is byte or short, it may be widened to char.
- If it is byte, it may be widened to short.

A narrowing conversion may be used in an assignment under very limited conditions; for example, if the expression on the right is a constant expression and the value of the expression is representable in the type of the variable on the left.

Such problems necessitated the development of the lint application which "examines C programs for potential errors, portability problems, and dubious construction" [Kernighan and Pike, 1984].

Thus, given a list d of *Declarations* d[i], the method typing returns a Java TypeMap whose keys are the declared variables d[i].v and whose values are their respective types d[i].t.[4],[5] For example, the program in Figure 6.1 has the following TypeMap:

```
{<n, int>, <i, int>, <result, int>}
```

In the remainder of this section, we define each of the remaining rules in the Clite type system (plus the two added constraints on identifiers) in English, alongside a discussion of its implementation.

Type Rule 6.1 *All referenced variables must be declared.*

---

4. The list d may be implemented as a Java ArrayList, for example, and a TypeMap may be implemented as an extension of a Java HashMap.

5. The size of an *ArrayDecl* is ignored here, since it can be a dynamically determined value.

Enforcement of this rule is shared among the type checking functions for different kinds of Clite statements and expressions, as we shall see below.

Type Rule 6.2 *All declared variables must have unique names.*

This rule can be enforced by checking that every distinct pair of variables in a declaration list must have mutually different identifiers. This particular validity rule addresses only the mutual uniqueness requirement for variables. In general, this function should also specify that the type of each variable be taken from the set of available types in the language (such as {int, float, char, bool} for Clite). We omit this requirement here because it has already been enforced by the Clite syntax.

Assuming that the abstract syntax category Declarations is implemented as a Java ArrayList, the method V for Declarations can be specified as follows:[6]

```
public static void V (Declarations d) {
    for (int i=0; i<d.size() - 1; i++)
        for (int j=i+1; j<d.size(); j++) {
            Declaration di = d.get(i);
            Declaration dj = d.get(j);
            check( ! (di.v.equals(dj.v)),
                "duplicate declaration: " + dj.v);
        }
}
```

For example, the declarations for the program in Figure 6.1 are named n, i, and result, which are mutually unique names. So the method *V* for this particular set of declarations should return normally (the check condition is true for all pairs). The implementation of the V function in Java returns void, instead stopping execution on the first instance of a duplicate pair. This practice relies on the short circuit evaluation of the *and* operator in which:

a and b ≡ *if not a then false else b*

That is, once a validity check fails, the program being checked continues to be invalid despite the truth or falsity of later validity checks.

Finally, we note that this method does not exactly mirror the definition given for uniqueness among declared variable names. That is, the rule suggests that *all* distinct pairs should be checked (i.e., d[i] vs d[j] *and* d[j] vs d[i]). We have omitted this computational redundancy by performing a diagonalization on the looping code.

To complete the type system for Clite, a set of functions *V* is defined for each abstract syntactic class, including the most general class *Program.* A complete program from the

6. In our implementation of the function *V*, the boolean result is replaced with a call to a *check* function, which throws an exception. Thus, if the type checker terminates normally, the compiler can be sure that the abstract syntax tree is valid with respect to the type rules.

abstract syntax point of view has two parts, a series of *Declarations* and a *Block*:

```
class Program {
    // Program = Declarations decpart ; Block body
    Declarations decpart;
    Block body;
}
```

Type Rule 6.3 *A Program is type valid if its Declarations* decpart *is valid and its Block* body *is valid with respect to the type map for those particular Declarations.*

Since these two parts are implemented as Java classes, this specification is straightforward to implement.

```
public static void V (Program p) {
    V (p.decpart);
    V (p.body, typing (p.decpart));
}
```

For the example program in Figure 6.1, this means that the *Declarations* (n, i, and result) are valid, and that the block that begins with the *Assignment* n = 8; is valid. Notice that the type validity of the program's body can be checked only in relation to the particular type map that represents its decpart.

To ensure the type validity of a *Block*, we must, of course, ensure the type validity of each of its individual statements. The rules defining the type validity of a *Statement* are expressed in Type Rule 6.4.

Type Rule 6.4 *A Statement is valid with respect to the program's type map if it satisfies the following constraints:*
1 *A Skip is always valid.*
2 *An Assignment is valid if all the following are true:*
   (a) *Its* target *Variable is declared.*
   (b) *Its* source *Expression is valid.*
   (c) *If the type of its* target *Variable is* float, *then the type of its* source *Expression must be either* float *or* int.[7]
   (d) *Otherwise, if the type of its* target *Variable is* int, *then the type of its source Expression must be either* int *or* char.
   (e) *Otherwise, the type of its* target *Variable must be the same as the type of its* source *Expression.*
3 *A Conditional is valid if its* test *Expression is valid and has type* bool, *and both its* thenbranch *and* elsebranch *Statements are valid.*
4 *A Loop is valid if its* test *Expression is valid and has type* bool, *and its Statement* body *is valid.*
5 *A Block is valid if all of its Statements are valid.*

---

7. We are excluding *ArrayRef*'s from this definition, since they are left as an exercise.

Referring again to our example program in Figure 6.1, note that its abstract *Block* contains four *Statement*s; three *Assignment*s and a *Loop*. Thus, according to Type Rule 6.4, the validity of this program depends upon the validity of each of these individual statements and, recursively, on the validity of the other *Block* that is the body of the *Loop* itself. Moreover, for each *Assignment*, like n = 8;, Type Rule 6.4 requires that:

- The target *Variable* n is declared,
- The source *Expression* 8 is valid, and
- The type of 8 is either int or char.

To complete this type checking activity, we must therefore have a clear definition of what we mean by an *Expression* being valid.

Implementing the above rules based on the abstract syntax of Clite is straightforward, as suggested in the sketch in Figure 6.2. There, the first if statement mirrors Type Rule 6.4.1 about the validity of *Skip* statements, and the logic for the *Assignment* statement faithfully follows Type Rule 6.4.2.

The observant reader will note the use of several defensive programming techniques in Figure 6.2. The first statement checks that the *Statement* is not the Java null object. Another check at the end of the method ensures that no case was left out, and, hence, control should *not reach here*.[8]

Next, we specify the validity rule for an *Expression*.

Type Rule 6.5 *The validity of an Expression is defined using the program's type map and each of the Expression's subclasses:*

1 *A Value is valid.*

2 *A Variable is valid if its* id *appears in the type map.*[9]

3 *A Binary is valid if all the following are true:*
(a) *Its Expressions* term1 *and* term2 *are valid.*
(b) *If its BinaryOp* op *is arithmetic (+, -, *, /), then both its Expressions must be either* int *or* float.
(c) *If* op *is relational (==, !=, <, <=, >, >=), then both its Expressions must have the same type.*
(d) *If* op *is boolean (&&, ||), then both its Expressions must be* bool.

4 *A Unary is valid if all the following are true:*
(a) *Its Expression* term *is valid.*
(b) *If its UnaryOp* op *is* !, *then* term *must be* bool.
(c) *If* op *is* -, *then* term *must be* int *or* float.
(d) *If* op *is the type conversion* float() *or* char(), *then* term *must be* int.
(e) *If* op *is the type conversion* int(), *then* term *must be* float *or* char.

The implementation of this *V* function is sketched in Figure 6.3. The fragment given mirrors the rules 1–3 above, with the implementation of *Unary* expressions omitted.

Finally, the result type of an *Expression* must be defined for all its variations.

---

8. An object-oriented programmer should observe that the if statements could have been avoided had we used a more object-oriented approach. However, at this point we are trying to faithfully implement the formal model of Section 6.3, which, being mathematical, is functional in nature.

9. Again, we are excluding *ArrayRef*'s from this definition; they are left as an exercise.

```
public static void V (Statement s, TypeMap tm) {
    if ( s == null )
        throw new IllegalArgumentException(
            "AST error: null statement");
    if (s instanceof Skip) return;
    if (s instanceof Assignment) {
        Assignment a = (Assignment)s;
        check( tm.containsKey(a.target)
                , " undefined target in assignment: " +
                a.target);
        V(a.source, tm);
        Type ttype = (Type)tm.get(a.target);
        Type srctype = typeOf(a.source, tm);
        if (ttype != srctype) {
            if (ttype == Type.FLOAT)
                check( srctype == Type.INT
                        , "mixed mode assignment to " +
                        a.target);
            else if (ttype == Type.INT)
                check( srctype == Type.CHAR
                        , "mixed mode assignment to " +
                        a.target);
            else
                check( false
                        , "mixed mode assignment to " +
                        a.target);
        }
        return;
    }
    ...

    throw new IllegalArgumentException(
        "should never reach here");
}
```

| **Figure 6.2**   **Validity Function *V* for *Statement***

Type Rule 6.6 *Every Expression's result type is determined as follows:*

1 *If the Expression is a Value, then its result type is the type of that Value.*

2 *If the Expression is a Variable, then its result type is the type of that Variable.*

3 *If the Expression is a Binary, then:*

  (a) *If the Operator is arithmetic ($+$, $-$, $*$, or $/$) then its result type is the type of its operands. For example, the Expression* x+1 *requires* x *to be* int *(since* 1 *is* int*), so its result type is* int*.*

```
public static void V (Expression e, TypeMap tm) {
    if (e instanceof Value)
        return;
    if (e instanceof Variable) {
        Variable v = (Variable)e;
        check( tm.containsKey(v)
                , "undeclared variable: " + v);
        return;
    }
    if (e instanceof Binary) {
        Binary b = (Binary) e;
        Type typ1 = typeOf(b.term1, tm);
        Type typ2 = typeOf(b.term2, tm);
        V (b.term1, tm);
        V (b.term2, tm);
        if (b.op.ArithmeticOp( ))
            check( typ1 == typ2 &&
                (typ1 == Type.INT || typ1 == Type.FLOAT)
                , "type error for " + b.op);
        else if (b.op.RelationalOp( ))
            check( typ1 == typ2 , "type error for " + b.op);
        else if (b.op.BooleanOp( ))
            check( typ1 == Type.BOOL && typ2 == Type.BOOL,
                    b.op + ": non-bool operand");
        else
            throw new IllegalArgumentException(
                    "should never reach here");
        return;
    }
    ...
    throw new IllegalArgumentException("should never reach here");
}
```

| **Figure 6.3**   **Validity Function** *V* **for** *Expression*

    (b) *If the Operator is relational* ($<, <=, >, >=, ==, !=$) *or boolean* (&&, ||), *then its result type is* `bool`.
   4   *If the Expression is a Unary, then:*
    (a) *If the Operator is* ! *then its result type is* `bool`.
    (b) *If the Operator is* - *then its result type is the type of its operand.*
    (c) *If the Operator is a type conversion, then the result type is given by the conversion.*

As an example, readers should see that the *Expression* `result*i` which is the `source` in the fourth *Assignment* of the sample Clite program in Figure 6.1 is valid. That is, by Rule 6.5, `result*i` is a *Binary*, its *Operator* is arithmetic, and both its operands are type `int` (using Rule 6.6).

```
public static Type typeOf (Expression e, TypeMap tm) {
    if (e instanceof Value) return ((Value)e).type;
    if (e instanceof Variable) {
        Variable v = (Variable)e;
        check (tm.containsKey(v), "undefined variable: " + v);
        return (Type) tm.get(v);
    }
    if (e instanceof Binary) {
        Binary b = (Binary)e;
        if (b.op.ArithmeticOp( ))
            if (typeOf(b.term1,tm) == Type.FLOAT)
                return (Type.FLOAT);
            else return (Type.INT);
        if (b.op.RelationalOp( ) || b.op.BooleanOp( ))
            return (Type.BOOL);
    }
    if (e instanceof Unary) {
        Unary u = (Unary)e;
        if (u.op.NotOp( )) return (Type.BOOL);
        else if (u.op.NegateOp( )) return typeOf(u.term,tm);
        else if (u.op.intOp( )) return (Type.INT);
        else if (u.op.floatOp( )) return (Type.FLOAT);
        else if (u.op.charOp( )) return (Type.CHAR);
    }
    throw new IllegalArgumentException(
        "should never reach here");
    }
```

| **Figure 6.4**   The `typeof` **Function**

A partial implementation of the `typeof` function that implements this rule is given in Figure 6.4; again the code for the type of a *Unary* expression is omitted. The code attempts to faithfully mirror Type Rule 6.6.

6.2   IMPLICIT TYPE CONVERSION

As suggested in Section 6.1, Clite supports some implicit type conversions in an *Assignment*, all of which are widening conversions. All other conversions require the program to include an explicit type conversion function, which is a *Unary* expression, since both operands in the implementation of a *Binary* expression must have the same type.

In the semantics of an *Assignment*, the value of the source *Expression* replaces that of the target *Variable*. If necessary, the type of the source must be implicitly converted, again using the widening conversions specified in Rule 6.4.2 and governed by the type of the target. Otherwise the types of the target and the source must be the same.

As an example of implicit type conversion, consider the following abstract syntax tree:

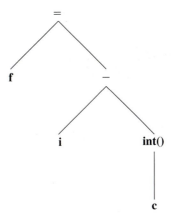

In this tree we are using implicit typing with the first letter of each variable indicating its type; for example, variable f is of type float. The tree is considered type valid because annotating it with the following type information:

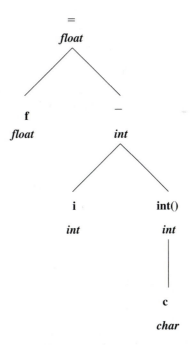

forces an implicit widening conversion in the assignment statement, which is allowed by Type Rule 6.4.2. Finally, we transform the tree so that all operators are explicitly typed and implicit conversions are made explicit:

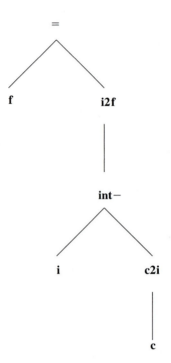

Here, `c2i` denotes character-to-integer conversion, `int-` denotes integer subtraction, and `i2f` denotes integer-to-float conversion. In a real system, the assignment operator `=` would be replaced by a type specific assignment, such as `float=`.

Thus, the transformed abstract syntax tree replaces all the overloaded operators with type specific operators and inserts explicit type conversions in place of the implicit ones wherever they are needed.

The transformations are implemented as a set of functions *T* (for *transform*) which convert an abstract syntax tree and a type map into another abstract syntax tree with all implicit type conversions removed:

$$T : AbstractSyntaxClass \times TypeMap \rightarrow AbstractSyntaxClass$$

The transform function *T* for *Program* constructs a new *Program* which consists of the original[10] *Declarations* and a transformed body (a *Block*):

```
public static Program T (Program p, TypeMap tm) {
    Block body = (Block)T(p.body, tm);
    return new Program(p.decpart, body);
}
```

The key transformations are the ones for an *Assignment* statement and *Expression*. The former must insert explicit conversions for both `int` to `float` and `char` to `int`, as

---

10. No such transformation is needed for the category *Declarations*, since it contains no operators.

```
if (s instanceof Assignment) {
   Assignment a = (Assignment)s;
      Variable target = a.target;
      Expression src = T (a.source, tm);
      Type ttype = (Type)tm.get(a.target);
      Type srctype = StaticTypeCheck.typeOf(a.source, tm);
      if (ttype == Type.FLOAT) {
      if (srctype == Type.INT) {
          src = new Unary(new Operator(Operator.I2F), src);
          srctype = Type.FLOAT;
          }

      }
      else if (ttype == Type.INT) {
          if (srctype == Type.CHAR) {
              src = new Unary(new Operator(Operator.C2I), src);
              srctype = Type.INT;
          }

      }
      StaticTypeCheck.check( ttype == srctype,
              "type error in assignment to " + target);
      return new Assignment(target, src);

}
```

| **Figure 6.5   Assignment Transformation**

shown in Figures 6.5 and 6.6. Otherwise, the type checking rules assure that the types are the same and so no further transformation is needed. Note also in Figure 6.6 that we do not transform the assignment operator by type, because it is not required for the run-time semantic model. For most machines, the assignment operator would need to be distinguished by type (at least by the memory size of the type) as discussed in Section 5.3.

The bulk of the work of transforming operators by type is done by the *T* function for an *Expression*, which is sketched in Figure 6.6. For binary operators, a type-specific map is used to translate the operator. For example, in i - int(c) the operand type is int, so the operator - is translated to int- using the integer operator map intMap( ).

For *Unary* expressions (not shown), the operator is the main governor in determining the operator transformation. However, for unary - and the type conversion int( ), type-dependent type maps are used. That is, the integer type map intMap( ) is used to transform an int( ) conversion on a character into a c2i operator.

The transformed abstract syntax tree serves as the basis for a specification and implementation of a run-time semantics function in Chapter 8. As described here, that function presumes the type-safety of the translated abstract syntax tree.

6.3   FORMALIZING THE CLITE TYPE SYSTEM

Below are the formal rules for static type checking for Clite; they are naturally written as predicates. Discussion and implementations of these rules as a collection of Java

π

```
public static Expression T (Expression e, TypeMap tm) {
    if (e instanceof Value)
        return e;
    if (e instanceof Variable)
        return e;
    if (e instanceof Binary) {
        Binary b = (Binary)e;
        Type typ1 = StaticTypeCheck.typeOf(b.term1, tm);
        Type typ2 = StaticTypeCheck.typeOf(b.term2, tm);
        Expression t1 = T (b.term1, tm);
        Expression t2 = T (b.term2, tm);
        if (typ1 == Type.INT)
            return new Binary(b.op.intMap(b.op.val), t1,t2);
        else if (typ1 == Type.FLOAT)
            return new Binary(b.op.floatMap(b.op.val), t1,t2);
        else if (typ1 == Type.CHAR)
            return new Binary(b.op.charMap(b.op.val), t1,t2);
        else if (typ1 == Type.BOOL)
            return new Binary(b.op.boolMap(b.op.val), t1,t2);
        throw new IllegalArgumentException(
                "should never reach here");
    }
    ...
    throw new IllegalArgumentException(
            "should never reach here");
}
```

| **Figure 6.6**   **Expression Transformation**

methods were already shown in Section 6.1. Readers who are not interested in the underlying mathematics of type system specification may omit this section.[11]

The *type map* of a *Program* is a set of ordered pairs, each pair having a *Variable v* and its declared *Type t*.

$$tm = \{\langle v_1, t_1 \rangle, \langle v_2, t_2 \rangle, \ldots, \langle v_n, t_n \rangle\}$$

The function *typing* creates a *TypeMap* from a series of *Declarations* and corresponds to Type Rule 6.1. Since individual identifiers are unique, the set union ensures that all declared variables and their types are represented.

typing: *Declarations* → *TypeMap*

$$typing\,(Declarations\ d) = \bigcup_{i \in \{1,\ldots,n\}} \langle d_i.v, d_i.t \rangle$$

---

11. The type validity of *ArrayDecl*'s and *ArrayRef*'s is ignored here, since it is ignored in Section 6.2.

A series of *Declarations* is valid if its variable names are mutually unique (Type Rule 6.2). Note that the functional definition checks all pairs of identifiers.

V: *Declarations* → **B**

V (*Declarations* d) = $\forall i, j \in \{1, \ldots, n\}(i \neq j \Rightarrow d_i.v \neq d_j.v)$

A program is valid if its *Declarations* are valid (V(p.decpart)) and its *Block* is valid (V(p.body, typing(p.decpart))) for the *TypeMap* defined by those *Declarations* (Type Rule 6.3).

V: *Program* → **B**

V (*Program* p) = V(p.decpart) $\wedge$ V(p.body, *typing*(p.decpart))

The validity check for a *Statement* depends on the kind of statement; for example, a *Skip* statement is always valid, while an *Assignment* statement requires checking both the target variable and the source expression. The function below is equivalent to Type Rule 6.4.

V: *Statement* $\times$ *TypeMap* → **B**

V (*Statement* s, *TypeMap* tm)

$= true$ if s *is a Skip*

$= s$.target $\in$ tm $\wedge$ V(s.source, tm)
   $\wedge((tm(s.\text{target}) = \text{float} \wedge typeOf(s.\text{source}, tm) \in \{\text{float, int}\})$
   $\vee(tm(s.\text{target}) = \text{int} \wedge typeOf(s.\text{source}, tm) \in \{\text{int, char}\})$
   $\vee(tm(s.\text{target}) = typeOf(s.\text{source}, tm))$

     if s *is an Assignment*

$= V($s.test, tm$) \wedge typeOf(s.\text{test, tm}) = \text{boolean}$
   $\wedge V($s.thenbranch, tm$) \wedge V($s.elsebranch, tm$)$

     if s is a *Conditional*

$= V($s.test, tm$) \wedge typeOf(s.\text{test, tm}) = \text{boolean}$
   $\wedge V($s.body, tm$)$

     if s is a *Loop*

$= V(b_1, \text{tm}) \wedge V(b_2, \text{tm}) \wedge \ldots \wedge V(b_n, \text{tm})$

     if s is a *Block* $= b_1 b_2 \ldots b_n$
   $\wedge n \geq 0$

An *Expression* is valid if it is a *Value*, a *Variable* in the program's type map, or a *Binary* or *Unary* expression whose operands satisfy additional constraints. The function below is equivalent to Type Rule 6.5.

V: *Expression* $\times$ *TypeMap* → **B**

V (*Expression* e, *TypeMap* tm)

$= true$ if e is a *Value*
$= e \in$ tm   if e is a *Variable*

$= V(e.\text{term1}, tm) \wedge V(e.\text{term2}, tm)$
   $\wedge \ typeOf(e.\text{term1}, tm) \in \{\text{float, int}\} \wedge typeOf(e.\text{term2}, tm) \in \{\text{float, int}\}$

$$\wedge\ typeOf\,(e.\text{term1, tm}) = typeOf\,(e.\text{term2, tm})$$
$$\text{if } e \text{ is a } Binary \wedge e.op \in \{ArithmeticOp\}$$
$$= V(e.\text{term1}, tm) \wedge V(e.\text{term2}, tm)$$
$$\wedge\ typeOf\,(e.\text{term1, tm}) = typeOf\,(e.\text{term2, tm})$$
$$\text{if } e \text{ is a } Binary \wedge e.op \in \{RelationalOp\}$$
$$= V(e.\text{term1}, tm) \wedge V(e.\text{term2}, tm)$$
$$\wedge\ typeOf\,(e.\text{term1}, tm) = \text{boolean} \wedge typeOf\,(e.\text{term2}, tm) = \text{boolean}$$
$$\text{if } e \text{ is a } Binary \wedge e.op \in \{BooleanOp\}$$
$$= V(e.\text{term}, tm)$$
$$\wedge\ ((e.op = !\ \wedge\ typeOf\,(e.\text{term}, tm) = \text{boolean})$$
$$\vee\ (e.op = -\ \wedge\ typeOf\,(e.\text{term}, tm) \in \{\text{float, int}\})$$
$$\vee\ (e.op = \text{float()}\ \wedge\ typeOf\,(e.\text{term}, tm) \in \{\text{int}\})$$
$$\vee\ (e.op = \text{char()}\ \wedge\ typeOf\,(e.\text{term}, tm) \in \{\text{int}\})$$
$$\vee\ (e.op = \text{int()}\ \wedge\ typeOf\,(e.\text{term}, tm) \in \{\text{float, char}\}))$$
$$\text{if } e \text{ is a } Unary$$

The auxiliary function *typeOf* defines the type of an *Expression*, as defined by Rule 6.6. Here, the expression *e*.type denotes the type of either a value or a variable *e* in the type map.

$$typeOf : Expression \times TypeMap \rightarrow Type$$
$$typeOf\,(Expression\ e,\ TypeMap\ \text{tm})$$

$= e.\text{type}$	if e is a *Value*
$= e.\text{type}$	if e is a *Variable* $\wedge\ e \in$ tm
$= typeOf\,(e.\text{term1}, tm)$	if e is a *Binary* $\wedge\ e.op \in \{ArithmeticOp\}$
$= \text{boolean}$	if e is a *Binary* $\wedge\ e.op \in \{BooleanOp, RelationalOp\}$
$= \text{boolean}$	if e is a *Unary* $\wedge\ e.op = !$
$= typeOf\,(e.\text{term}, tm))$	if e is a *Unary* $\wedge\ e.op = -$
$= \text{float}$	if e is a *Unary* $\wedge\ e.op = \text{float()}$
$= \text{char}$	if e is a *Unary* $\wedge\ e.op = \text{char()}$
$= \text{int}$	if e is a *Unary* $\wedge\ e.op = \text{int()}$

This completes the formal definition of the type system of Clite. Both the formal English rules and the Java implementation shown in Section 6.1 are based on this definition. This definition illustrates how a language's type system can be defined rigorously using conventional mathematical tools. Such rigor helps ensure that the informal understandings and the implementation of a language's type system are valid and consistent.

6.4 SUMMARY

With a strong type system, many run-time errors can be prevented at compile time, or at least more clearly understood at run time. The small language Clite provides a good medium for developing and implementing a complete type system for a language. The formal treatment of type systems, using mathematical functions and predicates, is also illustrated.

EXERCISES

6.1 Expand Type Rule 6.2 for *Declaration*s so that it defines the requirement that the type of each variable be taken from a small set of available types, {float, int, bool, char}. Use the same rule style and abstract syntax for *Declaration*s used in this chapter.

6.2 Expand the Java method that implements the function *V* for *Declaration*s so that it implements the additional requirement stated in Exercise 6.1.

6.3 Argue that the Java method that implements the function *V* for *Declaration*s is correct, in the sense that it covers all the cases that the Type Rule itself covers.

6.4 For each of the following statements using the implicit typing rules of Section 6.1, first draw the untyped abstract syntax tree, then add type information, as done in Section 6.2. If any typed abstract syntax tree is type invalid, clearly indicate where and why.
(a) f = −3;
(b) f = −3.5;
(c) i = −2;
(d) i = −2.5;
(e) f = c;
(f) i = c;
(g) i = i + 1;
(h) i = i + c;
(i) f = f + i;
(j) if (b) i = 1;
(k) if (f) i = 1;
(l) if (f1 > f2) f3 = f4 + f5;

6.5 Add line and column number information to the information displayed by the checks in the V function implementations. Hint: to do this, you will need to modify the Lexer, Token, Abstract-Syntax classes.

6.6 Modify Type Rule 6.5 to allow implicit char to int and int to float conversions. Modify the V function for expressions to implement the type rules.

6.7 Add a put( ) statement to Clite, where put( ) takes an expression as an argument and writes the value of the expression to stdout. For this new statement:
(a) Define its EBNF and abstract syntax,
(b) Modify Type Rule 6.4 to define the necessary validity checks, and
(c) Modify the V function for statements to implement the type rules.

6.8 Add getInt( ), getFloat( ) functions to Clite, where a getInt/getFloat takes the next value from stdin and returns the value read as an int/float, respectively. For this new expression:
(a) Define its EBNF and abstract syntax,
(b) Modify Type Rule 6.5 to define the necessary validity checks,
(c) Modify the V function for expressions to implement the type rules.

6.9 Modify the type transformer class so that the implicit conversions of Exercise 6.6 are converted to explicit conversions.

6.10 Modify the mathematical V functions of Section 6.3 so that the implicit conversions of Exercise 6.6 are included.

6.11 Modify Type Rule 6.5 so that it checks the validity of an *ArrayRef* (see Figure 2.14).

6.12 Modify Type Rule 6.6 so that it computes the type of an *ArrayRef* (see Figure 2.14).

6.13 Implement type checking for array references by modifying the *V* methods for *Statement* and *Expression* and the *Type Of* method.

Semantics

7

"Ishmael: 'Surely all this is not without meaning.'"
Herman Melville, Moby Dick

CHAPTER OUTLINE

In the early days of language design, it was possible to write a syntactically correct program in a particular language that would behave differently when run with the same input on different platforms. This situation arose because the language's run-time behavior (semantics) was not defined precisely enough. Different compilers translated a program to nonequivalent machine language versions.

Since that time, language designers have gradually realized that a rigorous treatment of semantics is as important as a formal treatment of syntax. A fully rigorous semantics should ensure that any particular program "means" the same thing regardless of the platform run-time.

A middle ground in dealing with cases where different implementations may produce different results would identify those cases in the language definition and specify that their meaning is left up to the implementation. This occurs in C, for instance, for the order of function argument evaluation.

7.1   MOTIVATION

The main motivations for precisely defining the semantics of a programming language are threefold:

1   To provide programmers with an authoritative definition of the meaning of all the language constructs.[1]
2   To provide compiler writers with an authoritative definition of the meaning of all constructs, thus avoiding implementation differences.
3   To provide a basis for standardizing the language.[2]

A programming language is well-defined only when its semantics, as well as its syntax and type system, is fully defined. Recall from Chapter 2 that the *semantics* of a programming language is a precise definition of the *meaning* of any program that is syntactically and type-wise correct. Three different approaches have been used extensively to define the semantics of a programming language.

The most straightforward idea of program meaning is "whatever happens when the program is compiled by compiler C and run on machine M." In the late 1950s, Fortran was originally defined this way, using the Fortran compiler on a IBM 709 computer. A precise characterization of this idea is called *operational semantics*.[3]

A second way to view program meaning is to axiomatize the meaning of each statement in the language. Then, given this formal specification of what a program is supposed to do, one can rigorously prove that the program does that by using a systematic logical argument. This approach is called *axiomatic semantics*, and is used in Chapter 18.

A third way to view semantics is to define the meaning of each type of statement that occurs in the (abstract) syntax as a state-transforming mathematical function. Thus, the meaning of a program can be expressed as a collection of functions operating on the program state. This approach is called *denotational semantics*, and is used in Chapter 8.

Each of these approaches to semantics has advantages and disadvantages. Operational semantics has the advantage of representing program meaning directly in the code of a real (or simulated) machine. But this is also a potential weakness, since defining the semantics of a programming language on the basis of any particular architecture, real or abstract, limits the utility of that definition for compiler-writers and programmers working with different architectures. Moreover, the virtual machine on which instructions

---

1. People who are well versed in the nuances of the meaning of a language are often called *language lawyers*.

2. PL/I was the first language in which a precise model served as the basis for its ANSI/ISO standard.

3. Technically, there are two kinds of operational semantics, called "traditional" and "structured" operational semantics (sometimes called "natural semantics").

execute also needs a semantic description, which adds complexity and can lead to circular definitions.

Axiomatic semantics is particularly useful in the exploration of formal properties of programs. Programmers who must write provably correct programs from a precise set of specifications are particularly well-served by this semantic style. The usefulness of axiomatic semantics is illustrated in Chapter 18.

Denotational semantics is valuable because its functional style brings the semantic definition of a language to a high level of mathematical precision. Through it, language designers obtain a functional definition of the meaning of each language construct that is independent of any particular machine architecture. The denotational model is also valuable because it allows us to actively explore language design concepts in a laboratory setting.

This chapter has an informal operational semantics flavor, so that it can address not only the fundamental semantics of assigment, expressions, and control flow, but also the broader semantic issues involving such features as input/output and exception handling.

7.2   EXPRESSION SEMANTICS

In programming languages, the evaluation of expressions is fundamentally important. In this section, we explore the semantics of expressions, including operators and their associativity and precedence, the role of different evaluation orders, and the importance of precision.

In mathematics, expressions are pure in the sense that they have no side effects. So the order in which subexpressions are evaluated is unimportant. Some functional programming languages mirror this purity, since they make side effects illegal. Chapter 14 explores this idea more fully.

Many imperative languages are impure in this sense, since their expressions (particularly those which have function calls) can have side effects.

7.2.1 Notation

Consider the expression tree in Figure 7.1. Following conventional mathematical notation, most programming languages use *infix* notation for binary operations; that is, each binary operator is written between its operands. In infix notation, the expression of Figure 7.1 would be written as a fully parenthesized expression as:

```
(a + b) - (c * d)
```

Assuming the normal associativity and precedence of the operators +, -, and *, the expression could also be written as:

```
a + b - c * d
```

Figure 7.1   Sample Expression Tree

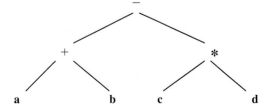

This raises an important point. Operator precedence and associativity often vary from one language to another, as we shall see in Section 7.2.2. Even in a single language or family of languages, the precedence table may be quite large (see, for example, Table 2.4). In most cases, however, parentheses may be inserted to achieve the desired semantic structure.

Absent associativity and precedence rules, infix notation is inherently ambiguous. Assigning associativity and precedence to the operators is one way of eliminating ambiguity.

An alternative way to eliminate semantic ambiguity is to use *Polish notation*. The semantics of this notation is inherently unambiguous. In *Polish prefix notation* a binary operator is always written in front of its two operands. For example, the expression of Figure 7.1 in prefix notation would be written:

```
- + a b * c d
```

Given an expression tree, its prefix notation can be generated using a "prefix walk" (sometimes called a "preorder traversal") of the tree. This algorithm can be expressed as follows, beginning at the root node:

1. Generate the value of the node.
2. Visit the left subtree.
3. Visit the right subtree.

Another variant is called *Polish postfix notation*, in which an operator always follows its operands. The expression of Figure 7.1 in postfix notation would be written:

```
a b + c d * -
```

Postfix notation is used in the languages Forth and Postscript (a printer control language).

Given an expression tree, the expression in postfix notation can be generated using a postfix walk (postorder traversal) of the tree. This algorithm can be expressed as follows, again starting at the root:

1. Visit the left subtree.
2. Visit the right subtree.
3. Generate the value of the node.

One of the limitations of Polish notation is that the same symbol cannot be used for an operation with different numbers of arguments (arity). For instance, in ordinary mathematics the symbol - is used for both unary and binary minus. One solution is to choose a different symbol for unary minus, such as tilde ($\sim$).

Cambridge prefix notation avoids this problems by having an operator always precede its operands and enclosing the entire expression in parentheses. The expression of Figure 7.1 in Cambridge prefix notation would be written:

```
(- (+ a b) (* c d))
```

Table 7.1	Language	+ - * /	Unary -	**	== != etc.
Associativity	C-like	left	right		left
of Operators	Ada	left	non	non	non
by Language	Fortran	left	right	right	left

An advantage of Cambridge prefix notation is that operators like + and - become naturally n-ary. The expression:

```
a + b + c + d
```

can thus be written:

```
(+ a b c d)
```

This also allows natural interpretations for (+), namely 0, and (+ a), namely a. Cambridge prefix notation is used by both Lisp and Scheme (see Section 14.2).

7.2.2 Associativity and Precedence

Most languages use infix notation for expressions involving unary and binary operators. They also follow the ordinary mathematical conventions for associativity and precedence wherever possible. Thus, the semantics reflected in the expression tree of Figure 7.1 can usually be obtained in the following way:

```
a + b - c * d
```

Table 7.1 shows the associativity of some common operators by language.[4] The column header for the relational operators uses the C representation. For the common additive and multiplicative operators there is agreement across the languages shown. However, for unary minus and Boolean negation, C-like languages and Fortran make them right associative, while Ada makes them nonassociative.

C-like languages have no exponentiation operator (** in Fortran and Ada). Fortran makes it right associative, consistent with mathematics. Ada makes exponentiation nonassociative, thereby forcing the programmer to clarifying such an expression by the use of parentheses.

We have already discussed the problems of associativity of relational expressions, but it bears repeating here. C-like languages make the relational operators left associative. However, the expression a < x < b is not equivalent to:

```
a < x && x < b
```

as one would expect. Instead in C and C++ it is equivalent to:

```
if (a < x) 1 < b else 0 < b
```

---

4. The representation of the relational operators varies widely by language with the representation of *not equals* varying the most.

Table 7.2

Precedence
of Operators
by Language

Operators	C-like	Ada	Fortran
Unary −	7	3	3
**		5	5
* /	6	4	4
+ −	5	3	3
== !=	4	2	2
< <= > >=	3	2	2
Unary not	7	2	2
Logical and	2	1	1
Logical or	1	1	1

which is not what one expects. Making the relational operators nonassociative, as Ada does, is a clearly superior design decision.

Table 7.2 shows the precedence of various operators by language. The table shows there is general agreement on the relative ordering of binary arithmetic operators, that relationals have lower precedence than the arithmetic operators, and that the binary Boolean operators have the lowest precedence.

However, there is wide disagreement on the placement of the unary operators in this hierarchy. Finally, C-like languages split the equality operators (equals and not equals) from the other four relationals, as well as the logical operators.

Not all languages use common mathematical conventions for defining operator precedence. For example, the language Smalltalk (see Section 13.3) uses straight left-to-right evaluation, assigning a single precedence level and left associativity to all the operators. APL uses straight right-to-left evaluation.

7.2.3 Short Circuit Evaluation

Following mathematical convention, early compilers would evaluate a Boolean expression such as A and B by first evaluating each of A and B separately. Short-circuit evaluation evaluates a Boolean expression from left to right and stops as soon as the truth of the expression can be determined.

Thus, a short-circuit definition of A and B is:

```
if (! A) false else B
```

Similarly, a short-circuit definition of A or B is:

```
if (A) true else B
```

Unlike mathematics, B can be undefined in these cases, since it may not be evaluated.

A classic example occurs in searching a linked list, with starting pointer `head`, to find a particular key value. Using Java syntax for this code fragment, we can write:

```
Node p = head;
while (p != null && p.info != key)
    p = p.next;
if (p == null) // not in list
    ...
else // found it
    ...
```

The test `p.info != key` will throw an exception when p is `null`. However, under short-circuit evaluation, the test `p.info != key` will not be performed whenever `p == null`.

The advantage is that the programmer is able to write shorter, clearer code by taking advantage of short-circuit evaluation. Without short-circuit evaluation, the above loop can be rewritten using a `break` statement:

```
while (p != null) {
    if (p.info == key)
        break;
    p = p.next;
}
```

Avoiding the `break` statement entirely requires introducing a Boolean variable:

```
boolean found = false;
while (p != null && ! found) {
    if (p.info == key)
        found = true;
    else
        p = p.next;
}
```

Introducing a Boolean variable makes the code harder to understand relative to the original short-circuit evaluation version.

A disadvantage of short-circuit expressions is that it breaks the commutative law. It is not true that `a && b` is the same as `b && a`. When `a` evaluates to false and `b` to undefined, `a && b` is false, while `b && a` is undefined.

7.2.4 The Meaning of an Expression

In a programming language, the meaning of an expression should depend only on the values of its subexpressions and the meaning of its operator. For the sake of simplicity, we assume here that the expression has been statically type checked.

One complication is that in mathematics there is no largest or smallest number. Computers and their programming languages support two types of numbers (in various precisions): integer numbers and floating point numbers. Both have a largest/smallest value.

Because of the finiteness of any given representation, the associative law does not hold for computer arithmetic. In particular:

$$(a + b) + c = a + (b + c)$$

is not true for all a, b, c. For integer arithmetic, if a is the largest possible positive integer, b is 3, and c is -5, then the left side of the equality evaluates to an error (integer overflow), while the right side evaluates to the largest integer minus 2.

Another problem occurs if any subexpression has a side effect. For example, consider the expression a + b, where a and b are floating point values and + denotes a floating point addition. The meaning of the expression, that is, its value, should depend only on the values of a and b. In particular, if both a and b themselves are subexpressions involving operators and functions, the order of evaluation of a and b should not affect the value of the expression.

Consider the C-style operators ++ and --, which can be problematic when they occur inside a larger expression. For example, after the following statements are executed:

```
i = 2; b = 2; c = 5;
a = b * i++ + c * i;
```

what is the resulting value of a? In fact, C-like languages define the above expression as semantically undefined, since a can be 14 (increment i after its second reference) or 19 (increment i before its second reference). The two interpretations depend on which of the two subexpressions b * i++ and c * i is evaluated first.

In most languages subexpressions in separate subtrees may be evaluated in any order. If the meaning of the program depends on the order, then the program is semantically undefined. A compiler is not required by the language design to detect such semantic errors.

7.3 PROGRAM STATE

To truly understand semantics, the concept of a program's state is fundamental.

Definition: The *state* of a program is the binding of all active objects to their current values.

The state has two maps: (1) the pairing of active objects with specific memory locations, (2) and the pairing of active memory locations with their current values. The current statement (portion of an abstract syntax tree) to be executed in a program is interpreted relative to the current state. The individual steps that occur during a program run can be viewed as a series of state transformations.

For example, suppose we have variables i and j with values 13 and -1 at some time during the execution of a program. Suppose that the memory locations are serially numbered beginning at 0, and the variables i and j are associated with the memory locations 154 and 155 at that time. Then the state represented by this configuration can be expressed as follows:

$$environment = \{\langle i, 154\rangle, \langle j, 155\rangle\}$$
$$memory = \{\langle 0, undef\rangle, \ldots, \langle 154, 13\rangle, \langle 155, -1\rangle, \ldots\}$$

```
1    // compute the factorial of n
2    void main ( ) {
3       int n, i, f;
4       n = 3;
5       i = 1;
6       f = 1;
7       while (i < n) {
8          i = i + 1;
9          f = f * i;
10      }
11   }
```

| **Figure 7.2**   **Factorial Program**

The special value *undef* is used to denote the value of a memory address that is currently undefined (not yet assigned a value).

Thus, the *state* of a program is the product of its active objects, their memory locations, and associated values. It can be viewed as the functional composition of the two maps *environment* and *memory* as: *state = memory × environment*. This formal treatment will be visited in Chapter 9.[5]

For the purposes of this chapter, it is convenient to represent the state of a program in a more simplified form. This representation takes the memory addresses out of play and simply defines the *state* of a program as a mapping from the declared variables to their currently assigned values at some point during the program run.

The state is like a *watch window* in an integrated development environment (IDE). It is always tied to a particular statement in the program source and shows for each program variable its current value.

Before a C/C++ program begins execution, each declared variable has the value *undef* consistent with its type. Any operation on an undefined value renders the program semantically undefined.

As an example, consider the program in Figure 7.2, which computes the factorial of 3. Table 7.3 shows a run-time trace of this program in a style that can be produced by most debuggers. The first line in the trace shows the program state before statement 4 (the first executable statement) is executed. Rather than showing the state here as a set of variable-value pairs, the table uses the familiar labeled column display. Note that there are three separate states associated with the `while` loop test on statement 7.

One feature that the trace table highlights is that an assignment modifies the program's state. In contrast, since the *while* loop test is free of side effects, it cannot modify the program's state. On the other hand, the *while* loop test does determine whether the loop body is executed next (lines 8 and 9) or the statement after the loop is executed next (line 11).

---

5. In Chapters 10 and 11, it will be important to represent the environment in a more realistic fashion, allowing us to precisely characterize the roles of the run-time stack and the heap. This allows us to deal effectively with procedure call, object creation, parameter passing, recursion, and so on.

Table 7.3

Trace of the
Factorial Program

	Before	Variables		
Step	Statement	n	i	f
1	4	*undef*	*undef*	*undef*
2	5	3	*undef*	*undef*
3	6	3	1	*undef*
4	7	3	1	1
5	8	3	1	1
6	9	3	2	1
7	7	3	2	2
8	8	3	2	2
9	9	3	3	2
10	7	3	3	6
11	11	3	3	6

7.4 ASSIGNMENT SEMANTICS

The assignment statement is fundamental to the imperative paradigm, and its newer offshoot, the object-oriented paradigm. In this section, we examine three assignment issues:

1   Multiple assignment,
2   Assignment statements vs. assignment expressions, and
3   Copy vs. reference semantics in assignments.

Recall the abstract syntax for a Clite assignment given in Chapter 2:

Assignment = *Variable* target; *Expression* source

The semantics of an assignment is as follows:

The source expression is evaluated in the current state, resulting in a value, which replaces the value of the target variable, resulting in a new state.

Throughout this section, we use the terms *target variable* and *source expression* with this particular semantic interpretation.

7.4.1 Multiple Assignment

Many languages support multiple target variables for a single source expression. A common use of such a construct is to initialize two or more variables to the same value, as in:

```
a = b = c = 0;
```

This assignment statement initializes all three variables to zero.

7.4.2 Assignment Statements vs. Assignment Expressions

Even with a multiple target assignment, in most languages an assignment is a statement. Like any other statement, it cannot be placed inside an expression.

However, in C-like languages an assignment is an expression rather than a statement. Thus, the assignment operator is little different than any other operator, such as +, -, etcetera. In C the following construct:

```
if (a = 0) ... else ...
```

is both syntactically and semantically meaningful.[6] It results in the value zero being assigned to the variable `a`, and the `else` part of the `if` being executed next, since zero is interpreted as false. In C, an assignment expression's value is just the value of the source expression.

There are many practical uses of the assignment expression in C and C++:

- Copy a string: for example, `while (*p++ = *q++) ...`
- Read characters until end of file: for example, `while (ch = getc(file)) ...`
- Traverse a linked list: for example, `while (p = p->next) ...`

However, offsetting this convenience is the common error given above of inadvertently mistyping the assignment operator (=) instead of the equals relation (==). For this reason, Java broke with C/C++ and required all such tests to be of type `boolean`.

7.4.3 Copy vs. Reference Semantics

Most imperative languages, including C/C++ use copy semantics for assignments, in which a copy of the value of the source expression is assigned to the target variable. By contrast, many object-oriented languages, including Java, use *reference* semantics for object assignments, in which a reference (pointer) to the value of the source expression is assigned to the target variable.

For example, under copy semantics the assignment:

```
a = b;
```

leaves `a` and `b` with two copies of the same value. Changes to either `a` or `b` have no effect on the other.

Under reference semantics the same assignment leaves `a` and `b` pointing to the same object, which is the original value of `b`. Thereafter, changing the value (internal state) of either `a` or `b` will have the side effect of changing the other. That is, the above assignment makes the variables `a` and `b` into two aliases for the same object.

---

6. Although the programmer presumably wanted to test if the variable a equals zero. Compilers often issue a warning to alert the programmer that == may have been intended instead of =.

A more illuminating example is method `add` from [Tucker and Noonan, 2002, p. 191]:

```java
public void add (Object word, Object number) {
    Vector set = (Vector) dict.get(word);
    if (set == null) { // not in Concordance
        set = new Vector( );
        dict.put(word, set);
    }
    if (allowDupl || !set.contains(number))
        set.addElement(number);
}
```

The first statement assigns to `set` the value of the entry with the key `word` in the hash table `dict`. If that key is not in the hash table, `set` is assigned the value `null`, in which case a new `set` is created and put into the hash table with the key `word`. In either case, the last statement of the method adds the integer `Number` to the `set` in the hash table. Under copy semantics, this last statement would not update the hash table properly.

7.5 CONTROL FLOW SEMANTICS

According to the Böhm-Jacopini Theorem [Böhm and Jacopini, 1966], a language is Turing complete if, in addition to an assignment statement, it has the following control structures: sequence, a conditional statement, and a looping statement.

> **Definition**: A programming language is *Turing complete* if its programs are capable of computing any computable function.

Each of these will be discussed in the sections that follow. Function/method calls and returns are discussed in Chapter 9.

Any other type of statement increases the automation or convenience of a programming language and its expressiveness, but ultimately not its computational power.

7.5.1 Sequence

The ability to write a sequence of statements in a language is so natural and basic that it is rarely discussed. In the simplest case, a sequence has two statements juxtaposed:

$s_1 s_2$

The semantics of such a sequence is intuitive. In the absence of some form of branch statement, first s_1 is executed and then s_2 is executed.

As we saw in Table 7.3, the output state of s_1 is the input state of s_2.

Branching statements include: `return`, `break`, `continue`, and the unrestricted `goto` statement. This last statement and its associated problems are discussed in Section 7.5.4. The others are restricted forms of `goto` statements.

The `return` statement is used to immediately terminate a function or method and is discussed more fully in Chapter 9. The `break` and `continue` statements are used primarily in loops and are discussed in Section 7.5.3.

7.5.2 Conditionals

The conditional statement is used to select alternative paths during program execution. In most languages it comes in two varieties: the basic `if` statement and the `case` (or `switch`) statement.

As we saw in Chapter 2, the `if` statement (using C syntax) comes in two varieties:

IfStatement → `if` (*Expression*) *Statement*1 [`else` *Statement*2]

which are often referred to as the *if-then* and the *if-then-else*. The semantics of an *IfStatement* can be defined as follows:

> If the value of the *Expression* is `true`, the meaning is the state resulting from evaluating *Statement1* in the current state. Otherwise, the meaning is the state resulting from evaluating *Statement2* in the current state.

Recall from Chapter 2 that the *if-then* can be viewed as an *if-then-else* with a skip statement inserted for the missing else part. Thus, the existence of an *if-then* statement is just a convenient shorthand.

An example of an *if-then-else* is the following code fragment (in C syntax) to compute the maximum of two numbers:

```
if (a > b)
    z = a;
else
    z = b;
```

An interesting question is how to specify that either *Statement1* or *Statement2* has more than a single statement. Two general approaches have been used.

The Algol 60 approach is to limit both the then-part and the else-part to a single statement. Since this is clearly inconvenient, Algol 60 also had a grouping mechanism that permitted a sequential sequence of statements to be considered syntactically as a single statement. Algol 60 used `begin` and `end` to denote such a sequence, which it called a compound statement. C-like languages and Perl follow this tradition but use a left brace for `begin` and a right brace for `end`.

Algol 68 viewed *Statement1* and *Statement2* as naturally compound, needing only a keyword to terminate *Statement2* (if present), or *Statement1* (if *Statement2* is absent). Algol 68 introduced the convention of using the beginning keyword spelled backwards. So an *if* statement was terminated with a *fi*. Ada follows this convention but uses two keywords to terminate, namely, *end if*. Python also follows this tradition, but uses indentation for *Statement1* and *Statement2*.

In order to simplify the closing of a nest of if statements, languages that follow the Algol 68 convention often have an `elseif` construct in their `if` statements. Using Ada as an example, the syntax of an `if` statement is:

IfStatement → `if` *Expression* `then` *Statements*
　　　　　　　　{ `elsif` *Expression* `then` *Statements* }
　　　　　　　　[`else` *Statement*]
　　　　　　　　`end if` ;

The spelling of the keyword `elseif` varies by language; even Perl, which follows the C tradition, has an `elsif`.

The switch (or case) statement started out as a jump table and was implemented as an indexed goto or jump. The individual cases did not have to be physically adjacent, but rather could be scattered throughout the code. An example from Fortran is:

```
goto (100, 200, 300, 400), i
```

If the variable `i` has the value 1, the next statement executed is the statement labelled 100; if `i` has the value 2, then 200; and so on. If `i` is not in the range 1 to 4, then the `goto` statement is skipped, and control passes to the next statement.

Because of this tradition and associated implementation, most languages limit the switch to type integer (including single characters). If the cases exceed a small range of values, many compilers implement a switch using an if.

An example of a switch statement in C-like languages appears in the tokenizer class in Figure 3.5. One unfortunate design decision for switch statements in C-like languages is the requirement that each case end with an explicit `break` statement to prevent one case from accidentally falling into the next case. This has proved to be very error prone; thus, it is unfortunate that newer languages such as Java and C# have continued this design.

In non-C-like languages, such as Ada, there is an implicit break at the end of each case. Furthermore, Ada also allows a case label to be an entire subrange of values. Thus, the switch of Figure 3.5 would appear in Ada:

```
case ch is
    when 'A' .. 'Z' | 'a' .. 'z' => -- identifier
        ...
    when '0' .. '9' => -- numeric literal
        ...
    when
        ...
    when others => -- default
        ...
end case;
```

Note that the first two cases are more conveniently written as if statements in Java. Note also that Ada uses `--` to begin a comment and `end case` to terminate the `case` statement.

7.5.3 Loops

The basic *begin test loop* is adequate for all looping needs. In C-like languages this loop is written as:

WhileStatement → `while ( ` *Expression* ` )` *Statement*

and is referred to as a `while` loop. Its meaning is summarized below:

The *Expression* is evaluated. If it is `true`, the *Statement* is executed and the *Loop* is executed again. Otherwise, the loop terminates.

In contrast, the *end test loop* in C-like languages appears syntactically as follows:

> *DoWhileStatement* → do *Statement* while (*Expression*)

Its meaning is slightly different from that of the *begin test loop*:

> The *Statement* is executed once and then the *Expression* is evaluated. If the *Expression* is true, the *Statement* is executed again, and so on. Otherwise, the loop terminates.

Such a construct is thus semantically equivalent to:

> { *Statement* while (*Expression*) *Statement* }

Hence, the *end test loop* is convenient but it is redundant.

Even more convenient is the *counting loop*. An example from C to sum the elements of an array is as follows:

```
sum = 0.0;
for (i = 0; i < SIZE; i++)
    sum += a[i];
```

In the language C, the variable i would have to be declared at the beginning of the block in which this code appears. Newer languages such as C++, Java, and C# allow the declaration of i to occur as part of the for loop initialization. In this case, the scope of i is limited to the *for* statement itself. As with the *end test loop*, the *counting loop* is also convenient but redundant.

Even more convenient are for-each loops which use some form of iterator to traverse a data structure, accessing each element of the data structure one time.

> **Definition**: An *iterator* is any finite set of values over which a loop can be repeated.

As an example, consider printing the keys and values of an associative array (or hash table). In the language Perl, this would be written:

```
foreach $key (sort keys %list) {
    print $key, "\t", $list{$key}, "\n";
}
```

Similar for-each loop constructs appear in Python, Java (as of version 1.5), and C#.

Many languages provide two forms of limited goto statement to make loop control more flexible. The first of these is referred to as a break statement in C-like languages. The purpose of the break statement is to enable a loop to be terminated from anywhere in the body of the loop.

One natural use of such a construct is in displaying menus or dialog boxes and getting the user's response. An outline of such code in the language C is:

```
while (1) {
    resp = displayMenu( );
    if (resp == QUIT)
        break;
    ...
}
```

The other form of limited branch is called a `continue` statement in C-like languages. Its purpose is to abort the current iteration of a loop and begin the next iteration. The `continue` statement can be thought of as a branch to the bottom of the loop.

An example of the use of a `continue` statement is the following Java snippet. This loop is reading a configuration file a line at a time. Each line is processed for the information it contains. However, blank lines and lines beginning with a pound sign (#) are ignored.

```
while (true) {
    String line = infile.readLine( );
    if (line == null) // end of file
        break;
    line = line.trim( );
    if (line.length == 0) continue;
    if (line.startsWith("#")) continue;
    ...
}
```

7.5.4 Go To Controversy

The `goto` statement controversy began with a letter to the editor of the *Communications of the ACM* from Edsger Dijkstra [Dijkstra, 1968b], entitled "GoTo Considered Harmful." With that letter, the *structured programming* revolution was launched.

In general, structured programming was all about designing programs from first principles, using only three basic control structures: the sequence, the conditional, and the while loop. In particular, structured programming advocated a ban on the use of any form of `goto` statement, since it was unnecessary and it encouraged writing incomprehensible code. Böhm and Jacopini [Böhm and Jacopini, 1966] showed that the `goto` statement was logically unnecessary. Since then, some languages (such as Ada and Java) have excluded the `goto` statement from their vocabularies.

In the 1960s, the primary program design tool was the flowchart (see Figure 12.1 for an example). The use of flowcharts for program design encouraged so-called *spaghetti code*, that is, code whose structure was all intertwined. The presence of logical loop and conditional structures was often difficult to discern. One aspect of structured programming was to make the logical structure of programs more obvious by eliminating spaghetti code.

Consider the Fortran program fragment in Figure 7.3 that sums the nonnegative values in a set of numbers. A count of the numbers summed is also computed.[7] A careful

---

7. In Fortran, the `continue` statement is used to mark the end of a loop, or any other branch point, which is different from its use in C-like languages.

```
        i = 0
        ct = 0
        sum = 0.0
100     if (i .ge. n) goto 300
        i = i + 1
        if (a(i) .lt. 0) goto 100
        ct = ct + 1
        sum = sum + a(i)
        goto 100
300     continue
```

| **Figure 7.3**   **Spaghetti Code Fortran**

reading should convince us that the program works, but the control structure is not obvious. A while loop would have provided a simpler, more readable solution.

The development in the late 1960s of the languages C and Pascal abetted the development of structured programming. Unlike Fortran 66 they had the necessary loop and conditional structures, including both begin test and end test loops, for loops, if-then-else statements, and switch/case statements, together with the compound statement which allowed nesting of these constructs. C also added restricted forms of `goto` statements, including the `return`, `break`, and `continue` statements, as discussed earlier.

However, Dijkstra and Wirth were primarily interested in replacing the flowchart with better methods of program design that facilitated demonstrating the correctness of programs (see Chapter 18). Wirth's text [Wirth, 1973] and Dijkstra's report [Dijkstra, 1972] were extremely influential in this regard.

Overall the structured programming revolution was a success. Programmers abandoned the unrestricted `goto` statement in favor of explicit looping and conditional constructs. It is extremely rare today to see an unconditional `goto` statement, although its use is still occasionally defended [Rubin, 1987]. While structured programming as a design methodology lies firmly within the imperative programming paradigm, its utility is less obvious in the object-oriented world.

7.6 INPUT/OUTPUT SEMANTICS

All practical programming requires a mastery of techniques for retrieving data from a remote permanent source and storing data in a remote permanent destination. Collectively, these techniques are called *input/output*, or *I/O* for short. The sources and destinations for input and output operations are called *files*. The media where files are stored are many and varied, including for instance, the keyboard, the display screen, a magnetic disk, or a removable memory stick. In this section, we review some of the semantic features that underlie I/O programming in various languages.

Over the years, language designers have taken very different approaches to the incorporation of input/output features into their languages. The designers of Algol, for instance, viewed I/O to be so implementation-dependent that they omitted its definition from the Algol 60 specification. Later language designs, however, were forced to include I/O specifications, usually choosing to include them in their standard function libraries.

7.6.1 Basic Concepts

Before a program can begin accessing a file, the file must be located and opened. Once opened, a file's information can be accessed in one of two ways: *sequentially* or *randomly*. A sequentially accessed file is one in which each entity is stored in the same order in which it is read/written by the program. A randomly-accessed file is one whose entities can be read/written in some nonserial order, so that a single entity can be read/written 0, 1, or any number of times while the file is open.

When a program finishes reading/writing entities in a file, the file is "closed." Thereby, the program relinquishes control so that the file can be accessed by other programs at later times. Typically, no file is opened by more than one program at a time.[8]

The entities in a sequentially accessed file may be retrieved/written by a program either as a *stream* of characters or as a series of fixed-length *records*, each of which shares the same layout, or *format*, as the others. Entities in randomly accessed files are typically read and written as fixed-length records.

Standard Files   One fundamental requirement in programming is the ability to read data from a keyboard and display it on a screen. These two media are identified as "standard files" in C-like languages. These languages also provide a "standard error file," where error messages that occur during the program run are serially stored. Java identifies these three standard files as System.in, System.out, and System.err, respectively. This convention is adapted from C, where these files are named stdin, stdout, and stderr, respectively.

Java, C++, and Ada require the program to explicitly name the standard I/O packages (java.io, iostream and, Ada.Text_IO, respectively) before it can open any of these files for reading or writing. A Fortran, C++, or Ada program can access data using either formatted or unformatted I/O.

Figure 7.4 shows an example C++ program that reads eight integer values into an array a using standard input, and then displays the values in a list using standard output.

```
#include <iostream.h>
main()
{
    int i, a[8];
    cout << "Enter a series of eight integers: \n";
    for (i=0; i<8; i++)
        cin >> a[i];
    for (i=0; i<8; i++)
        cout << a[i] << '\n';
}
```

| **Figure 7.4**   **Example Use of Standard I/O in C++**

---

8. There are exceptions, as in the case of a bank database being accessed simultaneously by programs serving customers at different automatic teller machines (ATMs) at the same time.

Java 1.5 supports reading a numeric value from the keyboard in an unformatted style, via the class `Java.util.Scanner`. This class parses an input stream into a series of tokens as it is read. The convention for doing this is to use the `nextInt` method, which finds the next token, converts it to `int`, and returns it.

```
Scanner reader = new Scanner(System.in);
int i = reader.nextInt();
```

Earlier versions of Java required that the input pass through an `InputStreamReader` and `BufferedReader`, and then be parsed before it could be assigned to an `int` variable. That is, the following code would be required:

```
BufferedReader br = new BufferedReader(
                        new InputStreamReader(System.in));
String str = br.readLine();
int i = Integer.parseInt(str);
```

Input/Output Streams   As a default, languages support sequential input and output in an "unformatted" style. That is, information is read/written as a stream of characters, from which individual token values are distinguished, converted to the appropriate type, and assigned to variables in the order that the variables are listed in the read or write statement. This style of I/O programming is especially useful for beginning programmers, as illustrated in Figure 7.4.

Unformatted input/output in Fortran is called "list-directed," which is analogous to a C++ or Java I/O "stream." The layout of an unformatted Fortran READ or WRITE statement using standard I/O is:

```
READ (*, *) variable-list
WRITE (*, *) expression-list
```

Below is a Fortran program that mimics the C++ code in Figure 7.4.

```
INTEGER :: i, a(8)
WRITE (*, *) "Enter a series of eight integers: "
READ (*, *) a
WRITE (*, *) a
```

The references to `a` in the READ and WRITE statements designate implied loops of the form `(a(i), i=1,8)`. Such a reference can be used whenever the loop covers the entire array.

In Java, the library `java.io` provides many different types of streams for sequential input/output, including file streams, pipe streams, memory streams, and filter streams. A *file stream* is used to transfer data to or from the native system file system. A *pipe stream* allows data from one stream to be fed directly into another stream. This allows a program to avoid storing data in intermediary data structures. *Memory streams* are used to transfer data between arrays and the program, while *filter streams* provide Java support for formatting input and output.

I/O streams in Java also support a `mark` method, which tags the current location in a stream. If a `reset` method is later called, the program will resume reading at the tagged location in the stream. *Reader streams* have `read` methods which either get a character from the stream, store all available input into an array of characters, or store input into a specified portion of an array of characters. *Writer streams* support similar `write` methods for writing to streams. *Writer streams* use a character encoder to convert data between character format and byte format. *Array* readers and writers are used to perform I/O operations on whole blocks of memory.

Java also has conventions for *serializing* objects using streams. Serialization is a process by which objects may be archived either for instantiation later in the same program or for transmission between computers via sockets. By casting values fetched from the input stream for object serialization, either as strings or as their original object type, they can be retrieved and recreated later in their original form.

The Java `StreamTokenizer` class provides four tools that are useful for various stream tokenizing activities: `nextToken`, `TT_EOF`, `sval`, and `nval`. The method `nextToken` scans the stream serially, starting from the current position and skipping whitespace, until it locates and returns the next token it finds. `TT_EOF` is a special constant indicating that the end of the file has been reached. The values `sval` and `nval` contain the value of the next token parsed as a `String` and as a `double`, respectively.

Ada's procedures for opening, closing, and accessing sequential files mirror those of C++ and Java. In Ada, `Open` associates a program-defined file name with an external file that already exists, whereas `Create` makes a new external file. `Close` breaks the association between the program and the file, and `Delete` breaks this association and deletes the external file as well.

For an Ada program to determine the current status of a file, the `Is_Open`, `Name`, `Form`, or `Mode` functions are provided. `Is_Open` returns a boolean describing whether the file is open or not, while `Name` returns the name associated with the file. `Form` gives operating-system-specific information about the file, such as read/write privileges and the amount of disk space initially allocated for it. `Mode` tells whether the file is of type `In_File`, `Out_File`, or `Inout_File`. The latter mode is reserved for random-access files, which are discussed later in this section.

Formatted Sequential I/O Formatted I/O is provided in C, Fortran, Java 1.5, and Ada. However, it takes a different form in each of these languages. Below is a summary.

In C, the `fopen` statement provides the file name and the permissions under which the file is to be opened. Reading and writing to a file (once opened) can be performed by using the library functions `fscanf` and `fprintf`. Here is a C example that reads information into an array from a file called `input.asc`.

```
FILE* input;
input = fopen("input.asc", "r");
for (i=0; i<8; i++)
    fscanf(input, "%d", &a[i]);
```

Here, the `%d` in the second parameter is a cue that the `fscanf` function should scan for an integer (as opposed to `%f` for a float or `%s` for a string), skipping whitespace in the interim. This process is a kind of hybrid between unformatted and formatted I/O: unformatted because arbitrary amounts of whitespace (spaces, new lines, etc.) can occur between adjacent values, and formatted because the values read must be of the type specified.

In addition to `fscanf` and `fprintf`, C provides the functions `getc` and `putc` which input and output a single character, and `fgets` and `fputs` which input and output an entire line of characters from/to a file to/from a string variable. All the input functions among these return `EOF` when the end of the file is reached.

In Fortran, formatted I/O is more strict than in C, since whitespace is not automatically skipped between input entities. The layout of a Fortran READ or WRITE statement is:

```
READ (file_unit, format_expression) variable-list
WRITE (file_unit, format_expression) expression-list
```

If `file_unit` is an asterisk, standard input or output is assumed. Otherwise, `file_unit` is an integer identifying a file other than the standard input buffer, in which case an OPEN statement must precede the READ statement:

```
OPEN (UNIT=file_unit, FILE='f', STATUS='OLD', &
      ACTION='READ',IOSTAT=s)
```

Here, the following information is provided:

> `file_unit` connects the file to subsequent `READ` statements.

> The file name 'f' is the external name of the file on the medium where it permanently resides.

> The file must be `OLD`, indicating that it already exists.

> Optionally the integer-valued `IOSTAT` variable `s` can be set to indicate the status of the i/o operation (e.g., that the file was successfully opened).

The FORMAT statement lets Fortran programs control the location and layout of individual data values in an input or output stream. Many different kinds of format descriptors are available for this purpose. The following four are frequently used:

> In—indicates an n-position integer.

> Fn.d—indicates an n-position floating point value, with d digits to the right of the decimal point.

> An—indicates an n-character string value.

> nX—indicates skipping n characters.

When printing, the first position in each output line must contain a control character that defines vertical spacing for that line (single space, double space, etc.).[9] Here is a Fortran variant of the above C code for initializing array `a` from the input file `input.asc`.

---

9. This is a holdover from the days when Fortran was outputting primarily to line printers, which could print exactly 132 characters per line and each character was in fixed font (like today's courier font).

```
OPEN (UNIT=3, FILE='input.asc', STATUS='OLD', &
    ACTION='READ', IOSTAT='ioerror')
IF (ioerror == 0) READ (3, 110) a
    110 FORMAT ( 8I5 )
```

Here, the FORMAT statement says that each value read and stored in a is retrieved as a 5-digit integer from the file, and there are eight of these.

A character string may be placed in the FORMAT expression to provide documentation for the output. The following statement displays a message followed by the eight values from a in the standard output file; each value takes five decimal positions on the line.

```
WRITE (*, 120) a
120 FORMAT ( 'Contents of array a are: ', 8I5 )
```

Note the blank space at the beginning of the message, indicating that this output line be single spaced.

Before version 1.5, Java used FilterOutputStreams and FilterInputStreams to manage its I/O formatting. The basic versions of these classes provide another input/output stream through which programmers could subclass filter streams to define their own filter streams. This method is clumsy at best, and it leads to inconsistencies among different Java applications for I/O formatting.

The release of Java 1.5 includes the class java.util.Formatter, which contains output formatting methods similar to those found in C. This feature may lead to easier and more standardized formatting conventions for Java programs. For example, the following Java 1.5 code displays a string and a 3-digit integer:

```
System.out.printf("%s %3d", name, age);
```

In Ada, the library Text_IO provides two heavily overloaded procedures, Get and Put, which allow programs to specify formatted input and output for various types of values. For instance, here are some variants of the Get procedure for inputting Character, Integer, and String values, respectively.

```
procedure Get (File: in File_Type; Item: out Character);
procedure Get (File: in File_Type; Item: out Integer);
procedure Get (File: in File_Type; Item: out String);
```

Here, the out parameter designates a variable where the character/string/integer value is to be stored.

Each of these has an optional Width parameter that allows the program to specify the number of characters to read from a file before it encounters a line terminator. This is similar to the Fortran convention of defining the width of a field containing a data value. If Width=0 is specified, the program will try to read as many characters as it can interpret to be of the appropriate type. For example, suppose i is an Integer variable and:

```
myFile: File_type;
Get (myFile, Item => i, Width => 0);
```

is performed on the input stream:

```
213a345
```

This will retrieve the value 213 from the input and assign it to i.

Ada formatted I/O also allows the program to specify the number of digits before and after the decimal, the number of exponential digits to include, and the base (binary, hexadecimal or octal) to use for displaying the value. For instance, the following statement:

```
Put (myFile, Item => 1024, Base => B);
```

displays

```
10000000000
```

which is the integer 1024 in binary notation.

We conclude this section with an observation. That is, while formatted and unformatted sequential I/O is a fairly straightforward and central programming activity, its programming details and idiosyncrasies are highly variable among different languages.

7.6.2 Random Access Files

Sequential I/O has two serious limitations when processing large files. First, not all applications access the information in a file in the same sequence in which it is stored. Second, since individual records in a sequential file are stored adjacent to each other, any attempt to replace a record with a larger one risks overwriting the initial portion of the next record in the sequence.

Random access (*or direct access*) files allow for nonsequential processing of information in a file. Such files occur in directories and other applications that need to avoid processing all records serially from the beginning just to find or update a single entry.

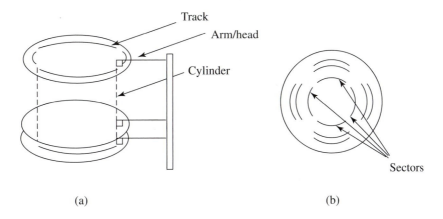

(a)   (b)

| **Figure 7.5**   **The Structure of Disk Storage Devices**

Disk storage devices are designed to handle random file access. Figure 7.5a shows the structure of such a device. A disk has multiple platters, each having several concentric circular tracks. Each track has the same number of fixed-length sectors (Figure 7.5b). A series of read/write heads, one per platter surface, is positioned to read/write information on a single cylinder before the arm moves them all to another cylinder. This arm movement is called a "seek."

In C programs, a `struct` can be used to define an individual record in a random access file application. As we saw in Chapter 5, a `struct` is simply a label for a collection of variables with different types.[10] Here is an example of a C `struct` that defines an entry of fluid flow data stored in an `nRows` x `nCols` array of such entries in a random access file.

```
typedef struct grid_t {
  float nRows, nCols;
  int noData;
  int dir;
} grid_entry;
```

The standard C libraries contain the following methods for randomly accessing data: `fseek`, `ftell`, `rewind`, `fgetpos`, and `fsetpos`. These allow C programs to seek to a specific record, tell which record it is currently about to read or write, seek back to the beginning of the file, retrieve the current file position, or reassign the current file position, respectively.

When randomly accessing a record in a file, the `fseek` statement is first used to reposition the read/write arm at the cylinder where the record is stored. An `fseek` statement is of the form:

```
fseek(FILE *stream, long offset, int origin)
```

Here, `offset` is the displacement in bytes of the next record from the file's `origin`, from which the distance for repositioning the read/write arm can be calculated.

The C `sizeof` function returns the number of bytes that a `struct` will require when stored in a file, and so the `offset` parameter for `fseek` to seek the nth record in the file can be written as `(n-1) * sizeof(struct)`.

The `origin` parameter can have one of three constant values, defining either the current position (SEEK_CUR) in the file, the beginning (SEEK_SET) of the file, or the end (SEEK_END) of the file. The program then seeks by moving from the given `origin` to an `offset` number of bytes in preparation for the next `fscanf` or `fprintf` operation in that file.

Figure 7.6 shows an application of random access in GIS, where an entry in the NORTHWEST direction from the current entry in the file `GIS.data` is retrieved in a nonsequential fashion. Here, x and y define the coordinates of the current entry, whose information is stored in the `struct grid_entry` defined above.

The `fseek` function here repositions the file to the beginning of that entry which is in the previous row and column (i.e., the pair x-1 and y-1 designates NORTHWEST). The entire grid is stored on the disk in row-major order (similar

---

10. Ada has the type `record`, which serves the same purpose as the C `struct`.

```
FILE* input;
input = fopen("GIS.data", "r");
...
x = /* column of entry */;
y = /* row of entry */;
/* seek to the "dir" variable NORTHWEST of grid_entry */
fseek(input, sizeof(grid_entry) * ((y-2) * nCols
    + (x-1)) + 2 * sizeof(float) + sizeof(int), SEEK_SET);
fscanf(input, "%d", &temp);
if (temp == SOUTHEAST)
    return true;
...
```

| **Figure 7.6**   **C code Segment That Randomly Accesses an Entry in a Grid**

to the storage scheme for arrays discussed in Chapter 5). Thus, the calculation `offset = sizeof(grid_entry)*((y-2)*nCols+(x-1))` identifies the beginning of that entry and the incremental value `2*sizeof(float)+sizeof(int)` moves past the first three variables in that entry. Thus, the `fscanf` function that follows `fseek` in Figure 7.6 retrieves the `dir` value for the grid entry in the NORTHWEST direction from the current entry.

In Fortran, programmers use a `RECL` and `ACCESS = DIRECT` clause in the `OPEN` statement to specify that the file will be accessed randomly. `RECL` is used to specify the length of an individual record in the file that is being opened. Thereafter, every READ or WRITE statement that accesses a record in the file must specify the record number, using the `REC` parameter to specify position of the record within the file.

Below is a FORTRAN statement pair that simulates the `fopen`, `fseek`, and `fcanf` statements in Figure 7.6, assuming `x` and `y` represent the column and row of the current entry.

```
OPEN(7, ACCESS='DIRECT', RECL=16)
READ(7, REC = (y-1)*nCols + x) nCols, nRows, noData, dir
```

The record length represented here assumes that each REAL and INTEGER value occupies 4 bytes of memory, so that the FORTRAN equivalent of the entire C `struct` `grid_entry` occupies 16 bytes altogether.[11]

We note finally that the FORTRAN solution automatically performs a seek within the READ statement, where the record number of the sought entry is specified to facilitate the seek. That is, the file position of the record is computed by the system as `rec*RECL`.

7.6.3 I/O Error Handling Semantics

Most run-time errors in practical programming situations occur during input and output operations. The hackneyed phrase "garbage in, garbage out" (GIGO, for short) was

---

11. Recall that FORTRAN array indexing begins at 1 (rather than 0) so that the calculation of the relative record number is slightly different than in Figure 7.6.

coined to denote that if a program received bad data input, it was bound to produce bad results. However, early languages provided few programming tools for trapping I/O errors. More recent languages incorporate more sophisticated tools to support on-the-fly I/O error detection and correction. Thus, the phrase GIGO is less likely to characterize programs written in modern languages, provided those programs effectively utilize the available error-handling facilities.

In this section, we summarize the I/O error handling features of recent versions of Fortran, C++, and Ada. This treatment provides a convenient prelude to Section 7.7, which covers the more general topic of exception handling semantics.

Figure 7.7 shows a small Fortran program that tries to open and read an integer value from a file and writes the outcome of that effort on the screen. Fortran's vehicle for I/O error handling is the IOSTAT clause, where an integer variable is designated to monitor the status of an OPEN, READ or WRITE operation. When used in an OPEN statement, the value 0 means that the file was opened successfully; otherwise a positive integer is assigned.

When a READ or WRITE statement encounters format errors, end-of-file, or end-of-record conditions, the program will abort unless the IOSTAT clause is present. In that case, the IOSTAT variable is assigned a negative value if the end of a file is reached, a positive value if an input error occurs, or zero if neither the end of the file nor an input error occurs.

Since Fortran, more recent language designs support I/O error handling through the use of "exception" mechanisms. These mechanisms support not only the handling of unexpected I/O events, but also the handling of a variety of other unexpected run-time events. We treat the use of exception handling for I/O errors in the remainder of this section, while leaving a broader treatment of exception handling for other types of events to Section 7.7.

```
PROGRAM main
 INTEGER :: error
 OPEN(UNIT=7,FILE='myData',STATUS='OLD',IOSTAT=ioerror)
 IF (ioerror==0) THEN
   WRITE (*, '(1X,A)') 'opened without errors'
   READ (7, *, IOSTAT=ioerror) InValue
   IF (error < 0)
     WRITE (*, '(1X,A,I3)') 'End of file : ',ioerror
   ELSE IF (ioerror > 0)
     WRITE (*, '(1X,A,I3)') 'error on READ: ',ioerror
   ELSE WRITE (*, '(1X,I3,A)') InValue,' was read'
   END IF
  CLOSE (UNIT=7)
 ELSE IF (ioerror > 0) THEN
   WRITE (*, '(1X,A,I4,A)') 'error on OPEN ',ioerror, &
        ': file does not exist'
 END IF
END PROGRAM main
```

| **Figure 7.7**   **Fortran I/O Error Handling Example**

| **Table 7.4** | Predefined I/O Exceptions in Ada |

Exception	Meaning
Status_Error	Attempt to read or write to a file that is not open
Mode_Error	Attempt to read from an output file or write to an input file
Name_Error	Use of an improper file name in an open command
Use_Error	Attempt to output on an input device (e.g., the keyboard)
Device_Error	Hardware malfunction
End_Error	Attempt to read past end of file
Data_Error	Value read is incompatible with the type of the target variable
Layout_Error	Attempt to set column or line number outside its boundary

C++, Ada, and Java have comprehensive exception handling mechanisms, while Fortran, Pascal, and C do not. C++ exception handling fills the gap between a class definition and its client. That is, while a class has detailed information as to what type of error may occur, it does not know where such an error will occur—only the client program knows that.

Ada supports a number of predefined exceptions, I/O and otherwise. Like C++, Ada also allows programmers to define their own exceptions. However, Ada does not handle exceptions by default, so if one is raised the program will terminate and display information about the type and location of the exception.

Table 7.4 lists the predefined I/O exceptions in Ada, with a brief description of each. For example, the Ada exception handling code in Figure 7.8 simulates some of the behavior of the Fortran code in Figure 7.7.

These C++ and Ada examples illustrate the progress that has taken place in I/O error handling since the design of Fortran. Specifically, handling errors through a language's exception mechanism can result in cleaner code and a more powerful suite of alternatives for the program to respond to I/O errors. This flexibility extends to the more general issue of handling exceptions that occur in other-than-I/O parts of the program, as we discuss in Section 7.7.

7.7 EXCEPTION HANDLING SEMANTICS

Robustness has become critically important as computers have been embedded in real-time devices such as car engines, aircraft control systems, home security systems, and so forth.

> **Definition**: Applications are *robust* when they continue to operate under all conceivable error situations.

A computer that assists in running a car engine or flying an aircraft cannot be allowed to stop simply because an exceptional condition has occurred.

Exception handling provides a means for a program to deal with unexpected run-time errors, I/O and otherwise. It is usually essential for a program to be able to respond to run-time errors when they occur, rather than to let errors terminate the program prematurely.

> **Definition**: An *exception* is an error condition occurring from an operation that cannot be resolved by the operation itself.

```
with Ada.Text_IO, Ada.Integer_IO;
use Ada.Text_IO, Ada.Integer_IO;
procedure main is
begin
   error: Integer;
   inValue: Integer;
   myData: File_Type;
   Open (Unit7, In_File, "myData");
   Get (Unit7, inValue);
   Put ("Opened file without errors");
   New_Line;
   Put ("Value read is: "); Put (inValue);
exception
   when Name_error =>
      Put ("Error on open: improper file name");
   when Data_error =>
      Put ("Error on read: invalid integer");
end;
end main;
```

| **Figure 7.8   Ada I/O Error Handling Example**

Exceptions can occur at many levels of abstraction. At the hardware level, exceptions include illegal operations such as division by zero, and illegal memory references such as segmentation faults and bus errors. At the programming language level, exceptions can be caused by such events as an out-of-bounds array index, an attempt to read a value of the wrong type, or an attempt to access an object in the heap by using a null pointer. Higher level exceptions are also useful for specific kinds of data structures, like attempting to execute a pop operation on an empty stack.

For a long time, no language in widespread use provided a truly general and usable exception mechanism. A few languages (e.g., Cobol and PL/I) provided limited exception facilities. Cobol's exception facility was quite limited, but PL/I greatly extended the idea of exception handling.

PL/I provided a long list of predefined exceptions, as well as the ability for a program to define application-specific exceptions. The designers of Ada extended the PL/I approach, while also incorporating the exception handling ideas in the experimental languages CLU [Liskov and Snyder, 1979; Liskov and others, 1981] and Mesa [Mitchell *et al.*, 1979]. Modern languages (e.g., C++, Ada, and Java) now incorporate an extensive exception mechanism, in order to facilitate robust applications.

To *throw an exception* is to signal that the condition it represents has occurred. In the case of division by zero, the exception is thrown by the hardware. To *catch an exception* means to transfer control to an exception handler, which defines the response that the program takes when the exception occurs. In the case of division by zero, control can be transferred by the hardware interrupt to an interrupt handling routine, which might display a message and terminate the offending program.

Although a formal semantic model of exceptions based on denotational semantics exists [Alves-Foss (ed.), 1999], it is mathematically too formidable to be useful in this study. In Section 7.7.1, we give a more conceptual treatment of exception handling semantics, both in programming languages that do not have general exception facility and in those that do.

7.7.1 Strategies and Design Issues

How do programmers deal with exceptional situations in languages such as Pascal, C, and Fortran that do not have an exception mechanism? Typically, they invent a convention for dealing with the exception that allows the program to continue gracefully when it occurs.

One common technique is to define a function that returns an unusual or illegal value when a run-time failure occurs. For example, when searching an array for a specific value, if the value is found, typically the index of the value is returned. But if the value is not contained within the array, then (in the case of 0-indexed arrays) the value -1 can be returned, to indicate that the value was not found.

However, a programmer-defined mechanism is often a poor substitute for a built-in exception mechanism. Consider, for example, the following naive Pascal fragment that reads a series of numbers from a file and computes their sum:

```
sum := 0.0;
while not eof(file) do
begin
    read(file, number);
    sum := sum + number;
end;
```

Several different possible exceptions prevent this code from being robust. First, if white-space occurs after the last number, the end of file test will return *false*, but the read will skip that whitespace and raise a fatal error when the end of the file is reached. Another type of exception can occur if an input value is not a valid number, for example, the value contains a nondigit character. This also raises a fatal error. These types of errors are difficult to "program around."

Modern languages incorporate programming-level strategies into their function and class libraries. For instance, when Java's indexOf method is used for searching a Vector, it returns -1 when the search is unsuccessful.

Similar definitions occur in many other Java library functions. When retrieving the value associated with a given key in a hash table, Java returns a null object if the key is not found. Similarly, when reading lines from a BufferedReader using the readLine method, a null object is returned when end of file is reached. This approach is also used in the standard C libraries.

Another approach to programming for exceptions is to add an error parameter (or to return an error code for an otherwise void function). An example from Turbo Pascal is that the val function converts a string representation of a number to binary:

```
val(numberString, int, error);
```

If the variable `numberString` contains the value *'123'* before the call on `val`, then the resulting *int* has the value 123 and `error` has the value 0. If instead `numberString` contains the value *'1x3'*, then `int` is undefined and `error` has the value 2, which is the position in the string where the illegal character occurs.

Whether such situations are truly exceptions or just part of the normal processing of tables and files is a debatable question. In Java these situations are not considered exceptions, while in Ada, for example, one is expected to continue reading until encountering an end of file to trigger that exception.

One possible explanation for the difference in exception handling philosophies between Ada and Java is that in Java exceptions are objects. Thus, creating an exception involves a heap allocation that must eventually be garbage collected after the exception has been handled. However, an Ada exception is a primitive type built into the language, so the cost of generating and handling exceptions is less than it is in Java.

When an exception is triggered, the flow of control is transferred directly to an exception handling mechanism. Two major questions arise when designing an effective exception handling mechanism.

1 How is each handler associated with each possible exception that can be thrown?
2 Should an exception handler resume executing the code that throws the exception?

To address the first question, hardware-level exceptions are defined to correspond to specific hardware interrupts. There is basically one distinct interrupt handler for each type of interrupt. In a large application, such an arrangement is less useful than allowing different portions of an application to respond differently to a particular exception when it occurs.

Ada, C++, and Java all allow an exception handler to be associated with a block of code. Such a block can be an entire method or function, or simply a group of statements embedded in a larger construct, such as a statement sequence, a conditional, or a loop.

If no exception handler appears inside the function where the exception is thrown, the search for a handler is propagated up the call stack to the calling routine. If the method or function call is contained in a block with a handler for the given exception, then the exception is caught there. Otherwise the search continues up the call stack for the first appropriate exception handler.

In addressing the second question, two alternative approaches have been used. These are called the *resumption* model and the *termination* model, and are summarized pictorially in Figure 7.9 (using Java syntax).

Figure 7.9
Exception Handling
Models—Resumption
vs. Termination

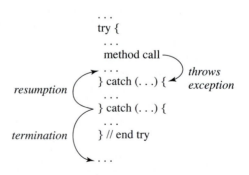

Interrupt handlers in an operating system implement the resumption model; that is, after dealing with the interrupt, the handler is free to resume whatever code threw the interrupt. PL/I uses the resumption model. Exception handling mechanisms in Ada, C++, and Java, however, all use the termination model; the code signaling the exception cannot be resumed.

PL/I programmers achieve the effect of the termination model by executing a return or nonlocal goto statement inside the exception handler. Similarly, careful programming in Ada, C++, and Java can be used to simulate the resumption model.

In general, the resumption model is more complex to implement, since it must restore the entire state of the program just before the exception was raised. This may include rolling back the run-time stack and restoring the values of certain variables. The termination model, of course, carries no such complexity.

7.7.2 Exception Handling in Ada, C++, and Java

An Ada program may contain code that responds to exceptions when they occur. When an exception occurs, the runtime system looks for an exception handler that corresponds to the exception thrown. If it does not find one, the current routine exits and passes the exception up to the routine that called it. This process continues until it either finds a handler that deals with the exception or exits the main routine in which case the program terminates.

If the system finds a handler for the exception, it executes the code in the handler, and then exits the current routine. If an exception is raised in the declarative portion of a routine, Ada abandons further processing of that declaration. The same holds for exceptions raised inside an exception handler itself, thus eliminating the danger of infinite exception handling loops.

An Ada program may raise an exception explicitly with the `raise` statement. This exception may be either a predefined Ada exception or one defined in the program itself. However, since Ada exceptions are broadly defined, a more specific program-defined exception is often more useful. Within an exception handler, the exception `raise with no condition` may be employed to propagate the exception to a higher level in the calling sequence. This can be useful for ensuring graceful recovery at all levels when an exception is fatal to the program.

Exceptions in C++ and Java are defined as classes. These two languages contain similar facilities for defining, throwing, and catching an exception.

C++ uses the following keywords for exception handling: `try`, `throw`, and `catch`. The syntax of an exception-handling statement is:

```
try {
   // code that may throw an exception
}
catch ( // exception type )
{
   // code executed when that exception type occurs
}
```

The semantics of a C++ exception handler is straightforward. First, the code within the `try` block is executed normally. If no exception occurs, the `catch` block is skipped. If an exception does occur (i.e., a `throw` function is executed for that exception), the `catch` block's code is executed immediately and control does not return to the statement where the exception was thrown.

Below is a C++ example, where the program can catch an instance of an array index out of range and display a message when that occurs.

```
#include <iostream.h>
int main () {
  char A[10];
  cin >> n;
  try
  {
    for (int i=0; i<n; i++)
    {
      if (i>9) throw "array index out of range";
      A[i]=getchar();
    }
  }
  catch (char * s)
  {
    cout << "Exception: " << s << endl;
  }
  return 0;
}
```

Once the exception is caught, the program executes the catch block and returns 0. In general, the parameter for `catch` can be of any valid type. Moreover, `catch` can be overloaded so that it can accept different types as parameters. In that case, the `catch` block executed is the one that matches the exception raised. If an exception is not caught by any `catch` statement, the program will terminate and display an "Abnormal termination" error message.

The C++ standard library predefines some exceptions that can be caught when they occur within a `try` block. The following exceptions are subclasses of the class `std::exception`:

C++ Exception	Thrown When:
bad_alloc	Heap storage cannot be allocated for a `new`
bad_cast	A cast cannot be completed
bad_exception	An exception doesn't match any catch
bad_typeid	A type cannot be determined by `typeid`
logic_error	A programming error (e.g., index out of range) occurs
runtime_error	A circumstance outside the program's control occurs

Figure 7.10 Java Exception Class Hierarchy

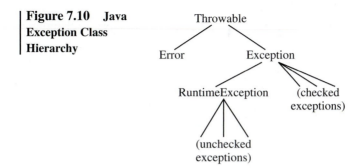

Since Java is a newer language than C++, its support for exceptions is more well-developed. Figure 7.10 shows the Java *Exception* class and some of its related classes.

Some Java exceptions are predefined within the class hierarchy. All Java exceptions are subclasses of `Throwable` and are divided into three categories:

1 Errors in the virtual machine (`Error` and its subclasses);
2 Run-time exceptions (`RuntimeException` and its subclasses) such as access through a null object or an illegal subscript; and
3 All others.

The latter two categories are subclasses of the class `Exception` and, by convention, have the word *Exception* as part of their name. Similarly, virtual machine errors, by convention, all have the word *Error* as part of their name.[12]

Exceptions, as opposed to virtual machine errors, are divided into *checked* and *unchecked* exceptions. Formally, a checked exception is an instance of the class `Exception` or a subclass that is not an instance of `RuntimeException`. Checked exceptions are application-level exceptions. The Java class libraries contain a wide variety of exceptions, including I/O exceptions, network exceptions, and so on.

An unchecked exception is an instance of the class `RuntimeException` or one of its subclasses. Java requires that checked exceptions be caught by an exception handler, while an exception handler is optional for an unchecked exception. Examples of unchecked exceptions include substring or array indices out of bounds, access through a null object, and division by zero.

A programmer-defined exception in Java is an object of class `Exception` or one of its subclasses; thus, a programmer-defined exception can be checked or unchecked. An exception may contain an arbitrary string message. Thus, the class `Exception` has two constructors, whose signatures are:

```
public Exception( );
public Exception(String s);
```

Thus, one creates a new exception by subclassing `Exception` or one of its subclasses, as shown below.

---

12. Java exceptions of type `Error` are not normally the concern of the programmer; they include such virtual machine errors as out of memory, run-time stack overflow, and so on.

```
class StackUnderflowException extends Exception {
    public StackUnderflowException() {super(); }
    public StackUnderflowException(String s){super(s); }

}
```

A typical use of such an exception would be:

```
if (stack == null)
    throw new StackUnderflowException();
```

Exception objects (as opposed to subclasses) are rarely named, since their only purpose is to be thrown. Subclasses of Exception may hold additional information or provide specialized behavior. However, in most cases they exist only to provide new exception subclasses. The most common subclass is the IOException and its subclasses in the package java.io.

A Java method is required to specify via a throws clause in its header for any checked exception that it does not catch itself. An example is the readLine method of a BufferedReader:

```
public String readLine( ) throws IOException;
```

Thereby, the Java compiler can ensure that each checked exception is caught and handled by the application.

Exceptions are caught in one of two ways. Either a call to a method that potentially throws an exception must appear in a try statement or the method containing the call must declare which exceptions it throws. Consider the following code which, given a *filename*, attempts to open that file for input:

```
try { BufferedReader infile = new BufferedReader(
                                new FileReader(filename));
    ... // process file
} catch (FileNotFoundException e) {
    System.out.println("File not found: " + filename);
    System.exit(1);
} // try
```

A Java catch is similar to a method header, in the sense that its formal argument specifies the type (or supertype) of the exception that it is catching, which can be used like any object.[13] In this case if the exception is thrown, a message is printed and the application terminated via a nonzero (error) exit. If there were no exit, the flow of control would continue with the next statement after the try; that is, Java uses the termination model for handling exceptions. The general form of a Java try statement is:

---

13. This similarity is limited, however, since a catch has no return type or visibility modifiers.

```
try {
    // code that can throw one or more exception types
    ...
} catch (Exception type e) {
    ...
} catch (Exception type e) {
    ...
} finally {
    ...
}
```

If an exception is thrown, each `catch` clause is evaluated in order until a match occurs. Then the block associated with that `catch` clause is executed. Each `try` can have as many `catch` clauses as desired. Note that a single `try` can be used to catch multiple exceptions across a group of statements, provided that every possible checked exception is caught. A simple way to simulate a single generic `catch` for every checked exception is to use `catch (Exception)` as the last (or only!) `catch` clause.

The `finally` clause, if present, is always executed, whether an exception is thrown or not. It is not possible to avoid executing the code in the `finally` clause. This clause is often used for closing files that had been opened and processed inside its `try` statement.

The other alternative to using a `try` on calls to methods that throw exceptions is to have the containing method itself propagate the exception via a `throws` clause:

```
public void readFile (BufferedReader infile)
                        throws IOException {
    String line;
    while ((line = infile.readLine()) != null) {
        ... // process line
    }
}
```

This routine reads lines via the `readLine` method of class `BufferedReader`, which can throw an `IOException`. Because the call to `readLine` does not appear in a `try` statement, the `readFile` method must declare that it does not handle the exception.

Note that at end of file, the `readLine` method returns a null value, rather than throwing an end of file exception. In contrast, other Java read methods throw an exception at end of file, as does Ada.

Java exceptions are thrown with a *throw* statement:

```
throw new Exception( );
```

At this point the normal flow of control is terminated, with control being transferred to the matching `catch` of the nearest surrounding `try`. If one does not exist, the called method propagates the exception and the process continues up the run-time stack (for more details on the dynamics of the run-time stack, see Chapter 10).

Note that the exception thrown above is anonymous, in that no named reference to it is kept. Since the flow of control does not continue past this point, it usually serves no purpose to keep a reference to the exception.

Normally, the exception thrown would be one of the subclasses of `Exception`, perhaps even with a message attached:

```
throw new StackUnderflowException("pop on an empty stack");
```

The major purpose of creating new exceptions is to name a category that is meaningful to the application and to group exceptions by category. An example of the latter is `IOException` which is the parent class of all of the input/output exceptions.

Example: Handling Input Robustly   Exceptions causing termination of a Java input process occur often in applications that use a command line argument to identify an input file.

A typical `main` method for handling such a scenario is shown in Figure 7.11. When the user supplies a valid file name at run time, the file is opened and processed normally. However, several other events could occur. For instance, the user could forget to supply an argument, or else the user could supply an argument that is either an invalid file name or the name of a file that cannot be read by the application. The program is designed to respond to any of these events.

If no argument is supplied on the command line, then the reference `arg[0]` throws an `ArrayIndexOutOfBoundsException`, since the index 0 exceeds the actual size of the array. Normally, indexing need not appear in a `try` statement; doing so in this case allows the application to supply an application-specific error message, rather than the Java language error message. The latter would presumably be unintelligible to the user.

In response, the `catch` catches an `IndexOutOfBoundsException`, which is the parent class of the exception actually thrown. Other than the relative brevity of the parent class name, there seems little reason in this case to prefer one versus the other. One use of

```
public static void main(String[] arg) {
   BufferedReader rdr = null;
   try {
     rdr = new BufferedReader(new FileReader(arg[0]));
   } catch (IndexOutOfBoundsException e) {
     System.err.println("Missing argument");
     displayUsage( );
     System.exit(1);
   } catch (FileNotFoundException e) {
     System.err.println("Cannot open file: " + arg[0]);
     System.exit(1);
   }
   process(rdr);
}
```

| **Figure 7.11   Robust Input Handling in Java**

this feature is to list all specific exceptions first and then use a parent class (for example, `Exception`) effectively as a catch-all for all other exceptions.

Another event that can occur is that the file cannot be opened for reading. This can be caused by any number of situations, as explained above. In any of these cases, the class `FileReader` throws a `FileNotFoundException`. In this case, the exception is caught in the `main` method and an appropriate error message is displayed. Note that in this example each `catch` ends with a nonzero error exit.

The solution given above has one other notable aspect. That is, the call to the method `process` cannot be included inside the `try` block. If it were, any uncaught index bounds exception in the method `process` would result in the "Missing argument" message, which would be misleading. Keeping the call to `process` outside the `try-catch` block requires declaring the `BufferedReader` variable outside the `try-catch` block and explicitly initializing it to `null`.

Example: Screening for Invalid Keyboard Input   In this example, we explore how the resumption model of handling exceptions can be simulated in Java using a loop. This example typifies applications that prompt a user for input and a keying error occurs. A simple expedient response is to notify the user of the error and prompting the user to try again.

Prior to version 1.5, Java provided no overloaded *read* method for the different primitive data types that convert from the text representation of, for example, an integer to its internal representation (32-bit binary for integers), as there is for `print`.[14] Instead, a string representation of the number is read and converted to (for example) an `int`. Assuming that a `BufferedReader` object `in` has been created using:

```
BufferedReader in = new BufferedReader(
                    new InputStreamReader(System.in));
```

then the required code is given in Figure 7.12.

```
while (true) {
  try {
    System.out.print ("Enter number : ");
    number = Integer.parseInt(in.readLine ( ));
    break;
  } catch (NumberFormatException e) {
    System.out.println ("Invalid number, please reenter.");
  } catch (IOException e) {
    System.out.println("Input error, please reenter.");
  } // try
} // while
```

| **Figure 7.12   Resumption Model Example**

14. Recall our earlier discussion of the introduction of formatted I/O in Java 1.5.

If a valid number is entered, no exception is thrown and the loop is terminated normally. However, if an invalid number is entered, an exception is thrown, an error message is printed, and the loop is repeated, reprompting the user for a number. In this code, the `readLine` method may throw an `IOException`, which must be caught by the `try` statement.

The invalid input example uses a potentially infinite loop to circumvent the termination model employed by Java for handling exceptions. The loop here can be terminated only if no exception is thrown. Thus, use of the loop allows the programmer to effectively achieve a resumption model of exception handling.

Example: Defining an Application-Specific Exception In developing a reusable class or method, errors may occur that the class developer would like the client to handle. Most languages that provide exception handling allow the programmer to create such application-specific exceptions and throw them under the appropriate conditions. These usually represent conditions from which the client may wish to recover.

A typical example occurs in the development of a stack class. Assume that we have the `StackUnderflowException` class given at the beginning of Figure 7.13. When the stack is empty, a `pop` operation cannot be defined. Thus, the typical code for `pop` on a `Stack` class of `ints` using an array implementation is given in the remainder of Figure 7.13.

The code declares the array `stack` with some maximum capacity; the variable `top` keeps track of the current top of the stack. `StackUnderflowException` is declared as a subclass of the class `Exception` and relies on that parent class for its methods.

The method `pop` is simple; first, it decrements `top` and then returns the value of `stack[top]` using the decremented value of `top`. However, this operation is unsafe; if the original value of `top` is less than or equal to zero, an `ArrayIndexOutOfBoundsException` will be thrown.

```
class StackUnderflowException extends Exception {
  public StackUnderflowException( ) { super(); }
  public StackUnderflowException(String s){ super(s);}
}
...
class Stack {
  private int stack[];
  private int top = 0;
  ...
  public int pop() throws StackUnderflowException {
    if (top <= 0)
        throw new StackUnderflowException("pop on empty stack");
    return stack[--top];
  }
  ...
}
```

| **Figure 7.13**   **Defining and Using an Application-Specific Exception**

However, the caller of this method shouldn't have to deal with the exception. So instead a `StackUnderflowException` is created and thrown, as needed, by the `pop` method. The header of this method must list any exception that it can throw in a `throws` clause. Thus, any call to the `pop` method must explicitly catch this exception.

As this example illustrates, creating a new exception is a simple yet powerful tool in Java.

7.7.3 Exceptions and Assertions

I/O error handlers and exceptions are two distinct devices that programmers can use to respond to unexpected run-time events. A third device, which is especially useful during program development, is the so-called *assertion*,[15] which is a predicate inserted at some point in a program which describes a state that the active variables should satisfy whenever that point is reached at run time. If that state is not satisfied, the assertion is said to "fail" and execution can be interrupted. Thus, assertions are somewhat like exceptions in the sense that they can define and respond to unexpected run-time events.

The language Eiffel was the first language to fully incorporate assertions into the language. Later versions of Java also include assertions. In this section we examine Java's mechanism (added in version 1.4) for defining and handling assertions. We also examine the challenge of implementing an assertion mechanism in earlier versions of Java.

In general, assertions are useful in program verification because they can represent so-called "preconditions," "postconditions," and "loop invariants." A careful treatment of using assertions in program verification is the focus of Chapter 18.

Informally, a function's *precondition* is a constraint on the values of its arguments that must be met in order for the function to perform its task. Similarly, a *postcondition* is a kind of "promise" that, if the call provides arguments that satisfy the precondition, the result will satisfy the postcondition. A *loop invariant* is an expression about what must be true before (and after) each repetition of the body of a loop. All three of these are written in the form of a Boolean expression in languages like Java, C++, and Ada.

For example, consider the calculation of the *n*th Fibonacci number shown in Figure 7.14—which is a Java variant of the C++ program from Figure 10.5. This program reads an integer as a command-line argument and reports a problem if that integer is negative. As shown there, the function `fibonacci`'s precondition is that the integer value of n provided by any call must be nonnegative, and its postcondition is a promise to return the *n*th Fibonacci number for that particular value of n.

The EBNF syntax of a Java assert statement is defined below:

AssertStatement → `assert` *booleanExpression* [`:` *stringExpression*] `;`

Here, the optional *stringExpression* defines the message that will be displayed whenever the *booleanExpression* is `false` at the time the *AssertStatement* is reached during run time.

Semantically, an *assertStatement* will interrupt program execution if its *booleanExpression* is `false` at the time it is reached during program execution, in which case its *stringExpression* is also displayed. If its *booleanExpression* is `true`, the

---

15. The term is formally defined in Chapter 18.

```
public class assertTest {
  public static int fibonacci (int n) {
    int fib0, fib1, temp, k;
    // precondition: n >= 0
    assert n >= 0 : "Invalid argument for fibonacci" ;
    fib0 = 0; fib1 = 1; k = n;
    while (k > 0) {
      temp = fib0;
      fib0 = fib1;
      fib1 = fib0 + temp;
      k = k - 1;
    }
    // postcondition: fib0 is the nth Fibonacci number.
    return fib0;
  }
  public static void main (String[] args) {
    int answer;
    answer = fibonacci(Integer.parseInt(args[0]));
  }
}
```

| **Figure 7.14   Java 1.4 Program with an AssertStatement**

assert statement's message will not be printed and program execution will continue normally.

In Java, an *AssertStatement* can be placed anywhere among the executable statements in a method, but not among the declarations.[16] For our example, the program will deliver the following error message if the argument for fibonacci is negative:

```
Exception in thread "main" java.lang.AssertionError: Invalid
        argument for fibonacci
    at assertTest.fibonacci(assertTest.java:4)
    at assertTest.main(assertTest.java:16)
```

In versions of Java prior to Java 1.4, we can implement assertion checking by defining an AssertException class [Fowler, 2000] as a special kind of exception.

```
class AssertException extends RuntimeException {
  public AssertException( ) { super( ); }
  public AssertException(String s) { super(s); }
}
```

---

16. To enable assertions in a Java 1.4 or 1.5 program, the run requires the -enableassertions (-ea for short) option. To disable assertion checking at run time, the -disableassertions (-da for short) option is used.

To avoid having to add lots of try-catch statements, we make `AssertException` a subclass of `RuntimeException`. Logically, an assert is like an index out of bounds: we expect it to occur only if the programmer has made an error. Thus, we should be able to make assertions without needing to include try-catch statements.

Next we consider the `Assert` class itself. Since there is no data to be stored within an assertion object, we opt to make the class a simple library of static methods. One method clearly required is to assert that a particular boolean condition is true.

The code for this method is straightforward; if the condition is false, the method throws an `AssertException`. Another useful method asserts that execution should not reach this point; the implementation always throws an exception. Finally, we include a boolean constant which, if desired, can be used to optimize assertions out of the client's code. Our `Assert` class is given in Figure 7.15.

As an example of the use of this class, consider the revised stack class given below:

```java
class Stack {
    int stack[];
    int top = 0;
    ...
    public boolean empty() { return top <= 0; }
    public int pop() {
        Assert.isTrue(!empty());
        return stack[--top];
    }
    ...
}
```

In this version, it is the caller's responsibility to check that a stack is not empty before invoking a `pop` operation. Therefore, the programmer merely asserts that the stack is not empty as part of the `pop` operation. In the event that a run-time exception is ever triggered by the assert, this would be considered a bug in the client code.

Note that since the `pop` method throws a `RuntimeException`, a `throws` clause is not needed in the method header. The philosophy used here is quite different than the one

```java
class Assert {
    static public final boolean ON = true;
    static public void isTrue(boolean b) {
        if (!b) {
        throw new AssertException("Assertion failed"); }
    }
    static public void shouldNeverReachHere() {
        throw new AssertException("Should never reach here");
    }
}
```

| **Figure 7.15   An Assert Class**

used earlier. Here, the developer of the class imposes certain restrictions on the clients of the class and these restrictions are enforced through the use of assertions.

Should a client of our stack class ever logically execute the following code sequence:

```
Stack stack = new Stack();
stack.pop();
```

a run-time exception will be thrown, resulting in a message like the following:

```
AssertException: Assertion failed
        at Assert.isTrue(Assert.java:4)
        at Stack.pop(Stack.java:13)
        at ...
```

Adequate testing should eliminate the possibility of such assertion exceptions ever being triggered. Inserting them into code serves partially to document assumptions made about the state of a method or object. Our assertion class allows such assumptions to be explicitly stated, thus aiding the detection of subtle run-time errors.

7.8 SUMMARY

This chapter introduces the semantics of programming languages from an informal point of view. An operational approach to semantics is used, highlighting the semantic features of several popular languages. The semantics of expressions, assignments, conditionals, branching, and looping statements are considered, along with those of input/output and exception handling.

This treatment focuses on the behavior of programs at run time. In later chapters, we shall consider the implementation of language semantics, as well as their denotational and operational definitions.

EXERCISES

7.1 Consider the following sequence of C/C++ statements, which are syntactically valid but have no reasonable semantic interpretation (assuming that i and j have been declared as int variables):

```
j = 0;
i = 3/j;
for (i=1; i>-1; i++)
    i--;
```

How are these situations handled when executed by your C/C++ system?

7.2 Give other kinds (beyond those illustrated in the previous question) of C/C++ statements that are syntactically valid but whose meaning cannot be reasonably defined in the semantics of a programming language.

7.3 (a) How does Java define the numerical idea of infinity? (You should look at the *Java Language Specification* [Gosling *et al.*, 1996] for the details.)

(b) Looking at the specifications in the *Java Language Definition* [Arnold and Gosling, 1998], can you explain in plain English the meaning of the statement i = 3/j; for all possible values of j, including 0?

7.4 Consider the expression x + y/2 in the language C. How many different meanings does this expression have, depending on the types of x and y?

7.5 Rewrite the factorial program of Figure 7.2 in Java so that the the initial value of n is read as input, and the final value of f is written to the screen. Now run the program for the values 2, 3, ... until the value of f overflows the size of an int value. What is the value of n for which this occurs? How is this error treated by Java?

7.6 For your C/C++ compiler, verify whether or not the cast of the integer 257 to a char results in an error.

7.7 For your Java compiler/interpreter, verify whether or not the cast of the integer 65537 to a char results in an error.

7.8 For both C/C++ and Java, write a program to compute $2^{30} + 65534$. Then convert this integer (or long int) to floating point by adding 1.0. Next convert the floating point number back to an integer and subtract 1. Do you get back the same integer you started with? Do *not* use double precision floating point.

7.9 Suggest a general strategy by which the various languages' (Fortran, C, Ada, and Java) formatted I/O conventions could become more unified. That is, can you design a generalized format expression to which a format expression in each of these languages could be mapped in a meaning-preserving way? What are the difficult challenges for creating such a mapping?

7.10 Answer the above question again, but for unformatted I/O.

7.11 Consider the C program fragment in Figure 7.6 that illustrates random access.

(a) Is this valid C++ code? Why or why not?

(b) Write a small C or C++ program that creates a modest representative random access file GIS.data that can be used as input by this code.

(c) Complete this program in such a way that it navigates the grid beginning from the upper left-hand (NORTHWEST) corner and displays each x-y coordinate pair that it encounters at each step.

7.12 Consider the Ada I/O errors summarized in Table 7.4. Using Web-based sources, determine if a similar collection of I/O errors is defined for C. What about C++?

7.13 Using Web-based sources, examine the C++ and Ada exception handling models in more detail.

(a) How does the C++ model for exception handling differ from the Java model discussed in this chapter?

(b) How does the Ada model for exception handling differ from the Java model?

7.14 Modify the invalid numeric input example of Section 7.7.2 so that the user has at most three tries to input a valid integer.

7.15 Incorporate the invalid numeric input example of Section 7.7.2 into a program that reads a sequence of numbers from the user until a negative number is entered and then computes the sum and average of the sequence of numbers. Verify that the application behaves correctly in the presence of invalid numeric input.

7.16   Consider the stack class of Section 7.7.2.

(a) Extend this class with an appropriate constructor and a main method to test the stack.

(b) Extend this class with a push method that throws a stack overflow exception if a push is made onto a full stack.

(c) Extend the stack class of Section 7.7.2 with an appropriate constructor and a main method to test the stack using the `assert` statement of Java 1.4.

7.17   Extend the stack class of Section 7.7.2 with a push method that throws a stack overflow exception if a push is made on a full stack.

Semantic Interpretation

"To understand a program you must become both the machine and the program."
Attributed to Alan Perlis

CHAPTER OUTLINE

This chapter has both an operational and a denotational semantics flavor. It begins by describing the state of a computation rather carefully, which provides a basis for the detailed discussion of Clite semantics in Sections 8.1 and 8.2.

Sections 8.2 and 8.3 have an operational semantics flavor. They discuss the details of Clite semantics, with static and dynamic typing respectively, using an informal style supplemented by pieces of Java code. A complete interpreter for Clite provides a ready test bench to explore these semantic ideas in detail.

Section 8.4, which is optional, takes a more formal denotational semantics pass through the same topic. It provides insight into the mathematical rigor needed to fully expose the semantics of a complete programming language.

8.1 STATE TRANSFORMATIONS AND PARTIAL FUNCTIONS

The individual steps that occur during a program run can be modeled as a series of state-transforming functions. Recall from Chapter 7 that the *state* of a program is the collection of all active objects and their current values.

> **Definition**: The *denotational semantics* of a language defines the meanings of abstract language elements as a collection of state-transforming functions.

In order to specify the semantics of a language, we first need a small collection of mathematical entities and their properties as a basis. For example, the integers, real numbers, characters, and booleans and their properties provide a basis for studying the semantics of Clite.

These mathematical assumptions are tempered by the constraints of real computers, as discussed in Chapter 5. The integers, for example, constitute a semantic domain for programming languages, but the type `int` in C-style languages does not include the full range of integer values.

> **Definition**: A *semantic domain* is a set of values whose properties and operations are independently well-understood and upon which the rules that define the semantics of a language can be based.

The second element we need is a precise model of a state, including the values that can be stored there, which was introduced in Chapter 7. For the simple language Clite, whose environment is static, the state can be represented as a set of variable-value pairs. That is:

$$state = \{\langle var_1, val_1 \rangle, \langle var_2, val_2 \rangle, \ldots, \langle var_m, val_m \rangle\}$$

Here, each var_i denotes a variable and each val_i denotes its currently assigned value.

We shall expand this definition of state in Chapters 10 and 11, when it will be important to represent the environment in a more dynamic fashion. There, a dynamic environment allows us to precisely characterize the ideas of run-time stack and heap, and thus deal effectively with procedure call, object creation, parameter passing, recursion, and so on.

The third element we need is the idea that the state-transforming functions in the semantic definition are necessarily *partial functions*.

> **Definition**: A *partial function* is one that is not well-defined for all possible values of its domain (input state).

That is, certain program constructs in certain states cannot have meaning representations, even though those constructs are valid with respect to their syntax and type characteristics.

For example, consider the following (insidious) Clite program fragment.

```
i = 1;
while (i > 0)
    ;
```

Assuming that i is an int variable, this fragment has no final state, since the value of i never changes and the loop repeats itself endlessly.

The meaning of a Clite *Expression* is also a partial function. For example, division by zero is undefined for many computers and programming languages. Similarly, adding 1 to the largest int value on a machine cannot be defined semantically, since the result is a value outside the semantic domain of the machine.

8.2   SEMANTICS OF CLITE

With this background, we can define the meaning of an abstract Clite program[1] as a set of functions *M* (for meaning) that transform the program state. These functions individually define the meaning of *Program* and of every kind of statement that occurs in the abstract syntax: *Skip, Block, Conditional, Loop, Assignment.*

These functions are implemented as a Java class Semantics which, combined with the AbstractSyntax class, forms an interpreter for Clite. Such an interpreter is valuable to the language designer because:

- It can be used to test the validity of the semantic definitions, and

- It can reveal the trade-offs that occur among alternative semantic definitions.

However, a Java interpreter for Clite, to be completely valid, must assume that Java itself has been completely defined. In fact, that is nearly the case—a formal definition of Java has been proposed in recent research papers. Interested readers are referred to [Alves-Foss (ed.), 1999] for more information.

8.2.1 Meaning of a Program

Let *State* represent the set of all program states. Then the meaning *M* of an abstract Clite *Program* is defined by the following three functions:

$$M: Program \rightarrow State$$
$$M: Statement \times State \rightarrow State$$
$$M: Expression \times State \rightarrow Value$$

That is, the meaning of a *Program* is a function that produces a *State*. Similarly, the meaning of a *Statement* is a function that, given a current *State*, produces a new *State*. Finally, the meaning of an *Expression* is a function that, given a current *State*, produces a *Value*.

Note that the meaning of an *Expression* is normally a *Value*. This makes intuitive sense since an expression is normally a constant *Value* (e.g., 1), a *Variable* (e.g., n), a *Binary* (e.g., i + 1), a *Unary* (e.g., -x), or some combination thereof. The *Value* of a *Variable* is its value in the current state.

---

1. The semantics of Clite arrays is omitted from this discussion, since arrays require a dynamic memory model (see Chapter 11).

Since the abstract syntax of a Clite program is a tree structure whose root is the abstract element *Program,* the meaning of a Clite program can be defined by the application of a series of functions to the tree. Recall from Chapter 2 that the abstract syntax of a *Program* is:

Program = Declarations decpart; *Block* body

> **Meaning Rule 8.1** *The meaning of a Program is defined to be the meaning of its* body *when given an initial state consisting of the variables of the* decpart, *each initialized to the undef value corresponding to its declared type.*

The rule defines the meaning of a program using the abstract syntax definitions of the constituents of *Program.* So this rule says that the meaning of a program is the meaning of the program's body with the initial state where all the declared variables have undefined values of the appropriate type. As the meaning of the program unfolds, this initial state will change as variables are assigned and reassigned values, as shown, for example, in Table 7.3.

This functional style for defining the meaning of a program is particularly straightforward to implement in Java. An implementation is as follows:

```
State M (Program p) {
    return M (p.body, initialState(p.decpart));
}
```

The method initialState( ) constructs a state holding each declared variable initialized to the value undef appropriate to its type.

Since a state is a set of unique key-value pairs, it is naturally implemented as a hash table, using Java's HashMap class:

```
public class State extends HashMap { ... }
```

Recalling that *Declarations* is implemented as a Java ArrayList and that the abstract syntax for *Declaration* is defined:

Declaration = Variable v; *Type* t;

The necessary implementation of initialState is:

```
State initialState (Declarations d) {
    State state = new State();
    for (Declaration decl : d)
        state.put(decl.v, Value.mkValue(decl.t));
    return state;
}
```

The variable-value pairs are entered into the hash table using HashMap's put method. The method Value.mkValue, given the type, returns an undefined value of the appropriate type.

8.2.2 Statement Semantics

The meaning of an abstract *Statement* is a state-transforming function of the form:

M: *Statement* × *State* → *State*

There are five kinds of statements in Clite, identified in the abstract syntax as:

Statement = Skip | Assignment | Conditional | Loop | Block

Thus, the meaning of any Clite *Statement* is the meaning of the particular type of statement that it represents. An implementation consists of a method with an if statement for each type:

```
State M (Statement s, State state) {
    if (s instanceof Skip) return M((Skip)s, state);
    if (s instanceof Assignment)
        return M((Assignment)s, state);
    if (s instanceof Conditional)
        return M((Conditional)s, state);
    if (s instanceof Loop) return M((Loop)s, state);
    if (s instanceof Block) return M((Block)s, state);
    throw new IllegalArgumentException(
        "should never reach here");
}
```

Note our use of the throw statement as a defensive programming technique to catch both logical errors in the semantic model and errors in the implementation of the model.

Skip A Clite *Skip* statement does nothing to the state, and so its meaning is simple.

> **Meaning Rule 8.2** *The meaning of a Skip statement is an identity function on the state; that is, the state is unchanged.*

Implementation of the semantics of a Skip is also simple; it returns the *State* it was passed:

```
State M (Skip s, State state) {
    return state;
}
```

While a *Skip* statement does nothing, it still plays an important role in programming. For instance, C and C++ allow side effects in loop tests, so that a loop body can be a *Skip*. For example, see Figure 5.6. Another use of a *Skip* statement in Clite is that the parser converts all if-then statements in the concrete syntax to if-then-else statements in the abstract syntax by inserting a *Skip* as the else branch of an abstract *Conditional* statement.

Assignment   The abstract syntax of a Clite *Assignment* has the following parts:

> *Assignment = Variable* target; *Expression* source

Informally, the meaning of an *Assignment* evaluates the expression in the current state and produces a new value for the target variable in the output state.

> **Meaning Rule 8.3** *The meaning of an assignment statement is the result of replacing the value of the* target *Variable by the value of the* source *Expression in the current state.*

The meaning of an *Assignment* assumes the type constraints discussed in Chapter 6. Recall the following example from Figure 7.2:

```
f = f * i;
```

Since Clite is strongly typed, this *Assignment* is type valid by the time the following meaning function is applied. That is, the result type of the expression is guaranteed to be the same as the type of the target variable. Thus, run-time type errors (such as assigning a boolean value to a floating point target) cannot occur.

Table 7.3 shows that, when statement 4 is executed, the integer value 3 replaces the *undef* value for the variable n. The values of the other variables are unchanged by this *Assignment*.

Implementation of an *Assignment* uses a method named onion( )[2] to replace the value of the variable in the hash table implementation of the *State*.

```
State M (Assignment a, State state) {
    return state.onion(a.target, M (a.source, state));
}
```

Basically, the onion method executes a put to replace the value of the target *Variable* in the hash table (state) with the value of the source *Expression*.

Conditional   A Clite *Conditional* statement has three parts:

> *Conditional = Expression* test; *Statement* thenbranch, elsebranch

In the case that the elsebranch is omitted in the concrete syntax, the *Conditional* has a *Skip* statement in its place.

> **Meaning Rule 8.4** *The meaning of a Conditional depends on the truth or falsity of its boolean* test *in the current state. If* test *is true, then the meaning of the Conditional is the meaning of the* thenbranch *Statement; otherwise, it is the meaning of the* elsebranch *Statement.*

---

2. The reason for this rather odd name is explained in Section 8.4, which defines the mathematics and the formal model underlying the implementation.

Consider the following code to compute the maximum of two numbers a and b:

```
if (a > b)
    max = a;
else
    max = b;
```

If it is true that a > b, then the meaning of the *Conditional* is defined as the meaning of max = a. Otherwise, it is that of max = b. So, regardless of the outcome of the test a > b, the output state reflects an assignment to max as either the value of a or the value of b.

The implementation mimics the above rule:

```
State M (Conditional c, State state) {
    if (M(c.test, state).boolValue( ))
        return M (c.thenbranch, state);
    else
        return M (c.elsebranch, state);
}
```

The *Conditional*'s boolean test is evaluated in the current state. If the test is true, the meaning of the *Conditional* is the state returned by the thenbranch; otherwise, the meaning is the state returned by the elsebranch.

Loop   The Clite *Loop* has a test and a body:

> *Loop = Expression test; Statement body*

> **Meaning Rule 8.5** *If the test is false, the meaning (output state) of a Loop is the same as the input state. Otherwise, the meaning is the result of applying this rule again to the meaning of its body in the current state.*

This is a recursive definition. Intuitively, a *Loop* specifies the repetition of the body zero or more times, each iteration beginning with the state that results from the previous one.

Consider again the loop (statements 7–10) in the factorial program of Figure 7.2. The first time this loop is executed, the program state is

$$\{\langle n, 3 \rangle, \langle i, 1 \rangle, \langle f, 1 \rangle\}$$

(see Table 7.3). So this state becomes the input state to the loop body, effectively statements 8–9, whose output state is

$$\{\langle n, 3 \rangle, \langle i, 2 \rangle, \langle f, 2 \rangle\}$$

This state becomes the input state to a recursive meaning function for the loop. And so the process repeats until the state

$$\{\langle n, 3 \rangle, \langle i, 3 \rangle, \langle f, 6 \rangle\}$$

which results in the third iteration of the loop returning the input state as its output state, since i < n is false. At that point the recursion unwinds with this state as the output state of the meaning of the *Loop*.

The implementation of a *Loop*'s meaning is a direct encoding of Rule 8.5:

```
State M (Loop l, State state) {
    if (M (l.test, state).boolValue( ))
        return M(l, M (l.body, state));
    else return state;
}
```

Notice that if the *Loop* never terminates, neither does this recursion (since it never reaches the `else` clause). This reflects the fact that the semantics of a program is a partial function.

Block   Abstractly, a Clite *Block* is just a sequence of statements to be executed in the order in which they occur.

*Block = Statement**

> **Meaning Rule 8.6** *The meaning of a Block is the aggregated meaning of its statements when applied to the current state. If a Block has no statements the state is not changed. Otherwise, the state resulting from the meaning of the first Statement in the Block becomes the basis for defining the meaning of the rest of the block.*

This is also a recursive definition. For example, consider the *Block* consisting of statements 8–9 of Figure 7.2 with the initial state:

$$\{\langle n, 3 \rangle, \langle i, 2 \rangle, \langle f, 2 \rangle\}$$

The output state of the *Block* is to first determine the output state from the *Assignment* `i = i + 1`, which is:

$$\{\langle n, 3 \rangle, \langle i, 3 \rangle, \langle f, 2 \rangle\}$$

This output state becomes the input state to the *Assignment* `f = f * i`, whose output state is:

$$\{\langle n, 3 \rangle, \langle i, 3 \rangle, \langle f, 6 \rangle\}$$

This last state becomes the output state of the *Block*.

The implementation:

```
State M (Block b, State state) {
    for (Statement s : b.members)
        state = M (s, state);
    return state;
}
```

uses a loop to traverse the *Statements* of the *Block*, using the output state of one *Statement* as the input state to the next.

This completes the definitions of the various Clite statement types. Now we turn to defining the meaning of an expression.

8.2.3 Expression Semantics

The meaning of an *Expression* is complicated. On the one hand, the primary mission of an *Expression* is to deliver a value, either to be assigned to a variable in an assignment or to be used as a test in a *Conditional* or *Loop* statement. On the other hand, *Expressions* may have so-called *side effects*:

> **Definition**: A *side effect* occurs during the evaluation of an expression if, in addition to returning a value, the expression alters the state of the program.

Because the treatment of side effects is an important topic in language semantics, we discuss it more fully in Section 8.2.4.

So, for now, the meaning of a Clite *Expression* is a *Value*:

$$M : Expression \times State \rightarrow Value$$

An *Expression* is always evaluated in the current state, because it may contain variables whose *Value*s might have changed in earlier states.

Recall that a Clite *Expression* has the following abstract syntax:

$$Expression = Variable \mid Value \mid Binary \mid Unary$$
$$Binary = BinaryOp \text{ op}; \; Expression \text{ term1, term2}$$
$$Unary = UnaryOp \text{ op}; \; Expression \text{ term}$$
$$Variable = String \text{ id}$$
$$Value = IntValue \mid BoolValue \mid FloatValue \mid CharValue$$

where *Binary* and *Unary* expressions involve binary and unary operators and their operands, respectively.[3] The meaning of an *Expression* is thus defined on the basis of its four alternative forms:

> **Meaning Rule 8.7** *The meaning of a Expression in a state is a Value defined as follows:*
>
> **1** *If the Expression is a Value, then its meaning is the meaning of the Value itself. An example of a Value is the integer 3.*
>
> **2** *If the Expression is a Variable, then its meaning is the Value of the Variable in the current state. In Table 7.3 the meaning of variable* i *in state*
>
> $$\{\langle n, 3 \rangle, \langle i, 2 \rangle, \langle f, 2 \rangle\}$$
>
> *is 2.*
>
> **3** *If the Expression is a Binary, then the meaning of each of its operands* term1 *and* term2 *is first determined. Then Rule 8.8 determines the meaning of the expression by applying the Operator* op *to the Values of those two operands.*
>
> **4** *If the Expression is a Unary, then the meaning of its operand* term *is determined. Then Rule 8.9 determines the meaning of the expression by applying the Operator* op *to the Value of the operand.*

---

3. To keep focussed on the main issues, we assume in the following discussion that all of the Clite operators except assignment are type specific, so there is no overloading of operators (see Chapter 4) and integer addition + is different from floating point addition +. The state-transforming rules also assume that some primitive types and transformations are predefined, and thus constitute a semantic domain for Clite.

This rule has a straightforward implementation:

```
Value M (Expression e, State state) {
    if (e instanceof Value)
        return (Value)e;
    if (e instanceof Variable)
        return (Value)(state.get(e));
    if (e instanceof Binary) {
        Binary b = (Binary)e;
        return applyBinary (b.op,
            M(b.term1, state), M(b.term2, state));
    }
    if (e instanceof Unary) {
        Unary u = (Unary)e;
        return applyUnary(u.op, M(u.term, state));
    }
    throw new IllegalArgumentException(
        "should never reach here");
}
```

In the implementation, the meaning of a *Value* or a *Variable* is exactly as specified in the above rule. For a *Binary* expression, both operands are evaluated in the current state, and then the method `applyBinary` is called to apply the operator `op` to the values of the two operands. The explanation of the evaluation of a *Unary* expression is similar.

Consider, for example, evaluating the `source` *Expression* of statement 8 in Figure 7.2:

```
i = i + 1;
```

with the input state shown in step 5 of Table 7.3. The value of `i` is 1 (Rule 4.7.2) and the value of 1 is 1 (Rule 4.7.2). So the value of `i + 1` is 2 (Rules 4.7.3 and 4.8).

Recall from Chapter 6 that the overloaded concrete operators in Clite were transformed into type specific, abstract operators. For example, the binary arithmetic operators `+`, `-`, `*`, `/` were converted to type specific operators `int+`, `int-`, `int*`, `int/` for `int` operands and `float+`, `float-`, `float*`, `float/` for `float` operands. Further, any necessary type conversions were inserted into the abstract syntax tree. So a `float+`, for example, is guaranteed that both of its operands are of type `float`.

Meaning Rule 8.8 *The meaning of a Binary expression is a Value defined as follows:*

1 *If either operand* `term1` *or* `term2` *is undefined, the program is semantically meaningless.*

2 *If the operator is an integer arithmetic operator, then an* `int+`, `int-`, `int*` *perform an integer add, subtract, or multiply on its integer operands, resulting in an integer result. If the operator is* `int/`, *then the result is the same as a mathematical divide with truncation toward zero. For example, a mathematical value of* −3.9 *is truncated toward zero, resulting in an* `int` *value of* −3. *Similarly, a mathematical result of 3.9 is truncated to 3.*

3 *If the operator is a floating point operator, then floating point arithmetic using the IEEE standard is performed on the* float *operands, resulting in a* float *result.*

4 *If the operator is a relational operator, then the operands are compared with a result of either* true *or* false. *The result is the same as the corresponding mathematical result, except that* false < true.

5 *If the operator is a Boolean operator, then:*
   (a) *The operator && is interpreted as:*

$$a \text{ \&\& } b \equiv \text{if } a \text{ then } b \text{ else } false$$

   (b) *The operator || is interpreted as:*

$$a \text{ || } b \equiv \text{if } a \text{ then } true \text{ else } b$$

The implementation below shows only the integer arithmetic operators on integer operands. The remaining cases would constitute a giant switch statement.

```
Value applyBinary (Operator op, Value v1, Value v2) {
    StaticTypeCheck.check( ! v1.isUndef( ) &&
        ! v2.isUndef( ), "reference to undef value");
    if (op.val.equals(Operator.INT_PLUS))
        return new IntValue(
        v1.intValue( ) + v2.intValue( ));
    if (op.val.equals(Operator.INT_MINUS))
        return new IntValue(
        v1.intValue( ) - v2.intValue( ));
    if (op.val.equals(Operator.INT_TIMES))
        return new IntValue(
        v1.intValue( ) * v2.intValue( ));
    if (op.val.equals(Operator.INT_DIV))
        return new IntValue(
        v1.intValue( ) / v2.intValue( ));
    ...
}
```

Thus, the full implementation would mimic what a real machine does, except that real computers do not trap uninitialized variables as our model is required to do.

In this code, each integer operator has a corresponding Java operator applied to the integer operands, yielding a new integer *Value* which is the result. Our interpreter traps an attempt to interpret a character or floating point value as an integer, which would be a type error in the implementation. C++, and hence Clite, defines false to be less than true, which can be implemented in Java by mapping the value false to 0 and true to 1. Other than our implementation of relational operators on boolean operands, our type checker does not permit booleans to be interpreted as integer values, which is a departure from C/C++.

Meaning Rule 8.9 *The meaning of a Unary expression is a Value defined as follows:*

1 *If the operand* term *is undefined, the meaning of the expression is undefined.*

2 *If the operator is* ! *(not), then the boolean operand is inverted.*

3 *If the operator is* int-/float-, *then the integer/floating point operand's sign is inverted.*

4 *If the operator is* i2f, *then the integer operand is converted to floating point. For example, the value 2 would be converted to 2.0.*

5 *If the operator is* c2i, *then the* char *operand is converted to integer using the ASCII code for the character. Effectively, except for adding leading zero bits, the value is unchanged except for its type.*

6 *If the operator is* i2c, *then the integer operand is converted to character. If the integer operand is either greater than 255 or less than zero, the meaning of the expression is undefined. If the conversion is successful, then except for the loss of leading zero bits, the value's bit pattern is the same, only the type is changed.*

7 *If the operator is* f2i, *then the floating point value is converted to integer by discarding the places after the decimal point, that is, it is truncated toward zero. For example, the value 2.9 is converted to 2 and −2.9 to −2. If the integer part of the floating point value is too large to store in an integer, the meaning of the expression is undefined.*

The implementation follows from the above rule:

```
Value applyUnary (Operator op, Value v) {
    StaticTypeCheck.check( ! v.isUndef( ),
        "reference to undef value");
    if (op.val.equals(Operator.NOT))
        return new BoolValue(!v.boolValue( ));
    else if (op.val.equals(Operator.INT_NEG))
        return new IntValue(-v.intValue( ));
    else if (op.val.equals(Operator.FLOAT_NEG))
        return new FloatValue(-v.floatValue( ));
    else if (op.val.equals(Operator.I2F))
        return new FloatValue((float)(v.intValue( )));
    else if (op.val.equals(Operator.F2I))
        return new IntValue((int)(v.floatValue( )));
    else if (op.val.equals(Operator.C2I))
        return new IntValue((int)(v.charValue( )));
    else if (op.val.equals(Operator.I2C))
        return new CharValue((char)(v.intValue( )));
    throw new IllegalArgumentException(
        "should never reach here");
}
```

Unlike the implementation of applyBinary, all of the cases are shown.

This completes the definition and implementation of the run-time semantics of Clite. A formal description of the semantics is given in Section 8.4.

8.2.4 Expressions with Side Effects

In addition to returning a value, an expression may have a side effect on the state of the computation. For example, the appearance of a function call `f(x)` in an expression like `f(x) + x` seems innocuous enough under normal circumstances. However, if this call alters the value of `x` in the state in which it is evaluated, the value returned by the expression will differ, depending on the order in which the two operands are evaluated, left-to-right or right-to-left.

Notice in Meaning Rule 8.7 that the order of evaluation of operands in a *Binary* is unspecified. However, the Java code which accompanies this definition clearly evaluates the operands in a left-to-right manner, since the Java function call:

```
applyBinary(b.op, M(b.term1, state), M(b.term2, state)
```

evaluates its arguments from left to right.

Side effects can trickle into the normal behavior of *Conditional* and *Loop* statements, as well. For instance, suppose the function call `g(x)` delivers a boolean result, and has a side effect on `x` as well. Then the following:

```
if (g(x))
    y = x;
```

may or may not assign to `y` the *a priori* value of `x` when `g(x)` is true.

A naive way to deal semantically with side effects in a language is simply to outlaw them. However, this would have serious consequences in languages like C, where even expressions like `x++` inside a larger expression would not be allowed.

Another way to deal with side effects is to expand the definition of the meaning of an expression so that it delivers both a *Value* and a *State*. Below is a revision of Meaning Rule 8.7 that allows an *Expression* to have a state-altering side effect.

$$M : Expression \times State \rightarrow Value \times State$$

Meaning Rule 8.10 *The meaning of an Expression in a state is a Value and a State, defined as follows:*

1. *If the Expression is a Value, then its meaning is the meaning of the Value itself and the current state is unchanged.*

2. *If the Expression is a Variable, then its meaning is the Value of the Variable in the current state, which remains unchanged.*

3. *If the Expression is a Binary, the meaning of* `term1` *in the current state is first determined, giving a value v_1 and a state s_1. Then the meaning of* `term2` *in state s_1 is determined, giving a value v_2 and a state s_2. Then Rule 8.8 determines the meaning of the expression by applying the Operator* `op` *to the resulting values v_1 and v_2 in state s_2, and the resulting state is s_2.*

4. *If the Expression is a Unary, then the meaning of its operand* `term` *in the current state is determined, giving value v_1 and state s_1. Then Rule 8.9 determines the meaning of the expression by applying the Operator* `op` *to the Value of the operand, and the resulting state is s_1.*

Note that the third step in this rule defines left-to-right evaluation. Moreover, the third and fourth steps assume that the binary and unary operators in the language have no side effects themselves. If they do, then Meaning Rules 8.8 and 8.9 would need to be expanded so that they deliver a value-state pair as well.

Finally, note that the introduction of side effects in this way will impact even the meaning of *Conditional* and *Loop* statements. For instance, when a *Loop*'s test *Expression* evaluation has a side effect, the values of some variables may be altered before its body begins to be interpreted.

8.3 SEMANTICS WITH DYNAMIC TYPING

Here we consider the semantics of a dynamically typed language in order to examine the difference between statically and dynamically typed languages more fully. We use the same method of presentation as in Section 8.2.

Many different dynamically typed languages could serve as a vehicle for this study, including JavaScript, Perl, Python, and Scheme. However, we prefer to use a modified version of Clite for this discussion, because it is familiar and it is sufficient to illustrate the main points behind dynamic typing.

We call this version Clite$_D$, since it uses the same lexer, parser, and abstract syntax as was used for Clite. Our semantic model for Clite$_D$ interprets the abstract syntax directly without preprocessing by either a type checker or a type transformer.

Consider the factorial program presented in Figure 8.1. It looks very much like the one in Figure 7.2, except for the absence of declarations. Other than eliminating declarations, what other features should Clite$_D$ have?

For example, Perl has distinct operators for string versus numeric comparisons. In Perl, $2 < 10$ is true using a numeric test, but 2 lt 10 is false since the test is a string comparison, that is, "2" lt "10" is the test actually performed. In contrast, Python overloads the operators like C/C++; for overloaded operators such as comparisons, if one operand is a string, the other must be also. In specifying the semantics of Clite$_D$, we will largely use Python as our model.

In this presentation, we discuss only the parts of Clite$_D$ semantics that differ from the semantics of Clite. The abstract syntax of a *Program* in Clite$_D$ is:

Program = Block body

```
1 int main ( ) {
2    n = 3;
3    i = 1;
4    f = 1.0;
5    while (i < n) {
6       i = i + 1;
7       f = f * float(i);
8    }
9 }
```

| **Figure 8.1**   Clite$_D$ **Factorial Program**

The first difference between the two semantic models is in the meaning of a program itself. Recall from Rule 8.1 that the interpretation of a *Program* began with a *State* in which all the declared variables were initialized to the special value *undef.* Here there are no variables declared, so the *Program* begins with an empty *State.*

> **Meaning Rule 8.11** *The meaning of a Program is defined to be the meaning of its* body *when given an empty initial state.*

Using this rule, Table 8.1 shows a trace for the factorial program of Figure 8.1. Note that the state in step 1 is empty. As assignment statements are executed, new `target` variables are added to the state. The type of the variable is the type of its value in the current state. For example, in step 4 the variables n and i have type integer, while the variable f is floating point.

Recall that for dynamically typed languages, no type checking is performed on the program. Despite this, the meaning of an *Expression* in the two languages (Rule 8.7) is almost identical. For example, the meaning of a *Value*, since the *M* function is supposed to return a *Value*, is the *Value* itself. In defining the meaning of a *Variable* in Clite$_D$, we insist that the *Variable* have a *Value*. Here is the complete definition:

> **Meaning Rule 8.12** *The meaning of an Expression in a state is a Value defined as follows:*
> 1 *If the Expression is a Value, then its meaning is the meaning of the Value itself.*
> 2 *If the Expression is a Variable, then its meaning is the Value of the Variable in the current state. If the Variable is not defined in the current state, the program is semantically meaningless. For instance, in Table 8.1 the variable f in step 2 does not occur in the current state; therefore, a reference to f in statement 4 would be an error.*
> 3 *If the Expression is a Binary, then the meaning of both of its operands* term1 *and* term2 *is determined. Then Rule 8.13 determines the meaning of the Expression by applying the Operator* op *to the Values of the operands.*

Table 8.1

Trace of the Factorial Program

Step	Statement	State
1	3	
2	4	<n, 3>
3	5	<n, 3>, <i, 1>
4	6	<n, 3>, <i, 1>, <f, 1.0>
5	7	<n, 3>, <i, 1>, <f, 1.0>
6	8	<n, 3>, <i, 2>, <f, 1.0>
7	6	<n, 3>, <i, 2>, <f, 2.0>
8	7	<n, 3>, <i, 2>, <f, 2.0>
9	8	<n, 3>, <i, 3>, <f, 2.0>
10	6	<n, 3>, <i, 3>, <f, 6.0>
11	10	<n, 3>, <i, 3>, <f, 6.0>

4 *If the Expression is a Unary, then the meaning of its operand* term *is determined. Then Rule 8.14 determines the meaning of the Expression by applying the Operator* op *to the Value of the operand.*

This rule has a straightforward implementation:

```
Value M (Expression e, State sigma) {
    if (e instanceof Value)
        return (Value)e;
    if (e instanceof Variable) {
        StaticTypeCheck.check( sigma.containsKey(e),
            "reference to undefined variable");
        return (Value)(sigma.get(e));
    }
    if (e instanceof Binary) {
        Binary b = (Binary)e;
        return applyBinary (b.op,
                M(b.term1, sigma), M(b.term2, sigma));
    }
    if (e instanceof Unary) {
        Unary u = (Unary)e;
        return applyUnary (u.op, M(u.term, sigma));
    }
    throw new IllegalArgumentException(
        "should never reach here");
}
```

In this implementation, the meanings of a *Binary* and a *Unary* are deferred to the methods applyBinary and applyUnary respectively. For the meaning of a *Variable* in Clite$_D$ the semantic interpreter makes the check that the current *State* contains the variable at the time it is referenced in an *Expression*.

For a *Binary*, both operands are evaluated in the current state and then the method applyBinary is called to apply the operator op to the values of the two operands. The explanation of the evaluation of a *Unary* expression is similar.

Recall from Chapter 6 that the overloaded operators in Clite are transformed into type dependent operators. No such phase exists for a dynamically typed language. Instead, the operators remain overloaded in the abstract syntax, just as they were constructed by the parser. So the check that both operands of a binary operator are the same type and are compatible with the operator must be performed by the meaning rule (i.e., at run time).

Meaning Rule 8.13 *The meaning of a Binary is a Value, defined as follows:*
1 *If the operator is an arithmetic operator, then:*
    (a) *If either operand is of integer type, the other operand must be of integer type as well. If the operator is an* +, -, *, *the result is the integer sum, difference, or product of the operands. If the operator is* /, *then the result is the mathematical quotient with truncation toward 0. For example, the quotient −3.9 is truncated to* int *value of −3.*

    (b) *If either operand is of floating point type, the other operand must be of floating point type as well. Floating point arithmetic using the IEEE standard is performed on the* float *operands, resulting in a* float *result.*

2 *If the operator is a relational operator, then the operands are compared with a result of either* true *or* false. *The result is the same as the corresponding mathematical result. Following C/C++,* false < true.

3 *If the operator is a Boolean operator, then:*
    (a) *The meaning of* && *is:* if *a* then *b* else *false*
    (b) *The meaning of* || *is:* if *a* then *true* else *b*
    where both a and b must be of type boolean.

4 *Any other operator/type combination is illegal.*

Below is an implementation of the integer arithmetic semantics in Clite$_D$:

```
Value applyBinary (Operator op, Value v1, Value v2) {
    StaticTypeCheck.check( v1.type( ) == v2.type( ),
                          "mismatched types");
    if (op.ArithmeticOp( )) {
        if (v1.type( ) == Type.INT) {
            if (op.val.equals(Operator.PLUS))
                return new IntValue(
            v1.intValue( ) + v2.intValue( ));
            if (op.val.equals(Operator.MINUS))
                return new IntValue(
            v1.intValue( ) - v2.intValue( ));
            if (op.val.equals(Operator.TIMES))
                return new IntValue(
            v1.intValue( ) * v2.intValue( ));
            if (op.val.equals(Operator.DIV))
                return new IntValue(
            v1.intValue( ) / v2.intValue( ));
        }
        ...
}
```

Note the test on the type of the left operand v1 to determine if it is an integer. Only the first few cases are shown of what is essentially a giant case statement.

    For each integer operator, the corresponding Java operator is applied to the integer operands, and then a new integer *Value* is constructed which contains the result. Our interpreter traps an attempt to interpret a character or floating point value as an integer, which would be a type error in the implementation.

    Meaning Rule 8.14 *The meaning of a Unary is a Value defined as follows:*
1 *If the operator is* ! *(not), then the boolean operand is inverted.*
2 *If the operator is unary* -, *then the integer/floating point operand has its sign inverted.*
3 *If the operator is* float, *then the integer operand is converted to floating point. For example, the value 2 would be converted to 2.0.*

4 *If the operator is* int, *then:*

(a) *A* char *operand is converted to integer using the ASCII code for the character. Effectively, except for adding leading zero bits, the value is unchanged except for its type.*

(b) *A* float *value is converted to integer by discarding the fractional part. For example, the value* −2.9 *to* −2. *If the integer part of the floating point value is too large to store as an* int, *the result is undefined.*

5 *If the operator is* char, *then the integer operand is converted to character. If the integer operand is either greater than 255 or less than zero, the result is undefined. If the conversion is successful, then except for the loss of leading zero bits, the value's bit pattern is the same; only the type is changed.*

6 *Any other operator/type combination is illegal.*

The implementation of this rule is also straightforward:

```
   ...
      else if (op.val.equals(Operator.FLOAT))
         return new FloatValue((float)(v.intValue( )));
      else if (op.val.equals(Operator.INT))
         return new IntValue((int)(v.floatValue( )));
      else if (op.val.equals(Operator.INT))
         return new IntValue((int)(v.charValue( )));
      else if (op.val.equals(Operator.CHAR))
         return new CharValue((char)(v.intValue( )));
      throw new IllegalArgumentException(
         "should never reach here");
   ...
```

As with the implementation of applyBinary, only a few cases are shown of what is essentially a giant case statement.

π 8.4 A FORMAL TREATMENT OF SEMANTICS

This section presents the semantics of Clite using a formal denotational style. It mirrors the meaning rules for statements and expressions given in Section 8.2.

The purpose of this presentation is to show how the semantics of a programming language can be defined with mathematical precision. Such a definition can persuade language designers and implementors that a language is well-defined. Well-definedness is an essential characteristic for programming languages, especially those whose programs must be proved correct (see Chapter 18).

Readers who choose to cover this section should be familiar with the requisite mathematical topics that are reviewed in Appendix B.

8.4.1 State and State Transformation

In determining the meaning of a variable in Section 8.2, we had to access the value of the variable in the current state. As with types in Chapter 5, a variable and its value are modeled as an ordered pair, for example, $\langle x, 3 \rangle$.

Thus, a state is a set of ordered pairs, where the first element is the variable name and the second element is its value. For example, the expression below describes the state of our factorial program corresponding to line 8 of Table 7.3:

$$state = \{\langle n, 3\rangle, \langle i, 2\rangle, \langle f, 2\rangle\}$$

For this particular state, we can retrieve the value of a variable, say f, by writing the expression $state(f)$, which gives the value 2. Since the variable names are unique, a state, as a set of ordered pairs, is equivalent to a function. Thus, the expression $state(v)$ denotes the function that retrieves the value of the variable v from the current $state$.

A state transformation occurs whenever an assignment is interpreted in an imperative or object-oriented program. For example, consider the following assignment:

```
i = i + 1;
```

whose effect is to change the above state as follows:

$$state = \{\langle n, 3\rangle, \langle i, 3\rangle, \langle f, 2\rangle\}$$

In Clite the target variable always occurs in the state. In contrast, an assignment in Clite$_D$, such as:

```
f = 1;
```

may have the effect of transforming the state from:

$$state = \{\langle n, 3\rangle, \langle i, 1\rangle\}$$

to the state:

$$state = \{\langle n, 3\rangle, \langle i, 1\rangle, \langle f, 1\rangle\}$$

The latter can be modeled using ordinary set union. However, using set union for the former would create the state:

$$state = \{\langle n, 3\rangle, \langle i, 3\rangle, \langle i, 2\rangle, \langle f, 2\rangle\}$$

which is clearly incorrect.

State transformations that represent both types of assignments can be represented mathematically by a special function called the *overriding union,* represented by the symbol $\overline{\cup}$. This function is similar to the ordinary set union, except when it changes the value of a variable that is already present in the current state.

> **Definition**: The *overriding union* of X and Y, written $X \overline{\cup} Y$, is the result of replacing in X all pairs $\langle x, v\rangle$ whose first member matches a pair $\langle x, w\rangle$ from Y by $\langle x, w\rangle$ and then adding to X any remaining pairs in Y.

For example, suppose $state_1 = \{\langle x, 1\rangle, \langle y, 2\rangle, \langle z, 3\rangle\}$ and $state_2 = \{\langle y, 9\rangle, \langle w, 4\rangle\}$. Then $state_1 \overline{\cup} state_2 = \{\langle x, 1\rangle, \langle y, 9\rangle, \langle z, 3\rangle, \langle w, 4\rangle\}$.

Another way to visualize the overriding union is through the natural join of these two sets. The *natural join* $state_1 \otimes state_2$ is the set of all pairs in $state_1$ and $state_2$ that have the same first member. For example,

$$\{\langle x, 1\rangle, \langle y, 2\rangle, \langle z, 3\rangle\} \otimes \{\langle y, 9\rangle, \langle w, 4\rangle\} = \{\langle y, 2\rangle, \langle y, 9\rangle\}$$

Recall that the set difference, $state_1 - (state_1 \otimes state_2)$ effectively removes every pair from $state_1$ whose first member is identical with the first member of some pair in

$state_2$. Now the the overriding union can be defined in terms of this set difference as follows:

$$state_1 \; \overline{\cup} \; state_2 = (state_1 - (state_1 \otimes state_2)) \cup state_2$$

Readers may have observed that the operator $\overline{\cup}$ is a formal and generalized model of the familiar assignment operation in imperative programming. It thus plays a pivotal role in the formal semantics of imperative and object-oriented languages like C/C++, Ada, and Java. We illustrate this characteristic below.

8.4.2 Denotational Semantics of a Program

Recall from Section 8.2 that the meaning function M is a mapping:

$$M : Program \rightarrow State$$
$$M : Statement \times State \rightarrow State$$
$$M : Expression \times State \rightarrow Value$$

That is, the meaning of a *Program* is a function that produces a *State* from a *Program*. Similarly, the meaning of a *Statement* is a function that produces a *State* from that *Statement* and a *State*. Finally, the meaning of an *Expression* is a function which, given an expression and a *State*, produces a *Value*.[4]

Recall also from Section 8.2 that these functions are *partial* functions, since they are not well-defined for all members of their domain. Thus, the abstract representations of certain program constructs in certain states do not have finite meaning representations, even though those constructs are syntactically valid.

Since the abstract syntax of a Clite program is a tree structure whose root is the abstract element *Program,* the meaning of a Clite program can be defined by a series of functions, the first of which defines the meaning of *Program*. Readers should recognize this function as a mathematical restatement of Meaning Rule 8.1.

$$M : Program \rightarrow State$$
$$M(Program \; \text{p}) = M(\text{p.body}, \; InitialState(\text{p.decpart}))$$

The first line of this definition is a prototype function M, while the second line defines the function itself, using the abstract syntax definitions of the direct constituents of *Program*:

$$Program = Declarations \; \texttt{decpart}; \; Block \; \texttt{body}$$
$$Declarations = Declaration^*$$
$$Declaration = Variable \; \texttt{v}; \; Type \; \texttt{t}$$

So this functional definition says that the meaning of a program is the meaning of the program's body with the initial state produced by the function *InitialState* applied to the list of declarations.

The function *InitialState*, given a list of declarations, produces:

$$\{\langle v_1, \; undef_{t_1} \rangle, \ldots, \langle v_m, \; undef_{t_m} \rangle\}$$

That is, all of the program's declared variables are stored in the initial state with their values set to the special value *undef* appropriate for each type.

---

4. For simplicity, this definition excludes the issue of side effects covered in Section 8.2.4.

8.4.3 Denotational Semantics of Statements

Recall that a Clite *Statement* is defined in the abstract syntax as:

$$Statement = Skip \mid Block \mid Assignment \mid Conditional \mid Loop$$
$$Skip =$$
$$Block = Statement^*$$
$$Assignment = Variable \ \texttt{target}; \ Expression \ \texttt{source}$$
$$Conditional = Expression \ \texttt{test}; \ Statement \ \texttt{thenbranch}, \ \texttt{elsebranch}$$
$$Loop = Expression \ \texttt{test}; \ Statement \ \texttt{body}$$

The meaning of a statement is, thus, the meaning of the particular type of statement that it represents:

$$M : Statement \times State \rightarrow State$$

$$
\begin{aligned}
M(Statement \ s, State \ state) &= M((Skip)s, state) & &\text{if } s \text{ is a } Skip \\
&= M((Assignment)s, state) & &\text{if } s \text{ is an } Assignment \\
&= M((Conditional)s, state) & &\text{if } s \text{ is a } Conditional \\
&= M((Loop)s, state) & &\text{if } s \text{ is a } Loop \\
&= M((Block)s, state) & &\text{if } s \text{ is a } Block
\end{aligned}
$$

Skip   The meaning of a *Skip* statement is effectively the identity function, since it does not change the current state of the computation (recall Meaning Rule 8.2).

$$M(Skip \ s, State \ state) = state$$

Assignment   The meaning of an *Assignment* can be expressed as an overriding union (recall Meaning Rule 8.3):

$$M : Assignment \ \times State \rightarrow State$$

$$M(Assignment \ a, State \ state) = state \ \overline{\cup} \ \{\langle a.target, M(a.source, state)\rangle\}$$

This is a formal way of defining the state that results from transforming the current *state* into a new state that differs from the old *state* only by the pair whose first member is the *Assignment*'s target *Variable* a.target. That pair's second member is the value of the *Assignment*'s source *Expression* a.source. The meaning of that *Expression* will be formally defined by another function *M* in Section 8.4.4.

Consider the example in Figure 8.2, and assume that the current *state* is:

$$state = \{\langle x, 2\rangle, \langle y, -3\rangle, \langle z, 75\rangle\}$$

Intuitively, we expect that the meaning of the source expression in this state, or

$$M(a.source, state) = M(x + 2 * y, \{\langle x, 2\rangle, \langle y, -3\rangle, \langle z, 75\rangle\})$$

is the *Value* -4. Thus,

$$
\begin{aligned}
M(z = x + 2 * y, \{\langle x, 2\rangle, \langle y, -3\rangle, \langle z, 75\rangle\}) &= \{\langle x, 2\rangle, \langle y, -3\rangle, \langle z, 75\rangle\} \\
&\quad \times \ \overline{\cup} \ \{\langle z, -4\rangle\} \\
&= \{\langle x, 2\rangle, \langle y, -3\rangle, \langle z, -4\rangle\}
\end{aligned}
$$

which completes the state transformation for this assignment.

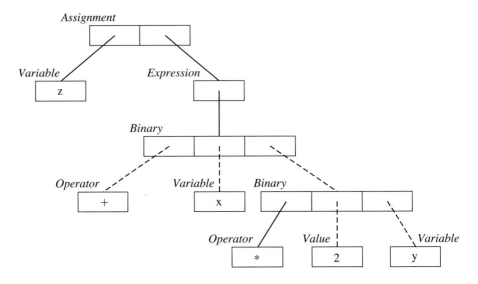

| **Figure 8.2** **Abstract Syntax for the Assignment z = x + 2 * y;**

Conditional The meaning of a *Conditional* is the meaning of one or the other of its branches, depending on whether the test is *true* or not (see Meaning Rule 8.4).

$$M(\textit{Conditional } c, \textit{State state}) = M(c.\text{thenbranch}, \textit{state}) \text{ if } M(c.\text{test}, \textit{state}) \text{ is true}$$
$$= M(c.\text{elsebranch}, \textit{state}) \text{ otherwise}$$

Consider the following code to compute the maximum of two numbers a and b:

```
if (a > b)
    max = a;
else
    max = b;
```

Given the state *state* = {⟨a, 3⟩, ⟨b, 1⟩}, the meaning of this conditional gives the following interpretation:

$$M(\text{if } (a > b) \text{ max } = a; \text{ else max } = b;, \textit{state})$$
$$= M(\text{max } = a;, \textit{state}) \text{ if } M(a > b, \textit{state}) \text{ is } \textit{true}$$
$$= M(\text{max } = b;, \textit{state}) \text{ otherwise}$$

Using the definition of $M(\textit{Expression}, \textit{state})$, we see that $M(a > b, \textit{state})$ is *true* in this particular state, so that the meaning of this Conditional is the same as that of the first *Assignment,* or $M(\text{max} = a;, \textit{state})$. Knowing what we do about the meaning of *Assignment*s, we see that the final state becomes:

$$\textit{state} = \{⟨a, 3⟩, ⟨b, 1⟩, ⟨\text{max}, 3⟩\}$$

Block   The meaning of a *Block* is either the identity function (if it has no statements), or the meaning of the rest of the *Block* applied to the new state achieved by computing the meaning of the *Block*'s first statement.

$$M(\textit{Block } b, \textit{State state}) = state \qquad\qquad\qquad \text{if } b = \{\}$$
$$= M(b_n, M(\ldots, M(b_1, state)\ldots)) \text{ if } b = \{b_1 b_2 \ldots b_n\}$$

This is a formal way of expressing Meaning Rule 8.6.

For example, consider the *Block* in Figure 7.2. Here is a summary of its meaning for $state = \{\langle i, 2\rangle, \langle f, 2\rangle, \langle n, 3\rangle\}$, as defined by the above function.

$$M(\{i = i + 1; f = f * i;\}, state)$$
$$= M(\{f = f * i;\}, M(i = i + 1;, \{\langle i, 2\rangle, \langle f, 2\rangle, \langle n, 3\rangle\}))$$
$$= M(\{\}, M(f = f * i;, M(i = i + 1;, \{\langle i, 2\rangle, \langle f, 2\rangle, \langle n, 3\rangle\})))$$
$$= M(\{\}, M(f = f * i;, \{\langle i, 3\rangle, \langle f, 2\rangle, \langle n, 3\rangle\}))$$
$$= M(\{\}, \{\langle i, 3\rangle, \langle f, 6\rangle, \langle n, 3\rangle\})$$
$$= \{\langle i, 3\rangle, \langle f, 6\rangle, \langle n, 3\rangle\}$$

The first two lines and the last line in this interpretation unravel the meaning of a *Block*, while the remaining lines apply the two assignments to the original state in the order that they appear in the *Block*. This illustrates that we can formally explain what happens when any sequence of statements is executed.

Loop   The meaning of a *Loop* is either the identity function (if the boolean `test` is not *true*) or the meaning of the same loop when applied to the state resulting from executing its body one time (see Meaning Rule 8.5).

$$M(\textit{Loop } l, \textit{State state}) = M(l, M(l.\text{body}, state)) \quad \text{if } M(l.\text{test}, state) \text{ is } \textit{true}$$
$$= state \qquad\qquad\qquad \text{otherwise}$$

For example, consider the *Loop* in Figure 7.2. It should be clear that the two statements that precede that loop in this example leave $state = \{\langle i, 1\rangle, \langle f, 1\rangle, \langle n, 3\rangle\}$. Recalling what we know about the meaning of the block $\{i = i + 1; \ f = f * i; \}$ from the previous paragraph, we can begin the analysis as follows:

$$M(\text{while}(i < n)\{i = i + 1; f = f * i;\}, state)$$
$$= M(\text{while}(i < n)\{i = i + 1; f = f * i;\}, M(\{i = i + 1; f = f * i;\}, \{\langle i, 1\rangle, \langle f, 1\rangle, \langle n, 3\rangle\}))$$

That is, we interpret the body once in the given state, and then pass the resulting state back to the function M for the *Loop* itself. This gives the following series of state transformations:

$$M(\text{while}(i < n)\{i = i + 1; \ f = f * i;\}, state)$$
$$= M(\text{while}(i < n)\{i = i + 1; f = f * i;\}, M(\{i = i + 1; f = f * i;\}, \{\langle i, 1\rangle, \langle f, 1\rangle, \langle n, 3\rangle\}))$$
$$= M(\text{while}(i < n)\{i = i + 1; f = f * i;\}, M(\{i = i + 1; f = f * i;\}, \{\langle i, 2\rangle, \langle f, 2\rangle, \langle n, 3\rangle\}))$$
$$= M(\text{while}(i < n)\{i = i + 1; f = f * i;\}, M(\{i = i + 1; f = f * i;\}, \{\langle i, 3\rangle, \langle f, 6\rangle, \langle n, 3\rangle\}))$$
$$= \{\langle i, 3\rangle, \langle f, 6\rangle, \langle n, 3\rangle\}$$

For each of the middle three lines, the function *M* for *Block, Assignment,* and *Expression* is used to transform the state that is shown on the line below it. The last line results from the test i < n becoming *false*, in which case the state is unchanged. This function is, of course, a partial function, since a *Loop* can be written that never halts. In that case, it should be clear that the last line in interpretations like the one above will never be reached.

8.4.4 Denotational Semantics of Expressions

Recall that a Clite *Expression* has the following abstract syntax:

$$Expression = Variable \mid Value \mid Binary \mid Unary$$
$$Binary = BinaryOp \text{ op}; \ Expression \text{ term1, term2}$$
$$Unary = UnaryOp \text{ op}; \ Expression \text{ term}$$
$$Variable = String \text{ id}$$
$$Value = IntValue \mid BoolValue \mid FloatValue \mid CharValue$$

The meaning of an *Expression* in a *State* depends on its type:

$$M : Expression \times State \rightarrow Value$$
$$M(Expression\ e, State\ state)$$

$= e$	if *e* is a *Value*
$= state(e)$	if *e* is a *Variable*
$= ApplyBinary(e.\text{op}, M(e.\text{term1}, state), M(e.\text{term2}, state))$	if *e* is a *Binary*
$= ApplyUnary(e.\text{op}, M(e.\text{term}, state))$	if *e* is a *Unary*

This function is a formalization of Meaning Rule 8.7.

The function *ApplyBinary* computes a *Value* when given a binary *Operator* and two *Value*s that are its operands (see Meaning Rule 8.8).

$$ApplyBinary : Operator \times Value \times Value \rightarrow Value$$
$$ApplyBinary(Operator\ op, Value\ v1, Value\ v2)$$

$= v1 + v2$	if $op = $ int+
$= v1 - v2$	if $op = $ int-
$= v1 \times v2$	if $op = $ int*
$= floor\left(\left\lvert\dfrac{v1}{v2}\right\rvert\right) \times sign(v1 \times v2)$	if $op = $ int/

. . .

This function assumes that the operators int+, int-, . . . carry their usual meanings in the semantic domains of integers **I**, floating point numbers **F**, strings **S**, and booleans **B**.[5] It also assumes that the types of $v1$ and $v2$ must be the same and agree with the type required by the operator. As in Section 8.2.3, we show only the first few cases of a rather large semantic definition given the number of distinct operators.

The function *ApplyUnary* computes a *Value* when given a unary *Operator* and one *Value* that is its operand (see Meaning Rule 8.9).

---

5. Note the definition of the operator int/ is a mathematical way of specifying the integer quotient of $v1$ and $v2$ (the Java implementation is simpler to express).

$$ApplyUnary : Operator \times Value \rightarrow Value$$
$$ApplyUnary\ (Operator\ op,\ Value\ v)\quad = \neg v\quad \text{if } op = !$$
$$= -v\quad \text{if } op = \texttt{int-}$$
$$= -v\quad \text{if } op = \texttt{float-}$$
$$\ldots$$

where the type of v must agree with the type required by the operator. As in Section 8.2.3, we show only the first few cases of a rather large semantic definition given the number of distinct operators.

To illustrate how these functions work, consider again the expression x+2*y whose abstract syntax is shown in Figure 8.2. Assume that this expression is evaluated in state $state = \{\langle x, 2\rangle, \langle y, -3\rangle, \langle z, 75\rangle\}$. That is, we want to use these functional definitions to show that:

$$M(x + 2 * y, \{\langle x, 2\rangle, \langle y, -3\rangle, \langle z, 75\rangle\}) = -4$$

Since this expression is a *Binary*, we have:

$$M(x + 2 * y, \{\langle x, 2\rangle, \langle y, -3\rangle, \langle z, 75\rangle\}) = ApplyBinary(+, A, B)$$
$$\text{where } A = M(x, \{\langle x, 2\rangle, \langle y, -3\rangle, \langle z, 75\rangle\})$$
$$\text{and } B = M(2 * y, \{\langle x, 2\rangle, \langle y, -3\rangle, \langle z, 75\rangle\})$$

Now the meaning of A is the value of x in $state = \{\langle x, 2\rangle, \langle y, -3\rangle, \langle z, 75\rangle\}$, or 2, since x is a *Variable*. The meaning of the *Binary B*, however, comes from another application of the function M, which is:

$$M(2 * y, \{\langle x, 2\rangle, \langle y, -3\rangle, \langle z, 75\rangle\}) = ApplyBinary(*, C, D)$$
$$\text{where } C = M(2, \{\langle x, 2\rangle, \langle y, -3\rangle, \langle z, 75\rangle\})$$
$$\text{and } D = M(y, \{\langle x, 2\rangle, \langle y, -3\rangle, \langle z, 75\rangle\})$$

Here, the meaning of C is 2, since 2 is a *Value*, and the meaning of D is -3, since y is a *Variable* in $state = \{\langle x, 2\rangle, \langle y, -3\rangle, \langle z, 75\rangle\}$.

With this information, the definition of *ApplyBinary* gives us the meaning of $2 * y$:

$$M(2 * y, \{\langle x, 2\rangle, \langle y, -3\rangle, \langle z, 75\rangle\}) = ApplyBinary(*, 2, -3)$$
$$= -6$$

Thus, the meaning of our original expression unravels as follows:

$$M(x + 2 * y, \{\langle x, 2\rangle, \langle y, -3\rangle, \langle z, 75\rangle\}) = ApplyBinary(+, 2, -6)$$
$$= -4$$

Note that this example uses only the functions *ApplyBinary* and M defined above, along with the mathematical properties of integer arithmetic, to derive this result. It should be clear to readers that the meanings of more complex *Expressions* with binary operations and integer operands are fully defined by these functions.

This completes our formal treatment of semantics for the language Clite. A complete Java implementation of Clite syntax, type system, and semantics can be found at the book's website given in the Preface. These tools can be used to exercise the functions discussed in this chapter with various sample Clite programs.

8.4.5 Limits of Formal Semantic Models

Formal semantics is difficult to apply to some language constructs, like transfers of control (the `goto`, `break`, and `continue` statements), throwing and catching exceptions, and dynamic memory activities surrounding function call and object creation.

In denotational semantics, transfers of control are handled by a device known as a *continuation* (see, for example, [Tennent, 1981]), whose coverage is beyond the scope of this text.

A language feature that currently cannot be defined by a denotational semantic model is concurrency. In denotational semantics the meaning of a *Program* is a state. Since meaning is a function, given the same input state and the same program, the result is always the same output state. However, the meaning of a concurrent program may be a slightly different state each time the program is run.

8.5 SUMMARY

This chapter introduces the idea of semantics by presenting a complete semantic description for Clite, first in an operational style and then in a formal denotatonal style. The advantages and limitations of formal semantic models for programming languages are also summarized.

Many of the exercises below ask you to run or modify the Clite interpreter to explore various semantic features. This interpreter can be downloaded from the book's website mentioned in the Preface.

EXERCISES

8.1 Discuss adding ++ and -- operators to Clite. Assume they are allowed only as free-standing statements.
   (a) Discuss the changes required to the type checker and type transformer.
   (b) Add new rules for statements that define the semantics of these operators.
   (c) Modify the Clite$_D$ interpreter to implement these new statements.
   (d) Discuss why we do not add these operators to expressions in general. Hint: think about how it changes the interpreter.

8.2 Add C++ style `cin/cout` I/O statements to Clite by:
   (a) Defining their concrete syntax,
   (b) Defining their abstract syntax,
   (c) Modifying the lexer and parser to recognize them, and
   (d) Adding these statements to the Clite$_D$ interpreter.

8.3 Discuss the advantages and disadvantages of disallowing assignment statements of the form b = a, where a has the value *undef*. What changes would you have to make to the Clite semantic rules and interpreter to enforce this change?

8.4 Add the operator % to Clite by:
   (a) Defining its concrete syntax,
   (b) Defining its abstract syntax,
   (c) Modifying the lexer and parser to recognize it, and
   (d) Adding it to the Clite$_D$ interpreter.

8.5 Modify the definition of the operators && and || so that they do not use short circuit evaluation. Give the new semantic rules. Discuss the needed modifications to the implementation.

8.6 Modify the Clite interpreter so that the current state is displayed immediately before each statement is executed. Extra credit: include the statement number in the trace.

8.7 Modify the Clite interpreter so that an error termination identifies the line number of the statement in which the error occurs.

8.8 Using Table 7.3 as a guide, write a trace table for the Clite program:

```
1 void main ( ) {
2     int i, a, z;
3     i = 5;
4     a = 2;
5     z = 1;
6     while (i > 0) {
7         if (i - i / 2 * 2 == 1)
8             z = z * a;
9         i = i / 2;
10        a = a * a;
11    }
12 }
```

8.9 For the program of Exercise 8.8:
(a) Give the abstract syntax of statement 8 as it is produced by the parser.
(b) Give the abstract syntax of statement 8 as it is produced by the type transformer.
(c) According to the semantic rules of Section 8.2.3, explain *precisely* how the value of the expression in statement 8 is computed.

8.10 Modify the interpreter for Clite so that integer overflow (as seen in Exercise 7.5) terminates the interpreter with an appropriate error message. Demonstrate that your modification works on the factorial program.

8.11 Modify the Clite interpreter so that expressions with side effects are supported. Use the definitions in Section 8.2.4 as a guide.

8.12 Using Table 7.3 as a guide, write a trace table for the Clite$_D$ program:

```
1 void main ( ) {
2     i = 5;
3     a = 2.0;
4     z = 1.0;
5     while (i > 0) {
6         if (i - i / 2 * 2 == 1)
7             z = z * a;
8         i = i / 2;
9         a = a * a;
10    }
11 }
```

8.13 For the program of Exercise 8.12, give:
(a) Give the abstract syntax of statement 7 as it is produced by the type transformer.
(b) According to the semantic rules of Section 8.2.3, explain **precisely** how the value of the expression is computed.

8.14 Modify the Clite$_D$ interpreter so that implicit integer to floating point conversions are permitted.

8.15 Suppose $state_1 = \{\langle x, 1 \rangle, \langle y, 2 \rangle, \langle z, 3 \rangle\}$, $state_2 = \{\langle y, 5 \rangle\}$, and $state_3 = \{\langle w, 1 \rangle\}$. What are the results of the following operations? Note: the symbol $\overline{\cup}$ denotes the `onion` method introduced in Section 8.4.
(a) $state_1 \; \overline{\cup} \; state_2$
(b) $state_1 \; \overline{\cup} \; state_3$
(c) $state_2 \; \overline{\cup} \; state_3$
(d) $\phi \; \overline{\cup} \; state_2$
(e) $state_1 \otimes state_3$
(f) $state_2 \otimes state_3$
(g) $(state_1 - (state_1 \otimes state_3)) \cup state_3$

8.16 Show how the meaning of each of the following expressions and given states are derived from the semantic rules given in Section 8.2.3. (The abstract syntax for each of these expressions was developed as an exercise in Chapter 2.)
(a) $M((z + 2) * y, \{\langle x, 2 \rangle, \langle y, -3 \rangle, \langle z, 75 \rangle\})$
(b) $M(2 * x + 3/y - 4, \{\langle x, 2 \rangle, \langle y, -3 \rangle, \langle z, 75 \rangle\})$
(c) $M(1, \{\langle x, 2 \rangle, \langle y, -3 \rangle, \langle z, 75 \rangle\})$

8.17 Show all steps in the derivation of the meaning of the following assignment statement when executed in the given state, using the semantic rules given in Section 8.2.3.

$$M(z = 2 * x + 3/y - 4, \{\langle x, 6 \rangle, \langle y, -12 \rangle, \langle z, 75 \rangle\})$$

8.18 Complete the semantic rules for the arithmetic, boolean, and logical operators of Clite that were introduced in Section 8.2.3.

π **8.19** Modify the denotational semantic functions for statements and expressions as needed to disallow an assignment b = a, where a has the value *undef*.

π **8.20** Modify the denotational semantic functions for expressions so that side effects are supported. Use the definitions in Section 8.2.4 as a guide.

π **8.21** Give a denotational semantic function for the operators ++ and - - as discussed in Exercise 8.1.

π **8.22** Give a denotational semantic function for the statements cin and cout as discussed in Exercise 8.2.

9

Functions

"It is better to have 100 functions operate on one data structure than 10 functions on 10 data structures."

Alan Perlis

C H A P T E R   O U T L I N E

Functions are a fundamental element in every programming language, since they are an essential tool for abstraction in programming. In different languages, functions are known variously as procedures, subroutines, subprograms, or methods. These have several characteristics in common as well as some important differences across different languages.

225

The behavior of functions is tightly intertwined with dynamic memory management. The characteristics of a fundamental memory structure, the stack, help clarify our understanding of how memory is organized to implement functions, particularly recursive functions.

This chapter discusses the key elements of functions in programming languages, including call and return, parameters and arguments, and recursion. The implementation of functions is discussed in Chapter 10.

9.1   BASIC TERMINOLOGY

Fortran and Ada make a distinction between functions that return a value and those that do not. The former are termed *functions* and the latter termed *subroutines* in Fortran and *procedures* in Ada. C-like languages make no such distinction; both are termed functions. In C++ and Java, a *method* is a function which is declared inside a class.

Some have argued that functions should be like mathematical functions. They should have no side effects and their only return value should be the value of the function itself. Calls to functions, as in mathematics, appear as a part of an expression. An example from Fortran is the formula for computing a solution x to a quadratic equation, $ax^2 + bx + c$:

```
x = (b*b - sqrt(4*a*c))/(2*a)
```

In this case, the `sqrt` function computes the square root of its argument and has no side effects.

Some have also argued that subroutines and procedures should not return a value, except by modifying one or more of its arguments. A subroutine or procedure may also read input or write output or modify one or more global variables, which are side effects. In C-like languages, a procedure is a function with a `void` return type. In contrast, Fortran and Ada have a distinct syntax for functions versus procedures.

Procedure calls appear as separate statements, rather than as parts of an expression. Even in C, a function call can appear as a separate statement, in which case its return type is normally `void`. An example of a C call appears below:

```
strcpy(s1, s2);
```

This call copies a string of characters from `s1` to `s2`.

The above arguments aside, most imperative and object-oriented languages make no attempt to enforce the no-side-effect rule on functions. In keeping with the C convention, we shall use the term *function* to denote both procedures and functions.

9.2   FUNCTION CALL AND RETURN

The program in Figure 9.1, first introduced in Chapter 4, can illustrate the dynamics of function call and return. In this program, `main` is initially called, and the global variables `h` and `i` are available to it, along with with the local variables `a` and `b`. After the first three assignment statements in `main` are executed, the variables `h`, `a`, and `b` have the values 5, 3, and 2, respectively.

```
int h, i;
void B(int w) {
    int j, k;
    i = 2*w;
    w = w+1;
}
void A(int x, int y) {
    bool i, j;
    B(h);
}
int main() {
    int a, b;
    h = 5; a = 3; b = 2;
    A(a, b);
}
```

| **Figure 9.1**   **Example C/C++ Program**

When A is called by main, its parameters x and y obtain the values 3 and 2, and A also has access to the global variable h. A's local variables i and j are also accessible at this point, as is the global variable h. However, the global variable i is not accessible to A, as outlined in the discussion of scope in Chapter 4.

At the time B is called by A, the parameter w becomes accessible (with the value 5), as do the local variables j and k and the globals h and i. Thus, the first assignment within B assigns the value 10 to the global variable i.

Control returns from a called function in either of two ways. For a void function or procedure, control returns either when the end of the function body is reached or when a return statement is encountered. For a non-void function, control returns when a return statement is encountered. In this case, the return statement has an expression which designates the value to be returned.

Pascal functions designate a returned result through an assignment statement whose target variable is identically the name of the function itself. Haskell functions designate the result by writing an expression. Many examples of the Haskell style of writing functions appear in Chapter 14.

9.3 PARAMETERS

Functions derive their great usefulness in both mathematics and programming languages by their ability to accept parameters. For example, a square root function would not be very useful if it lacked the ability to accept an argument specifying the value whose square root is to be computed.

> **Definition**: An expression which appears in a function or procedure call is termed an *argument*.

Definition: An identifier which appears in a function or procedure declaration is termed a *parameter*.

The Algol/Pascal tradition is to use the term *actual parameter* for an expression in the call and *formal parameter* for a parameter in a function declaration. The C/Java tradition is to use the terms *argument* for the former and *parameter* for the latter. Some texts use parameter as a synonym for argument. This text follows the C/Java tradition.

Following mathematical convention, most programming languages match arguments in the function call with parameters in the function declaration by position. Thus, in Figure 9.1, the call in `main` to function A:

```
A(a, b)
```

matches the argument `a` with the parameter `x`, and the argument `b` with the parameter `y`, and never vice versa.

Except for overloaded function names (see Chapter 4), the arguments must match the parameters in number and type. Exceptions to this rule occur for the languages Perl, Ada, and Smalltalk.

Perl does not permit the declaration of parameters in a function header. Instead, Perl makes the parameters available in an array named @_. The parameters can be accessed positionally using the above array. This convention was adapted from the Unix shell script. Perl is discussed in Section 12.7.

As optional alternatives to the strict matching by position, Ada provides two mechanisms. In the first, parameters may be declared with default values:

```
function sum(list : realList;
    length : integer := list'length) return real is
    ...
```

In this example, if the second parameter is omitted, it defaults to the declared length of the first parameter. Once a parameter is declared with a default value, all succeeding parameters must also have default values. This feature is desirable because it helps reduce the number of arguments in a call. A number of scientific library functions in earlier languages, primarily Fortran, had double-digit parameter counts.

The other mechanism provided by Ada allows arguments to have an order different than the positional order by using the parameter names in the call. In Figure 9.1, the call on A in `main` can be written in any of the following ways:

```
A(a, b);
A(a, y => b);
A(x => a, y=> b);
A(y => b, x => a);
```

This mechanism is most useful when the parameter names are meaningful identifiers.

Smalltalk (see Section 13.3) provides an interesting mechanism. A call on the method `at:put` on an array `a` is written:

```
a at: i put: x + y
```

Assuming a colon is a legal identifier character, the Java equivalent would be:

```
a.at:put:(i, x+y);    // meaning a[i] = x+y
```

Strictly speaking, this does not deviate from the *match by position* rule, since the method `put:at:` may either not exist or have a different semantics.

9.4   PARAMETER PASSING MECHANISMS

The *values* associated with the parameters during the life of a called function are determined on the basis of how these arguments are *passed* to the function by the call. There are five principal ways to pass an argument to a function:

1   By *value*,
2   By *reference*,
3   By *value-result*,
4   By *result*, and
5   By *name*.

Among these, the first two are the most prominent.

9.4.1   Pass by Value

Pass by value (sometimes called *eager* evaluation) typically occurs when an argument provides an *input* value to the called function.

> **Definition**: Passing an argument *by value* means that the value of the argument is computed at the time of the call and copied to the corresponding parameter.

Using the example program from Figure 9.1, pass by value is illustrated in Figure 9.2, both in the call A(a,b) from main (part (b)) and in the call B(x) from A (part (c)). In these calls, each of the arguments a, b, and x is passed by value. Notice that the trace provided shows values 3 and 2 for A's parameters x and y. Now all references to x and y from within A use these copies of the values of arguments a and b, so that their original values are effectively write-protected for the life of the call.

Thus, the following C/C++ swap function will not exchange the values of the arguments associated with parameters a and b:

```
void swap(int a, int b) {
    int temp = a;
    a = b;
    b = temp;
}
```

Although the values of the parameters a and b are indeed swapped, these values are not *copied out* to the arguments. Hence, pass by value is often termed a *copy-in* mechanism.

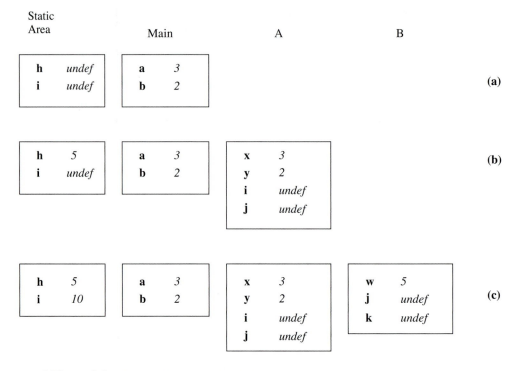

| Figure 9.2   **Passing Arguments by Value**

In C a swap function can be written using pointers as follows:

```
void swap(int *a, int *b) {
    int temp = *a;
    *a = *b;
    *b = temp;
}
```

In this case the values of the parameters are pointers to other variables. Consider the call:

```
swap(&x, &y);
```

The parameters a and b contain the addresses &x and &y respectively. Because the pointers are explicitly dereferenced, for example:

```
*a = *b;
```

the values of the arguments x and y are swapped.

As with C, all arguments in Java are passed by value. The value of a variable for so-called *reference types* (arrays and class objects) is actually an address rather than an ordinary value (as would be the case for int, float, char, etc.). Arguments which are reference types are passed by copying their reference (address) to the parameter rather than their value. Thus, the following Java swap function will not exchange the values of the arguments associated with parameters a and b:

```
void swap(Object a, Object b) {
    Object temp = a;
    a = b;
    b = temp;
}
```

The reasoning is basically the same as in C/C++.

However, the following Java swap function will exchange the values of the *i*th and *j*th entries in the array associated with the parameter A.

```
void swap(Object[ ] A, int i, int j) {
    Object temp = A[i];
    A[i] = A[j];
    A[j] = temp;
}
```

9.4.2 Pass by Reference

Pass by reference occurs when an argument provides an *output* variable to which the called function can assign a result.

> **Definition**: Passing an argument *by reference* (or *by address*) means that the *memory address* of the argument is copied to the corresponding parameter, so that the parameter becomes an indirect *reference* (pointer) to the actual argument.

Thus all assignments to the formal parameter within the life of the call directly affect the value of the argument. For example, suppose the program in Figure 9.1 had the argument for B's parameter w passed by reference rather than by value. Now the assignment

```
w = w+1;
```

inside B will directly increment the value of h rather than a copy of that value inside B's variable w.

One way to understand pass by reference is to view Figure 9.1 as a compiler might translate the program to C, as shown in Figure 9.3. In this example, the address of h, namely, &h, is passed to the pointer variable *w. Within function B, all occurrences of w are explicitly dereferenced as *w. Thus, in pass by reference the argument h is potentially changed by any assignment to the parameter w. Because of the dereferencing in the "compiled" version, it is not possible to change where w points. A trace of the "compiled" version of the program is given in Figure 9.4.

In languages that support multiple parameter passing mechanisms, the distinction between a value and a reference parameter must be made explicit within the function declaration. For instance, in C++ a preceding ampersand (&) is written to indicate a reference parameter, and its absence indicates a value parameter. For example, if

```
int h, i;
void B(int* w) {
    int j, k;
    i = 2*(*w);
    *w = *w+1;
    ...
}
void A(int* x, int* y) {
    bool i, j;
    B(&h);
    ...
}
int main() {
    int a, b;
    h = 5; a = 3; b = 2;
    A(&a, &b);
    ...
}
```

| **Figure 9.3**   **Pass by Reference Example**

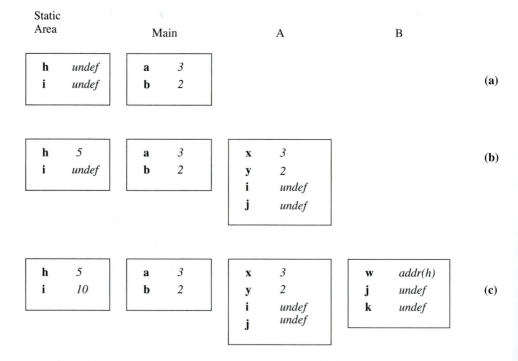

| **Figure 9.4**   **Passing an Argument by Reference Example**

function B in Figure 9.1 were written in C++, its first line would be altered as follows to indicate a reference parameter:

```
void B(int& w) {
```

and the call from A would remain B(h).

This declaration of w as a reference parameter in B requires that the argument in any call must have an address, that is, a variable, array, or structure, for instance, but not an expression with operators or a literal.

So arguments are passed by reference in cases when the actual value of the argument must be changed during the life of the call. Passing by reference is also preferred when the argument passed occupies a lot of memory, such as a large array. In these cases, the space and time overhead needed to create a complete copy of the object, if it were passed by value, is avoided by copying a single address into the parameter instead.

The main disadvantage of pass by reference is that side effects on the original value of the argument passed may not be desired by the caller. For instance, if the call of B by A with argument h does not want the value of h to be changed during the life of that call, passing h by reference should be avoided.

Fortran uses pass by reference exclusively, which caused some interesting side effects in older versions of Fortran. For example, the Fortran subroutine sub that adds 1 to its parameter p, along with the call `call sub(1)`, might leave the value of the "constant" 1 changed to 2 throughout the rest of the program run. Modern Fortran compilers evaluate each actual argument which cannot be interpreted as an lvalue and assign it to a temporary variable; the address of the temporary is then passed to the parameter.

9.4.3 Pass by Value-Result and Result

Pass by value-result is used when an argument provides both input to, and output from, the called function.

> **Definition**: An argument passed by *value-result* is implemented by copying the argument's value into the parameter at the beginning of the call and then copying the computed result back to the corresponding argument at the end of the call.

Because it is a *copy-in-copy-out* mechanism, pass by value-result combines *pass by value* and *pass by result*.

> **Definition**: An argument passed by *result* is implemented by copying the final value computed for the parameter out to the argument at the end of the life of the call.

Some Fortran compilers pass nonarray variables using pass by value-result. Pass by reference and by value-result are equivalent in the absence of aliasing.

> **Definition**: *Aliasing* occurs when, within a function or procedure, the same memory location can be accessed using different names.

Examples of aliasing include:

- Passing a variable as a parameter and referencing it as a global within the same function.
- Passing a variable as an argument two or more times using any parameter passing mechanism other than pass by value.

- Having two or more references (i.e., pointers) to the same location.

As a comparison of pass by reference versus pass by value-result, consider the following similar C++ and Ada functions:

```
void f (int& x, int& y)
{
    x = x + 1;
    y = y + 1;
}
```

```
procedure f (x, y: in out Integer) is
begin
    x := x + 1;
    y := y + 1;
end f;
```

The call `f(a, b)` has the effect in both cases of incrementing both a and b by one. However, the call `f(a, a)` will leave the *a priori* value of a incremented by 2 in the C++ (pass by reference) case and by 1 (pass by value-result) in the Ada case.[1]

However, as with many other issues, the standards for most languages specify that such programs are invalid. Although simple cases like the one above can be detected by many compilers, the aliasing problem is, in general, intractable.

9.4.4 Pass by Name

Pass by name is an example of *late binding*, in that the expression in the call is not evaluated until it is used by the function.

> **Definition**: An argument passed by *name* behaves as though it is textually substituted for each occurrence of the parameter.

One implementation view of pass by name is a macro expansion, effectively the #define mechanism of C/C++, but implemented dynamically for each call rather than at compile time as is used by #define.

Pass by name was originally used by Algol 60. In simple cases it was an inefficient mechanism to achieve call by reference. Unfortunately for Algol 60 it had several unforeseen consequences.

One of these was the inability to write a completely general swap procedure:

```
procedure swap(a, b);
    integer a, b;
begin integer t;
    t := a;
    a := b;
    b := t
end;
```

---

1. Technically an Ada `in out` parameter can be implemented either as pass by reference or as pass by value-result. In this example, we are assuming that the implementation is value-result.

The call `swap(a[i], i)` swaps the two values, but the call `swap(i, a[i])` does not, because the second assignment statement changes the value of `i`.

Even more interesting is Jensen's device [Knuth, 1967]. Consider the following summation function:

```
procedure sigma (a, j, m) : integer;
    integer a, j, m;
begin integer s;
    s := 0; j := 1;
    while (j <= m) do
    begin
        s := s + sigma;
        j := j + 1;
    end;
    sigma := s;
end;
```

On the surface, it appears to be an expensive way to compute the quantity $m \times a$.

Consider, however, each of the following invocations:

```
s := sigma (z, i, n);
s := sigma (x[i], i, n);
s := sigma (x[i] * y[i], i, n);
```

These invocations compute, respectively:

$$n \times z$$

$$x_1 + \ldots + x_n$$

$$x_1 \times y_1 + \ldots + x_n \times y_n$$

With the advent of structured programming (see Chapter 7.5.4), a premium was put on writing clear, easily understood code. Jensen's device provided clear evidence that functions using pass by name could not be totally understood independently of calls on those functions. None of Algol's successors used pass by name.

However, late binding can be implemented using a mechanism called *lazy evaluation*, which is very important in functional languages. These ideas are discussed in Chapter 14.

9.4.5 Parameter Passing in Ada

Among all of the languages discussed in this book, Ada is unique in that it does not specify how parameters are passed, but rather how they are used: in, out, or in-out. In Ada an *in parameter* is one that is referenced, but is not modified. As such, either pass by value or by reference can be used depending on the size of the argument.

In contrast, an *out parameter* is one whose value must be set by the called routine before it can be referenced. In particular, the called routine must assign a value to an *out parameter* before either referencing it or returning. Another way of viewing an out parameter is that its input value is never referenced. An out parameter could be implemented using either call by result or by reference, depending on its size.

Finally, an *in-out parameter* is one whose value may be referenced before it is assigned and one whose value may be reassigned before returning. *In-out parameters* may be implemented using either pass by value-result for primitive data types or pass by reference for arrays and records.

As expected, the Ada language standard specifies that a program is illegal if the actual implementation mechanism changes the result of the computation. Ada is the only language discussed here that specifies the usage of a parameter, rather than the implementation mechanism.

9.5 ACTIVATION RECORDS

To implement a function call, the notion of an activation record has become widely accepted. This section summarizes the basic ideas, in preparation for a more complete treatment of function call in Chapter 10.

> **Definition**: An *activation record* is the block of information associated with a function activation, including the function's parameters and local variables.

The basic structure of an *activation record* is shown in Figure 9.5. An individual activation record has space for:

- The called function's *parameters* and *local variables*.
- A return address.
- A copy of the calling function's *saved registers*.
- *Temporary values*.
- The called function's *return value*, if any.
- A *static link* pointer to the function's static parent.
- A *dynamic link* pointer to the activation record of the calling function.

The need for most of the items in the activation record should be obvious. For example, the return address is needed so that the called function can return properly

Figure 9.5 Structure of a Called Function's Activation Record

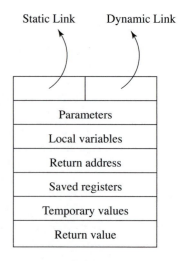

to its caller. The dynamic link is used to facilitate information flow between the called function and its caller.

The static link is usually only present in those languages which permit a function to be statically nested within another function. For example, C does not need a static link, since it does not permit such nesting. However, Algol, Pascal, Ada, and Java do require a static link, since in these languages the caller may not be the static parent of the called function. Without the static link, the called function is unable to locate the activation record of its static parent. An example of the need for the static link is given in Section 9.7.

In languages which do not support recursive functions (e.g., Fortran), activation records can be statically allocated. Doing so is very efficient in time, but not necessarily in space. The time efficiency results from the direct access to both local and global variables. However, it is inefficient in space because space is allocated for functions that may never be called.

More commonly, activation records are allocated dynamically on a run-time stack when a function is called and deallocated when the function's return is executed. In such cases, the term *stack frame* is commonly used. A *stack frame* is a synonym for activation record when the latter is allocated and deallocated dynamically using a stack. In Section 9.6 we examine recursive functions in order to motivate the need for a run-time stack of activation records.

9.6   RECURSIVE FUNCTIONS

Recursive functions have a natural implementation using a run-time stack that records the status of all active calls by associating an activation record with each call. Most current languages (C, C++, Java, Ada) support recursion, and indeed many languages have recursion as a core control structure (Scheme, Haskell, Prolog). Consider the following recursive C++ function that computes the factorial of a nonnegative integer n:

```
int factorial (int n) {
// computes the factorial of n, given n >= 0
    if (n < 2)
        return 1;
    else
        return n*factorial(n-1);
}
```

Suppose some function executes the call factorial(n), where n has the value 3. This will result in recursive calls to compute factorial(2) and factorial(1), as given in the call tree in Figure 9.6. Since the original call used a variable, whose value could have read from the keyboard, a compiler cannot determine how many simultaneous activation records may be needed for a given recursive function.

The solution is to dynamically allocate (push) activation records on a stack as functions are called, and deallocate (pop) them off of the stack as functions return to their callers. Figure 9.7a shows an activation record for the call factorial(3) being pushed onto the run-time stack.

The else part initiates a new call, factorial(2), causing one more activation record to be pushed onto the stack, as shown in Figure 9.7b. At this point, the activation record for the first call remains in the stack waiting for the second call to complete.

| **Figure 9.6** **Call Tree for** factorial(3)

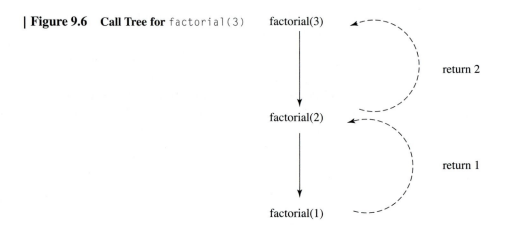

However, the second call initiates a third call, since the condition n < 2 is not yet satisfied, as shown in Figure 9.7c. Notice that the three activation records now on the stack hold different values for the parameter n, since each call is effectively calculating a different factorial.

Now the third call returns 1 to the second call, which can then complete the calculation 2*factorial(1) = 2 and return 2 to the original call, as shown in Figure 9.7c and d. At that point, the top two activation records have been removed (popped) from the stack and the original call returns 3*factorial(2) = 6 to the original caller and its activation record is popped from the stack.

This example illustrates how the general concept of a run-time stack is an effective model for recursive functions. Each recursive call pushes a new activation record onto the stack and each return pops that activation record while returning its result to the caller.

9.7 RUN-TIME STACK

A natural way to model the semantics of function call and return is by using a stack to store each called function's activation record. A *push* of an activation record occurs

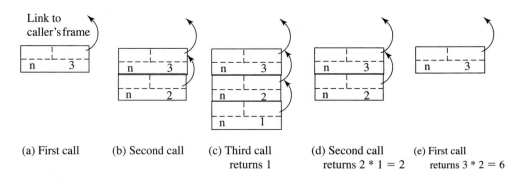

| **Figure 9.7** **Stack Activity for the Recursive Call** factorial(3)

whenever a function is called, and a *pop* occurs whenever control returns from a called function.

> **Definition**: A *run-time stack* is a stack of activation records used to model the semantics of function call and return.

When a called function returns control to the caller, its activation record is removed from the stack. Since a called function can (and usually does) call another function, many activation records can be active on the run-time stack at any one time. The fact that activation records are removed in the reverse order in which they are pushed onto the stack provides a model consistent with the fundamental ideas of scope and visibility.

Consider the C/C++ program in Figure 9.1 whose run-time stack can be modeled as shown in Figure 9.8. Here, we see on the left the single activation record on top of the globals h and i at the time the main function is entered. The middle snapshot shows the stack at the time function A is called from main.

The right-hand snapshot in Figure 9.8 shows the stack at the time function B is called from A. Three activation records are now on the stack, reflecting that all three functions are active. Each activation record contains a static link to the globals h and i and a dynamic link back to the activation record for the function that called it. Each activation record also contains its own function's parameters and local variables.

Finally, consider the Ada program given in Figure 9.9. Consider the chain of calls: Quicksort, Sort, Sort, Swap. Even without explicitly drawing the run-time stack, it should be clear that the dynamic link is inadequate to locate the static parent of Swap. Hence, the need for the *static link* pointer.

Java has exactly the same problem with inner classes, which are commonly used for event handlers which need access to the instance variables of their outer class. These event handlers can be invoked by some user action, such as clicking on a button. Without the static link, the run-time stack would need to be sequentially searched to locate the static parent. Several examples of such event handlers occur in the Controller class of Section 16.3.3, which discusses the graphical interface to a game of *TicTacToe*.

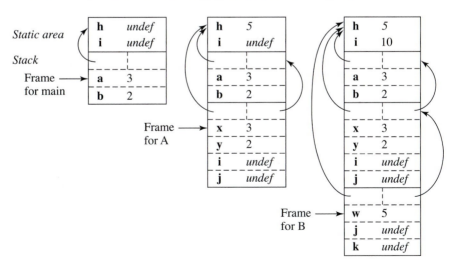

| **Figure 9.8**   **Run-Time Stack of Activation Records**

```
procedure Quicksort(List : in out Intarray;
                    Length: Integer := List'Length) is
    procedure Swap(I,J : Integer) is
      Temp : Integer;
    begin
      Temp := List(I);
      List(I) := List(J);
      List(J) := List(I);
    end Swap;

    procedure Sort (M, N : Integer) is
      I, J, Key : Integer;
    begin
      if M < N then
        I := M; J := N + 1;
        Key := List(M);
        loop
          I := I + 1;
          exit when List(I) >= Key;
        end loop;
        loop
          J := J + 1;
          exit when List(J) <= Key;
        end loop;
        Swap (I, J);
        Sort (M, J-1);
        Sort (J+1, N);
      end if;
    end Swap;

begin
    Sort(1, Length);
end Quicksort;
```

| **Figure 9.9**   **Need for a Static Link Pointer**

9.8 SUMMARY

This chapter studies the important subject of functions, their parameter passing mechanisms, and activation records. A run-time stack facilitates the normal run-time management of local variables and parameter passing for function calls, as well as for recursion. Its dynamic behavior is explored more fully in Chapter 10, where we discuss a complete implementation of functions in Clite.

EXERCISES

9.1 Consider the following C-like program:

```
void swap(int[] list, int i, int j) {
    int temp = list[i];
    list[i] = list[j];
    list[j] = temp;
}
void main() {
    int x[3] = {5, 2, 4};
    swap(x, 1, 2);
}
```

What is the final value of the array x for each of the following parameter passing assumptions?
(a) Argument x is passed by value.
(b) Argument x is passed by reference.
(c) Argument x is passed by value-result.

9.2 Using the accompanying software for this book, exercise the Clite interpreter for the program functions.cpp. What are the values of the global variables h and i in this program when each of the functions main, A, and B begin executing?

9.3 In the accompanying software for this book, exercise the program recFib.cpp.
(a) What is the value of the parameter n in the program recFib.cpp in the topmost stack activation record each time the function fibonacci is called?
(b) How many stack activation records are activated for the call fibonacci(13)?
(c) Can you think of a different way to define the function fibonacci so that fewer stack activation records are activated?

9.4 The following C/C++ program solves the Towers of Hanoi problem for three disks.

```
void moveTower (int disks, char start, char end,
               char temp) {
    if (disks == 1)
        cout << "Move a disk from " << start <<
                "to" << end << endl;
    else {
        moveTower (disks-1, start, temp, end);
        // move one disk from start to end
        cout << "Move a disk from " << start <<
                "to" << end << endl;
        moveTower (disks-1, temp, end, start);
    }
}
int main() {
    int totalDisks;
    totalDisks = 3;
    moveTower(totalDisks, 'A', 'B', 'C');
}
```

Using your favorite C++ compiler, trace the values of the parameters disks, start, end, and temp in all of the stack activation records that are pushed onto the stack as the program executes.

9.5 Modify the program in Figure 9.1 so that the function B has no side effects on the global variable i. Instead, B should return an int value, which is the calculation 2*w. Also, the call to B from A should be modified so that this result is assigned to the global variable i. The local variable declaration of i within A should be removed. Run this modified program using your favorite C++ compiler and answer the following questions:

(a) Describe graphically (draw) the abstract subtree that represents your modified call to B from A.

(b) Describe the activation record that occurs when this call is interpreted.

(c) This modified program has the same global effect as the original program in Figure 9.1. What would have happened if you had not removed the declaration of the local variable i from A?

9.6 The run-time stack strategy discussed in this chapter is particularly robust for supporting recursive functions. Run the Clite interpreter using the program gcd.cpp, which contains the following recursive functions for computing the greatest common divisor of two integers x and y.

```
int rem(int x, int y) {
    return x - x/y*y;
}
int gcd(int x, int y) {
    if (y==0) return x;
    else return gcd(y, rem(x, y));
}
```

What stack activation records are generated by the call gcd(24,10) and subsequent recursive calls to gcd? Include in each stack activation record the return value as well as the argument values for its call.

9.7 Consider the Ada program in Figure 9.9.

(a) Show the contents of the new stack frame when the call Quicksort(a) is initiated, for the array a = {4, 2, 5, 1}.

(b) Show the contents of each new stack frame added when each of the next four calls is initiated (i.e., to Sort, to Swap, and twice to Sort again).

9.8 How can the Ada procedure in Figure 9.9 be rewritten in C, which does not allow nesting of functions? What parameter passing mechanism is needed in the C version for the parameter List in the function Quicksort?

Function Implementation

10

"In theory, there is no difference between theory and practice, but not in practice."

Anonymous

CHAPTER OUTLINE

Functions are the key element of procedural abstraction in programming. Thus, language designers and implementors must treat functions as a central concern. Language designers must take into account both the design of functions so that programmers may use them effectively and the implementation of functions so that compiler-writers may implement them effectively and efficiently.

To illustrate the design and implementation of functions in depth, this chapter develops a full definition and implementation of the syntax, type system, and semantics for an extension of Clite that permits programs to have global variables, function declarations, and calls.

As an optional study, this chapter also provides a formal definition for the type system and semantics of functions in Clite. This treatment provides readers with a perspective on the mathematical rigor required for a full and complete specification of a modern programming language.

10.1   FUNCTION DECLARATION AND CALL IN CLITE

In this section, we focus on the concrete and abstract syntax, type system, and semantics that incorporate the principle of function declaration, call, scope, and visibility discussed in earlier chapters. The syntax of Clite provides a starting point for this discussion.

Recall the example Clite program in Figure 10.1, which was first introduced in Chapter 4. In this program, main is initially called and the global variables h and i are available to it, along with the local variables a and b.

After the first three assignment statements in main are executed, the variables h, a, and b have the values 5, 3, and 2, respectively. Thereafter, main calls A and A calls B, each call associating itself with an activation record that contains a different set of locals and parameters alongside the globals h and i. Part of our purpose in this chapter is to explain how these semantic features can be implemented in the setting of a run-time stack.

10.1.1 Concrete Syntax

The concrete syntax of this Clite extension allows a *Program* to declare functions and global variables in addition to a main function. The top half of Figure 10.2 shows those grammar rules that, when added to the grammar in Figure 2.7, define the syntax of

```
int h, i;

void B(int w) {
    int j, k;
    i = 2*w;
    w = w+1;
}
void A(int x, int y) {
    bool i, j;
    B(h);
}
int main() {
    int a, b;
    h = 5; a = 3; b = 2;
    A(a, b);
}
```

| **Figure 10.1   Example Clite Program**

$$Program \rightarrow \{ \textit{Type Identifier FunctionOrGlobal} \} \; \textit{MainFunction}$$
$$Type \rightarrow \texttt{int} \mid \texttt{boolean} \mid \texttt{float} \mid \texttt{char} \mid \underline{\texttt{void}}$$
$$\underline{FunctionOrGlobal} \rightarrow (\textit{Parameters}) \{ \textit{Declarations Statements} \} \mid \textit{Global}$$
$$\underline{Parameters} \rightarrow [\textit{Parameter} \{ , \textit{Parameter} \}]$$
$$\underline{Parameter} \rightarrow \textit{Type Identifier}$$
$$\underline{Global} \rightarrow \{ , \textit{Identifier} \} ;$$
$$MainFunction \rightarrow \texttt{int main ( )} \{ \textit{Declarations Statements} \}$$

$$Statement \rightarrow ; \mid Block \mid Assignment \mid \textit{If Statement}$$
$$WhileStatement \mid \underline{CallStatement} \mid \underline{ReturnStatement}$$
$$\underline{CallStatement} \rightarrow Call ;$$
$$\underline{ReturnStatement} \rightarrow \texttt{return} \; Expression ;$$
$$Factor \rightarrow \textit{Identifier} \mid Literal \mid (Expression) \mid \underline{Call}$$
$$\underline{Call} \rightarrow \textit{Identifier} (\textit{Arguments})$$
$$\underline{Arguments} \rightarrow [Expression \{ , Expression \}]$$

| **Figure 10.2   Grammar Rules for Clite Extension**

functions and globals. Underlining indicates additions to the original rules for Clite given in Chapter 2.

In this definition, the *MainFunction* is identical to the original notion of *Program* defined in Chapter 2. Here, however, the *MainFunction* can be preceded by any number of function and/or global variable declarations to form a complete *Program*. The new *Type* void designates a function that returns no result.[1]

The program in Figure 10.1 follows this new syntax. It has two global variables h and i and two functions A and B, in addition to its *MainFunction*. The functions A and B both have *Type* void, indicating that they return no result and are called by standalone *Call* statements. Function A has two int parameters and B has one.

The syntax of Clite allows a function call to appear either as a separate *CallStatement* or as a *Call* alternative within a *Factor*. In the latter case, the body of the called function, which is a *Block*, must contain a *ReturnStatement*. The bottom half of Figure 10.2 shows grammar rules that accomplish these goals.

For instance, the program in Figure 10.1 has two *CallStatements*, one from main to A and one from A to B. The first has two *Arguments* a and b, and the second has a single *Argument* h. This program has no *Calls* as instances of *Factor*, since both A and B are void functions. As in C++, a *ReturnStatement* can only appear in functions that do not have *Type* void.

---

1. It may be puzzling to see that the main function is non-void, since it appears to return no result. This is consistent with C, in which the main function returns an integer to tell the operating system whether the program executed correctly. In C, a default value of 0 (absent a return statement) means that it did, while a nonzero value is normally a programmer-defined error code. For simplicity, the main function in Clite will have no return statement, even though its return type is non-void.

Since a called function may or may not have type `void`, it is important to ensure that a `return` statement appears in every non-`void` function. This requirement is enforced by the Clite type system, which is presented later.

10.1.2 Abstract Syntax

The next step in this study is to examine how the abstract syntax of Clite is extended to cover these new ideas. This additional view of abstract syntax provides a foundation for extending the idea of type validity to programs with globals, function declarations, and calls. It also provides the basis for defining an interpreter that transforms the run-time stack when each function call is initiated or terminated.

Refinements to the abstract syntax of Clite given in Chapter 2 that will support globals, function declarations, and calls are summarized in Figure 10.3. Underlined portions indicate additions to the original abstract syntax. These additions mirror those that occur within the concrete syntax presented above.

Notice the two different ways in which a *Call* can appear in a program—as a separate statement or inside an expression. In the first case, the *Call* is used to call a function whose type t is `void`. In the second case the called function should return a result. Hence, a *Return* statement should appear in the body of a non-void function, but not in the body of a void function. This important distinction will be both enforced in the type checking rules and used in the definition of the interpreter for Clite.

Figure 10.4 provides a sketch of the abstract syntax for the program shown in Figure 10.1. Here, the dotted arrows indicate abbreviations of parts of the abstract syntax tree. Only the key elements of functions, locals, parameters, and calls are shown in detail here.

To work with these definitions, we implemented a recursive descent parser for this extension of Clite. That parser can be downloaded from the book's website and run with the program in Figure 10.1 as input.

The inclusion of function call and return in a programming language carries a distinct set of type checking and semantic requirements. In the following sections, we develop type checking and and semantic rules for Clite programs that have static scoping.

$$Program = Declarations \text{ globals; } \underline{Functions} \text{ functions}$$

$$\underline{Functions} = Function^*$$

$$\underline{Function} = Type \text{ t; } String \text{ id; } Declarations \text{ params, locals; } Block \text{ body}$$

$$Type = \text{int} \mid \text{boolean} \mid \text{float} \mid \text{char} \mid \underline{\text{void}}$$

$$Statement = Skip \mid Block \mid Assignment \mid Conditional \mid Loop \mid \underline{Call} \mid \underline{Return}$$

$$\underline{Call} = String \text{ name; } Expressions \text{ args}$$

$$\underline{Expressions} = Expression^*$$

$$\underline{Return} = Variable \text{ target; } Expression \text{ result}$$

$$Expression = Variable \mid Value \mid Binary \mid Unary \mid \underline{Call}$$

| **Figure 10.3** **Abstract Syntax of Clite Functions, Globals, and Calls**

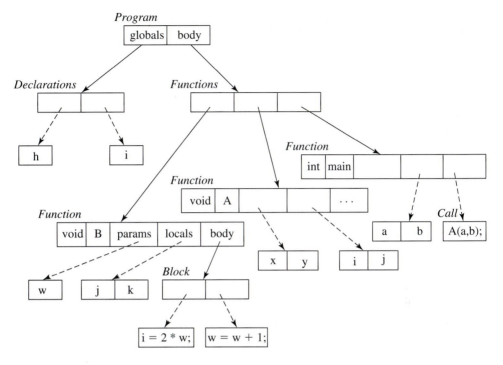

| **Figure 10.4**   **Abstract Syntax Sketch for a Clite Program**

This discussion makes clear how the run-time stack is deployed to support scoping, functions, calls, and parameter-argument linkage.

10.2   COMPLETING THE CLITE TYPE SYSTEM

The type system for Clite has rules that prevent type errors from occuring during a function call. These rules complement the original Clite type checking rules (see Chapter 6) to ensure that any syntactically correct Clite program is type safe in this new regard.

Type Rule 10.1 *Every function and global* id *must be unique.*

Consider the program in Figure 10.1. This rule prevents a program from having two different functions named A, for example. The concrete syntax of Clite cannot by itself ensure this uniqueness, any more than it can ensure that all the variables in a declaration are uniquely named.

Type Rule 10.2 *Every Function's* params *and* locals *must have mutually unique* id*'s.*

For example, this rule ensures that the list of parameter and local variable id's in function A—x, y, i, and j—has no duplicates.

Type Rule 10.3 *Every Statement in the* body *of each function must be valid with respect to the function's local variables, parameters, and visible globals.*

```
int fibonacci (int n) {
    int fib0, fib1, temp, k;
    fib0 = 0; fib1 = 1; k = n;
    while (k > 0) {
        temp = fib0;
        fib0 = fib1;
        fib1 = fib0 + temp;
        k = k - 1;
    }
    return fib0;
}
int main () {
    int answer;
    answer = fibonacci(8);
}
```

| **Figure 10.5**   **A Clite Function to Compute a Fibonacci Number**

The list of locals, parameters, and globals that are within the scope of A's body contains x, y, i, j, and h, but not the global i. Every statement in A's body may reference only those names, and no others. For instance, a cross-reference from a statement in A to the local variable k in B would be an error by this rule.

> **Type Rule 10.4** *A Return statement must appear in the* body *of every non-void function except* main, *and its Expression must have the same Type as that function.*

For example, consider the Clite program in Figure 10.5. This program computes the 8th fibonacci number by calling the function fibonacci. Here, the function fibonacci is called by the main program with the argument 8. Since that function contains a return statement, and the type of that expression (int) is the same of the type of the function, this rule is satisfied.

> **Type Rule 10.5** *No Return statement can appear in a* void *function.*

On the other hand, the body of each void function A and B in Figure 10.1 properly contains no *Return* statement.

> **Type Rule 10.6** *Every Call Statement must identify a void Function, and every Call Expression must identify a non-void Function.*[2]

The two *Call* statements in the program of Figure 10.1 identify the void function A and the void function B. The one *Call* in the program of Figure 10.5 is an expression that identifies the non-void function fibonacci. While the abstract syntax of this program isn't shown here, readers may wish to run the Clite interpreter to see that the expression fibonacci(8) parses to a *Call* to a function with a return type int.

> **Type Rule 10.7** *Every Call must have the same number of* args *as the number of* params *in the identified Function, and each such* arg *must have the same type as its corresponding* param, *reading from left to right.*

---

2. This rule is a departure from C/C++.

Let's look at the *Call* A(a,b) in Figure 10.1. The two arguments a and b are both type int, which agrees with the types of the two parameters x and y, respectively. If this *Call* had a different number of arguments, or if one of the arguments had type float (say), this rule would have trapped such an error.

> **Type Rule 10.8** *The type of a Call is the type of the function identified, and the expression in which it appears must be valid according to Type Rules 6.5 and 6.6.*

For example, the expression fibonacci(8) that appears in Figure 10.5 has the type int, which is valid in the context of the *Assignment* in which it appears.

Altogether, these type rules combine with the earlier rules in Chapter 6 to ensure that Clite is type safe. If these rules are enforced by a type checker, no program should fail because of a type error. Of course, to be fully rigorous, any claim of type safety for a language design must be formally proved.

10.3 SEMANTICS OF FUNCTION CALL AND RETURN

The semantics of Clite can be extended by defining a collection of meaning rules that extend those in Chapter 7. The programs in Figure 10.1 and Figure 10.5 are used to provide illustrations of the key features of these extensions.

Whenever a *Call* is executed, a new activation record is placed on the stack and filled with the called function's parameters, locals, and a variable to hold the return result. Each parameter is assigned a copy of the value of the corresponding argument, assuming that arguments are passed by value. The following rule fully defines the meaning of a *Call*:

> **Meaning Rule 10.1** *The meaning of a Call c to Function f has the following steps:*
> 1 *Make a new activation record, add f's* params *and* locals *to it.*
> 2 *Evaluate each of c's* args *and assign its Value to f's corresponding* param *in the activation record.*
> 3 *If the function is non-void, add to the activation record a result variable identical with the function's name and type.*
> 4 *Push that activation record onto the run-time stack.*
> 5 *Interpret the statements in f's* body.
> 6 *Pop the activation record from the run-time stack.*
> 7 *If the function is non-void, return the value of the result variable to the call.*

To illustrate this rule in action, let's consider again the Clite program in Figure 10.1. When the program begins running, the stack has only the global variables h and i. The first call comes from the system to the main function, in which case Meaning Rule 10.1 is invoked. Steps 1 and 2 combine to push the first activation record onto the stack, as shown on the on the left-hand side of Figure 9.8, and then the body of main is interpreted.

The variables that are visible for the life of this call, which we call the *visible state*, are shown on the first line of Figure 10.6. These include the parameters and locals, together with any global variables whose names are distinct from those of the parameters and locals.

The first three *Assignments* in main are interpreted as they were in Clite using the semantic rules in Chapter 7. These statements change the value of global variable h, as well as local variables a and b.

Calling	Returning	Visible State
main		$\langle h, undef \rangle, \langle i, undef \rangle, \langle a, undef \rangle, \langle b, undef \rangle$
A		$\langle h, 5 \rangle, \langle x, 3 \rangle, \langle y, 2 \rangle, \langle i, undef \rangle, \langle j, undef \rangle$
B		$\langle h, 5 \rangle, \langle i, undef \rangle, \langle w, 5 \rangle, \langle j, undef \rangle, \langle k, undef \rangle$
	B	$\langle h, 5 \rangle, \langle i, 10 \rangle, \langle w, 6 \rangle, \langle j, undef \rangle, \langle k, undef \rangle$
	A	$\langle h, 5 \rangle, \langle x, 3 \rangle, \langle y, 2 \rangle, \langle i, undef \rangle, \langle j, undef \rangle$
	main	$\langle h, 5 \rangle, \langle i, 10 \rangle, \langle a, 3 \rangle, \langle b, 2 \rangle$

| **Figure 10.6**   **Trace for a Program with Function Calls**

The fourth statement in main is a *Call*, and so Meaning Rule 10.1 is invoked again. This creates a second activation record, as shown in the middle of Figure 9.8, and then the body of A begins executing.

At that point, interpretation of the body of main is suspended until all the statements in the body of A are completed. The visible state for this call is shown in the second line of Figure 10.6; notice that the global variable *i* becomes hidden, since another variable with that name is redeclared locally within A.

Since A's body has a call to B, Meaning Rule 10.1 applies again, adding a third activation record to the stack as shown in Figure 9.8. The visible state for this call is shown in the third line of Figure 10.6; notice that the global variable *i* is now visible within B.

When B's body is fully interpreted, its activation record is first popped from the stack and the call from A to B is thus completed. Similarly, when A's body is fully interpreted, the *Call* from main to A is completed and that activation record is popped from the stack. Finally, main's activation record is popped from the stack and control returns to the system. The visible state before each of these calls completes is shown in the last three lines of Figure 10.6.

10.3.1 Non-Void Functions

The meaning of a *Call* for a non-void *Function* is similar, except that the *Value* returned is obtained by executing a *Return* statement. This outcome is defined in steps 3 and 7 of Meaning Rule 10.1. The type system guarantees that a non-void function contain a *Return* statement which, when encountered, acts like an assignment. The target of this assignment is the result variable identified by the function name in the activation record.

> **Meaning Rule 10.2** *The meaning of a Return is computed by replacing the value of the* result *Variable (the name of the called function) in the activation record by the value of the* result *Expression.*

Since *Return* statements can occur anywhere within the function's body, Meaning Rule 8.6 for a *Block* must also be modified so that it terminates as soon as a *Return* statement is encountered.

> **Meaning Rule 10.3** *The meaning of a Block is the aggregated meaning of its statements when applied to the current state, up to and including the point where the first Return is encountered. If there are nested Blocks, the first Return encountered signals termination of the outermost Block. That is, the first Return encountered terminates the body of the function.*

For instance, suppose we call the function `fibonacci` that returns an `int` value as shown in Figure 10.5. This function is called from `main` as the source *Expression* inside the following assignment:

```
answer = fibonacci(8);
```

Thus, the result of the *Call* `fibonacci(8)` is returned as a *Value* that will become that of the *Variable* `answer` when the *Assignment* is interpreted.

The activation record for this *Call* contains six entries; four for the function's local variables, one for the parameter `n`, and one for the result variable `fibonacci`. In step 2 of Meaning Rule 10.1, `n` is assigned the value 8. Since `fib0` is the *Expression* in the *Return* statement, the meaning of this *Call* is the value of `fib0` at the time that *Return* statement is interpreted.

The function's body is a block with five statements: three *Assignments*, a *While*, and a *Return*. Thus, the first four statements in the *Block* are interpreted as they would be in Clite. When the *Return* is interpreted, the value of `fib0` is returned and the *Call*'s activation record is popped from the stack.

To exercise this program, we can run the Clite interpreter again and obtain results like those shown in Figure 10.7. Notice here that the result variable `fibonacci` appears in the activation record to store the result returned to the *Call*.

Finally, we note that passing arguments by reference could be added to the definition in Meaning Rule 10.1 by modifying step 2 to require that each `arg` passed by reference have its address assigned to the corresponding param. We would also have to define the dereferencing of a reference parameter in an *Assignment* and an *Expression*. Finally, we would need to modify the concrete and abstract syntax of Clite to incorporate this additional feature properly.

10.3.2 Side Effects Revisited

Readers may have noticed that the above definitions place no constraints on how and when functions with side effects can occur in Clite. In particular, any function that alters the value of a global variable during the life of its call has a side effect. That is the case, for example, for function B in the program in Figure 10.1, which alters the value of global variable `i` when it is called.

Moreover, if B had been declared as a non-void function, this side effect will subtly impact the result returned by an expression like `B(h) + i`, where `i` denotes the same global variable mentioned above.

Calling	Returning	Visible State
main fibonacci		$\langle answer, undef \rangle$ $\langle n, 8 \rangle, \langle fib0, undef \rangle, \langle fib1, undef \rangle, \langle temp, undef \rangle,$ $\langle k, undef \rangle, \langle fibonacci, undef \rangle$
	fibonacci	$\langle n, 8 \rangle, \langle fib0, 21 \rangle, \langle fib1, 34 \rangle, \langle temp, 13 \rangle,$ $\langle k, 0 \rangle, \langle fibonacci, 21 \rangle$
	main	$\langle answer, 21 \rangle$

| **Figure 10.7**   **Program Trace for a Non-Void Function Call**

Recall that, in Chapter 8, we were careful to define the order of evaluation of operands in a `Binary` operation (such as this one) as left to right, so that the meaning of an expression containing a call with a side effect would be well-defined. That definition also guarantees that the result returned by `B(h) + i` will be different than that returned by `i + B(h)`.

A main problem with side effects is that they create more distance between the semantics of mathematical expressions when they appear in a program than when they appear in mathematics. For example, in Clite, addition is clearly not commutative, whereas in mathematics it normally is.

We note finally that programming languages without side effects do exist, especially in the functional programming paradigm. For example, our treatment of the language Haskell in Chapter 14 shows that programming and mathematical principles need not be disparate.

10.4 FORMAL TREATMENT OF TYPES
π AND SEMANTICS

This section repeats the above two sections using a formal mathematical style. Its purpose is to illustrate the power of denotational semantics to enable the full specification of a programming language's type system and semantics. Since it is machine independent, this notation can be used by language and compiler designers as they define and implement new programming languages.

10.4.1 Type Maps for Clite

The notion of "type map" for a Clite program with functions is more complex than what was represented in Chapter 6. For instance, static scoping allows multiple definitions of the same *Identifier* to occur but only one to be accessible by any particular statement in the program.

Thus, while Chapter 6 discussed a single type map, a proper treatment of scope and visibility requires that a different type map be defined for every different function in the program.

> **Definition**: The *type map* for a function f is defined as a collection of pairs and triples, each representing a global variable, a global function, a parameter, or a local variable.

Let tm_G, tm_F, *f.locals*, and *f.params* denote the global variable type map, the prototypes for all functions, the local variable and parameter type maps, respectively, for any particular function f. Then we can define the type map tm_f for f as the overriding union of $tm_G \cup tm_F$ and the set of all pairs of f's local variables and parameters with their respective types. That is:

$$tm_f = (tm_G \cup tm_F) \,\overline{\cup}\, (f.locals \cup f.params)$$
$$= \{\langle v.id_1, v.t_1\rangle, \langle v.id_2, v.t_2\rangle, \ldots, \langle v.id_n, v.t_n\rangle,$$
$$\langle f.id_1, f.t_1, \{\langle p_{11}, t_{11}\rangle, \ldots, \langle p_{1n_1}, t_{1n_1}\rangle\}\rangle,$$

$$\langle f.id_2, f.t_2, \{\langle p_{21}, t_{21}\rangle, \ldots, \langle p_{2n_2}, t_{2n_2}\rangle\}\rangle,$$

$$\ldots$$

$$\langle f.id_m, f.t_m, \{\langle p_{m1}, t_{m1}\rangle, \ldots, \langle p_{mn_m}, t_{mn_m}\rangle\}\rangle\} \; \overline{U} \; (f.locals \cup f.params)$$

Each pair is a variable identifier $v.id$ and type $v.t$, and each triple is a function identifier $f.id$, type $f.t$, and a sequence of parameters with their types.

Consider the example program in Figure 10.1. There, tm_G and tm_F would have the following values:

$$tm_G = \{\langle h, int\rangle, \langle i, int\rangle\}$$
$$tm_F = \{\langle B, void, \{\langle w, int\rangle\}\rangle, \langle A, void, \{\langle x, int\rangle, \langle y, int\rangle\}\rangle, \langle main, int, \{\}\rangle\}$$

This definition ensures that the visibility of globally defined variables and functions is appropriately limited in cases where a new local variable or parameter with the same name is defined inside a function.

For instance, each function in our example program has a distinct type map, as defined below:

$$tm_B = (tm_G \cup tm_F) \; \overline{U} \; \{\langle w, int\rangle, \langle j, int\rangle, \langle k, int\rangle\}$$
$$= \{\langle h, int\rangle, \langle i, int\rangle, \langle w, int\rangle, \langle j, int\rangle, \langle k, int\rangle,$$
$$\langle B, void, \{\langle w, int\rangle\}\rangle, \langle A, void, \{\langle x, int\rangle, \langle y, int\rangle\}\rangle, \langle main, int, \{\}\rangle\}$$
$$tm_A = (tm_G \cup tm_F) \; \overline{U} \; \{\langle x, int\rangle, \langle y, int\rangle, \langle i, boolean\rangle, \langle j, boolean\rangle\}$$
$$= \{\langle h, int\rangle, \langle x, int\rangle, \langle y, int\rangle, \langle i, boolean\rangle, \langle j, boolean\rangle,$$
$$\langle B, void, \{\langle w, int\rangle\}\rangle, \langle A, void, \{\langle x, int\rangle, \langle y, int\rangle\}\rangle, \langle main, int, \{\}\rangle\}$$
$$tm_{main} = (tm_G \cup tm_F) \; \overline{U} \; \{\langle a, int\rangle, \langle b, int\rangle\}$$
$$= \{\langle h, int\rangle, \langle i, int\rangle, \langle a, int\rangle, \langle b, int\rangle,$$
$$\langle B, void, \{\langle w, int\rangle\}\rangle, \langle A, void, \{\langle x, int\rangle, \langle y, int\rangle\}\rangle, \langle main, int, \{\}\rangle\}$$

With this background, we can extend the function *typing* given in Chapter 8 so that it generates type maps like the ones shown above for any Clite program with globals G, functions F, and individual function f:

$$typing : Declarations \times Functions \times Function \rightarrow TypeMap$$
$$typing(G, F, f) = (tm_G \cup tm_F) \; \overline{U} \; tm_F, \text{ where}$$
$$tm_G = \cup_{i \in 1, \ldots, n} \langle G_i.id, G_i.t\rangle$$
$$tm_F = \cup_{i \in 1, \ldots, m} \langle F_i.id, F_i.t, F_i.params\rangle$$
$$tm_f = f.params \cup f.locals$$
$$f.params = \cup_{i \in 1, \ldots, p} \langle param_i.id, param_i.t\rangle$$
$$f.locals = \cup_{i \in 1, \ldots, l} \langle local_i.id, local_i.t\rangle$$

That is, tm_G is the union of all pairs of global variables and their types, tm_F is the union of all function declarations and their types, and tm_f contains the function's own parameters and local variables and their types.

The overriding union $\overline{U}$ that appears in the expression $(tm_G \cup tm_F) \; \overline{U} \; tm_f$ realizes the idea that a function's parameters and locals can limit the scope of any identically named globals and other functions for the duration of the call. For example, notice that in tm_A, the scope of global variable i excludes the body of function A because A has a local variable declared with the same name.

10.4.2 Formalizing the Type Rules for Clite

With a definition of type maps in hand, we can now formalize the idea of type validity for any Clite program. Many of the functions defined below mirror ideas expressed in the type rules presented in Section 10.2.

Working from the top down, here is a formal definition of type validity for a Clite program.

$$V: Program \rightarrow \mathbf{B}$$
$$V(p) = V(tm_{p.globals} \cup tm_{p.body}) \wedge \forall f \in p.body : V(f, typing(G, F, f))$$

That is, a program is *valid* if its global variable and function declarations are valid and each of its functions (including main) is valid with respect to its type map.

This means that the sample program in Figure 10.1 is valid if the following conditions are simultaneously satisfied:

$$V(tm_G \cup tm_F)$$
$$V(A, typing(G, F, A))$$
$$V(B, typing(G, F, B))$$
$$V(main, typing(G, F, main)), \text{ where}$$
$$\quad tm_G = \{\langle h, int \rangle, \langle i, int \rangle\}$$
$$\quad tm_F = \{\langle B, void, \{\langle w, int \rangle\}\rangle, \langle A, void, \{\langle x, int \rangle, \langle y, int \rangle\}\rangle, \langle main, int, \{\}\rangle\}$$

The validity of a type map requires that all global variable and function identifiers be mutually unique, and no variable have type void. Finally, there must be exactly one function with the name main. The following definitions capture these ideas.

$$V : Declarations \rightarrow Boolean$$
$$V(d) = \forall i, j \in \{1, \ldots, n_d\} : i \neq j \Rightarrow (d_i.id \neq d_j.id \wedge d_i.t \neq void)$$

$$V : Functions \rightarrow Boolean$$
$$V(f) = \forall i, j \in \{1, \ldots, n_f\} : i \neq j \Rightarrow f_i.id \neq f_j.id \wedge$$
$$\exists i \in \{1, \ldots, n_f\} : f_i.id = main$$

Validity of a Function   The validity of an individual function in a program carries several requirements.

1   A function's parameters and locals must have mutually unique names.
2   The statements in the function's body must be valid with respect to its type map.
3   A non-void function (except main) must contain at least one *Return* statement and a void (or main) function must not.

Here is a formalization of these requirements, where G and F denote the program's global variables and functions, respectively:

$$V : Function \times TypeMap \rightarrow \mathbf{B}$$
$$V(f, tm) = V(f.params \cup f.locals) \wedge V(f.body, tm) \wedge$$
$$(f.t \neq void \wedge f.id \neq main \wedge \exists s \in f.body : s \text{ is a } Return$$
$$\wedge \; typeOf(s.result) = f.t) \vee$$
$$((f.t = void \vee f.id = main) \wedge \nexists s \in m.body : s \text{ is a } Return), \text{ where}$$
$$tm = typing(G, F, f)$$

For example, in the above program we require that $V(A, tm_A)$, $V(B, tm_B)$ and $V(main, tm_{main})$.

Validity of Call and Return   To complete the type checking requirements for Clite, we need to specify type validity for the new statements *Call* and *Return*.

Each *Call* must have its name identical with the id of some void function in the type map *tm* of the function f where the *Call* appears. Moreover, that function, say g, must have the same number of parameters (np) as the *Call* has arguments (na). Finally, for each argument-parameter pair between that function and the *Call*, both members of the pair must have the same type.

$$V : Call \times TypeMap \rightarrow \mathbf{B}$$
$$V(c, tm) = \exists g \in tm : (c.name = g.id \wedge np = na \wedge$$
$$\forall i \in \{1, \ldots, np\} : typeOf(c.args_i) = typeOf(g.params_i)), \text{ where}$$
$$tm = typing(G, F, f)$$

For a *Return* statement, the type of its result expression must match the type of the function in which the statement appears.

$$V : Return \times TypeMap \rightarrow \mathbf{B}$$
$$V(r, tm) = typeOf(r.result) = f.t, \text{ where } tm = typing(G, F, f)$$

The remaining type checking functions V for Clite are those defined in Chapter 6 for the various other statements and expressions considered in the original Clite subset. A full integration of these type specifications with the original functions V is left as an exercise.

10.4.3 Formalizing the Semantics of Clite

To formalize the full semantics of Clite, the notions of static memory, activation record, and run-time stack need to be formally defined. Moreover, a more detailed concept of state is needed in order to properly characterize the dynamic behavior of the stack as function calls are initiated and terminated.

Definition: The *environment* γ_f of an active function f is a set of pairs that unites variables whose scope includes f with specific *memory addresses*.

Definition: The *memory* μ is a set of pairs that relate addresses with values.

Definition: *Memory addresses* are typically a contiguous subset $\{0, \ldots, n\}$ of the integers, and are often called the program's *address space*.

By convention, each memory address to which no variable has yet been allocated is marked *unused*, and each address to which a variable has been allocated but no value has been assigned is marked *undefined*.

For example, suppose we have a program whose variables i and j have values 13 and -1 at some time during execution of function f, that k has no value yet assigned, and that these variables are assigned memory locations 154, 155, and 156. The state of f represented by this configuration can be expressed as follows:

$$\gamma_f = \{\langle i, 154\rangle, \langle j, 155\rangle, \langle k, 156\rangle\}$$
$$\mu = \{\langle 0, undef\rangle \ldots \langle 154, 13\rangle, \langle 155, -1\rangle, \langle 156, undef\rangle \ldots \langle a-1, undef\rangle,$$
$$\langle a, unused\rangle \ldots \langle n, unused\rangle\}$$

Here, $a - 1$ is the address of the top of the run-time stack, which contains f's activation record among others. Variables i, j, and k are either local variables or parameters of f (if addresses 154–156 are within f's activation record), or else global variables (if they are not).

The *address* of a variable v in f's environment is given by the function $\gamma_f(v) = \max x : \langle v.id, x\rangle \in \gamma_f$.[3] The *value* of that variable is given by $\mu(\gamma_f(v))$, which is equivalently denoted by $\sigma_f(v)$. For this example, we have

$$\gamma_f(i) = 154, \quad \text{and}$$
$$\sigma_f(i) = \mu(\gamma_f(i)) = 13$$

Now the *assignment* of a value to a variable can be defined using the overriding union operator introduced in Chapter 7. For example, suppose we want to assign the value 20 to the variable i in the example above. The memory change resulting from that assignment can be described by:

$$\mu' = \mu \,\overline{\cup}\, \{\langle \gamma_f(i), 20\rangle\}$$
$$= \mu \,\overline{\cup}\, \langle 154, 20\rangle$$
$$= \{\langle 0, undef\rangle \ldots \langle 154, 20\rangle, \langle 155, -1\rangle, \langle 156, undef\rangle \ldots \langle a-1, undef\rangle,$$
$$\langle a, unused\rangle \ldots \langle n, unused\rangle\}$$

The *state* σ_f of an active function f in a program can be viewed as the product of f's environment γ_f, the memory μ, and an integer a that marks the top of the run-time stack. That is, $\sigma_f = \gamma_f \times \mu \times a$.

Allocation of variables to addresses in the static area and the run-time stack is serial, beginning at address 0. At any time during the run of a program, the range of active addresses in these two areas is $\{0, \ldots, a-1\}$, where a is the number of active variables. In this model, we make the strong assumption that every variable's value takes exactly one addressable unit of memory.[4]

---

3. The reason for using "max" to find the value of variable v is that there may be more than one variable with the same *id* allocated at one time. The nature of our stack allocation scheme assures us that the function "max" retrieves that variable whose scope includes the statements of f, and not some other variable in the stack with the same *id*.

4. In Chapter 5, we saw that this is not the case in real systems; a char value, for instance, requires one byte while a float value requires four. We make this assumption here in order to keep the discussion simple.

The function *allocate* defines the change in state when a group of new variable *Declarations* $d_1, d_2, \ldots, d_k$ is added to the static area or the run-time stack:

$$allocate(d_1, d_2, \ldots, d_k, \sigma) = \gamma' \times \mu' \times a'$$
$$\text{where } \gamma' = \gamma \cup \{\langle d_1.v.id, a \rangle, \langle d_2.v.id, a + 1 \rangle, \ldots,$$
$$\langle d_k.v.id, a + k - 1 \rangle\}$$
$$\mu' = \mu \,\overline{\cup}\, \{\langle a, undef \rangle, \langle a + 1, undef \rangle, \ldots,$$
$$\langle a + k - 1, undef \rangle\}$$
$$a' = a + k$$

giving the new state $\sigma' = \gamma' \times \mu' \times a'$. Notice that the creation of γ' is an ordinary set union rather than an overriding union, since variable id's are not necessarily unique in the stack.

Removing a group of k variables from the top of the run-time stack reverses the process, and is defined by the *deallocate* function:

$$deallocate(d_1, d_2, \ldots, d_k, \sigma) = \gamma' \times \mu' \times a'$$
$$\text{where } \gamma' = \gamma - \{\langle d_k.v.id, a \rangle, \langle d_{k-1}.v.id, a - 1 \rangle, \ldots,$$
$$\langle d_1.v.id, a - k + 1 \rangle\}$$
$$\mu' = \mu \,\overline{\cup}\, \{\langle a, unused \rangle, \langle a - 1, unused \rangle, \ldots,$$
$$\langle a - k + 1, unused \rangle\}$$
$$a' = a - k$$

Thus, the creation of γ' is an ordinary set difference, and the function *deallocate* is well-defined as long as $a - k \geq 0$, which avoids stack underflow.

The state resulting from executing a *Call c* to a void *Function f* in a Clite program is defined in a way that mirrors Meaning Rule 10.1.

$$M : Call \times Function \times State \rightarrow State$$
$$M(c, f, \sigma) = removeactivationrecord(f.params, f.locals,$$
$$M(f.body,$$
$$ByValue(f.params, c.args,$$
$$addactivationrecord(f.locals, f.params, \sigma))))$$

The functions *removeactivationrecord* and *addactivationrecord* effectively hide the caller's locals and parameters from access by the called function for the duration of the call. The function *ByValue* assigns the values of the caller's arguments to the corresponding parameters just before the function's body is interpreted.

The initial state σ_0 for any Clite program has an empty environment γ_0, a memory whose locations are all marked *unused*, and $a = 0$:

$$\sigma_0 = \gamma_0 \times \mu(0) \times 0 = \{\} \times \{\langle 0, unused \rangle, \langle 1, unused \rangle \ldots \langle n, unused \rangle\} \times 0$$

The meaning of a complete program is its global state, $\sigma_G = allocate(p.\text{globals}, \sigma_0)$, that results when the following function is evaluated:

$$M : Program \times State \rightarrow State$$

$$M(p, \sigma_0) = M(p.main(), allocate(p.\text{globals}, \sigma_0))$$

where $p.main()$ denotes a 0-argument call to the function inside of p whose id is *main*. This is essentially what happens when any C/C++ program or Java application begins execution.

Here is a summary of the results of evaluating the function M for that sample program that appears in Figure 10.1. First, we establish σ_G as follows:

$$\sigma_G = \gamma_G \times \mu \times 2$$
$$= \{\langle h, 0 \rangle, \langle i, 1 \rangle\} \times \{\langle 0, undef \rangle, \langle 1, undef \rangle, \langle 2, unused \rangle \ldots \langle n, unused \rangle\} \times 2$$

after the function *allocate* is applied to $p.globals$ and σ_0.

The state achieved when function main begins execution is thus defined by the meaning of a call, which allocates a new activation record with 0 parameters and two local variables a and b. That is:

$$\sigma_{main} = \gamma_G \cup \{\langle a, 2 \rangle, \langle b, 3 \rangle\} \times \mu' \times 4$$
$$= \{\langle h, 0 \rangle, \langle i, 1 \rangle, \langle a, 2 \rangle, \langle b, 3 \rangle\} \times \mu' \times 4$$
where $\mu' = \{\langle 0, undef \rangle, \langle 1, undef \rangle, \langle 2, undef \rangle, \langle 3, undef \rangle, \langle 4, unused \rangle \ldots$
$$\langle n, unused \rangle\}$$

Except for the links "slink" and "dlink" and the values assigned to a and b by the first three statements in main, this structure corresponds to the initial state of the run-time stack shown on the left in Figure 9.8. In general, the formal semantics of this program mirrors the intuitive picture of function call and return shown in that figure.

The first three statements in main leave the values of h, a, and b at 5, 3, and 2, as shown in the state that occurs just before main calls A.

$$\sigma_{main} = \gamma_G \cup \{\langle a, 2 \rangle, \langle b, 3 \rangle\} \times \mu \times 4$$
$$= \{\langle h, 0 \rangle, \langle i, 1 \rangle, \langle a, 2 \rangle, \langle b, 3 \rangle\} \times \mu_{main} \times 4$$
where $\mu_{main} = \{\langle 0, 5 \rangle, \langle 1, undef \rangle, \langle 2, 3 \rangle, \langle 3, 2 \rangle, \langle 4, unused \rangle \ldots \langle n, unused \rangle\}$

Upon entry to A via the call A(a, b) from main, the following state change occcurs:

$$\sigma_A = \gamma_{main} - main.locals \cup \{\langle x, 4 \rangle, \langle y, 5 \rangle, \langle i, 6 \rangle, \langle j, 7 \rangle\} \times \mu_A \times 8$$
$$= \{\langle h, 0 \rangle, \langle i, 1 \rangle, \langle x, 4 \rangle, \langle y, 5 \rangle, \langle i, 6 \rangle, \langle j, 7 \rangle\} \times \mu_A \times 8$$
where $\mu_A = \{\langle 0, 5 \rangle, \langle 1, undef \rangle, \langle 2, 3 \rangle, \langle 3, 2 \rangle, \langle 4, 3 \rangle, \langle 5, 2 \rangle, \langle 6, undef \rangle, \langle 7, undef \rangle,$
$$\langle 8, unused \rangle \ldots \langle n, unused \rangle\}$$

This configuration corresponds to the middle diagram of the run-time stack shown in Figure 9.8. Note here that the global variable i has become hidden from the active state for this call, since another variable with the same name has a higher address within γ_A. The local variables a and b within main are also inaccessible to A, since they have been temporarily removed from A's environment while A is active.

Upon entry to B, another activation record is added to the environment, leaving the following state:

$$\sigma_B = \gamma_A - A.locals - A.params \cup \{\langle w, 8 \rangle, \langle j, 9 \rangle, \langle k, 10 \rangle\} \times \mu_B \times 11$$
$$= \{\langle h, 0 \rangle, \langle i, 1 \rangle, \langle w, 8 \rangle, \langle j, 9 \rangle, \langle k, 10 \rangle\} \times \mu_B \times 11$$
$$\text{where } \mu_B = \{\langle 0, 5 \rangle, \langle 1, undef \rangle, \langle 2, 3 \rangle, \langle 3, 2 \rangle, \langle 4, 3 \rangle, \langle 5, 2 \rangle, \langle 6, undef \rangle, \langle 7, undef \rangle,$$
$$\langle 8, undef \rangle, \langle 9, undef \rangle, \langle 10, undef \rangle, \langle 11, unused \rangle, \dots \langle n, unused \rangle\}$$

This configuration corresponds to the right-hand diagram of the run-time stack shown in Figure 9.8.

Execution of the body of B in this state changes the value of the global variable i, leaving the following state upon return to A. Notice that the activation record for B has disappeared and the state of its memory locations are returned to *unused*.

$$\sigma_A = \{\langle h, 0 \rangle, \langle i, 1 \rangle, \langle x, 4 \rangle, \langle y, 5 \rangle, \langle i, 6 \rangle, \langle j, 7 \rangle\} \times \mu_A \times 8$$
$$\text{where } \mu_A = \{\langle 0, 5 \rangle, \langle 1, 10 \rangle, \langle 2, 3 \rangle, \langle 3, 2 \rangle, \langle 4, 3 \rangle, \langle 5, 2 \rangle, \langle 6, undef \rangle, \langle 7, undef \rangle,$$
$$\langle 8, unused \rangle \dots \langle n, unused \rangle\}$$

Finally, when control returns to main, the state now includes the new value of global variable i and reflects the abandonment of the activation record for A, which has terminated, and the restoration of main's local variables:

$$\sigma_{main} = \{\langle h, 0 \rangle, \langle i, 1 \rangle, \langle a, 2 \rangle, \langle b, 3 \rangle\}$$
$$\text{and } \mu_{main} = \{\langle 0, 5 \rangle, \langle 1, 10 \rangle, \langle 2, 3 \rangle, \langle 3, 2 \rangle, \langle 4, unused \rangle, \dots, \langle n, unused \rangle\}$$

The meaning of a *Call c* to a non-void *Function f* is a *Value*. For instance, suppose we define the function fibonacci that returns an int value. This function is called in the context of a larger *Expression*, such as:

```
answer = fibonacci(8);
```

In this case, the result fibonacci(8) is returned as a new *Value* to the current state, rather than affect a state transition (as would a separate *Call* statement). This suggests the following alternative definition for a call to a non-void function:

$$M : Call \times Function \times State \rightarrow Value$$
$$M(c, f, \sigma) = \sigma(f.id, remove activation \ record(f.params, f.locals,$$
$$M(f.body,$$
$$allocate(f.id,$$
$$ByValue(f.params, c.args,$$
$$addactivationrecord(f.locals, f.params, \sigma)))))$$

Note that we have introduced allocation of an additional local variable on the stack, with *allocate*$(f.id, \sigma)$, to accommodate the value returned by the call.

This allows the meaning of a *Return* statement to be defined as a special kind of assignment — one that assigns the value of its `result` to this additional variable *f.id*.

$$M : Return \times \Sigma \rightarrow \Sigma$$

$$M(r, \sigma) = \sigma \; \overline{\cup} \; \{\langle f.id, M(r.result, \sigma) \rangle\}$$

Finally, the meaning of the function's body, which is a *Block*, must be changed from its original definition in Chapter 8 to accommodate the dynamics of a *Return* statement. Here is a redefinition of the meaning of *Block* from that takes the *Return* into consideration:

$$M : Block \times State \rightarrow State$$

$$
\begin{aligned}
M(b, \sigma) &= \sigma & &\text{if } b = \emptyset \\
&= M(b_1, \sigma) & &\text{if } b = b_1 b_2 \ldots b_n \wedge b_1 = Return \\
&= M((Block)b_{2\ldots n}, M(b_1, \sigma)) & &\text{otherwise}
\end{aligned}
$$

That is, if the first statement remaining in *Block* of statements is a *Return*, its meaning limits the meaning of the entire *Block* in which it occurs.

10.5 SUMMARY

This chapter has considered the implementation of programming languages with functions. The dynamic aspects of the run-time stack that support function call and return have been discussed.

A working interpreter for the entire Clite language provides a useful tool for exploring these characteristics with real programs. Many of the exercises below require students to continue that exploration in a laboratory setting.

A formal treatment of the type system and semantics of Clite concludes the chapter. It allows interested readers to understand more fully the mathematical dimensions of language design.

EXERCISES

10.1 Consider Type Rules 10.4 and 10.5, in which a return statement's presence is tightly associated with whether a function is non-`void`. Suppose we wanted to loosen these rules a bit so that a return statement could appear in either a `void` or non-`void` function. The presence of a return statement in a `void` function would simply indicate return of control to the caller, without returning a result.
(a) What concrete and abstract syntax changes would be required for this change?
(b) What changes to Type Rules 10.4 and 10.5 would be required?
(c) What changes to Semantic Rule 10.2 would be required?

10.2 Using the example Clite functions defined in Figures 10.1 and 10.5, construct three different calls; each call should violate one of the Type Rules 10.6, 10.7, and 10.8, but not the other two.

10.3 Consider the statement `k = k - 1;` inside the `while` loop in the program of Figure 10.5. Remove this statement from the program.
(a) Will this change raise a syntax or type error for this modified program? Explain.
(b) Now run the `Clite` interpreter on this modified program. Briefly describe what happens.

     (c) Can Meaning Rule 10.1 somehow be changed so that this problem can be avoided? If so, explain how. If not, explain why not.

10.4 Associate each of the type validity functions *V* in Section 10.2 with one or more Type Rules in Section 10.4.2. Are there any functions *V* for which there is no Type Rule, or vice versa? Explain.

10.5 Can Meaning Rule 10.1 be revised so that functions with side effects are disallowed? Explain.

10.6 Consider Meaning Rule 10.1 in Section 10.3 that informally defines the meaning of a Clite function call. Note, however, there are two different functions *M* in Section 10.4.3 that formalize this definition. Suggest how these two can be combined into a single rule that more directly mirrors the single Meaning Rule 10.1.

10.7 Complete the formal definition of type checking for Clite by integrating the validity rules *V* defined in this chapter with those given in Chapter 6.

10.8 Complete the formal definition of semantics for Clite by integrating the semantic functions *M* defined in this chapter with those given in Chapter 8.

Memory Management

11

"C makes it easy to shoot yourself in the foot; C++ makes it harder,
but when you do it blows your whole leg off."

Attributed to Bjarne Stroustrup

CHAPTER OUTLINE

The run-time management of dynamic memory is a necessary activity for modern programming languages. For a long time, the automation of this activity has been a key element in the implementation of functional and logic programming languages, beginning with Lisp in the 1960s.

C and C++ have allowed the run-time management of dynamic memory to be assumed by either the programmer or the system. While there are several automatic memory management routines available for C and C++, their use by the programmer is entirely optional. Java, on the other hand, insists that memory management is too tricky and error-prone to be left to the programmer; only the system can be responsible for memory management.

In either case, memory management is a key area in the study of programming languages, since it is tightly intertwined with the meaning of programs. While the run-time stack helps to clarify our understanding of how memory is organized to implement functions, a different memory area, called the *heap*, helps us understand the run-time behavior dynamic objects.

This chapter discusses the implementation of dynamic arrays and other objects using conventional techniques for managing heap memory. Especially important in this context is the notion of *heap overflow*, along with strategies for dealing with heap overflow when it occurs at run time. We discuss three key algorithms for heap memory management, which are affectionately known as *garbage collection* algorithms.

11.1 THE HEAP

In languages like C, C++, and Java, memory at run time can be viewed as having three parts, the *static area,* the *run-time stack*, and the *heap*.[1] This is pictured in Figure 11.1.

Static memory contains values whose storage requirements are known before run time and remain constant throughout the life of the running program. As we saw in Chapter 10, the *run-time stack* is the center of control for dispatching active functions, locally-declared variables, and parameter-argument linkage.

By contrast, the *heap* contains values that are dynamically allocated and structured while the program is running, such as strings, dynamic arrays, objects, and various dynamic data structures like linked lists. By its nature, the heap becomes fragmented as it is used for the dynamic allocation and deallocation of storage blocks of different sizes. For that reason, many languages use garbage collection algorithms to manage heap memory so that the available space is efficiently utilized. We address the issue of garbage collection later in this chapter.

As Figure 11.1 indicates, the memory address space $\{0, \ldots, n\}$ is partitioned in a way that anticipates the dynamic behavior of the program. At the beginning of run time, the size of the static area is fixed, the top of the stack is marked by address $a - 1$, and the beginning and end of the heap is marked by the fixed addresses h and n.

In this model, the stack grows upward toward the high end of the address space. In many real systems, the stack grows toward the low end instead. The following invariant relation must hold throughout the program run, to avoid raising a *stack overflow* error:

$$0 \leq a \leq h \leq n$$

Here, we assume that each memory word in the heap can have one of three states— *unused, undef,* or an elementary value (such as int or float).[2] Intuitively, *unused* means that the word is not allocated to the program, while *undef* means that it is allocated to the program but has, as yet, not been assigned a value. A typical snapshot of the heap is shown in Figure 11.2.

---

1. Other languages treat memory management differently. For instance, Fortran does not rely on the run-time stack for program control. Fortran programs use static memory for program and data control, and they use the heap mainly for allocating variable-sized arrays.

2. In reality, this assumption is simplistic. For instance, a memory word can often hold two or more values, and the value *undefined* is often not used as an initial value. However, we shall retain this assumption in order to keep our discussion simple.

Figure 11.1
The Structure of
Run-Time Memory

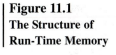
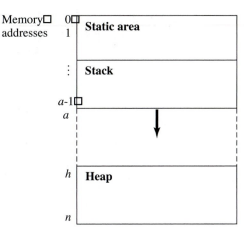

Heap management functions *new* and *delete* allow the program to obtain and release a contiguous block of memory words in the heap. Individual blocks of heap space are addressed using pointer variables, whose values are addresses.

The function *new* returns the address of the first word in a contiguous block of *k unused* words and marks them *undef.*

> **Definition**: *Heap overflow* occurs when a call to *new* occurs and the heap does not contain a contiguous block of unused words large enough to satisfy the call.

If no such *k*-word block exists, the *new* function fails. Otherwise, the value returned is a pointer to the beginning of the heap block thus allocated.

For example, the effect of the function call *new*(5) is shown on the right-hand side of Figure 11.2, given the arbitrary heap state shown on the left. The shaded blocks on the right indicate the five heap blocks that are marked *undef*ined. The address $h + 10$ is returned by *new* in this example.

The function *delete* undoes the effect of *new*, since it returns to *unused* status a contiguous block of words beginning at a designated address.

For example, the effect of the call *delete*($h + 10, 5$) is shown in Figure 11.2 by reading the right-hand heap as the initial state and the left-hand heap as the final state after the call.

h

7	*undef*	12	0
3	*unused*	*unused*	*unused*
undef	0	*unused*	*unused*
unused	*unused*	*unused*	*unused*

...

n

h

7	*undef*	12	0
3	*unused*	*unused*	*unused*
undef	0	*undef*	*undef*
undef	*undef*	*undef*	*unused*

...

n

| **Figure 11.2** **The** *New* **(5) Heap Allocation Function Call: Before and After**

11.2 IMPLEMENTATION OF DYNAMIC ARRAYS

Objects that require heap space include variable-sized arrays and record structures. It is important to note that variable-sized arrays and structures are not always allocated in the heap. For instance, they may be allocated to a stack frame at run time. If a small array or structure is passed to a parameter by value, for instance, stack allocation can yield an efficient alternative to heap allocation.

However, in the interest of introducing the behavior of dynamic objects in the heap, we will use arrays as an example. This is a continuation of the discusssion of arrays and structures begun in Chapter 5, where we first made oblique references to the heap. Here, we hope to expose more fully the role of the heap when dynamic arrays are created and destroyed at run time.

Consider the need to allocate a block of memory for an array whose size is not known until run time, such as the following declaration.

```
int A[n];
```

Static allocation is not appropriate here. In general, an array requires space in both the stack and the heap. The stack holds a reference to the address of a heap block that holds the array's first entry, while the heap holds the array's entries. This is illustrated in Figure 11.3.

Since the heap is used, the *new* function comes into play and the array is allocated space as shown in Figure 11.3. There, we see that the address of A[0] is stored in the stack along with the rest of the array's dope vector, while the array's entries, A[0] through A[n-1], is stored in a contiguous block of the heap.

The semantics of dynamic arrays utilize the *new* and *delete* functions discussed previously. The following rule describes the semantics of an array declaration.

Meaning Rule 11.1 *The meaning of an ArrayDecl* ad *is:*
1 *Compute addr (*ad[0]*) = new(*ad.size*), where the value of the Expression* ad.size *is computed as described in Chapter 5.*
2 *Push addr (*ad[0]*) onto the stack.*

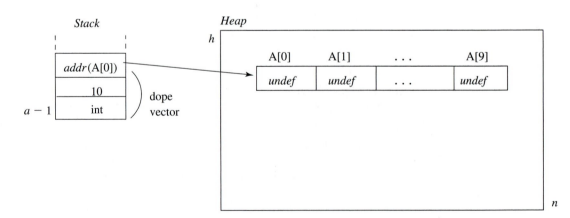

| **Figure 11.3**   **Allocation of Stack and Heap Space for the Declaration of Array A**

3 *Push* ad.size *onto the stack.*
4 *Push* ad.type *onto the stack.*

This rule would naturally be incorporated with the meaning of a *Call* in Clite. That is where the stack frame is created for the declarations in the called function. An *ArrayDecl* could be handled as a special case in this setting.

Notice that steps 2–4 here create the dope vector for the *ArrayDecl* ad, as illustrated in Figure 11.3 for the particular array A with size 10. Note also that the function *new* used in step 1 may or may not succeed. If it does not succeed, an exceptional condition called "heap overflow" occurs and the array cannot be allocated immediately. We return to this problem in the next section.

When a function in a Clite program returns control to the caller, any dynamically allocated array for that function must be deallocated by restoring all entries in its heap block to the *unused* state. Thus, the semantics of a function call must be changed to incorporate this consideration. Such a change would naturally utilize the *delete* function discussed above. The details of this change are left as an exercise.

The semantics of expression evaluation in Clite can be extended to cover array references ar in the following way.

> **Meaning Rule 11.2** *The meaning of an ArrayRef* ar *is:*
> **1** *Compute addr*(ad[ar.index]) = *addr*(ad[0]) + ad.index − 1.
> **2** *If addr*(ad[0]) ≤ *addr*(ad[ar.index]) < *addr*(ad[0]) + ad.size, *return the value at addr* (ad[ar.index]).
> **3** *Otherwise, signal an index-out-of-range error.*

Note that this definition includes run-time range checking for array references. It uses the full dope vector for the array as stored in the run-time stack when the array declaration is processed by Meaning Rule 11.1.

For example, suppose we have the *ArrayRef* A[5]. Then the value of A[5] is retrieved from the heap block allocated for A by retrieving the address of A[0], adding 4 (denoted by *addr* (ad[ar.index]) −1), and retrieving the value stored there.

Finally, the meaning of an *Assignment* statement as whose target is an *ArrayRef* ar, can be defined as follows:

> **Meaning Rule 11.3** *The meaning of an Assignment* as *is:*
> **1** *Compute addr*(ad[ar.index]) = *addr*(ad[0]) + ad.index − 1.
> **2** *If addr*(ad[0]) ≤ *addr*(ad[ar.index]) < *addr*(ad[0]) + ad.size, *then change the value at addr*(ad[ar.index]) *to the value of* as.source.
> **3** *Otherwise, signal an index-out-of-range error.*

For example, suppose we have the assignment A[5] = 3. Here, we will change the value in the heap addressed by A[5] (that is, *addr*(ad[0]) + 4) by the value of the expression 3 (denoted by as.source).

11.2.1 Heap Management Problems: Garbage

Garbage is any block of heap memory that cannot be accessed by the program. That is, there is no pointer accessible to the program whose value references that block.

Garbage can be easily created. For example, garbage can occur when a dynamically allocated array, like A in the foregoing section, has its dope vector removed from the stack (when the stack frame is popped) before its heap block is returned via a *delete*.

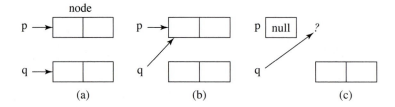

| Figure 11.4   **Creating Orphans and Widows: A Simple Example**

For further illustration, consider the following simple Java-like example, which initiates the creation of nodes in a linked list:

```
class node {
      int value;
      node next;
}
...
node p, q;
p = new node();
q = new node();
q = p;
```

The last statement creates a "memory leak" as shown in Figure 11.4b. In this situation, the node that had been referenced by q in Figure 11.4a has now become an *orphan,* or garbage. Moreover, adding, at the end of this program fragment, the following statement

```
delete(p);
```

creates a dangling reference, or *widow,* out of q, as illustrated in Figure 11.4c.

C and C++ default the garbage collection responsibility to the programmer. That is, they provide explicit tools (like the `delete` function above) to explicitly return heap blocks to the system for reuse.[3] Java, Lisp, and other languages provide automatic garbage collection and take the responsibility for heap memory management out of the hands of programmers.

11.3   GARBAGE COLLECTION

As mentioned at the beginning of the chapter, garbage collection algorithms have been in use for over 40 years in the functional and logic programming communities. A renewed shift of attention toward garbage collection occurred in other communities with the emergence of object-oriented programming in the 1990s. This shift recognized the need for effective heap management, since the heap is the place where objects reside at run time.

As suggested in Section 11.2, the heap contains both active and inactive objects—blocks that had been allocated during an earlier stage of program execution and then relegated to the status of "no longer needed." Altogether, inactive objects are known as

---

3. Recent implementations of C and C++ have begun to provide garbage collection options, thereby relieving the programmer from this responsibility.

garbage, since they continue to occupy valuable heap space after their useful life has expired.

Once the heap becomes full, it is important to have a strategy to reclaim all blocks of memory that are garbage, so that these blocks can be reused by new objects that require heap blocks of their own. For instance, the semantics of dynamic array allocation discussed in Section 11.2 will not function normally when the heap overflows (as in the call *new(n)* when a contiguous block of *n* words is not available).

The term *garbage collection* refers to any strategy for reclamation of unused heap blocks for later use by the program. Several garbage collection algorithms have been used more-or-less successfully over the last 40 years. The first languages that needed garbage collection were the functional languages (notably Lisp), since their run-time activities were dominated by the need to dynamically create, destroy, and change the structure of linked lists. The main garbage collection algorithms in use today are derived from those of the functional languages.

Three major strategies have served as a foundation for modern garbage collection algorithms. These are called *reference counting*, *mark-sweep*, and *copy collection*. We summarize these three strategies in the following sections.

11.3.1 Reference Counting

Reference counting assumes that the initial heap is a continuous chain of nodes called the *free_list*, each node having an additional integer field that contains a count of the number of pointers referencing that node (initially 0). As the program runs, nodes are taken from the free list and connected to each other via pointers, thus forming chains. Figure 11.5 is an example heap in which each node's reference count (RC) is shown as an integer inside a dotted line.

At this moment, there are four nodes and three are active, and the *free_list* contains all other nodes in the heap that are available for future use. Thus, three nodes are directly or indirectly accessible from p or q (which are assumed to be static global variables or local variables allocated within a stack frame).

The reference counting algorithm is applied dynamically; that is, whenever a `new` or `delete` operation occurs on a pointer, the algorithm is activated and as many orphans as possible are returned to the *free_list*. In this scheme, an orphan is simply a node whose

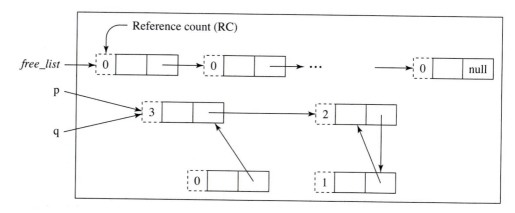

| **Figure 11.5** **Node Structure and Example Heap for Reference Counting**

reference count becomes zero, or any of its descendents (in the chain) whose reference count becomes zero as a result of a `delete` operation.

When a `new` operation occurs in the program, the algorithm allocates a heap node from the *free_list* and initializes its reference count to 1 (since this is the first reference to that node). Whenever a pointer assignment occurs in the program, such as

```
q = p;
```

some book-keeping on the reference counts must be done:

1 The reference count for p's node is increased by 1.
2 The reference count for q's node is decreased by 1.
3 If the reference count for q's node becomes 0, the reference count for each of its descendents is decreased by 1, q's node is returned to the *free_list*, and this step is repeated for each of q's node's descendents.
4 The pointer q is assigned the (reference) value of p.

When a `delete q` operation occurs, step 3 in the above algorithm is applied and q's node is returned to the *free_list*.

A careful examination of the reference counting algorithm reveals its fundamental weakness as a garbage collector. That is, it fails to return to the *free_list* any garbage that occurs in the form of an isolated circular chain. For instance, look at the effect of applying the above algorithm to the heap shown in Figure 11.5 when the following statement is executed:

```
p.next = null;
```

This statement leaves the active heap from Figure 11.5 in the following condition:

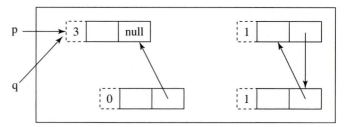

Here, two nodes are in an isolated chain pointing to each other (each of their reference counts is 1). However, the algorithm cannot return either of these to the *free_list*, since neither node's reference count is 0. A more detailed treatment of this algorithm is given as an exercise.

Overall, reference counting has one major advantage and three major disadvantages as a garbage collection algorithm. Its advantage is that it occurs dynamically, whenever a pointer assignment or other heap action is triggered by the program. Thus, the overhead associated with garbage collection is naturally distributed over the run-time life of the program. Its disadvantages are (1) its failure to detect inaccessible circular chains, as illustrated above, (2) the storage overhead created by appending an integer reference count to every node in the heap, and (3) the performance overhead created by the above algorithm whenever a pointer is assigned or a heap block is allocated or deallocated.

11.3.2 Mark-Sweep

Unlike reference counting, the *mark-sweep* algorithm is called into action only when the heap is full (i.e., the *free_list* is empty). Thus, several thousand pointer assignments and heap block allocations and deallocations can take place with no garbage-collection overhead occurring. Once mark-sweep is invoked, however, a more elaborate and time-consuming process interrupts the program, as explained below.

An example initial configuration for the mark-sweep algorithm is shown in Figure 11.6, where the dotted line surrounds a "mark bit" (MB) which is attached to each heap node and initialized at 0.

The mark-sweep algorithm makes two passes on the heap. It is invoked whenever a new node is requested by the program and the heap is full. Thus, when the assignment on the left is executed, the meaning on the right is implied:

```
q = new node();    if (free_list == null)
                       mark_sweep();
                   if (free_list != null) {
                       q = free_list;
                       free_list = free_list.next;
                   }
                   else abort('heap full')
```

Here, the final else clause reflects the event that garbage collection fails to reclaim any blocks for the `free_list`, which forces abnormal termination of the program.

During Pass I, the "mark" pass, every heap block that can be reached by following a chain of pointers originating in the run-time stack is marked as accessible (its MB is set to 1). That is, all references R in the run-time stack to heap addresses cause the following function to be invoked:

```
Mark(R):     if (R.MB == 0)
                 R.MB = 1;
             if (R.next != null)
                 Mark(R.next);
```

All blocks that remain unmarked (MB = 0) in Pass I are thus identified as orphans.

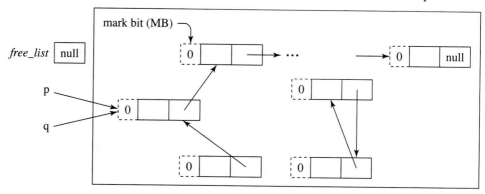

| **Figure 11.6**   Node Structure and Example for Mark-Sweep Algorithm

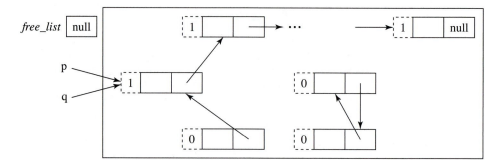

| **Figure 11.7** **Heap after Pass I of Mark-Sweep**

In our example, suppose that p and q are the only stack variables that reference the heap. Pass I would leave the heap in the configuration shown in Figure 11.7.

Pass II, the "sweep pass," traverses the entire heap, returning all unmarked nodes to the *free_list* and unmarking all blocks that had been marked in Pass I. Recall that h and n denote the bottom and top of the heap, as originally defined in Figure 11.1.

```
Sweep():  i=h;
          while (i<=n) {
             if (i.MB == 0)
                free(i);
             else i.MB = 0;
             i = i + 1;
          }
```

The function free(N) restores the node referenced by N to the *free_list*. That is,

```
free(N):  N.next = free_list;
          free_list = N;
```

The result of Pass II on our example heap is shown in Figure 11.8. Here we assume that the beginning and end of the heap are in the upper-left and lower-right corners of

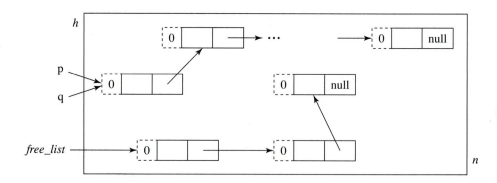

| **Figure 11.8** **Heap after Pass II of Mark-Sweep**

the figure, so that the bottom-most nodes that appear in the picture are the last nodes to be returned to the *free_list*.

Now that the *free_list* is nonempty, the original assignment q = new node() that invoked the mark-sweep algorithm can be resumed and completed. The main advantages of mark-sweep over reference counting are: (1) it reclaims *all* garbage in the heap, and (2) it is only invoked when the heap is full.

11.3.3 Copy Collection

Copy collection represents a kind of time-space compromise when compared with mark-sweep. Like mark-sweep, copy collection is called only when the heap is full. Unlike mark-sweep, copy collection makes only one pass on the heap, so it is significantly faster. However, copy collection requires significantly more memory because only half the entire heap space is actively available for allocating new memory blocks to the program at any one time.

For copy collection, the heap is divided into two identical blocks, called the *from_space* and the *to_space*, as shown in Figure 11.9. Here, no extra field is required in each node for a reference count or mark bit, and no *free_list* is needed. Instead, a pointer free to the end of the allocated area in the *from_space* is maintained.

At the beginning of program execution, all of the active nodes are resident in the *from_space* and the *to_space* is unused. Heap initialization is accomplished by the following algorithm:

```
from_space = h;
top_of_space = h + (n - h)/2;
to_space = top_of_space + 1;
free = from_space;
```

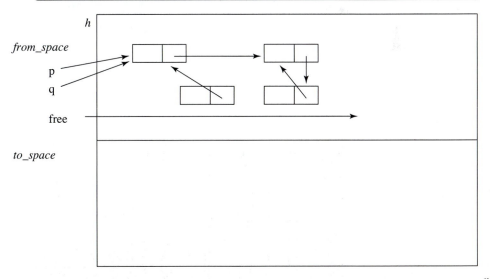

| **Figure 11.9**   **Heap Organization before Copy Collection**

Whenever a new node is allocated during program execution, the next available block referenced by free is allocated and the value of free is updated. If none is available, copy collection is invoked, causing the allocated blocks to be copied and repacked into the *to_space*, and the roles of *from_space* and *to_space* are reversed. That is, when the program statement on the left below is executed, the actions on the right are invoked:

```
q = new node();   if (free + 1 > top_of_space)
                      flip();
                  if (free + 1 > top_of_space)
                      abort('heap full')
                  q = free;
                  free = free + 1;
```

The functions *flip* and *copy* accomplish this role reversal as follows:

```
flip():     from_space, to_space = to_space, from_space;
            top_of_space = to_space + (n - h)/2;
            free = to_space;
            for R in roots
                R = copy(R);
copy(R):    if (atomic(R) || R == null)
                return R;
            if (!forwarded(R)) {
                R' = free;
                free = free + 2;
                forwarding_address(R) = R';
                R' = copy(R.value);
                R'+1 = copy(R.next);
            }
            return forwarding_address(R);
```

Flip reassigns the top_of_space pointer and copy repacks the active blocks into the beginning of the *to_space*. During this process, a referenced node R in the *from_space* can be either "forwarded" (copied to the *to_space*) or not. If it has been forwarded, each successive reference to node R is assigned its new address in the *to_space*. If it has not been forwarded, copy(R) copies it to the *to_space* using the next available node in the *free_list*. This is a recursive process, since node R may have descendants in the *from_space* that need to be forwarded.

Copy collection thereby eliminates all inaccessible nodes in *from_space* and tightly repacks the active nodes in *to_space*, as shown in Figure 11.10.

11.3.4 Comparison of Strategies

The performance trade-offs between copy collection and mark-sweep have been carefully studied, including a detailed discussion of garbage collection algorithms and their performance [Jones and Lins, 1996]. These trade-offs are summarized in the following way. If R is the number of active heap blocks and the "residency" r is defined as the ratio of R to the heap size $n - h$, then the efficiency e (measured as the amount of memory reclaimed per unit time) is greater for copy collection when r is much less

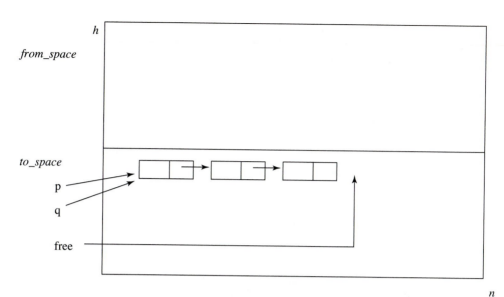

| **Figure 11.10**   **Heap Reorganization after Copy Collection**

than $(n - h)/2$. However, mark-sweep becomes more efficient than copy collection as r approaches $(n - h)/2$.

Dozens of different garbage collection algorithms are in use today, and most of them are more complex than the three simple strategies discussed above. For example, some language implementations use a hybrid strategy, selecting between mark-sweep and copy collection depending on the residency r in the heap at the time garbage collection is invoked.

In Sun's Java system, the garbage collector runs as a low-priority process called a "thread," which executes whenever demand on processing time from other threads is low.[4] This reduces the number of garbage collection calls needed during peak processing times. Also in Java, the program can explicitly call the garbage collector using the call `System.gc()`. This invokes garbage collection immediately, regardless of the state of the heap at the time of the call.

11.4 SUMMARY

This chapter studies the important subject of memory management for dynamic objects in programming languages. The semantics of dynamic array declarations and references are used to illustrate the main principles. The semantics of run-time array index checking is also covered.

The chapter pays special attention to exceptional situations that occur in dynamic memory, including memory leaks, widows, and orphans. Because garbage collection algorithms have become a staple of life in all programming paradigms, these algorithms are naturally included in this discussion.

---

4. We discuss Java threads in detail in Chapter 17.

EXERCISES

11.1 C has functions `malloc` and `free` that allow programmers to dynamically allocate and deallocate heap space. Research these two functions and compare their similarities and differences with the functions *new* and *delete* discussed in this chapter.

11.2 Determine the status of garbage collection in the current version of the Perl language. Is garbage collection built into the language? Are there separate garbage collection algorithms available to Perl programmers? How do Perl programmers typically manage heap memory leaks, widows, and orphans?

11.3 Identify all of the possible run-time errors that can occur for the array declaration or reference `A[n]` when it is encountered during the interpretation of a program.

11.4 Array indices in Clite must be checked at run time, since the size of an array cannot be statically determined. Use the indexing errors that you identified in the previous question, along with the heap-based model for array allocation discussed in this chapter, as a basis for your expanded rule definitions.

11.5 Expand the meaning rule for a *Call* in Clite to incorporate the idea of heap memory allocation and recovery for an array parameter or local variable. This change will naturally utilize the *new* and *delete* functions discussed at the beginning of this chapter.

11.6 Dynamic arrays in Clite can be allocated in the run-time stack rather than the heap. Discuss the impact of this choice on the semantics of array declarations and references, using the semantic framework presented in Chapter 8.

11.7 What are the trade-offs, in time and space, when the allocation of dynamic arrays occurs in the run-time stack rather than the heap?

11.8 (Team project) Extend the implementation of Clite so that it supports dynamic arrays. Use the concrete and abstract syntax, type-checking rules, and meaning rules for arrays that are defined in this and earlier chapters. This will require extending the definition of state so that the memory includes the heap, the heap bounds m and n, and the heap management functions *new* and *delete*.

11.9 (Team Project) Design a complete reference counting garbage collection algorithm in C++, using the discussion and elementary node structure given in this chapter. *Hint:* assume that the heap's address range is $\{h, \ldots, n\}$ and that each node has three addressable units of memory: one for the reference count, one for the value stored, and one for a pointer to another node in the heap. Consider the following auxiliary functions:

> `free(N)`: restore the node referenced by N to the *free_list*.
>
> `delete(N)`: decrement the reference count for node N; if its reference count becomes 0, then `delete(N.next)` and `free(N)`. (This one's recursive.)
>
> `N = M`: `delete(N)`, increment the reference count for M, and assign N = M.

Imperative Programming

"I really hate this darn machine; I wish that they would sell it.
It won't do what I want it to, but only what I tell it."

Programmer's lament (anonymous)

CHAPTER OUTLINE

Imperative programming is the oldest and most well-developed programming paradigm. It emerged with the first computers in the 1940s, and its elements directly mirror the architectural characteristics of modern computers as well.

In this chapter, we discuss the key features of imperative languages. Next, we focus on the role that function libraries have played. We conclude the chapter by considering three very different languages: C, Ada, and Perl.

12.1 WHAT MAKES A LANGUAGE IMPERATIVE?

In the mid 1940s, John von Neumann and others recognized that both a program and its data could reside in the main memory of a computer, an idea implicit in Turing's earlier work [Turing, 1936]. Early computers had stored their programs outside the computer's memory, typically using a wire plug-board. The idea of storing a program in the computer's memory led to an enormous increase in the potential power and versatility of computers.

The architecture of the so-called von Neumann-Eckert model (see Chapter 1) is the basis for the imperative programming paradigm. The machine's memory contains both program instructions (the *program store*) and data values (the *data store*). At the heart of this architecture is the idea of *assignment*—changing the value of a memory location and destroying its previous value.

Since they emerged out of the von Neumann-Eckert model, all imperative languages include assignment as a central element. In addition, they support variable declarations, expressions, conditional statements, loops, and procedural abstraction. Declarations assign names to memory locations and associate types with the stored values. Expressions are interpreted by retrieving the current values of the named variables from their respective memory locations and computing a result from those values. Given any reference to a variable x, the memory returns the current value in the location associated with x.

Commands are normally executed in the order they appear in the memory, while conditional and unconditional branching statements can interrupt this normal flow of execution. Because of their extensive use of branching, early imperative programs were often modeled with the aid of a special kind of graph known as a *flowchart*. An example flowchart for the Fibonacci program discussed in earlier chapters appears in Figure 12.1.

Originally, the commands in an imperative language were simple abstractions of the instructions in standard von Neumann-Eckert machines; these included assignment statements, conditional statements, and branching statements. Assignment statements provided the ability to dynamically update the value stored in a memory location, while conditional and branching statements could be combined to allow a set of statements to be either skipped or repeatedly executed. These constructs alone made the language *Turing complete*.[1]

An imperative language is said to be *Turing complete* if it provides an effective basis for implementing any algorithm that can be designed. Imperative languages containing integer variables and values, basic arithmetic operations, assignment statements,

---

1. Turing completeness is important because it provides a measure by which a minimal collection of language features can express all algorithms that can be conceived. Turing completeness is not exclusive to imperative languages—functional, logic, and object-oriented languages are also Turing complete, in the sense that any of these languages are equally capable of expressing any algorithm.

Figure 12.1
Example Flowchart
for Computing
Fibonacci Numbers

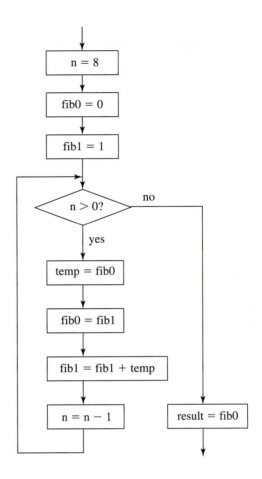

memory-based statement sequencing, conditionals, and branching statements are Turing complete.

The language Clite contains all these features except branching statements. However, Dijkstra [1968b] showed that excessive use of the branching (or "go to") statement was harmful to the process of developing reliable programs. Nonetheless, it is well-known that any statement sequence in an imperative program that included branching statements could be written equivalently using only conditionals and while loops in their place. Thus, Clite is also Turing complete.

An *imperative programming language* is thus one which is Turing complete and also supports certain common features that have emerged with the evolution of the imperative programming paradigm:

- Control structures.
- Input/output.
- Error and exception handling.
- Procedural abstraction.
- Expressions and assignment.
- Library support for data structures.

The first three of these features have been discussed extensively in earlier chapters. The remaining three are discussed below. Together, all six of these features appear in a variety of languages and a wide range of complex applications. This chapter addresses the use of these features, using examples from C, Ada, and Perl.

12.2 PROCEDURAL ABSTRACTION

In the imperative programming paradigm, programs are modeled as "algorithms plus data structures" [Wirth, 1976]. The algorithms are developed into programs using two complementary ideas: procedural abstraction and stepwise refinement.

Very early in the development of imperative languages the value of libraries of reusable functions was recognized. Even in the 1950s, Fortran and Algol included a number of standard mathematical functions, including `sin`, `cos`, `sqrt`, and so on. Programmers exploit the availability of predefined functions by using procedural abstraction.

> **Definition**: The process of *procedural abstraction* allows the programmer to be concerned mainly with the interface between the function and what it computes, ignoring the details of how the computation is accomplished.

A systematic way of producing a program [Wirth, 1973] is called *stepwise refinement* (or, sometimes, *functional decomposition*). That is, the programmer starts with a description of the function computed by a program, together with its input and output, and then systematically breaks the function down into a collection of more primitive functions using sequencing, iteration, and selection. This process is repeated until all the functions to be computed and their data can be realized by the primitive statements and data types in the language itself.

> **Definition**: The process of *stepwise refinement* utilizes procedural abstraction by developing an algorithm from its most general form into a specific implementation.

A familiar example is the development of a sorting function, in which the program needs an algorithm to sort an array of numbers, while ignoring the details of how the sort is to be performed. Thus, any given implementation of the sorting algorithm could be later replaced by a different one. The interface to such a sort routine would be:

```
sort(list, len);
```

where `list` is the array of numbers to be sorted and `len` contains the number of numbers in the list.

A first approximation to this algorithm might be expressed as:

```
foreach i in the sequence of indices of list {
    list[i] = minimum element in remaining list
}
```

The second statement could then be refined as:

```
foreach i in the sequence of indices of list {
    foreach j > i in the sequence of indices of list {
        list[i], list[j] = min, max of list[i], list[j]
    }
}
```

Recognizing that the third statement can be accomplished by an if and a swap, we get:

```
foreach i in the sequence of indices of list {
    foreach j > i in the sequence of indices of list {
        if list[j] < list[i] { swap list[i], list[j] }
    }
}
```

This refined algorithm now takes a form that can be coded fairly directly in an imperative language. A C-style encoding of this might look like:

```
void sort(Type list, int len) {
    for (int i = 0; i < len; i++)
        for (int j = i+1; j < len; j++)
            if (list[j] < list[i]) {
                Type t = list[j];
                list[j] = list[i];
                list[i] = t;
            }
}
```

This is the heart of stepwise refinement in an imperative language. While not shown here, additional levels of procedural abstraction could have been used during this refinement process, for instance to abstract the last three lines of code above into a call to a `swap` procedure.

12.3 EXPRESSIONS AND ASSIGNMENT

Fundamental to all imperative languages is the assignment statement, which takes the general form:

```
target = expression
```

There are a variety of assignment operator symbols; the two most popular are the Fortran-style = and the Algol-style :=.

The semantics of an assignment are simple. In the absence of errors, the expression is evaluated to a value, which is then *copied* to the target. That is, most imperative languages use *copy semantics*.

Expressions are written using familiar arithmetic and logical operators, as well as occasional calls to standard functions provided by the language. As Table 2.4 suggests, a rich variety of operators is available for use in imperative languages like C and

Table 12.1 Some Standard Mathematical Functions			
Function	**Fortran**	**C/C++**	**Ada**
Sine of x	sin(x)	sin(x)	Sin(x)
Cosine of x	cos(x)	cos(x)	Cos(x)
Tangent of x	tan(x)	tan(x)	Tan(x)
Arcsine of x	asin(x)	asin(x)	Arcsin(x)
Arccosine of x	acos(x)	acos(x)	Arccos(x)
Arctangent of x	atan(x)	atan(x)	Arctan(x)
Hyperbolic sine of x	sinh(x)	sinh(x)	Sinh(x)
Hyperbolic cosine of x	cosh(x)	cosh(x)	Cosh(x)
Hyperbolic tangent of x	tanh(x)	tanh(x)	Tanh(x)
Exponential: e^x	exp(x)	exp(x)	Exp(x)
Natural logarithm: $ln(x)$	log(x)	log(x)	Log(x)
Logarithm: $log_{10}(x)$	log10(x)	log10(x)	Log(x,10)
x^y	x**y	pow(x,y)	x**y
$\sqrt{x}$	sqrt(x)	sqrt(x)	Sqrt(x)
$\lceil x \rceil$	ceiling(x)	ceil(x)	Float'Ceiling(x)
$\lfloor x \rfloor$	floor(x)	floor(x)	Float'Floor(x)
$\lvert x \rvert$	abs(x)	fabs(x)	abs(x)

C++. In addition, imperative languages provide libraries of "standard functions" that can perform various computations during the evaluation of an expression. A summary of some Fortran, C/C++, and Ada mathematical functions is provided in Table 12.1.

The list in Table 12.1 provides only a sampling of all the functions available. For instance, Fortran has many more so-called "intrinsic functions" beyond those listed in Table 12.1. C, C++, and Ada standard functions are organized into predefined libraries. We discuss the C++ standard libraries later in this chapter. The C and Ada standard libraries are identified in Table 12.2.

The IMSL libraries (**www.vni.com/products/imsl/**) provide thousands of mathematical and statistical functions for Fortran and C programmers beyond those provided in their respective standard libraries. These functions perform a wide range of calculations in areas such as differential equations, fast Fourier transforms (FFTs), correlation, regression, time series analysis, optimization, and many more.

Table 12.2 A Few of the Many Function Libraries in C and Ada		
C Library	**Ada Library Unit**	**Functions Provided**
math.h	Ada.Numerics	Mathematical functions (Table 12.1)
ctype.h	Ada.Characters	Character classification functions
string.h	Ada.Strings	String manipulation functions
stdlib.h	Ada.Numerics	Utility functions
time.h	Ada.Calendar	Date and time functions

Table 2.4 reveals a lot about the evolution of imperative programming languages over the last four decades. The Fortran operators are a subset of the C operators, which are in turn a subset of the C++ operators, reflecting the evolution of these three languages as the range of programming applications expanded over the last three decades.

However, it is also important to examine language dependent libraries that facilitate the organization of data into flexible arrays, stacks, queues, graphs, hash tables, and other useful forms.

12.4   LIBRARY SUPPORT FOR DATA STRUCTURES

The basic data structures in imperative languages—arrays and record structures—were discussed in Chapter 5. Beyond these, modern languages have extensive libraries of functions that facilitate the development of complex applications. In practice, programmers rely on these libraries to avoid "reinventing the wheel" every time a common function or data structure is needed by an application.

The current ANSI/ISO standard version of C++ includes the "Standard C++ Library," a large collection of classes and functions designed to support the management of complex data structures, I/O functions, exceptions, and so forth. This library has the following major parts:

1 A collection of functions for defining and manipulating data structures,
2 A collection of I/O functions,
3 A string class,
4 A complex number class,
5 A framework for fitting the program to an execution environment, such as the implementation details for each elementary data type on a particular architecture,
6 Memory allocation and deallocation functions,
7 Exception handling functions, and
8 A class optimized for matrix arithmetic.

Before the current C++ standard was adopted in the late 1990s, many of these items had been known as the *Standard Template Library*, or *STL* for short. That portion of the Standard C++ Library contains data structures and functions that manipulate those data structures. In this sense, the library is designed for imperative programming rather than object-oriented programming, as would be characteristic of the Java or Eiffel class library, for example. Thus, programmers who prefer an imperative style over an object-oriented style can easily exploit the functionality provided by the Standard C++ Library.

The following list summarizes the main elements provided by the Standard C++ Library:

- Iterators.
- Vectors.
- Lists.
- Stacks, queues, dequeues, and priority queues.
- Sets and multisets.
- Maps.

- Graphs.
- Strings.
- Complex numbers.
- Overloading.
- Generics.

The following list summarizes some of the major functions that can be used to manipulate these data structures:

- Subscripting a vector.
- Resizing vectors and lists.
- Inserting and removing elements from vectors, lists, and maps.
- Vector, list, set, map, graph, and string searching.
- Vector and list sorting.
- List, set, and map insertion and deletion.
- Queue and stack operations (push, pop, etc.).
- Graph functions (shortest paths, etc.).
- String functions (substring, insertion, etc.).
- Arithmetic, comparison, and I/O functions for complex numbers.

For more details, an excellent reference on the Standard C++ Library can be found in [Josuttis, 1999].

12.5 IMPERATIVE PROGRAMMING AND C

In order to understand the design of C, it helps to understand the circumstances which led to its development. According to Kernighan and Ritchie [1978]:

> C was originally designed for and implemented on the UNIX operating system on the DEC PDP-11, by Dennis Ritchie. The operating system, the C compiler, and essentially all UNIX applications programs (including all of the software used to prepare this book) are written in C. Production compilers also exist for several other machines, including the IBM System/370, the Honeywell 6000, and the Interdata 8/32. C is not tied to any particular hardware or system, however, and it is easy to write programs that will run without change on any machine that supports C.

At that time, Ken Thompson and Dennis Ritchie had been involved at Bell Laboratories in the development of an advanced operating system named Multics, which unlike previous operating systems was being written largely in PL/I rather than assembly code. Bell Labs dropped out as one of the partners in the Multics project and forbade further work on it. Thompson and Ritchie then proposed developing a typesetting documentation system that would be machine-independent and would run on inexpensive minicomputers of the late 1960s. Thus was born Unix, which was a pun on the word Multics.

A typical 16-bit minicomputer like the PDP-11 might have 32KB of memory, of which the operating system took half, and an application like a C compiler took the other half. C was initially based on a language named BCPL, which was typeless. However, the portability problems of dealing with both big-endian and little-endian machines necessitated some minimal type system. However, the lack of a Boolean data type, pointer arithmetic (i.e., treating pointer as though they were integers), and so on, are all remnants of the original typeless design.

The other important design feature was that virtually all of Unix and its utilities were written in C. That meant that the C compiler had to generate very good code but had minimal memory in which to optimize the code generated. The solution was to design a relatively low level language, to which were added language features, such as the ++ and -- operators, that were directly supported by the PDP-11 hardware. Thus, C was able to achieve its goal of supporting the coding of the Unix operating system.

Currently, the popularity of C seems to have lost some ground in favor of languages like C++, Java, C#, Perl, and Python. However, C still thrives in two areas. C is often treated as a universal machine language; most of the Unix kernel, for example, is written in C. Moreover, the first C++ compiler, named `cfront`, translated C++ to C, rather than machine code. Another continuing use of C is in developing software for memory- or power-limited environments, such as cell phones.

C has had an enormous impact on language design. For instance, the languages C++, Java, and C# all look very much like C, both syntactically and semantically. Most of their operators are copied directly from C. Even Perl uses statements whose syntax is a variant of C.

12.5.1 General Characteristics

The syntax of C was examined in Chapters 2 and 3. Its operators and their precedence was given in Table 2.4. C introduced the cast operation, whose syntax is a parenthesized type name preceding an expression which causes conversion of the value of the expression to that type. C also introduced the use of braces in place of Algol's `begin` and `end`.

C has assignment statements; statement sequencing; if and switch conditional statements; while, for, and do loops; and function calls. In the area of data structures, C has arrays, pointers, structures (records), and union data types. In keeping with being a low level language, it has a compile time macro facility and conditional compilation.

As an imperative language, C lacks:

- Iterators,
- Exception handling,
- Overloading, and
- Generics.

Some have argued that several C operators, like *bitwise inclusive or* and 11 different variations of the assignment operator, have questionable value in practical programming. However, one of C's design goals was to facilitate programming at the operating system level, where the strategic use of bitwise operations that save a few nanoseconds of running time is a valuable exercise.

In C the assignment is an operator, which allows an assignment to occur in any context where an expression can occur. This is a strict departure from Pascal, Ada, Algol, and Fortran, where assignment is a separate statement type and nothing more. The implication of treating assignment as an operator is that intermediate assignments can be embedded within an expression while it is being evaluated. Consider the following implementation of the C strcpy function (which also appears as Figure 5.6):

```
void strcpy (char *p, char *q) {
    while (*p++ = *q++)  ;
}
```

In effect, three statements appear in the while loop test: the copying of one character, the post-increment assignment of p, and the post-increment assignment of q. The loop is very efficient, terminating when a NUL character is copied. This idiom is fairly standard, but it is also fraught with peril.

This function reveals many of the problems of programming in C. No check is made that the memory space referenced by p does not overflow. Such problems in C are responsible for many of the *buffer overflow* security problems on the Internet. Also, the code itself is very cryptic.

C supports dynamic array allocation via the malloc function. Consider the case where a program has determined that it needs an integer array of size positions. This would be accomplished as described in the first edition of Kernighan and Ritchie's C text (which we call K&R C) via:

```
int *a;
...
a = malloc(sizeof(int)   *size);
/*  ANSI C: a = (int *) malloc(sizeof(int)   *size);
    C++: a = new int[size]; */
```

Suppose the type of a changes to something larger than an int. We must change not only the declaration, but also the reference to the type of a in the call to sizeof. K&R C does not report an error in such a case. In contrast, ANSI C (the first comment line) detects the cast error, but if that is fixed, it misses the sizeof error. C++ (the second comment line) requires that the type in the new match the declared type. Unfortunately, most of Unix is written in K&R C, while some utilities are written in a pre-K&R C dialect and others are written in ANSI C.

All three C variants require the programmer to explicitly deallocate memory when it is no longer needed. This was discussed in Chapter 11. A subtle bug occurs when the program continues to use the storage allocated to the variable a after it is deallocated.

Sections 12.5.2 and 12.5.3 present some simple imperative programming examples. The development of a stack type in C is presented in Chapter 13.

12.5.2 Example: Grep

In this section we develop a C version of the Unix utility named grep, which is used to search for strings within a text file. The actual grep utility has a myriad of options and allows the use of regular expressions (see Chapter 3) for command-line text searching.

Our simple version, given in Figure 12.2, takes two command line arguments. The first argument is a string which much be matched exactly. The second argument is the name of the file which is to be searched.

In this example, each line that is matched is written to the console, preceded by its line number. If no lines match, there is no output.

```
#include <stdio.h>
#include <stdlib.h>
#include <string.h>
#define SIZE 1024
FILE *in;
void find(char* string);

int main(int argc, char *argv[ ]) {
    char *string;

    if (argc < 3) {
        fprintf(stderr, "Usage: %s string file\n", *argv);
        exit(1);
    }

    string = *++argv;

    if ((in = fopen(*++argv, "r")) == NULL) {
        fprintf(stderr, "Cannot open: %s\n", *argv);
        exit(1);
    }
    find(string);
    return 0;
}

void find(char *string) {
    char line[SIZE];
    int count;
    count = 0;
    while (fgets(line, SIZE, in)) {
        count++;
        if (strstr(line, string))
            printf("%5d:\t%s\n", count, line);
    }
}
```

| **Figure 12.2   A Simple Version of Grep**

The first three lines of the program import header files for three different libraries. Header files contain type signatures for various functions. Line 6 is an example of a function signature.

Definition: A *function signature* is a declaration of the function's name along with its return type and the types and ordering of its parameters. Sometimes this is called a *function prototype*.

The program itself consists of two functions. The function `main` is responsible for processing the command line arguments. Errors are reported if either the command line contains fewer than two arguments or if the input file named on the command line cannot be opened. In either case, the program halts.

The function `find` is responsible for reading the file, searching each line for an occurrence of the `string`, and writing the line, if the string is found. Here, the call `strstr(line, string)` returns a pointer to the first occurrence of `string` within `line`. Note also that lines are restricted to 1023 characters, one less than the declared size to allow for a `NUL` byte at the end. Fortunately, one of the arguments to `fgets` is the size of the line buffer, thus preventing a buffer overflow.

The counterpart to `fgets` for reading from standard input (the console) has no such argument. Its use often leads to buffer overflow hacks. Fortunately, `fgets` can be used with a third argument of `stdin` to read from the console. One of the problems is that even ANSI C provides no standard function to determine the length of an input line, even though it is fairly easy to write one.

12.5.3 Example: Average

In this example we read a sequence of numbers and compute their minimum, maximum, and average. This would be a typical sample program for explaining the use of a `while` loop in an introductory programming course.

The program, given in Figure 12.3, basically consists of a loop that reads numbers one at a time and then counts the number, sums it, and checks to see if the number is a new minimum or maximum. The numbers are read from the console (`stdin`).

```c
#include <stdio.h>
int main(int argc, char *argv[ ]) {
    int ct, number, min, max, sum;
    sum = ct = 0;
    printf("Enter number: ");
    while (scanf("%d", &number) != EOF) {
        if (ct == 0)
            min = max = number;
        ct++;
        sum += number;
        min = number < min ? number : min;
        max = number > max ? number : max;
        printf("Enter number: ");
    }
    printf("%d numbers read\n", ct);
    if (ct > 0) {
        printf("Average:\t%d\n", sum / ct);
        printf("Maximum:\t%d\n", max);
        printf("Minimum:\t%d\n", min);
    }
}
```

| Figure 12.3   **Program to Compute Average**

The program uses a multiple assignment statement to initialize sum and ct and later, min and max. Conditional assignments are used to update min and max. Input and output using format codes are also used.

A potential problem occurs in the call to scanf. The second argument must be the address of an int variable. Since C only supports call-by-value, it is the programmer's responsibility to supply the address by using the address-of operator (&). Failure to do so on older machines usually led to subtle run-time errors. On most modern computers the bug is either caught at compile time (by the gcc compiler) or generates a segmentation violation (memory protection violation) at run time. This situation exposes a weakness in C's typing system.

12.5.4 Example: Symbolic Differentiation

This example implements symbolic differentiation of simple calculus formulae. Some familiar rules for symbolic differentiation are given in Figure 12.4.

For example, differentiating the function $2 \cdot x + 1$ with respect to x using these rules gives:

$$\frac{d(2 \cdot x + 1)}{dx} = \frac{d(2 \cdot x)}{dx} + \frac{d1}{dx}$$
$$= 2 \cdot \frac{dx}{dx} + x \cdot \frac{d2}{dx} + 0$$
$$= 2 \cdot 1 + x \cdot 0 + 0$$

which would ordinarily simplify to 2.

In such an application, it is convenient to design the representation of expressions using abstract syntax. The abstract syntax of Clite programs was discussed in Section 2.5.3. Here the needed abstract syntax, summarized in Figure 12.5, is adapted from the abstract syntax of a Clite expression. The primary differences from Clite are that there is only a single type of value, and the abstract syntax classes Binary, Variable, and Value are types of an Expression.

In an imperative language, a class in the abstract syntax cannot be mapped to a class in the implementation. Instead, a physical or logical union type is used. Since C lacks tagged unions, the implemetation here (see Figure 12.6) uses a logical union, combining the three kinds of expressions into one record, together with a tag field (named kind).

Figure 12.4
Symbolic
Differentiation
Rules

$$\frac{d}{dx}(c) = 0 \qquad\qquad c \text{ is a constant}$$

$$\frac{d}{dx}(x) = 1$$

$$\frac{d}{dx}(u + v) = \frac{du}{dx} + \frac{dv}{dx} \qquad\qquad u \text{ and } v \text{ are functions of } x$$

$$\frac{d}{dx}(u - v) = \frac{du}{dx} - \frac{dv}{dx}$$

$$\frac{d}{dx}(uv) = u\frac{dv}{dx} + v\frac{du}{dx}$$

$$\frac{d}{dx}\left(\frac{u}{v}\right) = \left(v\frac{du}{dx} - u\frac{dv}{dx}\right)\bigg/ v^2$$

Figure 12.5
Abstract Syntax
of *Expressions*

$Expression = Variable \mid Value \mid Binary$

$Variable = char$ id

$Value = int$ value

$Binary = char$ op; $Expression$ left, right

As in an object-oriented language, a function is needed to make each of the three kinds of nodes. Since C lacks both object constructors and user overloaded functions, each function name must be unique and returns a pointer to the node constructed (see Figure 12.7).

Two other functions are defined (see Figure 12.8). The function `diff` takes two arguments: the variable in the differentiation and a pointer to an expression tree. It returns an expression tree representing the differentiated (but not simplified) expression. The function `dump` prints an expression tree in Polish prefix form.

Note the use of `switch` statements in both the `diff` and the `dump` functions. This is one of the hallmarks of imperative programming, namely, distributed switch statements, that object-oriented programming largely does away with. Of the four arithmetic operators, only + and * are presented; the others are left as exercises.

The first rule in Figure 12.4 says that the differentiation of a constant with respect to x is 0. This is implemented by the case `value` in the function `diff`, which returns a zero.

Similarly, the addition rule of Figure 12.4 (rule three) says to differentiate an addition, you first differentiate each term and then add the results. The case where `op` is a + in function `diff` does precisely that, constructing a new expression (abstract syntax tree) to hold the result.

An application of the `diff` method to the expression $2 \cdot x + 1$ gives:
+ + * 2 1 * x 0 0 representing the expression $2 \cdot 1 + x \cdot 0 + 0$. A better formatter, together with an algebraic simplifier, are left as exercises.

12.6 IMPERATIVE PROGRAMMING AND ADA

Ada was developed in the late 1970s by the Department of Defense for both large command and control systems, as well as embedded, real-time systems. According to

```
enum nodekind {binary, var, value};

struct node {
    enum nodekind kind;
    char op;
    struct node *term1, *term2;
    char id;
    int val;
};
```

| **Figure 12.6**   **Symbolic Differentiation Header File**

```
#include <stdio.h>
#include <stdlib.h>
#include "node.h"

struct node *mknodebin(char op1, struct node *left,
                       struct node * right) {
    struct node *result;
    result = (struct node*) malloc(sizeof(struct node));
    result->kind = binary;
    result->op = op1;
    result->term1 = left;
    result->term2 = right;
    return result;
}


struct node *mknodevar(char v) {
    struct node *result;
    result = (struct node*) malloc(sizeof(struct node));
    result->kind = var;
    result->id = v;
    return result;
}

struct node *mknodeval(int v) {
    struct node *result;
    result = (struct node*) malloc(sizeof(struct node));
    result->kind = value;
    result->val = v;
    return result;
}
```

| **Figure 12.7**   **Node Construction Functions**

one study, DoD was spending billions of dollars on software, a figure that was projected to rise significantly. What was worse, the study found that over 450 languages were then in use, many of them highly specialized and idiosyncratic.

The solution was obvious; standardize on one language. But which one? Thus was born the *Higher Order Language Working Group*, whose task was to identify a language generally suitable for DoD's requirements. This eventually led to the development and standardization in 1983 of the Ada programming language. The Ada 95 standard added object-oriented extensions to Ada 83.

The timing of the development of Ada was unfortunate for two reasons. Ada 83 was a very large language. At that time, a typical Pascal compiler written in Pascal ranged

```
struct node *diff(char x, struct node *root){
    struct node *result;
    switch (root->kind) {
    case value: result = mknodeval(0);
        break;
    case var:
        result = mknodeval(root->id == x?1:0);
        break;
    case binary:
        switch (root->op) {
        case '+':
            result = mknodebin(plus,
                        diff(x, root->term1),
                        diff(x, root->term2));
            break;
        case '*':
            result = mknodebin(plus,
                        mknodebin(times, root->term1,
                                diff(x, root->term2)),
                        mknodebin(times, root->term2,
                                diff(x, root->term1)));
            break;
        }
    }
    return result;
}

void dump(struct node *root) {
    if (! root) return;
    switch (root->kind) {
    case value: printf("%d", root->val);
        break;
    case var: printf("%c", root->id);
        break;
    case binary: printf("%c", oper[root->op]);
        dump(root->term1);
        dump(root->term2);
        break;
    }
}
```

| **Figure 12.8**   **Symbolic Differentiation Implementation**

from 8K to 12K lines of code, while a typical Modula compiler ranged from 15K to 25K lines. A typical Ada 83 compiler had minimally 250K lines of Ada code.

Because of the language study done in the mid-1970s, DoD outlawed Ada subsets. However, in the 1980s personal computers were beginning to replace minicomputers and mainframe computers. Personal computers of the 1980s lacked the memory needed to host an Ada compiler.

The second reason for the unfortunate timing is that object-oriented languages were about to revolutionize language design. Had the Ada project started 5–10 years later, Ada might have been a vastly simpler language.

Ada fell on hard times during the 1990s, as the Department of Defense eliminated the requirement to use Ada in favor of commercial, off-the-shelf (COTS) software and languages. However, there now seems to be a resurgence of interest in Ada:

- COTS software has proved to be problematic in the command and control environment.

- The development of Spark Ada and its associated compile-time tools (see Chapter 18) has convincingly demonstrated that software can be developed at high reliability and lower cost than software using COTS languages such as C/C++.

- The development of NYU GNAT (Ada) compiler, now part of the GNU compiler collection, has made a high-quality Ada compiler available to educators and students at no cost.

In the sections that follow, we use the name Ada to refer to the imperative subset of Ada.

12.6.1 General Characteristics

The languages with the greatest influence on Ada were Algol and Pascal. Examples of this influence abound: from the use of the symbol := for assignment to the use of begin-end for blocks. Syntactically, the two biggest deviations from these predecessor languages was the use of unique ending symbols for compound structures and the use of the semicolon as a statement ending symbol rather than as a statement separator. Both of these were concessions to pragmatism, as the other conventions had been found to be problematic.

Even syntactically Ada is a large language. The EBNF grammar has almost 200 productions. Ada is case-insensitive with respect to the spelling of reserved words and identifiers.

Basic data types include: character, integer, floating point, fixed point, boolean, and enumeration. Aggregate data types include: arrays (single and multidimensional), strings, records, case-variant records, and pointers. Ada supports subtypes and derived types.

Unlike C, all array indexing errors are caught in Ada. The use of subranges allows many instances of indexing errors to be caught at compile time.

Similarly, as we saw in Section 5.4.6, although Ada supports the tagged case-variant record type (which is normally a hole in the type system), syntax is provided that permits both the variant and the tag to be assigned in one statement; any attempt to assign to either the variant or the tag separately results in a compile time error.

Each reference to a variant is checked to ensure that the reference is consistent with the tag:

```
type union(b : boolean) is
    record
        case b is
            when true =>
                 i : integer;
            when false =>
                 r : float;
        end case;
    end record;
tagged : union;
begin
    tagged := (b => false, r => 3.375);
    put(tagged.i);
```

In this case the reference `tagged.i` generates a run-time exception. A common practice in Ada is to embed such references in a case (or switch) statement in which access within the case is consistent with the case label.

The usual imperative statements are included in Ada: assignment, if, case (switch), loops (but not iterators), blocks, exit, return, and goto.

Both value-returning functions and non-value-returning procedures are supported. However, parameter passing in Ada is unusual in several respects. Ada specifies how the parameter is to be used (input, output, input-output) and leaves it to the compiler to decide which mechanism to use, for example, value, reference, result, and so on. Another unusual aspect of parameters is that formal parameters can specify default values if they are omitted. Also, a function call can use the formal parameter names and their values, in which case the parameter order is irrelevant. For example:

```
sort(list => student_array, length => n);
```

This use of formal parameter names makes call statements easier to understand.

Ada supports encapsulating data and functions that operate on that data into a so-called *package*, forming an abstract data type. This is discussed in detail in Chapter 13, with an example presented in Figures 13.4 and 13.5. In this sense, Ada is often characterized as an object-based language with static types.

Ada also supports exception handling, user-defined exceptions, generics and overloading.

A specification of a generic sort routine is given in Figure 12.9. To instantiate this routine, the client must supply an `element` type and a > (greater than) operation for that type. Thus, the sort routine can sort an arbitrary list of such elements.

Figure 12.10 provides the generic sort implementation. Unlike C header files, both the client and the implementation must reference the **same** package specification. The references `a'first` and `a'last` are instances of attributes, and denote the lower and upper values of the declared index range. Thus, the compiler can guarantee at compile time that no subscript error can occur.

Tasking is a built-in feature of Ada. Communication between tasks is accomplished via a mechanism called a rendezvous [Hoare, 1978] [Hoare, 1985].

```
generic
  type element is private;
  type list is array(natural range <>) of element;
  function ">"(a, b : element) return boolean;
package sort_pck is
  procedure sort (in out a : list);
end sort_pck;
```

| **Figure 12.9** **Generic Sort in Ada**

Ada 95 added new function libraries and support for object-oriented programming, thus making Ada a multiparadigm language. Given that its primary application area is real-time command and control, Ada programs need to be highly reliable, unlike most commercial software. The developers of one implementation, called Spark Ada, report defect rates as low as 0.04 defects per thousand lines of code (KLOC) versus standard rates of 1–7 defects per KLOC, with a productivity rate three times the industry norm [Croxford, 2005]. In contrast, about 15 years ago a missing break statement in a several-million-line C program caused a system-wide AT&T failure, costing about $1 billion.

12.6.2 Example: Average

In this example we read a sequence of numbers and compute their minimum, maximum, and average. This would be a typical sample program for explaining the use of a while loop. The interested reader may wish to compare the C version of the program in Figure 12.3 with the Ada version.

```
package body sort_pck is
procedure sort (in out a : list) is
begin
  for i in a'first .. a'last - 1 loop
    for j in i+1 .. a'last loop
      if a(i) > a(j) then
          declare t : element;
          begin
              t := a(i);
              a(i) := a(j);
              a(j) := t;
          end;
      end if;
    end loop;
  end loop;
end sort;
end sort_pck;
```

| **Figure 12.10** **Generic Selection Sort Implementation in Ada**

The program, given in Figure 12.11, basically consists of a loop that reads numbers one at a time, counting each number, summing it, and checking to see if it is a new minimum or maximum. The numbers are read from the console.

The program is basically a copy of the C version with a few improvements. First, the loop is basically an infinite one (since there is no test), relying on the fact that an attempt to read past end of file generates an `End_Error` exception.

Second, the loop contains an inner block which catches the exceptions generated by the `Get`. The first two generate an error message, and the loop is repeated starting at the prompt for another number. In the event an end of file is detected, the loop is exited.

The other feature of Ada to note, besides its robustness, is its wordiness versus C. For example, writing the average, minimum, and maximum takes three statements each in Ada versus one in C.

12.6.3 Example: Matrix Multiplication

Ada supports the redefinition of any arithmetic operator whenever its operands are not simple arithmetic types. We employ this strategy here to overload the multiplication operator to implement matrix multiplication.

Figure 12.12 shows an Ada implementation of matrix multiplication as an over-loading of the "*" operator when its operands are of type `Matrix`. When the number of columns in A is not the same as the number of rows in B, this algorithm raises the `Bounds_Error` exception.

The expressions `A'First(2)` and `A'Last(2)` denote the lower and upper limits of the index range in the second dimension of array A. The expression `A'Range(2)` denotes the range of index values for the second dimension of A.

Recall that the product of an $m \times n$ matrix and an $n \times p$ matrix is an $m \times p$ matrix. So the result C must be declared to have `A'Range(1)` for its first dimension and `B'Range(2)` for its second.

The `if` statement checks that the range of A's second dimension is identical to B's first dimension. Otherwise the matrices cannot be multiplied. In this case, the Ada program raises a `Bounds_Error` exception.

Like Pascal, Ada counting loops are restricted to counting up or down by one, with the number of times the loop is executed determined at loop entry time. Thus, any changes to the initial and final values of the counting variable inside the loop do not affect the number of times the loop is repeated. The variables i and j are implicitly declared by the `for` loop header; their scope is strictly that of the `for` loop itself. Unlike C, an illegal index cannot occur in either `for` loop, which can be verified at compile time.

Finally, Ada uses explicit end's for its `if` and `for` statements, as well as the function itself. This avoids the *dangling else* syntax problem discussed in Chapter 2.

12.7 IMPERATIVE PROGRAMMING AND PERL

Perl is a widely used scripting language, which is a high-level language that is interpreted at run time rather than compiled into machine language. Early scripting languages were used to automate job control tasks that a user might perform at the keyboard. Examples include MS-DOS batch files, Unix Bourne shell scripts, and Apple HyperCard scripts.

```
with Ada.Text_IO;  with Ada.Integer_Text_IO;
procedure Average is
   Ct, Number, Min, Max : Integer;
begin
   Sum := 0;
   Ct := 0;
   Ada.Text_IO.Put("Enter number: ");
   loop
      begin
         Ada.Integer_Text_IO.Get(Number);
         if Ct = 0 then
            Min := Number;
            Max := Number;
         end if;
         Count := Count + 1;
         Sum := Sum + Number;
         if Number < Min then
            Min := Number;
         elsif Number > Max then
            Max := Number;
         end if;
      exception
         when Constraint_Error =>
            Ada.Text_IO.Put("Value out of range. ");
         when Ada.Text_IO.Data_Error =>
            Ada.Text_IO.Put("Value not an integer. ");
         when Ada.Text_IO.End_Error =>
            exit;
      end;
      Ada.Text_IO.Put("Enter number: ");
   end loop;
   Ada.Integer_Text_IO.Put(Ct, 5);
   Ada.Text_IO.Put(" numbers read");
   Ada.Text_IO.New_Line;
   if Ct > 0 then
      Ada.Text_IO.Put("Average: ");
      Ada.Integer_Text_IO.Put(Sum / Ct);
      Ada.Text_IO.New_Line;
      Ada.Text_IO.Put("Maximum: ");
      Ada.Integer_Text_IO.Put(Maximum);
      Ada.Text_IO.New_Line;
      Ada.Text_IO.Put("Minimum: ");
      Ada.Integer_Text_IO.Put(Minimum);
      Ada.Text_IO.New_Line;
   end if;
end Average;
```

| **Figure 12.11**   **Ada Program to Compute Average**

```
type Matrix is
   array (Positive range <> of Float,
          Positive range <> of Float);
function "*" (A, B: Matrix) return Matrix is
   C: Matrix (A'Range(1), B'Range(2));
   Sum: Float;
begin
   if A'First(2) /= B'First(1) or
      A'Last(2) /= B'Last(1) then
      raise Bounds_Error;
   end if;
   for i in C'Range(1) loop
      for j in C'Range(2) loop
         Sum := 0.0;
         for k in A'Range(2) loop
            Sum := Sum + A(i,k) * B(k,j);
         end loop;
         Result(i,j) := Sum;
      end loop;
   end loop;
   return C;
end "*";
```

| **Figure 12.12**   **Overloading of the "*" Operator for Matrix Multiplication**

On most computers a Perl program is dynamically compiled to byte code, which is then interpreted. However, there are Perl compilers that produce an executable program (similar to C compilers).

According to Schwartz [1993]:

> Larry Wall ... created Perl when he was trying to produce some reports from a Usenet-news-like hierarchy of files for a bug-reporting system, and *awk* ran out of steam. Larry, being the lazy programmer that he is, decided to over-kill the problem with a general purpose tool that he could use in at least one other place. The result was the first version of Perl.

Although Perl has its roots as a Unix scripting language, it is now widely available for most major computing systems, including Linux, Mac OS X, and MS Windows.

Scripting languages allow applications to be *glued* together, in the sense that scripts are widely used to take output data from one application and reformat it into a form appropriate for input into a different application. Although there is a performance penalty for scripting a *glued* application, most of the time is spent in the applications themselves compared to the script. And as computers have grown faster, scripts that tie applications together have proven to be "fast enough."

Languages generally included in the scripting category include the Unix Bourne shell for job control, Javascript for web pages, and PHP for server-side web applications. General purpose scripting languages comparable to Perl include Python, Ruby, and Tcl.

12.7.1 General Characteristics

Like most scripting languages, Perl is dynamically typed. It supports numbers, both integer and floating point, strings, and regular expressions. Data structures include dynamic arrays (with integer indices) and associative arrays (with string indices).

Perl and Python (see Section 13.5) take opposite approaches to basic types and data structures. Perl performs implicit conversions between basic data types on an as-needed basis. The result is that Perl has a distinct operator for most operations. Thus, Perl uses a period (with required surrounding whitespace) for string concatenation. Thus,

```
"abc" . "def"
```

produces the string "abcdef", while:

```
123 . 4.56
```

produces the string "1234.56"; note the two uses of the period in the last example. As a binary operator the period is interpreted as string concatenation, and the operands are converted as needed to strings.

The policy of having unique operators for strings carries over to relationals. The usual relational operators are reserved for numbers; string relationals are the operators eq, ne, lt, le, gt, and ge. The example below gives various examples with the result cited as a comment (following the pound symbol #):

```
10 < 2       # false
10 < "2"     # false
"10" lt "2"  # true
10 lt "2"    # true
```

In the second example, the string is converted to the number 2, while in the last example the 10 is converted to a string. The truth of the last two expressions follows from the fact that the character 1 is less than the character 2, so the 0 in the 10 is irrelevant; this is analogous to comparing the string ax to the string b.

Variables are either scalars, which must be prefixed with a dollar sign ($), arrays (prefixed by a @), or associative arrays (prefixed by a %). An indexed occurrence of an array or an associative array is usually a scalar value and is, thus, prefixed with a $. Because of complaints within the Perl community, Perl 6 breaks with this tradition.

Perl is equally permissive with arrays (which use zero indexing by default). If we declare the array:

```
@a = (2, 3, 5, 7);
```

then the size of a is 4 and the value of a[3] is 7. However, if we then execute:

```
$a[7] = 17;
```

the assignment is legal and the size of a becomes 8. However, indicies 4, 5, and 6 of a have the special value `undef`, which is interpreted as false (as a Boolean), the empty string (as a string), and 0 (as a number).

The developer of Perl, Larry Wall, feels that the three great virtues of a programmer are *laziness*, *impatience*, and *hubris*. As a linguist, Wall is strongly in favor of permitting many different ways of "saying the same thing." Thus, much of the syntax of Perl is optional, which makes it difficult for a beginner to understand. Perl's most common syntax error message is:

Syntax error near line *x*

where *x* is some line number. This recalls the quote by Niklaus Wirth at the start of Chapter 3: if the parser cannot give a precise error message and location, maybe the fault is with the syntax of the language.

As a dynamically typed language, Perl lacks both generics and overloading. It also lacks exception handling and user-defined iterators. Perl added support for classes in version 5, making it a multiparadigm language.

One of the great strengths of Perl is its support for regular expressions, which are used both for simple pattern matching and for substitution of one string for another. Indeed, many Perl programs exploit this feature.

However, Perl is irregular in this respect; regular expressions are not first class objects. They cannot generally be assigned to variables or passed as parameters. This is just one of many irregularities in the language. As the examples show, Perl is a large language with a lot of optional or alternative syntax and many irregularities.

12.7.2 Example: Grep

In this section we develop a Perl version of the Unix utility named `grep`, which was developed in C in an earlier section. This version, given in Figure 12.13, takes two command line arguments, a string to be matched exactly and the name of the file to be searched for the string.

```
#! /usr/bin/perl

die "Usage mygrep string \n" if @ARGV < 1;
use strict;
my $string = shift;
my $ct = 0;

while (<>) {
    $ct++;
    print "$ct:\t$_" if /$string/;
}
exit;
```

| **Figure 12.13**   **A Simple Version of Grep**

In this example, each line that is matched is written to the console, preceded by its line number. If no lines match, there is no output.

Comments begin with the symbol # and continue until the end of the line. The first line of the program is a special comment (the ! after the comment symbol # is important) that gives the location of the Perl interpreter. In Unix, if such a file is marked as executable, it may be invoked directly as a command.

The second statement is a backwards if statement that terminates the program if there is not at least one command line argument to the command. This argument is shifted off the front end of the @ARGV array and stored in the scalar variable $string. Array references are prefixed by the at symbol (@), while scalar references are prefixed by a dollar sign ($).

The use strict directive requires that each variable be declared via a my directive. Although unnecessary in small scripts such as this one, it is indispensable in catching spelling errors in variable names in larger scripts.

The syntax of the while loop is conventional, except that Perl requires the use of the braces for both loops and normal if statements. Note the required parentheses surrounding the while loop test, just as in C.

The angle operator (<>) represents a read line on a input file handle. If the file is at end of file, an undef is returned which is interpreted as false, terminating the loop. Otherwise, the line read is returned, including any operating system dependent end of line characters. Hence, the line is always non-empty and is interpreted as true.

But what file is being read? And is the line read merely thrown away? The answer is that the test is interpreted as follows:

```
while ($_ = <>) {
    ...
}
```

According to the "Camel book" ([Wall *et al.*, 1996, p. 53]), the most authoritative reference on Perl:

> The most heavily used input operator is the line input operator, also known as the angle operator. ... Ordinarily you would assign the input value to a variable, but there is one situation where an automatic assignment happens. If and only if the input line operator is the only thing inside the conditional of a while loop, the value is automatically assigned to the variable $_.

Unfortunately, Perl is riddled with such rules making it a difficult language to know well. The file being read is ([Wall *et al.*, 1996, p. 15]):

> all the files on the command line, or STDIN, if none were specified.

Assuming the command was named mygrep, any of the following invocations would work in Unix

```
mygrep xxx aFile
cat aFile | mygrep xxx
mygrep xxx < aFile
```

```
#! /usr/bin/perl

if (@ARGV < 1) {
    die "Usage mygrep string \n" ;
}
use strict;
my $string = shift(@ARGV);
my $ct = 0;
my $line;

while ($line = <>) {
    $ct++;
    if ($line =~ m/$string/) {
        print STDOUT $ct, ":\t", $line;
    }
}
exit;
```

| **Figure 12.14**   **Alternate Version of the grep Program**

for an arbitrary string ×××. The first command invocation is comparable to the C version. The second has some command (or commands) generating input that is sent to mygrep via a Unix pipe. The third uses input redirection to have mygrep read the file from stdin. Only the first of these works for the C version of Section 12.5.2.

In the rewrite of the while loop test, note the implied subject named $_. Many commands make this interpretation if no subject is provided. For example,

```
print; #interpreted as: print $_;
```

the simple print with no object is interpreted to mean print the $_ scalar. Similarly, the backward if statement inside the while loop is interpreted as follows:

```
print "$ct:t$_" if $_ =~ m/$string/;
```

That is, the line is printed if the string matches part of the line. The scalar $_ is the subject $(=~)^2$ of a simple pattern match (m) where the pattern is conventionally enclosed in / symbols. So some pattern match special characters (such as the single wildcard character .) will work, while others will not.

Note also that scalar references can be embedded in a double quoted string, but not in a string enclosed in single quotes.

A more conventional version of the grep program is given in Figure 12.14. In this version, only conventional if statements are used, and the version tries to make everything explicit.

---

2. Many programmers find this symbol confusing since it looks like an assignment operator. The language *awk* uses just the tilde (˜).

Both versions have a subtle bug. Try executing the following command:

```
altgrep string mygrep.c mygrep.c
```

It is left as an exercise to describe and fix this bug.

Another irregularity in Perl is that the variable $_ has global scope. Overuse of this implied subject may have a subroutine accidentally change its value, leading to subtle bugs.

Finally, the `exit` statement in each script is unnecessary.

12.7.3 Example: Mailing Grades

A typical "glue" script moves data from one application to another. Student grades are often kept in a spreadsheet. After every project or test, the instructor wants to email a copy of the grades and their average to each student. Of course, for privacy reasons, each student should receive a copy of only their own grades. In addition, it is useful to include the class average on each project and test, as well as the overall class average.

In writing such an application, it is useful to know that different instructors may use either different spreadsheet applications or different versions of the same spreadsheet application. Such spreadsheet applications usually can export their data to ordinary text files in a form referred to as *comma-separated values* (CSV). Spreadsheet rows become text lines, with each column separated by a separator (by default, a comma). Since commas may occur naturally in some fields, better choices (depending on the spreadsheet used) include the tab character, the colon, and the semicolon. Some spreadsheet applications may quote some or all of the values with either single or double quotes, which need to be deleted. Thus, each spreadsheet application may have a slightly different definition of CSV format.

An example of this format as it is used in this application appears in Figure 12.15. The separator used in this example is a colon, since the comma can't be used (it appears within the name field) and student names are stored as *Last name, first name*.

In this spreadsheet, the first two columns contain student names and email addresses, while the last two contain the total points and averages. The middle columns contain the grades themselves; some columns are empty because the projects or tests have not yet been assigned. The first row contains the project or test name, while the second row contains the total number of points assigned to the project. The last row contains the column averages. The middle rows contain the individual students; in the example in Figure 12.15, there are two students. Computed values may appear as either integer or floating point values; the latter may contain an excessive number of decimal digits.

Figure 12.15
Student Grades in CSV Format

```
::Proj1:Test1:::::Total:Average
::50:100:::::::150:
Tucker:atuck@college.edu:48:97:::::145:96.66666666
Noonan:rnoon@college.edu:40:85:::::125:83.33333333
Average::88:91:::::135:90
```

```perl
#! /usr/bin/perl

use strict;
my $class = shift;
my $suf = ".csv";
open(IN, "<$class$suf") || die "Cannot read: $class$suf\n";
my $sep = ":";
my $tab = 8;
my $q = '"';

# read header lines: titles, max grades
my @hdr = &readSplit();
my @max = &readSplit();
push(@max, '100%');

# read students
my @student;
while (<IN>) {
    chomp;
    tr /"//d; # "
    push(@student, $_);
}
my @ave = split(/$sep/, pop(@student));

# gen mail for each student
my $ct = 0;
foreach (@student) {
    my @p = split(/$sep/);
    $ct += &sendMail(@p);
}
$ave[1] = $ENV{"USER"};
&sendMail(@ave);
print "Emails sent: $ct\n";
exit;
```

| **Figure 12.16**   **Example: Main Program of** `mailgrades`

The program is presented in two figures. The main program appears in Figure 12.16. It is divided into four parts, each separated by a blank line.

The first part retrieves the class designation from the command line and opens the CSV file for input. It is also responsible for "declaring" some global constants that are subject to change.

The second part reads and processes the first two header lines. These are stored as arrays, one array element per column.

The third part of the program reads all the student data using the Perl while loop idiom for reading and processing lines in a file. Each line is stored in an array using the push function to append the line to the array @student. Of course, the last line is not a student, but rather the line of column averages, so it is popped off the array, split into columns, and stored into the array @ave. Thus, the entire file must be read in order to email the column averages to each student.

The last part iterates over the list of students, generating email for each student using the routine sendMail. The foreach loop is like a Java iterator that processes one array value per iteration. Since no explicit iteration variable is given, the implicit (and global) variable $_ is used, and implicitly referenced in the split operator. The latter uses the separator (the colon) to split the line up into an array, one column per array element. The trailer after the foreach loop emails the column averages to the person running the script.

The remainder of the program is given in Figure 12.17 and consists of the two helper routines. Notice that neither routine declares formal parameters; routine readSplit has none, but routine sendMail has two. In the absence of comments, one has to read the code to determine these facts.

The routine readSplit consists of five lines of code. The first statement reads a line from the input file, and the second statement deletes the end of line character or characters, which is operating system dependent. The variable $_ must be explicit in the first statement, but is optional in the second.

Another irregularity of Perl is demonstrated by rewriting the second statement (with or without parentheses after the chomp) as:

```
$_ = chomp $_;
```

The operator chomp modifies its argument and returns the characters deleted as the value of the function, so this modified version is totally incorrect.

The third statement in readSplit uses the tr operator to delete all double quotes from the line. Since no subject or object is stated, the variable $_ is assumed.

The last two lines of the routine bring up another, sometimes confusing feature. Many operators can be evaluated in either list context or in scalar context. The split operator scans a string for delimiters as given in the pattern (in this case, colons) and divides the string into an array of substrings. In list context this array of substrings is the result, while in scalar context the size of the array of substrings is the result. As an exercise, try various modifications to these last two lines.

The details of generating an email message to the student are hidden inside the sendMail routine. It returns 1 if the message is sent, and 0 otherwise. The first two statements shift the arguments to the routine off the array @_; this effectively provides call by value. An alternative is to use the names $_[0] for $name and $_[1] for $email; this effectively provides call by reference. For this routine, call by value is sufficient, and significantly more readable. Approximately 40 percent of the statements in this program are in this routine, most of which are associated with generating and formatting the email message.

The third statement returns if the email address field is empty. This mechanism supports keeping the student in the spreadsheet even if the student drops the course.

```perl
sub readSplit {
    $_ = <IN>;
    chomp;
    tr /$q//d;
    my @r = split(/$sep/);
    return @r;
}

sub sendMail {
    my $name = shift;
    my $email = shift;
    return 0 unless $email;
    open(MAIL, "| mail -s '$class Grades' $email")
        || die "Cannot fork mail: $!\n";
    print MAIL "GRADE\t\tYOUR\tMAX\tCLASS\n",
                "NAME\t\tSCORE\tSCORE\tAVE\n\n";

    my $ct = 1;
    foreach (@_) {
        $ct++;
        next unless $hdr[$ct];
        print MAIL "$hdr[$ct]\t";
        print MAIL "\t" if length($hdr[$ct]) < $tab;
        if (/^\d/) { print MAIL int($_ + 0.5); }
        else { print MAIL $_; }
        print MAIL "\t$max[$ct]\t";
        if ($ave[$ct] =~/^\d/) {
            print MAIL int($ave[$ct] + 0.5);
        } else { print MAIL $ave[$ct];}
        print MAIL "\n";
    }
    return 1;
}
```

| **Figure 12.17**   **Support Routines for Emailing Grades**

The next statement opens an output file as a pipe to the Unix/Linux (Berkeley) mail command. When the file is closed, what was written to the file becomes the body of the email message. A better implementation would use a Perl module for interfacing to a pop mail server. After printing some column headers, the following `foreach` loop processes the remaining columns, formatting the mail message.

This concludes our brief examination of Perl. Despite our criticism of the language design, the authors wrote five "quick and dirty" programs to support the writing of this book; all five were written in Perl.

12.8 SUMMARY

Imperative programming is the oldest and most well established of the language paradigms, mimicking the design of early computers. Many of the key features of imperative languages were discussed in earlier chapters.

In this chapter, we shifted our attention to an examination of program development in the imperative paradigm. Next we considered the assignment statement and the importance of built-in operators and functions.

Finally, we examined briefly the languages C, Ada, and Perl. C, the oldest of these, is weakly typed, while Ada is strongly typed. Perl is a scripting language that is very useful for "quick and dirty" applications despite its many idiosyncracies.

EXERCISES

12.1 Discuss the advantages and disadvantages of having case-sensitive identifiers in a programming language, with respect to program reliability, type checking, and compile-time complexity.

12.2 Starting from Table 2.4, show the operators and their precedence for C, Ada, and Perl.

12.3 Prepare a table comparing the standard C, Ada, and Perl string libraries. Ignore regular expressions in Perl.

12.4 Write a paper which compares and contrasts arrays (with integer subscripts) in C, Ada, and Perl.

12.5 By using programs for which source code is available, discuss by example the major differences between pre-K&R C, first edition K&R C, and ANSI C.

12.6 By using programs for which source code is available, discuss by example how string utility programs like grep avoid the buffer overflow problem in C.

12.7 What other ANSI C standard functions require the address of a variable like scanf?

12.8 For the language C, use a simple sort routine to demonstrate that it is possible to have a client and an implementation use distinct header files with disasterous consequences.

12.9 Write the eight queens program of Section 13.4.2 in C.

12.10 Compile and execute the Ada average program. What happens if you enter nonnumeric values? Integer values greater than $2^{31} - 1$? Values whose sum exceeds 2^{32}?

12.11 Write a test driver for the Ada matrix multiplication routine.

12.12 Extend the Ada matrix multiplication routine into a matrix package supporting, in addition, matrix addition and subtraction.

12.13 Extend the Ada matrix package to support matrix creation.

12.14 Reimplement the eight queens program of Section 13.4.2 in Ada.

12.15 Using the Perl mygrep program, test which characters in the string are interpreted as regular expression sequences, rather than as themselves.

12.16 Demonstrate the bug described in Section 12.7.2. Then fix it.

12.17   Construct a Perl program showing the global scope of the scalar variable $_.

12.18   For the language Perl, modify the `mailgrades` program to demonstrate, using the function `split`, the difference between list context and scalar context.

12.19   Reimplement the eight queens program of Section 13.4.2 in Perl.

Object-Oriented Programming

"I am surprised that ancient and modern writers have not attributed greater importance to the laws of inheritance..."
Alexis de Tocquevile, Democracy in America, 1840

CHAPTER OUTLINE

In this chapter we present the object-oriented (OO) programming paradigm, including its history and impact, its design issues, and examples of its use. We first describe the idea of abstract data types, an idea that predated and greatly influenced the idea of object-oriented programming. Next, we describe the object-oriented paradigm as an extension of data abstraction. This discussion includes the pertinent history and core design issues that surround object-oriented programming languages, such as inheritance and polymorphism. Third, we present some interesting examples of object-oriented programming in Smalltalk, Java, and Python.

13.1 PRELUDE: ABSTRACT DATA TYPES

A key development in imperative programming was an effort, beginning with Simula 67, to extend procedural abstraction, as described in Section 12.2 to include *data abstraction* or *abstract data types*. Good examples of data abstraction occur among the primitive data types.[1] For example, the type `float` has encapsulated with it the standard arithmetic (addition, subtraction, etc.) and relational (less than, greater than, etc.) operations. It is abstract because the use of type `float` in programs does not depend on the concrete representation of its values or the details of how its operations are computed.

Data abstraction extends the notion of type by providing the programmer with an *encapsulation* mechanism for defining new data types that are close to the application at hand.

> **Definition**: *Encapsulation* is a mechanism which allows logically related constants, types, variables, methods, and so on, to be grouped into a new entity. Examples include procedures, packages, and classes.

By utilizing this mechanism, the program can limit the scope and visibility of the data values and encapsulated functions for this newly defined data type. Thus, we have the notion of an *abstract data type*.

Consider, for example, the definition of a stack. An abstraction of this notion should encapsulate a representation of the stack, together with its fundamental operations: `push`, `pop`, `top`, and `empty`. Other operations, such as the ability to initialize or display the contents of the stack, may also be desirable. Consider the implementation for a stack of integers in the language C given in Figure 13.1.

In C, a separate header file provides the specification of the *interface* for the stack abstraction. An interface contains only the *signature* for each function, which includes its name, its return type, and the types of each of its parameters. Omission of a function or global data variable from the header file effectively hides the details of its implementation from use by other parts of the program.[2]

The use of independent compilation to provide an encapsulation mechanism for a stack does not, by itself, give us a true abstract data type. The difficulty results from the fact that, in C, we cannot declare variables to be of type stack. The code presented in Figure 13.1 defines only a single instance of a stack, not a *type* stack. Also, the code is restricted to a stack of integers; if a stack of `float`s is wanted, we will most likely copy and edit the code.

In contrast, Figure 13.2 defines a type stack that allows the programmer to declare variables of this type. This header file gives a specification of the type `STACK`; it would normally be included in two places—the implementation file (Figure 13.3) and any client program that uses this type. In this case the stack is actually a pointer to a record

---

1. Recall from Chapter 5 that a *type* is a set of data values together with a set of operations on those data.

2. Note that C allows both global data and functions to be declared `static`, which enforces this hiding. However, use of the keyword `static` for this role can be criticized as misleading. This use of the keyword `static` to enforce information hiding in C does not appear to be widespread.

```c
#include "stack.h"

struct Node {
    int val;
    struct Node* next;
};
typedef struct Node* STACK;

STACK theStack = NULL;

int empty( ) {
    return theStack == NULL;
}

int pop( ) {
    STACK temp;
    int result = theStack->val;
    temp = theStack;
    theStack = theStack->next;
    free(temp);
    return result;
}

void push(int newval) {
    STACK temp = (STACK)malloc(sizeof(struct Node));
    temp->val = newval;
    temp->next = theStack;
    theStack = temp;
}

int top( ) {
    return theStack->val;
}
```

| **Figure 13.1**   **A Simple Stack in C**

that implements a linked list. The operations given here restrict the view of the linked list to be that of a stack. Also, this implementation requires that the stack must be explicitly initialized (operation `newstack`), and the stack itself must be passed as an explicit argument to each function.

The use of independent compilation and pointers in C allows for the construction of a type stack, which encapsulates both data and operations (or functions) on that data. However, C suffers from the fact that it permits access by stack clients (called *public access*) to the underlying representation of the stack as a linked list. This can be a particular problem if the client needs to extend the *abstract data type* but does not have access to the source code; in this case the temptation to directly access the underlying representation can be overwhelming.

```
struct Node {
    int val;
    struct Node* next;
};
typedef struct Node* STACK;

int empty(STACK theStack);
STACK newstack( );
int pop(STACK* theStack);
void push(STACK* theStack, int newval);
int top(STACK theStack);
```

| **Figure 13.2   A STACK Type in C**

```
#include "stack.h"

int empty(STACK theStack){
    return theStack == NULL;
}

STACK newstack( ) {
    return (STACK) NULL;
}

int pop(STACK* theStack) {
    STACK temp;
    int result = (*theStack)->val;
    temp = *theStack;
    *theStack = (*theStack)->next;
    free(temp);
    return result;
}

void push(STACK* theStack, int newval) {
    STACK temp;
    temp = (STACK)malloc(sizeof(struct Node));
    temp->val = newval;
    temp->next = *theStack;
    *theStack = temp;
}

int top(STACK theStack) {
    return theStack->val;
}
```

| **Figure 13.3   Implementation of the STACK Type in C**

The key goal of data abstraction is to package the data type and its functions together in a single module so that the functions provide a public interface to the type. Direct support for this concept can be found in "modules" in Modula and in "packages" in Ada. The use of modules/packages allows for the separation of the logical interface (often called the "specification") from its detailed implementation. That is, modules/packages allow the programmer to restrict access to the underlying concrete representation of the abstract data type and the implementation details of its functions. This is called *information hiding*.

Ada uses packages to encapsulate data and operations on the data, in short, to encapsulate an abstract data type. Ada divides a package into a definition or specification part and an implementation or body part. Unlike C and C++, these separate compilation facilities ensure full type checking of packages. This has the additional advantage of eliminating the need for recompiling abstract data type implementations for every new client.

An Ada package definition and implementation of the type STACK comparable to the one given in C appears in Figure 13.4 and Figure 13.5. One major difference, however, results from Ada's support for generics. Instead of a stack of integers, the Ada implementation supports stacks of any type.

Let us ignore the generic type element for the moment in Figure 13.4. Except for the syntax, the procedure declarations look like a header file. The type stack is public (it appears in the parameter list of every procedure), but is declared to be private. And, indeed, the private portion of the specification declares a stack to be a pointer (type access) to a node. The latter is a record containing a value of type element and a next pointer. Because these are declared to be private, the client programmer cannot access portions of the node nor dereference a stack pointer. Only the compiler may use this knowledge, which is a compromise here between a desire to completely hide the information and the requirement that the language be implementable.

```
generic
   type element is private;

package stack_pck is
   type stack is private;
   procedure push (in out s : stack; i : element);
   function pop (in out s : stack) return element;
   function empty(in s : stack) return boolean;
   function top(in s : stack) return element;

private
   type node;
   type stack is access node;
   type node is record
      val : element;
      next : stack;
   end record;
end stack_pck;
```

| **Figure 13.4   Generic Stack Specification in Ada**

```
package body stack_pck is
    procedure push (in out s : stack; i : element) is
        temp : stack;
    begin
        temp := new node;
        temp.all := (val => i, next => s);
        s := temp;
    end push;

    function pop (in out s : stack) return element is
        temp : stack;
        elem : element;
    begin
        elem := s.all.val;
        temp := s;
        s := temp.all.next;
        dispose(temp);
        return elem;
    end pop;

    function empty(in s : stack) return boolean is
    begin
        return s = null;
    end empty;

    function top(in s : stack) return element is
    begin
        return s.all.val;
    end top;
end stack_pck;
```

| **Figure 13.5**   **Generic Stack Implementation in Ada**

Figure 13.5 gives the stack implementation. Other than the syntax, the code looks very similar to the C implementation. Examining the code for a push, we see that the variable temp is assigned the pointer returned by the new node expression; recall that type stack is access node, that is, a pointer to a node. Instead of C's access via the ->, Ada uses the all specifier.

Similarly, the pop code should be familiar except for the syntax. First, a copy of the value to be returned is made. Next, a temporary is set to point to the current head of the list, so that the stack pointer s can be advanced one node. The dispose operation frees the node originally at the front of the list. And the copy of the value originally at the front of the list is returned.

Note that neither pop nor top check for an empty stack; that is the client's responsibility. Either operation on an empty stack will throw an exception, which can be caught by the client. This, again, emphasizes Ada's ability to write robust, reliable software.

To actually use this code, the generic stack must be instantiated for some type. If we want to mimic the C code which uses a stack of integers, we can instantiate the package via:

```
package int_stack is new stack_pck(element => integer);
```

Thus, we can create a stack of any single type, that is, the stack must be homogeneous.

13.2 THE OBJECT MODEL

Even with the evolution of modules and packages in the 1980s, problems remained. One such problem was that no mechanism for automatic initialization and finalization of a value of the given type was provided. Initializations that are commonly needed include opening of a file, memory allocation, and initialization of variables local to the module. Important finalizations include closing files and deallocating memory. Another problem with modules was that they provided no simple way to extend a data abstraction by adding new operations. Both of these problems were solved by the introduction of the idea of a "class," the main building block for object-oriented languages.

However, a more important problem emerged in the 1980s as programmers and language designers began to realize that a significant range of applications were not well served by the imperative paradigm of functional decomposition and data abstraction. More was needed. For example, the programming of embedded computers and graphical user interfaces (GUIs) could be much better modeled as a collection of objects, communicating with each other by sending and receiving messages. A GUI application, for instance, is most naturally modeled as a collection of different types of objects— buttons, text areas, images, video clips, and pull-down menus—each communicating with the program and the user by sending and receiving messages. For large programs in general, the object-oriented paradigm is a fundamentally different way of thinking about programs. For a complete treatment of object-oriented design and programming see [Budd, 2000] and [Horstmann, 2004].

Thus, *object-oriented programming* emerged as a popular[3] programming style in which object decomposition became a central concern, rather than functional decomposition and data abstraction. In the sections that follow, we use Java to explain the major features of an object-oriented language. Our purpose is not to explain Java, but rather to identify the major ideas in object-oriented languages, such as encapsulation, visibility, and inheritance.

13.2.1 Classes

An object-oriented language supports both the encapsulation of the data type with its functions and the information hiding features of data abstraction.

> **Definition**: A *class* is a type declaration which encapsulates constants, variables, and functions for manipulating these variables.

---

3. While these ideas had been around for a long time—since the design of Simula in the 1960s and the development of Smalltalk in the 1970s—a clear practical mandate for using the object-oriented paradigm did not appear until later.

A class is itself an abstract data type and a mechanism for defining an abstract data type in a program. In the vernacular of object-oriented programming, the local variables of a class are called *instance variables,* their initializations are accomplished by special functions called *constructors,* their finalizations by *destructors*, and other functions are implemented by *methods*. Each instance of a class is an *object*.

An implementation of the abstract data type `stack` as a Java class `MyStack` is given in Figure 13.6.

Java also supports the idea of an *inner class*.

> **Definition**: An *inner class* is a class definition that is fully embedded within another class.

The `Node` class is an example of an inner class but, since it has no methods other than constructors, it is closer to being a C `struct` than a true class.

The inner class `Node` has two instance variables (`val` and `next`) and a constructor named `Node`, with no explicit return type. Similarly, the class `MyStack` has an instance variable (`theStack`), a constructor (`MyStack`), and methods (`empty`, `top`, `push`, and `pop`). No destructors are present for either class, since Java performs automatic garbage collection of memory and, unfortunately, does not support destructors.

An advantage of the object-oriented approach to data abstraction is that it provides a *constructor,* in which heap space is allocated for the object and the instance variables of the object can be initialized. In the constructor for `Node` both instance variables are given

```java
class MyStack {
    class Node {
        Object  val;
        Node next;
        Node(Object v, Node n) { val = v; next = n; }
    }

    Node theStack;

    MyStack( ) { theStack = null; }

    boolean empty( ) { return theStack == null; }

    Object pop( ) {
        Object result = theStack.val;
        theStack = theStack.next;
        return result;
    }

    Object top( ) { return theStack.val; }

    void push(Object v) {
        theStack = new Node(v, theStack);
    }
}
```

| Figure 13.6   A Simple Stack Class in Java

values. Indeed, a primary use of a constructor is ensuring that all instance variables are properly initialized.

> **Definition**: A *client* of a class C is any other class or method that declares or uses an object of class C.

The declaration and initialization of such a variable in Java creates an *object* in the heap, since Java uses reference semantics for objects. Notice that class `MyStack` is a client of class `Node`, since the instance variable `theStack` is a `Node`.
Consider the following client code:

```
MyStack s = new MyStack();
```

Note that class `MyStack` has a zero-argument constructor explicitly defined.
Following this declaration, a client can now specify any number of `push` and `pop` operations on this object (using dot notation in Java). For example, here is a sequence of statements that leaves `MyStack` `s` with the values 1 and 5 (5 at the top):

```
s.push(1);
s.push(2);
s.pop();
s.push(5);
```

The effect of this declaration and four statements is shown in Figure 13.7. Note here that three nodes now exist in the heap, one of which has become "garbage" as a result of the call `s.pop()`. The most recently pushed `Node` is at the top of the stack and is referenced by `s`.
In languages that support destructors, an object's destructor is automatically called when the object is deallocated. For objects of classes like `MyStack`, one use of a destructor is to deallocate memory for objects that can no longer be referenced. Languages with automatic garbage collection, such as Java, do not need a destructor in this case. Another use of a destructor would be to release resources and close files.
Constructors are one example of *class methods*, sometimes also (unfortunately) known as *static methods*. Constructors are usually invoked through the `new` operation. Other class methods can be invoked through the class name (e.g., `Math.max`), with the address effectively computed at compile time.
The opposite of static or class methods are *instance methods*, which must be invoked through an object. Uses of instance methods are discussed in Section 13.2.3 on inheritance and their implementation in Section 13.2.9. In the remainder of Section 13.2, the reader should assume that all methods, other than constructors, are instance methods unless stated otherwise.

Figure 13.7   Creation of a Stack with Two Values

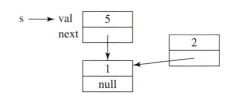

An important way to view an object-oriented program is that it is a collection of interacting objects that communicate via message passing. In effect, each object can be viewed as a separate machine having both data and operations on that data. In particular, several objects can be different instantiations of the same class; in that case, the operations are the same while the data is distinct. In our stack example the program could declare several objects of type `MyStack`, each with its own collection of data.

Objects communicate by passing messages among themselves. At most, one machine (object) can be executing at a time. When a machine passes a message to another machine, it invokes a particular method (function) of the receiving machine, passes the parameters (message contents) appropriate to the method, and then waits until the receiving machine returns a response (return value).

The set of behaviors that allows a program to create any number of instances of an abstract data type is often characterized as an *object-based language*. Even this is a new way of thinking about programming, since data is no longer passively acted upon by functions, but it becomes active.

Classes play two important and complementary roles in object-based languages. First, they determine the type of an object, so that they determine what messages (method calls) are legal and precisely which method is being called. Second, they permit full type checking. In a statically typed language like Java, these checks are performed at compile time, while in a dynamically typed language like Smalltalk, the checks are performed at run time.

13.2.2 Visibility and Information Hiding

Information hiding is made explicit by requiring that every method and instance variable in a class have a particular level of visibility—`public`, `protected`, or `private`—with regard to its subclasses and client classes.

A `public` variable or method is visible to any client and subclass of the class. The public methods of a class define the interface of the class to the outside world. Most methods of a class are public.

A `protected` variable or method is visible only to a subclass of the class.[4] This provides subclasses with direct access to the class's protected instance variables and methods. We shall illustrate the utility of this level of access when we discuss *inheritance* in Section 13.2.3.

A `private` variable or method is visible to the current class, but not to its subclasses or its clients. Following good software design practice, it is common to make instance variables private and allow subclass access only through the use of public or protected methods. This minimizes the changes that would need to be made if the concrete representation of the abstract data type were to change.

To illustrate these ideas more concretely, a reimplementation of class `MyStack` (Figure 13.7) with visibility modifiers added is presented in Figure 13.8. In the class `MyStack`, the instance variable `theStack` is private, and thus accessible only within the class itself. The constructor and methods are public, accessible to both subclasses and clients.

---

4. In an unfortunate design choice, Java makes protected objects and methods accessible to every class defined within the same package. By default, this choice breaks encapsulation, since any class can be declared as part of a package. For a more complete discussion of this issue, see [Niemeyer and Knudsen, 2002, Ch. 6].

```
public class MyStack {
    protected class Node {
        public Object  val;
        public Node next;
        public Node(Object v, Node n) {
            val = v; next = n;
        }
    }
    private Node theStack;

    public MyStack( ) { theStack = null; }

    public boolean empty( ) { return theStack == null; }

    public Object top( ) { return theStack.val; }

    public Object pop( ) {
        Object result = theStack.val;
        theStack = theStack.next;
        return result;
    }

    public void push(Object v) {
        theStack = new Node(v, theStack);
    }
}
```

| **Figure 13.8**   A Stack Class with Visibility Modifiers

The embedded or inner class Node is protected, which means it is accessible to subclasses but not to clients. But its instance variables and constructor are public. If they are to be accessible to subclasses, they cannot be either protected or private.

13.2.3 Inheritance

The object-oriented paradigm supports code reuse through *inheritance.* Classes exist in an object-oriented language in a class hierarchy. A class can be declared as a *subclass* of another class, which is called the *parent class* or *superclass.* Within this hierarchy, each subclass is able to inherit variables and methods from its parent simply by virtue of the fact that it is a subclass.

In object-oriented design, the relationship between a subclass and a superclass is established largely by whether a so-called *is-a* relationship exists between them. For instance, a stack *is-a* certain kind of list, and so is a queue, a deque, and a priority queue. Moreover, a priority queue *is-a* kind of queue.

A common mistake made by object-oriented beginners is to confuse the *is-a* relationship with the *has-a* relationship. The latter does not identify a subclass-superclass relationship; rather it identifies a class as a client of another class, usually termed *aggregation.*

| **Figure 13.9** **A Simple Class Hierarchy**

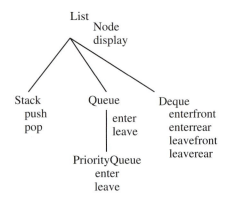

Definition: A class C_1 is an aggregation of a class C_2 if C_1 contains objects of type C_2.

For example, a program that declares a variable of class Stack is a client, not a subclass, of class Stack.

Thus, we expect that an object-oriented design might implement these various classes in a hierarchy like the one shown in Figure 13.9.

Inheritance comes in two varieties: *single inheritance* and *multiple inheritance*. These are distinguished from each other by whether or not a class may have just one or more than one parent class, respectively. C++, Python, and Eiffel support multiple inheritance, while Java and Smalltalk support only single inheritance.

In single inheritance, the class hierarchy forms a tree rooted in the most general class, for example, *Object*. A class D is a subclass of another class C when it extends or specializes the meaning of class C by adding new instance variables or methods, or by modifying the definitions of C's public and protected methods. A Java class definition uses the extends keyword to identify its superclass; if this keyword is omitted, the class is implicitly a subclass of the most general class *Object*.

Definition: Assume a simple subclass D extends a class C; subclass D is said to *inherit* all C's instance variables and methods, including constructors and destructors.

Of course, if some of these inherited variables or methods are declared private, direct reference by subclass D would not be possible. However, access to private objects and methods may be possible through protected methods.

For example, assume class C had instance variables i and j and subclass D had an instance variable k. A client object y of class D creates an object with the instance variables shown in Figure 13.10. This is true independent of the visibility of i and j, so long as the variables are not declared static (or class variables).

| **Figure 13.10** **Initialization of an Object with Inherited Features**

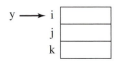

For a more concrete example, consider the partial class definitions for List, Stack, Queue, Deque, and PriorityQueue given in Figure 13.11. This hierarchy positions the definition of inner class Node so that it can be utilized by all of the classes shown in Figure 13.9. That is, all of the subclasses of class List inherit class Node and its features.

Note that the only features of these classes that clients can see and utilize are the public methods pop, push, enter, leave, and so forth. Note also in this example that enter and leave are redefined in the PriorityQueue class, since their semantics is different than the Queue class. That is, an extra parameter is needed for the enter method, and the choice of which node to select on a leave is different for a PriorityQueue than for a simple Queue. Finally, note that the Queue and PriorityQueue classes require the variables front and rear, which PriorityQueue can inherit from the class Queue. Stack does not require these variables; instead, its local variable theStack is defined and used privately by its methods. Each subclass therefore has a different configuration of public methods and instance variables, identifying both the unique and the overlapping ways in which it accesses the elements in the basic List data structure. *This is the essence of the idea of code reuse via inheritance in object-oriented programming.*

In passing, it is worthwhile to point out that Java's built-in Stack class is a subclass of its Vector class. Thereby, not only can the Stack class call the usual push and pop methods, but also it can call methods like insertElementAt and elementAt, which are publicly available and inherited from the parent class Vector. These latter methods allow insertion and retrieval of objects at an arbitrary point in the stack. Because such arbitrary insertion and deletion of elements is not "stack-like" behavior, Java's Stack class has been criticized for violating the *is-a* relationship. Instead, Java's Stack class should have used *aggregation*, in which the stack has an instance variable of type Vector.

While we are criticizing class hierarchies, the one presented in Figure 13.11 uses inheritance where it should use *aggregation*, that is, declare an instance variable of a general list implementation such as ArrayList or LinkedList. In such a case virtually all the methods of each class can be implemented in a single statement; for example:

```
public class LinkedStack( ) {
    private LinkedList stack = new LinkedList( );
    public void push(Object val) { stack.addFirst(val); }
    public Object pop( ) { return stack.removeFirst( ); }
    ...
}
```

It should not be inferred from this discussion that aggregation is to be preferred over inheritance. Each has its place. A good programmer recognizes which is appropriate in a given context.

13.2.4 Multiple Inheritance

In contrast to single inheritance languages, some object-oriented languages support *multiple inheritance* which allows a class to be a subclass of one *or more* superclasses.

Under multiple inheritance, a class may inherit instance variables and methods from several distinct classes. There are many practical situations in which this is a useful modeling tool. Consider, for instance, the hierarchy in Figure 13.12. There, we see

```
public class List extends Object {
    protected class Node {
        public Object val;
        public int priority;
        public Node prev, next;
        public Node (Object v, Node p) {
            val = v; prev = p; next = null; priority = 0; }
        public Node (Object v, Node p, Node n ) {
            val = v; prev = p; next = n; priority = 0; }
        public Node (Object v, int pr, Node p, Node n) {
            val = v; priority = pr; prev = p; next = n; }
    }
}
public class Stack extends List {
    private Node theStack;
    public MyStack( ) { theStack = null; }
    public Object pop( ) {
        Object result = theStack.val;
        theStack = theStack.next;
        return result;
    }
    public void push(Object v) {
        theStack = new Node(v, theStack);
    }
    ...
}
public class Queue extends List {
    protected Node front = null, rear = null ;
    public void enter(Object v) { ... }
    public Object leave( ) { ... }
    ...
}
public class PriorityQueue extends Queue {
    public void enter(Object v, int pr) { ... }
    public Object leave( ) { ... }
    ...
}
public class Deque extends List {
    public void enterfront(Object v) { ... }
    public void enterrear(Object v) { ... }
    public Object leavefront( ) { ... }
    public Object leaverear( ) { ... }
    ...
}
```

| **Figure 13.11** **Partial Java Implementation of the Hierarchy in Figure 13.9**

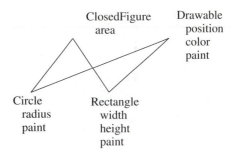

**Figure 13.12
An Example
of Multiple
Inheritance**

ClosedFigure
area

Drawable
position
color
paint

Circle
radius
paint

Rectangle
width
height
paint

the modeling of circles and rectangles as particular types of closed figures. Simultaneously, if we add features from the class `Drawable`, circles and rectangles will gain features (position and color) that allow them to be drawn on a graphics screen. Thus, for instance, a `Circle` inherits the features area, position, color, and paint from two different superclasses simultaneously.

Multiple inheritance has advantages and disadvantages. As this simple example shows, it facilitates code reuse by allowing a subclass to inherit features from several parent classes.

One disadvantage of multiple inheritance is that its semantics becomes very complicated in certain circumstances. For example, if a class E has superclasses B and C, and a method M is defined differently in B and C, which implementation of M should be inherited by E: the one in B, the one in C, or both?

Moreover, suppose method M is virtual. Can class E override B's version of method M but not C's version? Can class E override both versions of method M? If so, how are calls to the two versions distinguished?

While it is clear that these issues are resolvable, doing so complicates the semantics of a language with multiple inheritance. It also complicates the implementation of such a language. A final complication is that the experience base of designing class hierarchies with multiple inheritance is not as extensive as the experience base for single inheritance. For example, the book *Design Patterns* [Gamma *et al.*, 1995] mentions multiple inheritance in conjunction with only two of its many patterns.

At this point, we have summarized all of the essential features of an object-oriented language.

Definition: A language is *object-oriented* if it supports an encapsulation mechanism with information hiding for defining abstract data types, virtual methods, and inheritance.

Most of the remaining subsections of this section discuss useful additions to the object model, particularly for statically typed languages.

13.2.5 Polymorphism

According to the dictionary, the term *polymorphic* means "having many forms."

Definition: In object-oriented languages *polymorphism* refers to the late binding of a call to one of several different implementations of a method in an inheritance hierarchy.

Such methods must be instance methods. As we shall see in Chapter 14, this use of the term *polymorphism* is distinct from its use in functional programming. See also the discussion in Sections 4.8.

As an example, suppose we have an object `obj` of a declared (or apparent) type `T` whose actual type may vary at run time. Consider the following method call:

```
obj.m();
```

The type `T` of `obj` guarantees that all subtypes of `T` implement an appropriate method `m`; a statically typed language verifies this at compile time. The actual instance of the method `m` that is called will vary depending on the *actual* type of the object `obj` that occurs at run time. Thus, method `m` is polymorphic.

For example, consider the class hierarchy shown in Figure 13.13, along with the Java declaration:

```
Expression e;
```

During the course of analyzing a Clite program, the parser may assign to `e` a value in one of several different subclasses: `Variable`, `Binary`, `Unary`, and so on. Eventually, `e` must be displayed, using the call:

```
e.display( );
```

One of several different implementations of `display`, corresponding to the actual subclass of `Expression` to which the value of `e` belongs, determines the action responding to this call. The instance method `display` in this case is polymorphic.

For another example, suppose we have an application that implements a drawing program or an algorithm animation system. In such a program, different kinds of graphical objects (circles, rectangles, etc.) must be capable of being drawn in a window. Assume each graphical object of class `Drawable` has a `paint` method (following the Java AWT convention). Somewhere the system keeps a list (`myList`) of these objects and periodically asks every object to redraw itself:

```
for (Drawable obj : myList)
    obj.paint();
```

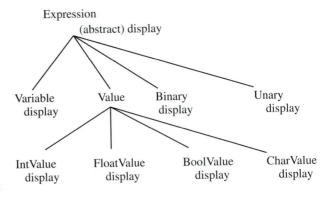

**Figure 13.13
Implementation
of Clite Expression as
an Abstract Class**

When this code is executed, each graphical object paints itself according to its own logic; squares are drawn differently from circles, for example. So the actual `paint` method being called varies according to the actual (dynamic) type of the graphical object being drawn. Yet, abstractly, each one is merely asked to paint itself. *This is the essence of polymorphism in object-oriented programming.*

To be truly polymorphic, the various instances of the `paint` method must uphold the principle of *substitutability* [Liskov and Guttag, 2001]. That is, each instance must perform the same abstract function, with only the code being particularized for the graphical object being painted.

> **Definition**: A subclass method is *substitutable* for a parent class method if the subclass's method performs the same general function.

Thus, for each different kind of graphical object, the logical behavior of the paint function must be transparent to the caller. Without the principle of substitutability, the code given above would not work.

In Java, for example, the declared type of object that is involved in the polymorphic method call can be either a concrete type, an abstract type, or an interface type. The compiler verifies at compile time that a method with the appropriate signature exists for the specified object, using its declared type and the class hierarchy within which its type exists. However, a compiler cannot ensure that the abstract function performed is logically equivalent; that is, it cannot verify that the methods as implemented uphold the principle of substitutability. That is the responsibility of the programmer.

13.2.6 Templates

A convenient feature of a statically typed object-oriented language is support for *templates*, also known as *generics*. As Java demonstrated prior to version 1.5, the absence of templates in an object-oriented language creates significant programming overhead in terms of the need for casting. Templates are well supported in Java (called generics in version 1.5), Ada (also called generics), and C++. The discussion below uses Java 1.5 to illustrate the basic ideas.

> **Definition**: A *template* defines a family of classes parameterized by one or more types.

Collection classes are commonly used to illustrate this concept, where a *collection class* is one which is used to store object values for efficient retrieval. Examples of collections include lists, stacks, queues, trees, and hash tables.

In Java prior to version 1.5, programmers had to explicitly monitor the class of each element stored in a collection, both at the time of its entry and at the time of its examination or removal. For example, let us expand on the `Drawable` graphics example of Section 13.2.5:

```
1 ArrayList myList = new ArrayList( );
2 ...
3 for (Iterator i = myList.iterator( ); i.hasNext( ); ) {
4     Drawable obj = (Drawable) i.next( );
5     obj.paint( );
6 }
```

The variable myList is intended to hold Drawable objects, that is, squares, circles, and the like. However, the type signatures of the various methods which add objects to an ArrayList allow any subclass of type Object, that is, any object at all. Should the programmer insert an object that is not Drawable or one of its subclasses, the cast in line 4 will fail and throw a run-time exception. The programmer must then find the point in the program where an object of the wrong type was inserted into myList.

In statically typed languages, templates can be used to identify the type of object stored in a collection, for example:

```
ArrayList<Drawable> myList = new arrayList<Drawable>( );
```

Now any attempt to add a non-Drawable object to myList generates a compile-time error. Explicit casting is no longer needed in retrieving a value from myList.

In both single and multiple inheritance languages that support templates, new parameterized classes can be written. Consider the following:

```
import java.util.ArrayList;
public class MyList<T> {
    private ArrayList<T> list;
    public MyList( ) { list = new ArrayList<T>( ); }
    public void add(T obj) { list.add(obj); }
    ...
}
```

The name T is arbitrary and merely refers to the type or class of object that each instance of MyList will hold. Note the use of the name T in method add.

13.2.7 Abstract Classes

Abstraction is a fundamental feature of object-oriented programming and design. This feature allows large systems to be specified at a very general level, long before the implementation of individual methods takes place.

Many object-oriented languages allow a class to be declared *abstract*, a condition that automatically occurs whenever one or more of its methods is abstract.

> **Definition**: An *abstract class* is one that is either declared to be abstract or has one or more abstract methods.

> **Definition**: An *abstract method* is a method that contains no code beyond its signature.

Any subclass of an abstract class that does not provide an implementation of an inherited abstract method is itself abstract. Because abstract classes have methods that cannot be executed, client programs cannot initialize an object that is a member an abstract class. This restriction ensures that a call will not be made to an abstract (unimplemented) method.

A class may be explicitly declared to be abstract even though it has no abstract methods. Such a case occurs when the class represents an abstract concept which unifies several concrete classes.

Our implementation of a Clite *Expression* of Figure 2.14, provides an example of an abstract class whose subclasses are *Binary*, *Unary*, *Variable*, and *Value*. Pictorially, this structure is summarized in Figure 13.13. Here, the presence of an abstract `display` method signature makes `Expression` itself an abstract class and requires all subclasses of `Expression` to implement a method with the same signature. This is appropriate for our `Expression` class, since each of its subclasses needs to display a different configuration of data. Note, however, that the `Value` subclass of `Expression` is also declared abstract. Even without the `display` method, both `Expression` and `Value` should remain abstract since each represents an abstraction of several concrete classes.

In this example, a client cannot create a concrete `Expression` object. Any attempt to do this would be identified at compile time as an error. The following skeleton Java code realizes the class structure in Figure 13.13.

```
abstract class Expression { ... }
    class Variable extends Expression { ... }
    abstract class Value extends Expression { ... }
        class IntValue extends Value { ... }
        class BoolValue extends Value { ... }
        class FloatValue extends Value { ... }
        class CharValue extends Value { ... }
    class Binary extends Expression { ... }
    class Unary extends Expression { ... }
```

13.2.8 Interfaces

In addition to abstract classes, Java also supports a related construct called an interface. Logically, an interface can be thought of as an extension of C's `typedef` facility.

> **Definition**: An *interface* encapsulates a collection of constants and abstract method signatures. An interface may not include either variables, constructors, or nonabstract methods.

Syntactically an interface declaration looks like an abstract class definition, except that the word `interface` replaces the word `class`. As an example, consider the definition of the Java `Map` interface and some of its principal methods:

```
public interface Map {
    public abstract boolean containsKey(Object key);
    public abstract boolean containsValue(Object value);
    public abstract boolean equals(Object o);
    public abstract Object get(Object key);
    public abstract Object remove(Object key);
    ...
}
```

The main difference between an interface and an abstract class is that *all* the methods in an interface must be abstract; only constants (`final` variables) may be concretely declared there. However, in an abstract class, objects can be declared and some methods may be fully implemented. Because it is not a class, an interface does not have a constructor, but an abstract class does.

Some like to think of an interface as an alternative to multiple inheritance. Strictly speaking, however, an interface is not quite the same since it doesn't provide a means of reusing code; that is, all of its methods must be abstract. An interface is similar to multiple inheritance in the sense that an interface is a type. A class that implements multiple interfaces appears to be many different types, one for each interface.

The Java class HashMap is a subclass of the abstract class AbstractMap and also draws features from three distinct interfaces. Thus, HashMap can be viewed as using multiple inheritance to obtain various method signatures from different sources. The methods entrySet and keySet are obtained from the superclass AbstractMap, while the methods containsKey and containsValue are obtained from the interface Map. A client of the class HashMap, therefore, has access to a combination of features drawn from four different classes. An object of class HashMap can be viewed as being any of the following types: AbstractMap, HashMap, Map, Cloneable, Serializable.

Thus, a common use of interfaces in Java is to simulate the effect of multiple inheritance while avoiding the pitfall of multiple inheritance mentioned above. That is, the interface ensures that any class that implements it must provide concrete definitions for *all* its methods; none are predefined. In other words, if both a superclass and an interface implemented by a class contain a method with the same signature, the class itself is thus obligated to (re)implement that method, thus avoiding the confusion that would arise under multiple inheritance.

A class is said to implement an interface, rather than extend it. To implement an interface, a concrete class must implement all the methods of an interface, in the same way as if it were making an abstract class concrete. Failure to implement all the methods of an interface makes the resulting class abstract.

A commonly implemented interface in Java is Comparable:

```
public interface Comparable {
    public abstract int compareTo(Object obj);
}
```

The compareTo returns a negative integer value if the receiver is less than obj, 0 if equal, and a positive value (≥ 1) if greater. Thus, a class Student that permits sorting by name might appear:

```
public class Student implements Comparable {
    private String lastName;
    private String firstName;
    ...
    public int compareTo(Object obj) {
        Student other = (Student) obj;
        int comp = lastName.compareTo(other.lastName);
        if (comp != 0)  return comp;
        return firstName.compareTo(other.firstName);
    }
}
```

In the above compareTo method, the parameter must be of type Object, as specified in the Comparable interface. However, a Student can only be compared to another Student, hence, the cast on the first line of the method. It is the client's responsibility to ensure that the cast does not fail.

An array of students (studentList) could then be easily sorted using:

```
java.util.Arrays.sort(studentList);
```

where the signature is: sort(Comparable[ ] obj). That is, the sort method does not care about the true type of objects being sorted, only that they implement the compareTo method.

Another example of the use of interfaces is given in the Eight Queens program in Section 13.4.2.

13.2.9 Virtual Method Table

The purpose of this section is to explain how the appropriate virtual method is called at run time. For this purpose, recall our example in Figure 13.11, where an object declared to be of class MyList may at run time be *any* subclass of MyList, such as MyStack or Queue. Consider the following:

```
MyList myList;
...
System.out.println(myList.toString( ));
```

At compile time, the run-time class of myList is unknown; it could be a MyList, a MyStack, or some other subclass of MyList. So the actual toString method invoked may be the one that is defined in the MyList class, or else it may be the one defined in one of its subclasses, depending on the run-time class of myList. This is distinctly different from statically typed imperative languages, where the actual function being invoked is determined at compile time.

Dynamic dispatching on a method-by-method basis can be implemented by a device called the *Virtual Method Table* (*VMT* for short). Abstractly, consider the following implementation. Each class has its own VMT, with each instance of the class having a reference (or pointer) to the VMT. A simple implementation of the VMT would be a hash table, using the method name (or signature, in the case of overloading) as the key and the run-time address of the method invoked as the value.

However, for statically typed languages, the VMT is kept as an array. The method being invoked is converted to an index into the VMT at compile time. Consider the following example:

```
class A {
    Obj a;
    void am1( ) { ... }
    void am2( ) { ... }
}
class B extends A {
    Obj b;
    void bm1( ) { ... }
    void bm2( ) { ... }
    void am2( ) { ... }
}
```

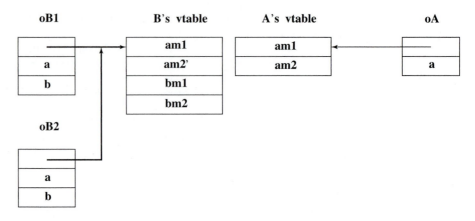

| **Figure 13.14** **VMT Implementation in Statically Typed Languages**

Class B is a subclass of A. Classes A and B both have one instance variable and two virtual methods. In addition, class B overrides method am2 in class A.

Figure 13.14 depicts the situation where the program has two B objects, oB1 and oB2, and one A object, oA1. Note that the entries of oB1 and oB2 of class B each contain their own unique copies of the nonstatic instance variables for both classes A and B; in addition, each object contains a reference to a shared virtual method table. This table contains an entry containing a reference for each virtual method, including those of the superclass (and so on, recursively). This occurs independent of the visibility of superclass methods. Recall that class B overrides inherited method am2; this is depicted in the diagram by adding a prime (') to the entry in B's vtable to indicate that it is distinct from the one in A's vtable. This example clearly indicates why a class needs a copy of its parent's vtable, rather than merely a reference.

As depicted in Figure 13.14, both methods am2 in class A and am2' (the overridden am2) in class B are stored at vtable[1]. Thus, given the code snippet:

```
A b = new B( );
...
b.am2( );
```

the compiler will correctly call B's am2, since the method invoked in this case is whatever method is stored at vtable[1] of object b.

The implementation depicted in Figure 13.14 works well for statically typed languages with single inheritance. Ellis and Stroustrup [1990] provide a similar implementation for languages with multiple inheritance.

Thus, the compiler maps the signature of each virtual method into an index into the VMT. The run-time cost of using an instance method (vs. a class method) is the run-time cost of using a pointer (to access the VMT) plus an array indexing operation (to access the method's address).

13.2.10 Run-Time Type Identification

Run-time type identification (RTTI) is the ability of the language to identify at run time the actual type or class of an object. Recall from Chapter 5 that all dynamically typed languages have this ability, whereas most statically typed imperative languages, such as C, lack this ability. At the machine level, recall that data is basically untyped (Section 5.1).

In Java, for example, given any object reference `obj`, we can determine its class via:

```
Class c = obj.getClass( );
```

where `getClass` is an inherited method from the `Object` class.[5]

One of the common uses of RTTI occurs when we must determine whether two objects are equal. Assume that we are writing such a method for class `MyObject`, which has subclasses. The prototypical code for an `equals` method in Java is:

```
1  public boolean equals(Object obj) {
2      if (obj == null) return false;
3      if (this == obj) return true;
4      if (getClass( ) != obj.getClass( ))  return false;
5      MyObject other = (MyObject) obj;
6      // test contents of this vs. other
7      ...
8  }
```

Line 3 is an optimization that says if the receiver of the message and the parameter refer to the same object, then they must be equal. Line 4 ensures that the receiver of the message and the parameter are objects of the same class. Assuming the parameter is a subtype of `MyObject`, then line 4 ensures that:

- The cast on line 5 does not throw an exception, and
- That if `x.equals(y)` then `y.equals(x)`.

13.2.11 Reflection

Reflection is a mechanism whereby a program can discover and use the methods of any of its objects and classes. Reflection is essential for programming tools that allow plug-ins (such as Eclipse—**www.eclipse.org**) and for JavaBeans components.

We saw in the last section that RTTI provides the ability to identify at run time the class of an object. In Java the `Class` class provides the following information about an object:

- The superclass or parent class.
- The names and types of all fields.
- The names and signatures of all methods.
- The signatures of all constructors.
- The interfaces that the class implements.

---

5. This discussion assumes that no superclass has overridden the `getClass` method.

```
Class class = obj.getClass( );
Constructor[ ] cons = class.getDeclaredConstructors( );
for (int i=0; i < cons.length; i++) {
    System.out.print(class.getName( ) + "(" );
    Class[ ] param = cons[i].getParameterTypes( );
    for (int j=0; j < param.length; j++) {
        if (j > 0) System.out.print(", ");
        System.out.print(param[j].getName( );
    }
    System.out.println( ")" );
}
```

| **Figure 13.15**   **Reflection on Constructors**

For example, the code given in Figure 13.15 writes to the console the type signatures of all constructors of an arbitrary object `obj`.

Similarly, we can obtain the names and method signatures for the methods of an arbitrary class as objects of class `Method`. One of the methods of class `Method` is the `invoke` method, which allows us to call the method:

```
Method printString = PrintStream.class.getDeclaredMethod(
    "print", new Class[ ] {String.class});
printString(System.out, new Object[ ] { "Tucker and Noonan"});
// same as: System.out.print("Tucker and Noonan");
```

Note that the first statement gets the method with the desired signature. The second statement invokes the method, where the first argument is an object which has the desired method and the second argument is the parameters, passed as an array of `Object`s.

The JUnit testing framework (**www.junit.org**) dynamically finds all the methods in a test case whose name starts with `test`. All such methods are automatically executed and their results displayed (success or failure) without the tester having to explicitly call any of them. The JUnit implementation relies on reflection.

In Sections 13.3–13.5, we introduce three object-oriented languages (Smalltalk, Java, and Python, respectively), briefly discuss the characteristics of each language, and then look at some interesting examples.

13.3 SMALLTALK

Smalltalk [Goldberg and Robson, 1989] was the original object-oriented language, having been developed at Xerox PARC (Palo Alto Research Center) during the 1970s. The Smalltalk system was hosted on the Xerox Alto, and consisted of an operating system, an integrated development environment, a class browser, and so on, together with support for a mouse-based GUI. Most of the Smalltalk system was written in Smalltalk itself.

Steve Jobs, after visiting Xerox PARC, used the Smalltalk-based GUI as the basis for the design of the GUIs for the Apple Lisa and Macintosh computers. Similarly, Microsoft licensed this same interface from Xerox as the basis for Windows.

As a language, Smalltalk was based on the simulation language Simula 67. Smalltalk suffered a decline in interest in the 1990s due to the development of other object-oriented languages, like Objective-C (used in the development of the Next computer), Eiffel, and Java. However, the development of Squeak [Guzdial and Rose, 2000], an open source implementation, seems to have rekindled an interest in Smalltalk. Squeak is available for a wide variety of platforms. GNU Smalltalk (**www.gnu.org**) is also usable.

13.3.1 General Characteristics

Smalltalk is a very simple language, both syntactically and semantically. The power of Smalltalk comes from its class libraries, most of which are written in Smalltalk itself. Interestingly, even control structures are objects in Smalltalk.

Excluding the lexical part, the grammar for Smalltalk consists of 21 productions (three pages). Compare this to the figures given in Table 2.2. For example, the rules for the evaluation of the syntax of object expressions are as follows [Guzdial and Rose, 2000]:

- The value of every variable is an object; every object is an instance of some class.
- A method is triggered by sending a message to an object. The object responds by evaluating the method of the same name, if it has one. Otherwise the message is sent to the parent object. The process continues until the method is found; otherwise an error is raised.
- In order of precedence, highest to lowest, there are the following types of messages:
  — Unary messages, such as `negated` as in:
    `x negated.`
  — Binary messages, such as + as in:
    `x + y.`
  — Keyword messages, such as `go:` as in:
    `Turtle go: length.`
  In the absence of parentheses, code is evaluated from left to right. Parentheses may be used freely to improve readability.

Here are some examples:

- `x + y * z squared` is interpreted as:
  `(x + y) * (z squared)`,
  since the unary message `squared` has the highest precedence, and then the binary messages/operators are executed from left to right, that is, first +, then *.
- `a max: b - c` is interpreted as:
  `a max: (b - c)`,
  or the maximum of the quantities `a` and `b - c`.
- `anArray at: i put: (anArray at: i + 1)`
  sends the message `at:put:` to the object `anArray` with the values
  `(i, anArray at: (i + 1))`.

Assuming `anArray` is an array, it is interpreted as the assignment `anArray[i] = anArray[i + 1]`.

By default, Smalltalk uses infinite precision fractional arithmetic, so the expression `1/3 + 2/6 + 3/9` evaluates to 1. This eliminates a number of problems ordinarily introduced by computer arithmetic:

- The differences between integer and floating point arithmetic.
- The concerns about whether numbers such as 0.2 have an exact representation in binary (see Section 5.3).
- Overflow problems, such as computing the factorial of 100.

Smalltalk is a dynamically typed language, so virtual method dispatching requires some form of dictionary lookup based on the method name; an efficient such implementation would be a hash table. However, any form of dictionary lookup is considerably more expensive at run time than the array implementation given in Section 13.2.9. Unlike statically typed languages, calls to non-existing virtual methods cannot be detected until they are made. As a dynamically typed language, Smalltalk supports both run-time type identification and reflection; for example, `1 class is Integer`.

There is some support for abstract methods, which are implemented by throwing an exception. However, one can usually still create an object as an instance of an abstract class, and possibly use it without throwing an error.

An assignment statement is written, for example, as:

```
a := b.
```

but the assignment operator is usually displayed as a left arrow ←. Smalltalk uses reference semantics for all objects. Smalltalk requires that variables be declared before they are used; temporary variables are declared using:

```
| a b |
```

which declares temporary variables `a` and `b`. Since Smalltalk is a dynamically typed language, no types are declared with `a` and `b`.

What we normally think of as control structures are block objects in Smalltalk. A block is denoted by square brackets and encloses unevaluated code. Blocks can have arguments. An if statement to compute the maximum of `a` and `b` would be written:

```
(a > b) ifTrue: [ max := a ]
        ifFalse: [ max := b ].
```

Because of the precedence rules, the parentheses surrounding the condition are unnecessary. The `ifTrue:` and `ifFalse:` arguments must both be blocks.

This code sequence is evaluated as follows. First, the expression `a<b` is evaluated resulting in a Boolean value, true or false. This value is sent the message `ifTrue:ifFalse:`, with the two unevaluated blocks as arguments. For example, if the value true is sent the message, then it forces the first block to evaluate itself.[6]

---

6. Interestingly, the value true is an object of the `True` class, so the receiver of the message does not need to test whether the condition is true or false.

Similarly, blocks are used in the construction of loops. Consider the following C fragment to compute the sum of an array of elements:

```
sum = 0;
for (i = 0; i < n; i++)
    sum += a[i];
```

The Smalltalk equivalent[7] is:

```
sum := 0.
1 to: n do: [ :i | sum := sum + (a at: i) ].
```

However, the following is also possible:

```
sum := 0.
a do: [ :x | sum := sum + x ].
```

In each case, the block has a parameter (i and x respectively), which is used in the subsequent computation. The do: method over the array is analogous to a Java iterator; it is not built-in but written entirely in Smalltalk. In this case, the array a responds to the do: message by iterating over itself, executing the block once for each value, effectively a at: i, in the array.

To investigate blocks further, consider the following rewrite of the summation example using a while loop:

```
sum := 0.
i := 1.
[ i <= n ] whileTrue: [ sum := sum + (a at: i).
        i := i + 1].
```

The code looks similar to C except for the syntactic differences. But, unlike the earlier if statement, this time the condition is written as a block. If the condition were not written as a block, the condition would only be evaluated once, not once per iteration. Again, blocks are built-in to Smalltalk, while control structures such as the while loop above is not. We examine a possible implementation of the method whileTrue for a block after a brief digression.

First, we examine the nature of Booleans in Smalltalk. Interestingly, the class Boolean has two subclasses, True and False. The values true and false are objects of their respective classes. Consider the implementation below of the method ifTrue:ifFalse: for class True which implements an if-else construct:

```
ifTrue: trueBlock ifFalse: falseBlock
    ^ trueBlock value
```

The first line is the method header which takes two arguments, the unevaluated true and false blocks, trueBlock and falseBlock respectively. Since this is a class True method,

---

7. Smalltalk arrays begin at index one.

it should execute the `trueBlock`. This is accomplished in the second line by sending the `trueBlock` the `value` message, which causes the block to execute itself one time. The method then returns, indicated by the caret (^), which is displayed as an up arrow (↑), whatever the `trueBlock` returns.

A use of the `ifTrue:ifFalse:` method would occur in computing the `max:` method:

```
max: b
    self > b ifTrue: [ ^self ] ifFalse: [ ^b ]
```

Note that even though `self` and `b` have already been evaluated, the `ifTrue:ifFalse:` method must be passed blocks, indicated by the brackets, not numbers. The reserved word `self` is the same as `this` in C++ or Java.

Note that what we show syntactically as the overall structure of a class or method definition is somewhat arbitrary, since defining a class is accomplished through the Smalltalk class browser. The form used here is based on the display (printed) version of class definitions of one of the Smalltalk systems we have used.

Other class `True` methods include:

```
ifTrue: aBlock
    ^ aBlock value

ifFalse: aBlock
    ^ nil

ifFalse: falseBlock ifTrue: trueBlock
    ^ trueBlock value
```

where the reserved word `nil` is analogous to the reserved word `null` in Java. Note that the `ifFalse:` method does nothing except return an empty reference (`nil`).

A block's `whileTrue:` method would look as follows:

```
whileTrue: aBlock
    (self value) ifFalse: [ ^ nil ].
    aBlock value.
    ^ self whileTrue: aBlock
```

The first line of the method body has the condition block evaluate itself, and if false, return. Otherwise, it executes the block body once and then calls itself recursively.

13.3.2 Example: Polynomials

In this section we develop a class to represent polynomials; for example:

$$3x^2 + 5x - 7$$

For this application, we will represent a polynomial by an array of its coefficients starting with the coefficient of x^0 and proceeding up to the highest power with a nonzero coefficient. So the above polynomial would be represented by the array #(-7 5 3).

The `Polynomial` class (given in Figure 13.16) is a subclass of `Magnitude` and has a single instance variable named `coefficient`. The methods for creating an instance of the

```
Magnitude subclass: #Polynomial
    instanceVariableNames: 'coefficient'
    classVariableNames:: ''
    poolDictionaries: ''

new
    "Unary class constructor: return 0*x^0"
    ^ self new: #( 0 )

new: array
    "Keyword class constructor"
    ^ (super new) init: array

init: array
    "Private: initialize coefficient instance variable"
    coefficient := array deepCopy

degree
    "Highest power with a non-zero coefficient"
    ^ coefficient size - 1

coefficient: power
    "Coefficient of given power"
    (power >= coefficient size) ifTrue: [ ^ 0 ].
    ^ coefficient at: power + 1

asArray
    ^ coefficient deepCopy

= aPoly
    ^ coefficient = aPoly asArray

!= aPoly
    ^ (self = aPoly) not

< aPoly
    "not defined"
    ^ self shouldNotImplement
```

| **Figure 13.16   Polynomial Class in Smalltalk**

class are: new and new:. The class method new creates the polynomial $0x^0$ using the new: method. The latter expects an array as its argument and uses that as its coefficient array.

In Figure 13.16, the first line of each method gives the method signature. The lines of what appear to be double-quoted strings are actually Smalltalk comments.

Consider the method coefficient:. If the argument (power) is too big, the actual coefficient is zero. Otherwise it returns the actual coefficient from the list (method at:), adjusting the index power to compensate for Smalltalk's use of one-based array indexing.

The asArray method is interesting in that it returns not the list of coefficients themselves, but a copy of the list. This prevents a client from changing the actual coefficients.

Note also that two polnomials p and q can be compared for equality using p = q. The method works by comparing the two lists of coefficients for equality. Note that there is no mathematical definition for p < q. The remaining method implementations are left as exercises.

13.3.3 Example: Complex Numbers

In this section we develop a complex number class based on the notion of complex numbers in mathematics of the form $a + b \cdot i$, where $i = \sqrt{-1}$. Do not worry if you do not remember anything about complex numbers; this example is more about writing a class than about mathematics.

Our first observation is that this class needs two instance variables, usually referred to as the real and imaginary parts, corresponding to a and b above respectively. We shall call these instance variables `realpart` and `imagpart`; all instance variables in Smalltalk are private.

Class `Complex` is a subclass of the `Number` class. The next design decision is to make objects of the class immutable. Objects of an *immutable class* cannot be changed once they have been created. That is, once we have created a complex number, we cannot change it, only create new ones. Adding two numbers (e.g., $x + y$), even if using a keyword message should not change x, but rather create a new complex number.

The first task is to write the class methods (given in Figure 13.17). The usual `new` method is here but effectively disabled, by calling `Object`'s `error:` method. Thus, uninitialized complex numbers are not allowed. The second class method (or constructor) assumes it is passed a complex number and makes a copy of it. The third class method uses `Number`'s `new` method to create a complex number and then initializes it using `Complex`'s `setReal:setImaginary:` instance method. Thus, given two numbers a and b, the way to create $a + b \cdot i$ is:

```
Complex real: a imaginary: b
```

The method `setReal:setImaginary:` should be declared private, because it allows us to change the value of a complex number. However, all methods are public; the comment that says it is private does not make it so. As is typical of an initialization method, the first two statements are assignments to the instance variables. It is expected, but not enforced, that this method is only called from the class method `real:imaginary:`.

Figure 13.17 outlines a few of the methods needed to fully implement complex numbers. The accessor methods `real` and `imaginary` return the real and imaginary parts of the complex number.

Note that addition, subtraction, and so on, can be implemented using the ordinary infix operators. Addition of two complex numbers is defined as:

$$(a + b \cdot i) + (c + d \cdot i) = (a + b) + (c + d) \cdot i$$

The binary method + implements this definition by constructing a new complex number. Note that much like computer hardware, subtraction of two complex numbers a - b is implemented as `a + b negated`, where `negated` is the unary minus operator.

For the relations, equality of two complex numbers is defined:

$$(a + b \cdot i) = (c + d \cdot i) \equiv (a = b) \text{ and } (c = d)$$

```
Object subclass: #Complex
    instanceVariableNames: 'realpart imagpart'
    classVariableNames:: ''
    poolDictionaries: ''

new
    "Unary constructor: invalid"
    ^ self error: 'use real:imaginary:'
new: aComplex
    "Class constructor: aComplex"
    ^ (super new) copy: aComplex
real: r imaginary: i
    "Class constructor"
    ^ (super new) setReal: r setImaginary: i

setReal: r setImaginary: i
    "Private instance method to initialize self"
    realpart := r.
    imagpart := i.
    ^ self
real
    "Return real part"
    ^ realpart
imaginary
    "Return imaginary part"
    ^ imagpart
+ val
    "Return new complex number: self + val"
    ^ Complex real: realpart + val real
        imaginary: imagpart + val imaginary
- val
    "Return new complex number: self - val"
    ^ self + val negated
negated
    "Return new complex number: - self"
    ^ Complex real: realpart negated imaginary: imagpart negated
= val
    "Return: self = val"
    ^ (realpart = val real) & (imagpart = val imaginary)
< val
    "Not mathematically defined"
    ^ self shouldNotImplement
```

| **Figure 13.17   Complex Number Methods**

```
Object subclass: #Account
    instanceVariableNames: 'bal'
    classVariableNames:: ''
    poolDictionaries: ''
new
    "Constructor"
    ^ (super new) init
init
    "Private instance method"
    bal := 0

balance
    ^ bal

deposit: amount
    (amount < 0) ifTrue: [ ^ self error: 'Invalid amount' ].
    bal := bal + amount

withdraw: amount
    (amount < 0) ifTrue: [ ^ self error: 'Invalid amount' ].
    (bal < amount) ifTrue: [ ^ self error: 'Insufficient funds' ].
    bal := bal - amount
```

| Figure 13.18   **An Account Class**

That is, two complex numbers are equal if their real and imaginary parts are equal. The relationals <, <=, >, >= are not defined for complex numbers. The relational != is left as an exercise.

13.3.4 Example: Bank Account

In this section we develop a simple bank account class, which has `Object` as its parent class. A bank account has a single instance variable `balance` which holds the amount of money in the account. The balance may never become negative.

Figure 13.18 shows the account class. The method `init` sets the balance to zero, while the `balance` method returns the current account balance.

The keyword methods `deposit:` and `withdraw:` are used respectively to put money into and take money out of the account. Both check to make sure that the amount is not negative. Method `withdraw:` further checks to ensure the account is not overdrawn.

13.4   JAVA

Java 1.0 was released in 1995, with Java 1.5 (now denoted Java 5) released in 2004. The language has been remarkably stable, with most of the changes occurring in Java 1.1. The same cannot be said about the changes in the Java Standard Edition (SE) class libraries, which have grown steadily with each release.

Java is a mixed language containing both primitive data types, such as `int`, and objects. Java uses copy semantics for primitive data types and reference semantics for objects (see Section 7.4). All methods must exist as part of some class and are virtual by default. Java (and its cousin, C#) benefit by not trying to remain totally backward compatible with C, unlike C++. Java uses automatic garbage collection, which greatly simplifies the task of memory management for the programmer.

Java is a statically typed, single inheritance object-oriented language. As we saw in Section 13.2, Java has direct support for:

- Inner classes.
- Public, protected, and private visibility of both variables and methods.
- Abstract classes.
- Interfaces.
- Templates.
- Run-time type identification.
- Reflection.

Since Java was used as the example language of Section 13.2, we shall not repeat that discussion here.

At this point in its life, Java has to be judged a success. Two of its major application areas are computer science education and server-side web programming.

Two examples are presented in Sections 13.4.1 and 13.4.2 below. The first example draws upon the abstract syntax discussion of Clite, providing a good illustration of encapsulation and inheritance. The second example shows the application of a general backtracker class to an object-oriented solution of the eight queens problem. Both of these examples recur in the next two chapters. Other Java examples can be found in Chapter 16 on event-driven programming.

13.4.1 Example: Symbolic Differentiation

This example implements symbolic differentiation of simple calculus formulae. Some familiar rules for symbolic differentiation are given in Figure 13.19.

$$\frac{d}{dx}(c) = 0 \qquad\qquad\qquad c \text{ is a constant}$$

$$\frac{d}{dx}(x) = 1$$

$$\frac{d}{dx}(u + v) = \frac{du}{dx} + \frac{dv}{dx} \qquad\qquad u \text{ and } v \text{ are functions of } x$$

$$\frac{d}{dx}(u - v) = \frac{du}{dx} - \frac{dv}{dx}$$

$$\frac{d}{dx}(uv) = u\frac{dv}{dx} + v\frac{du}{dx}$$

$$\frac{d}{dx}\left(\frac{u}{v}\right) = \left(v\frac{du}{dx} - u\frac{dv}{dx}\right)\Big/ v^2$$

| **Figure 13.19**   **Symbolic Differentiation Rules**

$$Expression = Variable \mid Value \mid Binary$$
$$Variable = String \text{ id}$$
$$Value = \text{int } value$$
$$Binary = Add \mid Subtract \mid Multiply \mid Divide$$
$$Add = Expression \text{ left, right}$$
$$Subtract = Expression \text{ left, right}$$
$$Multiply = Expression \text{ left, right}$$
$$Divide = Expression \text{ left, right}$$

| Figure 13.20   Abstract Syntax of *Expressions*

For example, differentiating the function $2 \cdot x + 1$ with respect to x using these rules gives:

$$\frac{d(2 \cdot x + 1)}{dx} = \frac{d}{dx}(2 \cdot x) + \frac{d}{dx}1$$
$$= 2 \cdot \frac{d}{dx}x + x \cdot \frac{d}{dx}2 + \frac{d}{dx}1$$
$$= 2 \cdot 1 + x \cdot 0 + 0$$

which would ordinarily simplify to 2.

In Java it is convenient to represent expressions using abstract syntax. An example is the abstract syntax of a Clite program discussed in Section 2.5.3. Here the needed abstract syntax, summarized in Figure 13.20, is adapted from the abstract syntax of a Clite expression. The primary differences from Clite are that there is only a single type of value, and the classes Add, Subtract, and so on, are subclasses of a Binary expression.

As before, each class in the abstract syntax becomes a class in Java, with the classes Expression and Binary declared abstract. Each concrete class has three methods:

- A constructor.
- A diff method which implements the appropriate rule.
- A toString method for printing both the original expression and the result.

Our implementation is presented in Figure 13.21, with the toString methods omitted. Of the four arithmetic operators, only the Add class is presented; the other three are left as exercises.

The first rule in Figure 13.19 says that the differentiation of a constant with respect to x is 0. This is implemented by the diff method of class Value, which returns a zero.

Similarly, the addition rule of Figure 13.19 (rule three) says to differentiate an addition, you first differentiate each term, and then add the results. The diff method of class Add does precisely that, constructing a new expression (abstract syntax tree) to hold the result.

An application of the diff method to the expression $2 \cdot x + 1$ gives:
`(((2) * (1)) + ((x)*(0))) + (0))`. A better formatter, together with an algebraic simplifier, are left as exercises.

```java
public abstract class Expression {
    public abstract Expression diff(Variable x);
}
class Value extends Expression {
    private int value;
    public Value(int v) { value = v; }
    public Expression diff(Variable x) {
        return new Value(0);
    }
}
class Variable extends Expression {
    private String id;
    static final private Value zero = new Value(0);
    static final private Value one = new Value(1);
    public Variable(String s) { id = s; }
    public Expression diff(Variable x) {
        return id.equals(x.id) ? one : zero;
    }
}
abstract class Binary extends Expression {
    protected Expression left, right;
    protected Binary(Expression u, Expression v) {
        left = u; right = v;
    }
}
class Add extends Binary {
    public Add(Expression u, Expression v) {
        super(u, v);
    }
    public Expression diff(Variable x) {
        return new Add(left.diff(x), right.diff(x));
    }
}
```

| **Figure 13.21** **Symbolic Differentiation in Java**

13.4.2 Example: Backtracking

In this example we develop an object-oriented version [Noonan, 2000] of Wirth's *backtracking algorithm* [Wirth, 1976, p. 137]:

> A particularly intriguing programming endeavor is the subject of "general problem solving." The task is to determine algorithms for finding solutions to specific problems not by following a fixed rule of computation, but by trial and error. The common pattern is to decompose the trial-and-error process into partial tasks. Often

these tasks are most naturally expressed in recursive terms and consist of the exploration of a finite number of subtasks.

As we shall see in Chapter 15, backtracking is the basis for logic programming. It is also used in a wide variety of graph algorithms and artificial intelligence applications.

The general solution that Wirth presents is a recursive procedure that iterates through a series of trial moves. Each move is tested to see if it satisfies an appropriate *validity* criterion. If it does, the move is recorded, and if the problem is not yet solved, the procedure calls itself recursively to try the next level; if the recursive call fails, then the current move is undone and an alternative move is tried. The process of trying moves continues until either a completely successful solution is found or all the moves at the current level are unsuccessfully tried.

An object-oriented version of this algorithm is presented in Figure 13.22. Abstractly, the method `attempt` implements the general algorithm. The formal parameter `level` is used to keep track of the recursive level. The local variable `successful` is used to keep track of whether a solution to the entire problem has been solved; thus, at each recursive level `successful` is initially set to false. Within a level, moves are successively generated, tested, and, if valid, recorded; only then is the next level tried recursively. Moves that do not result in a solution to the general problem are undone. The process terminates when either a solution is found or the set of moves at the current level is exhausted.

The `Backtrack` constructor takes a single parameter `b` which encapsulates the details of the problem to be solved. As defined by the `Backtracker` interface in Figure 13.23, these methods are:

1. An Iterator `moves`, which is the set of all possible trial solutions on a given level.
2. A Boolean function `valid`, which determines whether the current move satisfies the validity criteria.
3. A method `record`, which records the current move on the current recursive level.
4. A boolean method `done`, which determines whether the solution as recorded solves the problem.
5. A method `undo` that undoes a move at the current level.

For an application of backtracking, consider the *n-queens* problem where *n* mutually antagonistic queens must be placed on an $n \times n$ chess board in a configuration where no queen can capture any other queen in a single turn.[8] Even though a chess board normally has 8×8 squares, we consider the more general $n \times n$ case, letting *n* be a run-time parameter that can be set to any integer value greater than zero. Consider the following (arbitrary) position for the 4×4 chess board shown below:

	0	1	2	3
0	Q			
1				
2		Q		
3				

8. A queen can legally move any number of squares horizontally, vertically, or on either diagonal in a single turn, provided it does not pass or cross over another chess piece in the process. A chess piece that lands on a square occupied by another chess piece is said to *capture* that piece.

```
import java.util.Iterator;

public class Backtrack {

Backtracker b;

public Backtrack (Backtracker b) { this.b = b; }

public boolean attempt (int level) {
    boolean successful = false;
    Iterator i = b.moves(level);
    while (!successful && i.hasNext()) {
        Object move = i.next();
        if (b.valid(level, move)) {
            b.record(level, move);
            if (b.done(level))
                successful= true;
            else {
                successful = attempt(level+1);
                if (!successful)
                    b.undo(level, move);
            } // if done
        } // if valid
    } // while
    return successful;
} // attempt
}
```

| **Figure 13.22   Object-Oriented Backtracking Algorithm**

```
import java.util.Iterator;

public abstract interface Backtracker {
    public abstract Iterator moves(int level);
    public abstract boolean valid(int level, Object move);
    public abstract void record(int level, Object move);
    public abstract boolean done(int level);
    public abstract void undo(int level, Object move);
}
```

| **Figure 13.23   Backtracker Interface**

Suppose the `level` represents the current column number, which in this example is set at 2.[9] The set of possible `moves` represents all the valid row numbers, namely, {0...3}. For instance, it is easy to see in this example that no queen can be validly placed in column 2. Hence, the search for a solution has to backtrack to column 1 and relocate that queen from row 2 to row 3, before proceeding forward again.

In designing the `Queens` class, we need to decide on a representation for the chess board. One possibility is an $n \times n$ square matrix. However, a little investigation reveals that such a representation is fairly cumbersome in checking the validity or "safeness" of a new position. Instead, we use a set of four one-dimensional arrays.

The first array named `rowPos` takes a column number as an index and indicates for that column the row number, or position, of a queen, if it contains one. For the sample board shown above:

```
rowPos[0] = 0
rowPos[1] = 2
```

This array is used for displaying a successful board configuration. A row is defined to be "safe" if no queen occupies that row. This information can be represented by a Boolean array named `row` which takes a row number as an index and indicates whether there is a queen in that row. For the sample board above:

```
row[0] = true      row[2] = true
row[1] = false     row[3] = false
```

indicating that rows 0 and 2 have queens and the other rows do not. We next note that in a southwest diagonal[10] the sum of the row and column numbers is constant:

	0	1	2	3
0	0	1	2	3
1	1	2	3	4
2	2	3	4	5
3	3	4	5	6

This information is captured by a Boolean array named `swDiag`, which takes the sum of the row and column numbers as an index and indicates whether a queen occupies that southwest diagonal. For an $n \times n$ board the set of indices ranges from 0 to $2n - 1$. For our sample board above we have a 7-entry array `swDiag` in which:

```
swDiag[0] = true
swDiag[3] = true
```

and all the other entries are `false`, indicating that the southwest diagonals 0 and 3 have queens and the other southwest diagonals do not.

---

9. Note that an equivalent solution scheme could proceed row by row rather than column by column.

10. A southwest diagonal is one that extends from upper right to lower left on the board.

Finally, we note that in a southeast diagonal[11] the difference between the row and column numbers is constant:

	0	1	2	3
0	0	−1	−2	−3
1	1	0	−1	−2
2	2	1	0	−1
3	3	2	1	0

This information can be captured by a $(2n-1)$-entry Boolean array named seDiag which takes the difference of the row and column numbers as an index and indicates whether a queen occupies that southeast diagonal. For an $n \times n$ board the set of indices ranges from $-n+1 \ldots n-1$; since all Java arrays are 0-based, we add $n-1$ to the difference, giving a range of $0 \ldots 2(n-1)$. For our sample board above, we have a 7-entry array seDiag, in which:

```
seDiag[3] = true     (southeast diagonal 0 + 3)
seDiag[4] = true     (southeast diagonal 1 + 3)
```

marks the presence of queens on southeast diagonals 0 and 1, and the remaining entries are false. This completes our design of the chess board.

With this board design, the methods of the Queens class can be implemented. The constructor is passed the value n, the size of the chess board; this value is stored as the variable MAXROW and is used to allocate the arrays cited above. However, the actual row and column numbers used are 0-based to simplify their use as array indices.

Implementing the Backtracker interface methods to solve the eight queens problem is straightforward:

- A move varies from 0 to $n-1$ to accommodate Java's 0-based arrays; a trial move corresponds to a potential row position within a column. So the enumerator moves must simply iterate over the values $0 \ldots n-1$.

- The method done checks to see if column number (its parameter) plus one is at least MAXROW.

- The method valid checks to see if the row, southwest diagonal, and southeast diagonal are all empty (i.e., all false).

- Recording a move (the method record) is accomplished by marking the row, the southwest diagonal, and the southeast diagonal for the occupied (i.e., true) square; undoing a move corresponds to marking these three as unoccupied (i.e., false). The variable rowPos records, for each column, the row position of the queen occupying that column, and is later used for display purposes. A private method setPosition is used for both recording and undoing moves.

The complete Queens class is shown in Figure 13.24. It also includes a display method for printing the solution. A simple driver that can be used to run the simulation

---

11. A southeast diagonal is one that extends from upper left to lower right.

```java
import java.io.*;
import java.util.Iterator;

public class Queen implements Backtracker {

int MAXROW = 8;         // board size
boolean swDiag[];
boolean seDiag[];
boolean row[];
int rowPos[];

public Queen(int n) {
    MAXROW = n;
    swDiag = new boolean[2*MAXROW-1];
    seDiag = new boolean[2*MAXROW+1];
    row = new boolean[MAXROW];
    rowPos = new int[MAXROW];
}

private void setPosition(int rowNo, int colNo,
        boolean occupied) {
    row[rowNo] = occupied;
    swDiag[rowNo+colNo] = occupied;
    seDiag[rowNo-colNo+MAXROW-1] = occupied;
}

public boolean valid(int colNo, Object move) {
    int rowNo = ((Integer)move).intValue();
    System.out.println("Try: " + rowNo + ", " + colNo);
    return (!row[rowNo])
        && (!swDiag[rowNo+colNo])
        && (!seDiag[rowNo-colNo+MAXROW-1]);
}

public boolean done(int colNo) {
    return colNo + 1 >= MAXROW;
}

public void record(int colNo, Object move) {
    int rowNo = ((Integer)move).intValue();
    System.out.println("Record: " + rowNo + ", " + colNo);
    rowPos[colNo] = rowNo;
    setPosition(rowNo, colNo, true);
}
```

| Figure 13.24   Object-Oriented n-Queens Program

```java
public void undo(int colNo, Object move) {
    int rowNo = ((Integer)move).intValue();
    System.out.println("Undo: " + rowNo + ", " + colNo);
    rowPos[colNo] = 0;
    setPosition(rowNo, colNo, false);
}

public void display( ) {
    for (int i = 0; i < MAXROW; i++) {
        for (int j = 0; j < MAXROW; j++)
            if (rowPos[j] == i)
                System.out.print("Q");
            else
                System.out.print(".");
        System.out.println();
    }
} // display

public Iterator moves(int level) {
    return new QueenIterator( );
}

private class QueenIterator
        implements Iterator {
    int cursor = 0;

    public boolean hasNext( ) {
        return cursor < MAXROW;
    }

    public Object next( ) {
        return new Integer(cursor++);
    }
    public void remove() { }
} // QueenIterator

} //class Queen
```

| **Figure 13.24**   (*Continued*)

for different values of *n* can be found at the book website. The output for running this program with $n = 4$ appears below:

```
Try:    0, 0      Record:   1, 2      Try: 3, 1
Record:   0, 0    Try:   0, 3         Record: 3, 1
Try:    0, 1      Try:   1, 3         Try: 0, 2
Try:    1, 1      Try:   2, 3         Record: 0, 2
Try:    2, 1      Try:   3, 3         Try: 0, 3
Record:   2, 1    Undo:  1, 2         Try: 1, 3
Try:    0, 2      Try:   2, 2         Try: 2, 3
Try:    1, 2      Try:   3, 2         Record: 2, 3
Try:    2, 2      Undo:  3, 1          .  .  Q  .
Try:    3, 2      Undo:  0, 0         Q  .  .  .
Undo:   2, 1      Try:   1, 0          .  .  .  Q
Try:    3, 1      Record:   1, 0       .  Q  .  .
Record:   3, 1    Try:   0, 1
Try:    0, 2      Try:   1, 1
Try:    1, 2      Try:   2, 1
```

This output shows the dynamics of backtracking and exhaustive search. For example, an attempt to position the first column's queen at (0,0) is tried in the first step and then finally abandoned in step 26 after unsuccessful attempts to locate the second column's queens at (2,1) and (3,1). Relocating the first column's queen at (1,0) results in a successful relocation of the second column's queen at (3,1), as well as the other two queens at (0,2) and (2,3) after several additional steps.

Solutions to other backtracking problems, such as *knight's tour,* graph reachability, running a maze, and so forth, can be produced by implementing the methods defined by the Backtracker interface in appropriate ways. With this approach, the process of implementing a particular backtracking algorithm is reduced to filling in the details of the five methods in the Backtracker interface.

13.5 PYTHON

Many authors (e.g., [Lutz and Ascher, 1999, p. 4]), view Python as an object-oriented language. However, your authors have the somewhat broader view that Python is a multiparadigm language supporting the following programming styles:

- Imperative
- Object-oriented
- Functional[12]

In this sense, Python is closer to C++ (which is also multiparadigm) than it is to Smalltalk.

---

12. See Chapter 14.

Python, like Perl, is a scripting language (see Section 12.7) and is part of the LAMP (Linux, Apache, MySQl, Perl/Python/PHP) movement. Characteristics of scripting languages are:

- They are often used to "glue" two or more applications together by transforming the output of one application into a form appropriate as input to another application.
- They are typically interpreted rather than compiled.
- They are dynamically typed.

In this discussion we focus on the object-oriented features of Python. However, in order to understand the sample programs, we first explain the basic syntax and semantics of the language.

13.5.1 General Characteristics

Compared with Java, Python has many more built-in types (ints, floats, infinite precision integers, complex numbers, strings, etc.) and basic data structures, including:

- Lists or expandable arrays: `[1, [2, "allen"], "bob", 3.54];`
- Dictionaries or associative arrays, that is, arrays with string indices: `{"Tucker": "Bowdoin", "Noonan": "William and Mary"};`
- Tuples, that is, structures accessed by position rather than field name: `(238111, "allen", "bob")`.

While some of these may be implemented as classes, they do not appear to be classes. The arithmetic data types have the usual operators and functions, as do strings. Some math, string, and other functions are provided through modules, which have to be explicitly imported.

Python strings are viewed as a list of characters, so list operators applied to strings have the expected effect. For example, if we index into a string, we get a character; if we take a slice of a string, we get a substring.

However, in general, Python is less forgiving than Perl. We cannot do string operations on numbers, nor can we do arithmetic operations on strings whose values look like numbers. We cannot index past the end of a list. To grow a string or list, we must append to the end of the list.

Python statements are fairly conventional, except for the syntax of compound statements or blocks. In Python, the header of a compound statement or block ends in a colon and the body is indented and ends when the indentation ends. Compound statements include: class definitions, method or function definitions, if statements, and loops. So the `if` ambiguity problem in other languages, where a statement looks like it is part of an `if` statement but is not, cannot occur in Python.

Like most object-oriented languages, Python uses reference semantics. In the following example:

```
x = [1, 2, 3]
y = x
x[0] = "abc"
```

the last assignment changes both x and y. Note also that list indexing begins at zero.

Python supports multiple inheritance. All methods and instance variables are public. A simple class would be declared:

```
class MyClass:
    def set(self, value):
        self.value = value
    def display(self):
        print self.value
```

As a compound statement `class` ends in a colon (`:`), and its body, consisting of the methods named `set` and `display`, is indented; also, the body of each method is indented. `MyClass` has no super class. Of the two methods, the first has one real parameter and the other none, since the first parameter of each method is the receiver of the message. Conventionally, the name `self` is used for the receiver of the message.

The following code declares three objects and then sets their instance variable `value`:

```
x = MyClass( )
y = MyClass( )
z = MyClass( )
x.set(123);
set(y, "allen")
z.value = "bob"
```

In Python all variables must be set before being referenced; except for parameters, variables are declared by assigning a value to them. Declaring an instance variable outside a constructor, as is done by method `set`, is a questionable programming decision, since a call to method `display` before any call to method `set` will result in a run-time error.

Classes in Python may have constructors, destructors, and class variables. All instance methods are public; all class and instance variables are also public. As a dynamically typed language, Python also supports run-time type identification and reflection, but lacks both abstract classes and interfaces.

13.5.2 Example: Polynomials

In this section we develop a class to represent polynomials, such as:

$$3x^2 + 5x - 7$$

For this application, we will represent a polynomial by an array of its coefficients starting with the coefficient of x^0 and proceeding up to the highest power with a nonzero coefficient. So the above polynomial would be represented by the array [-7 5 3].

The `Polynomial` class does not have a superclass and has a single instance variable named `coefficient`. The class definition is given in Figure 13.25.

A constructor is always named `__init__` and may have as many arguments as desired; in this case, one argument is passed and used to initialize the instance variable `coefficient`. Here, the list concatenate operator (+), together with an empty list, is used to force a shallow copy to be made of the argument. A destructor, if used, would be named `__del__`.

A triple quoted string immediately follows each method header; such strings can extend over multiple lines. Strictly speaking, they are strings, not comments. However,

```
class Polynomial:
    def __init__(self, coef):
        """constructor"""
        self.coefficient = [ ] + coef

    def degree(self):
        """Highest power with a non-zero coefficient"""
        return len(coefficient)

    def coefficient(self, power):
        """Coefficient of given power"""
        if power > len(coefficient):
            return 0
        return coefficient[power]

    def asList(self):
        """return copy of coefficient"""
        return [ ] + coefficient

    def __eq__(self, aPoly):
        """return self == aPoly"""
        return coefficient == aPoly.asList( )

    def __ne__(self, aPoly):
        """return self <> aPoly.asList( )"""
        return coefficient <> aPoly.asList( )

    def __str__(self):
        """return string representation"""
        r = ""
        p = len(coefficient) + 1
        while p > 0:
            p = p - 1
            if coefficient[p] == 0: continue
            if p < len(coefficient): r = r + "+"
            r = r + str(coefficient[p])
            if p == 0: continue
            r = r + "x"
            if p <= 1: continue
            r = r + "^" + str(p)
        return r
```

| **Figure 13.25   Polynomial Class in Python**

the Python documentation utililty `pydoc`, analogous to Java's `javadoc` utility, looks for such strings and uses them to generate documentation. An ordinary comment begins with a pound sign (#) and extends to the end of the line.

The methods `degree` and `coefficient` are similar to their equivalents in Smalltalk (Section 13.3.2), except that lists in Python start at index zero. The method `asList` returns a shallow copy of the `coefficient` list; an alternative is to import and use the `copy` method from module `copy`. This alternative would be necessary if we had to make a `deepcopy`.

By defining methods `__eq__` and `__ne__`, we can compare two polynomials p and q for equality by writing p == q. The method `__eq__` works by comparing the coefficients of the two polynomials for equality. A somewhat subtle bug is left as an exercise.

The method `__str__` is analogous to Java's `toString` method. It is called whenever Python needs a string representation of an object. The method works from the highest list index to zero. For the set of coefficients [3, 0, 5], it generates the string:

```
5x^2+3
```

rather than the less readable:

```
5x^2+0x^1+3x^0
```

where the caret (^) is used to denote the exponent. Note that the plus operator used is the string concatenation operator. Also note that a one-line block body, in this case the `if` statement body, can be written on the same line as the block header.

13.5.3 Example: Fractions

In this section we develop a fractional arithmetic class so that the expression 1/3 + 2/6 + 3/9 evaluates to 1. In our implementation we use Python integers. A fraction such as 2/6 has a numerator (2) and a denominator (6). The implementation works by storing fractions in normalized form:

1 In the case of a negative number, the sign is stored with the numerator. So, the fraction 1/-3 would be stored as -1/3.
2 A fraction is stored such that the largest factor of both the numerator and the denominator is one. So, the fraction 2/6 would be stored as 1/3.

Figure 13.26 gives a partial implementation of the fraction class. The constructor has default values for the numerator and denominator. The latter is checked for a zero value; if found, an exception is thrown. Otherwise the fraction is converted to normalized form as defined above. A better solution would ensure that both parts of the fraction are long integers.

The methods `numerator` and `denominator` return the corresponding parts of the fraction.

```
class Fraction:
    def __init__(self, numer=1, denomin=1):
        """constructor: default value is 1/1"""
        if denomin == 0:
            raise ZeroDivisionError, "Divide by 0"
        div = gcd(numer, denomin)
        self.num = abs(numer / div)
        self.denom = abs(denomin / div)
        if numer * denomin < 0: self.num = - self.num

    def numerator(self):
        return self.num

    def denominator(self):
        return self.denom

    def __add__(self, other):
        return Fraction(other.denom * self.num
                        + self.denom * other.num,
                        self.denom + other.denom)

    def __neg__(self):
        return Fraction(- self.num, self.denom)

    def __sub__(self, other):
        return - other + self

    def __eq__(self, other):
        return (self.num == other.num and
                self.denom == other.denom)

    def __str__(self):
        return str(self.num) + "/" + str(self.denom)
```

| **Figure 13.26**   **Fraction Class in Python**

The addition of two fractions $\frac{a}{b}$ and $\frac{c}{d}$ is defined as:

$$\frac{a}{b} + \frac{c}{d} = \frac{d \times a + b \times c}{b \times d}$$

The code merely implements this definition (method __add__), returning a new fraction. Unary negation (method __neg__) is implemented by negating the numerator.

Subtraction can then be implemented (method _ _sub_ _) by negating the second operand and adding it to the first.

Two fractions $\frac{a}{b}$ and $\frac{c}{d}$ are equal (method _ _eq_ _) if:

$$a = c \text{ and } b = d$$

This follows because the fractions are stored in normalized form. The remaining arithmetic and logical operators are left as exercises.

The final method implemented is the string conversion function (method _ _str_ _) which converts the fraction $\frac{a}{b}$ to the string a/b.

Running the program:

```
print Fraction(1, 3) + Fraction(-2, -6) + Fraction(3, 9)
```

prints the value 1/1, as expected.

This concludes our brief tour of the object-oriented features of Python. One of your authors writes all his real programs in either Perl or Python, but he greatly prefers Python to Perl.

13.6 SUMMARY

An object-oriented language supports both the encapsulation of a data type with its functions and the information hiding features of data abstraction. The primary mechanism for doing this is the class, which defines a type. Instances of a class are known as *objects*. Classes provide a mechanism for defining an abstract data type in a program. An advantage of the object-oriented approach to data abstraction is that it provides a constructor, in which memory is allocated for the object and the instance variables of the object can be initialized.

In languages that support destructors, an object's destructor is automatically called when the object is deallocated. Uses of a destructor include the deallocation of memory for objects that can no longer be referenced, the release of resources, and the closing of files.

Classes play two important and complementary roles in object-based languages. First, they determine the type of an object so that they determine what messages (method calls) are legal and precisely which method is being called. Second, they permit full type checking.

The object-oriented paradigm supports code reuse through inheritance. Classes exist in an object-oriented language in a class hierarchy. A class can be declared as a subclass of another class, which is called the parent class or superclass. Within this hierarchy, each subclass is able to inherit variables and methods from its parent simply by virtue of the fact that it is a subclass.

A common mistake made by object-oriented beginners is to confuse the *is-a* relationship with the *has-a* relationship. The latter does not identify a subclass-superclass relationship; rather it identifies a class as a client of another class, usually termed an *aggregation*.

In object-oriented languages polymorphism refers to the late binding of a call to one of several different implementations of a method in an inheritance hierarchy. Such methods must be instance methods.

Run-time type identification (RTTI) is the ability of the language to identify at run time the actual type or class of an object. RTTI is also a necessary feature to support reflection, which is a mechanism whereby a program can discover and use the methods of any of its objects and classes.

The last three sections considered the history and general object-oriented characteristics of Smalltalk, Java, and Python. For each language, at least two example classes are presented.

EXERCISES

13.1 Give an example of a feature from Java or C++ that promotes each of the following object-oriented design principles: code reuse, type safety, abstraction, and encapsulation. Give another example that violates each of these principles.

13.2 Complete the Java implementation of the classes `Queue`, `Deque`, and `PriorityQueue` that is sketched in Figure 13.11.

13.3 Sketch a Java class and interface that captures the specific idea of multiple inheritance displayed in Figure 13.12.

13.4 The Java `Collection` classes have some idiosyncrasies. We noted one of them, in that class `Stack` is a subclass of class `Vector`. Moreover, there is no class `Queue` or `PriorityQueue` predefined in Java, even though these collections are very important modeling tools in computer science.

(a) What other weaknesses do you find with the Java `Collection` classes?

(b) What similar data structures are predefined in the C++ standard library? Is this library more complete than Java's? Explain the basic differences between the two.

(c) Perform the same comparison as in part (b), except between Java and Ada.

13.5 Based on the definitions given in this chapter, conduct some modest research to determine whether or not Ada is an object-oriented language. What about CLOS? Perl? Ruby?

13.6 Implement the remaining operators for the Smalltalk polynomial class.

13.7 Implement a polynomial method `differentiate` in Smalltalk that creates a new polynomial which is the differentiation $\frac{d}{dx}$ of the receiver of the message.

13.8 Implement the remaining operators for the Smalltalk complex number class.

13.9 Considering the complete implementation of Clite abstract syntax, parser, type checker, and semantics, identify opportunities for using templates. Reimplement the Clite interpreter in Java 1.5 in a way that takes advantage of these opportunities.

13.10 Complete the object-oriented implementation of the `Expression` class and its subclasses for Clite by redefining the type checking function `V` so that it becomes polymorphic over the subclasses of `Expression`. Also redo all the parser and type checking for expressions in this more object-oriented style, using the same approach as used in Section 13.4.1.

13.11 Using the changes you made in Exercises 13.9 and 13.10, test your code by interpreting the following Clite program (provided in the software distribution):

```
int main() {
    float a, b, c, d, x, y;
    a = 4.0; b = 8.0; c = 3.0;
    x = 1.0;
    y = b*b - 4*a*c;
    while (x*x > y+0.0001 || x*x < y-0.0001 )
        x = (x + y/x)/2.0;
    d = (- b + x) / 2*a;
}
```

What does this program compute (approximately)?

13.12 Consider the unary negation operator (-) used in the example above. What would be an alternative to defining Unary as a subclass of Expression, as is now implemented in the Clite interpreter? For example, what implementation changes would be needed if we just added unary negation as another operator for the Binary class?

13.13 Using the Concordance example from the book website, extend the program so that it can report, for each word in the list, its frequency (number of occurrences) in addition to the line numbers where it occurs.

13.14 Using the following test driver, compile and run the Concordance classes provided at the book website.

```
import java.io.*;

class MakeConcordance {
  public static void main (String[] args) {
    Concordance dict = new Concordance( );
    if (args.length < 1) {
    System.err.println("No file name provided: ");
    System.exit(1);
    }
    try {
    BufferedReader in = new BufferedReader(
                       new FileReader(args[0]));
    Document doc = new Document(in, true, dict);
    } catch (Exception e) {
    System.err.println("File open or read error: " + e);
    System.exit(1);
    }
        Report r = new Report(dict, System.out);
  }
}
```

Use a simple text file as input to corroborate that the program works properly, both with and without the option of showing duplicate line numbers.

13.15 Using the Concordance program again, carry out the following experiments. For each experiment carry out the specified task and answer the associated questions as needed. For any experiment that fails (gets a compilation error), undo the change before proceeding with the next experiment.

(a) In the class Concordance change its superclass from HashMap to Hashtable. Then recompile and rerun Concordance. Has anything changed? Why or why not? Explain.

(b) In the call to add in the Document class, remove the first argument's cast to String, and in the declaration of add in the Concordance class, change the type of word from String to Object. Then recompile and rerun Concordance. Has anything changed? Why or why not? Explain.

(c) In the call to add in the Document class, eliminate the conversion of the value of number to Integer (via the newInteger(number)), and in the declaration of add change the type of the parameter line from Integer to int. Then recompile and rerun Concordance. Has anything changed? Why or why not? Explain.

(d) In the Report class, change f.next() to f.next.toString(), then recompile and rerun Concordance. Has anything changed? Why or why not? Explain.

13.16 Implement knight's tour [Wirth, 1976, p. 137] in Java using the Backtrack class and its associated Backtracker interface. Note that the smallest chess board (greater than 1) for which a solution exists is 5 × 5; verify this.

Given is a $n \times n$ board. A knight—allowed to move according to the rules of chess—is placed on the board with initial coordinates (x_0, y_0). The problem is to find a covering of the entire board, if there exists one, that is, to compute a tour of $n^2 - 1$ moves such that every square of the board is visited exactly once.

13.17 Modify the Backtrack class's attempt method so that it generates all solutions. Test your modification on eight queens.

13.18 Consider all the classes that define the abstract syntax of Clite .

(a) Find a class that is a client of another class.

(b) Find a class that is a subclass of another class.

13.19 Add display methods to the Clite abstract syntax so that the call p.display(), where p is a Clite abstract program, displays all the elements of the program.

13.20 Classes in Java 1.4 are not *generic* as they are in Ada, C++, and Java 1.5. Thus, the latter allow us to specify Vector<int> v to define a vector of int's. This allows us to extract the ith value from v and immediately do arithmetic with that value without an explicit cast. Briefly list the advantages and disadvantages of templates, both in programming and in language design.

13.21 Consider the possibility of designing a complete object-oriented implementation of Clite, incorporating all of its type checking and meaning rules inside the classes of its abstract syntax.

(a) Determine which of these rules would appear with each class.

(b) What simplifications of these rules are achieved by this change?

(c) Complete the implementation (Team Project).

13.22 Using the Stack class in Section 7.5 as a guide, add a display method and give its pre- and postconditions.

13.23 Rewrite the code for the pop method given in Figure 7.31 so that it uses the top method. Does the postcondition for pop need to be altered? Why or why not?

13.24 Implement the remaining operators for the Python polynomial class.

13.25 Implement a polynomial method `differentiate` in Python that creates a new polynomial which is the differentiation $\frac{d}{dx}$ of the receiver of the message.

13.26 Implement the remaining operators for the Python fraction class.

13.27 The class `Set` is an important abstract class in Java. Its implementations include `HashSet` and `SortedSet`. Do some research to answer the following questions:

(a) What is the difference between a `HashSet` and a `HashMap`? Would the former be a candidate for implementation of the `Concordance` class instead of the latter? Why or why not?

(b) What comparable classes exist in the C++ Standard Library for the Java `HashSet` and `HashMap`? What are the major differences in their design?

(c) What comparable classes exist in Ada for the Java `HashSet` and `HashMap`? What are the major differences in their design?

Functional Programming

"It is better to have 100 functions operate on one data structure than 10 functions on 10 data structures."

Attributed to Alan Perlis

CHAPTER OUTLINE

Functional programming emerged as a distinct paradigm in the early 1960s. Its creation was motivated by the needs of researchers in artificial intelligence and its subfields—symbolic computation, theorem proving, rule-based systems, and natural language processing. These needs were not particularly well met by the imperative languages of the time.

The original functional language was Lisp, developed by John McCarthy [McCarthy, 1960] and described in the *LISP 1.5 Programmer's Manual* [McCarthy and others, 1965]. The description is notable for both its clarity and its brevity; the manual has only 106 pages! It contains not only a description of the Lisp system but also a formal definition of Lisp itself. To quote the authors [McCarthy and others, 1965, p. 1]:

> The Lisp language is primarily for symbolic data processing. It has been used for symbolic calculations in differential and integral calculus, electrical circuit design, mathematical logic, game playing, and other fields of artificial intelligence.

Recall from Chapter 1 that the essential feature of *functional programming* is that a computation is viewed as a mathematical function mapping inputs to outputs. Unlike imperative programming, there is no notion of state and therefore no need for an assignment statement. Thus, the effect of a loop is achieved via recursion, since there is no way to increment or decrement the value of a variable in the state, since there are no variables. As a practical matter, however, most functional languages do support the notions of variable, assignment, and looping. The point here is that these elements are not part of the "pure" functional programming model, and so we will not emphasize them in this chapter.

Because of its relative purity, which we will explain shortly, functional programming is viewed by some as a more reliable paradigm for software design than imperative programming. This view is difficult to document, however, since the vast majority of (artificial intelligence) applications for which functional programming is used are not readily amenable to solutions in the imperative paradigm, and conversely. For a more careful discussion of the merits of functional programming versus imperative programming, see [Hughes, 1989].

14.1 FUNCTIONS AND THE LAMBDA CALCULUS

A typical mathematical function such as the square of a number is often defined by:

```
Square(n) = n * n
```

This definition gives the name of the function, followed by its arguments in parentheses, followed by an expression that defines the meaning of the function. Square is understood to be a function that maps from the set of real numbers **R** (its *domain*) to the set of real numbers **R** (its *range*), or more formally:

Square: **R** → **R**

> **Definition**: A function is said to be *total* if it is defined for all elements in its domain, and *partial* otherwise.

The Square function is total over the set of real numbers.

In imperative programming languages, a variable such as x denotes a location in memory. So the statement:

```
x = x + 1
```

literally means "update the program state by adding 1 to the value stored in the memory cell named x and then storing that sum back into that memory cell." Thus, the name x is used to denote both a value (as in x + 1), often called an *r-value*, and a memory address, called an *l-value*.[1] (See Section 7.4.)

In mathematics, variables are somewhat different in their semantics: they always stand for actual expressions and are immutable. In mathematics there is no concept of "memory cell" or updating the value of a memory cell. So-called *pure* functional programming languages eliminate the memory cell notion of a variable in favor of the mathematical notion; that is, a variable names an immutable expression, which also eliminates the assignment operator. A functional language is *pure* if there is no concept of an assignment operator or a memory cell; otherwise, it is said to be *impure*. However, most functional programming languages retain some form of assignment operator and are, thus, *impure*.

One consequence of the lack of memory-based variables and assignment is that functional programming has no notion of state, as was used in defining the meaning of the imperative language Clite. The value of a function such as *Square* depends only on the values of its arguments and not on any previous computation or even the order of the evaluation of its arguments. This property of a functional language is known as *referential transparency*. A function has *referential transparency* if its value depends only on the values of its arguments.

The foundation of functional programming is the *lambda calculus*, developed by Church [1941]. A lambda expression specifies the parameters and definition of a function, but not its name. For instance, here is a lambda expression that defines the function `square` discussed above.

$$(\lambda x \cdot x * x)$$

The identifier x is a parameter used in the (unnamed) function body $x * x$. Application of a lambda expression to a value is denoted by:

$$((\lambda x \cdot x * x)2)$$

which evaluates to 4.

This example is an illustration of an applied lambda calculus. What Church actually defined was a *pure* or *uninterpreted* lambda calculus, in the following way:

1   Any identifier is a lambda expression.
2   If M and N are lambda expressions, then the *application* of M to N, written $(M\ N)$, is a lambda expression.
3   An *abstraction*, written $(\lambda x \cdot M)$, where x is an identifier and M is a lambda expression, is also a lambda expression.

A simple set of BNF grammar rules for the syntax of this pure lambda calculus can be written as:

$$LambdaExpression \rightarrow variable\ |\ (\ M\ N\ )\ |\ (\ \lambda\ variable \cdot M\ )$$
$$M \rightarrow LambdaExpression$$
$$N \rightarrow LambdaExpression$$

---

1. The terms *r-value* and *l-value* were originally coined because they referred to the values returned by the right- and the left-hand sides of an assignment, respectively.

Examples of lambda expressions are:

x

$(\lambda x \cdot x)$

$((\lambda x \cdot x)(\lambda y \cdot y))$

In the lambda expression $(\lambda x \cdot M)$, the variable x is said to be *bound* in the subexpression M. A *bound variable* is one whose name is the same as a parameter; otherwise the variable is said to be *free*. Any variable not bound in M is said to be *free*. Bound variables are simply placeholders, like function parameters in the imperative and object-oriented paradigms. Any such variable can be renamed consistently with any variable free in M without changing the meaning of the lambda expression. Formally, the free variables in a lambda expression can be defined as:

$$free(x) = x$$
$$free(MN) = free(M) \cup free(N)$$
$$free(\lambda x \cdot M) = free(M) - \{x\}$$

A substitution of an expression N for a variable x in M, written $M[x \leftarrow N]$, is defined as follows:

1. If the free variables of N have no bound occurrences in M, then the term $M[x \leftarrow N]$ is formed by replacing all free occurrences of x in M by N.
2. Otherwise, assume that the variable y is free in N and bound in M. Then consistently replace the binding and corresponding bound occurrences of y in M by a new variable, say u. Repeat this renaming of bound variables in M until the condition in step 1 applies, then proceed as in step 1.

The following examples illustrate the substitution process:

$$x[x \leftarrow y] = y$$
$$(xx)[x \leftarrow y] = (yy)$$
$$(zw)[x \leftarrow y] = (zw)$$
$$(zx)[x \leftarrow y] = (zy)$$
$$(\lambda x \cdot (zx))[x \leftarrow y] = (\lambda u \cdot (zu))[x \leftarrow y] = (\lambda u \cdot (zu))$$
$$(\lambda x \cdot (zx))[y \leftarrow x] = (\lambda u \cdot (zu))[y \leftarrow x] = (\lambda u \cdot (zu))$$

The meaning of a lambda expression is defined by the following reduction rule:

$$((\lambda x \cdot M)N) \Rightarrow M[x \leftarrow N]$$

This is called a *beta-reduction*, and can be read "whenever we have a lambda expression of the form $((\lambda x \cdot M)N)$, we may simplify it by the substitution $M[x \leftarrow N]$." A beta-reduction therefore represents a single function application.

An *evaluation* of a lambda expression is a sequence $P \Rightarrow Q \Rightarrow R \Rightarrow \cdots$ in which each expression in the sequence is obtained by the application of a beta-reduction to the previous expression. If P is a lambda expression, then a *redux* of P is any subexpression obtained by a beta-reduction. A lambda expression that does not contain a function application is called a *normal form*.

An example of an evaluation is:

$$((\lambda y \cdot ((\lambda x \cdot xyz)a))b) \Rightarrow ((\lambda y \cdot ayz)b) \Rightarrow abz$$

In this example, we evaluated the innermost λ expression first; we could have just as easily done the outermost reduction first:

$$((\lambda y \cdot ((\lambda x \cdot xyz)a))b) = ((\lambda x \cdot xbz)a) = abz$$

The equality of lambda expressions is termed *beta-equality* both for historical reasons and because the term suggests beta-reducibility from one expression to the other. Informally if two lambda expressions M and N are equal, written $M = N$, then M and N can be reduced to the same expression (up to renaming their variables). Beta-equality deals with applying an abstraction $(\lambda x \cdot M)$ to an argument N, and so it provides a fundamental model for the notions of function call and parameter passing in programming languages.

A functional programming language is essentially an applied lambda calculus with constant values and functions built in. The pure lambda expression (xyx) can just as easily be written $(x \times x)$ or $(x * x)$. Moreover, this last form can be written in prefix style like $(*xx)$. When we add constants such as numbers with their usual interpretation and definitions for functions, such as *, we obtain an applied lambda calculus. For instance, $(*2\,x)$ is an expression in an applied lambda calculus. As we shall see, pure Lisp/Scheme and Haskell are examples of applied lambda calculi.

An important distinction in functional languages is usually made in the way they define function evaluation. In languages such as Scheme, all arguments to a function are normally evaluated at the time of the call. This is usually referred to as *eager evaluation*, or *call by value* (as discussed in Chapter 9). *Eager evaluation* in functional languages refers to the strategy of evaluating all arguments to a function at the time of the call. With eager evaluation, functions such as if and and cannot be defined without potential run-time errors, as in the Scheme function:

```
(if (= x 0) 1 (/ 1 x))
```

which defines the value of the function to be 1 when x is zero and 1/x otherwise. If all arguments to the if function are evaluated at the time of the call, division by zero cannot be prevented.

> **Definition**: An alternative to the eager evaluation strategy is termed *lazy evaluation*, in which an argument to a function is not evaluated (it is deferred) until it is needed.

As an argument passing mechanism lazy evaluation is similar (but not identical) to call by name, and it is the default mechanism in the language Haskell. Scheme also has mechanisms which permit the programmer to specify the use of lazy evaluation, but we shall not explore these mechanisms in this chapter.

An advantage of eager evaluation is efficiency in that each argument passed to a function is only evaluated once, while in lazy evaluation an argument to a function is reevaluated each time it is used, which can be more than once. An advantage of lazy evaluation is that it permits certain interesting functions to be defined that cannot be implemented in eager languages. Even the above definition of the function if becomes error-free with a lazy evaluation strategy, since the division (/ 1 x) will only occur when $x \neq 0$.

In the pure lambda calculus, the function application:

$$((\lambda x \cdot {}^*x\ x)5) = (* 5\ 5)$$

does not give any interpretation to either the symbol 5 or the symbol *. Only in an applied lambda calculus would we achieve a further reduction to the number 25.

A key aspect of functional programming is that functions are treated as first-class values. A function name may be passed as a parameter, and a function may return a function as a value. Such a function is sometimes termed a *functional form*. An example of a functional form would be a function g that takes as parameters both a function and a list (or sequence of values) and applies the given function to each element in the list returning a list. Using Square as an example then:

```
g(f, [x1, x2, ...]) = [f(x1), f(x2), ...]
```

becomes

```
g(Square, [2, 3, 5]) = [4, 9, 25]
```

In Sections 14.2 and 14.3, we explore the use of these and many other useful functional forms.

14.2   SCHEME

As the original functional programming language, Lisp has many features that carried over into later languages, and so Lisp provides a good basis for studying other functional languages. Over the years a number of variants of Lisp were developed; today only two major variants remain in widespread use: Common Lisp [Steele, 1990] and Scheme [Kelsey *et al.*, 1998] [Dybvig, 1996]. As languages which attempt to unify a number of variants, both Scheme and Common Lisp contain a number of equivalent functions. This chapter presents a purely functional subset of Scheme.

When viewed as a pure functional language, our Scheme subset[2] has no assignment statement. Instead programs are written as (recursive) functions on input values which produce output values; the input values themselves are not changed. In this sense Scheme notation is much closer to mathematics than are the imperative and object-oriented programming languages like C and Java.

Without an assignment statement, our Scheme subset makes heavy use of recursive functions for repetition, instead of the *while* statement that we find in imperative languages. Despite the absence of while statements, it can be proved that such a subset is *Turing complete*, meaning that any computable function can be implemented in that subset. That is, a functional language is Turing complete because it has integer values and operations, a way of defining new functions using existing functions, conditionals (if statements), and recursion.

---

2. The full language Scheme has an assignment statement called set!, which we shall avoid using in this discussion.

A proof that this definition of Turing completeness is equivalent to the one in Chapter 12 for imperative languages is beyond the scope of this text. However, the use of Scheme to implement the denotational semantics of Clite given in this chapter should provide convincing, although informal, evidence that a purely functional language is at least as powerful as an imperative language. The converse is also true, since Scheme and Lisp interpreters are implemented on von Neumann machines which underlie the imperative paradigm.

14.2.1 Expressions

Expressions in Scheme are constructed in Cambridge-prefix notation, in which expressions are surrounded by parentheses and the operator or function precedes its operands, as in the example:

```
(+ 2 2)
```

If this expression is presented to a Scheme interpreter, it returns the value 4.

An advantage of this notation is that it allows arithmetic operators like + and * to take an arbitrary number of operands:

```
(+)                    ; evaluates to 0
(+ 5)                  ; evaluates to 5
(+ 5 4 3 2 1)          ; evaluates to 15
(*)                    ; evaluates to 1
(* 5)                  ; evaluates to 5
(* 1 2 3 4 5)          ; evaluates to 120
```

Note that a semicolon in Scheme starts a comment, which continues until the end of the line.

These arithmetic expressions are examples of Scheme lists; both data and programs (functions) are represented by lists. When a Scheme list is interpreted as a function, the operator or function name follows the left parenthesis and the remaining numbers are its operands. More complicated expressions can be built using nesting:

```
(+ (* 5 4) (- 6 2))
```

which is equivalent to $5 * 4 + (6 - 2)$ in infix notation, and evaluates to 24.

Global variables are defined in Scheme using the function define. To define a variable f equal to 120 we would enter the expression:

```
(define f 120)
```

The function define is the only one that we will examine that changes its environment, rather than merely returning a value. However, we will not treat define as an assignment statement in our Scheme subset;[3] we only use it to introduce a global name for a value, as in mathematics.

---

3. The function set! is a true assignment in Scheme in that it may be used to change the value of an existing variable. Many Scheme texts use the set! function at a global level as equivalent to define.

14.2.2 Expression Evaluation

To understand how Scheme evaluates expressions, three major rules apply.

First, names or symbols are replaced by their current bindings. Assuming the definition of the variable f from the previous section:

```
f                       ; evaluates to 120
( + f 5)                ; evaluates to 125
                        ; using the bindings for +, f
```

This use of f is an example of the first rule.

The second rule is that lists are evaluated as function calls written in Cambridge prefix notation:

```
(+)                     ; calls + with no arguments
(+ 5)                   ; calls + with 1 argument
(+ 5 4 3 2 1)           ; calls + with 5 arguments
(+ (5 4 3 2 1))         ; error, tries to evaluate 5 as
                        ; a function
(f)                     ; error; f evaluates to 120, not
                        ; a function
```

The third rule is that constants evaluate to themselves:

```
5                       ; evaluates to 5
#f                      ; is false, predefined
#t                      ; is true, predefined
```

One can prevent a symbol or list from being evaluated by quoting it using the quote function or the apostrophe ('), as in:

```
(define  colors  (quote  (red  yellow  green)))
(define  colors  '(red  yellow  green))
```

Note that there is no closing apostrophe; the apostrophe quotes the symbol or list immediately following it. You can also quote symbols:

```
(define  x  f)          ; defines x to be 120 (value of f)
(define  x  'f)         ; defines x to be the symbol f
(define acolor 'red)    ; defines acolor to be red
(define acolor red)     ; an error, symbol red not defined
```

14.2.3 Lists

As we have seen, the fundamental data structure of Scheme is the list; it is used for both commands and data. We have seen a number of examples of constant lists. In this section we shall see how to put things into lists and how to retrieve them.

**Figure 14.1
Structure of a List in
Scheme**

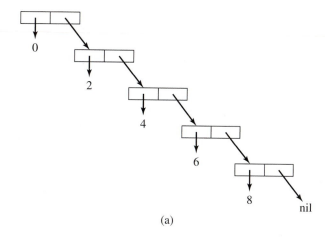

(a)

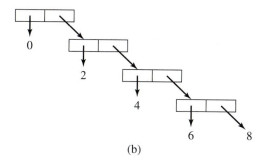

(b)

First, let us define some lists of numbers:

```
(define  evens  '(0  2  4  6  8))
(define  odds  '(1  3  5  7  9))
```

Pictorially, the list `evens` would be represented as shown in Figure 14.1a.

The symbol ( ) denotes an empty list; by convention Scheme lists usually end with
( ).[4] In imperative linked list terms, the ( ) can be thought of as a `null` pointer. If the ( )
had been missing from the end of the list, Scheme would display it as:

```
(0 2 4 6 . 8)
```

This sort of structure can be generated by some of the Scheme functions discussed below.
Figure 14.1 shows the difference in memory representation between a list that has ( ) as
its last element (Figure 14.1a) and one that does not (Figure 14.1b).

---

4. The value ( ) is implemented by the null reference, as discussed earlier in Chapter 5.

The basic function used for constructing a list is `cons`, which takes two arguments, the second of which should be a list:

```
(cons 8 ())                       ; gives (8)
(cons 6 (cons 8 ()))              ; gives (6 8)
(cons 4 (cons 6 (cons 8 ())))     ; gives (4 6 8)
(cons 4 (cons 6 (cons 8 9)))      ; gives (4 6 8 . 9)
```

Notice that the last example creates a dotted list, since the second argument of the innermost `cons` is not a list.

A node in a Scheme list has two parts, the first element or the "head" of the list, and the list of remaining elements or its "tail." The function `car` returns the head of the list, while the function `cdr` returns the tail.[5] Referring again to the list `evens` pictured in Figure 14.1, the following examples illustrate these functions:

```
(car evens)           ; gives 0
(cdr evens)           ; gives (2 4 6 8)
(car (cdr evens))     ; gives 2
(cadr evens)          ; gives 2
(cdr (cdr evens))     ; gives (4 6 8)
(cddr evens)          ; gives (4 6 8)
(car '(6 8))          ; gives 6
(car (cons 6 8))      ; gives 6
(cdr '(6 8))          ; gives (8)
(cdr (cons 6 8))      ; gives 8, not (8)
(car '(8))            ; gives 8
(cdr '(8))            ; gives ()
```

Note that Scheme allows sequences of `car`'s and `cdr`'s (up to five) to be abbreviated by including only the middle letter; thus, `cadr` is a `car` of a `cdr`, `cddr` is a `cdr` of a `cdr`, and so on.

Higher level functions for putting lists together include the `list` and `append` functions. The `list` function takes a variable number of arguments and constructs a list consisting of those arguments:

```
(list 1 2 3 4)            ; gives (1 2 3 4)
(list '(1 2) '(3 4) 5)    ; gives ((1 2) (3 4) 5)
(list evens odds)         ; gives ((0 2 4 6 8) (1 3 5 7 9))
(list 'evens 'odds)       ; gives (evens odds)
```

---

5. The terms `car` and `cdr` are remnants from earlier days when Lisp was implemented on the IBM 704. That machine's address registers had two parts, the *address* part and the *decrement* part. Thus, the original Lisp terms `car` and `cdr` were acronyms for "contents of the address part of the register," and "contents of the decrement part of the register," respectively. While the 704 has slipped into obscurity, these two acronyms remain.

In contrast, the `append` function takes two arguments both of which should be lists and concatenates the second list onto the end of the first list:

```
(append '(1 2) '(3 4))    ; gives (1 2 3 4)
(append evens odds)       ; gives (0 2 4 6 8 1 3 5 7 9)
(append '(1 2) '())       ; gives (1 2)
(append '(1 2) (list 3))  ; gives (1 2 3)
```

To add a single number to the front of the list of even numbers, we would use the `cons` function:

```
(cons 10 evens)           ; gives (10 0 2 4 6 8)
```

The empty list `()` at the end of the list is important; in recursively traversing a list, we always check for the empty list at the end.

Since Scheme was designed to process lists, it contains a number of special list processing functions. Because the need frequently arises, there is a special function named `null?` to test for an empty list:

```
(null?  '())              ; returns #t
(null?  evens)            ; returns #f
(null?  '(1 2 3))         ; returns #f
(null?  5)                ; returns #f
```

Scheme contains a number of functions for testing if one object is equal or equivalent to another. These are `equal?`, `=`, and `eqv?`. Rather than enumerating their differences, we will rely on the `equal?` function, which is fairly general. This function returns *true* (#t) if the two objects have the same structure and content; otherwise it returns *false*:

```
(equal? 5 5)                    ; returns #t
(equal? 5 1)                    ; returns #f
(equal? '(1 2) '(1 2))         ; returns #t
(equal? 5 '(5))                 ; returns #f
(equal? '(1 2 3) '(1 (2 3)))   ; returns #f
(equal? '(1 2) '(2 1))         ; returns #f
(equal? '() '())               ; returns #t
```

14.2.4 Elementary Values

So far, all of the elementary values we have seen in Scheme are either numbers or symbols (names). There are actually quite a few different types of numbers, including integers, rationals, and floating point numbers. Other types of Scheme elementary values include characters, functions, symbols, and strings. Each of these types can be distinguished using an appropriate predicate; for example, all of the following return #t:

```
(pair?   evens)
(list?   evens)
(symbol? 'evens)
(number?  3)
```

In addition to the types of values listed above, there are also Boolean values: #t which stands for *true* and #f which stands for *false*. All values except #f and the empty list () are interpreted as #t when used as a predicate.

14.2.5 Control Flow

The two control-flow constructs we will use are the if and the case.

The if function comes in the usual two flavors: the if-then and the if-then-else. Abstractly these appear as:

```
(if    test   then-part)
(if    test   then-part   else-part)
```

An example of each is:

```
(if (<   x   0) (- 0 x))
(if (<   x   y) x y)
```

The first if function returns the negative of x if x is less than zero. The second function returns the smaller of the two values of x and y.

The case function is much like the case in Ada and the switch in Java; the case function has an optional else which, if present, must be the last case. A simple case to compute the number of days in a month (ignoring leap years) is:

```
(case   month
        ((sep apr jun nov) 30)
        ((feb) 28)
        (else  31)
)
```

Note that each specific case takes an unquoted list of constants, except the else.

14.2.6 Defining Functions

Scheme functions are defined using define, which has the following general form:

```
(define   name   (lambda ( arguments )   function-body ))
```

Thus, a minimum function can be defined by:

```
(define min (lambda (x y) (if (< x y) x y)))
```

In other words, Scheme (like its ancestor Lisp) is an applied lambda calculus with the ability to give names to specific lambda definitions.

Since programmers quickly tire of entering the word lambda and the extra set of parentheses, Scheme provides an alternative way of writing the define function:

```
(define ( name arguments )   function-body )
```

Using this alternative, the minimum function can be rewritten more simply:

```
(define (min  x  y) (if (< x y) x y))
```

The following function computes the absolute value of a number:

```
(define (abs x) (if (< x 0) (- 0 x) x))
```

More interesting functions occur when we use recursion to define a function in terms of itself. One example from mathematics is the venerable factorial function, which can be defined in Scheme as follows:

```
(define (factorial n)
   (if (< n 1) 1 (* n (factorial (- n 1)))
))
```

For example, the function application (factorial 4) evaluates to 24 using the above definition in the following way:

```
(factorial 4) = (* 4 (factorial 3))
             = (* 4 (* 3 (factorial 2)))
             = (* 4 (* 3 (* 2 (factorial 1))))
             = (* 4 (* 3 (* 2 (* 1 (factorial 0)))))
             = (* 4 (* 3 (* 2 (* 1 1))))
             = (* 4 (* 3 (* 2 1)))
             = (* 4 (* 3 2))
             = (* 4 6)
             = 24
```

Even simple iterative tasks such as adding a list of numbers are accomplished recursively in Scheme. Here, we assume that the numbers form a list (a1 a2...an) whose elements are to be summed:

```
(define (sum alist)
   (if (null? alist) 0
        (+ (car alist) (sum (cdr alist)))
))
```

Note that this sum function is similar in effect to Scheme's built-in addition function (+).

The sum function exhibits a pattern common to a wide variety of Scheme functions. The function recurses through the list after first testing for an empty list. This test is often called the *base case* in recursive definitions. The *recursive step* proceeds by adding the first element of the list to the sum of the remainder of the list (the recursive application of the function). The function is guaranteed to terminate because at each recursive step of the computation, the list argument becomes shorter by taking the cdr of the list.

Other interesting Scheme functions manipulate lists of symbols, rather than numbers. All of the following functions presented here are already defined in Scheme; we show them here because they represent recurring patterns in Scheme programming.

The first example computes the length of a list, that is, its number of elements, counting sublists as single elements. Examples of the use of the `length` function include:

```
(length '(1 2 3 4))           ; returns 4
(length '((1 2) 3 (4 5 6)))   ; returns 3
(length '())                  ; returns 0
(length 5)                    ; error
```

The definition of the `length` function closely follows the pattern set by the `sum` function with only minor differences:

```
(define (length alist)
    (if (null? alist) 0 (+ 1 (length (cdr alist))))
))
```

The function application `(length '((1 2) 3 (4 5)))` yields:

```
(length '((1 2) 3 (4 5)))
    = (+ 1 (length '(3 (4 5))))
    = (+ 1 (+ 1 (length '((4 5)))))
    = (+ 1 (+ 1 (+ 1 (length ()))))
    = (+ 1 (+ 1 (+ 1 0)))
    = (+ 1 (+ 1 1))
    = (+ 1 2)
    = 3
```

Another common built-in function is the `member` function which tests to see whether an element `elt` (which can be a list) occurs as a member of a given list. If not, the function returns #f. Otherwise it returns the remainder of the list starting at the element found, which can be interpreted as #t. Examples of the use of the `member` function include:

```
(member 4 evens)          ; returns (4 6 8)
(member 1 evens)          ; returns #f
(member 2 '((1 2) 3 (4 5)))   ; returns #f
(member '(3 4) '(1 2 (3 4) 5))  ; returns ((3 4) 5)
```

The `member` function is most commonly used as a predicate. Again, the definition starts with the base case, namely an empty list, in which case `member` returns the empty list. Otherwise, it tests to see if the head of the list is equal to the element sought; if so, it returns the list and otherwise it recurses on the tail of the list.

```
(define (member elt alist)
    (if (null? alist) '()
        (if (equal? elt (car alist)) alist
            (member elt (cdr alist))
)))
```

Our last simple function is subst, which is used to substitute its first argument for all occurrences of its second argument in a list (its third argument). Like the member function, the checking for equal objects is only done at the top level of the list:

```
(subst 'x 2 '(1 2 3 2 1))        ; returns (1 x 3 x 1)
(subst 'x 2 '(1 (2 3) 2 1))      ; returns (1 (2 3) x 1)
(subst 'x 2 '(1 (2 3) (2)))      ; returns (1 (2 3) (2))
(subst 'x '(2 3) '(1 (2 3) 2 3)) ; returns (1 x 2 3)
(subst '(2 3) 'x '(x o x o))     ; returns ((2 3) o (2 3) o)
```

This function is interesting since it must build the output list as the result of the function, rather than simply returning one of its arguments. Otherwise, this function is similar in structure to the member function:

```
(define (subst y x alist)
   (if (null? alist) '()
       (if (equal? x (car alist))
           (cons y (subst y x (cdr alist)))
           (cons (car alist) (subst y x (cdr alist)))
)))
```

14.2.7 Let Expressions

Commonly, in defining a function a subexpression may occur several times. Scheme follows the convention in mathematics of allowing the introduction of a name for a subexpression. This is accomplished via the let function which has the following general form:

```
(let (( var1   expr1 ) ( var2 expr2 )  ... )  body )
```

Judicious use of a let function can improve the readability of a function definition. A side effect of using a let is that Scheme only evaluates the expression once, rather than once for every time it occurs in the definition. An example of the use of a let function follows:

```
(let ((x 2) (y 3)) (+ x y))       ; returns 5
(let ((plus +) (x 2)) (plus x 3)) ; returns 5
```

A more interesting use of a let function occurs when it appears inside the definition of a function:

```
(define (subst y x alist)
   (if (null? alist) '()
       (let ((head (car alist)) (tail (cdr alist)))
           (if (equal? x head)
               (cons y (subst y x tail))
               (cons head (subst y x tail))
))))
```

As in mathematics, a `let` function merely introduces a set of names for common expressions. The names are bound to their values only in the body of the `let` function. A more extensive example of the `let` function occurs in Section 14.2.7.[6]

In all of the above examples, the arguments to a function are either atoms or lists. Scheme also allows a function to be a formal parameter to another function being defined:

```
(define (mapcar fun alist)
   (if (null? alist) '()
       (cons (fun (car alist)) (mapcar fun (cdr alist)))
))
```

The `mapcar` function has two parameters, a function `fun` and a list `alist`; it applies the function `fun` to each element of a list, building a list from the results. As an example, consider a function of one argument which squares the argument:

```
(define (square x) (* x x))
```

The `square` function can be used with `mapcar` in either of the following two varations to square all of the elements of a list:

```
(mapcar square '(2 3 5 7 9))
(mapcar (lambda (x) (* x x)) '(2 3 5 7 9))
```

In the first variation, the first parameter is a defined function. In the second variation, a nameless function is passed using lambda notation for defining it. Both variations yield the result (4 9 25 49 81).[7]

This ease of defining functional forms gives functional languages like Scheme, Lisp, and Haskell an ease of extensibility. With such a facility users can easily add many apply-to-all functional forms. Many simple Scheme functions are defined this way.

Sections 14.3.8–14.3.10 develop several interesting examples that combine to illustrate the unique value of functional programming in Scheme. The first example revisits the semantics of Clite, which was originally discussed and implemented in Java (see Chapter 8). The second example, symbolic differentiation, is a rather classic one, while the third example reconsiders the eight queens problem that was originally implemented in Java (see Chapter 13).

---

6. In Scheme, the order of evaluation of the values `expr1`, `expr2`, and so on in a `let` is not implied. In other words, each value is evaluated independently of the bindings of the names `var1`, `var2`, and so on. If it is necessary to refer to an earlier name in a later expression within a `let`, the `let*` function should be used instead.

7. The built-in Scheme function `map` is equivalent to `mapcar`.

Observation

Tracing

Most Scheme interpreters provide a tracing, or single-stepping, facility to aid in understanding the details of a function's behavior. This is particularly useful in debugging. Unfortunately, no particular tracing function is part of Standard Scheme, so its use varies from one slightly from one implementation to another. Below we give an example of the use of a tracing function to single-step the activation and deactivation of calls in the factorial function discussed above:

```
> (trace factorial)              Trace: Value = 1
> (factorial 4)                  Trace: Value = 1
Trace: (factorial 4)             Trace: Value = 2
Trace: (factorial 3)             Trace: Value = 6
Trace: (factorial 2)             Trace: Value = 24
Trace: (factorial 1)             24
Trace: (factorial 0)             > (untrace factorial)
                                 > (factorial 4)
                                 24
```

For some Scheme implementations, the effect of tracing can be achieved via the standard imperative technique of embedding debugging print commands. One convenient function to use is printf, which is similar to the function of the same name in C. The printf function takes as its first argument a string which specifies how the output is to be displayed; the code ~a is used to display a value, while ~n is used to represent an end of line code. Using this, we can rewrite the factorial function to get output similar to that above using:

```
(define (factorial n)
   (printf "(factorial ~a ~n)" n)
   (if (<= n 0) 1
      ; else
      (let ((x (* n (factorial (- n 1)))))
         (printf "(factorial ~a) = ~a ~n" n x)
         x
      )
))
```

Below is an example of the output for this modified factorial function:

```
> (factorial 3)                  (factorial 1) = 1
(factorial 3)                    (factorial 2) = 2
(factorial 2)                    (factorial 3) = 6
(factorial 1)                    6
(factorial 0)
```

This works easily because both the define and let functions allow a sequence of functions as a body and return the value of the last function computed.

14.2.8 Example: Semantics of Clite

In this section we implement much of the semantics of Clite using Scheme. Recall from Chapter 8 that for the elementary language Clite, the environment is static, so the state can be simply represented as a collection of variable-value pairs. This is expressed as follows:

$$state = \{\langle var_1, val_1 \rangle, \langle var_2, val_2 \rangle, \ldots, \langle var_m, val_m \rangle\}$$

Here, each var_i denotes a variable and each val_i denotes its currently assigned value.

The state is like a *watch window* in an integrated development environment (IDE). It is always tied to a particular statement in the program source and shows for each program variable its current value. In our Java implementation, the state was implemented as a hash table in which the variable identifier was the key and the associated value was the current value of the variable (see Chapter 8 for the details).

A fundamental idea in the Scheme implementation is that a state is naturally represented as a list, with each element of the list being a pair representing the binding of a variable to its value. So the Clite state:

$$\{\langle x, 1 \rangle, \langle y, 5 \rangle\}$$

can be represented as the Scheme list:

```
((x 1) (y 5))
```

First, we implement the state access functions `get` and `onion` (overriding union) from the Java implementation (see Chapter 8). Recall that `get` is used to obtain the value of a variable from the current state. In Scheme, the code needed is similar to the `member` function:

```
(define (get id state)
  (if (equal? id (caar state)) (cadar state)
      (get id (cdr state))
))
```

Since the Clite type system requires that all variables used in a program be declared and we assume that the abstract syntax has been statically verified as described in Chapter 6, there cannot be a reference to a variable that is not in the state. Thus, the function `get` is simpler than the `member` function in this regard, since it does not need to check for a null list. An example of the `get` function is:

```
(get 'y '((x 5) (y 3) (z 1)))
    = (get 'y '((y 3) (z 1)))
    = 3
```

A good model for the `onion` (overriding union) function is the previously defined `subst` function, with one difference being the structure of the lists and the other being that there must be exactly one occurrence of each variable in the state:

```
(define (onion id val state)
  (if (equal? id (caar state))
        (cons (list id val) (cdr state))
        (cons (car state) (onion id val (cdr state)))
))
```

The `onion` function can thus make the simplifying assumption that the variable for which we are searching occurs within the state since we assume static semantics verification as described in Chapter 6. Hence, there is no need to check for a null list as the base case. The `onion` function can also stop recursing once the variable is found. An example of the `onion` function is:

```
(onion 'y 4 '((x 5) (y 3) (z 1)))
  = (cons '(x 5) (onion 'y '((y 3) (z 1)))
  = (cons '(x 5) (cons '(y 4) '((z 1))))
  = '((x 5) (y 4) (z 1))
```

In developing semantic functions for Clite, we assume that statements in Clite abstract syntax (see Figure 2.14) are represented as Scheme lists as follows:

```
(skip)
(assignment target source)
(block s1 ... sn)
(loop test body)
(conditional test thenbranch elsebranch)
```

Here, each individual field for an abstract statement type is not named, as it was in Java, but rather is identified by its a position in the list. Thus, in a `loop` statement the `test` is the second element (i.e., the `cadr`) of the list, while the `body` is the third element (the `caddr`).

The meaning function for a Clite statement can be written as a simple Scheme case statement:

```
(define (m-statement statement state)
  (case (car statement)
        ((skip) (m-skip statement state))
        ((assignment) (m-assignment statement state))
        ((block) (m-block (cdr statement) state))
        ((loop) (m-loop statement state))
        ((conditional) (m-conditional statement state))
        (else ())
))
```

The meaning of an abstract *Statement* is a state-transforming function of the form which takes a *State* as input and produces a *State* as output. The implementation of these meaning functions follows directly from the rules given in Chapter 8 (and summarized here). We also asssume that a static semantics verification, as described in Chapter 6, has been performed.

A *Skip* statement corresponds to an empty statement. As such, it leaves the state unchanged; the output state is a copy of the input state.

```
(define (m-skip statement state) state)
```

The meaning of a *Block* is just that of its statements applied to the current state in the order they appear. That is, if a *Block* has no statements the state is not changed. Otherwise, the state resulting from the meaning of the first *Statement* in the *Block* becomes the basis for defining the meaning of the rest of the block. This is a recursive definition.

This is implemented in Scheme by first interpreting the meaning of the first statement in the list, and then recursively applying this function to the remainder of the list. We have already stripped the block tag from the head of the list in the m-statement function.

```
(define (m-block alist state)
  (if (null? alist) state
      (m-block (cdr alist) (m-statement (car alist) state))
))
```

A *Loop* statement has a boolean test, which is an *Expression*, and a *Statement* body. If the boolean test is not *true*, the meaning (output state) of a *Loop* is the same as the input state, otherwise the meaning is the state resulting from first executing its body one time, then passing the resulting state to the re-execution of the *Loop*.

The Scheme implementation follows almost directly from this definition:

```
(define (m-loop statement state)
  (if (m-expression (car statement) state)
      (m-loop statement (m-statement (cdr statement) state))
      state
))
```

Finally, consider the Scheme meaning function for Clite expression evaluation for the integers only. To facilitate this, we use the following list representation for each type of abstract Clite expression:

```
(value val), where val is an integer
(variable id), where id is a variable name
(operator term1 term2), where operator is one of:
    plus, minus, times, div -- arithmetic
    lt, le, eq, ne, gt, ge -- relational
```

The meaning function for a Clite abstract expression is implemented using a case on the type of expression. The meaning of a value expression is just the value itself (i.e., the cadr). The meaning of a variable is the value associated with the variable's identifier (the the cadr) in the current state.

The meaning of a binary expression is obtained by applying the operator to the meanings of the operands (the `cadr` and the `caddr`):

```scheme
(define (m-expression expr state)
  (case (car expr)
        ((value) (cadr expr))
        ((variable) (get (cadr expr) state))
        (else (applyBinary (car expr) (cadr expr)
                           (caddr expr) state))
))
```

The function `applyBinary` defined in Chapter 8 restricted to the integers is easily implemented as a case on the operator. Here we show only the arithmetic operators, leaving the implementation of relational operators as an exercise:

```scheme
(define (applyBinary op left right state)
  (let ((leftval (m-expression left state))
        (rightval (m-expression right state)))
    (case op
      ((plus)   (+ leftval rightval))
      ((minus)  (- leftval rightval))
      ((times)  (* leftval rightval))
      ((div)    (/ leftval rightval))
      (else #f))
))
```

The implementation of relational operators, as well as the assignment statement itself, is left as an exercise.

As an application of the `m-expression` function to the expression y+2 in the state {<x,5>, <y,3>, <z,1>}, consider the following:

```scheme
(m-expression '(plus (variable y) (value 2)) '((x 5) (y 3) (z 1)))
= (applyBinary '(plus (variable y) (value 2)) '((x 5) (y 3)
    (z 1)))
= (+ (m-expression '(variable y) '((x 5) (y 3) (z 1)))
     (m-expression '(value 2) '((x 5) (y 3) (z 1))))
= (+ (get 'y '((x 5) (y 3) (z 1)))
     (m-expression '(value 2) '((x 5) (y 3) (z 1))))
= (+ 3
     (m-expression '(value 2) '((x 5) (y 3) (z 1))))
= (+ 3 2)
= 5
```

This development of even this small fraction of the semantics of Clite should be convincing that a full semantic model for an imperative language can be implemented in Scheme.

Thus, via interpretation, Scheme is capable of computing any function that can be programmed in an imperative language. The converse is also true since modern computers are fundamentally imperative in nature. Since Scheme interpreters are implemented on these machines, any function programmed in Scheme can be computed by an imperative program. Thus, in fact, imperative languages and functional languages are equivalent in computational power.

14.2.9 Example: Symbolic Differentiation

The utility of Scheme for symbol manipulation is widespread, as the previous example suggests. This next example further illustrates some of the power of Scheme by doing symbolic differentiation and simplification of simple calculus formulae. Some familiar rules for symbolic differentiation are given in Figure 14.2.

For example, differentiating the function $2 \cdot x + 1$ with respect to x using these rules gives:

$$
\begin{aligned}
\frac{d(2 \cdot x + 1)}{dx} &= \frac{d(2 \cdot x)}{dx} + \frac{d1}{dx} \\
&= 2 \cdot \frac{dx}{dx} + x \cdot \frac{d2}{dx} + 0 \\
&= 2 \cdot 1 + x \cdot 0 + 0
\end{aligned}
$$

which would ordinarily simplify to 2.

$$\frac{d}{dx}(c) = 0 \qquad\qquad\qquad\qquad c \text{ is a constant}$$

$$\frac{d}{dx}(x) = 1$$

$$\frac{d}{dx}(u + v) = \frac{du}{dx} + \frac{dv}{dx} \qquad\qquad u \text{ and } v \text{ are functions of } x$$

$$\frac{d}{dx}(u - v) = \frac{du}{dx} - \frac{dv}{dx}$$

$$\frac{d}{dx}(uv) = u\frac{dv}{dx} + v\frac{du}{dx}$$

$$\frac{d}{dx}\left(\frac{u}{v}\right) = \left(v\frac{du}{dx} - u\frac{dv}{dx}\right)\bigg/ v^2$$

| **Figure 14.2   Symbolic Differentiation Rules**

In Scheme it is convenient to represent expressions using Polish prefix notation:

```
(+ term1 term2)
(- term1 term2)
(* term1 term2)
(/ term1 term2)
```

The required function to do symbolic differentiation first tests to see if the expression is either a constant or the variable being differentiated, as in the first two rules above. Otherwise, the expression is a list starting with an operator, and the code applies one of the remaining four rules using a case on the operator. A let function has been used to make the Scheme code look as much like the rules in Figure 14.2 as possible.

```
(define (diff x expr)
  (if (not (list? expr))
    (if (equal? x expr) 1 0)
    (let ((u (cadr expr)) (v (caddr expr)))
      (case (car expr)
        ((+) (list '+ (diff x u) (diff x v)))
        ((-) (list '- (diff x u) (diff x v)))
        ((*) (list '+
               (list '* u (diff x v))
               (list '* v (diff x u))))
        ((/) (list 'div (list '-
               (list '* v (diff x u))
               (list '* u (diff x v)))
               (list '* u v)))
))))
```

An application of the diff function to the expression $2 \cdot x + 1$ gives:

```
(diff 'x '(+ (* 2 x) 1))
  = (list '+ (diff 'x '(* 2 x)) (diff 'x 1))
  = (list '+ (list '+ (list '* 2 (diff 'x 'x))
                      (list '* x (diff 'x 2)))
            (diff 'x 1))
  = (list '+ (list '+ (list '* 2 1) (list '* x (diff 'x 2)))
            (diff 'x 1))
  = (list '+ (list '+ '(* 2 1) (list '* x (diff 'x 2)))
            (diff 'x 1))
  = (list '+ (list '+ '(* 2 1) (list '* x 0)) (diff 'x 1))
  = (list '+ (list '+ '(* 2 1) '(* x 0)) (diff 'x 1))
  = (list '+ '(+ '(* 2 1) '(* x 0)) (diff 'x 1))
  = (list '+ '(+ '(* 2 1) '(* x 0)) 0)
```

which, in infix form, is $2 * 1 + 0 * x + 0$. The normal result, 2, would occur after simplifying this expression. Writing an expression simplifier is left as an exercise.

14.2.10 Example: Eight Queens

In Chapter 13, we developed an object-oriented version of Wirth's backtracking algorithm [Wirth, 1976]. The general solution that Wirth presents is a recursive procedure that iterates through a series of trial moves. Each move is tested to see if it satisfies an appropriate *validity* criterion. If it does, the move is recorded, and if the problem is not yet solved, the procedure calls itself recursively to try the next level. If the recursive call fails, then the current move is undone and the next move is tried. The process of trying moves continues until either a completely successful solution is found or all of the moves at the current level have been unsuccessfully tried.

The general iterative solution for this problem, according to [Wirth, 1976, p. 136], can be achieved in the following C-like notation:

```
boolean try(Solution) {
  boolean successful = false;
  initialize moves;
  while (more moves && !successful) {
    select next move;
    if (move is valid) {
      record move in Solution;
      if (Solution not done) {
        successful = try(Solution);
        if (!successful)
          undo move in Solution;
      }
    }
  }
  return successful;
}
```

This section develops a purely functional version of this algorithm and then specializes it to solve the eight queens problem. This solution is interesting because it shows some of the positive and negative aspects of functional programming, in contrast with imperative and object-oriented programming.

There are effectively two problems we must solve in converting this general, imperative model into a purely functional one. The first problem is that the function `try` returns two results: whether or not a solution was successfully found and the solution itself.

In the imperative version outlined above, the function `try` returns `successful` as the value of the function, and the *Solution* is returned as a reference parameter: the commands *record* and *undo* are generalized assignments implemented as function calls. A purely functional language does not have reference parameters and assignments, nor can it return more than a single result. To solve this problem in Scheme, we can `cons` the value of the variable `successful` onto the front of the solution itself.

The second problem is that Wirth's model uses a while loop to iterate through a series of moves until either a completely successful solution is found or there are no more moves at this level. A direct Scheme encoding of this problem could use the imperative features of Scheme to essentially duplicate Wirth's algorithm. However, to present a purely functional equivalent to the imperative loop structure, we shall replace the loop by a recursive function.

We develop this algorithm in bottom-up or inside-out fashion, depending on your point of view. This means that we shall attack the inner if statements first, then the while loop, and finally the overall function. Functions particular to the actual problem being solved, such as when the solution is done, when there are no more moves, and so forth, will be left unspecified for now.

The first function, denoted `tryone`, was developed to solve the *if move is valid* statement in the above model:

```
(define (tryone move soln)
  (let ((xsoln (cons move soln)))
    (if (valid move soln)
    (if (done xsoln) (cons #t xsoln)
        (try xsoln))
    (cons #f soln)
)))
```

The function `tryone` is only called if the variable `successful` is *false*; so the parameter `soln` does not have the value of `successful` on the front of the list. However, it returns a solution with the value of `successful` on the front of the list.

Note that we used a `let` function as a functional shorthand to avoid computing the extended solution `xsoln` twice. The function first checks if the current move is valid given the current partial solution. If it is not valid, then it returns *false* for `successful` and the current solution via `(cons #f soln)`. If the move is valid, then it checks to see if the extended solution solves the problem (function `done`). In this case, it returns true for `successful` and the extended solution. Otherwise it recursively calls `try` with the extended solution to attempt to continue extending the solution.

Next we convert the while loop to a recursive function, using the following strategy. That is, any imperative while loop of the form:

```
while (test) {
    body
}
```

can be converted to a recursive function of the form:

```
(define (while test body state)
    (if (test state)
        (let ((onepass (body state)))
            (while test body onepass)
        )
        state
))
```

Here, the variable `onepass` delivers the state that results from executing the body of the while loop one time. So if the test is *true*, the while statement is reexecuted after making one pass on the body. Otherwise, the current state is returned.

The program state for eight queens is a little more complicated, but this general loop conversion strategy produces the following function:

```
(define (trywh move soln)
  (if (and (hasmore move) (not (car soln)))
      (let ((atry (tryone move (cdr soln))))
        (if (car atry) atry (trywh (nextmove move) soln))
   )
  soln
))
```

Note that the `let` function appears as a functional shorthand to avoid writing the call on the `tryone` function twice. Note also that the `trywh` function expects the value of the variable `successful` to be on the front of the list, while the `tryone` function does not, since `tryone` is called only when `successful` is *false*.

Finally, we implement the `try` function. It is called with a partial solution without the variable `successful`, and returns the `cons` of the variable `successful` and the solution found. It is responsible for getting the first move to initialize the while loop:

```
(define (try soln) (trywh 1 (cons #f soln)))
```

To specialize this general strategy for solving a particular problem, we must implement several functions.

- The functions `hasmore` and `nextmove` are concerned with generating trial moves.
- The function `valid` is concerned with whether a trial move validly extends the current partial solution.
- The function `done` tests whether an extended solution solves the problem.

We illustrate implementations of these functions by developing a solution for the eight queens problem.

An initial concern for the eight queens problem is how to store the (row, column) position of each of the queens. Recall from Section 13.4.2 that we developed the solution one column at a time, storing the row position for each column using an array. In the solution developed here, we store the row position for each column using a list, but with one fundamental difference. We store the list in reverse order so that the most recently added row is at the head of the list at all times. For example, the board with three queens in the (row, column) positions shown in Figure 14.3 is represented as the following list:

```
(5 3 1)
```

If the variable N represents the number of rows and columns of the chess board, we can define the functions for generating moves as:

```
(define (hasmore move) (<= move N))
(define (nextmove move) (+ move 1))
```

Figure 14.3   Three Queens on an 8 × 8 Chess Board

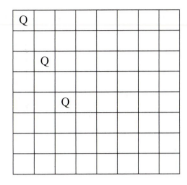

which generates row numbers in the sequence from 1 to N. Similarly, we can define a solution to be "done" in the following way:

```scheme
(define (done soln) (>= (length soln) N))
```

Now all that remains is to define whether or not a trial row validly extends the current partial solution. Recall from Chapter 13 that three conditions must hold:

1   The trial row must not be occupied. This means that the trial row (or move) must not be a member of the current solution.
2   The southwest diagonal formed by the trial row and column must not be occupied. The southwest diagonal is the sum of the row and column numbers.
3   The southeast diagonal formed by the trial row and column must not be occupied. The southeast diagonal is the difference of the row and column numbers.

Given a row and column number, the southwest and southeast diagonals are easily computed as:

```scheme
(define (swDiag row col) (+ row col))
(define (seDiag row col) (- row col))
```

To test a trial solution, we must first convert a list of row positions into a list of southwest and southeast diagonal positions. For a given trial `soln` the row position of the trial move is `(car soln)` and the associated column number is `(length soln)`. The functions `selist` and `swlist` develop these lists for any trial solution.

```scheme
(define (selist alist)
  (if (null? alist)
      '()
      (cons (seDiag (car alist) (length alist))
            (selist (cdr alist)))))
(define (swlist alist)
  (if (null? alist)
      '()
      (cons (swDiag (car alist) (length alist))
            (swlist (cdr alist)))))
```

Finally, the three conditions for the trial solution can be tested using the function `valid`. This function checks that the current trial move representing a row position validly extends the current partial solution. That is, the move (row) is not a member of the solution, and the move (row position and associated column) is not a member of either the southeast or southwest diagonal.

```
(define (valid move soln)
   (let ((col (length (cons move soln))))
      (and (not (member move soln))
         (not (member (seDiag move col) (selist soln)))
         (not (member (swDiag move col) (swlist soln)))
)))
```

This program can be tested using the call `(try ())`, where the global variable N defines the size of the problem. For example, the declaration:

```
(define N 8)
```

will specialize the solution for an 8×8 board. This concludes our functional implementation of the backtracking and eight queens problem.

This exercise has been interesting for a number of reasons. On the one hand, it shows the power of functional programming. On the other hand, our solution shows some of the weaknesses of pure functional programming:

1 Converting a program that has an iterative loop to a recursive function can be unnecessarily tedious.
2 Using a list to return multiple values from a function is clumsy when compared to using reference parameters or returning an object with named instance variables.

To compensate for the first weakness (and also for the sake of efficiency), Scheme extends "pure Lisp" by including imperative features such as local variables, assignment statements, and iterative loops. The second weakness is really a weakness of Scheme's type system, one that is substantially corrected in later functional languages like Haskell. We shall discuss Haskell's type system in the next section.

14.3 HASKELL

A number of recent developments in functional programming are not well-captured by the traditional languages, Common Lisp and Scheme. In this section, we introduce a more modern functional language, Haskell [Thompson, 1999], whose features signal more clearly the present and future directions in functional programming research and applications. The distinct and salient features of Haskell include its lazy evaluation strategy and its type system. While Haskell is a strongly typed language (all type errors are identified), sometimes a type error is not detected until the program element that contains the error is actually executed.

14.3.1 Introduction

Haskell has a minimalist syntax for writing functions. Consider the factorial function, which can be written in any one of the following ways:

```
-- equivalent definitions of factorial
fact1 0 = 1
fact1 n = n * fact1 (n - 1)

fact2 n = if n == 0 then 1 else n * fact2 (n - 1)

fact3 n
    | n == 0 = 1
    | otherwise = n * fact3 (n - 1)
```

A double dash (--) starts a Haskell comment, which continues to the end of the line. The first version, fact1, is written in a generative style, in that the special cases are defined first followed by the general case. The second version, fact2, uses the more traditional if-then-else style of definition. The third version, fact3, uses guards on each definition; this style is useful when there are more than two alternatives. In the example applications, all three styles will be used.

Note the minimalist syntax. Unlike Scheme there is no define introducing the function definition, no parentheses surrounding the formal arguments, no commas separating the arguments. Furthermore, there is neither an explicit continuation symbol (as in Unix shell programming) nor an explicit terminator (the semicolon in C/C++/Java). Instead, like Python, Haskell relies on indentation of continued constructs. In fact3, since it is written over more than one line, the guards (|) must all be indented by the same amount. However, the equals signs need not be aligned. A long definition for a guard would conventionally start on a new line and be indented from the guard symbol.

In Haskell the arguments to a function are not surrounded by parentheses, either in the definition of the function or its invocation. Furthermore, function invocation binds more tightly than infix operators. So the normal interpretation of fact n - 1 is $fact(n) - 1$, which is not what is desired. So the quantity n - 1 must be parenthesized, since it is a single argument to fact in all three variants. The mathematical quantity $fact(n - 1) * n$ would be written:

```
fact (n - 1) * n
```

where the parentheses are needed so that the quantity n - 1 is interpreted as the single argument to fact.

Haskell is case-sensitive. Functions and variables must start with a lowercase letter, while types start with an uppercase letter. Furthermore, a function may not redefine a standard Haskell function. As we shall see, functions in Haskell are strongly typed and polymorphic.

Also, like most functional languages, Haskell uses infinite precision integers by default:

```
> fact2 30
265252859812191058636308480000000
```

an answer which clearly exceeds the largest int value in a C/C++/Java program.

In Haskell, as with any functional language, functions are first-class objects, in that unevaluated functions may be passed as arguments, and constructed and returned as values of functions. Furthermore, functions may be *curried* in that an *n* argument function may have some of its arguments fixed. A *curried function* is an *n* argument function in which some of its arguments are fixed. As an example of the latter, suppose we want to define a function which doubles its argument:

```
double1 x = 2 * x
double2 = (2 *)
```

The functions `double1` and `double2` are equivalent; the second is an example of a curried function.

With this brief introduction, let us begin a more systematic exploration of Haskell.

14.3.2 Expressions

Expressions in Haskell are normally written in infix notation, in which the operator or function appears between its operands, as in the example:

```
2+2       -- compute the value 4
```

When this expression is presented to a Haskell interpreter, it computes the value 4. The usual arithmetic and relational operators are provided in Haskell, and more complicated expressions can be built using parentheses and the built-in precedence relationships among these operators. Here, for instance, is a Haskell expression that computes the value 48.

```
5*(4+6)-2
```

which would be equivalent to the Scheme expression `(- (* 5 (+ 4 6) 2))`. Moreover, we may write Haskell expressions using prefix notation, provided that we parenthesize all operators and nonatomic operands. This is illustrated by the following expression (equivalent to the above infix expression).

```
(-) ((*) 5 ((+) 4 6)) 2
```

A more complete summary of the Haskell operators and their precedence relationships is given in Table 14.1.

The right-associative operators are evaluated from right to left when they are adjacent in an expression at the same level of parenthesization; the left-associative operators are evaluated from left to right. For instance, the Haskell expression

```
2^3^4
```

denotes raising 2 to the 3^4 power (or 2^{81} or 2417851639229258349412352), rather than raising 2^3 to the 4th power (or 2^{12} or 4096). The non-associative operators cannot appear adjacent in an expression. That is, the expression a+b+c is permissible, but a<b<c is not.

| Table 14.1 | Summary of the Haskell Operators and Their Precedences

Precedence	Left-Associative	Non-Associative	Right-Associative
9	!, !!, //		.
8			**, ^, ^ ^
7	*, /, `div`, `mod`, `rem`, `quot`		
6	+, -	:+	
5	\\		:, ++
4		/=, <, <=, ==, >, >=, `elem`, `notElem`	
3			&&
2			||
1	», »=	:=	
0			$, `seq`

The meanings of many of these operators should be self-explanatory. Many of the others will be explained in the discussion below.[8]

14.3.3 Lists and List Comprehensions

Like Lisp and Scheme, the fundamental data structure of Haskell is the list. Lists are collections of elements with a given type. Lists can be defined by enumerating their elements, as shown in the following definitions for two small lists of numbers:

```
evens = [0, 2, 4, 6, 8]
odds = [1, 3 .. 9]
```

The list odds is defined by the familiar mathematical convention of using ellipses (..) to omit all the intermediate elements when the pattern is obvious. Pictorially, the list evens is represented in Figure 14.1(a).

Alternatively, a list can be defined using a so-called generator which takes the following form:

```
moreevens = [2*x | x <- [0..10]]
```

This literally says, "the list of all values 2*x such that x is an element in the list [0..10]." The operator <- represents the mathematical symbol ∈, which denotes list membership.

---

8. Haskell also supports the definition of additional operators, provided that they are formed from the following symbols: # $ % * + . / < = > ? \^| | : ~.

A list *comprehension* can be defined using a generator, and the list it defines may be infinite. For instance, the following defines the infinite list containing all the even nonnegative integers:

```
mostevens = [2*x | x <- [0,1 .. ]]
```

Here, the generator is the expression x <- [0,1 ..]. Alternatively, this infinite list could have been defined by:

```
mostevens = [0,2 .. ]
```

This example illustrates a strong departure of Haskell from the traditional functional languages. Infinite lists, and functions that compute values from them, are common in Haskell. They are possible because of Haskell's general commitment to *lazy evaluation*, which says simply to evaluate no argument to a function until the moment it is absolutely needed.[9] For infinite lists, this means that they are stored in unevaluated form; however the *n*th element, no matter how large the value of *n*, can be computed whenever it is needed.

Generators may have conditions attached to them, just as in mathematics. The following function computes the factors of a number:

```
factors n = [ f | f <- [1..n], n 'mod' f == 0]
```

This can be read as the factors of n are all numbers f in the range from one to n such that f divides n evenly. Note that the expression:

```
n 'mod' f == 0
```

could also have been written:

```
mod n f == 0
```

When a function name is used as an infix operator, the name must be enclosed in backquote characters.

The basic function for constructing a list is the infix operator : , which takes an element and a list as its two arguments.[10] Here are some examples, where [] denotes the empty list:

```
8:[]        -- gives [8]
6:8:[]      -- gives 6:[8] or [6,8]
4:[6,8]     -- gives [4,6,8]
```

A Haskell list has two parts, the first element or the *head* of the list, and the list of remaining elements or its *tail*. The functions head and tail return these two parts,

---

9. Recall the distinction between "eager" and "lazy" evaluation first made in Chapter 9, where parameter passing was discussed. It should be clear that eager evaluation of arguments to a function would prohibit the definition of infinite lists or functions that operate on them.

10. This operator is like the Scheme cons function.

respectively. Referring to the list `evens` pictured in Figure 14.1, the following examples illustrate these functions:

```
head evens              --gives 0
tail evens              --gives [2,4,6,8]
head (tail evens)       --gives 2
tail (tail evens)       --gives [4,6,8]
head [6,8]              --gives 6
head 6:[8]              --gives 6
tail [6,8]              --gives [8]
tail [8]                --gives []
```

Combining generators and list concatenation, the set of prime numbers using a sieve can be defined:

```
primes = sieve [2..]
    where
    sieve (p:xs) = p : sieve [ a | a <- xs, a 'mod' p /= 0]
```

First, note the use of the `where` clause, which makes the definition of `sieve` local to the definition of `primes` (analogous to the use of `let` in Scheme or mathematics). The definition says that the list of primes up to n is returned by `sieve` on the list of numbers from two through n. The function `sieve`, given a list consisting of a head `p` and a tail `xs` (which is a list), consists of the list whose head is `p` (which must be prime) and whose tail is the value of `sieve` applied to `xs` with all the multiples of `p` removed. The second definition of `sieve` is an example of a pattern match and is explained in Section 14.3.6.

The principal operator for putting lists together is ++.[11] This operator is illustrated by the following examples:

```
[1,2]++[3,4]++[5]    -- gives [1,2,3,4,5]
evens ++ odds        -- gives [0,2,4,6,8,1,3,5,7,9]
[1,2]++[]            -- gives [1,2]
[1,2]++3:[]          -- gives [1,2,3]
1++2                 -- error; wrong type of arguments for ++
```

Since Haskell was designed to process lists, it contains a number of special list processing functions. Because the need frequently arises, there is a special function `null` to test for an empty list:

```
null []          -- gives True
null evens       -- gives False
null [1,2,3]     -- gives False
null 5           -- error; wrong type of argument for null
```

Haskell contains functions for testing if one object is equal or equivalent to another. The main function is embodied in the infix operator ==, which is fairly general. This

---

11. This operator is like the Scheme `append` function.

function returns `True` if the two objects have the same structure and content; otherwise it returns `False` or a type error:

```
5==5                     -- returns True
5==1                     -- returns False
[1,2]==[1,2]             -- returns True
5==[5]                   -- error; mismatched argument types
[1,2,3]==[1,[2,3]]       -- error; mismatched argument types
[1,2]==[2,1]             -- returns False
[]==[]                   -- returns True
```

List types can be defined and then later used in the construction of functions. To define a list type `IntList` of `Int` values, for instance, the following statement is used:

```
type IntList = [Int]
```

Notice that the use of brackets signals that the type being defined is a particular kind of list—one whose entries are of type `Int`.[12]

14.3.4 Elementary Types and Values

So far, all of the values we have seen in Haskell are integers, predefined symbols (function names), and type names. Haskell supports various types of elementary values, including booleans (called `Bool`), integers (`Int` and `Integer`), characters (`Char`), character strings (`String`), and floating point numbers (`Float`).

As noted above, the boolean values are `True` and `False`. The `Int` type supports a finite range of values (-2^{31} through $2^{31} - 1$, the usual range for 32-bit representation). However, the `Integer` type supports integers of any size, and hence contains an infinite set of values.

Characters in Haskell are represented inside single quotes, as in 'a', and familiar escape conventions are used to identify special characters, like '\n' for newline, '\t' for tab, and so forth. Strings are represented either as series of characters inside double quotes (") or as lists of `Char` values. That is, the type `String` is equivalent to the type `[Char]`. So the list `['h','e','l','l','o']` is equivalent to the String "hello". That is, the following type definition is implicit in Haskell:

```
type String = [Char]
```

Because of this equivalence, many String operators are the same as list operators. For instance, the expression

```
"hello" ++ "world"
```

represents string concatenation, and yields the result "helloworld".

---

12. Haskell type names are distinguished from other names by the fact that they begin with an upper-case letter.

Floating point values are written in either decimal notation or scientific notation. Each of the following represents the number 3.14.

```
3.14
0.000314e4
```

Various functions are available for transforming floating point values in Haskell, including the following, whose meanings are fairly self-explanatory (arguments to trigonometric functions are expressed in radians):

```
abs acos atan ceiling floor cos sin
log logBase pi sqrt
```

14.3.5 Control Flow

The major control flow constructs in Haskell are the guarded command and the if-then-else.[13] The guarded command is a generalization of a nested if-then-else, and can be written more briefly. For instance, suppose we want to find the maximum of three values, x, y, and z. Then we can express this as an if-then-else as follows:

```
if x >= y && x >= z then x
else if y >= x && y >= z then y
     else z
```

Alternatively, we can express this as a guarded command in the following way:

```
| x >= y && x >= z = x
| y >= x && y >= z = y
| otherwise = z
```

The guarded command is widely used when defining Haskell functions, as we shall see below.

14.3.6 Defining Functions

Haskell functions are defined in two parts. The first part identifies the function's name, domain, and range, and the second part describes the meaning of the function. That is, a function definition has the following form:

```
name :: Domain -> Range
name x y z
        | g1 = e1
        | g2 = e2
        :
        | otherwise = e
```

13. Haskell also has a case function, which is similar to the case in Ada and the switch in Java and C. However, this function seems to be relatively unimportant in Haskell programming, as its meaning is subsumed by the guarded command.

Figure 14.5   Three Queens on an 8 × 8 Chess Board

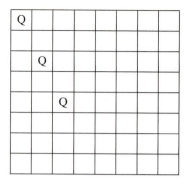

move. In developing the solution we shall use the same encodings of the diagonals as in Section 13.4.2. However, rather than attempting to convert Wirth's backtracking algorithm [Wirth, 1976] and then adapting it to the eight queens problem, we develop a purely functional version from scratch.

The first decision is that the desired function produce a list of all possible solutions, where each solution lists the row position of each queen in order by column. For example, the board with three queens in the (row, column) positions shown in Figure 14.5 is represented as the following list:

```
[0, 2, 4]
```

However, the program is best understood as working from right to left.

In attempting to extend a partial safe solution, we first construct new lists with a trial row number (taken from the sequence `[0..n-1]`). Recall from Section 13.4.2 that such a (*row, col*) is safe:

- If the trial row is not an element of the existing solution.
- If the southwest and southeast diagonals are unoccupied. Section 13.4.2 the southwest diagonal was computed as *row + col* and the southeast diagonal as *row − col*.

This *safe* check is embodied in the functions `safe` and `checks`. The function `safe` is passed a board b and a next trial row q. In this program the board is constructed from right to left; since solutions are symmetrical, which direction to work from is purely a matter of preference or efficiency.

Row q is safe relative to the current board if the conditions above are met. In this case, `checks` is called once per index value of b, that is, from 0 to `length b` - 1. The row check for each i is simply: `q /= b!!i`. The southwest diagonal check for each i should be `q+n /= b!!i - (n-i-1)` which simplifies to `q - b!!i /= -i-1`. By a similar analysis, the southeast diagonal check for each i simplifies to `q - b!!i /= i+1`. The check in the program combines the two cases by taking the absolute value.

In a functional program there is no global storage to store and access the diagonals. Even the occupied rows are stored as a list and passed as an argument. Thus, we prefer to dynamically compute the diagonal information as needed, rather than pass it in the argument list.

The solution for this problem is:

```
queens n = solve n
    where
    solve 0 = [ [ ] ]
    solve (k+1) = [ q:b | b <- solve k,
           q <- [0..(n - 1)], safe q b ]
    safe q b = and [not (checks q b i) |
            i <- [0..(length b - 1)] ]
    checks q b i = q == b!!i || abs(q - b!!i) == i+1
```

Notice the use of the where clause to hide the definitions of the helper functions solve, safe, and checks. Also note that the formal argument to queens, namely n, is referenced in solve. Note both the brevity and simplicity of this solution.

Note that this program computes all solutions for a given *n* as a list of row lists. Thus, solve 0 returns a list consisting of the empty list, since this can be interpreted as a valid solution. The function solve extends each previous valid solution (inner list) by filtering each legal row number with each valid solution to see if it is safe. The function safe uses the function checks to see if the row or diagonals are occupied, producing for each trial extended solution a list of booleans which is first inverted and then the list is anded together. In this case an occupied row or diagonal produces true, which is inverted to false. Any false in the list makes the *and* false, resulting in the rejection of the trial extended solution.

Execution of this program for various values of n include:

```
> queens 0
[[]]
> queens 1
[[0]]
> queens 2
[]
> queens 3
[]
> queens 4
[[2,0,3,1],[1,3,0,2]]
```

which says that:

- For $n = 0$ a solution consists of placing no queens.
- For $n = 1$ a solution consists of placing a queen at $(0, 0)$.
- For $n = 2, 3$ there are no solutions.
- For $n = 4$ there are two solutions, but one is a mirror image of the other.

14.4 SUMMARY

This chapter covers the principles and surveys the applications of the functional programming paradigm. Functional programming is distinct from other paradigms because it closely models the mathematical idea of a function.

The applications of functional programming are largely rooted in artificial intelligence. This chapter illustrates these applications in both Scheme and Haskell. Scheme is a derivative of Lisp, the first major functional programming language. Haskell is a more recent language whose distinctions benefit from its lazy evaluation strategy.

EXERCISES

14.1 Evaluate the following lambda expressions using *eager* beta-reduction (use the standard interpretations for numbers and booleans wherever needed).

(a) $((\lambda x \cdot x * x)5)$

(b) $((\lambda y \cdot ((\lambda x \cdot x + y + z)3))2)$

(c) $((\lambda v \cdot (\lambda w \cdot w))((\lambda x \cdot x)(y(\lambda z \cdot z))))$

14.2 Evaluate the expressions in the previous exercise using *lazy* beta-reduction. Do you get the same results?

14.3 Evaluate the following expressions using your Scheme interpreter:

(a) `(null? ())`

(b) `(null? '(a b c d e))`

(c) `(car '(a (b c) d e))`

(d) `(cdr '(a (b c) d e))`

(e) `(cadr '(a (b c) d e))`

14.4 Evaluate the Scheme expression `(sum 1 2 3 4 5)`, showing all the steps in the expansion of the sum function given in this chapter.

14.5 Write a Scheme function named `elements` which counts the number of elements in a list; for example: `(elements '(1 (2 (3) 4) 5 6))` is 6, while the length of the same list is 4.

14.6 In the Clite interpreter of Section 14.2.8, manually trace:

```
(m-expression '(plus (times (variable a) (variable b))
                     (value 2)) '((a 2) (b 4)))
```

14.7 For the Clite interpreter discussed in this chapter, implement in Scheme the meaning of the relational and Boolean operators.

14.8 For the Clite interpreter discussed in this chapter, implement in Scheme the meaning of the assignment statement.

14.9 Add an implementation of the unary operator `not` to the Clite interpreter.

14.10 (Team Project) Rewrite the abstract syntax of Clite as Scheme lists. Then use these definitions to implement a type checker for Clite in Scheme using the Java implementation as a model.

14.11   (Team Project) Rewrite the abstract syntax of Clite as Scheme lists. Then use these definitions to implement the run-time semantics for Clite in Scheme using the Java implementation as a model.

14.12   Extend the symbolic differentiation program so that it differentiates functions with exponents as well as sums and products. This extension should rely on the following knowledge:

$$\frac{du^n}{dx} = nu^{n-1}\frac{du}{dx} \qquad \text{for integers } n > 0$$

14.13   Use your extended symbolic differentiation program to differentiate the following functions:
(a) $x^2 + 2x + 1$
(b) $(5x - 2y)/(x^2 + 1)$

14.14   Consider the problem of simplifying an algebraic expression, such as the result of symbolic differentiation. We know that mathematical identities like $x + 0 = x$ and $1 \cdot x = x$ are used in simplifying expressions.
(a) Design a set of rules for simplification, based on the properties of 0 and 1 when added or multiplied with another expression.
(b) Write a Scheme function that simplifies an arbitrary algebraic expression using these rules.
(c) Design a set of rules for simplification based on adding and multiplying constants.
(d) Write a Scheme function that simplifies an arbitrary algebraic expression using these rules.
(e) Extend the Scheme functions above so that the rules are applied repeatedly until no further simplification results. Hint: apply the simplifications and test to see if the "simpler" expression is different from the original.

14.15   Consider the eight queens backtracking problem. Turn on tracing for the functions `try`, `trywh`, and `tryone`.
(a) Show that there is no solution when N is 3.
(b) Show that when N is 5, the solution is found without backtracking.
(c) Is a solution found when N is 6? Is backtracking used?

14.16   Implement knight's tour in Scheme for a board of size 5 when the knight begins at square (1, 1). For a description of knight's tour, see Exercise 13.16.

14.17   Write a Scheme program using backtracking to solve (easy) Sudoku puzzles (**www.sudoku.com**).

14.18   Using the Haskell generative solution to the eight queens problem (Section 14.3.10) as a model, write a generative solution to the eight queens problem in Scheme.

14.19   Evaluate the following expressions using your Haskell interpreter:
(a) `[1,2,3,4,5]!!2`
(b) `[1,2,3,4,5]!!5`
(c) `head [1,2,3,4,5]`
(d) `tail [1,2,3,4,5]`

14.20   For the phonebook example discussed in Section 14.3.7, evaluate the following functions assuming that the list `pb` has the initial values shown there.
(a) `addEntry pb` "Jane" `1223345`
(b) `deleteEntry pb` "Bob" `2770123`

14.21   Rewrite the `deleteEntry` function in Section 14.3.7 so that it deletes all entries for a given person. For example, if `pb` is as defined there, then the function

```
deleteEntry "Bob"
```

will delete *all* entries from pb for the person named "Bob" and not just one.

14.22 Write a Haskell function named elements which counts the number of elements in a list. It should produce the same results as the length function.

14.23 Implement the Haskell meaning function for a Clite *Block*, using the following mathematical definition:

$$M(Block\ b,\ State\ \sigma) = \sigma \qquad\qquad\qquad\qquad\quad \text{if } b = \phi$$
$$= M((Block)b_{2...n},\ M((Statement)b_1,\sigma)) \qquad \text{if } b = b_1 b_2 \ldots b_n$$

14.24 In the Haskell interpreter discussed in Section 14.3.8, implement meaning functions for the Clite arithmetic, relational, and boolean operators.

14.25 Add an implementation of the Clite unary operator ! to the Haskell version of the Clite interpreter.

14.26 After completing the previous two exercises, derive all steps in the application of the Haskell function eval to the *Expression* y+2 in the state {<x,5>, <y,3>, <z,1>}. That is, show all steps in deriving the following result:

```
eval(Binary "+" (Vary) (Lit (Intval 2)))[("x",(Intval 5)),
            ("y",(Intval 3)),("z",(Intval 1)))]
= (Value 5)
```

14.27 Give a recursive definition of the Haskell function length, which computes the number of entries in a list.

14.28 Consider the following (correct, but inefficient) Haskell implementation of the familiar Fibonacci function:

```
fibSlow n
    | n == 0 = 1
    | n == 1 = 1
    | n >  1 =  fibSlow(n-1) + fibSlow(n-2)
```

The correctness of this function is apparent, since it is a direct encoding of the familiar mathematical definition.

$$fib(0) = 1$$
$$fib(1) = 1$$
$$fib(n) = fib(n-1) + fib(n-2) \quad \text{if } n > 1$$

(a) But the efficiency of this function is suspect. Try running fibSlow(25) and then fibSlow(50) on your system and see how long these computations take. What causes this inefficiency?

(b) An alternative definition of the *fib* function can be made in the following way. Define a function fibPair that generates a two-element tuple that contains the *n*th Fibonacci number and its successor. Define another function fibNext that generates the next such tuple from the current one. Then the Fibonacci function itself, which we optimistically call fibFast, is defined by selecting the first member of the *n*th `fibPair`. In Haskell, this is written as follows:

```
fibPair n
    | n == 0    = (1,1)
    | n > 0     = fibNext(fibPair(n-1))
fibNext (m,n) = (n,m+n)
fibFast n = fst(fibPair(n))
```

Try running the function `fibFast` to compute the 25th and 50th Fibonacci numbers. It should be considerably more efficient than `fibSlow`. Explain.

14.29 Rewrite the Haskell formatter for symbolic differentiation to remove any unnecessary parentheses. Hint: avoid introducing them in the first place.

14.30 Write a Haskell expression simplifier for symbolic differentiation (see Exercise 14.14).

14.31 Using the eight queens solution as a model, write a Haskell program to solve (easy) Sudoku puzzles (**www.sudoku.com**).

14.32 (Team Project) Give a complete abstract syntax of Clite as Haskell recursive data types. Then use these definitions to implement a type checker for Clite in Haskell using the Java implementation as a model.

14.33 (Team Project) Give a complete abstract syntax of Clite as Haskell recursive data types. Then use these definitions to implement the meaning functions for Clite in Haskell using the Java implementation as a model.

14.34 (Team Project) Develop a concrete and abstract syntax for a small subset of Scheme or Haskell. Then use these definitions to implement a run-time semantics for Scheme or Haskell using Java as the implementation language.

Logic Programming

"Q: How many legs does a dog have if you call its tail a leg?
A: Four. Calling a tail a leg doesn't make it one."

Abraham Lincoln

CHAPTER OUTLINE

Logic (declarative) programming emerged as a distinct paradigm in the 1970s. Logic programming is distinct from the other paradigms because it requires the programmer to declare the goals of the computation, rather than the detailed algorithm by which these goals can be achieved. The goals are expressed as a collection of assertions, or rules about the outcomes and constraints of the computation. For this reason, logic programming is sometimes called *rule-based* programming.

Applications of declarative programming fall into two major domains: artificial intelligence and database information retrieval. Across the artificial intelligence area, Prolog has been influential. Some subfields of artificial intelligence enjoy the use of other declarative languages, as in the use of MYCIN for modeling expert systems. In the database area, the Structured Query Language (SQL) has been very popular.

In order to achieve depth of understanding, this chapter focuses only on logic programming with Prolog, studying its applications in natural language processing and problem solving.

Two interesting and distinguishing features of logic programs are *nondeterminism* and *backtracking*. A nondeterministic logic program may find several solutions to a problem rather than just one, as would be the norm in other programming domains. Further, the backtracking mechanism which enables nondeterminism is built into the Prolog interpreter, and therefore is implicit in all Prolog programs. By contrast, using other languages to write backtracking programs requires the programmer to define the backtracking mechanism explicitly, as is done in Section 13.4.2. We shall see the power of backtracking and nondeterminism throughout this chapter.

15.1 LOGIC AND HORN CLAUSES

A logic program expresses the specifications for problem solutions using expressions in mathematical logic. This style evolved out of the needs of researchers in natural language processing and automatic theorem proving. Conventional programming languages are not particularly well suited to these researchers' needs. However, writing down the specification of a theorem or a grammar (such as the BNF grammar used to define the syntax of Clite) as a formal logical expression provides an effective vehicle to study the process of theorem proving and natural language analysis in an experimental laboratory setting.

So propositional and predicate logic (see Appendix B for a review) provides the formal foundation for logic programming. The Horn clause is a particular variant of predicate logic that underlies the syntax of Prolog.

> **Definition**: A *Horn clause* has a head *h*, which is a predicate, and a body, which is a list of predicates $p_1, p_2, \ldots, p_n$.

Horn clauses are written in the following style:

$$h \leftarrow p_1, p_2, \ldots, p_n$$

This means that *h* is *true* only if $p_1, p_2, \ldots,$ and p_n are simultaneously *true*.

For example, suppose we want to capture the idea that it is snowing in some city *C* only if there is precipitation in city *C* and the temperature in city *C* is freezing. We can write this as the following Horn clause:

$$snowing(C) \leftarrow precipitation(C), freezing(C)$$

There is a limited correspondence between Horn clauses and predicates. For instance, the above Horn clause can be written equivalently as the predicate:

$$precipitation(C) \land freezing(C) \supset snowing(C)$$

This expression is logically equivalent to either of the following predicates, using the properties of predicates summarized in Appendix B.

$$\neg(precipitation(C) \land freezing(C)) \lor snowing(C)$$
$$\neg precipitation(C) \lor \neg freezing(C) \lor snowing(C)$$

Thus, any Horn clause can be written equivalently as a predicate.

Unfortunately, the converse is not true; not all predicates can be translated into Horn clauses. Below is a six-step procedure [Clocksin and Mellish, 1997, Chapter 10] that, whenever possible, translates a predicate p into a Horn clause.

1 Eliminate implications from p, using the implication property in Table B.5.
2 Move negation inward in p, using the deMorgan and quantification properties, so that only individual terms are negated.
3 Eliminate existential quantifiers from p, using a technique called *skolemization.* Here, the existentially quantified variable is replaced by a unique constant. For example, the expression $\exists x P(x)$ is replaced by $P(c)$, where c is an arbitrarily chosen constant in the domain of x. For each such existential quantifier, a different constant c must be chosen.
4 Move all universal quantifiers to the beginning of p; as long as there are no naming conflicts, this step does not change the meaning of p. Assuming that all variables are universally quantified, we can drop the quantifiers without changing the meaning of the predicate.
5 Use the distributive, associative, and commutative properties in Table B.5 to convert p to *conjunctive normal form.* In this form, the conjunction and disjunction operators are nested no more than two levels deep, with conjunctions at the highest level.
6 Convert the embedded disjunctions to implications, using the implication property. If each of these implications has a single term on its right, then each can be rewritten as a series of Horn clauses equivalent to p.

To illustrate this procedure, consider the transformation of the following predicate to conjunctive normal form:

$$\forall x(\neg literate(x) \supset (\neg writes(x) \wedge \neg \exists y(reads(x, y) \wedge book(y))))$$

Applying step 1 removes the implication, leaving

$$\forall x(literate(x) \vee (\neg writes(x) \wedge \neg \exists y(reads(x, y) \wedge book(y))))$$

Step 2 moves negations so that they are adjacent to individual terms:

$$\forall x(literate(x) \vee (\neg writes(x) \wedge \forall y(\neg(reads(x, y) \wedge book(y)))))$$
$$= \forall x(literate(x) \vee (\neg writes(x) \wedge \forall y(\neg reads(x, y) \vee \neg book(y))))$$

Since there are no existential quantifiers, skolemization is not necessary. Step 4 moves all quantifiers to the left and then drops them, giving:

$$\forall x \forall y(literate(x) \vee (\neg writes(x) \wedge (\neg(reads(x, y) \wedge book(y)))))$$
$$= literate(x) \vee (\neg writes(x) \wedge (\neg reads(x, y) \vee \neg book(y)))$$

Now we convert this to conjunctive normal form as follows:

$$literate(x) \vee (\neg writes(x) \wedge (\neg reads(x, y) \vee \neg book(y)))$$
$$= (literate(x) \vee \neg writes(x)) \wedge (literate(x) \vee \neg reads(x, y) \vee \neg book(y))$$
$$= (\neg writes(x) \vee literate(x)) \wedge (\neg reads(x, y) \vee \neg book(y) \vee literate(x))$$

These two conjuncts now convert back to implications,

$$(\neg writes(x) \lor literate(x)) \land (\neg reads(x, y) \lor \neg book(y) \lor literate(x))$$
$$= (writes(x) \supset literate(x)) \land (\neg(\neg reads(x, y) \lor \neg book(y)) \supset literate(x))$$
$$= (writes(x) \supset literate(x)) \land ((reads(x, y) \land book(y)) \supset literate(x))$$

which are equivalent to the following Horn clauses:

$$literate(x) \leftarrow writes(x)$$
$$literate(x) \leftarrow reads(x, y), book(y)$$

Unfortunately, conversion of a predicate to conjunctive normal form does not always ensure a series of equivalent Horn clauses. Consider the following predicate, which represents the statement "Every literate person reads or writes."

$$\forall x(literate(x) \supset reads(x) \lor writes(x))$$

which reduces to the following clausal form:

$$\neg literate(x) \lor reads(x) \lor writes(x)$$

But this converts to the following implication

$$literate(x) \supset reads(x) \lor writes(x)$$

which does not have a single term on the right. Thus, there is no equivalent Horn clause for this predicate.

15.1.1 Resolution and Unification

Making a single inference from a pair of Horn clauses is called *resolution*. The resolution principle is similar to the idea of transitivity in algebra.

> **Definition**: When applied to Horn clauses, *resolution* says that if h is the head of a Horn clause and it matches with one of the terms of another Horn clause, then that term can be replaced by h.

In other words, if we have the clauses

$$h \leftarrow terms$$
$$t \leftarrow t_1, h, t_2$$

then we can resolve the second clause to $t \leftarrow t_1$, *terms*, t_2. For instance, consider the following clauses:

$$speaks(Mary, English)$$
$$talkswith(X, Y) \leftarrow speaks(X, L), speaks(Y, L), X \neq Y$$

The first of these is a Horn clause with an empty list of terms, so it is unconditionally *true*. Thus, resolution allows us to deduce the following:

$$talkswith(Mary, Y) \leftarrow speaks(Mary, English), speaks(Y, English), Mary \neq Y$$

with the assumption that the variables X and L are assigned the values "Mary" and "English" in the second rule. Resolution thus helps to arrive at conclusions.

Definition: The assignment of variables to values during resolution is called *instantiation.*

Definition: *Unification* is a pattern matching process that determines what particular instantiations can be made to variables while making a series of simultaneous resolutions.

Unification is recursive, so it eventually finds all possible instantiations for which resolutions can be made. We illustrate unification in detail in Section 15.2.

15.2 LOGIC PROGRAMMING IN PROLOG

Prolog is the principal language used in logic programming. The development of Prolog is based on two powerful principles discovered by Robinson [Robinson, 1965] called *resolution* and *unification.* Prolog itself emerged in 1970, out of the work of Colmerauer, Rousseau, and Kowalski [Kowalski and Kuehner, 1970], and has been the major logic programming language to the present day. Applications of logic programming are widespread in the areas of natural language processing, automatic reasoning and theorem proving, database search, and expert systems.

15.2.1 Prolog Program Elements

Prolog programs are made from *terms,* which can be constants, variables, or structures. A *constant* is either an atom (like the, zebra, 'Bob', and '.') or a nonnegative integer (like 24). A *variable* is a series of letters (A-Z, a-z, _) that must begin with a capital letter (like Bob).[1] A *structure* is a predicate with zero or more arguments, written in functional notation. For example, the following are Prolog structures:

```
n(zebra)
speaks(Who, russian)
np(X, Y)
```

The number of arguments is called the structure's *arity* (1, 2, and 2 in these examples).

Prolog facts and rules are realizations of the formal idea of Horn clauses, as introduced in Section 15.1. A *fact* is a term followed by a period (.) and is similar to a Horn clause without a right-hand side; a variable cannot be a fact. A *rule* is a term followed by :- and a series of terms separated by commas and ended by a period (.). A rule has the following form:

term :- term$_1$, term$_2$, ..., term$_n$.

This is equivalent to the Horn clause:

term ← *term*$_1$, *term*$_2$, ..., *term*$_n$

Rules are interpreted as "only if" assertions, with the comma playing the role of the logical "and" operator. Thus, the above form asserts that term is *true* only if term$_1$, term$_2$, ..., and term$_n$ are simultaneously *true.*

---

1. A constant cannot begin with a capital letter unless it is enclosed in quotes.

A Prolog program is a series of facts and rules. Here is an example:

```
speaks(allen, russian).
speaks(bob, english).
speaks(mary, russian).
speaks(mary, english).
talkswith(Person1, Person2) :- speaks(Person1,L),
   speaks(Person2,L), Person1 \= Person2.
```

This program asserts four facts: that `allen` and `mary` speak `russian` and `bob` and `mary` speak `english`. It also has a rule that defines the relation `talkswith` between two persons, which is true exactly when they both speak the same language, denoted by the variable `L`, and they are different people. The operator `\=` specifies that `Person1` cannot be the same as (equal to) `Person2`.

A Prolog rule *succeeds* when there are instantiations (which are temporary assignments) of its variables for which all of the terms on the right of the :- operator simultaneously succeed for those assignments. Otherwise, the rule is said to *fail*. A fact always succeeds; that is, it is universally *true*. For example, the rule in the above example succeeds for the instantiations

```
Person1 = allen
Person2 = mary
```

since there is an instantiation of the variable `L` (=`russian`) for which the three predicates:

```
speaks(allen, L)
speaks(mary, L)
allen \= mary
```

simultaneously succeed. However, this rule fails for other instantiations, such as:

```
Person1 = allen
Person2 = bob
```

since they share no common instantiation of variable `L`.

To exercise a Prolog program, one writes *queries* in reply to the Prolog prompt ?-. Here is a simple query that asks the question "Who speaks Russian?"

```
?- speaks(Who, russian).
```

In reply, Prolog tries to satisfy a query by finding a fact or series of fact/rule applications that will answer the query, that is, an assignment of values to the variables in the query that causes a fact or rule to succeed, in the pattern-matching sense.

Loading and Running Programs   Loading files with Prolog function definitions has the same effect as typing them directly to the Prolog interpreter. For example, to load the file named `diff` that contains the function d, we can use the command:

```
?- consult(diff).
```

Prolog facts and rules are usually typed into a separate file, for which the `consult` command is used to load that file into the interpreter. The interpreter then asserts each of the facts and rules that are defined in the program. After program loading, queries to the interpreter can be made in the form of assertions with variables, and the interpreter will try to answer these queries.

Here are some general guidelines for writing Prolog programs:

1   Identifiers that begin with a capital letter or an underscore character are taken as variables; all other identifiers are treated as constants.
2   There must be no space between the name of the predicate and the left parenthesis that opens its argument list.
3   All facts, rules, and queries must end with a period.
4   A program file must end with an end-of-line.

For example, suppose we have the following Prolog program file called `speaks`:

```
speaks(allen, russian).
speaks(bob, english).
speaks(mary, russian).
speaks(mary, english).
talkswith(Person1, Person2) :-
    speaks(Person1, L), speaks(Person2, L), Person1 \= Person2.
```

Then we can load this program with:

```
?- consult(speaks).
speaks compiled, 0.00 sec, 1,312 bytes.

Yes
```

The `Yes` reply says that Prolog has successfully syntax-checked and loaded the file, so we can now go ahead and pose queries.

Unification, Evaluation Order, and Backtracking   Consider the following query:

```
?- speaks(Who, russian).
```

When searching for a solution, Prolog examines all the facts and rules that have a head that matches with the function mentioned in the query (in this case `speaks`). If there are more than one (in this case, there are four), it considers them in the order they appear in the program. Since `russian` is a constant, the only variable to be resolved is the variable `Who`. Using the first fact in the program, Prolog replies with:

```
Who = allen
```

since that assignment to the variable Who causes the first fact to succeed. At this point, the user may want to know if there are other ways of satisfying the same query, in which a semicolon (;) is typed. Prolog continues its search through the program, reporting the next success, if there is one. When there are no more successful instantiations for the variable Who, Prolog finally replies No and the process stops. Here is the complete interaction:

```
?- speaks(Who, russian).
Who = allen ;
Who = mary ;
No
```

Another sort of query that this program can handle is one that asks questions like "Does Bob talk with Allen?" or "Who talks with Allen?" or "Which persons talk with each other?" These can be written as the following Prolog queries, with the replies to the first two shown below them:

```
?- talkswith(bob, allen).
No
?- talkswith(Who, allen).
Who = mary ;
No
?- talkswith(P1, P2).
```

To see how these queries are satisfied, we need to see how the rule for talkswith is evaluated. Any query of the form talkswith(X, Y) appeals to that rule, which can be satisfied only if there is a common instantiation for the variables X, Y, and L for which speaks(X, L), speaks(Y, L), and X\=Y are simultaneously satisfied. These three terms are often called *subgoals* of the main goal talkswith(X, Y).

Prolog tries to satisfy the subgoals in a rule from left to right, so that a search is first made for values of X and L for which speaks(X, L) is satisfied. Once such values are found, these same values are used wherever their variables appear in the search to satisfy additional subgoals for that rule, like speaks(Y, L) and X\=Y.

The process of trying to satisfy the first query above is diagrammed in the *search tree* shown in Figure 15.1.

Figure 15.1
Attempting to
Satisfy the Query
talkswith(bob, allen)

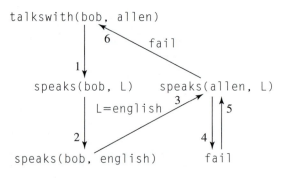

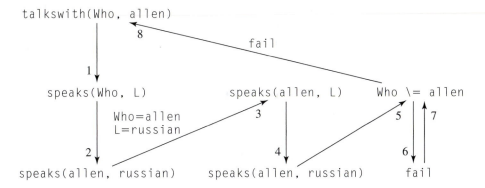

| **Figure 15.2** **First Attempt to Satisfy the Query** talkswith(Who, allen)

This process fails because the only instantiation of L that satisfies speaks(bob, L) does not simultaneously satisfy speaks(allen, L) for this program. The numbers assigned to the arrows in this diagram indicate the order in which subgoals are tried.

The response no indicates that Prolog can find no more solutions to a query. In general, Prolog operates under the so-called *closed world assumption,* which means that anything it has not been told is not *true.* In this example, the closed world contains only facts that have been stated about specific people speaking specific languages, and no others.

The process of satisfying the second query above is somewhat more complex. It first fails in the sequence shown in Figure 15.2. Although the subgoals speaks(Who,L) and speaks(allen,L) are satisfied by the instantiation Who=allen, the third subgoal fails, since allen\=allen fails.

Once this failure occurs, the process backtracks to the step labeled 2 in the figure and looks for other instantiations of Who and L that will satisfy all three of these subgoals simultaneously. Thus, the process eventually succeeds with the instantiations Who=mary and L=russian, but no others.

Database Search—The Family Tree   It may be apparent that Prolog is well-suited to solving problems that require searching a database. In fact, the development of expert systems during the 1970s and 1980s was facilitated in large part by Prolog programs. The program speaks in this section can be viewed as a very simple database search program, where the first four facts represent the database and the rule represents the constraints upon which a successful search can occur. A slightly different example appears in Figure 15.3.

This program models a small group of people whose family "tree" is shown in Figure 15.4.[2] The diagram confirms that "parent" relates two people at adjacent levels

---

2. Strictly speaking, this isn't really a tree structure since some nodes have more than one parent and there is more than one potential "root" node. But it is a "family tree" in the colloquial sense.

```
parent(A,B) :- father(A,B).
parent(A,B) :- mother(A,B).
grandparent(C,D) :- parent(C,E), parent(E,D).

mother(mary, sue).
mother(mary, bill).
mother(sue, nancy).
mother(sue, jeff).
mother(jane, ron).

father(john, sue).
father(john, bill).
father(bob, nancy).
father(bob, jeff).
father(bill, ron).
```

| **Figure 15.3   A Partial Family Tree**

in the tree and "grandparent" relates two people who are removed two levels from each other.

We can query this database in various ways to ask different questions. For instance, the question "Who is a grandparent of Ron" can be posed by:

```
?- grandparent(Who, ron).
```

Additional relationships can be defined to enable a wider variety of questions to be asked. For instance, the sibling relationship can be defined between two different people who share the same parent:

```
?- sibling(X, Y) :- parent(W, X), parent(W, Y), X \= Y.
```

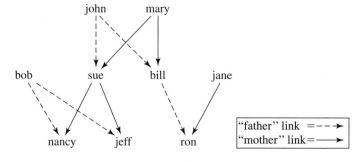

| **Figure 15.4   A Small Family "Tree"**

It should be noted that Prolog suffers from the *closed world* syndrome. A Prolog program only *knows* what it has been told. In this example a father could just as easily be a woman as a man. The system has no sense of gender; it does not understand that a biological father must be a man, nor that a person's parents must be distinct.

Lists The basic data structure in Prolog programming is the list, which is written as a series of terms separated by commas and enclosed in brackets [and]. Sentences are usually represented as lists of atoms, as in the following example:

```
[the, giraffe, dreams]
```

The empty list is denoted by [], while a *don't care* entry in a list is represented by an underscore (_). The following denote lists of one, two, and three elements, respectively.

```
[X]
[X, Y]
[_, _, Z]
```

The head (first) element of a list is distinguished from its remaining elements by a vertical bar. Thus,

```
[Head | Tail]
```

denotes a list whose first element is Head and whose remaining elements form the list [Tail], often termed the *tail* of the list.

Here is a simple Prolog function that defines the concatenation of two lists together to form one. The first two arguments for this function represent the two lists being concatenated, and the third represents the result.

```
append([], X, X).
append([Head | Tail], Y, [Head | Z]) :- append(Tail, Y, Z).
```

This rather odd-looking recursive definition has two parts. The "base case" is defined by the first line, which simply affirms that the empty list concatenated with any other list returns that other list as the result. The recursive case, defined by the second line, says that if Z is the result of concatenating lists Tail and Y, then concatenating any new list [Head | Tail] with Y gives the result [Head | Z].

It is important to understand the dynamics of execution for this function, since this form of recursive definition occurs often in Prolog. Consider the query

```
?- append([english, russian], [spanish], L).
```

which should yield the list L = [english, russian, spanish]. Figure 15.5 gives a partial search tree that traces the instantiations of H, T, X, Y, and Z as this result is developed.

The first two calls use the recursive rule, which strips the head H from the first argument and recalls append with a shorter list as first argument. The final call uses the base

```
append([english, russian], [spanish], L).
```

H = english, T = [russian], Y = [spanish], L = [english | Z]

1

```
append([russian], [spanish], [Z]).
```

H = russian, T = [], Y = [spanish], [Z] = [russian | Z']

2

```
append([], [spanish], [Z']).
```

X = [spanish], Z' = spanish

3

```
append([], [spanish], [spanish]).
```

| **Figure 15.5** **Partial Search Tree for** `append([english, russian], [spanish], L)`

case, which forces instantiation of the variable X = [spanish] and Z' = spanish.[3] Thus, the result [H | Z'] in the second call is resolved as [russian, spanish] and identified with the list Z in the first call. Finally, the list L is resolved to [english, russian, spanish], using this newly discovered value for Z as its tail.

Here are three more functions with lists that are very useful in Prolog programming. The first two, called *prefix* and *suffix*, mean exactly what their names suggest. X is a prefix of Z if there's a Y which we can append to X to make Z. The definition of Y as a suffix of Z is similar.

```
prefix(X, Z) :- append(X, Y, Z).
suffix(Y, Z) :- append(X, Y, Z).
```

The third useful function defines recursively the notion of membership in a list. X is a member of a list if it is identical to the first element or a member of the list's tail.

```
member(X, [X | _]).
member(X, [_ | Y]) :- member(X, Y).
```

Note here the use of the "don't care" notation in parts of the definition that don't affect the definition. In the first line, we don't care what the rest of the list looks like if X is identical with the first member. In the second, we don't care what's at the head of the list if X is a member of the tail.

---

3. The use of prime (') in this analysis, although not a legal character in a Prolog variable name, helps to distinguish the use of a variable in a rule at one level of recursion from the use of the same variable at another level.

To illustrate, suppose we have the following list assignments in Prolog:

```
L = [my, dog, has, many, fleas]
M = [many, fleas, spoil, the, picnic]
```

Then the following Prolog queries cause the responses shown below them:

```
? - prefix(Answer, L).
Answer = [];
Answer = [my];
Answer = [my, dog];
...
Answer = [my, dog, has, many, fleas];
No
? - suffix(Answer, L), prefix(Answer, M).
Answer = [];
Answer = [many, fleas];
No
? - member(spoil, L).
No
? - member(spoil, M).
Yes
```

15.2.2 Practical Aspects of Prolog

Prolog is not, in practice, an altogether "pure" logic programming language. In particular, it has some features designed to make programming more efficient and practical. In this section, we discuss several prominent features, among them: the "cut," the `is` operator and arithmetic, and the `assert` function.

Tracing Many Prolog implementations provide the predicates `trace` and `untrace`, which are used to turn on and off the tracing of other predicates. Because there can be different predicates with the same name and different arities (numbers of arguments), trace expects the name of a predicate to be followed by a slash and its arity. For example, consider the predicate `factorial` defined as follows:

```
factorial(0, 1).
factorial(N, Result) :- N > 0, M is N - 1,
          factorial(M, SubRes), Result is N * SubRes.
```

This predicate defines the factorial function recursively, with the first line defining the base case ($0! = 1$) and the second and third lines defining the recursive case ($n! = n(n - 1)!$). Notice that we need to introduce the intermediate variable M to force the evaluation of $N - 1$ before the recursive call.

To trace this function, we can do this:

```
?- trace(factorial/2).
factorial/2: call redo exit fail

Yes
?- factorial(4, X).
Call: (  7) factorial(4, _G173)
Call: (  8) factorial(3, _L131)
Call: (  9) factorial(2, _L144)
Call: ( 10) factorial(1, _L157)
Call: ( 11) factorial(0, _L170)
Exit: ( 11) factorial(0, 1)
Exit: ( 10) factorial(1, 1)
Exit: (  9) factorial(2, 2)
Exit: (  8) factorial(3, 6)
Exit: (  7) factorial(4, 24)

X = 24
```

In the first call, the first argument is bound to 4, and the second is bound to an anonymous variable (_G173). This same pattern is repeated for each of the next four recursive calls, until the base case occurs and the second argument _L170 is finally assigned the value 1. Now the recursion unwinds, assigning intermediate values to the anonymous variables and doing the multiplications.

The predicate listing, as in listing(factorial/2), will display all the current facts and rules for the argument predicate:

```
?- listing(factorial/2).
factorial(0, 1).
factorial(A, B) :-
        A>0,
        C is A-1,
        factorial(C, D),
        B is A*D.
Yes
```

The predicate listing with no arguments lists *all* the functions of the currently consulted program.

The Cut and Negation

Prolog provides a special function called the *cut*, which forces the evaluation of a series of subgoals on the right-hand side of a rule not to be retried if the right-hand side succeeds once. The cut is written by inserting an exclamation mark (!) as a subgoal at the place where the interruption is to occur.

To illustrate, consider the following program that performs a bubble sort on a list.

```
?- bsort([5,2,3,1], Ans).
Call:  (  7) bsort([5, 2, 3, 1], _G221)
Call:  (  8) bsort([2, 5, 3, 1], _G221)
Call:  (  9) bsort([2, 3, 5, 1], _G221)
Call:  ( 10) bsort([2, 3, 1, 5], _G221)
Call:  ( 11) bsort([2, 1, 3, 5], _G221)
Call:  ( 12) bsort([1, 2, 3, 5], _G221)
Redo:  ( 12) bsort([1, 2, 3, 5], _G221)
Exit:  ( 12) bsort([1, 2, 3, 5], [1, 2, 3, 5])
Exit:  ( 11) bsort([2, 1, 3, 5], [1, 2, 3, 5])
Exit:  ( 10) bsort([2, 3, 1, 5], [1, 2, 3, 5])
Exit:  (  9) bsort([2, 3, 5, 1], [1, 2, 3, 5])
Exit:  (  8) bsort([2, 5, 3, 1], [1, 2, 3, 5])
Exit:  (  7) bsort([5, 2, 3, 1], [1, 2, 3, 5])

Ans = [1, 2, 3, 5] ;

No
```

| **Figure 15.6**   Trace of `bsort` for the List [5, 2, 3, 1]

```
bsort(L, S) :- append(U, [A, B | V], L),
               B < A, !,
               append(U, [B, A | V], M),
               bsort(M, S).
bsort(L, L).
```

This program first partitions a list `L` by finding two sublists `U` and `[A, B | V]` for which `B < A` is *true*. Once such a partition is found, the list `M` is formed by appending the sublists `U` and `[B, A | V]` and then recursively bubble-sorted to form the new list `S`.

This process repeats until no more partitions of `L` can be found: until there is no sublist `[A, B | V]` of `L` in which `B < A`. This is a terse way of saying that the list `L` is sorted. At that point, the only remaining applicable rule is `bsort(L,L)`, which returns the sorted list as the answer. Figure 15.6 shows a trace of the program.

If the cut had not been present in this program, the search process would have continued with a `Redo` of the rule at level 11, since Prolog would be seeking all solutions:

```
Redo:  ( 11) bsort([2, 1, 3, 5], _G221)
```

and this would lead to the first of a series of incorrect answers. The cut is therefore useful when we want to cut off the search process after finding the first set of instantiations to the variables on the right that satisfy the rule, but no others.

```
factorial(0, 1).
factorial(N, Result) :- N > 0, M is N - 1,
                        factorial(M, P),
                        Result is N * P.
```

| **Figure 15.7** **The Factorial Function in Prolog**

```
?- factorial(4, X).                    N   M    P       Result
Call:  (  7) factorial(4, _G173)       4   3   _G173    4*P
Call:  (  8) factorial(3, _L131)       3   2   _L131    3*P
Call:  (  9) factorial(2, _L144)       2   1   _L144    2*P
Call:  ( 10) factorial(1, _L157)       1   0   _L157    1*P
Call:  ( 11) factorial(0, _L170)       0       _L170
Exit:  ( 11) factorial(0, 1)                            1
Exit:  ( 10) factorial(1, 1)                            1*1 = 1
Exit:  (  9) factorial(2, 2)                            2*1 = 2
Exit:  (  8) factorial(3, 6)                            3*2 = 6
Exit:  (  7) factorial(4, 24)                           4*6 = 24
```

| **Figure 15.8** **Trace of Factorial (4)**

The is, not, and Other Operators The infix operator is can be used to force instantiation of a variable:

```
?- X is 3+7.
X = 10
yes
```

Prolog provides arithmetic $(+, -, *, /, \char`\^)$ and relational operators $(<, >, =, =<, >=,$ and $\ =)$ with their usual interpretations. Note that, in order to keep $=>$ and $<=$ free for use as arrows, Prolog uses $=<$ for less-than-or-equal comparisons and $>=$ for greater-than-or-equal comparisons.

Consider the predicate factorial defined in Figure 15.7. This predicate defines the factorial function recursively, with the first line defining the base case $(0! = 1)$ and the second and third lines defining the recursive case $(n! = n \times (n-1)!$ when $n > 0)$. Notice that we need to introduce the intermediate variable M to force the evaluation of $N - 1$ before the recursive call. The is operator plays the role of an intermediate assignment operator by unifying a value with this variable.

A call to this function generates the series of assignments to different instantiations of the variables N, M, and P (shown with the aid of a trace output) in Figure 15.8. The anonymous variables _G173, _L131, ... are generated by the interpreter at each reinstantiation of the recursive rule in this definition. In the first call, the first argument is bound to 4, and the second is bound to an anonymous variable (_G173). This same pattern is repeated for each of the next four recursive calls, until the base case occurs and the second argument _L170 is finally assigned the value 1. Now the recursion unwinds, assigning intermediate values to the anonymous variables and doing the multiplications.

The operator not is implemented in Prolog in terms of goal failure. That is, the clause not(P) succeeds when resolution of P fails. Thus, not can be used to define a function in place of the cut. Consider the following alternative definitions of the factorial function given in Figure 15.7.

```
factorial(N, 1) :- N < 1, !.
factorial(N, Result) :- M is N - 1,
                        factorial(M, P),
                        Result is N * P.
factorial(N, 1) :- N < 1.
factorial(N, Result) :- not(N < 1), M is N - 1,
                        factorial(M, P),
                        Result is N * P.
```

The first definition shows how the cut (!) can be used to delineate the base case from the recursive call. The second shows how not removes the need for using the cut (although at the expense of some efficiency, since it evaluates the clause N < 1 twice for every different value of N). Nevertheless, it is usually better programming style to use not in place of the cut, since it enhances readability. Even better would be to invert the condition, in this case N >= 1, thus, avoiding the use of not.

It is important to point out that the not operator does not always act like logical negation. Sometimes, it will simply fail when one of the variables contained in its argument is uninstantiated.

The assert **Function**   Prolog applications often encounter situations where the program must "update" itself in response to the most recent query. For instance, in a database application like the one shown in Section 15.2.1 one might want to add a new member to the family tree and let that member play a role in the program's response to later queries. This can be done using the assert function, which essentially allows the program to dynamically alter itself by adding new facts and rules to the existing ones. For example, suppose we want to add the assertion to the program in Figure 15.3 that Jane is the mother of Joe. We would do this by the statement:

```
?- assert(mother(jane,joe)).
```

This fact is now added to all the others in that program, and will affect future queries such as the following:

```
?- mother(jane, X).

X = ron ;
X = joe ;
No
```

Moreover, the assert function can be added to the body of a function definition itself and dynamically add new facts and rules to the database. This kind of activity is important for programs that simulate learning in the sense that they can store new knowledge as they interact with the user.

15.3 PROLOG EXAMPLES

In the next several sections, we present examples of Prolog applications across a wide range of artificial intelligence applications: symbolic differentiation, solving word puzzles, natural language processing, semantics, and the eight queens problem.

Each of these examples highlights various strengths of declarative programming, and especially Prolog's built-in backtracking mechanism and resultant nondeterminism. While studying these examples, readers should think about what it would take to solve these kinds of problems in an imperative programming paradigm; normally the coding effort will be more substantial there than it is in Prolog.

15.3.1 Symbolic Differentiation

The use of Prolog for symbol manipulation and theorem proving is widespread. This example illustrates some of the natural deduction powers of Prolog in the area of logical reasoning by performing symbolic differentiation and simplification of simple calculus formulae. Figure 15.9 shows the familiar rules for differentiation.

For example, differentiating the function $2 \cdot x + 1$ using these rules leaves the (unsimplified) answer $2 \cdot 1 + x \cdot 0 + 0$, which simplifies to 2.

The Prolog solution mimics these rules one-for-one. They are intrinsically recursive, and so is the Prolog solution as shown in Figure 15.10.

The Prolog rules are written in this particular order so that the search process will analyze the expression recursively before getting down to the base case, where the individual terms and factors reside. A search tree for the query d(x, 2*x+1, Ans) is shown in Figure 15.11 (branches that lead to failure are not shown).

In this illustration, the temporary variables _G268, _G269, _G275, and _G278 represent anonymous variables generated by Prolog as it finds answers for the intermediate terms in the original expression.

$$\frac{dc}{dx} = 0 \qquad\qquad c \text{ is a constant}$$

$$\frac{dx}{dx} = 1$$

$$\frac{d}{dx}(u + v) = \frac{du}{dx} + \frac{dv}{dx} \qquad u \text{ and } v \text{ are functions of } x$$

$$\frac{d}{dx}(u - v) = \frac{du}{dx} - \frac{dv}{dx}$$

$$\frac{d}{dx}(uv) = u\frac{dv}{dx} + v\frac{du}{dx}$$

$$\frac{d}{dx}\left(\frac{u}{v}\right) = \left(v\frac{du}{dx} - u\frac{dv}{dx}\right)\Big/v^2$$

| **Figure 15.9** Symbolic Differentiation Rules

```
d(X, U+V, DU+DV) :- d(X, U, DU), d(X, V, DV).
d(X, U-V, DU-DV) :- d(X, U, DU), d(X, V, DV).
d(X, U*V, U*DV + V*DU) :- d(X, U, DU), d(X, V, DV).
d(X, U/V, (V*DU - U*DV)/(V*V)) :- d(X, U, DU), d(X, V, DV).
d(X, C, 0) :- atomic(C), C\=X.
d(X, X, 1).
```

| **Figure 15.10**   **Prolog Symbolic Differentiator**

Readers should note that the task of simplifying an algebraic expression is not covered by the rules for symbolic differentiation. For example, the following query

```
?- d(x, 2*x, 2).
```

fails to give the intuitive yes answer, since the symbolic result $2 * 1 + x * 0 + 0$ is not obviously equivalent to 2. The task of simplification relies on identities like $1 * x = x$ and $0 + x = x$, and so forth. An exercise at the end of the chapter provides an opportunity to extend the symbolic differentiation program in this way.

15.3.2 Solving Word Puzzles

Logic often asks us to solve problems that are word puzzles, which are series of assertions from which various inferences can be made and complex conclusions drawn. Here is a simple example:

Baker, Cooper, Fletcher, Miller, and Smith live in a five-story building. Baker doesn't live on the 5th floor and Cooper doesn't live on the first. Fletcher doesn't live on the

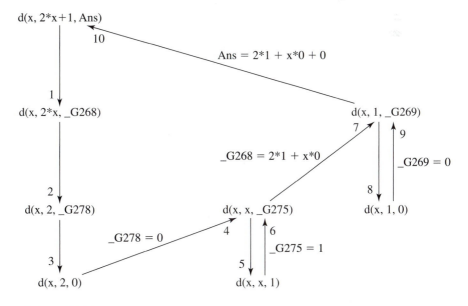

| **Figure 15.11**   **Search Tree for the Query d(x, 2*x+1, Ans)**

```
floors([floor(_,5),floor(_,4),floor(_,3),floor(_,2),floor(_,1)]).
building(Floors) :- floors(Floors),
        member(floor(baker, B), Floors), B \= 5,
        member(floor(cooper, C), Floors), C \= 1,
        member(floor(fletcher, F), Floors), F \= 1, F = 5,
        member(floor(miller, M), Floors), M > C,
        member(floor(smith, S), Floors), not(adjacent(S, F)),
        not(adjacent(F, C)),
        print_floors(Floors).
```

| **Figure 15.12**   **Prolog Solution for the Building Problem**

top or the bottom floor, and he is not on a floor adjacent to Smith or Cooper. Miller lives on some floor above Cooper. Who lives on what floors?

In Prolog, we can set up a list to solve this kind of problem, with one entry for each floor in the building. Since each floor has an occupant and a number, the function floor (Occupant, Number) can be used to characterize it. We can then fill in the facts that we do know for each floor using this particular list and function. Figure 15.12 shows a solution for this problem.

Each separate line in the Prolog rule contains subgoals that represent one of the sentences in the above problem statement; all of these subgoals must be satisfied simultaneously for the entire rule to succeed. The variables B, C, F, M, and S represent the different person's floor numbers, which the program seeks to instantiate. Their values are constrained to the integers 1 through 5 by the first statement.

The auxiliary function print_floors is a simple recursive routine to display the elements of a list on separate lines. All five persons live somewhere, so the member function is used to guarantee that.

```
print_floors([A | B]) :- write(A), nl, print_floors(B).
print_floors([]).

member(X, [X | _]).
member(X, [_ | Y]) :- member(X, Y).
```

The adjacent function succeeds whenever its two arguments X and Y differ by 1, so it defines what it means for two floors to be adjacent to each other.

```
adjacent(X, Y) :- X =:= Y+1.
adjacent(X, Y) :- X =:= Y-1.
```

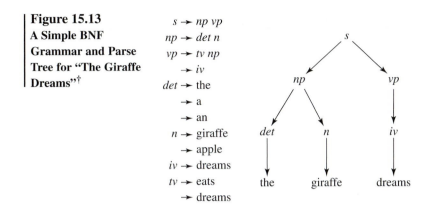

Figure 15.13
A Simple BNF
Grammar and Parse
Tree for "The Giraffe
Dreams"†

$$s \rightarrow np\ vp$$
$$np \rightarrow det\ n$$
$$vp \rightarrow tv\ np$$
$$\rightarrow iv$$
$$det \rightarrow the$$
$$\rightarrow a$$
$$\rightarrow an$$
$$n \rightarrow giraffe$$
$$\rightarrow apple$$
$$iv \rightarrow dreams$$
$$tv \rightarrow eats$$
$$\rightarrow dreams$$

The puzzle is solved by issuing the following query, which finds instantiations of the five variables that together satisfy all the constraints and assign a list of values to the array X.

```
? - building(X).
```

15.3.3 Natural Language Processing

We can write Prolog programs that are effectively BNF grammars which, when executed, will parse sentences in a natural language. An example of such a grammar along with a parse tree for the sentence "the giraffe dreams" is shown in Figure 15.13.

When using the list representation for sentences, we can write Prolog rules that partition a sentence into its grammatical categories, using the structure defined by the grammar rules themselves. For example, consider the following BNF grammar rule, where *s*, *np*, and *vp* denote the notions "sentence," "noun phrase," and "verb phrase."

$$s \rightarrow np\ vp$$

A corresponding Prolog rule would be:

```
s(X, Y) :- np(X, U), vp(U, Y).
```

The variables in this rule represent lists. In particular, X denotes the list representation of the sentence being parsed, and Y represents the resulting tail of the list that will remain if this rule succeeds. The interpretation here mirrors that of the original grammar rule: "X is a sentence, leaving Y, if the beginning of X can be identified as a noun phrase, leaving U, and the beginning of U can be identified as a verb phrase, leaving Y."

---

† The grammatical categories shown here are: *s* = "sentence," *np* = "noun phrase," *vp* = "verb phrase," *det* = "determiner" (or "article"), *n* = "noun," *iv* = "intransitive verb," and *tv* = "transitive verb." Terminal symbols are denoted by nonitalicized words. Parsing proceeds for these kinds of grammars exactly as it does for grammars that represent the syntax of programming languages, as presented in Chapter 2.

The Prolog program for the grammar in Figure 15.13 is shown below:

```
s(X, Y) :- np(X, U), vp(U, Y).


np(X, Y) :- det(X, U), n(U, Y).


vp(X, Y) :- iv(X, Y).
vp(X, Y) :- tv(X, U), np(U, Y).

det([the | Y], Y).
det([a | Y], Y).

n([giraffe | Y], Y).
n([apple | Y], Y).

iv([dreams | Y], Y).
tv([dreams | Y], Y).
tv([eats | Y], Y).
```

Note that the facts identifying terminal symbols (giraffe, eats, etc.) effectively strip those symbols from the head of the list being passed through the grammar.

To see how this works, consider the following Prolog query, which asks whether or not "the giraffe dreams" is a sentence.

```
?- s([the, giraffe, dreams], [])
```

Here, X and Y are identified with the two lists given as arguments, and the task is to find a list U that will satisfy, in the order given, each of the following goals (using the right-hand side of the first rule in the program).

```
np([the, giraffe, dreams],U) vp(U,[])
```

One way to see the dynamics of the entire parsing process is to run a trace on the query itself, which is shown in Figure 15.14. From this trace, we can see that the variables U and Y are instantiated to [dreams] and [] respectively, to satisfy the right-hand side of the first grammar rule. Notice that, upon exit from each level of the trace, one or more words are removed from the head of the list. A careful reading of this trace reveals a direct correspondence between the successful calls (rule applications) and the nodes of the parse tree shown in Figure 15.13 for this sentence. So reading a trace can be helpful when developing a complex parse tree for a sentence.

Using Prolog to encode complex grammars in this way is often more cumbersome than helpful. For that reason, Prolog provides a very compact notation that directly mimics the notation of context-free grammar rules themselves. This notation is called a *Definite Clause Grammar* (DCG), and is simple to assimilate.[4] The Prolog operator `-->`

---

4. DCG's are in general LL(n) for arbitrary lookahead n. Thus, it is necessary to eliminate left recursion in the grammar rules, to avoid infinite looping during resolution.

```
?- s([the, giraffe, dreams],[]).
Call:  (   7) s([the, giraffe dreams], []) ?
Call:  (   8) np([the, giraffe, dreams], _L131) ?
Call:  (   9) det([the, giraffe, dreams], _L143) ?
Exit:  (   9) det([the, giraffe, dreams], [giraffe, dreams]) ?
Call:  (   9) n([giraffe, dreams], _L131) ?
Exit:  (   9) n([giraffe, dreams], [dreams]) ?
Exit:  (   8) np([the, giraffe, dreams], [dreams]) ?
Call:  (   8) vp([dreams], []) ?
Call:  (   9) iv([dreams], []) ?
Exit:  (   9) iv([dreams], []) ?
Exit:  (   8) vp([dreams], []) ?
Exit:  (   7) s([the, giraffe, dreams], []) ?
Yes
```

| **Figure 15.14   Tracing Execution of a Prolog Query**

is substituted in place of the operator :- in each rule, and the list variables inside the rule
are thus dropped. For instance, the rule

```
s(X, Y) :- np(X, U), vp(U, V).
```

can be replaced by the following equivalent simplified version:

```
s --> np, vp.
```

In making this transformation, it is important to emphasize that we are not changing
either the arity of the function s (still 2) or the meaning of the original rule itself. This
notation is introduced as a kind of "macro" which allows Prolog rules to be written
almost identically to the BNF grammar rules which they represent. A complete rewriting
of the Prolog program for the grammar in Figure 15.13 is shown below:

```
s --> np, vp.

np --> det, n.

vp --> iv.
vp --> tv, np.

det --> [the].
det --> [a].
n --> [giraffe].
n --> [apple].
iv --> [dreams].
tv --> [dreams].
tv --> [eats].
```

An additional refinement to the grammar-writing rules provides the capability to generate a parse tree directly from the grammar. That is, the above grammar can be modified so that a query gives not just a Yes or No answer, but a complete parse tree in functional form as a response. For instance, the functional form of the parse tree in Figure 15.13 is:

```
s(np(det(the), n(giraffe)), vp(iv(dreams)))
```

This modification is accomplished by adding an additional argument to the left-hand side of each rule, and appropriate variables to hold the intermediate values that are derived in the intermediate stages of execution. For instance, the first rule in the grammar above would be augmented as follows:

```
s(s(NP,VP)) --> np(NP), vp(VP).
```

This means that the query needs an extra argument, alongside the sentence to be parsed and the empty list. That argument, appearing first in the query, is a variable that will hold the resulting parse tree, as shown below:

```
?- s(Tree, [the, giraffe, dreams], []).
```

A complete revision of the above grammar that accommodates this refinement is left as an exercise.

It is important to point out that Prolog can be used to generate sentences as well as parse them. For example, consider applying the following general query to the above Prolog program (grammar):

```
? - s(Sentence, []).
```

This query, when initiated, asks the search process to find all instantiations of the variable Sentence that will succeed with this grammar. In the list of responses, we'll find the following as well as all others that can be generated by this grammar:

```
Sentence = [the, giraffe, dreams] ;
Sentence = [the, giraffe, eats, the, apple] ;
...
```

where the semicolon can be interpreted as an *or*.

Natural language processing has been an on-going area of research since the late 1950s. The example presented here does not begin to explore the extreme difficulty of the subject. Many researchers in natural language processing continue to use Prolog as a vehicle to do their work.

15.3.4 Semantics of Clite

In this section we implement much of the formal semantics of Clite using Prolog. Recall from Chapter 8 that for the elementary language Clite, the environment is static, so the state can be simply represented as a collection of variable-value pairs. This is expressed as follows:

$$state = \{\langle var_1, val_1 \rangle, \langle var_2, val_2 \rangle, \ldots, \langle var_m, val_m \rangle\}$$

Here, each var_i denotes a variable and each val_i denotes its currently assigned value.

The state is like a *watch window* in an integrated development environment (IDE). It is always tied to a particular statement in the program source and shows for each program variable its current value. In our Java implementation, the state was implemented as a hash table in which the variable identifier was the key and the associated value was the current value of the variable.

A state here is naturally represented as a list, with each element of the list being a pair representing the binding of a variable to its value. So the Clite state:

$$\{\langle x, 1 \rangle, \langle y, 5 \rangle\}$$

can be represented as the Prolog list:

```
[[x,1], [y,5]]
```

Next we implement the state access functions named `get` and `onion` (overriding union) from the Java implementation. Recall that the `get` function in Java was used to obtain the value of a variable from the current state. The `get` function takes an input variable and an input state and produces an output value.

```
/* get(var, inState, outValue) */
```

Since the Clite type system requires that all variables used in a program be declared, there cannot be a reference to a variable that is not in the state. The base case is that the variable-value pair occurs at the front of the state list, in which case the value associated with the variable is the desired result value. Otherwise the search continues through the tail of the list.[5]

```
get(Var, [[Var, Val] | _], Val).
get(Var, [_ | Rest], Val) :- get(Var, Rest, Val).
```

An application of the `get` function is:

```
?- get(y, [[x, 5], [y, 3], [z, 1]], V).

V = 3.
```

The `onion` function takes an input variable, an input value, and an input state, and produces a new state with the value part of the matching variable-value pair replaced with the new value.

```
/* onion(var, val, inState, outState) */
```

Recall that the `onion` function is able to make the simplifying assumption that the variable for which we are searching occurs exactly once within the state. The base case is that the variable being matched occurs at the head of the list; the output state is just a new variable-value pair concatenated with the remainder of the input state. Otherwise the

---

5. An astute reader who has already read Chapter 14 may have noticed the similarity of this implementation to the Scheme implementation.

new state is constructed from the head concatenated with the output state resulting from the recursive application of onion on the tail of the input state.

```
onion(Var, Val, [[Var, _] | Rest], [[Var, Val] | Rest]).
onion(Var, Val, [Xvar | Rest], [Xvar | OState]) :-
    onion(Var, Val, Rest, OState).
```

An application of onion is:

```
?- onion(y, 4, [[x, 5], [y, 3], [z, 1]], S).
S = [[x, 5], [y, 4], [z, 1]].
```

Next, consider the meaning function for Clite expression evaluation for the integers only. To facilitate this, we choose an appropriate representation for a Clite expression in abstract syntax. One possibility is to use lists; instead, we prefer using structures:

```
value(val), where val is a number
variable(ident), where ident is a variable name
operator(term1, term2), where operator is one of:
    plus minus times div -- arithmetic
    lt, le, eq, ne, gt, ge -- relational
```

The implementation of these meaning functions follows directly from the rules given in Chapter 8. We also asssume that a static semantics verification has been performed. The meaning of a Clite abstract expression is implemented as a set of rules depending on the kind of expression. In Prolog, these rules take an input expression and an input state and return a value:

```
/* mexpression(expr, state, val) */
```

The meaning of a value expression is just the value itself.

```
mexpression(value(Val), _, Val).
```

The meaning of a variable is the value associated with the variable in the current state, obtained by applying the get function.

```
mexpression(variable(Var), State, Val) :-
    get(Var, State, Val).
```

The meaning of a binary expression is obtained by applying the operator to the meaning of the operands; below we show the meaning for plus:

```
mexpression(plus(Expr1, Expr2), State, Val) :-
    mexpression(Expr1, State, Val1),
    mexpression(Expr2, State, Val2),
    Val is Val1 + Val2.
```

This definition says first evaluate `Expr1` in `State` giving `Val1`, then evaluate `Expr2` in `State` giving `Val2`. Then add the two values giving the resulting value. The remaining binary operators are implemented similarly.

Finally, we need to pick a representation for the abstract syntax of Clite statements. Although we could use a list representation (as we did for Scheme), we prefer to use structures:

```
skip
assignment(target, source)
block([s1, ... sn])
loop(test, body)
conditional(test, thenbranch, elsebranch)
```

The meaning of an abstract *Statement* is a state-transforming function of the form which takes a *State* as input and produces a *State* as output. The implementation of these meaning functions follows directly from the rules given in Chapter 8 (and summarized here). We also asssume that a static semantics verification has been performed. The meaning function for a Clite statement (or instruction) can be written as a sequence of Prolog rules. Recall that the meaning function for an instruction takes an input statement and an input state and computes an output state:

```
/* minstruction(statement, inState, outState) */
```

A *Skip* statement corresponds to an empty statement. As such, it leaves the state unchanged; the output state is a copy of the input state.

```
minstruction(skip, State, State).
```

An *Assignment* statement consists of a target *Variable* and a source *Expression*. The output state is computed from the input state by replacing the *Value* of the target *Variable* by the computed value of the source *Expression*, which is evaluated using the input state. All other variables have the same value in the output state as they had in the input state.

Thus, the implementation of the meaning of an assignment evaluates the source expression in the current state, resulting in a value, and then uses that value to produce an output state (using onion).

```
minstruction(assignment(Var, Expr), InState, OutState) :-
    mexpression(Expr, InState, Val),
    onion(Var, Val, InState, OutState).
```

The remaining meaning rules are left as an exercise. Note that this solution is fundamentally functional in nature.[6] Nowhere did we require the automatic search ability of Prolog.

---

6. An astute reader who has read Chapter 14 may wish to compare this implementation to the Scheme or Haskell implementations.

This development of a small fraction of the formal semantics of Clite should be convincing that a full semantic model for an imperative language can be defined in Prolog. Thus, via interpretation, Prolog is capable of computing any function that can be programmed in an interpretative language. The converse is also true since most modern computers are fundamentally imperative in nature and since Prolog interpreters exist on these machines, any function programmed in Prolog can be computed by an imperative program. Thus, in theory, imperative languages and logic programming languages are equivalent in computational power.

15.3.5 Eight Queens Problem

Finally, we return to the backtracking problem of Section 13.4.2. Since backtracking is the natural control mechanism of Prolog, we can proceed to developing a solution to the *eight queens* problem without concern for the undoing of trial moves.

In general, the problem is to place N mutually antagonistic queens on an $N \times N$ chess board so that no queen can capture any other queen in a single move. In developing the solution we shall use the same encodings of the diagonals as was used in Section 13.4.2.

We shall develop the solution in a bottom-up fashion. One major problem in using Prolog is that there are no global data structures. As in functional programming, all needed information must be passed as arguments to any needed predicate. As before, we shall proceed column by column, looking for a row in which to safely place the next queen. If a safe row is found, we proceed to the next column; otherwise Prolog backs up and undoes the last move.

The occupied rows are stored as a list, with the most recent row number stored at the front of the list. Thus, for a 4×4 board, the list [2, 0] represents the board configuration:

	0	1	2	3
0	Q			
1				
2		Q		
3				

As in the Java solution, we number rows and columns starting at 0. So for an $N \times N$ chess board:

$$0 \le row, column < N$$

First we determine whether a trial row move is safe. This is done by passing as arguments the list of occupied rows, southwest diagonals, and southeast diagonals. In order to take advantage of the member predicate, these are passed as three separate lists. A trial row move is valid if the row number is not in the occupied row list and if its associated southwest and southeast diagonals are not members of the associated diagonals lists:

```
/* valid(TrialRow, TrialSwDiag, TrialSeDiag,
        RowlIst, SwDiagList, SeDiagList) */
valid(_, _, _, [ ]).

valid(TrialRow, TrialSwDiag, TrialSeDiag,
        RowList, SwDiagList, SeDiagList) :-
    not(member(TrialRow, RowList)),
    not(member(TrialSwDiag, SwDiagList)),
    not(member(TrialSeDiag, SeDiagList)).
```

Next, given a row and column, we need to compute the southwest and southeast diagonals. From Section 13.4.2. we recall that the former is the sum of the row and column numbers, while the latter is their difference:

```
/* compute SeDiag, SwDiag */
getDiag(Row, Col, SwDiag, SeDiag) :-
    SwDiag is Row + Col, SeDiag is Row - Col.
```

Next, we attempt for a given column to find a safe row to place the next queen. This is accomplished by iterating over the sequence of row numbers $0 \ldots N - 1$:

```
/* for current col, find safe row */
place(N, Row, Col, RowList, SwDiagList, SeDiagList, Row) :-
    Row < N,
    getDiag(Row, Col, SeDiag, SwDiag),
    valid(Row, SeDiag, SwDiag, RowList, SwDiagList, SeDiagList).

place(N, Row, Col, RowList, SwDiagList, SeDiagList, Answer) :-
    NextRow is Row + 1,
    NextRow < N,
    place(N, NextRow, Col, RowList, SwDiagList, SeDiagList, Answer).
```

The last argument is the row number where the queen was safely placed, if the predicate place succeeds. The first predicate for place succeeds if the current row is safe. Otherwise the second predicate is used to advance to the next row.

Basically, the same logic is applied to iterating over the columns. In this case, if the predicate `solve` succeeds, the last argument is the list of row placements in backwards order:

```
/* iterate over columns, placing queens */
solve(N, Col, RowList, _, _, RowList) :-
    Col >= N.

solve(N, Col, RowList, SwDiagList, SeDiagList, Answer) :-
    Col < N,
    place(N, 0, Col, RowList, SwDiagList, SeDiagList, Row),
    getDiag(Row, Col, SwDiag, SeDiag),
    NextCol is Col + 1,
    solve(N, NextCol, [Row | RowList], [SwDiag | SwDiagList],
        [SeDiag | SeDiagList], Answer).
```

Finally, we need the main driver itself, which allows us to solve for an arbitrary $N \times N$ board, for $N \geq 0$:

```
queens(N, Answer) :- solve(N, 0, [ ], [ ], [ ], Answer).
```

The second argument is the result containing the list of row placements in backward order. A sample execution of this program for $N = 0, 1, 2, 3, 4$ is given below:

```
| ?- queens(0, R).
R = [].
no
| ?- queens(1, R).
R = [0].
no
| ?- queens(2, R).
no
| ?- queens(3, R).
no
| ?- queens(4, R).
R = [2,0,3,1];
R = [1,3,0,2];
no
| ?-
```

15.4 SUMMARY

Logic programming languages such as Prolog provide a different way of thinking about problem solving. Following some early successes, some experts predicted that logic languages would largely replace imperative languages [Kowalski, 1988]. For example, Prolog was a cornerstone of the Japanese *Fifth Generation Computer* project [Shapiro, 1983] begun in the early 1980s. However, this project was abandoned after about 10 years [Fuchi *et al.*, 1993].

Despite the failure of such expectations, a number of other declarative languages have been used to build successful applications. For instance, the degree audit system at the college of one of the authors was a rule-based system used successfully for many years to certify undergraduates for graduation. Other successful rule-based systems include programs to identify drug interactions, diagnose diseases from symptoms, and configure computer installations.

Outside the area of artificial intelligence, research continues in the development of declarative languages. One example is the Datalog language [Ullman, 1989] which was developed for database systems. Datalog has also been used recently in the area of compiler code optimization [Waley and Lam, 2004]. The simplicity and understandability of the rules for code optimization in Datalog, as compared with C or Java, helps to explain the continuing interest in developing rule-based languages.

EXERCISES

15.1 Identify each of the clauses in the following statements by a logical variable, and then rewrite these statements as Horn clauses.
   (a) If "Phantom" is being performed and ticket prices are reasonable, then we'll go to the theater.
   (b) If the local economy is good or Webber is in town, then ticket prices will be reasonable.
   (c) Webber is in town.

15.2 (a) Write the following statements as a series of Prolog facts and rules. Mammals have four legs and no arms, or two arms and two legs. A cow is a mammal. A cow has no arms.
   (b) Can Prolog derive the conclusion that a cow has four legs? Explain.

15.3 Consider the family tree defined in Figure 15.4. Draw a search tree in the style of the one shown in Figure 15.2 for the query grandparent(Who, ron).

15.4 Reconsidering Figure 15.4, define a new relation "cousin" that defines the relationship between any two people whose parents are siblings. Write a query for this expanded program that will identify all people who are cousins of Ron.

15.5 Write a Prolog program to find the maximum, minimum, and range of the values in a list of numbers.

15.6 Write a Prolog program remdup that removes all duplicates from a list. For example, the query remdup([a,b,a,a,c,b,b,a], X) should return X = [a,b,c].

15.7 Extend the symbolic differentiation program so that it differentiates functions with exponents as well as sums and products. This extension should rely on the following knowledge:

$$\frac{du^n}{dx} = nu^{n-1}\frac{du}{dx} \quad \text{for integers } n > 0$$

In solving this problem, use the symbol ˆ to denote exponentiation. That is, the expression x^2 would be typed x^2.

15.8 Use your extended symbolic differentiation program d to differentiate the following functions:
(a) $x^2 + 2x + 1$
(b) $(5x - 2y)/(x^2 + 1)$

15.9 Consider the problem of simplifying an algebraic expression, such as the result of symbolic differentiation. We know that identities like $x + 0 = x$ and $1 \cdot x = x$ are used in simplifying expressions.
(a) Design a set of rules for simplification, based on the properties of 0 and 1 when added or multiplied with another expression, and then write a Prolog recursive function simp that simplifies an arbitrary algebraic expression.
(b) Show how simp can be used to simplify the result of differentiating the expressions a and b in the previous question.

15.10 Considering the append, prefix, and suffix functions defined in this chapter, draw a search tree for each of the following Prolog queries:
(a) suffix([a], L), prefix(L, [a, b, c]).
(b) suffix([b], L), prefix(L, [a, b, c]).

15.11 Consider the Prolog program to find the factorial of a number n, given in Section 15.2.2. Draw the search tree of subgoals that Prolog uses to compute the factorial of 4.

15.12 Consider adding the following fact and rule to the family tree program discussed in Section 15.2.1:

```
ancestor(X, X).

ancestor(X, Y) :- ancestor(Z, Y), parent(X, Z).
```

(a) Explain Prolog's response to the query ancestor(bill, X) using a search tree of subgoals.
(b) Describe the general circumstances under which an infinite loop can occur in a Prolog program.
(c) Suggest a slight revision of the fact and rule above that will avoid the problem you discovered in part (a) of this question.

15.13 (a) Run the natural language processing program in Section 15.3.3 to determine whether or not each of the following is a valid sentence (instance of the nonterminal symbol s):

```
The giraffe eats the apple.

The apple eats the giraffe.

The giraffe eats.
```

(b) Suggest a small change in the program that would make all three of the above sentences valid.

15.14 Revise the Prolog grammar for Figure 15.13 so that it produces a complete parse tree for the query s(Tree, [the, giraffe, eats, the, apple], []).

15.15 Complete the Clite semantic functions begun in Section 15.3.4.

15.16 (Team project) Design a complete interpreter for Clite in Prolog, beginning with the concrete syntax and including Prolog rules for the functions *V* and *M* that define Clite's type system and semantics.

15.17 Use Prolog to find all (zero or more) solutions to the following word puzzle: Mason, Alex, Steve, and Simon are standing in a police lineup. One of them is blond, handsome, and unscarred. Two of them who are not blond are standing on either side of Mason. Alex is the only one standing next to exactly one handsome man. Steve is the only one not standing next to exactly one scarred man. Who is blond, handsome, and unscarred?

15.18 Write a Prolog function "intersection" that returns a list containing only one instance of each atom that is a member of both of its two argument lists. For instance, the query:

```
?- intersection([a,b,a], [c,b,d,a], Answer)
```

should return the answer [b,a] or [a,b]. Hint: consider using a member function and other functions you have written to assist with this problem.

15.19 Write a Prolog program that solves the following problem:

Mr. and Mrs. Astor, Mr. and Mrs. Blake, Mr. and Mrs. Crane, and Mr. and Mrs. Davis were seated around a circular table. Mrs. Astor was insulted by Mr. Blake, who sat next to her on her left. Mr. Blake was insulted by Mrs. Crane, who sat opposite him across the center of the table. Mrs. Crane was insulted by the hostess, Mrs. Davis. The hostess was the only person to sit between each of a married couple. The hostess was insulted by the only person to sit betweeen two men. Who insulted the hostess?

Also print the seating order starting with the hostess.

15.20 Write a Prolog program that solves the problem below. As part of the solution, it should print **all** the crossings, with the paddler listed first.

Tom, Elliott, Bill, and Vic had to cross a river using a canoe that held only two persons. In each of three crossings from the left to the right bank, the canoe had two persons, and in each of the two crossings from the right to the left bank, the canoe had one person. Tom was unable to paddle when someone else was in the canoe with him. Elliott was unable to paddle when anyone else but Bill was in the canoe with him. Each person paddled for at least one crossing. Who paddled twice?

15.21 Discuss the basic differences between the object-oriented and logic programming paradigms. In what circumstances is each one particularly strong, and in what circumstances is each one particularly feeble?

15.22 Why is garbage collection important to logic programming languages? What garbage collection strategies are used in Prolog interpreters? Can you determine what strategies are used in the particular Prolog interpreter you are using?

15.23 (Team Project) Define and implement the concrete and abstract syntax, type system, and semantics of a small subset of Prolog using the notational style, and Java implementation developed for Clite.

15.24 Design a Prolog program that solves (easy) Sudoku puzzles (**www.sudoku.com**).

Event-Driven Programming

16

> *"Of all men's miseries the bitterest is this,*
> *to know so much and to have control over nothing."*
> **Herodotus (484–432 B.C.)**

A conventional model of computation has the program prescribe the exact order of input. This model is supported by the four programming paradigms—imperative, object-oriented, functional, and logic. In this model, the program controls the sequence of steps that occur at run time, and the ordering of input plays a passive role in regulating how those steps are carried out. Moreover, this model supports algorithms that terminate once the input is exhausted.

Event-driven programming turns this model inside out.

> **Definition**: Event-driven programs do not control the sequence in which input events occur; instead, they are written to react to any reasonable sequence of events.

In this control model, the input data govern the particular sequence of operations that is carried out by the program, but the program does not determine the input sequence order. Moreover, an event-driven program is usually designed to run indefinitely, or at least until the user selects an exit button.

The most widespread example of an event-driven program is the *graphical user interface* (GUI) found on most desktop and laptop computers in use today. Event-driven programs also drive web-based applications. For example, an online student registration system must be prepared to interact with a student no matter what her next action is: adding a course, dropping a course, determining the classroom where a course meets, and so forth. An online airline reservation system must be prepared to respond to various sequences of user events, like changing the date of travel, the destination city, or the seating preference.

Event-driven programming is also used in embedded applications for such devices as cell phones, car engines, airplane navigation and home security systems. In airplane navigation, the events that trigger programmed responses include a change in direction, wind speed, or temperature; by their nature these events also do not occur in any particular or predictable order.

To provide effective support for event-driven programming, some languages have added support for the model-view-controller (MVC) design pattern [Gamma *et al.*, 1995]. Java has classes that support an MVC design, though other languages like Visual Basic and Tcl/Tk also support event-driven programming. In this chapter, we use Java as the primary vehicle for illustrating the principles and practice of event-driven programming.

16.1 EVENT-DRIVEN CONTROL

Stein [1999, p. 1], explains event-driven programming by contrasting it with the traditional view of input-controlled computation;

> Computation is a function from its input to its output. It is made up of a sequence of functional steps that produce—at its end—some result as its goal .... These steps are combined by temporal sequencing.

Stein argues that many modern computations are embedded in physical environments where the temporal sequencing of events is unpredictable and (potentially) without an explicit end. In order to cope with this unpredictability, Stein claims that computation should be modeled as *interaction* [Stein, 1999, p. 8]:

> Computation is a community of persistent entities coupled together by their ongoing interactive behavior .... Beginning and end, when present, are special cases that can often be ignored.

This view is used by a wide range of applications for which computer programs are now designed, including robotics, video games, global positioning systems, and home security alarm systems.

Event-driven program control is different from the traditional input-driven program control, as summarized in Figure 16.1. Here we see that in the traditional imperative model, the program is designed so that the input order determines the computational

Imperative   **Event-Driven**

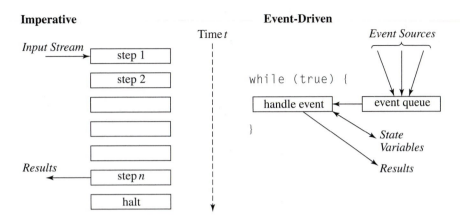

| **Figure 16.1**   Contrasting the Imperative and Event-Driven Models

design. In one variant of this model, input is gathered near the beginning of the computation and results are emitted near the end. In another variant, the computation consumes input data and produces results in a continuous loop. In either case, the programmer determines the order of the input data, which in turn determines the computational design.

By contrast, the input to an event-driven program comes from distinct autonomous *event sources,* which may be sensors on a robot or buttons in an interactive application. These events occur asynchronously, with each one entering an event queue when it occurs. As time passes, a simple control loop retrieves the next event from this queue and "handles" it. In the process of handling the event, the program may consult and/or change the value of a variable or produce intermediate *results.*

Importantly, we see two properties of event-driven programs:

1   An event-driven program typically has no preconceived stopping point, such as reaching the end of file in reading data.
2   The explicit read-evaluate-print loop present in traditional input-controlled programs does not explicitly appear in event-driven programs. Indeed, in Section 16.3.1 we will see an application that contains no loops.

16.1.1 Model-View-Controller

[Gamma *et al.*, 1995] discusses a number of design patterns for object-oriented programs. One design pattern, namely, model-view-controller (MVC), is particularly useful in the design of event-driven GUI applications.

> **Definition**: In MVC the model is the actual object being implemented, the controller is the input mechanism (buttons, menus, combo boxes, etc.) and the view is the output representation of the model.

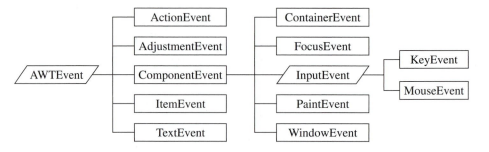

| **Figure 16.2   Java Class AWTEvent and Its Subclasses***

In applying the MVC pattern it is good practice to decouple the model, the view, and the controller as much as possible. In a given application a model may have multiple views and multiple controllers.

For example, in the familiar game of tic-tac-toe, the game is the model. It is the game's responsibility to determine whose turn it is, when a game is over, who has won, and so on. Thus, the state of the Game class consists of:

- Which player has the next move, X or 0.

- The current state of the board, that is, the contents of each square.

Other than returning a visual representation of a player's move, the game class (and its supporting classes) is not concerned with the visual aspects of the game. Nor is it concerned with how players indicate what square they choose to mark. An example model for tic-tac-toe is implemented in Section 16.3.3.

The Controller class is responsible for setting up the visual appearance of the game and for handling player input. The visual aspects are a TextArea for displaying messages, a new game button for initiating a new game, and the board itself. The primary responsibility of the controller is to handle each player's input.

Keeping track of the visual representation of the game board and displaying messages to the players is the responsibility of the *view*. If having multiple views of the game were desirable, the view would be decoupled from both the model/game and the controller. However, in our implementation the view is highly coupled with the controller, so much so that it is hard to separate the two.

A complete MVC implementation for the game of tic-tac-toe is developed in Section 16.3.3.

16.1.2 Events in Java

Java supports event-driven programming by providing certain classes and methods that can be used to design an interaction. Such a design needs to classify the events that can occur, associate those event occurrences with specific objects in the frame, and then handle each event effectively when it does occur.

---

* In these class diagrams, abstract classes are enclosed in parallelograms, while nonabstract classes are enclosed in rectangles. This notation is used by Flanagan [Flanagan, 1996] in his sequence of *Java in a Nutshell* books.

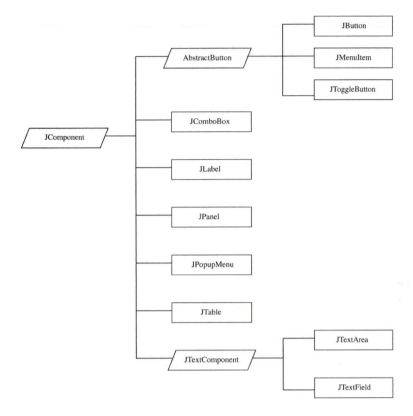

| Figure 16.3 Partial Event Source Class Hierarchy

The types of events that can occur in Java are defined by the subclasses of the predefined abstract class AWTEvent. These subclasses are summarized in Figure 16.2.

Every event source in an interaction can generate an event that is a member of one of these classes. For instance, if a button is an event source, it generates events that are members of the ActionEvent class. We shall discuss the details of this relationship in Section 16.2.

The objects themselves that can be event sources in the Swing framework are subclasses of the abstract class JComponent. A summary of some of these classes is given in Figure 16.3. Here we see, for example, that any button that can be selected by the user in an interaction is declared as an instance of the JButton class.

For a program to handle an event, it must be equipped with appropriate "listeners" that will recognize when a particular event, such as a mouse click, has occurred on an object that is an event source. The Event class has subclasses that play this role for each of the event classes identified above. These subclasses are summarized in Figure 16.4.

For example, to equip a button so that the program can "detect" an occurrence of that button's selection, the button needs to invoke its addActionListener method. If this is not done, button events will not be detected by the program. This is discussed in Section 16.2.

Figure 16.4 **Java EventListener Classes***

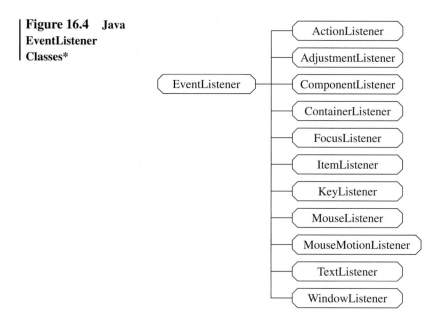

Finally, to respond to events initiated by objects in these classes, we need to implement special methods called *handlers*. Each class of events predefines the name(s) of the handler(s) that can be written for it. A summary of the handlers that are preidentified for button selections, combo box (menu) selections, text typing, and mouse events is given in Table 16.1.

| **Table 16.1** Components and Their Event Handlers |

Widget	Listener	Interface Methods
JButton	ActionListener	actionPerformed(ActionEvent e)
JComboBox	ActionListener	actionPerformed(ActionEvent e)
JLabel		
	MouseListener	mouseClicked(MouseEvent e)
		mouseEntered(MouseEvent e)
		mouseExited(MouseEvent e)
		mousePressed(MouseEvent e)
		mouseReleased(MouseEvent e)
	MouseMotion-Listener	mouseDragged(MouseEvent e)
		mouseMoved(MouseEvent e)
JTextArea	ActionListener	actionPerformed(ActionEvent e)
JTextField	ActionListener	actionPerformed(ActionEvent e)

---

* Enclosing a class in a hexagon distinguishes it as a class interface [Flanagan, 1996], rather than a regular class. Recall the distinction between classes and interfaces that was discussed in Chapter 13.

16.1.3 Java GUI Applications

Java provides a framework for programmers to build event-driven programs where the source of the events is a graphical user interface.

> **Definition**: A *graphical user interface (GUI)* application is a program that runs inside its own window and communicates with users using graphical elements such as buttons and menus.

Because they are designed to react to events rather than initiate them, GUI applications have a slightly different structure than other Java applications; this structure is sketched in Figure 16.5.

The first few lines shown in this figure are `import` directives which provide convenient access to the Java class libraries for both graphical widgets and event handlers. The `<instance variable declarations>` define various objects that can be placed in the application, as well as other values that help the program remember what has occurred so far. As with any other class, these variables collectively define the *state* of the interaction. They can be primitive data variables, objects, and arrays, just as in any Java application program or class. Some variables may represent colors, buttons, menus, text fields, and other objects that have special functions as the program and the user interact. The `main` method may be either included in the class or in a separate class by itself.

The constructor has the responsibility of placing objects in the frame, such as buttons, combo boxes, labels, and text fields. The constructor also attaches specific event listeners to different objects in the frame, so that these objects can be equipped to recognize when they have been selected by the user. Event listeners are nothing more than objects which implement a particular interface; they can be either the GUI application itself as indicated above, or they can be separate classes. As we will see, such classes often need access to various GUI application variables, so they are commonly implemented as inner classes.

A graphical user interface often has a paint method, which is invoked whenever the application needs to repaint itself. A repaint can occur for a number of reasons: another window partially obscures the application window for a time, the application window

```
import java.awt.*;
import java.awt.event.*;
import java.swing.*;

public class <classname> extends JPanel
                         implements <listeners> {
    <instance variable declarations>
    public <classname> ( ) {
        <code to initialize the GUI>
    }
    <event handlers>
}
```

| **Figure 16.5   Overall Structure of a GUI Java Application**

is first iconified and then de-iconified, and so forth. Components such as buttons, text fields, and so on will repaint themselves. However, anything done directly to the frame using `Graphics` methods will be lost during a repaint operation if not done in the paint method.

For each specific kind of event (like a button selection, a mouse click, or a combo box selection), the program must implement a special method called an `<event handler>`. The purpose of the handler is to change the state of the interaction so that it "remembers" that such an event has occurred. One handler may respond to the user pressing the mouse button, while another may respond to the user selecting a button in the frame. Whenever such an event actually occurs, its associated handler is executed one time.

The `<listeners>` that appear in the class header identify the *kinds* of events to which the application is prepared to respond. Four different kinds of user-initiated events can be handled by:

- Mouse motion events (handled by the `MouseMotionListener`).
- Mouse events (handled by the `MouseListener`).
- Button and text field selections (handled by the `ActionListener`).
- Selections from a combo box (handled by the `ActionListener`).

Importantly, the program cannot know, or predict, the order in which different events will occur, or the number of times each one will be repeated; it has to be prepared for all possibilities. That is the essence of event-driven programming. Another important difference is that the programmer writes each method to accomplish its task and exit. The loop that awaits events and dispatches them is part of the framework that Java provides.

16.2   EVENT HANDLING

In this section we describe the basic Java programming considerations for responding to various types of user-initiated events that occur while an event-driven application is running—mouse events, button selections, text field entries, and combo box (menu) selections.

16.2.1 Mouse Clicks

For the program to handle mouse clicks, the `MouseListener` interface must be implemented, either by the application itself or by a mouse handler class. If the listener is being handled directly by the class, then the class must specify the listener in its `implements` clause and activate the listener, usually inside the constructor:

```
public class MyApplication extends JPanel implements MouseListener {

    public MyApplication( ) {
        ...
        addMouseListener(this);
        ...
    }
```

The alternative is to use a separate class to handle mouse clicks. Commonly, this class is an inner class to the application, so that the mouse handler has access to all of the application's methods, particularly the graphics context:

```
public class MyApplication extends JPanel{

    public MyApplication( ) {
        ...
        addMouseListener(new MouseHandler());
        ...
    }

    private class MouseHandler implements MouseListener {
        ...
    }
}
```

If an external class is used, it is common for the class to pass itself in the call of the mouse handler constructor; the object can then be saved to an instance variable of the mouse handler class.

Whichever alternative is used, all of the following methods must be added to the class which implements the MouseListener, and at least one must have some statements that respond to the event that it represents:

```
public void mousePressed(MouseEvent e) { }
public void mouseReleased(MouseEvent e) { }
public void mouseClicked(MouseEvent e) { }
public void mouseExited(MouseEvent e) { }
public void mouseEntered(MouseEvent e) { }
```

An advantage to using a separate class is that Java provides a MouseAdapter class, which is precisely the trivial implementation of MouseListener given above. This means that the separate class can extend the MouseAdapter class (which an application cannot do), overriding exactly the methods for which actions are to be provided. In most instances, this is usually only the mouseClicked or mousePressed method.

```
public class MyApplication extends JPanel {

    public MyApplication( ) {
    ...
    addMouseListener(new MouseHandler());
    ...
    }

    private class MouseHandler extends MouseAdapter {
        public void mouseClicked(MouseEvent e) {
            <action>
        }
    }
}
```

A typical response to a mouse event is to capture the x-y pixel coordinates where that event occurs on the frame. To do this, the `getX` and `getY` methods of the `MouseEvent` class are used. For example, the following handler responds to a mouse click by storing the x-y coordinates of the click in the outer class's instance variables `x` and `y`.

```
public void mouseClicked(MouseEvent e) {
    x = e.getX();
    y = e.getY();
}
```

16.2.2 Mouse Motion

Similar to mouse clicks, to handle mouse motion, the `MouseMotionListener` interface must be implemented either by the application itself or a mouse motion handler class. To activate the listener, the following calls must be placed inside the constructor:

```
addMouseMotionListener(<listener>);
```

The class which implements the listener must implement all of the following methods; at least one must have some statements that respond to the event that the listener represents:

```
public void mouseDragged(MouseEvent e) { }
public void mouseMoved(MouseEvent e) { }
```

An advantage to using a separate class is that Java provides a `MouseMotionAdapter` class, which is precisely the trivial implementation of `MouseMotionListener` given above. This means that the separate class can extend the `MouseMotionAdapter` class (which a class that extends `JPanel` cannot do), overriding exactly the methods for which actions are to be provided. In most instances, this is usually the `mouseDragged` method.

16.2.3 Buttons

A *button* is a named object on the screen which can be selected by a mouse click. Because any number of variables can be declared with class `JButton` and placed in the application, button handlers are usually implemented via a separate class, rather than by the application itself. A button is declared and initialized as follows:

```
JButton <variable> = new JButton(<string>);
```

Here is an example:

```
JButton clearButton = new JButton("Clear");
```

A button is placed in the application by including the following inside the constructor in your program.

```
add(<variable>);
```

For example:

```
add(clearButton);
```

To be useful, a button needs to have a listener attached so that the button responds to mouse clicks. This is normally done by including the following inside the application's constructor:

```
<variable>.addActionListener(<listener>);
```

For example:

```
clearButton.addActionListener(new ClearButtonHandler());
```

The class which handles the user selecting the button must implement the `ActionListener` interface. The listener class must implement an `actionPerformed` method to handle the button selection event:

```
public void actionPerformed (ActionEvent e) {
    if (e.getSource() == <variable>) {
      <action>
    }
}
```

Here, `<variable>` refers to the name of the `JButton` variable as declared and initialized, and `<action>` defines what to do whenever that event occurs. If a unique handler is created for each button, the test to determine which button was selected can be omitted; this is normally preferred. Following, for example, is a handler written as an inner class to the application class that clears the screen whenever the `clearButton` is clicked by the user:

```
private class ClearButtonHandler implements ActionListener {
    public void actionPerformed(ActionEvent e) {
        repaint();
    }
}
```

Note that the `repaint` method is a `JPanel` method; thus, this class works as written only if it is an inner class to the application class which extends `JPanel`. Using an external class requires writing a constructor which takes the application as an argument. Using our clear button as an example, the `addActionListener` code in the application's constructor would appear as:

```
clearButton.addActionListener(new ClearButtonHandler(this));
```

The button handler class would then appear as:

```
public class ClearButtonHandler implements ActionListener {
    JPanel app;
    public ClearButtonHandler(JPanel a) { app = a; }
    public void actionPerformed(ActionEvent e) {
        app.repaint( );
    }
}
```

Note that using an external class makes it more difficult for a listener class to determine which button was selected since the buttons themselves are declared within the application class.

16.2.4 Labels, TextAreas, and TextFields

A JLabel is an object whose string value can be placed inside a frame to label another object, such as a JTextField. It can be added to the frame from within the constructor. For example, the statement

```
add(new JLabel("Fahrenheit"));
```

would place the message "Fahrenheit" in the frame. Labels are like buttons except that labels cannot have a listener attached to them.

A JTextArea is an object on the screen which is named and can hold multiline text messages. It is a scrollable object, so the object can hold more text than is visible on the screen at one time. A JTextField is an object which holds a single line of text. Either one can be used to gather text from the keyboard or merely to display messages from the application. In the former case, an ActionEvent is raised when the user types the return/enter key. JTextAreas and JTextFields are declared as follows:

```
JTextArea <variable>;
JTextField <variable>;
```

For example:

```
JTextArea echoArea;
JTextField typing;
```

JTextArea and JTextField objects are normally placed in the application as part of the constructor in the program. Initialization requires the number of lines of text (for JTextAreas) and the number of characters per line to be specified.

```
<variable1> = new JTextArea(<lines>, <chars>);
add(<variable1>);
<variable2> = new JTextField(<chars>);
add(<variable2>);
```

For example:

```
echoArea = new JTextArea(5, 40);
add(echoArea);
typing = new JTextField(40);
add(typing);
```

In this example, we declare and place a 5 line by 40 character JTextArea and a 40-character JTextField in the current panel.

When the user types in a JTextField or JTextArea and hits the return key, the application can handle that event by writing additional code in its actionPerformed event handler:

```
public void actionPerformed (actionEvent e) {
    if (e.getSource() == <variable>) {
        String s = <variable>.getText();
        <action>
    }
}
```

Here, <variable> refers to the name of the JTextArea or JTextArea variable that was declared and placed in the frame by the constructor, like typing in the example above. When the event occurs, the string value typed in the text area is assigned to the variable s and the <action> is then executed.

A better solution is to use an internal class that listens specifically to the JTextField typing:

```
private class TextHandler implements ActionListener {
    public void actionPerformed (actionEvent e) {
        String s = <variable>.getText( );
        <action>
    }
}
```

In this case, the handler need not check for the source of the triggering event; it must be the user pressing the return (or enter) key in the JTextField typing.

As an example of an <action>, the user's typing can be immediately echoed in the TextArea by concatenating it with the text that is already there. The getText and setText methods are useful for this purpose, as shown below:

```
echoArea.setText(echoArea.getText() + s + "\n");
```

If this line is added as the <action> in the above code, the user's typing will be echoed on a new line inside the JTextArea object named echoArea.

16.2.5 Combo Boxes

A *combo box* is an object on the screen that offers several options to be selected by the user; it is like a pull-down menu, but it can be placed anywhere within the application, not just at the top. A combo box is declared as follows:

```
JComboBox <variable> ;
```

For example:

```
JComboBox combo;
```

The combo box is named and placed in the frame as part of the constructor of your program. The different selections are assigned to the `JComboBox` variable either as part of the constructor or using the `addItem` method. Interaction is triggered by adding a listener to the frame for the combo box.

```
<variable> = new JComboBox( );
<variable>.addItem(<string1>);
...
add(<variable>);
<variable>.addActionListener(<listener>);
```

For example:

```
combo = new JComboBox( );
combo.addItem("North");
combo.addItem("East");
combo.addItem("South");
combo.additem("West");
add(combo);
combo.addItemListener(new ComboHandler());
```

In the case above, an inner class to the application itself is assumed to be handling the combo box event. The application listener event handler must implement `ActionListener`. When the user selects one of the combo boxes, the event is handled by an `actionPerformed` method:

```
private class ComboHandler implements ActionListener {
    public void actionPerformed (ActionEvent e) {
        String s = (String)combo.getItem( );
        if (s.equals(<string1>)) {
            <action1> in response to a selection of <string1>
        }
        else if (s.equals(<string2>)) {
            <action2> in response to a selection of <string2>
        }
        ...
    }
}
```

When the event of selecting a combo box occurs, this handler is executed. The String `s` gets the value of the choice the user has selected, which is accessible to the handler by way of the method call `combo.getItem( )`. This choice is used in a series of tests to select the appropriate `<action>`.

16.3   THREE EXAMPLES

In this section, we illustrate three problems that utilize event-driven programming. The first is the design of a simple GUI interface. The second is a Java applet, and the third involves the design of an interactive game using the Model-View-Controller (MVC) design pattern.

16.3.1 A Simple GUI Interface

Consider the design of a simple interface, in which the user can insert rectangles and place texts in arbitrary locations of the frame. The user should be able to accomplish this as simply as possible, and so providing buttons, menus, and text typing areas, as well as handling mouse-click actions on the screen is essential. An initial design to support this activity is shown in Figure 16.6.

This frame has four objects; a clear button, a combo box menu, a text area for communicating with the user as events are initiated, and a text field in which the user can enter messages. Thus, we can begin our design by defining the state of the computation with the following objects and interpretations:

`combo`   User can select Nothing, Rectangle, or Message from this menu.

`echoArea`   A text area for reporting the most recent event that has occurred.

`typing`   A text field for entering user input.

The button need not be part of the global state, since its function is merely to clear the screen, and this can be done completely within the event handler for the button. No other object or handler needs to be aware of the clear button.

The state of the computation for this application must also keep track of any information that is relevant to accomplishing the next task, be it drawing a rectangle or placing a text somewhere in the frame. To draw a rectangle, the system must have two pieces of information, the x-y coordinates of the upper left-hand corner of the rectangle and the

**Figure 16.6
Initial Design for a
Graphical Drawing
Tool**

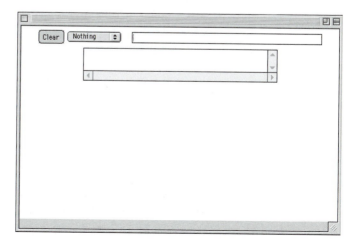

x-y coordinates of the lower right. These two points can be retrieved via a mouse event and the `mouseClicked` handler, but the first x-y coordinate pair must be stored globally within the application's state. Furthermore, a count of the mouse clicks must also be stored globally so that the first click can be distinguished from the second in determining the corners of the rectangle. Thus, additional global state information includes:

```
lastX, lastY    X-Y coordinates of last mouse click
clickNumber     The number of mouse clicks (odd or even)
```

The x and y coordinates of a mouse click are reported in the `JTextArea` by the program whenever a mouse click event occurs. Informative messages to the user are also displayed there.

The code that defines the state is shown in Figure 16.7, and the code that initializes the interaction is shown in Figure 16.8.

Designing the event handlers is a more intricate process. For each event that occurs, an appropriate handler must contain code to distinguish that event from the rest and then change the state and/or generate output into the frame appropriately. Consider the following scenario:

> The user first selects "Rectangle" from the combo box menu. To properly handle the event, the system must store that selection and then prompt the user to click the mouse at the point where the upper left-hand corner of the rectangle should be drawn, as shown in Figure 16.9.

What code do we write to respond to this selection? We write code inside an `actionPerformed` method of the `ComboHandler` event handler class, since the object selected is a `JComboBox`. The complete handler for this problem is shown in Figure 16.10.

While this code is a bit obscure, it does reveal that the `ActionListener` handler must prepare for *any* menu event that can occur. It distinguishes among the possibilities by checking the parameter e for the item selected, which is assigned to the state variable `combo`. If the choice is a `Rectangle`, the handler dutifully prompts the user to click to set the location where the upper left-hand corner of the rectangle should be located in the frame. If the choice is a `Message`, a different prompt goes to the user. In either case, this handler echoes the nature of this event in the `echoArea`.

Assuming that the user clicks the mouse in the frame, the system must respond by storing the x-y coordinates of that click in the application's state variables `lastX`, `lastY` and prompt the user to click to set the lower right-hand corner of the desired

```
private int lastX = 0; // first click's x-y coordinates
private int lastY = 0;
private int clickNumber = 0;
private JComboBox combo;
private String[ ] choices = {"Nothing", "Rectangle", "Message"};
private JTextArea echoArea;
private JTextField typing;
```

| **Figure 16.7   Defining the State for the Interaction**

```
public Skeleton( ) {
    // Set the background color and listen for the mouse
    setBackground(Color.white);
    addMouseListener(new MouseHandler());

    // Create a button and add it to the Panel.
    JButton clearButton = new JButton("Clear");
    clearButton.setForeground(Color.black);
    clearButton.setBackground(Color.lightGray);
    add(clearButton);
    clearButton.addActionListener(new ClearButtonHandler());

    // Create a menu of user combos and add it
    combo = new JComboBox(choices);
    add(combo);
    combo.addActionListener(new ComboHandler());

    // Create a TextField and a TextArea and add them
    typing = new JTextField(20);
    add(typing);
    typing.addActionListener(new TextHandler());
    echoArea = new JTextArea(2, 40);
    echoArea.setEditable(false);
    add(echoArea);
}
```

| **Figure 16.8   Code to Initialize the Interaction**

Figure 16.9   First Interaction Step: The User Selects Rectangle

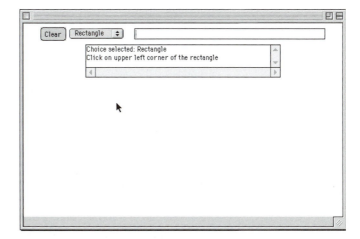

```
private class ComboHandler implements ActionListener {
    public void actionPerformed (ActionEvent e) {
        String c = (String) (combo.getSelectedItem());
        echoArea.setText("Combo selected: " + c);
        // prepare to handle first mouse click
        clickNumber = 0;
        if (c.equals("Rectangle"))
            echoArea.append("\nClick to set upper"
                + "left corner of the rectangle");
        else if (c.equals("Message"))
            echoArea.append(
                "\nEnter a message in the text area");
    }
}
```

| **Figure 16.10**   `ActionListener` **Handler for This Interaction**

rectangle. But that should be done *only* if the current choice is a `Rectangle`. By the time the mouse-click event happens, the only source of information about what event immediately preceded it comes from the application's state. That is, the click could have been preceded by a different event, which should provoke a different response from the interaction. Where is this all sorted out? In the `mouseClicked` handler, as shown in Figure 16.11.

This handler must also be prepared for anything, since it doesn't implicitly know what events occurred immediately before this particular mouse click. The state variable `clickNumber` helps sort things out, since its updated value will have an odd number for the first click of a pair and an even number for the second. Thus, the upper left-hand corner of a rectangle is indicated for odd values and the drawing of a complete rectangle, using the x and y coordinates of the current click together with the x and y coordinates of the previous click (stored in `lastX` and `lastY`), is indicated for even clicks.

The remainder of this event handler should be fairly readable. The effect of drawing a rectangle after the user has clicked twice is shown in Figure 16.12. Here, the arrow in the figure shows the location of the second click, whose x and y coordinates are 215 and 204, respectively.

The next task in designing this interaction is to implement the event handler that responds to the user selecting the clear button or typing text in the typing area. The `actionPerformed` method for this event is shown in Figure 16.13. Note here the simplicity of attaching a unique handler to the clear button; it does not have to test what triggers the event (the button or the enter key in the typing area); it clears the screen via a repaint.

Responding to a text typed by the user is straightforward; we need only to store the text for later use and prompt the user to click the mouse to locate the text in the frame, as shown in Figure 16.14.

Note that both the `TextHandler` and `ClearButtonHandler` classes implement the `ActionListener` interface and both have `actionPerformed` methods. Neither handler has to be aware of the other, as each is listening for separate events.

```
private class MouseHandler extends MouseAdapter {
  public void mouseClicked(MouseEvent e) {
    int x = e.getX();
    int y = e.getY();
    echoArea.setText("Mouse Clicked at " +
                e.getX() + ", " + e.getY() + "\n");
    Graphics g = getGraphics();
    if (combo.getSelectedItem().equals("Rectangle")) {
        clickNumber = clickNumber + 1;
        // is it the first click?
        if (clickNumber % 2 == 1) {
            echoArea.append("Click to set lower right"
                + "corner of the rectangle");
            lastX = x;
            lastY = y;
            }
            // or the second?
            else g.drawRect(lastX, lastY,
                Math.abs(x-lastX), Math.abs(y-lastY));
    }
    else if (combo.getSelectedItem().equals("Message"))
        // for a message, display it
        g.drawString(typing.getText(), x, y);
  } // mouseClicked
}
```

| **Figure 16.11**   Details of the `mouseClicked` **Handler**

Figure 16.12
Effect of Selecting
Rectangle Choice and
Clicking the Mouse
Twice

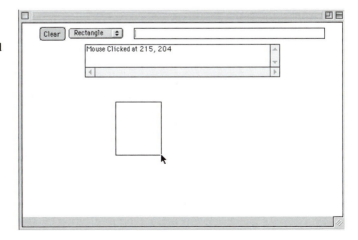

```
private class ClearButtonHandler implements ActionListener {
    public void actionPerformed (ActionEvent e) {
        echoArea.setText("Clear button selected ");
        repaint();
    }
}
```

| **Figure 16.13** **ActionPerformed Handler for the Clear Button**

```
private class TextHandler implements ActionListener {
    public void actionPerformed (ActionEvent e) {
        echoArea.setText("Text entered: " + typing.getText());
        if (combo.getSelectedItem().equals("Message"))
            echoArea.append("\nNow click to place this message");
    }
}
```

| **Figure 16.14** **ActionPerformed Handler for the Enter Key in the Typing Area**

Figure 16.15 Net Effect of User Placing a Text in the Frame

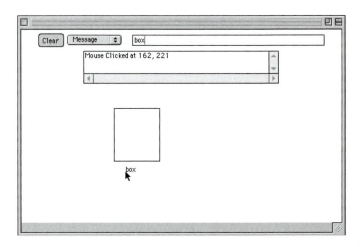

The net effect of typing text and clicking to locate it below the rectangle that had been placed in the frame is shown in Figure 16.15. There, the location of the mouse click is indicated by the arrow in the figure, which is at x-y coordinates 162 and 221.

Finally, we give the code for the main method in Figure 16.16. This code establishes the outer window as a JFrame and adds the skeleton's panel to its content pane. It then establishes a size for the frame and tells the frame to show itself.

This sketch provides a concrete example of the process of designing an event-driven program. The program runs indefinitely—the user can spend hours drawing rectangles, placing messages, and clearing the frame, and only the user decides what event sequence will occur at any particular point in time.

```
public static void main(String args[]) {
    JFrame frame = new JFrame();
    frame.setDefaultCloseOperation(JFrame.EXIT_ON_CLOSE);

    Skeleton panel = new Skeleton( );

    frame.getContentPane().add(panel);
    frame.setLocation(100, 100);  // needed by some window managers
    frame.setSize(500, 500);
    //frame.pack( );
    frame.show();
}
```

| **Figure 16.16**   The main **Method**

```
import java.awt.*;
import java.awt.event.*;
import javax.swing.*;
public class <classname> extends JApplet {
                        implements <listeners> {
  <state variable declarations>
  public void init ( ) {
    <code to initialize the applet>
  }
  <event handlers>
}
```

| **Figure 16.17**   **Overall Structure of a Java Applet**

None of the methods we have written has a loop. Thus, all methods appear to exit. Yet the program continues to run, responding to events. How is this accomplished? Control resides with the event loop discussed in Section 16.1 and provided by the Java Swing framework.

The observant reader will have noticed that this application has no paint method. Thus, iconifying the window or overlaying another window on top of this window will eventually necessitate a repaint, causing all the rectangles and messages to disappear. If the application needs to repaint what has been drawn on the screen, then the application has to remember what it has drawn. We will see examples of this in later programs.

16.3.2 Designing a Java Applet

In this section we convert the program of the previous section into an *applet*. An *applet* is a Java program designed to run inside a web browser. Many educators have developed interesting applets that help to illustrate difficult concepts in various fields.

In this section we outline how to convert the simple application of the previous section to an applet. The actual code is available on the book's website. It is not shown here, because the details of the code are the same as shown in the previous section. Only the structure is slightly different, as shown in Figure 16.17.

The major differences between an applet and a GUI application are:

1 The main class extends `JApplet` rather than either `JPanel` or `JFrame`.

2 An applet does not have a `static main` method.

3 An applet does not have a constructor. Instead, the applet framework provides equivalent functionality by calling the applet's `init` method, which is used to initialize the state of the applet, including GUI elements on the screen.

4 When the class extends `JPanel`, we can add components directly to the panel. Note that in the `main` method the panel itself has to be added to the frame's content panel via the method call `getContentPane( ).add(component)`. In an applet, the method `init` must create a `JPanel` and add all the widgets to the panel. The panel is, in turn, added to the applet's `contentPane`.

5 The `paintComponent` method of a panel must be converted to the `paint` method of an applet. The `Skeleton` class does not override the `paintComponent` of the panel.

Thus, to convert GUI application `Skeleton` to an applet `SkeletonApplet`, we carry out the above process. The result, with most of the actual code elided, is given in Figure 16.18. The details of the code are otherwise identical in the two programs.

The other major applet methods are:

- `start`: this method is invoked when the web page is visited. It is usually used to start any animation threads.

- `stop`: this method is invoked when the applet's web page is left or when the web browser is iconified. It is used to stop any animation threads.

- `destroy`: this method is the opposite of `init`. It is used to release resources held by the applet.

Thus, given Java's Swing framework, converting a GUI application to an applet is a simple process. The opposite conversion is equally straightforward.

16.3.3 Event-Driven Interactive Games

Consider designing an event-driven program that monitors an interactive game between two persons. We develop an implementation of the tic-tac-toe game here, and discuss the implementation of the game of Nim, both as event-driven programs.

Tic-Tac-Toe In the game tic-tac-toe, there is a 3 × 3 board and two players alternate turns. Each turn forces the board into a new state which differs from the old one by the contents of one square. A game is over when either the board is full or one of the players has placed three markers (X or O) in a row, either horizontally, vertically, or diagonally. The interaction should run indefinitely, so the players can clear the board and start a new game at any time. Thus, the *state* of a tic-tac-toe game naturally includes:

- The state of the board,

- Whose turn it is, and

- Whether the game has been won.

An *event* in this setting is either a player move (clicking the mouse in an unoccupied square to place the next X or O) or a player selecting the "new game" button. The sequencing of these events is entirely unpredictable by the program—either one can occur while a game is going on.

```
import java.awt.*;
import java.awt.event.*;
import javax.swing.*;

public class SkelApplet extends JApplet {
    // Global "state" of the interaction
    private int lastX = 0;      // first click's x-y coordinates
    private int lastY = 0;
    ...

    public void init( ) {
        JPanel panel = new JPanel( );
        ...
        // Create a button and add it to the Panel.
        JButton clearButton = new JButton("Clear");
        clearButton.setForeground(Color.black);
        clearButton.setBackground(Color.lightGray);
        panel.add(clearButton);
        clearButton.addActionListener(new ClearButtonHandler());
        ...
        getContentPane( ).add(panel);
    }

    private class ClearButtonHandler implements ActionListener {
        public void actionPerformed (ActionEvent e) {
            ...
        }
    }
    ...
}
```

| **Figure 16.18**   **The Skeleton Program as an Applet**

The results displayed by the program are the board itself and a message area which is used to report whose turn it is, the winner, and other information as the game proceeds.

The overall design of this GUI application follows the Model-View-Controller pattern introduced in Section 16.1.1.

Model The Game class has a very simple state. It must keep track of which player moves next and the state of the board. Players are represented by integers, and so the board is a one dimensional array of integers, where -1 represents an empty cell, 0 an X, and 1 an 0.

```
private int player = -1;    // Current player: EX, or OH
private int[ ] board = new int[9];
```

Although visually the board is two dimensional, it is simpler to use a one-dimensional representation. Thus, the squares are numbered from zero to eight, proceeding across each row from left to right.

The primary responsibility of the game is to record player moves, which is handled by the move(square) method. This method first switches to the next player (using modulo arithmetic) and then records the move. Finally, it returns a visual representation of the move (which is discussed below).

```
public CellIcon move(int square) {
    player = (player + 1) % 2;
    board[square] = player;
    return cell[player];
}
```

Another responsibility of the game is to discover when a player has won the game. This is implemented using a brute force approach. The array lines has a row with indices for each winning row, column, and diagonal in the game. The method won( ) checks each of these to see if the current player has a winning combination.

```
private int[ ][ ] lines = {
    {0, 1, 2}, {3, 4, 5}, {6, 7, 8}, //across
    {0, 3, 6}, {1, 4, 7}, {2, 5, 8}, //down
    {0, 4, 8}, {2, 4, 6}              //diagonal
};
public boolean won( ) {
    for (int i = 0; i < lines.length; i++)
        if (board[lines[i][0]] == player
            && board[lines[i][1]] == player
            && board[lines[i][2]] == player)
            return true;
    return false;
} // won
```

Another major responsibility of the game is to clear the board, when asked, and to reset the player. Recall that an empty square is represented by the integer −1.

```
public CellIcon[ ] clear( ) {
    for (int i = 0; i < board.length; i++)
        board[i] = -1;
    player = -1;
    return initial;
};
```

The final Game method is player( ), which returns a String representing the current player, that is, either X or O.

The other classes that are part of the model are the CellIcon class and its subclasses. An instance of the CellIcon class is returned by the Game so that the board position chosen by the player can be appropriately labeled with either an X or an O as appropriate.

Buttons and labels can be labeled with either text strings or icons. The latter can be images or any class which implements the Icon interface. Such a class must implement the paintIcon method for rendering the icon. We use icons so that the buttons have large x's and o's.

The `CellIcon` class is an abstract class that implements the basic functionality, including setting colors and sizes. The only method not implemented is the `paintIcon` method, which is unique to each icon being rendered. The code for the `CellIcon` class is given in Figure 16.19.

Three subclasses are provided: the empty cell, an `X`, and an `O`. The code for the class that provides an `X` icon is:

```java
import java.awt.*;
import java.awt.geom.*;
import javax.swing.*;

public class CellXIcon extends CellIcon {
    public CellXIcon(int size) { super(size); }

    public void paintIcon(Component c, Graphics g,
                int x, int y) {
        int size = size( );
        g.setColor(Color.white);
        g.fillRect(x, y, size, size);
        g.setColor(getColor( ));
        g.drawLine(x, y, x+size, y+size);
        g.drawLine(x+size, y, x, y+size);
        g.setColor(Color.black);
    }
}
```

Note that the `CellXIcon` class does not know (or care) that it is associated with an `X`; it just draws itself when asked. The remaining two classes, as well as the complete `Game` class, are provided at the book website.

```java
import java.awt.*;
import javax.swing.*;

public abstract class CellIcon implements Icon {

    private Color color = Color.black;
    private int size;

    public CellIcon (int size) { this.size = size; }

    public int size( ) { return size; }
    public Color getColor( ) { return color; }
    public void setColor(Color c) { color = c; }

    public int getIconWidth( ) { return size; }
    public int getIconHeight( ) { return size; }
}
```

| **Figure 16.19   The CellIcon Class**

The Controller Classes   Recognizing that many board games require a rectangular array, or "grid," of squares or "cells" into which moves can be placed, the class Keypad is designed to support these activities. Let us consider the concept of a cell first.

A *cell* is basically a square that is capable of displaying itself on the screen. As such, it has x-y coordinates and a size; it can be implemented using the java.awt class Rectangle. A cell has a value; to accommodate a variety of games, the constant cell values include OFF (no value or empty), ON, EX (for tic-tac-toe), and OH (a simple circle). A cell can also have a color.

A game designer might be tempted to implement a cell class. However, anyone familiar with the Java's Swing library would realize that a JButton has all the desired properties. Furthermore, once selected, it can be disabled so that it no longer responds to mouse clicks representing illegal moves. This simplifies the program logic, since the presence of an illegal move does not need to be checked.

An important aspect of the controller is the initialization code which creates a rectangular array of labeled buttons. As part of the constructor state it leaves behind buttons which respond to mouse clicks. This initialization code for the keypad method is given in Figure 16.20. Note that like the game class, a one dimensional array is used to represent the visual two dimensional array.

Any cell in the grid may be set by a single mouse click using the icon returned by the game's move method. For example, suppose we want to place an X in row 2, column 1 of the tic-tac-toe board. This is illustrated in Figure 16.21. Note that the game thinks that square 7 was selected.

The mouse listener assigned to the grid/board buttons is used to identify the square selected. The central event-driven code appears in this handler for mouse clicks. As each button is clicked, the actionPerformed method invokes the game's move method and marks the button with the result. The button is then disabled. Then a check is made to see if the game has been won. If so, the winner is announced and all the buttons are disabled. The mouse listener class for the board buttons is given in Figure 16.22.

Now with the the board and its mouse listener classes in hand, we can complete the design of the visual and event-handling parts of the tic-tac-toe program. The major visual design element is a 3 × 3 board, as seen in Figure 16.21.

```java
public JPanel keypad (int rows, int cols, Icon[ ] label) {
    JPanel panel = new JPanel( );
    panel.setLayout( new GridLayout(rows, cols, 2, 2) );
    square = new JButton[label.length];
    for (int i = 0; i < label.length; i++) {
        square[i] = new JButton(label[i]);
        square[i].addActionListener( new ActionHandler(i) );
        panel.add( square[i] );
    }
    return panel;
}
```

| Figure 16.20   The Keypad Class

Figure 16.21
Placement of an
X in the Grid

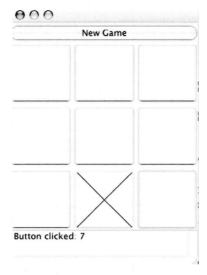

Each player takes a turn by clicking the mouse to place an X or O on one of the unoccupied squares; player X goes first. The winner is the player who first places three X's or 3 O's in a row, either horizontally, vertically, or diagonally. A tie game occurs when the board is full, and no one has three X's or O's in a row.

The program uses a TextArea for displaying appropriate messages (for instance, when a player has won). It allows each player in turn to click on an empty square and replace that square with an X or an O. The program thus keeps track of whose turn it

```
private class ActionHandler implements ActionListener {
    private int button;

    public ActionHandler(int button) {
        this.button = button;
    }

    public void actionPerformed(ActionEvent e) {
        Icon icon = game.move(button);
        square[button].setIcon(icon);
        square[button].setEnabled(false);
        if (game.won( )) {
            setButtons(false);
            echoArea.setText(game.player( ) + "wins!");
        } else
            echoArea.setText("Button clicked: " + button);
    }
}
```

Figure 16.22   The Mouse Listener Class for the Board Buttons

is and reports that information in the TextArea at the beginning of each turn. Thus, the state variables for this game include:

- A variable for the 3 × 3 buttons.
- A TextArea variable for sending messages to the players.
- A variable that represents the game.

These state variables are:

```
private TextArea echoArea;
private Game game;
private JButton[ ] square;
```

The constructor initializes the display by first adding a "New Game" button and attaching a mouse listener to it. Next it adds the board. And finally it adds the text area for messages. This initialization code is given in Figure 16.23.

Whenever a player decides to quit the current game, even perhaps before the game is over, the program should respond appropriately by clearing the board and re-enabling all the board buttons. The event handler must respond to a player's selection of the "new game" button whenever it occurs. It should re-initialize the board. This event handler is given in Figure 16.24.

The complete application is available at the website given in the Preface. It contains what is presented here, the complete Controller and Game classes, as well as the main program.

It should be noted that the Controller class itself and its event handling classes are largely unaware of the details of the game. They do not know about X's and O's, the

```
public Controller(Game game) {
    this.game = game;
    setLayout(new BorderLayout( ));

    // Add a new game button
    Button newGame = new Button("New Game");
    newGame.addActionListener(new NewGameHandler());
    add(newGame, BorderLayout.NORTH);

    // Place a 3x3 board to the panel
    Icon[ ] label = game.clear( );
    JPanel board = keypad(3, 3, label);
    add(board, BorderLayout.CENTER);

    // Add an echo area
    echoArea = new TextArea(2, 25);
    echoArea.setEditable(false);
    echoArea.setText("X goes first");
    add(echoArea, BorderLayout.SOUTH);
} // Controller
```

| **Figure 16.23** **Controller Initialization**

```
private class NewGameHandler implements ActionListener {
    public void actionPerformed (ActionEvent e) {
        echoArea.setText("New Game button selected");
        newGame( );
        repaint( );
    }
}
```

| **Figure 16.24**   **The New Game Event Handler**

size of the board, what icons are being put on the board buttons, and so on. They do not even know how many players are involved. The controller is largely decoupled from the game.

Nim   Designing other interactive games involves similar considerations, whether the game be Othello, Connect-4, or Nim. Each one requires that the program keep track of the state of the game by defining appropriate variables and event handlers so that the state is altered in exactly the right way when each event occurs.

Consider the two-player game of Nim, which can be played on a board that has three rows of pebbles, as shown below:

Each player takes her turn by removing one or more pebbles from any one of the three rows. The winner is the player who picks up the last pebble. A program can monitor this game by using a 7 × 7 board in which the first three rows contain O's in locations where the pebbles are initially placed, as shown below:

The program can conduct a dialogue with the two players using a TextArea for displaying appropriate messages. It should allow each player to click on the particular pebble(s) to be removed during that player's turn, but it should not allow a pebble to be picked up in two different rows in the same turn. To mark a "removed" pebble, the program can replace its O with a space (OFF) on the same position of the board.

To monitor this game, your program should be able to

1   Keep track of whose turn (Player 1 or Player 2) it is and report that information in the TextArea at the beginning of each turn;

2   Accept a series of mouse clicks that together constitute a legal move;

3 Determine when the game is over (and which of Player 1 or Player 2 is the winner) and report that event in the TextArea; and

4 Allow a new game to be started at any time, perhaps by providing a Combo Box or a Button that will cause a handler to restore the board to the state shown above.

The program should have a method GameOver that determines whether or not the game is over (the board contains only spaces). That method should be called by the mouseClicked handler to tell whether or not to report a winner.

The state of the program, including both game and controller, should include the following:

- A variable for the 7×7 board.
- A TextArea variable for sending messages to the players.
- A variable that determines whose turn it is; that variable flips back and forth whenever a player has completed a legal move.
- A variable that records the row in which a player has picked up her first pebble for a single move (since all subsequent pebbles must be picked up from the same row).

Completion of the design of this interaction is left as an exercise.

16.4 OTHER EVENT-DRIVEN APPLICATIONS

Event-driven programs occur in many other domains. Here are three examples:

- An ATM machine.
- A home security system.
- A supermarket checkout station.

In this section, we briefly describe the first two of these interactions, focussing on their state variables and the kinds of events that should be handled in the event loop to maintain integrity among the state variables.

16.4.1 ATM Machine

An ATM machine is driven by a program that runs seven days a week and 24 hours a day. The program must be able to conduct transactions with a user. The essential elements of a typical ATM machine display are shown in Figure 16.25. (In practice, the details are different, but the elements shown here are adequate to characterize what happens during an ATM transaction).

The state of this interaction is captured partially by the objects in this display and partially by other information that relates to the particular user at the machine. A basic collection of state variables required for an ATM transaction includes:

- The user's account number—account.
- The type of transaction (deposit, withdrawal, etc.)—type.
- The amount of the transaction—amount.
- A message from the bank to the user—message.
- The user's available balance—balance.

**Figure 16.25
Elements of an
ATM Machine User
Interface**

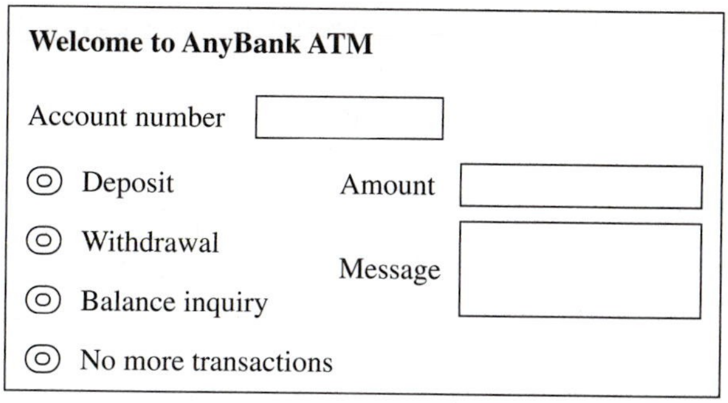

The last variable in this list, the available balance, brings into play a new dimension that we haven't encountered in our other event-driven programming examples. In this case, the program must interact not only with the user but also with the bank's database of all its accounts and current balances. A program that interacts with such a database, which may reside on an entirely different computer, or "server," on the bank's network, is called a *client-server* application. Client-server applications exist in a wide variety of systems, including airline reservation systems, online textbook ordering systems, and inventory systems. A client-server example is fully developed in Section 17.4.2.

Returning to this example, we can now characterize the different events that can occur, together with how they should be handled (that is, the effect they should have on the state of the interaction).

1 *Event:* User enters an account number (swipes her card).
   Handled by: Program checks that account is a valid number, sets balance, and issues the message, "Choose a transaction."
2 *Event:* User selects a button (deposit, withdrawal, etc.)
   Handled by: Program checks to see that a valid account has been entered. If so, save the type of button selected.

   - If deposit or withdrawal, issue the message, "Enter an amount."
   - If balance inquiry, display the balance.
   - If no more transactions, clear the account.

   If not, issue the message, "Enter an account number."
3 *Event*: User enters an amount.
   Handled by: Program checks that user has selected a deposit or withdrawal type. If deposit, add the amount to the balance. If withdrawal, then

   - If balance is greater than amount, subtract amount from balance.
   - Otherwise, issue the message, "Insufficient funds."

   Otherwise, issue the message, "Select a transaction type (deposit or withdrawal)."

The key insight with this design is that the system does not anticipate the type of transaction or the order in which the events will occur. It responds to every different possibility and updates the state of the interaction appropriately.

16.4.2 Home Security System

Home security systems provide homeowners with a modest warning that an unwanted event, such as a break-in, fire, or flood, has occurred. These systems are programmed to react to sensors which can detect smoke, water, or motion and are placed strategically around the house. They can be programmed by homeowners so that their own motion about the house is not taken as an unwanted break-in. They also can be connected to the local fire and police stations so that notification of an unwanted event can receive immediate response.

The overall design for such a system is sketched in Figure 16.26. Here, sensors and the user interface supply events to the program, while alarms and the user interface receive responses from the program. Responses at the user interface are displayed on an LCD display. Since this system must be able to handle events in parallel (e.g., signals from two different sensors may occur simultaneously), the program must handle both events (as discussed in this chapter) and concurrency (as discussed in Chapter 17). We ignore the concurrent programming dimensions of this problem in the current discussion.

The state variables for this program include:

- The user's password—password.
- The state of the user (here or away)—user.
- The state of the system (armed or unarmed)—armed.
- The state of each sensor (active or inactive)—sensors.
- The state of each alarm (active or inactive)—alarms.
- A message from the system to the control panel—message.

We have dramatically generalized this description in order to simplify the discussion and focus on the main ideas about event-driven programming that this problem evokes. In any case, here are some of the events that can reasonably occur, with a sketch of what should happen to the state in response to each event.

- *Event:* User enters password.
  Handled by: Program checks that password is valid and displays message.
- *Event:* User enters function "away."
  Handled by: Program checks password has been entered and changes the state of all sensors to "active," the state of the system to "armed," and displays message.

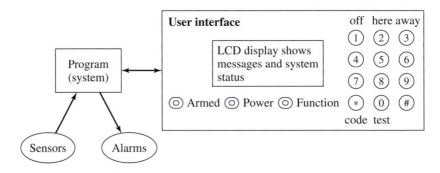

| **Figure 16.26** **Overall Design of a Home Security System**

- *Event:* Sensor receives signal.
  Handled by: If system is armed, program sends appropriate alarm and displays a message.
- *Event:* User enters function "test."
  Handled by: Program disarms system.
- *Event:* User enters function "here."
  Handled by: Program disables motion-detection sensors, enables all others, and changes state of the system to "armed."

16.5 SUMMARY

Event-driven programming has become pervasive in modern applications, largely due to the emergence of graphical user interfaces (GUIs). This design technique differs from the conventional paradigms because it allows input to occur in unpredictable sequences and because its programs are designed to run continuously.

Java provides strong support for event-driven programming, although it is not the only language used for this purpose. Several other languages, such as Tcl/Tk, also have facilities to support event-handling.

Event-driven GUI programs can be written for a wide range of applications, such as interactive games and on-line search engines. The Model-View-Controller (MVC) design pattern is particularly useful for the design of these programs.

EXERCISES

16.1 The TextArea variable happens to be scrollable, so that all actions in a run of this program can be echoed without a loss of information. How can you refine the interaction in Section 16.3.1 so that this happens?

16.2 Augment the simple event-driven interaction given in Section 16.3.1 so that the menu of combo boxes includes lines and ovals, in addition to rectangles and messages.

16.3 Consider augmenting this program again so that it has an erase function. Discuss the difference between erasing the most recently drawn shape on the screen and erasing objects in the reverse order in which they were drawn. What changes in the definition of the state of the program are needed to accomplish this more ambitious latter goal?

16.4 Write an application which implements the following:
- There are three choice popup menu boxes.
- One sets the color: red, green, yellow, blue.
- One sets the figure to be drawn: circle, square.
- One sets the size of a circle or square: 10, 20, 30 pixels. Size is the diameter of a circle or height and width of a square.
- When the mouse is clicked, a filled circle or square of the appropriate size and color is drawn at the mouse's (x,y) coordinates, if the figure to be drawn is either a circle or square.

- The figures drawn should survive a repaint, that is, the application being iconified and de-iconified. Hint: you will need a `List` of graphic figures; your `paintComponent` method should just ask each figure in the `List` to paint itself.

16.5 Consider the following tic-tac-toe board configuration.

Describe the sequence of events that should occur for this to be achieved, starting with an empty board. For each event, identify the handler that is called and the change that occurs among the state variables that are affected by that event.

16.6 Think of a strategy by which your program can support either a two-player or a one-player tic-tac-toe game. If the user chooses the one-player option (from, say, a menu), the program should assume the role of Player X and play a competitive game against the user—that is, Player X should never lose.

16.7 Implement the Nim event-driven program by declaring the state variables and implementing the `init`, `mouseClicked`, `actionPerformed`, and `gameOver` methods.

16.8 (Hard) Think of a strategy by which your Nim program assumes the role of Player 1 and plays a competitive game of Nim. You may want to research this problem before beginning to write the code. (Do this problem only after you have completed the previous question.)

16.9 The game Connect-4 has two players who alternately place X's and O's on an 8 × 8 grid, like the one shown below.

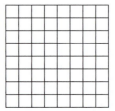

However, each move must be made at the bottom-most empty square of a column. The winner is the player who places four of her tokens (X or O) in a row, either horizontally, vertically, or diagonally. Design an event-driven interaction for this game. In doing this, start by designing the state variables, the objects in the frame, and finally the event-handlers that are required to effectively monitor the play of the game. Be sure to have a method that determines when the game is over (a player has placed four tokens in a row, or else the board has become full).

16.10 (Team project) Consider designing an event-driven interaction that demonstrates population growth. This interaction demonstrates a model of population growth and decay called the "Game of Life," which was designed by John Conway in 1970. It uses a grid to display a population of individuals in a single generation, such as the 8 × 8 grid shown below.

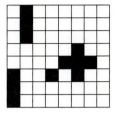

A square is filled in on the grid to indicate a living individual, and is left empty to indicate the absence of a living individual. Each square on the grid has up to eight immediate "neighbors," one on each side and one on each diagonal. For example, the eight neighbors of the cell at position (2, 3)—that is, row 2 and column 3—are the cells at positions (1, 2), (1, 3), (1, 4), (2, 2), (2, 4), (3, 2), (3, 3), and (3, 4).

The interaction tracks what happens to the grid from one generation to the next, over a series of generations. We start with an initial generation, such as the one shown above. To predict which cells will be living in the next generation, the following rules apply to each cell:

Survival. An individual survives into the next generation if it has two or three living neighbors in the current generation.

Birth. An individual is born in the next generation if (a) its cell is empty in the current generation, and (b) its cell has exactly three living neighbors in the current generation.

Death by loneliness. An individual dies in the next generation if it has fewer than two living neighbors in the current generation.

Death by overcrowding. An individual dies in the next generation if it has four or more living neighbors in the current generation.

The grid below shows the result of applying these four rules to each of the cells in the grid above.

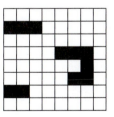

As you can see, various cells have survived [e.g., the one in position (1, 1)], been born [e.g., the one in position (1, 0)], died of loneliness [e.g., the one in position (3, 5)], or died of overcrowding [e.g., the one in position (5, 4)]. Other cells have remained unoccupied from the first generation to the second.

Repeating this process over a series of generations gives some interesting patterns of population growth and decay. For instance, the pattern in the upper left-hand corner of the grid will repeat itself over a series of generations, while the one in the lower left-hand corner will completely disappear after the second generation. The pattern in the middle of the screen will change its shape and position in an interesting way across a series of generations.

To visualize these population changes, your interaction should provide two grids side-by-side on the board, and then ask the user to define the first generation by clicking on a series of squares in the left-hand grid. Completion of that activity may be signaled by the user clicking outside the grid, or perhaps selecting a different alternative in a Combo Box menu on the screen. Next, the user should be able to ask the program to compute and display the second generation on the right-hand grid, the third generation on the left-hand grid, the fourth on the right, and so on. The end of the simulation occurs with one of the following states:

(1) The entire grid becomes empty (the whole generation has died);

(2) Two successive generations are identical in their populations; or

(3) The user selects a button that stops the simulation.

The user should also have the opportunity to start a new simulation; in this event, the program should clear both grids and allow the user to start a new game by selecting a different initial configuration in the left-hand grid.

16.11 Do some research on the Web and learn about the programming of a real home security alarm system. What programming language is used in implementing this system? How is the event-driven model used in the program that drives this system?

Concurrent Programming

"Two roads diverged in a yellow wood,
And sorry I could not travel both ..."
Robert Frost, The Road Not Taken

CHAPTER OUTLINE

On its surface, the idea of two program parts, or even two separate programs, executing *concurrently* seems simple enough. Programming for concurrency can occur at many levels of language—from the lowest level of digital logic to the application level (e.g., web browsing). Concurrency also occurs in all four programming paradigms—imperative, object oriented, functional, and logic.

483

No matter what the perspective, an introduction of concurrency into a complex application makes it more realistic, in the sense that it models reality better than if concurrency were ruled out. Moreover, the introduction of concurrency into a program can save enormous amounts of computing resources, both in space and in speed. Indeed, many important computing applications—like ocean modeling, web browsing, or even an operating system—would not be conceivable if concurrency were not a central element of their design.

However, concurrent programming at any level or application domain carries unique and fundamental complexities. In particular, if two concurrent program elements need to communicate with each other, how will such communication be coordinated? Moreover, if two such elements need to share a common data value, with the possibility that either one can overwrite that value, how will such sharing be rationalized?

Traditionally, the study of concurrency occurs in the setting of an operating systems course, where the management of simultaneous events in different active processes is a central concern. However, designing applications with concurrency built-in has become increasingly important, since software designers now routinely model systems with components that interact asynchronously and share data. Thus, it is important in the setting of a programming languages course to learn about the steps that language designers have taken to address this now-pervasive programming need.

Because of the vast range of topics that occur under the heading of concurrency, this chapter focuses only on concurrency at the language and software design levels, leaving other aspects of concurrency to other courses. Moreover, this chapter treats concurrency in just two settings:

- The single processor setting, and
- The interprocess communication (IPC) setting.

In the first case, a program runs on a single processor, but it can dynamically divide into concurrent *threads* of control from time to time. In the second case, a program is viewed as a collection of cooperating processes that run over a network and share data. One type of IPC application is called a *client-server* application, in which a single server process shares information with several client processes running simultaneously and autonomously on separate machines over the Internet.

This chapter illustrates each of these scenarios, along with the coordination and data sharing strategies that underlie their effective implementation. To provide a focus for this discussion, our examples favor Java as the language of illustration. Concurrency features in several other languages are summarized at the end of the chapter.

17.1   CONCURRENCY CONCEPTS

Chapter 13 suggested that a good way to think of an object-oriented program is as a collection of interacting objects that communicate using *message passing* via methods. Thus, each object is viewed as a separate machine that encapsulates both data and operations on that data. Different objects that are instances of the same class share the same set of operations, but they differ in their data.

For example, a program using the stack class can contain several different objects that are stacks, each with its own collection of data but sharing the same set of stack operations (push, pop, etc.) in common. Taking this model one step further, we can now explore how all stack objects can be executing simultaneously, sending and receiving messages with the other objects in the program.

A more practical example of a concurrent object-oriented program is the modern web browser. Concurrency in a web browser occurs when the browser begins to render a page. The page being rendered is a shared resource which must be cooperatively managed by the various threads involved in downloading and rendering its different aspects. For instance, while the browser is still downloading an image or graphics file, it may be rendering another image in a different location on the screen.

However, these various threads cannot all write to the screen simultaneously, especially if the image or graphic being downloaded causes the space allocated for the display of the image to be resized, thus affecting the text layout. While doing all this, various buttons such as the `Stop` button are still active and can be clicked by the user.

In this section, we explore how different threads can cooperate to accomplish a task such as web page rendering. Threads must at times have exclusive access to a shared resource, such as the display, in order to prevent other threads from interfering with it. For example, the thread that resizes a web page on the screen needs to have exclusive access to that page for the duration of time that it is performing the resizing task.

17.1.1 History and Definitions

Concurrent execution of the processes within a program can occur either by distributing them to separate processors or by interleaving them on a single processor using time slicing. Time slicing divides time into small blocks and distributes the blocks among the processes in an even-handed way. Early computers often had a single main processor and several other smaller processors for doing input and output separately. Programs on these early machines were executed in batch mode, with each program being executed to completion before the next program begins to execute.

Later, multiprogramming was introduced to increase efficiency. In *multiprogramming* several programs would be loaded into memory and executed in an interleaved fashion, with a *scheduler* being used to switch control from one program to another. As the cost of computing decreased relative to the cost of labor, the concept of *interactive time-sharing* was introduced. Time-sharing allows two or more people to use keyboards and monitors to simultaneously communicate with a computer. The Unix operating system was developed in the late 1960s to support time-shared operations on relatively inexpensive computers.

Concurrent programming was used in early operating systems to support parallelism in the underlying hardware and to support multiprogramming and time-sharing. But for a long time, concurrent programming was felt to be too difficult and error prone to be used by ordinary applications. However, both our understanding of concurrent programming and the programming language methods used to support it have evolved so that many modern applications are multithreaded. On computers with two or more processors, such applications can have each thread executed by a separate processor, thus achieving a significant speedup.

The following definitions and concepts are in widespread use. While a *program* denotes the execution of a sequence of statements, a *process* denotes a single sequence of statements in execution. As such, each process has its own state independent of the state of any other process, including operating system processes. A process also has attached resources, such as files, memory, and network ports. The state of a process includes both its memory and the location of the current instruction being executed. This extended notion of state is called an *execution context.*

> **Definition**: A *concurrent program* is a program designed to have two or more execution contexts. Such a program is said to be *multithreaded*, since more than one execution context can be active simultaneously.

A *parallel program* is a concurrent program in which several execution contexts, or threads, are active *simultaneously*. For our purposes, there is no difference between a concurrent program and a parallel one.

A *distributed program* is a concurrent program that is designed to be executed simultaneously on a network of autonomous processors that do not share main memory, with each thread running on its own separate processor. In a distributed operating system, for instance, the same program (e.g., a text editor) can be executed by several processors, each instance having in its own execution context separate from the others (e.g., its own window). This is not the same as a multithreaded program in which data can be shared among different execution contexts.

The term *concurrency* thus denotes a program in which two or more execution contexts can be active simultaneously. Each of the programs we have seen until now has a single execution context, and thus is called *single-threaded*. A program with multiple execution contexts is called *multi-threaded*. In a multi-threaded program, part of the program state is shared among the threads, while part of the state (including the flow of control) is unique to each thread.[1]

17.1.2 Thread Control and Communication

In both Java and Ada, a thread is associated with a separate method (function), rather than with a single statement. However, starting a thread requires additional actions beyond calling a function. First, the caller does not wait for the new thread to complete before continuing; it moves on to execute the statements that follow the call. Second, when the thread terminates, control does not return to the caller.

To understand thread control more concretely, we must introduce the idea of a thread's *state*. A thread can be in any one of the following states:

1 *Created*: the thread has been created, but is not yet ready to run.
2 *Runnable*: the thread is ready to run (sometimes this state is called *ready*). The thread awaits receiving a processor to run on.[2]
3 *Running*: the thread is executing on a processor.
4 *Blocked*: the thread is either waiting to enter a section of its code that requires exclusive access to a shared resource (variable), or else has voluntarily given up its processor.
5 *Terminated*: the thread has stopped and cannot be restarted.

---

1. If two or more communicating software components run concurrently, the result is a concurrent program if the pieces form a conceptual whole. Otherwise, the situation is viewed as two autonomous programs that may communicate through an agreed protocol such as a file system or network protocol. If the programs do communicate, they form a concurrent system.

2. From a programming language viewpoint, *Runnable* and *Running* can be combined into a single state.

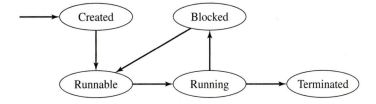

| **Figure 17.1** **States of a Thread**

A section of code that requires exclusive access to a shared variable is called a thread's *critical section.*

These states and the possible transitions among them are pictured in Figure 17.1. Notice in particular that a thread may transfer back and forth between the *Blocked* and *Running* states several times during its lifetime. For example, a thread may be sending several documents to a printer queue, but may need to wait until after the successful printing of one document before it sends a later one.

Concurrent programs require interthread communication or interaction. Communication occurs for the following reasons:

1 A thread sometimes requires exclusive access to a shared resource, like a printer queue, a terminal window, or a record in a data file.
2 A thread sometimes needs to exchange data with another thread.

In both cases the two communicating threads must synchronize their execution to avoid conflict when acquiring resources, or to make contact when exchanging data. A thread can communicate with other threads through:

1 Shared variables: this is the primary mechanism used by Java, and it can also be used by Ada.
2 Message passing: this is the primary mechanism used by Ada.[3]
3 Parameters: this is used by Ada in conjunction with message passing.

Threads normally cooperate with one another to solve a problem. However, it is highly desirable to keep communication between threads to a minimum; this makes the code easier to understand and allows each thread to run at its own speed without being slowed down by complex communication protocols.

17.1.3 Races and Deadlocks

Two fundamental problems that can occur while executing two different threads asynchronously are *race conditions* and *deadlocks.*

> **Definition**: A *race* condition (sometimes called a *critical race*) occurs when the resulting value of a variable, when two different threads of a program are writing to it, will differ depending on which thread writes to it first.

---

3. Ada uses an interthread communication mechanism known as a *rendezvous.* The design of this mechanism was heavily influenced by Hoare's work on Communicating Sequential Processes (CSP) [Hoare, 1978], [Hoare, 1985]. CSP provides a complete theory of concurrency, and current efforts are aimed at adding CSP-style programming features to Java.

That is, the result is determined by which of the threads wins a "race" between them, since it depends on the order in which the individual operations are interleaved over time.

For example, consider two threads sharing a variable c, and both trying to execute the following statement asynchronously:

```
c = c + 1;
```

On a JVM-style machine, the target code for this instruction might be:

```
1. load   c
2. add    1
3. store  c
```

Assume that each of the above instructions is atomic, but that a thread can be stopped between any two of them.

If the initial value of c is 0, then either of the final values 1 or 2 for c is possible. For instance, suppose the two threads are A and B. Then the resulting value of c depends critically on whether A or B completes step 3 before the other one begins step 1. If so, then the resulting value of c is 2; otherwise the resulting value of c is 1.

In fact, as the number of threads trying to execute this code increases, the resulting number of distinct values computed for c can vary between 1 and the number of threads! This is a computationally unacceptable situation.

A thread wishing to acquire a *shared resource*, such as a file or a shared variable (like c in the above example), must first acquire access to the resource. When the resource is no longer required, the thread must relinquish access to the resource so that other threads can access it. If a thread is unable to acquire a resource, its execution is normally suspended until the resource becomes available. Resource acquisition must be administered so that no thread is unduly delayed or denied access to a resource that it needs. An occurrence of the latter is often called *lockout* or *starvation*. We explore strategies for preventing lockout in the next section.

Errors that occur in a concurrent program may appear as *transient errors*. These are errors that may or may not occur, depending on the execution paths of the various threads. Finding a transient error can be extremely difficult because the sequence of events that caused the occurrence of the fault may not be known or reproducible. Unlike sequential programming, rerunning the same program on the same data may not reproduce the fault. Inserting debugging output itself may alter the behavior of the concurrent program so as to prevent the fault from reoccurring. Thus, an important skill in designing a concurrent program is the ability to express it in a form that guarantees the absence of critical races.

The code inside a thread that accesses a shared variable or other resource is termed a *critical section*. For a thread to safely execute a critical section, it needs to have access to a locking mechanism; such a mechanism must allow a lock to be tested or set as a single atomic instruction. Locking mechanisms are used to ensure that only a single thread is executing a critical section (hence accessing a shared variable) at a time; this can eliminate critical race conditions such as the one illustrated above. One such locking mechanism is called a *semaphore*, and is illustrated later.

Figure 17.2
Deadlock at an
Intersection

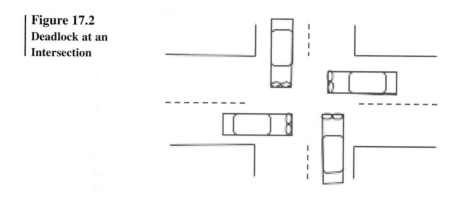

The second fundamental problem that can occur while executing two different threads asynchronously is called a *deadlock*.

> **Definition**: A *deadlock* occurs when a thread is waiting for an event that will never happen.

A deadlock normally involves several threads, each waiting for access to a resource held by another thread. A classical example of a deadlock is a traffic jam at an intersection where each car entering is blocked by another, as shown in Figure 17.2.

Four necessary conditions must occur for a deadlock to exist [Coffman *et al.*, 1971]:

1 Threads must claim exclusive rights to resources.
2 Threads must hold some resources while waiting for others; that is, they acquire resources piecemeal rather than all at once.
3 Resources may not be removed from waiting threads (no preemption).
4 A circular chain of threads exists in which each thread holds one or more resources required by the next thread in the chain.

Techniques for avoiding or recovering from deadlocks rely on negating at least one of these conditions. One of the best techniques for avoiding deadlock, although largely impractical, is the Banker's Algorithm [Dijkstra, 1968a]. Dijkstra also devised a problem known as the Dining Philosophers' Problem [Dijkstra, 1971], whose solution has since become a classical illustration of deadlock prevention. This problem is given as an exercise.

A thread is said to be *indefinitely postponed* if it is delayed awaiting an event that may never occur. Such a situation can occur if the algorithm that allocates resources to requesting threads makes no allowance for the waiting time of a thread. Allocating resources on a first-in-first-out basis is a simple solution that eliminates indefinite postponement.

Analogous to indefinite postponement is the concept of *unfairness*. In such a case no attempt is made to ensure that threads of equal status make equal progress in acquiring resources. Fairness in a concurrent system should be considered at the design level. A simple fairness criterion is that when several choices for an action can be made, every alternative should be equally likely. Neglecting fairness in designing a concurrent system may lead to indefinite postponement, thereby rendering the system unusable.

17.2 SYNCHRONIZATION STRATEGIES

Two principal devices have been developed that support programming for concurrency: semaphores and monitors. These are discussed separately in each of the following sections.

17.2.1 Semaphores

Semaphores were originally defined by Dijkstra [1968a]. Basically, a semaphore is an integer variable and an associated thread queueing mechanism. Two atomic operations, traditionally called *P* and *V*, are defined for a semaphore s:

- *P*(*s*)—if *s* > 0 then assign s = s - 1; otherwise block (enqueue) the thread that called *P*.

- *V*(*s*)—if a thread *T* is blocked on the semaphore s, then wake up *T*; otherwise assign s = s + 1.

The operations *P* and *V* are atomic in the sense that they cannot be interrupted once they are initiated. If the semaphore only takes on the values 0 and 1, it is called a *binary* semaphore. Otherwise, it is called a *counting semaphore.*

One use of a binary semaphore occurs when two tasks use semaphores to signal each other when there is work for the other to do; this process is sometimes termed *cooperative synchronization.* A classic example occurs in the case of producer-consumer cooperation, where a single producer task deposits information into a shared, single-entry buffer for a single consumer task to retrieve. The producer thread waits (via a *P*) for the buffer to be empty, deposits information, then signals (via a *V*) that the buffer is full. The consumer thread waits (via a *P*) for the buffer to be full, then removes the information from the buffer, and signals (via a *V*) that the buffer is empty. Code for this example in Concurrent Pascal is given in Figure 17.3.

A more complicated case occurs when we have several producers and consumers sharing a multiple-entry (but finite-sized) buffer. In this case, it is insufficient, for example, for a producer to know that the buffer is not full. It must also lock out other producers while depositing its information. The usual protocol for this is given in Figure 17.4, in which the producer first tests (via a *P*) that the buffer is not full and then locks the critical section (via another *P* on the lock semaphore). If the producer had taken these two steps in the opposite order, it would have produced a *deadlock,* since all other threads would be blocked from running. Note that the nonfull/nonempty semaphores are general counting semaphores, while the lock semaphore is a binary semaphore.

The producer first produces information locally. Then it ensures that the buffer is not full by doing a *P* operation on the `nonfull` semaphore; if the buffer is not full, one or more producers will continue. Next the producer needs exclusive access to the shared-buffer variables. To gain this access the producer performs a *P* operation on the binary `lock` semaphore. Getting past this point ensures exclusive access to the various shared-buffer variables. The producer deposits its information and exits the critical section by performing a *V* operation on the lock semaphore. Finally, the producer signals the consumer threads that the buffer is not empty via a *V* operation on the `nonempty` semaphore. The code for the consumer is similar.

While the semaphore is an elegant, low-level mechanism for synchronization control, we would not want to build a large, multitasking system, such as an operating

```
program SimpleProducerConsumer;
var buffer : string;
    full : semaphore = 0;
    empty : semaphore = 1;

procedure Producer;
var tmp : string
begin
    while (true) do begin
        produce(tmp);
        P(empty); { begin critical section }
        buffer := tmp;
        V(full); { end critical section }
    end;
end;

procedure Consumer;
var tmp : string
begin
    while (true) do begin
        P(full); { begin critical section }
        tmp := buffer;
        V(empty); { end critical section }
        consume(tmp);
    end;
end;

begin
    cobegin
        Producer; Consumer;
    coend;
end.
```

| **Figure 17.3** **Simple Producer-Consumer Cooperation Using Semaphores**

system, using semaphores. This results from the fact that omission of a single *P* or *V* operation could be catastrophic.

17.2.2 Monitors

Monitors [Hoare, 1974] provide an alternative device for managing concurrency and avoiding deadlock. Monitors provide the basis for synchronization in Java. The concept of a monitor is based on the monitor or kernel of early operating systems; there, it was used as a method of communication among operating system threads. These early monitors ran in privileged mode and were uninterruptible.

```
program ProducerConsumer;
const size = 5;
var buffer : array[1..size] of string;
    inn     : integer = 0;
    out     : integer = 0;
    lock    : semaphore = 1;
    nonfull : semaphore = size;
    nonempty : semaphore = 0;


procedure Producer;
var tmp : string
begin
    while (true) do begin
        produce(tmp);
        P(nonfull);
        P(lock); { begin critical section }
        inn := inn mod size + 1;
        buffer[inn] := tmp;
        V(lock); { end critical section }
        V(nonempty);
    end;
end;

procedure Consumer;
var tmp : string
begin
    while (true) do begin
        P(nonempty);
        P(lock); { begin critical section }
        out = out mod size + 1;
        tmp := buffer[out];
        V(lock); { end critical section }
        V(nonfull);
        consume(tmp);
    end;
end;
```

| **Figure 17.4   Multiple Producers and Consumers**

The monitor developed by Hoare is a decentralized version of early operating system monitors. Its purpose is to encapsulate a shared variable with primitive operations (signal and wait) on that variable, and then provide an automatic locking mechanism on these operations so that at most one thread can be executing an operation at one time. Our producer-consumer example is recast in Figure 17.5 using a monitor instead of semaphores.

```
monitor Buffer;
const size = 5;
var buffer  : array[1..size] of string;
    in      : integer = 0;
    out     : integer = 0;
    count   : integer = 0;
    nonfull : condition;
    nonempty : condition;

procedure put(s : string);
begin
    if (count = size) then
        wait(nonfull);
    in := in mod size + 1;
    buffer[in] := tmp;
    count := count + 1;
    signal(nonempty);
end;

function get : string;
var tmp : string
begin
    if (count = 0) then
        wait(nonempty);
    out = out mod size + 1;
    tmp := buffer[out];
    count := count - 1;
    signal(nonfull);
    get := tmp;
end;
end;
```

| **Figure 17.5**   **Producer-Consumer Monitor**

The critical section lock in the semaphore version is provided automatically by the monitor on each function or procedure. This means that a producer has to attempt a put operation before it can determine whether or not there is space in the buffer. In this case, after entering the put, a producer must check the value of the variable count which keeps track of the number of buffer entries that are in use. If the buffer is full, then the producer waits for the condition nonfull to occur. Thus, the previous general counting semaphore has been transformed into an integer variable and a condition. The changes to the function get are similar. Note that when a thread is forced to wait on a condition, the lock on the monitor is released.

The actual code for the producer and consumer threads is not given in Figure 17.5; it shows only the operations that are associated with the shared buffer. Monitors and semaphores are equivalent in power, since any monitor can be implemented using semaphores [Hoare, 1974] and vice versa [Ben-Ari, 1994].

17.3 SYNCHRONIZATION IN JAVA

In this section, we explore a modern implementation of concurrency control, using Java as the language of illustration. Other languages, such as Ada, provide similar facilities; these are summarized later in the chapter.

17.3.1 Java Threads

Recall from Figure 17.1 that a thread can be in one of five states: created, runnable, running, blocked, or terminated. In this section and the next one, we discuss how a thread makes transitions from one state to another, largely ignoring the transition from the runnable state to running, since this is handled by the underlying Java virtual machine. Figure 17.6 summarizes the states of a Java thread and the transitions between them.

In Java, every thread is an implementation of the `Runnable` interface, and so it must contain a `run()` method. The simplest way to create a thread is to define a subclass that inherits from the Java `Thread` class:

```
public class MyThread extends Thread {
    public MyThread( ) { ... }
    ...
}
```

An object of this subclass can then be created by declaring and constructing it using a `new` operation:

```
Thread thread = new MyThread( );
```

To make this thread runnable, its `start` method must be invoked:

```
thread.start( );
```

Starting a thread means transferring control to its `run` method and then continuing execution. Each class that extends the `Thread` class must thus provide a `run` method. However, it does not need to provide a `start` method, since one is provided by the `Thread` class.

A thread's `run` method normally contains a loop, since exiting the `run` method terminates the thread. In a graphics animation, for example, the `run` method would

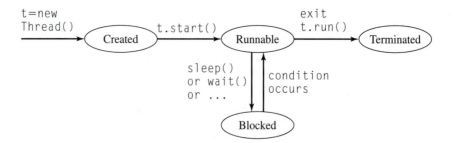

| **Figure 17.6** **States of a Java Thread**

repeatedly move the graphics objects, repaint the screen, and then sleep (to slow the animation down). Thus, a typical graphics animation might appear as:

```java
public void run () {
    while (true) {
        moveObjects( );
        repaint( );
        try { Thread.sleep(50);
        } catch (InterruptedException exc) { return; }
    }
}
```

Note that the method `sleep` potentially throws an `InterruptedException`, which must be caught using a `try-catch` statement.

Calling the `sleep` method moves the thread from the running state to a blocked state, where the thread awaits an interval timer interrupt. Sleeping is often done in visual applications to prevent the visualization from proceeding too quickly. Other forms of blocking include accessing shared variables, which is discussed below.

Finally, the terminated state is reached when the run method exits. One way to reach this state is for the thread to exit its `run` method, which will terminate the thread, for example:[4]

```java
public void run () {
    while (continue) {
        moveObjects( );
        repaint( );
        try { Thread.sleep(50);
        } catch (InterruptedException exc) { return; }
    }
}
```

To stop this thread, another thread can call a method to set the value of the instance variable `continue` to *false*. Such a variable is not regarded as shared; any potential race condition can safely be ignored, since at worst it only causes an extra iteration of the loop.

Sometimes it is inconvenient to subclass the `Thread` class; for example, we may want an applet to be a separate thread. In such cases, a class merely has to implement the `Runnable` interface directly; that is, implement a `run` method. The outline of such a class is:

```java
public class MyClass extends SomeClass implements Runnable {
    ...
    public void run( ) { ... }
}
```

---

4. Prior to Java 1.2, a thread could also be terminated by calling its `stop` method; however, for complicated reasons this turned out to be problematic and the `stop` method in the class `Thread` was deprecated in Java 1.2.

Making an instance of `MyClass` into a thread is accomplished using:

```
MyClass obj = new MyClass();
Thread thread = new Thread(obj);
thread.start( );
```

Note here that Java's use of interfaces eliminates the need for multiple inheritance.

Synchronization in Java is achieved by using the monitor concept and associating a lock with each object that may be shared. To implement a shared variable, we create a shared variable class and denote each method (other than the constructor) as `synchronized`:

```
public class SharedVariable ... {
    public SharedVariable (...) { ... }

    public synchronized ... method1 (...) { ... }
    public synchronized ... method2 (...) { ... }
    ...
}
```

To actually share a variable, we create an instance of the class and make it accessible to the separate threads. One way of accomplishing this is to pass the shared object as a parameter to the constructor for each thread. In the case of a producer-consumer shared variable, this might appear as:

```
SharedVariable shared = new SharedVariable( );
Thread producer = new Producer(shared);
Thread consumer = new Consumer(shared);
```

Here, it is assumed that both `Producer` and `Consumer` extend `Thread`. The complete bounded buffer example appears in the next section.

17.3.2 Examples

In this section, several examples of concurrency are developed and illustrated in Java. The first example, called "Bouncing Balls," uses threads to run a simple animation, but with no synchronization. The second example reimplements the bounded buffer problem in Java, highlighting the use of synchronizing primitives to control access to shared variables and avoid deadlock. The third example, called the "Sieve of Eratosthenes," illustrates the use of concurrency in scientific computing.

Bouncing Balls   In this example, we consider the simple case of using a thread to run an animation. The problem is to animate one or more balls bouncing around a window. When a ball reaches the edge of a window, it reverses direction; however, no attempt is made to be physically realistic.

Initially, we construct two classes, one which encapsulates the ball and the other the application itself. Let us consider the class `Ball` first.

What information must be kept about a ball in motion? If a ball is painted on the screen as a circle, then we should know:

- Its location, as an (x, y) coordinate pair within the animation window or frame.
- Its direction and velocity (*delta*), as a change in the (x, y) coordinates (dx, dy).
- Its size, as a diameter in pixels.
- Its color (to make the animation more fun).

Other than a constructor, two methods are provided:

- A `move` method, which moves the ball one step (*delta*). If the ball collides with the edge of the window frame, then its direction is reversed.
- A `paint` method, which draws the ball on the screen.

The constructor is passed only the initial position of the ball on the screen. The velocity and direction of motion and color are chosen as simple pseudo-random functions of these coordinates. The diameter is fixed; all balls are the same size. The complete code for the ball class is given in Figure 17.7.

Construction of an initial version of the application class, called `BouncingBalls`, is equally simple. Recall from Chapter 16 that a graphical application class should extend the class `JPanel` and have a `main` method similar to the one given in Figure 16.16. In this initial version, two other methods are provided:

- The constructor, which does some housekeeping by setting the width and height of the frame and places a single ball in the frame.
- A `paintChildren` method, which asks the ball to paint itself, in typical object-oriented fashion.

This simple, unanimated version is shown in Figure 17.8. Here, the width and height of the panel in which the balls are bouncing are declared as public constants.

Two problems remain: adding motion and adding more balls. There are a variety of ways to add more balls to the screen. One can randomly generate balls at random coordinates. An equally simple, and more fun, alternative is to insert a ball using a mouse click. However additional balls are added, each ball has to be recorded and the `paintChildren` method revised to ask each ball to paint itself. A solution is to insert each ball into a `Vector`.

The standard way of adding motion to computer graphics is to use a thread. One approach is to make each ball a separate thread whose `run` method moves and paints the ball. However, to make the move visible on the screen, the ball must call the application's repaint method. Upon reflection it seems excessive to require a repaint of the entire application after the movement of each ball.

A better approach is to have a thread class whose `run` method moves each ball one step and only then repaints the screen. This class is an inner class to the application itself. In order to make the movement of the balls more visible on a fast processor, the thread sleeps after each repaint.

The expanded set of instance variables and associated constructor for this revised bouncing balls applet is given in Figure 17.9.

Since the balls are now all in a vector, the `paintChildren` method (shown in Figure 17.10) must be revised. Instead of merely painting a single ball, we must iterate over all the objects in the vector `list`, asking each ball to paint itself.

```java
import java.awt.*;

public class Ball {

    Color color = Color.red;
    int x;
    int y;
    int diameter = 10;
    int dx = 3;
    int dy = 6;

    public Ball (int ix, int iy) {
        super( );
        x = ix;
        y = iy;
        color = new Color(x % 256, y % 256, (x+y) % 256);
        dx = x % 10 + 1;
        dy = y % 10 + 1;
    }

    public void move () {
        if (x < 0 || x >= BouncingBalls.width)
            dx = - dx;
        if (y < 0 || y >= BouncingBalls.height)
            dy = - dy;
        x += dx;
        y += dy;
    }

    public void paint (Graphics g) {
        g.setColor(color);
        g.fillOval(x, y, diameter, diameter);
    }
} // Ball
```

| **Figure 17.7** **Ball Class**

The application class also contains a `MouseHandler` inner class (shown in Figure 17.11) whose `mousePressed` method is invoked when a mouse click is detected. This method creates a new ball at the (x, y) coordinates of the click and inserts the ball into the vector.

Finally, the `BallThread` class is shown in Figure 17.12. This class consists of only a run method, which loops forever. On each iteration of the loop, each ball is moved, the entire frame repainted, and then the thread sleeps (to slow down the animation).

```
import java.awt.*;

public class BouncingBalls extends JPanel {
    public final static int width = 500;
    public final static int height = 400;
    private Ball ball = new Ball(128, 127);

    public BouncingBalls ( ) {
        setPreferredSize(new Dimension(width, height));
    }

    public synchronized void paintChildren(Graphics g) {
        ball.paint(g);
    }

    public static void main(String[] args) {
        JFrame frame = new JFrame("Bouncing Balls");
        frame.setDefaultCloseOperation(JFrame.EXIT_ON_CLOSE);

        frame.getContentPane().add(new BouncingBalls( ));
        frame.setLocation(50, 50);
        frame.pack();
        frame.setVisible(true);
    }
}
```

| **Figure 17.8**   **Initial Application Class**

```
public final static int width = 500;
public final static int height = 400;
private Ball ball = new Ball(128, 127);
private Vector<Ball> list = new Vector();

public BouncingBalls ( ) {
    setPreferredSize(new Dimension(width, height));
    list.add(ball);
    addMouseListener(new MouseHandler());
    BallThread bt = new BallThread();
    bt.start( );
}
```

| **Figure 17.9**   **Final Bouncing Balls Constructor**

```
public synchronized void paintChildren(Graphics g) {
    for (Ball b : list) {
        b.paint(g);
    }
}
```

| **Figure 17.10** **Final Bouncing Balls paintChildren Method**

```
private class MouseHandler extends MouseAdapter {
    public void mousePressed(MouseEvent e) {
        Ball b = new Ball(e.getX(), e.getY());
        list.add(b);
    } // mousePressed
} // MouseHandler
```

| **Figure 17.11** **Bouncing Balls Mouse Handler**

```
private class BallThread extends Thread {
    public boolean cont;
    public void run( ) {
        cont = true;
        while (cont) {
        for (Ball b : list) {
            b.move();
        }
        repaint( );
        try { Thread.sleep(50);
        } catch (InterruptedException exc) { }
        }
    } // run
} // BallThread
```

| **Figure 17.12** **Bouncing Balls Thread**

An observant reader of the material earlier in this chapter should be concerned about possible race conditions. In this simple application a race condition is unlikely to occur but may, depending on the implementation of the class Vector. It is theoretically possible that the implementation of Vector's add method creates an empty element in the vector and then inserts the appropriate information into the element. A check of the Java API for the class Vector shows that the add method is synchronized, thus locking the object from access by another thread (e.g., the thread that calls paintChildren).

Several additional imports must now be added to the header of this class:

```
import javax.swing.*;
import java.awt.event.*;
import java.util.*;
import java.awt.*;
```

A variety of possible modifications to this class are given as exercises.

Bounded Buffer In this section we revisit the bounded buffer example, only this time in Java. Recall that it allows at least two threads, a producer and a consumer. However, our solution will accommodate multiple producers and multiple consumers.

Recall from Section 17.2 that the producer and consumer communicate via a shared buffer of finite size. The buffer is effectively placed inside a monitor by declaring each of its public methods as synchronized. In this case Java creates a lock associated with each instance or object of the Buffer class; only a single thread is allowed to be executing any synchronized method for a given object.

Both the producer and the consumer access the buffer in a circular fashion. The producer deposits information (in this example, date strings) using a put method, while the consumer removes information via a get method.

In the monitor version, after entry into the method, the producer may have to wait (relinquish the monitor) on the condition nonfull, while the consumer may have to wait on the condition nonempty. In both cases, after depositing/receiving information the producer/consumer has to signal the other. Java provides for both waiting (method wait()) and signaling (method notify()), but not on a specific condition. A notify() signals a waiting thread, which can be either a producer or a consumer. Thus, the simple if statements of the monitor solution become while loops in Java. Otherwise the Java code for the Buffer class given in Figure 17.13 mimics the monitor solution fairly closely.

The producer and consumer are quite similar in construction. Both classes are sub-classes of Thread and take three arguments: an instance of the shared buffer, an integer telling the thread how long to sleep, and an iteration limit. Each class consists of only a constructor and a run method which are given in Figure 17.14 and Figure 17.15, respectively.

The main application (see Figure 17.16) is quite simple. It first constructs a buffer, then a producer and a consumer. The buffer is passed as an argument to the two threads, together with a time in milliseconds and an iteration count. In this example, the producer is set to produce a time stamp every second, but the consumer consumes the message only every three seconds. Because the buffer is finite in size, eventually the producer is slowed down to the rate of the consumer.

Sieve of Eratosthenes An area of increasing importance in concurrent/parallel programming is scientific computing. The idea is to take numerical algorithms and refor-mulate them so that portions of the problem can be solved in parallel. The development of powerful arrays of inexpensive workstations has made this approach very appealing to solve such "grand challenge" problems as structural analysis of aircraft, fluid dynamics, weather modeling, and so on.

```
class Buffer {
    private String[] buffer;
    private int in = -1;
    private int out = -1;
    private int count = 0;

    public Buffer(int size) { buffer = new String[size]; }

    public synchronized void put(String s) {
        while (count >= buffer.length)
        try{ wait(); } catch(InterruptedException e)
        { return; };
        count++;
        buffer[++in % buffer.length] = s;
        notifyAll();
    }

    public synchronized String get() {
        while (count == 0)
            try { wait(); }
                catch(InterruptedException e) { return; };
        count--;
        String s = buffer[++out % buffer.length];
        notifyAll();
        return s;
    }
} // Buffer
```

| **Figure 17.13   Buffer Class**

In this example we compute all the prime numbers less than a given input using the *Sieve of Eratosthenes.* Using sets, the abstract sequential algorithm works as follows:

```
Set s = {2..N}; // initialize s
while (|s| > 0) { // s is not empty
    int p = x in s      // x is the minimum value in s
    print(p);           // p is prime
    for (int i = p; i <= N; i += p) // each multiple of p
    s = s - {i}; // delete it from s
}
```

We initialize a set s to all the integers from 2 to N (our input value). Then while the set s is not empty, we first select the minimum value of s and call it p. The value p must be prime, so we output it. Then we remove from the set s all multiples of p, including p itself.

In converting this sequential algorithm to a concurrent one, we first note that the filtering of multiples of a given prime from the set can be done concurrently. Second,

```
import java.util.Date;

public class Producer extends Thread {
    private Buffer buffer;
    private int millisecs;
    private int iterations;

    public Producer(Buffer b, int s, int n) {
        buffer = b;
        millisecs = s; iterations = n;
    }

    public void run() {
        try {
            for (int i = 0; i<iterations; i++) {
                buffer.put(new Date().toString());
                Thread.sleep(millisecs);
            }
        } catch(InterruptedException e) { };
    }
} // Producer
```

| **Figure 17.14**   **Producer Class**

```
public class Consumer extends Thread {
    private Buffer buffer;
    private int millisecs;
    private int iterations;

    public Consumer(Buffer b, int s, int n) {
        buffer = b;
        millisecs = s; iterations = n;
    }

    public void run() {
        try {
            for (int i = 0; i<iterations; i++) {
                System.out.println(buffer.get());
                Thread.sleep(millisecs);
            }
        } catch(InterruptedException e) { };
    }
} // Consumer
```

| **Figure 17.15**   **Consumer Class**

```
public class BoundedBuffer {
    public static void main(String[] arg) {
        Buffer buffer = new Buffer(5);
        Producer producer = new Producer(buffer, 1000, 20);
        producer.start();
        Consumer consumer = new Consumer(buffer, 3000, 20);
        consumer.start();
    }
} // BoundedBuffer
```

| **Figure 17.16   Bounded Buffer Class**

```
class Sieve implements Runnable {
    Buffer in;

    public Sieve(Buffer b) { in = b; }

    public void run( ) {
        int p = in.get( );
        if (p < 0) return;
        System.out.println(p);
        Buffer out = new Buffer(5);
        Thread t = new Thread(new Sieve(out));
        t.start();
        while (true) {
            int num = in.get();
            if (num < 0) {
                out.put(num);
                return;
            }
            if (num % p != 0)
                out.put(num);
        }
    }
}
```

| **Figure 17.17   Sieve of Eratosthenes**

we note that the set itself can be implicit rather than explicit. That is each filter can pass whatever numbers are not eliminated from the set via a buffer to the next filter. Provided that the numbers are kept in numerical order, the first number sent to each concurrent thread must have passed all the previous filters and must be prime. Our solution to the Sieve of Eratosthenes as a concurrent program appears in Figure 17.17.[5]

---

5. [Dershem and Jipping, 1990, p. 210] present a solution to this problem in Ada.

In this solution the end of the sequence of numbers is marked with a negative number, say −1. All communication is through a `Buffer` object that we adapted from Figure 17.13 to accommodate integers rather than strings. The first number received through the input buffer is checked to see if it is less than 0; if so, the sequence is empty and the process of filtering should cease.

Otherwise the number is remembered in the variable p; as noted earlier, p must be prime so it is printed. An output buffer is created and passed to a new `Sieve`, started as a thread; hereafter, all communication to the thread started is through the output buffer.

Then we repeatedly get another number out of the input buffer. If the number is less than 0, then it marks the end of the sequence. In this case, the end marker is copied to the output buffer, and the thread terminates itself by exiting its `run` method. Otherwise the number is checked to see if it is a multiple of p; if it is not a multiple, then the number is passed through the sieve via the output buffer.

All that remains is to create a test driver (see Figure 17.18). In this test driver, the input number N is obtained from the command line. Then a buffer is created and passed to a sieve filter started as a thread. Then all the numbers from 2 to N are passed to the sieve filter via the buffer. Finally, the end of the number sequence is indicated by passing a negative one through the buffer.

As with our previous concurrent programs, this one assumes a shared memory through which the threads communicate. Without multiple processors, this program would run slower than the sequential version. With some effort, this program could be converted into a distributed program. In this case, the buffer would need to be replaced by a network socket, and the code that starts a new thread would be replaced by code

```java
public static void main (String[] arg) {
    if(arg.length < 1) {
        System.out.println("Usage: java Sieve number");
        System.exit(1);
    }
    try {
      int N = Integer.parseInt(arg[0]);
      Buffer out = new Buffer(5);
      Thread t = new Thread(new Sieve(out));
      t.start();
      for (int i = 2; i <= N; i++)
        out.put(i);
      out.put(-1);
    } (catch NumberFormatException e) {
      System.out.println("Illegal number: " + arg[0]);
      System.exit(1);
    }
  }
}
```

| **Figure 17.18**   **Test Driver for Sieve of Eratosthenes**

that obtains a network address of a waiting process. In the case of a distributed program, there is also the problem of reassembling the output into a coherent whole. However, the basic strategy of the program would remain intact.

17.4 INTERPROCESS COMMUNICATION

Several languages support the implementation of various models for realizing interprocess communication.

> **Definition**: *Interprocess communication (IPC)* occurs when two or more different programs simultaneously communicate with each other over a network.

The following discussion illustrates one model of IPC, commonly known as the *client-server* model.

> **Definition**: A *client-server architecture* is a network architecture in which each computer or process on the network is either a client or a server.

Servers are powerful computers or processes dedicated to managing databases (file servers), printers (print servers), or network traffic (network servers). Clients are PCs or workstations on which users run applications. Clients rely on servers for sharing resources such as files, devices, and even processing power.[6]

Thus, client-server applications reflect the features of client-server architectures. They have one program, usually residing on a single computer, that serves resources across the network to various clients simultaneously. Each client typically resides on a different computer connected to the server via a network. The clients are thus simultaneously accessing the resources provided by the server. This is visualized in Figure 17.19.

Concurrency occurs in a client-server application because client programs connect, disconnect, and access shared server resources in an unpredictable order. Thus, at a single moment in time any number of clients may be accessing the same service simultaneously. The server's task is to coordinate these accesses so that:

1 Deadlock and starvation are prevented, and
2 Critical races are avoided.

| **Figure 17.19**   **Client-Server Architecture**

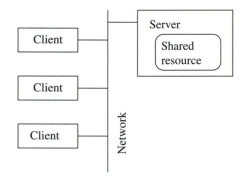

---

6. Client-server architecture is often contrasted with "peer-to-peer" architecture, in which each processor can act either as a client or as a server. Each of these two architectures has unique strengths and weaknesses, as well as a wide range of applications.

Deadlock and starvation are prevented when the server treats every client with equal fairness. Critical races are avoided when the server disallows two clients from accessing a shared resource (like the same database entry) at the same time.

To manage such an environment, the server starts a new thread of control every time a new client requests to connect and access its services. The server must follow basic networking conventions to guarantee that such connections are established with integrity. The following discussion explores these activities in more detail.

17.4.1 IP Addresses, Ports, and Sockets

Each computer on the Internet has a unique processor `id`, which is either a *IP address* (e.g., `139.140.1.1`) or a *domain name* (e.g., `bowdoin.edu`). It also has a series of so-called `ports`, which are access points through which data can be sent or received from the Internet. Each of these ports is identified by a unique number in the range 0–65,535.

> **Definition**: A *socket* is one end point of a dedicated communication link between two programs running on two different computers on a network.

For example, Java's `Socket` class is used to represent such an endpoint.

Two pieces of information are needed to properly define a socket for a program—its processor `id` and the `port` through which the socket connects to the network. Each socket remains dedicated to its assigned port throughout the life of the connection.

17.4.2 A Client-Server Example

To illustrate the elements of client-server computing, let's consider a simple application that tallies the ballots received by an electronic voting machine. We use Java as the language of illustration.

Each voter is a client, and may connect to the voting machine from any computer on the Internet. A typical interaction between the voting machine and a voter might be as follows:

```
> Vote for one or more: 1. Allen 2. Bob 3. Alan 4. Rebecca
3
> Do you want another vote? (y/n)
y
> Enter another number:
2
> Do you want another vote? (y/n)
n
> Bye
```

Until the client enters `n`, the options keep coming. Of course, the server must assure that no client can vote for the same person twice, and every client must cast at least one valid vote. A ballot is complete when the client enters `n`.

On the server side, the termination of each session is echoed and the current tally is reported as each voter finishes his/her session. Here is a sample output that can appear on the server side after four voters have completed sessions like the one above (some of the details are elided to save space).

```
Server listening on port 9600
Voter starting
Voter finishing
Current voting tally:
    candidate 1. 0
    candidate 2. 1
    candidate 3. 1
    candidate 4. 0
Voter starting
Voter finishing
. . .
Voter starting
Voter starting
Voter finishing
. . .
Voter finishing
Current voting tally:
    candidate 1. 3
    candidate 2. 2
    candidate 3. 2
    candidate 4. 1
```

While any of these sessions can overlap in time, after they are all finished the `Current voting tally` must reflect their collective voice. In particular, no voter's ballot should be skipped or double counted, as could occur if a critical race were allowed.

In this discussion, we want to focus on the concurrency aspects of client-server applications. Therefore, we will omit many of the programming details in favor of discussing issues of deadlock, starvation, and critical races. Readers interested in running the entire program can download it from the book's website.[7]

The Server Side When the server is started, its task is to initialize the vote tally, open a socket, and remain actively listening for new clients attempting to connect to that socket. Each request is satisfied by starting a new thread of control.

A thread always has a `run` method, as discussed in earlier sections. Each thread's task is to oversee an interaction with one particular voter and to share access to the resource `tally`. An example of this dynamic, when three active voters are simultaneously accessing the server, is shown in Figure 17.20.

The server's general strategy for initiating threads is summarized below.

1   Initialize a shared variable to tally the votes.
2   Open a new socket for communicating with clients.
3   Enter a loop that:
    (a) Listens for connection requests from clients through that socket.
    (b) Whenever a request arrives, accept it and start a new thread.

---

7. This application is adapted from a similar one in *The Java Tutorial* at the website
http://java.sun.com/docs/books/tutorial/networking/sockets/clientServer.html.

**Figure 17.20
Client-Server
Architecture for
Tallying Votes**

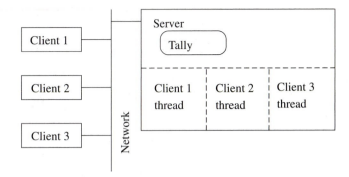

This loop continues until the server is shut down. The essential server code is shown in Figure 17.21. Comments in this code identify the above steps.

The shared variable `tally` behaves like the bounded buffer discussed in previous sections. It must not be accessed by two threads at the same time, since each thread can potentially update it. Thus, every update of `tally` must occur inside a thread's critical section. For this reason, `tally` is encapsulated within a `TallyBuffer` object whose methods are `synchronized`. This class is sketched in Figure 17.22.

Significantly, the methods in this class are `synchronized`, which guarantees that no two calls to either one can overlap in time. This constraint prevents critical races from

```
public class Server
    ...
// 1. Initialize a shared variable to tally the votes.
    TallyBuffer tally = new TallyBuffer();
    ...
// 2. Open a new Socket for communicating with clients.
        try {
            serverSocket = new ServerSocket(port);
            System.out.println(
            "Server listening on port " + port);
        } catch (IOException e) {
            System.err.println(
            "Port: " + port + " unavailable.");
            System.exit(-1);
        }
// 3. Listen for connection requests from clients
//      and start new threads.
        while (true) {
            ct = new ClientThread(
                serverSocket.accept(), tally);
            ct.start();
        }
    ...
```

| **Figure 17.21   Server for a Simple Client-Server Application**

```
public class TallyBuffer {
    int[] tally = {0,0,0,0};

    public synchronized void update(int[] aBallot) {
        for (int i=0; i<tally.length; i++)
            tally[i] = tally[i] + aBallot[i];
    }
    public synchronized void display() {
        ...
    }
}
```

| **Figure 17.22**   **Synchronizing Access to the Shared Variable** tally

occurring, since the private variable tally inside this class can be updated by no more than one call at a time.

Each client thread must communicate through the socket with its associated voter. It must also be able to update the shared variable tally that was declared and initialized by the server. The following general steps are required for a client thread to run properly:

1 Open a new input and output stream with the client.
2 Initialize a new ballot and protocol for interacting with the voter.
3 Enter a loop that:
   (a) reads a vote from the client,
   (b) processes that vote by updating the ballot, and
   (c) prompts for another vote.
4 Close the two streams, and finally the socket.

More details of a client thread are shown in Figure 17.23. The comments identify the code needed to implement the first three of these steps.

The Client Protocol   The Client Protocol voter referenced in this program is an object that keeps track of the interaction between a single client thread and the user who is voting. That is, it takes care of the details, like making sure a voter casts at least one valid ballot, does not vote twice for the same candidate, and so forth.

The logic of that protocol is to make a single transition between states of a voter's interaction each time its method processInput is called. The states of a voter's interaction are straightforward. The initial state is WAITING, while the intermediate states are SENTBALLOT (voter has been sent the ballot) and WANTANOTHER (voter has an opportunity to vote for a second, third, or fourth candidate). The final state is DONE, which terminates the voter's interaction and triggers the updating of the shared tally variable with this voter's ballot.

Some of the code in that protocol is shown in Figure 17.24, which identifies the potential transitions among states for a voter. Note also that, when a voter finally completes casting votes, her ballot is cast by calling the TallyBuffer's update method.

```
public class ClientThread extends Thread
...
//1. Open a new input and output stream with the client.
    PrintWriter out = new PrintWriter(
        socket.getOutputStream(), true);
    BufferedReader in = new BufferedReader(
        new InputStreamReader(socket.getInputStream()));

// 2. Initialize a new ballot and protocol.
    String inputLine, outputLine;
    ClientProtocol voter = new ClientProtocol();
    outputLine = voter.processInput(null, tally);
    out.println(outputLine);

// 3. Loop to read and process individual votes.
    while ((inputLine = in.readLine()) != null) {
        outputLine = voter.processInput(inputLine, tally);
        out.println(outputLine); // relay to client
        if (outputLine.equals("Bye"))
            break;

    }
...
```

| **Figure 17.23**   **Client Thread for a Simple Client-Server Application**

This step simulates the recording of a single voter's ballot in a conventional voting machine.

The Client Side   The client program is straightforward because the server is doing all the work.[8] The client acts as a relay between the client thread (on the server) and the user. It receives a message from the thread, passes it on to the user, retrieves the user's reply, and sends it on to the thread. One particular message, Bye, is agreed upon as the signal to terminate a client session. Here are the basic steps:

1. Open a socket.
2. Open input and output streams to socket and user.
3. Enter a loop that:
   (a) reads a message from the stream,
   (b) displays it to the user,
   (c) retrieves a reply from the user, and
   (d) writes that reply to the stream.
4. Close the two streams, and finally the socket.

---

8. Such a model is sometimes called a "thin client" system. The opposite case is where most of the work is done on the client side, in which case it is called a "fat client" system.

```
public class ClientProtocol
...
private int state = WAITING;
int[] ballot = {0,0,0,0};

public String processInput(String response,
                   TallyBuffer tally) {
    ...
    if (state == WAITING) {
        theOutput = "Vote for one or more: " +
            "1. Allen 2. Bob 3. Alan 4. Rebecca" ;
        state = SENTBALLOT;
    }
    else if (state == SENTBALLOT)
        if ...
            state = WANTANOTHER;
    ...
    else if (state == WANTANOTHER){
        if (response.equalsIgnoreCase("y")) {
            theOutput = "Enter another number: ";
            state = SENTBALLOT;
        }
        else {
            state = DONE;
            tally.update(ballot); // cast the ballot
            theOutput = "Bye";
        }
    ...
    return theOutput;
...
```

| **Figure 17.24   Elements of the ClientProtocol for a Single Voter**

The client code for the first three steps is given in Figure 17.25. The client program is a Java application whose command line argument must provide the host name and port where the server is running. This program cannot begin running until after the server has been activated on the host machine.

Here, in and out denote input and output messages coming from the server socket to this client. The client simply echoes these messages to the voter and passes the voter's replies back to the server. Terminal interaction with the voter is done via stdIn (which is System.in wrapped inside a BufferedReader) and System.out.

The simplicity of this code illustrates an advantage of a thin client architecture. A disadvantage, of course, is that a large number of simultaneous threads will place stress on the server side. A more careful treatment of the trade-offs among different client-server architectures is beyond the scope of this discussion.

```
public class Client
// 1. Open a socket.
   mySocket = new Socket(hostName, port);

// 2. Open input and output streams to socket and user.
   out = new PrintWriter(
           mySocket.getOutputStream(), true);
   in = new BufferedReader(new InputStreamReader(
           mySocket.getInputStream()));
   stdIn = new BufferedReader(
           new InputStreamReader(System.in));
   String fromServer;
   String fromUser;
// 3. Loop to relay messages from client thread
//    to user, and from user to client thread.
   while ((fromServer = in.readLine()) != null) {
       System.out.println(">" + fromServer);
       if (fromServer.equals("Bye"))
           break;
       fromUser = stdIn.readLine();
       if (fromUser != null)
           out.println(fromUser);
... }
```

| **Figure 17.25**   **Client Class for a Simple Client-Server Application**

17.5 CONCURRENCY IN OTHER LANGUAGES

Concurrency is supported in many other programming languages besides Java and in all other paradigms besides object-oriented. This section briefly summarizes the key language features for concurrency among the languages C#, C++, High-Performance Fortran, and Ada. This will provide the reader with a sampling of how concurrency is implemented to suit the needs of a wider range of programming applications and preferences beyond Java.

C#   C# is similar to Java in its approach to concurrency; its features reflect the monitor concept discussed above. C# has two operations, called `Monitor.Enter(o)` and `Monitor.Exit(o)`, which provide explicit entry and exit from an object's monitor, and thus a direct locking ability on the object. C# also supports locking an object in one method and releasing it from elsewhere in the code.

C++   The C++ Standard Library provides no support for concurrency. However, independent C++ library projects have extended the Standard Library in various ways. One such project is called ACE (ADAPTIVE Communication Environment), and it provides C++ support for networks, communication, and concurrency.

ACE has a set of C++ wrapper classes that include synchronization primitives (Semaphore class), interprocess communication with sockets and pipes (ACE_SOCK_Connector, ACE_SOCK_FIFO, and ACE_SOCK_Addr classes), and concurrency (Future and Servant thread classes). Ace has two classes, called *Reactor* and *Proactor*, that dispatch messages in an event-oriented fashion along with these synchronization classes.

More information about ACE can be obtained from the main Distributed Object Computing website at Washington University (**http://www.cs.wustl.edu/ doc/**).

High-Performance Fortran   High-Performance FORTRAN (HPF) has features that allow the programmer to supply the compiler with information that helps it optimize code in a multiprocessing environment. Here is a summary of some of those features:

Feature	HPF Specification
1. Number of processors	`!HPF$ PROCESSORS procs (n)`
2. Distribution of data	`!HPF$ DISTRIBUTE (type)`
	`ONTO procs :: identifiers`
3. Align two arrays	`ALIGN array1 WITH array2`
4. Concurrent looping	`FORALL (identifier = begin:end) statement`

In this table, `type` can be `BLOCK`, meaning "distribute to processors in blocks" or `CYCLIC`, meaning "distribute to processors serially."

Here is a brief example, in which `A`, `B`, `C`, and `D` are arrays being manipulated in a 10-processor environment. Here, we would like the arrays `A` and `B` to be distributed in blocks among the 10 processors.

```
REAL A(1000), B(1000)
!HPF\$ PROCESSORS p (10)
!HPF\$ DISTRIBUTE (BLOCK) ONTO p :: A, B
...
FORALL (i = 1:1000)
    A(i) = B(i)
```

The `FORALL` statement is used to specify a loop whose iterations can be executed concurrently. This one, in particular, specifies that all 1000 assignments `A(i) = B(i)` can be executed simultaneously.

Ada   A *rendezvous* is a concept developed during the design of Ada. It is a simple concept that suggests that two tasks can communicate only when both are ready. For instance, consider a car approaching an intersection with a stop light. The car can pass through the intersection only if both:

1   The light is green, and
2   The car is at the intersection.

If either of these conditions is false, then no rendezvous takes place (i.e., the car cannot pass through the intersection).

An Ada task (T) can have several alternative entry points (E) that that can be selected at run time:

```
task body T is
  loop
    select
      accept E1 (params) do
        ...
      end E1;
    or
      accept E2 (params) do
        ...
      end E2;
      ...
    end select;
  end loop;
end TASK_EXAMPLE;
```

Each entry point E has an associated queue of messages waiting for it. Initially, these queues are all empty, and the loop waits at the top of its select clause for the first message T to arrive. When one arrives, the appropriate entry point's code is executed and the caller (sender of the message) is suspended during that time. Parameters can be used to pass information in either direction—to the entry point or to the sender.

However, during execution of an entry point's code, other messages to the task T may arrive. Each of these is placed in the queue associated with its entry point. When an entry point's code completes, the sender is resumed and the top of the select clause is revisited. Now there may be more than one queue with an active message waiting for service, in which case one queue is chosen randomly (nondeterministically) to be the next one to receive services from task T. Thus, a *rendezvous* occurs whenever an entry point E begins processing a message that is at the front of its queue.

In addition to rendezvous, Ada includes two other features to support concurrency: (1) protected objects and (2) asynchronous communication. A protected object provides a more efficient way than rendezvous for implementing shared data. Asynchronous communication is provided through a refinement of the `select` structure. In the latter, either of two alternative activation mechanisms can be specified, an `entry` clause or a `delay` clause. The entry clause is activated when E is sent a message, and the delay clause is activated when E's specified time limit is reached.

17.6 SUMMARY

As this chapter suggests, concurrency is no longer the exclusive domain of operating systems or network designers. Concurrent programming has entered the programming mainstream in full force, and is an essential element of a modern programmer's repertoire.

Modern languages support concurrent programming in various ways. Synchronization to avoid deadlocks and races is a key element of concurrent programming. Language designers must continue to incorporate concurrent programming features in future programming languages.

EXERCISES

17.1 Consider the bouncing balls example. Make it more realistic by making the following modifications:

(a) Change the ball's `move` method so that a ball reverses direction as soon as it touches the window frame.

(b) Make the *reverse direction* more physically realistic (e.g., add gravity).

(c) Make the *delta* and color of a ball more truly random by using the low order bits of the time of day clock.

(d) Try removing the vector of balls, making each ball a `Component`. Can you now merely *add* each ball into the frame? Speculate as to what is truly happening based on other examples.

(e) Modify the example so that it can be run either as an application or as an applet.

17.2 In the bouncing balls example, remove the `BallThread`, and instead have the application implement the `Runnable` interface. Adjust the rest of the application as needed. Which is better?

17.3 Modify the bouncing balls example to use an array of size 5 instead of a `Vector`. Without any other changes, can you introduce a race condition? Demonstrate it.

17.4 Modify the bouncing balls example so that it will run either as an application or as an applet.

17.5 As an applet, the bouncing balls program is not well behaved in the sense that the animation continues to run, even when the browser is iconified or moves away from the page. Fix this problem by adding `start` and `stop` methods to the applet; in the former invoke the thread's `start` method. In the applet's `stop` method, use the ideas outlined in Section 16.3.2 to stop the thread. Have the applet's `start` and `stop` methods write the number of balls started/stopped (i.e., the size of the vector) to `System.out`.

17.6 Compile and run the bounded buffer example of Section 17.3. How many messages does it take before the producer slows down to the speed of the consumer?

17.7 Add a second producer and a second consumer to the bounded buffer example using the same parameters. Modify the messages so that it is clear which producer produced the date message, and which consumer is printing it. How many messages does it take before the producer slows down to the speed of the consumer?

17.8 In the multiple producer-consumer bounded buffer of Exercise 17.7, modify the code for the `put` method replacing the `while` with an `if`. Does this produce a race condition? Are you able to show it with experiments?

17.9 Modify the parameters of one of the consumers of Exercise 17.7 so that it only sleeps for two seconds and repeat the experiment.

17.10 Modify the stopping condition for the consumers of Exercise 17.7 so that each stops when there are no more messages. Can a race condition occur? Explain. If a race condition can occur, run the experiment 50 times to see if it actually ever occurs.

17.11 Modify the Sieve of Eratosthenes example so that all printing is done by a printserver, that is, a thread that loops through a buffer accepting prime numbers and printing them. Like the other threads, it should terminate when it receives a negative number.

17.12 (Dining Philosophers' Problem [Dijkstra, 1971]) Five philosophers wish to philosophize together. They each go through alternating periods of philosophizing and eating. Five bowls and five forks are arranged around a circular table, with each philosopher having her own place at the table. In the center is a large bowl of spaghetti, which is continually replenished. To eat, each philosopher needs both the fork on her left and the fork on her right. A fork may be used by only one philosopher at a time. The problem is to coordinate the use of the forks so that no philosopher dies of starvation.

This problem nicely exemplifies many problems and solutions found in concurrent programming. Deadlock can easily occur if each philosopher takes her left fork and refuses to relinquish it until she has eaten. Starvation can occur if two philosophers conspire against a third. Exclusive access to a fork illustrates mutual exclusion/synchronization problem.

17.13 (The Sleeping Barber Problem [Dijkstra, 1965]) A barbershop consists of a waiting room with n chairs and a barber room containing the barber chair. If there are no customers to be served, the barber goes to sleep. If a customer enters the barbershop and finds the barber asleep, he wakes him up. Write a program to coordinate the barber and the customers.

17.14 (Cigarette Smokers' Problem [Patil, 1971]) Consider a system with three smoker threads and one agent thread. Each smoker makes a cigarette and smokes it. To make a cigarette, three ingredients are needed: tobacco, paper, and matches. One of the smokers has tobacco, one has paper, and one has matches. The agent has an infinite supply of all three. The agent places two of the ingredients on the table. The smoker who has the third ingredient can then make and smoke a cigarette, signalling the agent upon completion. The agent then puts out two of the three ingredients, and the cycle repeats. Write a deadlock-free program to synchronize the agent and the smokers.

17.15 Download and run the client-server application in Section 17.4.2. To do this, start the server first, and then start four clients accessing the server from different machines on the network.
  (a) Can you recreate the voting results illustrated by the example in Section 17.4.2?
  (b) Now recreate the same voting results by varying the sequence in which the four voters start and finish their sessions.

17.16 Consider the client-server application in Section 17.4.2. Characterize each of the following modifications as "simple" or "complex" and briefly discuss how it could be accomplished.
  (a) Revise the program so that a voter may vote for only one candidate, rather than one or more.
  (b) Revise the program so that any number of candidates can be on the ballot, that number being provided by an argument to the server.
  (c) Revise the program so that each voter can see the current values of the shared variable `tally`, both at the beginning of the session and after casting the ballot.

17.17 If part c in the previous exercise isn't solved carefully, the value of `tally` displayed to the voter after casting a ballot might not accurately reflect that voter's vote in relationship to the value displayed at the beginning of the session. Explain the synchronization issue here.

18

Program Correctness

"To treat programming scientifically, it must be possible to specify the required properties of programs precisely. Formality is certainly not an end in itself. The importance of formal specifications must ultimately rest in their utility— in whether or not they are used to improve the quality of software or to reduce the cost of producing and maintaining software."

J. Horning

CHAPTER OUTLINE

Programming languages are powerful vehicles for designing and implementing software. Complex software systems are difficult to design well, and often the resulting system is full of errors. Much has been written about the need for better methodologies and tools

519

for designing reliable software, and in recent years some of these tools have begun to show some promise.

It is appropriate in our study of programming languages to examine the question of language features that support the design of reliable software systems and how those features extend the expressive power of conventional languages. This chapter addresses the issue of program correctness from the important perspective of language features and programming paradigms.

Intuitively, a "correct" program is one that does exactly what its designers and users intend it to do for all possible inputs. A "formally correct" program is one whose correctness can be proved mathematically, at least to a point that designers and users are convinced about its relative absence of errors.

For a program to be formally correct, there must be a way to specify precisely (i.e., mathematically) what the program is intended to do, for all possible legal input values. These so-called *specification languages* are based on mathematical logic, which is reviewed in Section B.3 of Appendix B. A programming language's specification language is based on a concept called *axiomatic semantics* [Hoare, 1969]. The use of axiomatic semantics for proving the correctness of small programs is introduced in Section 18.1.

Although we develop formal proofs of small programs and supporting exercises, our main interest is in developing an understanding of how to specify programs so that such proofs are possible. We believe that properly specifying program behavior will become increasingly important. Proving properties of programs will be accomplished either with compile time tools or with theorem provers such as PVS [Owre *et al.*, 1992]. Such tools may usher in a new era in software development in which programs with dramatically fewer bugs will be produced at lower cost than current practices.

Until recently, software modeling languages had been developed as separate tools, and were not fully integrated with popular compilers and languages used by real-world programmers. Instead, these languages, like the Universal Modeling Language (UML) [Blaha and Rumbaugh, 2005], provide a graphical tool that includes an Object Constraint Language (OCL) [Warmer and Kleppe, 1999] for modeling properties of objects and their interrelationships in a software design. Because of their separation from the compiled code and lack of a well-defined semantics, these modeling languages have served mainly as software documentation and as a tool for visualizing a software design.

In contrast, the emergence of Eiffel [Meyer, 1992], ESC/Java [Flanagan *et al.*, 2002], Spark/Ada [Barnes, 1997], JML [Leavens and Cheon, 2004], and the notion of *design by contract* [Meyer, 1997] is beginning to change this situation rapidly. These developments provide programmers with access to rigorous tools and verification techniques that are fully integrated with the run-time system itself. Design by contract is a formalism through which interactions between objects and their clients can be precisely described and dynamically checked. ESC/Java is a code-level language for annotating and statically checking a program for a wide variety of common errors.

The Java Modeling Language (JML) provides code level extensions to the Java language so that programs can include such formal specifications and enable their enforcement at run time. Spark/Ada is a proprietary system that provides similar extensions to the Ada language. To explore the impact of these developments on program correctness, we illustrate the use of JML in Section 18.2 and design by contract in Section 18.3.

```
int Max (int a, int b) {
    int m;
    if (a >= b)
        m = a;
    else
        m = b;
    fi
    return m;
}
```

| **Figure 18.1**   **A Max Function**

Functional programs, because of their close approximation to mathematical functions, provide a more direct vehicle for formal proof of program correctness. We discuss in Section 18.4 the application of proof techniques to functional programs using examples in Haskell.

18.1   AXIOMATIC SEMANTICS

While it is important for software designers to provide a good software design, it is also important to be able to *specify* what the program is *supposed* to do. For PVS or some other theorem prover to be able to prove, beyond a reasonable doubt, that the program and its specification are formally in agreement with each other, the programmer must be able to specify what the program is supposed to do. When the proof is complete, the program is said to be "correct."

For instance, suppose we want to prove that the function Max[1] in Figure 18.1 actually computes as its result the maximum value of any two arguments that correspond to its parameters a and b. Calling this function one time will obtain an answer for a particular pair of arguments for a and b, such as 8 and 13. But each of the parameters a and b defines a wide range of integer values—something like 4 million of them. So to call this function 16 trillion times, each with a different pair of values for a and b, to prove its correctness would be an infeasible task.

Axiomatic semantics provides a vehicle for reasoning about programs and their computations. This allows programmers to demonstrate a program's behavior in a more convincing way than running the program several times using random input values as test cases.

18.1.1 Fundamental Concepts

Axiomatic semantics is based on the notion of an *assertion*.

> **Definition**: An *assertion* is a Boolean predicate that describes the *state* of a program at a point in its execution.

---

1. For reasons that will become obvious, in this chapter we have changed the syntax of Clite slightly to eliminate the use of braces. We adopt an Algol 68-like convention (see Section 2.1.5) whereby *if* statements terminate with a fi and *while* statements with an od.

An assertion can define the meaning of a computation, as in for example "*m equals the maximum of a and b*," without concern for how that computation is accomplished.

The code in Figure 18.1 is just one way of algorithmically expressing the maximum computation; even for a function this simple, there are other variations. No matter which variation is used, the following assertion *Q* can be used to describe the function *Max* declaratively:

$$Q \equiv m = max(a, b)$$

That is, this predicate specifies the mathematical meaning of the function Max(a, b) for any integer values of a and b. It thus describes *what* should be the result, rather than *how* it should be computed. To prove that the program in Figure 18.1 actually computes $max(a, b)$, we must prove that the logical expression *Q* is valid for all values of a and b. In this formal verification exercise, *Q* is called a *postcondition* for the program Max.

> **Definition**: A program's *postcondition* is an assertion that states the program's result.

Axiomatic semantics allows us to develop a direct proof by reasoning about the behavior of each individual statement in the program, beginning with the postcondition *Q* and the last statement and working backwards. The final predicate, say *P*, that is derived in this process is called the program's *precondition*.

> **Definition**: A program's *precondition* is an assertion that expresses what must be *true* before program execution begins in order for the postcondition to be valid.

In the case of Max, the postcondition *Q* can be satisfied for any pair of integer values of a and b. This suggests the following precondition:

$$P \equiv true$$

That is, for the program to be proved correct, no constraints or preconditions on the values of a and b are needed. Such a weak precondition is not always appropriate. For instance, if we were trying to prove the correctness of a function Sqrt(x) that computes the float square root of the float value of x, an appropriate precondition would be $P \equiv x \geq 0$. We will return to this particular example later in the chapter.

One other consideration must be mentioned before we look at the details of correctness proofs themselves. That is, for *some* initial values of the variables that satisfy the program's precondition *P*, executing the program may *never* reach its last statement. This situation can occur when either of the following abnormal events occurs:

1   The program tries to compute a value that cannot be represented on the (virtual) machine where it is running, or
2   The program enters an infinite loop.

To illustrate the first event, suppose we write a program to compute the factorial of *n* for a large enough value of *n*. For example, $n = 21$ gives $n! = 51090942171709440000$, which cannot be computed using 32- or 64-bit integers. An attempt to perform such a calculation would cause normal execution to be interrupted by an integer overflow exception.[2]

---

2. The Java virtual machine, curiously, does not include integer overflow among its exceptions, although it does include division by zero. Thus, the computation of 21! by a Java program equivalent to the one in

In this section, we focus on proving program correctness only for those initial values of variables in which neither of these two abnormal events occurs and the program runs to completion. This constrained notion of correctness is called *partial correctness*. In a later section, we revisit the question of program correctness for cases where exceptions are raised at run time.

Recent research has developed tools and techniques by which exception handling can be incorporated into a program's formal specifications, thus allowing correctness to be established even when abnormal termination occurs. However, the second abnormal event noted above, where a program loops infinitely, cannot be covered automatically for the general case. That is assured by the unsolvability of the halting problem, a well-known result from the theory of computation that confirms the nonexistence of an algorithm which can determine whether an arbitrary program halts for all its inputs.

Proofs of termination for a particular program and loop can often be trivially constructed by the programmer. For instance, a C++/Java `for` loop that has explicit bounds and nonzero increment defines a finite sequence of values for the control variable. Thus, any such loop will always terminate. On the other hand, a proof of termination for a `while` loop, while often relatively simple, is not possible in the general case, since termination of a loop reverts ultimately to the question of solving the halting problem.

These considerations notwithstanding, we can prove the (partial) correctness of a program by placing its precondition in front of its first statement and its postcondition after its last statement, and then systematically deriving a series of valid predicates as we systematically derive the meaning of the program's code one instruction at a time. For any statement or series of statements s, the predicate

$$\{P\}\, s\, \{Q\}$$

formally represents the idea that s is partially correct with respect to the precondition P and the postcondition Q. This expression is called a *Hoare triple* since it first appeared in C. A. R. Hoare's proposal for axiomatizing the semantics of programming languages [Hoare, 1969].

> **Definition**: A program (or statement) s is *partially correct* with respect to assertions P and Q if, whenever s begins execution in a state that satisfies P, the resulting state satisfies Q (assuming statement s terminates).

> **Definition**: A program (or statement) s is *totally correct* with respect to assertions P and Q if s is partially correct with respect to assertions P and Q and if, whenever s begins execution in a state that satisfies P, s is guaranteed to terminate.

To prove the partial correctness of our example program, we need to show the validity of the Hoare triple

$$\{\textit{true}\}\ \text{max}\ \{m = \textit{max}(a, b)\}$$

where `max` represents the body of the function in Figure 18.1. We do this by deriving intermediate Hoare triples $\{P\}\, s\, \{Q\}$ that are valid for the individual statements s in

---

Figure 18.3 gives an incorrect result of -1195114496, and no run-time exception is raised! Haskell, however, does this calculation correctly for every value of n, since it supports arithmetic for arbitrarily large integers.

| **Table 18.1** Inference Rules for Different Types of Statements

Statement Type (s)	Inference Rule
1. Assignment	$\vdash \{Q[t \leftarrow (e)]\}\ t = e\ \{Q\}$
2. Sequence	$\{P\}\ s_1\ \{R\}, \{R\}\ s_2\ \{Q\} \vdash \{P\}\ s_1\ s_2\ \{Q\}$
3. Skip	$\{Q\}; \{Q\}$
4. Conditional	$\{test \wedge P\}\ s_1\ \{Q\}, \{\neg (test) \wedge P\}\ s_2\ \{Q\} \vdash$ $\{P\}$ if (test) s_1 else s_2 fi $\{Q\}$
5. Loop	$\{test \wedge P\}\ s_1\ \{P\}, P \wedge \neg(test) \Rightarrow Q \vdash$ $\{P\}$ while (test) s_1 od $\{Q\}$
6. Precondition Consequence Rule	$P \Rightarrow P', \{P'\}\ s\ \{Q\} \vdash \{P\}\ s\ \{Q\}$
7. Postcondition Consequence Rule	$\{P\}\ s\ \{Q'\}, Q' \Rightarrow Q \vdash \{P\}\ s\ \{Q\}$

the program, beginning with the last statement and the program's postcondition Q. This process continues until we have derived a Hoare triple like the one above, which completes the correctness proof.

How are these intermediate Hoare triples derived? That is done by using rules of inference that characterize what we know about the behavior of the different types of statements in the language. Programs in simple imperative languages have the following different types of statements: *Assignment, Sequence, Skip, Conditional,* and *Loop.* Each statement type has an *inference rule* which defines the meaning of that statement type in terms of the pre- and postconditions that it satisfies. The rules for these statement types are shown in Table 18.1.

As for the notation in Table 18.1, we note that these rules are of the form $p \vdash q$, which is similar to that used in the discussion of the predicate calculus in Section B.3. To interpret these rules, if the expression(s) on the left of $\vdash$ appears in a proof, it can be syntactically replaced by the expression on the right. Second, we note that the comma (,) in rules of the form $p_1, p_2 \vdash q$ denotes conjunction. Thus, this form should be read: "if p_1 and p_2 are valid, then q is valid."

Finally, we note that normally proofs proceed from the axioms and rules of inference to what must be proved. Instead, here everything proceeds backwards from what must be proved to what is known, usually termed a *proof derivation.* Once obtained, the proof derivation could be turned into a proof by reversing the steps. In the original proof derivation, if we are given r and to prove r we need to apply an inference rule of the form $p, q \vdash r$, this is written as:

$$\frac{p, q}{r}$$

The process is then repeated separately on p and q, thereby constructing a proof tree, until all assertions to be proved are equivalent to *true.*

18.1.2 The Assignment Rule

The *Assignment* inference rule has no premise, guaranteeing that we can always derive the conclusion. The notation $Q[t \leftarrow (e)]$ means "the predicate that results from replacing all occurrences of t in Q by (e)." The substitution is purely syntactic. The parentheses are given so that the meaning is not accidentally changed by the associativity or precedence of surrounding operators; in cases where the parentheses are unnecessary, they can be dropped.

Consider the examples below. The left column gives an assignment statement and its postcondition. The right column gives the precondition derived by applying the Assignment Rule. In the last example, $i!$ is the factorial function.

Example	$Q[t \leftarrow (e)]$
$\{?\}\ x = 1\ \{x = 1 \land y = 4\}$	$\{1 = 1 \land y = 4\}$
$\{?\}\ m = a\ \{m = max(a, b)\}$	$\{a = max(a, b)\}$
$\{?\}\ i = i + 1\ \{0 \leq i \land i < n\}$	$\{0 \leq i + 1 \land i + 1 < n\}$
$\{?\}\ x = a\ \{x \geq 0\}$	$\{a \geq 0\}$
$\{?\}\ i = i + 1\ \{f * i = i!\}$	$\{f * (i + 1) = (i + 1)!\}$

Several items should be noted here. As the third and fifth examples show, all occurrences of the target variable are simultaneously replaced by the source expression. The third example demonstrates that the source expression may contain several instances of the target variable, in this case, i. In the last example the parentheses are kept in order to preserve the correct meaning.

18.1.3 Rules of Consequence

The *Precondition Consequence Rule*, allows us to perform arithmetic and logical simplification in a predicate during the proof process. In particular, we can strengthen a statement's precondition (i.e., replace P by P' when $P \Rightarrow P'$) in order to match it better with the postcondition of the previous statement during the proof process.

In our example involving Figure 18.1, at some point we will need to show:

$$\{a \geq b\}\ m = a;\ \{m = max(a, b)\}$$

We can use precondition strengthening by applying rule 6:

$$
\frac{a \geq b \Rightarrow P' \qquad , \qquad
\begin{array}{c} \{P'\} \\ m = a; \\ \{m = max(a, b)\} \end{array}}
{\{a \geq b\} \qquad m = a; \qquad \{m = max(a, b)\}}
$$

for unknown assertion P'. The latter can be found by applying the Assignment Rule, resulting in:

$$
\frac{\begin{array}{c} a \geq b \Rightarrow \\ a = max(a, b) \end{array} \qquad , \qquad
\begin{array}{c} \{a = max(a, b)\} \\ m = a; \\ \{m = max(a, b)\} \end{array}}
{\{a \geq b\} \qquad m = a; \qquad \{m = max(a, b)\}}
$$

Since P' in the right-hand proof tree was obtained using the Assignment Rule, only the implication in the left-hand proof tree needs to be proved.

The precondition rule of consequence also suggests that any one of several alternatives might be derived from a given Hoare triple, using various properties that we know from the mathematical and logical domains of the variables that are in play. That precondition which is the *least* restrictive on the variables in play is called the *weakest precondition*. For instance, the precondition $\{a \geq b\}$ is the weakest precondition for the assignment m = a; and its postcondition $\{m = max(a, b)\}$. Finding weakest preconditions is important because it enables simplification of the proof at various stages.

Similarly, using inference rule 7, the Postcondition Consequence Rule, we can strengthen a postcondition (i.e., replace Q by Q' when $Q' \Rightarrow Q$) in order to match it better with the precondition of the next statement.

18.1.4 Correctness of the Max Function

A strategy for proving the partial correctness of the program in Figure 18.1 works systematically from the postcondition backwards through the if, and then through the two assignment statements in the then- and else-parts toward a derivation of the precondition for the program. If that strategy is successful, we have derived a proof tree, the reversal of which demonstrates that the program is *partially correct* with respect to its given pre- and postconditions.

We begin with the Hoare triple

$$\{ \ true \ \} \ max \ \{ \ m = max(a, b) \ \}$$

where max represents the body of the function in Figure 18.1. At the outermost level the program statement is an *if* statement. Therefore, we apply the inference rule for a *Conditional* statement, giving the partial proof tree:

$$\frac{\begin{array}{ccc} \{ \ true \land a > b \ \} & & \{ \ true \land \neg(a > b) \ \} \\ \text{m = a;} & & \text{m = b;} \\ \{ \ m = max(a, b) \ \} & , & \{ \ m = max(a, b) \ \} \end{array}}{\{ \ true \ \} \ \text{if} \ (a > b) \text{m = a; else m = b; fi} \ \{ \ m = max(a, b) \ \}}$$

Next we continue the proof of the left subtree by observing that the statement is an assignment statement. Thus, as we did in the previous section, we use inference rule 6 to replace the precondition $\{ \ true \land a > b \ \}$ with a new, unknown precondition, then use the Assignment axiom to generate the unknown precondition, leaving only an implication to be proved.

$$\frac{\frac{\begin{array}{c} true \land a > b \Rightarrow \\ a = max(a, b) \end{array} \quad , \quad \begin{array}{c} \{ \ a = max(a, b) \ \} \\ \text{m = a;} \\ \{ \ m = max(a, b) \ \} \end{array}}{\begin{array}{c} \{ \ true \land a > b \ \} \\ \text{m = a;} \\ \{ \ m = max(a, b) \ \} \end{array}} \quad , \quad \begin{array}{c} \{ \ true \land \neg(a > b) \ \} \\ \text{m = b;} \\ \{ \ m = max(a, b) \ \} \end{array}}{\{ \ true \ \} \ \text{if} \ (a > b) \text{m = a; else m = b; fi} \ \{ \ m = max(a, b) \ \}}$$

Given definitions of > and $max(a, b)$, it can be shown that $a > b \Rightarrow a = max(a, b)$. A complete proof tree is given in Figure 18.2. Thus, we have proven the correctness of the Hoare triple

$$\{ \ true \ \} \ \text{if} \ (a > b) \ \text{m = a; else m = b; fi} \ \{ \ m = max(a, b) \ \}$$

using the inference rules of Table 18.1.

$$\frac{\begin{array}{c} true \wedge a > b \Rightarrow \\ a = max(a,b) \end{array} \quad , \quad \begin{array}{c} \{\, a = max(a,b) \,\} \\ m = a; \\ \{\, m = max(a,b) \,\} \end{array}}{\begin{array}{c} \{\, true \wedge a > b \,\} \\ m = a \\ \{\, m = max(a,b) \,\} \end{array}} \qquad \frac{\begin{array}{c} true \wedge \neg(a > b) \Rightarrow \\ b = max(a,b) \end{array} \quad , \quad \begin{array}{c} \{\, b = max(a,b) \,\} \\ m = b; \\ \{\, m = max(a,b) \,\} \end{array}}{\begin{array}{c} \{\, true \wedge \neg (a > b) \,\} \\ m = b \\ \{\, m = max(a,b) \,\} \end{array}}$$

$$\{\, true \,\} \; if\,(a > b)\; m = a;\; else\; m = b;\; fi \; \{\, m = max(a,b) \,\}$$

| Figure 18.2   Partial Correctness of Max Function

18.1.5 Correctness of Programs with Loops

The (partial) correctness of a loop depends not only on logically connecting the pre- and postconditions of its Hoare triple with the rest of the program, but also on the correctness of each iteration of the loop itself. For that purpose, we introduce the idea of a *loop invariant*.

To illustrate these ideas, suppose we want to prove that the function Factorial in Figure 18.3 computes $n!$, for any integer n where $n \geq 1$, assuming the function terminates normally. By $n!$ we mean the product $1 \times 2 \times \cdots \times n$. We ignore here the possibility of integer overflow.

The precondition P for Factorial is $1 \leq n$, while the postcondition is $f = n!$. In general, a program involving a loop uses the Sequence Rule of Table 18.1 to break the code into two parts. As shown in Figure 18.4, there, P is the program's precondition, Q is its postcondition, and R is the *loop invariant*.

> **Definition**: A *loop invariant* is an assertion that remains *true* before and after every iteration of a loop.

The right side of Figure 18.4 applies the general schema on the left to the problem of proving the correctness of the factorial program to the two smaller problems, where R is the loop invariant and, in this case, the finalization part is empty. These subproblems may be proved in any convenient order.

```
int Factorial (int n) {
    int f = 1;
    int i = 1;
    while (i < n)
        i = i + 1;
        f = f * i;
    od
    return f;
}
```

| Figure 18.3   A Factorial Function

$$
\begin{array}{l|l l}
\{\,P\,\} & & \\
\text{initialization} & & \\
\{\,R\,\} & \{\,1 \le n\,\} & \{\,R\,\} \\
\text{while(test)} & \text{f} = 1; \text{i} = 1; & \text{while}\ldots\text{od} \\
\quad \text{loop body} & \{\,R\,\} & \{\,f = n!\,\} \\
\text{od} & \{\,1 \le n\,\}\,\text{Factorial}\,\{\,f = n!\,\} \\
\text{finalization} & & \\
\{\,Q\,\} & &
\end{array}
$$

| **Figure 18.4** **Hoare Triples for a Program with a Loop**

In general, there is no algorithmic way to derive a loop invariant from the program's pre- and postconditions.[3] However, it is necessary for the programmer to supply an invariant for every loop in a program if correctness of the whole program is to be proved.

One of the reasons for learning to prove a program correct is that often a loop invariant does not contain all the information needed to complete the proof. In such a case, a proof by an automatic theorem prover will fail. The programmer must then strengthen the loop invariant by adding new information. For the *Factorial* function given in Figure 18.3, the loop invariant is $R = \{\,1 \le i \wedge i \le n \wedge f = i!\,\}$. Leaving out any one of the three conjuncts will cause the proof to fail.

Starting at the bottom of the proof tree, the first step (as noted in Figure 18.4) is to break the problem into two parts. Proof of the initialization code is given in Figure 18.5. The first step applies the Sequence Rule and then the Assignment Rule to discover the linking intermediate assertion, which effectively proves the correctness of the right

$$
\begin{array}{c}
 & \{\,1 \le 1 \wedge 1 \le n \\
1 \le n & \wedge (1 = 1!)\,\} \\
\Rightarrow & \text{f} = 1; \\
\dfrac{1 \le 1 \wedge 1 \le n}{\wedge (1 = 1!)} \quad , \quad \dfrac{\{\,1 \le 1 \wedge 1 \le n}{\wedge (f = 1!)\,\}} \\
\dfrac{\{\,1 \le n\,\}}{\text{f} = 1;} \\
\dfrac{\{\,1 \le 1 \wedge 1 \le n}{\wedge (f = 1!)\,\}}
\end{array}
\quad
\begin{array}{c}
\{\,1 \le 1 \wedge 1 \le n \\
\wedge (f = 1!)\,\} \\
\text{i} = 1; \\
\{\,1 \le i \wedge i \le n \\
\wedge (f = i!)\,\}
\end{array}
$$

$$
\overline{\{\,1 \le n\,\}\,\text{f} = 1; \text{i} = 1; \{\,1 \le i \wedge i \le n \wedge (f = i!)\,\}}
$$

| **Figure 18.5** **Correctness Proof of Factorial—Initialization**

---

3. Finding a loop invariant is often tricky. Interested readers are encouraged to find additional sources (e.g., [Gries, 1981]) that develop this topic in more detail.

subtree. The process is repeated using the Precondition Consequence Rule to break the proof of the left subtree into two parts, where the linking assertion is derived in the right subtree using the Assignment Rule. That leaves only the proof of the implication:

$$1 = 1! \quad \equiv \quad true$$
$$1 \leq 1 \quad \equiv \quad true$$
$$1 \leq n \quad \Rightarrow \quad 1 \leq n$$

The second statement in the right half of Figure 18.4 is a loop, so we apply our Loop Rule, giving:

$$\frac{\{ (i < n) \wedge \atop 1 \leq i \wedge i \leq n \wedge f = i! \} \atop \frac{i = i + 1; \atop f = f * i;}{\{ 1 \leq i \wedge i \leq n \wedge f = i! \}}} , \quad \frac{\neg(i < n) \atop 1 \leq i \wedge \atop i \leq n \wedge \atop f = i! \Rightarrow \atop f = n!}{\{ 1 \leq i \wedge i \leq n \wedge f = i! \} \text{ while} \dots \text{od} \{ f = n! \}}}$$

The right side is easiest to prove, since it involves only an implication. In terms of Figure 18.4, we must show: $\neg test \wedge R \Rightarrow Q$. This can be shown by using our algebraic skills:

$$\neg(i < n) \wedge 1 \leq i \wedge i \leq n \wedge f = i! \Rightarrow$$
$$(i = n) \wedge f = i! \Rightarrow$$
$$f = n!$$

That is, since $\neg(i < n)$ and $i \leq n$, it follows that $i = n$.

That just leaves the proof that the loop predicate is indeed a loop invariant. This proof is given in Figure 18.6. Since the loop body is a sequence, we apply the Sequence Rule and then the Assignment Rule to derive the linking assertion. The process is then repeated using the Precondition Consequence Rule and again the Assignment Rule on the right subtree to derive the linking assertion. This leaves only an implication in the

$$\frac{\frac{i < n \wedge \atop 1 \leq i \wedge i \leq n \atop f * i = i! \atop \Rightarrow \atop i + 1 \leq n \wedge 1 \leq i + 1 \atop f * (i + 1) = (i + 1)!} , \frac{\{ i \leq n \wedge \atop 1 \leq i \wedge \atop f * (i + 1) = (i + 1)! \} \atop i = i + 1; \atop \{ i \leq n \wedge 1 \leq i \wedge \atop \wedge f * i = i! \}}{\{ i < n \wedge 1 \leq i \wedge i \leq n \wedge f = i! \} \atop i = i + 1; \atop \{ i \leq n \wedge 1 \leq i \wedge f * i = i! \}}}{\{ i < n \wedge 1 \leq i \wedge i \leq n \wedge f = i! \} i = i + 1; f = f * i; \{ 1 \leq i \wedge i \leq n \wedge f = i! \}}}, \frac{\{ i \leq n \wedge 1 \leq i \atop \wedge f * i = i! \} \atop f = f * i; \atop \{ i \leq n \wedge 1 \leq i \atop \wedge f = i! \}}{}$$

| **Figure 18.6**   Correctness Proof of Factorial—Loop Body

leftmost subtree to prove:

$$
\begin{aligned}
i < n &\implies i + 1 \leq n \\
1 \leq i &\implies i \leq i + 1 \\
f = i! &\implies f * (i + 1) = (i + 1)! \\
&\quad\text{since } 1 \leq i + 1
\end{aligned}
$$

This concludes our proof of the (partial) correctness of the *Factorial* function in Figure 18.3. To prove termination, we must only identify an integer quantity which decreases on every loop iteration and is bounded below by zero. Such a quantity is $n - i$ since the loop invariant includes the conjunct $i \leq n$ and i increases by 1 on each loop iteration. Thus, we have shown total correctness in the absence of exceptions.

Note that our proof does not address correctness when the calculation of $n!$ cannot be completed because too large a value for n was passed. We return to this issue in Section 18.2.

18.1.6 Perspectives on Formal Methods

Axiomatic semantics and the corresponding techniques for proving the correctness of imperative programs were developed in the late 1960s and early 1970s. At that time, many expected that most programs would routinely be proven correct, and that software products would become more reliable in general. Given the current state of the software industry today, it is clear that these expectations have come nowhere near to being fulfilled.

A field called *formal methods* in software design has emerged during the last 20 years. This field attempts to develop and apply correctness tools and techniques to two different phases of the software development process—software specification and software validation (testing). Tools like the Universal Modeling Language (UML) and the Java Modeling Language (JML), for example, have emerged to help designers specify more formally the behavior of components in large systems. Techniques like *design by contract* [Meyer, 1997] have been proposed to provide a basis upon which software components can be validated with a higher degree of reliability than the various testing techniques of the past.

Some computer scientists argue that formal proofs of program correctness are a useless exercise. The utility and importance of correctness proofs in software design has continued to be a subject of heated debate, especially throughout the most recent decade. Many software engineers reject the use of formal methods for software validation [Millo *et al.*, 1979], arguing that it is too complex and time-consuming a process for most programmers to master. Instead they suggest that more elaborate testing methods be used to convince designers and users that the software runs correctly most of the time.

A counter-argument to this view was made many years ago by Dijkstra [1972], who simply recognized that testing could only prove the presence of bugs, never their absence. For example, a simple program that inputs two 32-bit integers, computes some function, and outputs a 32-bit integer, has 2^{64} possible inputs (approximately 10^{20}), so that even if one could test and verify (!) 100 million test cases per second, a complete test of this simple program would take approximately 10^5 years. Imagine how long it would take to perform a complete test of a larger program using such exhaustive testing methods.

Of course, correctness proofs are also time-consuming and difficult. Most programmers and software engineers lack the mathematical training to incorporate such formal verification methods into their design process. There have been many software products designed with the careful use of formal methods, both in the verification phase and (most importantly, perhaps) in the design phase. The outcomes reported for these projects have been impressive—the resulting software exhibits a far higher standard of reliability and robustness than software designed using traditional techniques. However, some argue that this outcome is achieved at a price—increased design time and development cost overall, as compared with traditional testing methods.

Given these trade-offs, is it fair to ask whether there is a middle ground between complex and time-consuming formal verification of software, such as the one described above, and traditional testing methods which produce highly unreliable software? We believe so.

First, properties of programs other than correctness can be routinely proved. These include safety of programs where safety is a critical issue. Absence of deadlock in concurrent programs is also often formally proved.

Second, the methods that define the behaviors of a class in an object-oriented program are often quite small. Informal proofs of correctness for such methods are routinely possible, although they are not often practiced. One reason for this is that many programmers, who are mostly untrained in the use of formal logic, cannot even state the pre- and postconditions for the methods they write.

However, programmers trained in program correctness can and do state input-output assertions for the methods they write using formal English (or other natural language); this leads to vastly improved documentation.

As an example of how such formalism could be put to better use, consider Sun's `javadoc` documentation for the various `String` methods in JDK 1.1.[4] There, the defining comment for the `substring` method:

```
public String substring(int beginIndex, int endIndex);
```

reads:

> Returns a new string that is a substring of this string. The substring begins at the specified `beginIndex` and extends to the character at index `endIndex-1`. Throws `IndexOutOfBoundsException` if the `beginIndex` or the `endIndex` is out of range.

How would an implementor carry out a correctness proof for `substring`, given such a vague specification? This specification needs to be translated into a logical representation so that following questions can be answered clearly and precisely.

> What are the valid values for `beginIndex` and `endIndex`?
>
> For a given string $s = s_0s_1 \ldots s_{n-1}$, what result is normally returned?
>
> What happens in the abnormal case, when either index is not valid?

A programmer interested in producing even an informal proof of an implementation of `substring` would at least require a more formal description of this method's pre- and postconditions. Figure 18.7 shows one such description (which omits, for simplicity, the abnormal case). Unlike the informal description, this description formally specifies the acceptable values of *beginIndex*, *endIndex*, and the length *n* of the string *s* for which `substring` is well defined, as well as the exact nature of the result itself.

---

4. www.cs.wm.edu/~noonan/1.1.8/api/java.lang.String.html#substring(int,%20int)

$$\{\, 0 \leq beginIndex < endIndex \leq n \wedge s = s_0 s_1 \ldots s_{n-1} \,\}$$

s.substring(beginIndex, endIndex);

$$\{\, s = s_0 s_1 \ldots s_{n-1} \wedge result = s_{beginIndex} s_{beginIndex+1} \cdots s_{endIndex-1} \,\}$$

| **Figure 18.7** **Formal Specification of the Java** `substring` **Method**

In Section 18.2, we discuss recent improvements in language design and software methodology that are helping developers address these kinds of problems more effectively.

18.2 FORMAL METHODS TOOLS: JML

During the last several years, new tools and modeling techniques have been developed to assist software developers in making specifications more rigorous and designs more reliable. One such tool is the *Java Modeling Language* (JML for short), which is fully implemented and adaptable to a variety of software design and verification activities. A promising modeling technique is called *design by contract* [Meyer, 1997], which provides an operational framework within which object-oriented programs can be reliably designed.

These two work together. That is, JML provides a language for incorporating and checking formal specifications in Java programs, while design by contract provides the operational guidelines within which specifications can be used to ensure system integrity when classes interact with each other.

In this section, we introduce the features of JML as they apply to the formal specification and verification of an individual function, such as the *Factorial* function that we specified and verified by hand in the previous section. We also show how JML allows us to specify run-time exceptions, providing a more robust vehicle than the pure Hoare triples in a real computational setting where exceptions actually occur.

Consider the JML-annotated version of the *Factorial* function shown in Figure 18.8. This version differs from the program in Figure 18.3 in only one significant way. That is, the function `Factorial` is annotated by two stylized comments (written /*@...@*/), one containing `requires` and `ensures` and the other beginning `loop_invariant`. The first comment is the JML encoding for the pre- and postconditions P and Q that are used to form a Hoare triple out of the `Factorial` function in preparation for its correctness proof. The second comment is the JML encoding of the assertion R that represents the loop invariant in that proof.

Each one of the `requires`, `ensures`, and `loop_invariant` clauses has a Java-style boolean expression as its main element. Variables mentioned in these clauses, like n, are the ordinary variables and parameters that are visible to the `Factorial` function's code itself. Additional names mentioned in these clauses are of two types, local variables (like i and j in this example) and JML reserved words (like \result and \product in this example). *An important caveat for JML clauses like these is that their execution must have no side effect on the state of the computation.*

```
public class myFactorial {

/*@ requires 1 <= n;
     ensures \result == (\product int i; 1<=i && i<=n; i);
  @*/
static int Factorial (int n) {
   int f = 1;
   int i = 1;
/*@ loop_invariant i <= n &&
           f == (\product int j; 1 <= j && j <= i; j);
  @*/
   while (i < n) {
      i = i + 1;
      f = f * i;
   }
   return f;
}
public static void main(String[] args) {
   int n = Integer.parseInt(args[0]);
   System.out.println("Factorial of " + n +
                      " = " + Factorial(n));
}
}
```

| **Figure 18.8   A JML-Annotated Java Version of Factorial**

In JML, the reserved word \result uniquely identifies the result returned by a non-void function. The reserved word \product is a mathematical quantifier (a summary of the key JML quantifiers and operators appears in Table 18.2), and carries the same meaning as Π in mathematical expressions. The rest of the ensures clause defines the limits on the controlling variable i and the expression that is the subject of the calculation of the product. Thus, the JML expression (\product int i; 1<=i && i<=n; i) is equivalent to the mathematical expression $\prod_{i=1}^{n} i$.

Two significant points need to be made about the JML requires, ensures, and loop_invariant clauses in relation to our verification exercise using the pre-and post-conditions P and Q and loop invariant R in the previous section. First, these three clauses are integrated with the Java compiler and run-time system, enabling their specifications to be checked for syntax, type, and run-time errors. Second, however, these three clauses do not by themselves provide a platform upon which the code will be automatically proved correct by an anonymous agent.[5]

---

5. However, research efforts have developed tools that work from JML specifications to perform various levels of formal verification. Examples of these tools are ESC/JAVA2 [Flanagan et al., 2002] and LOOP [van den Berg and Jacobs, 2001].

Table 18.2 Summary of JML Expressions	

JML Expression	**Meaning**
`requires p ;`	p is a precondition for the call
`ensures p ;`	p is a postcondition for the call
`signals (E e) p;`	When exception type E is raised by the call, then p is a postcondition
`loop_invariant p;`	p is a loop invariant
`invariant p ;`	p is a class invariant (see next section)
`\result == e`	e is the result returned by the call
`\old(v)`	the value of v at entry to the call
`(\ product int x ; p(x); e(x))`	$\prod_{x \in p(x)} e(x)$; i.e., the product of `e(x)`
`(\ sum int x ; p(x); e(x))`	$\sum_{x \in p(x)} e(x)$; i.e., the sum of `e(x)`
`(\ min int x ; p(x); e(x))`	$\min_{x \in p(x)} e(x)$; i.e., the minimum of `e(x)`
`(\max int x ; p(x); e(x))`	$\max_{x \in p(x)} e(x)$; i.e., the maximum of `e(x)`
`(\forall type x ; p(x) ; q(x))`	$\forall x \in p(x): q(x)$
`(\exists type x ; p(x) ; q(x))`	$\exists x \in p(x): q(x)$
`p ==> q`	$p \Rightarrow q$
`p <== q`	$q \Rightarrow p$
`p <==> q`	$p \Leftrightarrow q$
`p <=!=> q`	$\neg\,(p \Leftrightarrow q)$

So we can conclude that JML provides a formal language for defining the preconditions, postconditions, and loop invariants of an executable function, and for automatically checking at run time that a call to the function will:

1 Satisfy the precondition *P*,
2 Satisfy each loop invariant *R* during execution of the function, and
3 Return a result that satisfies the postcondition *Q*.

While this is not a formal verification *per se*, JML does provide a robust basis for integrating a program's specifications with its code. This occurs because JML specifications can be actively compiled and interpreted with each compile and run of the program.[6]

Here are the results of four different runs for the program in Figure 18.8 that illustrate various possible outcomes. In the first run, the program executes normally, with only the result and no errors reported.

```
% jmlrac myFactorial 3
Factorial of 3 = 6
```

---

6. To compile a Java program with JML specifications embedded, the command line `%jmlc -Q myProgram.java` is used. To run such a program, the command line `%jmlrac myProgram` is used. Interested readers should visit the website http://www.jmlspecs.org for a free download of the JML software and other documentation.

The second run, an attempt to compute the factorial of -5, is met with a `JMLEntryPreConditionError`. This says that the call to the method `myFactorial.Factorial` violates that method's precondition `1 <= n`; it reports that the actual argument 'n' is `-5`. Since this event is an instance of Java exception handling, a trace of the method calls that are active for this JML error is also provided.

```
% jmlrac myFactorial -5
Exception in thread "main"
    org.jmlspecs.jmlrac.runtime.JMLEntryPreconditionError:
    by method myFactorial.Factorial regarding specifications at
File "myFactorial.java", line 3, character 15 when
        'n' is -5
    at myFactorial.checkPre$Factorial$myFactorial
        (myFactorial.java:240)
    at myFactorial.Factorial(myFactorial.java:382)
    at myFactorial.main(myFactorial.java:24)
```

The third and fourth runs show some of the vulnerability of the specifications to idiosyncrasies in Java itself. Since Java has no `ArithmeticOverflow` exception, the calculation of any `int` value that exceeds $2^{31} - 1 = 2147483647$ will give an incorrect result.[7] The largest `int` value of n for which $n! \leq 2^{31} - 1$ is 12.

```
% jmlrac myFactorial 21
Factorial of 21 = -1195114496
% jmlrac myFactorial 32
Factorial of 32 = -2147483648
```

Looking at the results of the third and fourth runs, we can now understand how no error was reported. That is, the `while` loop gives the same spurious result as that calculated by the JML run-time check that was specified by the postcondition. Thus, two equally incorrect answers create the illusion that all is well with this function for the arguments 21 and 32. In Section 18.2.1, we revisit the handling of run-time exceptions using JML specifications.

The exception `JMLEntryPreConditionError` is just one of several types of exceptions that can occur when running JML-annotated programs. A brief description of this and other key JML exceptions is given in Table 18.3.

---

7. For Java type `long`, the maximum value is $2^{63} - 1 = 9223372036854775807$, and for type `BigInteger` the maximum value is unlimited. So practical applications that compute factorials will likely use `BigInteger` values in order to rule out possibilities for overflow. We have avoided using the `BigInteger` class here because to do so would have introduced an enormous amount of extra baggage into the Java code, making our discussion of formal specifications almost unreadable.

| Table 18.3 Some of the Predefined JML Exceptions

JML Exception	Meaning
JMLEntryPreconditionError	A method call's parameters do not satisfy the method's `requires` clause
JMLNormalPostconditionError	A method call exits normally, but its result does not satisfy the method's `ensures` clause
JMLExceptionalPostconditionError	A method call exits abnormally, raising an exception defined by the method's `signals` clause.
JMLLoopInvariantError	Some execution of a loop's body does not satisfy its `loop_invariant` clause
JMLInvariantError	Some call to a method or constructor does not leave the object in a state that satisfies the `invariant` clause

However, suppose the `while` loop in Figure 18.8 were changed slightly to introduce an error in calculating the factorial by replacing the line `while (i < n)` with the line `while (i <= n)`. This would raise the following error when the loop invariant is checked:

```
% jmlrac myFactorial 3
Exception in thread "main"
    org.jmlspecs.jmlrac.runtime.JMLLoopInvariantError:
       LOOP INVARIANT:
    by method myFactorial.Factorial regarding specifications at
File "myFactorial.java", line 9, character 24 when
       'n' is 3
       at myFactorial.internal$Factorial(myFactorial.java:102)
       at myFactorial.Factorial(myFactorial.java:575)
       at myFactorial.main(myFactorial.java:211)
```

Here, the message `'n' is 3` indicates that the resulting value of n does not satisfy the loop invariant specified in Figure 18.8. The information given in this message doesn't really tell the whole story. That is, it would have been useful to see the value of i and the loop invariant, as well as n, since it is that value which causes the invariant to become *false*.[8]

---

8. In fairness, we must emphasize that JML is a work in progress at this writing. Perhaps in a later version, JML will report the values of all variables in such expressions when such an error is raised.

If we had not included the loop invariant in the program at all, the following exception would have been raised by the erroneous line `while (i <= n)`:

```
% jmlrac myFactorial 3
Exception in thread "main"
    org.jmlspecs.jmlrac.runtime.JMLNormalPostconditionError:
    by method myFactorial.Factorial regarding specifications at
File "myFactorial.java", line 4, character 23 when
    'n' is 3
    '\result' is 24
    at myFactorial.checkPost$Factorial$myFactorial
        (myFactorial.java:321)
    at myFactorial.Factorial(myFactorial.java:392)
    at myFactorial.main(myFactorial.java:24)
```

This message signals disagreement between the `ensures` clause and the result actually returned by the function, as reported by the line `'\result' is 24`. Here again, the programmer learns only that there is either something wrong with the specification or something wrong with the program code (or both).

A disagreement between a loop's invariant and its code could very well signal an error in the invariant and not the code. For example, if we insert an incorrect invariant into Figure 18.4, such as mistakenly writing `j <= i` as `j < i`, a loop invariant exception is raised again:

```
% jmlrac myFactorial 3
Exception in thread "main"
    org.jmlspecs.jmlrac.runtime.JMLLoopInvariantError:
        LOOP INVARIANT:
    by method myFactorial.Factorial regarding specifications at
File "myFactorial.java", line 9, character 24 when
        'n' is 3
        at myFactorial.internal$Factorial(myFactorial.java:101)
        at myFactorial.Factorial(myFactorial.java:573)
        at myFactorial.main(myFactorial.java:209)
```

But this time, it is the invariant that needs to be corrected and not the code.

Another benefit of run-time pre- and postcondition checking is that the programmer can slide a different implementation of a function into the program, and then test it using the same pre- and postconditions. For example, suppose we decide to implement `Factorial` recursively rather than iteratively, with the following code:

```
static int Factorial (int n) {
    if (n < 2) return n;
    else return n*Factorial(n-1);
}
```

```
/*@ requires 1 <= n;
    ensures \result == (\product int i; 1<=i && i<=n; i);
    signals (ArithmeticException) n > 12;
@*/
static int Factorial (int n) {
    if (n > 12) throw new ArithmeticException();
    else {
        int f = 1;
        int i = 1;
        /*@ loop_invariant i <= n &&
                f == (\product int j; 1 <= j && j <= i; j);
        @*/
        while (i < n) {
            i = i + 1;
            f = f * i;
        }
        return f;
    }
}
```

| **Figure 18.9**   **Adding Exception Handling to a JML Specification**

Both of the JML `requires` and `ensures` clauses remain intact while we compile and run this version; thus its satisfaction of the preconditions and postconditions can be immediately tested.

18.2.1 JML Exception Handling

Formal methods for program correctness should support the specification of conditions under which exceptions occur. To that end, JML provides a `signals` clause:

```
signals (exception) expression ;
```

that can appear together with a function's `requires` and `ensures` clauses. When that `exception` occurs, the `expression` is checked; if that `expression` is not true, the `exception` is displayed and the program is interrupted. Figure 18.9 shows a variant of the `Factorial` function that incorporates these ideas.

Now when we run this program to compute the factorial of a number that will cause arithmetic overflow, an exception is raised:

```
% jmlrac myFactorial 13
Exception in thread "main" java.lang.ArithmeticException
        at myFactorial.internal$Factorial(myFactorial.java:9)
        at myFactorial.Factorial(myFactorial.java:610)
        at myFactorial.main(myFactorial.java:213)
```

Observant readers will notice that `signals` clauses can be avoided in many cases simply by writing stronger preconditions—ones that so constrain the input to the call that the exception cannot occur. For instance, in the `Factorial` function, we can just as easily replace the `signals` clause by the following enhancement to the `requires` clause:

```
requires 1 <= n && n < 13;
```

Now the call `Factorial(13)` will raise a `JMLEntryPrecondition` error rather than a Java `ArithmeticException` error.

In more complex software design situations, the need for JML specifications to signal exceptions explicitly is more compelling than in this simple example. For example, consider the task of defining complete JML specifications for all the classes and methods in the Java class library. Among these methods is the `substring` method, whose informal and formal specifications were discussed earlier in this chapter (see Figure 18.7).

Below is a JML-style rendition of those formal specifications, with `signals` clauses added to describe actions when the preconditions are not met by the call.

```
/*@ requires 0 <= beginIndex && beginIndex < endIndex &&
        endIndex <= s.length();
    ensures \result ==
        "s[beginIndex] s[beginIndex+1] ... s[endIndex-1]";
    signals (StringIndexOutOfBoundsException)
        0 > beginIndex || beginIndex >= endIndex ||
        endIndex > s.length();
  @*/
    s.substring(intbeginIndex, intendIndex)
        throws StringIndexOutOfBoundsException
```

This specification is a slight abbreviation of the full JML specifications for `substring` used to define the entire Java class library. In particular, the line "`s[beginIndex] s[beginIndex+1]...s[endIndex-1]`" is our informal algebraic specification for the value of the string object that is returned by `substring`. In fact, that line appears in the JML specification as:

```
this.stringSeq.subsequence(beginIndex,endIndex);
```

Here, `stringSeq` is a JML class that defines strings as sequences of characters, and `subsequence` is a method in that class. Interested readers should consult **http://www.jmlspecs.org** for more details about these conventions.

18.3 CORRECTNESS OF OBJECT–ORIENTED PROGRAMS

Object-oriented programs are collections of classes. Each class defines a kind of object and a set of features (methods) that can transform that kind of object. When implementing an object-oriented program, the programmer needs to have standards, or tools by which s/he can formally specify what each class is intended to do. In addition to the formalization of individual functions, as described in Section 18.2, object-oriented programs provide two additional tools by which programmers can ensure correctness.

First, each interaction in which an object in one class is accessed or modified by a method call from a so-called *client* class must be guided by certain "rules of engagement." These rules ensure that the client provides the called method with appropriate values for its parameters, and that the called method returns a result to the client that is consistent with the purpose of the method. These rules of engagement are called a *contract* between the class and the client. When all the interactions among classes in a software design follow these rules, the software is said to have been *designed by contract.*

Second, whenever an object in a class is transformed, it must maintain the same set of properties that identifies it as a member of that particular class, and that it had when it was created. This set of properties is known as the *class invariant.*

We define and illustrate the use of design by contract and the class invariant in Sections 18.3.1 and 18.3.2.

18.3.1 Design By Contract

The methodology of design by contract was developed by Bertrand Meyer [Meyer, 1997].

> **Definition**: *Design by contract* is a formal framework that establishes so-called obligations and benefits (responsibilities and rights) between each supplier/client pair that occur during the life of a software product.

This framework helps software designers to document constraints that appear at the interface between interacting classes, and to effectively assign blame when things go wrong.

The structure of the design by contract framework is a 2×2 table that identifies obligations and benefits in one dimension and client and supplier classes in the other, as shown in Table 18.4. Typically, the client is about to call a public method that is implemented within the supplier class. At that time, the client is obligated to pass arguments that satisfy the method's precondition. If that is done, the client can be confident that the desired result will be computed. If, on the other hand, the client's parameters do not satisfy the method's precondition, no confidence can be had for the veracity of the result. If this event causes an error, then blame for the error is squarely in the lap of the client.

For the same call, the supplier has the obligation to compute a result that satisfies the method's postcondition, and to leave the object in a state in which the so-called *class invariant* is satisfied (see Section 18.3.2 for a discussion of the class invariant). The supplier benefits from the contract by not having to include code that explicitly checks

Table 18.4

The Design by Contract Framework

	Obligations	Benefits
Client	Satisfy precondition	Result is computed
Supplier	Satisfy postcondition	Simpler coding

that the argument satisfies the precondition. If an error occurs and/or the postcondition is not met, the blame is squarely in the lap of the supplier.

Let's look at a simple example of how the design by contract framework plays out for the factorial computation discussed in Section 18.2.

	Obligations	Benefits
Client	Pass $n > 0$	Receive $n!$ computed
Supplier	Compute $n!$	Can assume that $n > 0$

If either the client or the supplier fails to meet its obligations, it is responsible for any error that occurs during the call. If a precondition error occurs, the client is responsible for the error. If a postcondition error occurs, the supplier is responsible.

If neither type of error occurs during the call, then both the client and the supplier receive appropriate benefits. Specifically, the client can be confident that the value $n!$ is returned correctly, and the supplier need not explicitly check for $n > 0$ within its own code.

18.3.2 The Class Invariant

A class invariant is a tool for ensuring that all objects in the class retain their integrity throughout their lifetime, no matter what methods are applied to them. In discussing class invariants, we follow the approach of [Meyer, 1997]. We illustrate this approach with the formalization of the `MyStack` class that was originally introduced in Chapter 13 (Figure 13.6).

A *class invariant* is a Boolean-valued expression that specifies the conditions under which an object in that class remains well-defined. This expression describes the *internal state* of the object using the class's public and private instance variables. An expression *INV* is a correct class invariant for class *C* if it meets the following two conditions:

- Every call to a constructor *C* with arguments that satisfy *C*'s precondition, creates a new object with a state that satisfies *INV*.
- Every call to a public method *M* with arguments that satisfy *M*'s precondition leaves the object in a state that satisfies *INV*.

Thus, the class invariant must become *true* after the object is created by a constructor, and it must remain *true* after any public method in the class is called. During the execution of the code inside a method, the class invariant may be temporarily broken; however, such a condition must be repaired by the time the method is completed.

For example, reconsider the class `MyStack` in Figure 13.6, which we have recreated and expanded in Figure 18.11. This new version has a class invariant, an additional private instance variable n, three new public methods, and appropriate pre- and postconditions added to all methods. The new private instance variable n is a count of the number of elements in the stack, and the instance variable `theStack` is a reference to the topmost element in the stack.

For the time being, let us concentrate on the specification of the class invariant, which has the following general form in JML:

```
public invariant expression ;
```

The invariant is checked automatically by JML each time a constructor or method call is entered or exited, and a `JMLInvariantError` exception is raised whenever the invariant's `expression` is not *true*.

Consider the JML specification for the invariant for the class `myStack` in Figure 18.11:

```
/*@ public model Node S;
    private represents S <- theStack;
    public invariant S == null || n == this.size();
@*/
private /*@ spec_public @*/ Node theStack = null;
private /*@ spec_public @*/ int n = 0;
```

Here, we use a so-called *model variable* S, which is known only to the JML specifications and has no run-time functionality within the Java program. The purpose of a model variable is to facilitate writing JML specifications that are free from the details of the class implementation.

Our use of the model variable S frees the JML specifications from explicitly mentioning the variable `theStack` which is an implementation-dependent name. The clause that begins `private represents` identifies the relationship between the model variable and the actual variable that it represents.

The other JML clause that appears here is the `spec_public` clause. This clause allows a `private` variable to be treated as a public variable by the JML specifications themselves. Thus, a `private` variable's value can be accessed whenever it is mentioned by a JML specification, while it remains unaccessible to any client of the class at run time.

18.3.3 Example: Correctness of a Stack Application

As suggested above, any method in a class can be augmented with pre- and postconditions that constrain the range of values that its arguments and results can have. Consider, for example, the method `pop` that appears in the class `MyStack` in Figure 13.6:

```
public int pop( ) {
        int result = theStack.val;
        theStack = theStack.next;
        return result;
}
```

What would be an appropriate precondition for this method? That is, what would be required in order for the `pop` method to be able to complete its task successfully? Minimally, we would not want a `pop` method ever to be called when the stack is empty. That is, the references in the above code to `theStack.val` and `theStack.next` are meaningful only if the value of `theStack` is not `null` at the time of the call. So a good precondition for `pop` would require that $n > 0$.

What would we like to see for a postcondition? Informally, we know that the top element of the stack is removed and returned by this operation, so that the resulting stack might become empty. Beyond that, we can expect that the variable n will be decremented by 1 to signify removal of the top element.

```
/*@ requires n > 0;
   ensures \result==\old(S).val &&
            S==\old(S).next && n==\old(n)-1;
@*/
public /*@ pure @*/ int pop( ) {
    int result = theStack.val;
    theStack = theStack.next;
    n = n-1;
    return result;
}
```

| **Figure 18.10**   **Stack** pop **Method with Specifications Added**

These pre- and postconditions are formalized by adding JML specifications to pop as shown in Figure 18.10. There, we see a use of the special JML function \old to specify the *a priori* value of theStack and n upon entry to the pop method. Thus, the final value of a variable can be specified as a function of its value at entry to the method.

The JML specification /*@ pure @*/ is used for any method that has no nonlocal side effects and is provably nonlooping. That is, pure methods override, in some sense, the notion of partial correctness discussed in an earlier section. In order for a method to be used in the JML specification of the class invariant, it must be a pure method. This is the case, for instance, for the methods push, pop, and top in the MyStack class.

Using these conventions, a complete set of specifications for the methods in the MyStack class are shown in Figure 18.11. This includes pre- and postconditions for the push, pop, top, isEmpty, and size methods, the class invariant, and the use of the model variable S throughout.

Testing the Contract   Annotating the MyStack class with pre- and postconditions and a class invariant provides an executable environment in which the contract between the class and its clients can be continuously tested. Moreover, these annotations provide a mechanism for assigning blame when the contract is broken by the class or its client.

To illustrate this testing activity, the simple driver program shown in Figure 18.12 can exercise the methods of the MyStack class. The following command can be used to run the program.

```
% jmlrac myStackTest 4 5 6
Stack size = 3
Stack contents = 6 5 4
Is Stack empty? true
```

The parameters provide the values to be pushed onto the stack. The normal output produced by this program follows the command.

```
public class MyStack {
    private class Node {
        /*@ spec_public @*/ int val;
        /*@ spec_public @*/ Node next;
        Node(int v, Node n) {
            val = v; next = n;
        }
    }
    /*@ public model Node S;
        private represents S <- theStack;
        public invariant n == this.size();

    @*/
    private /*@ spec_public @*/ Node theStack = null;
    private /*@ spec_public @*/ int n = 0;
    /*@ requires n > 0;
        ensures \result==\old(S).val && S==\old(S).next;
    @*/
    public /*@ pure @*/ int pop( ) {
        int result = theStack.val;
        theStack = theStack.next;
        n = n-1;
        return result;
    }
    //@ ensures S.next==\old(S) && S.val==v;
    public /*@ pure @*/ void push(int v) {
        theStack = new Node(v, theStack);
        n = n+1;
    }
    /*@ requires n > 0;
        ensures \result==S.val && S == \old(S);
    @*/
    public /*@ pure @*/ int top() {
        return theStack.val;
    }
    //@ ensures \result == (S == null);
    public /*@ pure @*/ boolean isEmpty() {
        return theStack == null;
    }
    //@ ensures \result == n;
    public /*@ pure @*/ int size() {
        int count;
        Node p = theStack;
        for (count=0; p!=null; count++)
            p = p.next;
        return count;
    }
}
```

| **Figure 18.11   A Fully Specified Stack Class Using JML**

```
public class myStackTest {
public static void main(String[] args) {
   MyStack s = new MyStack();
   int val;
   for (int i=0; i<args.length; i++)
      s.push(Integer.parseInt(args[i]));
   System.out.println("Stack size = " + s.size());
   System.out.print("Stack contents =");
   for (int i=1; i<=n; i++) {
      System.out.print(" " + s.top( ));
      s.pop( );
   }
   System.out.println( );
   System.out.println("Is Stack empty?" + s.isEmpty( ));
}
}
```

| **Figure 18.12**   **A Driver Program for Testing the JML-Specified MyStack Class**

In order to exercise various aspects of the contract between the class and its client, we can run different tests. The first test, whose results are shown below, illustrates what happens when the top method erroneously removes the top element as well as returning it—that is, it incorrectly acts like a pop.

```
Exception in thread "main"
    org.jmlspecs.jmlrac.runtime.JMLNormalPostconditionError:
    by method MyStack.top regarding specifications at
File "MyStack.java", line 31, character 26 when
       '\old(S)' is MyStack$Node@5ff48b
       '\result' is 5
       'this' is MyStack@affc70
       at MyStack.checkPost$top$MyStack(MyStack.java:999)
       at MyStack.top(MyStack.java:1078)
       at myStackTest.main(MyStackTest.java:15)
```

To trigger this error, we added two extra lines to the top method in Figure 18.11 so that its body looked like that of the pop method. Since top's result now fails to satisfy its postcondition S == \old(S), a JMLNormalPostconditionError is raised and the values of \old(S) and \result are reported by JML. With this information, blame for the error can be assigned to to the top method rather than to its caller.

For the second test, we excluded the line n=n-1; from the pop method shown in Figure 18.11, thus creating a situation in which the method's postcondition is satisfied but the class invariant is violated. Below is the outcome.

```
Stack size = 3
Stack contents = 6
Exception in thread "main"
    org.jmlspecs.jmlrac.runtime.JMLInvariantError:
    by method MyStack.pop@post<File "MyStack.java", line 16,
            character 17>
    regarding specifications at
File "MyStack.java", line 11, character 30 when
        'this' is MyStack@9664a1
        at MyStack.checkInv$instance$MyStack(MyStack.java:102)
        at MyStack.pop(MyStack.java:525)
        at myStackTest.main(MyStackTest.java:21)
```

Here, we see that the program begins to run normally, but when the first call to the `pop` method is completed, the JML test of the class invariant `n==this.size();` fails. This causes the `JMLInvariantError` to be displayed, along with some useful tracing information. In order to check satisfaction of this invariant, JML calls the method `this.size()`, which recomputes the size of the stack independently by traversing its linked list representation.

The third test was created by adding a new final line `s.pop();` to the driver program so that it would try to pop an element from an empty stack. Here is the result.

```
Stack size = 3
Stack contents = 6 5 4
Is Stack empty? true
Exception in thread "main"
    org.jmlspecs.jmlrac.runtime.JMLEntryPreconditionError:
    by method MyStack.pop regarding specifications at
File "MyStack.java", line 16, character 21 when
        'this' is MyStack@9664a1
        at MyStack.checkPre$pop$MyStack(MyStack.java:330)
        at MyStack.pop(MyStack.java:479)
        at myStackTest.main(MyStacktest.java:24)
```

This run reports a `JMLEntryPreconditionError`, indicating that the precondition $n > 0$ for `pop` was violated. Thus, the blame for this error lies with the caller rather than with the `pop` method. The presence of an actively checked precondition protects the method itself from having to engage in "defensive programming," which would be necessary if the precondition were not there.

Correctness of the MyStack Class   What about the correctness of the `MyStack` class? Annotating it with pre- and postconditions and a class invariant, and then testing the contract with a driver program, surely doesn't guarantee correctness in a formal sense.

Informally, a class is *correct* if, for every object in the class and every constructor or method call that satisfies its precondition, completion of the call satisfies its postcondition and leaves the object's instance variables in a state that satisfies the class invariant. This idea assumes that no constructor or method call will result in an infinite loop, and thus it is a statement about partial correctness.

Let's try for a more formalized definition of class correctness,[9] using the notation of Hoare triples that we introduced at the beginning of the chapter. Let R denote a class's invariant, and P_i and Q_i denote the precondition and postcondition for its ith constructor C_i or method M_i. Then we can say that a class is *correct* with respect to its assertions if both:

1 For every set of valid arguments x to every constructor C_i,
   $\{\ P_i(x)\ \}\ C_i.body\ \{\ Q_i(x) \wedge INV\ \}$, and
2 For every set of valid arguments x to every method M_i,
   $\{\ P_i(x) \wedge INV\ \}\ M_i.body\ \{\ Q_i(x) \wedge INV\ \}$.

Rule 1 says, in effect, that execution of any constructor for an object in the class should establish the validity of the class invariant. Rule 2 says that execution of any method call in which the class invariant is valid at the outset should preserve the validity of the invariant upon completion of the call. Thus, this definition requires us to prove the correctness of every constructor and public method individually. Each such proof is conducted in a way similar to that developed for the `Factorial` method in Section 18.1.5.

Let us illustrate these ideas by developing some of the proof that our linked list implementation of the `MyStack` class is formally correct. First, we note that the default class constructor `MyStack()` establishes the values `theStack==null` and `n==0`. The class invariant *INV* itself is stated in terms of the public method `size`. Verification of the body of the `size` method with this invariant established should therefore satisfy its postcondition and preserve the invariant. Formally, we want to prove:

$$\{theStack = null \wedge n = 0\}\ size.body\ \{theStack = null \wedge n = 0 \wedge \backslash result = n\}$$

Informally, we note that the local variables `p` and `count` for `size` are initialized at `null` and 0, respectively. So the loop is not executed at all and the result 0 is returned, establishing the validity of the above Hoare triple. (A formal proof would have more rigorously applied all of the steps of the proof method described in Section 18.1.5; we have short-circuited that process here in order to keep our main focus on class verification.)

Now we need to verify all of the methods in the class. Let's illustrate this by verifying the `pop` method. That is, we need to establish the validity of the following Hoare triple:

$$\{n > 0 \wedge n = this.size()\}$$

pop.body

$$\{\backslash result = \backslash old(S).val \wedge S = \backslash old(S).next \wedge n = this.size()\}$$

The precondition `n > 0` states that the stack cannot be empty; that is equivalent to requiring that `S` not be `null`.

The series of assignments in `pop.body` lead directly to the validity of the postcondition. That is, the first element is removed from the linked list and the resulting list is returned. More precisely, note that the postcondition for `pop` specifies its effect in

---

9. This formalization is adapted from [Meyer, 1997].

terms of the model variable S, which is a surrogate for the instance variable `theStack`. Since `\old(S)` identifies the value of S at the beginning of the call to `pop`, the expression `S ≡ \old(S).next` asserts that the resulting stack S is identical to the input stack with the first element removed. Concurrently, the value of instance variable n is decremented, so as to preserve the validity of the invariant $n = this.size$.

Finally, the correctness of the `MyStack` class depends implicitly on the assumption for correctness of the `Node` class. In a formal verification setting, the `Node` class would need to be formally specified and proved correct as well.

18.3.4 Final Observations

We have sketched enough of the formal correctness procedures for a reasonably complex class to suggest that proof of correctness of any substantially large program is tedious (at best). What are the prospects for the effective use of formal methods in software design?

First, many believe that other software design techniques have more promise for solving the current software crisis than formal methods. For instance, the so-called capability maturity model (CMM) [Ahern and *et al.*, 2004] focuses on the refinement of software management processes as the key to improving software quality.

Second, it is also true that formal methods have been effectively used to verify components of safety-critical software products. For instance, a secure certification authority for smart cards was developed by Praxis Critical Systems [Hall and Chapman, 2002], using formal methods to establish correctness of the system's critical security properties. There are many other examples of the effective use of formal methods in the practice of software design.

Third, it is widely believed that the cost of developing a system that is provably correct is high, relative to the cost of using traditional test-and-debug methods. However, Praxis Critical Systems is now developing systems with 100 times fewer bugs at lower cost than conventional software by using formal methods. The bigger problem is that most programmers are not well trained in the use of mathematical logic to reason about their programs. They need to be trained in logic and the use of advanced software tools that assist with formal verification.

In summary, we conclude that the community of interest in developing better formal methods for software design has gained substantial momentum in the recent past. Surely the use of formal methods by itself is no panacea for the software crisis, but it does provide a level or rigor for the software design process that is badly needed. For that reason alone, we expect that more programming language tools like JML, ESC/JAVA, and LOOP will continue to evolve and make an impact on the software design process in the future.

18.4 CORRECTNESS OF FUNCTIONAL PROGRAMS

This section addresses the question of program correctness functional programming. We visit the question of how to prove a program correct for the special case when it is written in a pure functional program—one that is state-less and relies instead on functional composition and recursion as a foundation for its semantics.

Section 18.4.1 illustrates this process by making a strong connection between a recursive function and an inductive proof of its correctness. Section 18.4.2 provides three additional examples, paying particular attention to the use of structural induction—that is, induction on data structures like lists and strings, rather than on the integers.

18.4.1 Recursion and Induction

When considering the question of correctness for programs written in a pure functional language, such as Haskell, we find ourselves in a very different place. First, absent the notion of program state and assignment, we need not write Hoare triples to keep track of the state transformations as we would with programs written in imperative and object-oriented languages.

Instead, functional programs are written as collections of functions that are well grounded in the mathematics of functions and recurrence relations. This allows us to base correctness proofs for Haskell functions on the well-worn technique of mathematical induction, rather than direct proofs that rely on reasoning about state transformations at every step. Overall, the verification of functional programs is a more straightforward process than the verification of imperative and object-oriented programs.

For a simple example, consider the Haskell function that computes the factorial of a nonnegative integer n:

```
>    fact n
>        | n == 1  = 1                      -- fact.1  (basis step)
>        | n > 1   = n*fact(n-1)   -- fact.2  (induction step)
```

Suppose we want to prove that this function computes the product of the first n nonnegative integers, given n. That is, we want to prove that:

$$fact(1) = 1$$
$$fact(n) = 1 \times 2 \times \ldots \times (n-1) \times n \quad \text{when } n > 1$$

For an inductive proof, recall that we need to show both of the following:

1 (Basis step) That the function computes the correct result for $n = 1$.
2 (Induction step) Assuming the hypothesis that the function computes the correct result for some integer $n = k - 1$, we can conclude that the function computes the correct result for the next integer $n = k$.

Since the function `fact` is recursively defined, its guarded commands naturally delineate the basis step from the induction step, as indicated by the comments on the right. So the basis step is handled by the first line of the function definition, and the induction step is handled by the second.

The function definition satisfies the basis step by observation. That is, when $n = 1$ we have `fact(1)` = 1, using the line annotated `fact.1`.

For the induction step, assume that $n > 1$ and $fact(n-1) = 1 \times 2 \times \ldots \times (n-1)$. Then correctness is established for `fact(n)` by using the line annotated `fact.2` and the hypothesis, followed by an algebraic simplification:

```
fact(n) = n*fact(n-1)
        = n*(1 * 2 * ... * (n-1))
        = 1 * 2 * ... * (n-1) * n
```

From this particular example, readers should notice the relative ease with which the correctness of a program in a functional language can be proved in contrast with that of its counterpart in an imperative language. The latter's Hoare triples and proof techniques are replaced by a straightforward induction process in which the function's definition directly mirrors the proof.

18.4.2 Examples of Structural Induction

An induction strategy can also be used to prove properties of Haskell functions that operate on lists and strings. Induction on list-processing and string-processing functions is often called "structural induction" because it simplifies the structure (size) of a list or string as it defines the hypothesis and shows the validity of the induction step.

This section provides examples of induction proofs for various Haskell functions involving list concatenation, reversal, and length. Because a Haskell string is a list of characters, these proofs apply to strings as well as lists.

List Reversal and Concatenation   Consider the following functions defined for list concatenation and reversal (these mirror the standard Haskell functions ++ and `reverse`, respectively):

```
>   cat [] ys      = ys                    -- cat.1
>   cat (x:xs) ys = x : (cat xs ys)        -- cat.2
>
>   rev []      = []                       -- rev.1
>   rev (x:xs) = cat (rev (xs)) [x]        -- rev.2
```

Suppose we want to prove the following property about the relationship between these two functions:

```
rev (cat xs ys) = cat (rev ys) (rev xs)
```

For instance, if the two lists (strings) are "hello " and "world," then the following is true:

```
rev (cat "hello " "world")
    = cat (rev "world") (rev "hello ")
    = "dlrow olleh"
```

To prove this property by induction, we begin with the basis step and use the definitions of these two functions. So we first need to show that:

```
rev ([] ++ ys) = rev (ys) ++ rev ([])
```

Using various lines in the definitions of these functions, we prove this by substitution as follows (justifications for each step are shown on the right):

```
rev (cat [] ys) = rev (ys)                        (from cat.1)
                = cat (rev (ys) [])               (from rev.2)
                = cat (rev (ys) rev [])           (from rev.1)
```

The induction hypothesis for this proof is written by stating the conclusion for any two lists xs and ys.

```
rev (cat xs ys) = cat reverse(ys) reverse(xs)
```

Now the induction step can be completed by showing how a slightly longer (by 1 element) list x:xs obeys the same rule, as follows:

```
rev (cat (x:xs) ys) = cat (rev ys) (rev (x:xs))
```

Here, we transform the left-hand side of this expression using our hypothesis and various lines in the definitions of the functions rev and cat, to achieve the following:

```
rev (cat (x:xs) ys) = rev (x : (cat xs ys)) (from cat.2)
      = rev (cat (cat xs ys) [x])            (from rev.2)
      = cat (cat (rev ys) (rev xs)) [x]      (from our hypothesis)
      = cat (rev ys) (cat (rev xs) [x])      (associativity of cat)
      = cat (rev ys) (rev (x:xs))            (from rev.2)
```

Finally, notice that the fourth line in this derivation assumes associativity for the operator cat, which can be separately proved by induction. This is left as an exercise.

List Length and Concatenation Consider the following Haskell function, which explicitly computes the length of a list. Because this is predefined in Haskell as length, we redefine it here with a slightly different name. Again, the comments on the right will be used in proofs about the properties of this function.

```
> len []     = 0                    -- len.1
> len (x:xs) = 1 + (length xs)       -- len.2
```

For this function, the first line defines the length, 0, of an empty list and the second shows how to compute the length of a list based on the known length of a list slightly smaller than it. For example,

```
len [1,3,4,7]
   = 1 + len [3,4,7]
   = 1 + (1 + len [4,7])
   = 1 + (1 + (1 + len [7]))
   = 1 + (1 + (1 + (1 + len [])))
   = 1 + (1 + (1 + (1 + 0)))
   = 4
```

The first four calls use the second line of the `len` function, while the fifth call uses the first line.

Here is an inductive proof that the length of two concatenated strings is identical to the sum of their individual lengths.

```
len (cat xs ys) = len xs + len ys
```

Notice in this proof that a familiar pattern is used: the basis step uses the first line in the recursive definition, and the induction step in the proof uses the second line. This proof provides another example of structural induction.

For the basis step, we need to show that:

```
len (cat [] ys) = len [] + len ys
```

This is done by the following two lines:

```
len (cat [] ys) = len ys             by cat.1
                = 0 + len ys         by arithmetic
                = len [] + len ys    by len.1
```

For the inductive step, we assume the hypothesis is true for arbitrary strings xs and ys:

```
len (cat xs ys) = len xs + len ys for lists xs and ys.
```

Now let's see what happens when we add an additional character to the first string.

```
len (cat x:xs ys) = len x: (cat xs ys)   by cat.2
                  = 1 + len (cat xs ys)   by len.2
                  = 1 + len xs + len ys   by hypothesis
                  = len x:xs + len ys     by len.2
```

This completes the proof.

As these examples illustrate, Haskell provides especially strong support for correctness proofs. While, unfortunately, not a large number of software systems are implemented in Haskell, those that are enjoy a generally high level of reliability.

However, functional languages like Haskell are being considered more and more seriously by software designers as vehicles for defining precise specifications for software prototypes. Conventional languages like C++ and Ada have been inadequate for this purpose [Hudak, 2000].

18.5 SUMMARY

This chapter considers program correctness and its impact on the design of programming languages. Correctness of imperative and OO programs is rooted in axiomatic semantics.

The use of tools for specifying and checking the correctness of programs is illustrated through the Java Modeling Language (JML). The connection between JML and the concept of design by contract is also explained. Other languages also support formal methods in programming, such as Spark/Ada and Haskell.

A full treatment of program correctness would more naturally occur in a software design course. This chapter only introduces the idea, placing a focus on the theoretical foundations and the basic language design and programming issues.

EXERCISES

18.1 Suggest a different way to write the function Max(a, b) in Figure 18.1 without changing the meaning of the function.

18.2 Below is a Hoare triple that includes a C-like program fragment to compute the product z of two integers x and y.

$$\{y \geq 0\}$$
z = 0;
n = y;
while (n > 0)
  $z = z + x$;
  $n = n - -1$;
od
$$\{z = x \times y\}$$

(a) What inference rules in Table 18.1 and additional knowledge about algebra can be used to infer that the precondition in this Hoare triple is equivalent to the assertion $\{y \geq 0 \wedge 0 = x(y-y)\}$?

(b) Using the assignment inference rule, complete the following Hoare triple for the first two statements in this program fragment:

$$\{y \geq 0 \wedge 0 = x(y - y)\}$$
z = 0;
n = y;
$$\{y \geq 0 \wedge \qquad\qquad\qquad \}$$

(c) Explain how the following can be an invariant for the while loop in this program fragment.

$$\{y \geq 0 \wedge n \geq 0 \wedge z = x(y - n)\}$$

That is, why is this assertion *true* before execution of the first statement in the loop, and why must it be *true* before execution of every successive repetition of the loop?

(d) Show that this invariant holds for a single pass through the loop's statements.

(e) Using the inference rule for loops, show how the invariant is resolved to an assertion that implies the validity of the postcondition for the entire program.

18.3 The following C++ function approximates the square root of a to within a small error epsilon, using Newton's method.

```
float mySqrt (float a, float epsilon) {
    float x;
    x = 1.0;
    while (x*x > a+epsilon || x*x < a-epsilon)
        x = (x + a/x)/2.0;
    return x;
}
```

(a) Describe a precondition and a postcondition, P and Q, that would serve as appropriate formal specifications for this function.
(b) Describe a loop invariant that would serve to describe the loop in this function.
(c) Are there any special circumstances under which a call to this function will not terminate or satisfy its postcondition? Explain.
(d) Prove the (partial) correctness of this function.

18.4 Suppose the function in Exercise 18.3 were part of a Java class that supported mathematical functions. Describe a contract that would be appropriate for any client of that class with regard to their use of the mySqrt function. Give JML requires and ensures clauses that specify this contract.

18.5 Write a Java function that computes the sum of a series of integers stored as a linked list (similar to the class MyStack and Node discussed in this chapter). Write pre- and postconditions for this function, and then develop a proof of its correctness using the inference rules in Table 18.1.

18.6 In the spirit of designing software from formal specifications, find a precise English-language definition at the Java website for the method indexOf(String) in the class java.lang.String.
(a) Translate that definition to a formal pre- and postcondition.
(b) Now translate your specification into JML requires and ensures clauses.

18.7 Give a recursive C/C++ implementation of the function Factorial in Figure 18.3. Prove the partial correctness of your recursive implementation for all values of $n > 0$. *Note*: to prove the correctness of a recursive function, induction must be used. That is, the base case and recursive call in the function definition correspond with the basis step and induction step in the proof.

18.8 A program has *total correctness* if it (completes its execution and) satisfies its postcondition for *all* input values specified in its precondition. Suppose we altered the function Factorial in Figure 18.3 so that its argument and result types are long rather than int.
(a) Experimentally determine the largest value of n for which your altered version of Factorial will deliver a result. What happens when it does not?
(b) Refine the precondition for this version of Factorial so that its correctness proof becomes a proof of total correctness.
(c) How is the correctness proof itself altered by these changes, if at all? Explain.

18.9 Alter the JML version of the Factorial function definition in Figure 18.8 so that its argument and result types are long rather than int. Add exception generating capabilities to this function so that it raises an ArithmeticError exception whenever the factorial cannot be correctly computed. Finally, add a JML signals clause to the specification that covers this event.

18.10   Reimplement the `Factorial` function so that it returns a value of type `BigInteger`. In what ways is this implementation superior to the version presented in Figure 18.8?

18.11   Reimplement the `Factorial` function in Haskell. In what ways is this implementation superior to the Java variations in Figure 18.8 and question 18.10? In what ways is it inferior?

18.12   Give an induction proof for the correctness of your Haskell implementation of the `Factorial` function in Exercise 18.11. For this, you should rely on the mathematical definition of factorial.

18.13   Discuss the trade-offs that exist between the choices of refining the precondition and adding a `signals` clause when specifying a function's response to an input value for which it cannot compute a meaningful result. For example, these choices are illustrated in Exercises 18.8 and 18.9.

18.14   Consider the correctness of the class `MyStack` in Section 18.3.
  (a) The method `size` was verified in consort with initialization of an object using the class constructor. Write an appropriate Hoare triple and then verify the method `size` for all other states that the object may have.
  (b) Write an appropriate Hoare triple and then verify the method `push`.

18.15   Prove by induction that the Haskell operator ++ is associative, using its recursive definition named `cat` that is given in this chapter. That is, show that for all lists xs, ys, and zs:

```
cat (cat xs ys) zs = cat xs (cat ys zs)
```

That is, this is equivalent to $(xs\ ++\ ys)\ ++\ zs\ =\ xs\ ++\ (ys\ ++\ zs)$.

18.16   Given the definition of the Haskell function `len` in this chapter, prove by induction the following:

```
len (reverse xs) = len xs
```

18.17   Consider the following (correct, but inefficient) Haskell implementation of the familiar Fibonacci function:

```
> fibSlow n
>    | n == 0  = 1                          -- fib.1
>    | n == 1  = 1                          -- fib.2
>    | otherwise  = fibSlow(n-1) + fibSlow(n-2)    -- fib.3
```

The correctness of this function can be proved quickly, since it is a direct transcription of the familiar mathematical definition below, and since the Haskell type Integer is an infinite set:

$$fib(0) = 1$$
$$fib(1) = 1$$
$$fib(n) = fib(n - 1) + fib(n - 2) \quad \text{if } n \geq 2$$

Give an induction proof of correctness for `fibSlow`.

18.18   As sugggested by its name, the efficiency of the `fibSlow` function in Exercise 18.17 is suspect.
  (a) Try running `fibSlow(25)` and then `fibSlow(50)` on your system and see how long these computations take. What causes this inefficiency?
  (b) An alternative definition of the Fibonacci calculation can be made in the following way. Define a function `fibPair` that generates a two-element pair that contains the nth Fibonacci number

and its successor. Define another function `fibNext` that generates the next such tuple from the current one. Then the Fibonacci function itself, optimistically named `fibFast`, can be defined by selecting the first member of the nth `fibPair`. In Haskell, this is written as follows:

```
> fibPair n
>      | n == 0   = (1,1)
>      | n > 0    = fibNext(fibPair(n-1))
> fibNext (m,n) = (n,m+n)
> fibFast n = fst(fibPair(n))
```

Try running the function `fibFast` to compute the 25th and 50th Fibonacci numbers. It should be considerably more efficient than `fibSlow`. Explain.

(c) Prove by induction that $\forall n \geq 0 : fibFast(n) = fibSlow(n)$.

Definition of Clite   **Appendix** A

CHAPTER OUTLINE

This appendix provides a complete definition of the syntax, type system, and semantics of Clite. The first four sections define, respectively, the lexical and concrete syntax, abstract syntax, type system, and semantics of the core language Clite. These are the definitions first presented in Chapters 2, 6, 8, and 11. The fifth section supplements that core language definition by adding global variables and functions to Clite, as introduced in Chapter 10.

This appendix serves as a ready cross-reference to the precise definition of Clite features as readers work on various exercises throughout the text. For more detailed discussions of any particular feature, readers are encouraged to refer back to the chapter where it is first introduced.

A.1 LEXICAL AND CONCRETE SYNTAX OF CLITE

$Program \rightarrow$ `int main ( ) {` *Declarations Statements* `}`

$Declarations \rightarrow$ **{** *Declaration* **}**

$Declaration \rightarrow$ *Type Identifier* **[[** *Integer* **]] { ,** *Identifier* **[[** *Integer* **]] };**

$Type \rightarrow$ `int` **|** `bool` **|** `float` **|** `char`

$Statements \rightarrow$ **{** *Statement* **}**

$Statement \rightarrow$ **;** **|** *Block* **|** *Assignment* **|** *If Statement* **|** *WhileStatement*

$Block \rightarrow$ **{** *Statements* **}**

$Assignment \rightarrow$ *Identifier* **[[** *Expression* **]]** = *Expression*;

$If Statement \rightarrow$ `if (` *Expression* `)` *Statement* **[** `else` *Statement* **]**

$WhileStatement \rightarrow$ `while (` *Expression* `)` *Statement*

$Expression \rightarrow$ *Conjunction* **{ ||** *Conjunction* **}**

$Conjunction \rightarrow$ *Equality* **{** `&&` *Equality* **}**

$Equality \rightarrow$ *Relation* **[** *EquOp Relation* **]**

$EquOp \rightarrow$ `==` **|** `!=`

$Relation \rightarrow$ *Addition* **[** *RelOp Addition* **]**

$RelOp \rightarrow$ `<` **|** `<=` **|** `>` **|** `>=`

$Addition \rightarrow$ *Term* **{** *AddOp Term* **}**

$AddOp \rightarrow$ `+` **|** `-`

$Term \rightarrow$ *Factor* **{** *MulOp Factor* **}**

$MulOp \rightarrow$ `*` **|** `/` **|** `%`

$Factor \rightarrow$ **[** *UnaryOp* **]** *Primary*

$UnaryOp \rightarrow$ `-` **|** `!`

$Primary \rightarrow$ *Identifier* **[[** *Expression* **]]** **|** *Literal* **|** **(** *Expression* **)**
 | *Type* **(** *Expression* **)**

$Identifier \rightarrow$ *Letter* **{** *Letter* **|** *Digit* **}**

$Letter \rightarrow$ `a` **|** `b` **|** `...` **|** `z` **|** `A` **|** `B` **|** `...` **|** `Z`

$Digit \rightarrow$ `0` **|** `1` **|** `...` **|** `9`

$Literal \rightarrow$ *Integer* **|** *Boolean* **|** *Float* **|** *Char*

$Integer \rightarrow$ *Digit* **{** *Digit* **}**

$Boolean \rightarrow$ `true` **|** `false`

$Float \rightarrow$ *Integer* `.` *Integer*

$Char \rightarrow$ `'` *ASCIIChar* `'`

A.2 ABSTRACT SYNTAX OF CLITE

$$
\begin{aligned}
\textit{Program} &= \textit{Declarations} \;\texttt{decpart};\; \textit{Statements} \;\texttt{body}; \\
\textit{Declarations} &= \textit{Declaration}^* \\
\textit{Declaration} &= \textit{VariableDecl} \mid \textit{ArrayDecl} \\
\textit{VariableDecl} &= \textit{Variable} \;\texttt{v};\; \textit{Type} \;\texttt{t} \\
\textit{ArrayDecl} &= \textit{Variable} \;\texttt{v};\; \textit{Type} \;\texttt{t};\; \textit{Integer} \;\texttt{size} \\
\textit{Type} &= \texttt{int} \mid \texttt{bool} \mid \texttt{float} \mid \texttt{char} \\
\textit{Statements} &= \textit{Statement}^* \\
\textit{Statement} &= \textit{Skip} \mid \textit{Block} \mid \textit{Assignment} \mid \textit{Conditional} \mid \textit{Loop} \\
\textit{Skip} &= \\
\textit{Block} &= \textit{Statements} \\
\textit{Conditional} &= \textit{Expression} \;\texttt{test};\; \textit{Statement} \;\texttt{thenbranch, elsebranch} \\
\textit{Loop} &= \textit{Expression} \;\texttt{test};\; \textit{Statement} \;\texttt{body} \\
\textit{Assignment} &= \textit{VariableRef} \;\texttt{target};\; \textit{Expression} \;\texttt{source} \\
\textit{Expression} &= \textit{VariableRef} \mid \textit{Value} \mid \textit{Binary} \mid \textit{Unary} \\
\textit{VariableRef} &= \textit{Variable} \mid \textit{ArrayRef} \\
\textit{Binary} &= \textit{BinaryOp} \;\texttt{op};\; \textit{Expression} \;\texttt{term1, term2} \\
\textit{Unary} &= \textit{UnaryOp} \;\texttt{op};\; \textit{Expression} \;\texttt{term} \\
\textit{Operator} &= \textit{BooleanOp} \mid \textit{RelationalOp} \mid \textit{ArithmeticOp} \mid \textit{UnaryOp} \\
\textit{BooleanOp} &= \texttt{\&\&} \mid \texttt{||} \\
\textit{RelationalOp} &= \texttt{=} \mid \texttt{!=} \mid \texttt{<} \mid \texttt{<=} \mid \texttt{>} \mid \texttt{>=} \\
\textit{ArithmeticOp} &= \texttt{+} \mid \texttt{-} \mid \texttt{*} \mid \texttt{/} \\
\textit{UnaryOp} &= \texttt{!} \mid \texttt{-} \\
\textit{Variable} &= \textit{String} \;\texttt{id} \\
\textit{ArrayRef} &= \textit{String} \;\texttt{id};\; \textit{Expression} \;\texttt{index} \\
\textit{Value} &= \textit{IntValue} \mid \textit{BoolValue} \mid \textit{FloatValue} \mid \textit{CharValue} \\
\textit{IntValue} &= \textit{Integer} \;\texttt{intValue} \\
\textit{FloatValue} &= \textit{Float} \;\texttt{floatValue} \\
\textit{BoolValue} &= \textit{Boolean} \;\texttt{boolValue} \\
\textit{CharValue} &= \textit{Character} \;\texttt{charValue}
\end{aligned}
$$

A.3 TYPE SYSTEM OF CLITE

Type Rule A.1 *All referenced variables must be declared.*

Type Rule A.2 *All declared variables must have unique names.*

Type Rule A.3 *A Program is type valid if its Declarations* `decpart` *is valid and its Block* `body` *is valid with respect to the type map for those particular Declarations.*

Type Rule A.4 *A Statement is valid with respect to the program's type map if it satisfies the following constraints:*

1 *A Skip is always valid.*
2 *An Assignment is valid if all the following are true:*
   (a) *Its* target *Variable is declared.*
   (b) *Its* source *Expression is valid.*
   (c) *If the type of its* target *Variable is* float, *then the type of its* source *Expression must be either* float *or* int.
   (d) *Otherwise, if the type of its* target *Variable is* int, *then the type of its* source *Expression must be either* int *or* char.
   (e) *Otherwise, the type of its* target *Variable must be the same as the type of its* source *Expression.*
3 *A Conditional is valid if its* test *Expression is valid and has type* bool, *and both its* thenbranch *and* elsebranch *Statements are valid.*
4 *A Loop is valid if its* test *Expression is valid and has type* bool, *and its Statement* body *is valid.*
5 *A Block is valid if all of its Statements are valid.*

Type Rule A.5 *The validity of an Expression is defined using the program's type map and each of the Expression's subclasses:*

1 *A Value is valid.*
2 *A Variable is valid if its* id *appears in the type map.*
3 *A Binary is valid if all the following are true:*
   (a) *Its Expressions* term1 *and* term2 *are valid.*
   (b) *If its BinaryOp* op *is arithmetic (+, -, *, /), then both its Expressions must be either* int *or* float.
   (c) *If* op *is relational (==, !=, <, <=, >, >=), then both its Expressions must have the same type.*
   (d) *If* op *is boolean (&&, ||), then both its Expressions must be* bool.
4 *A Unary is valid if all the following are true:*
   (a) *Its Expression* term *is valid.*
   (b) *If its UnaryOp* op *is* !, *then* term *must be* bool.
   (c) *If* op *is* -, *then* term *must be* int *or* float.
   (d) *If* op *is the type conversion* float() *or* char(), *then* term *must be* int.
   (e) *If* op *is the type conversion* int(), *then* term *must be* float *or* char.

Type Rule A.6 *Every Expression's result type is determined as follows:*

1 *If the Expression is a Value, then its result type is the type of that Value.*
2 *If the Expression is a Variable, then its result type is the type of that Variable.*
3 *If the Expression is a Binary, then:*
   (a) *If the Operator is arithmetic (+, −, *, or /), then its terms must be the same type and its result type is the type of its operands. For example, the Expression* x+1 *requires* x *to be* int *(since* 1 *is* int*), so its result type is* int.

(b) *If the Operator is relational* ($<, <=, >, >=, ==, !=$) *or boolean* (&&, ||)*, then its result type is* `bool`.

4 *If the Expression is a Unary, then:*

(a) *If the Operator is* !*, then its result type is* `bool`.

(b) *If the Operator is* -*, then its result type is the type of its operand.*

(c) *If the Operator is a type conversion, then the result type is given by the conversion.*

A.4 SEMANTICS OF CLITE

Meaning Rule A.1 *The meaning of a Program is defined to be the meaning of its* `body` *when given an initial state consisting of the variables of the* `decpart`*, each initialized to the undef value corresponding to its declared type.*

Meaning Rule A.2 *The meaning of a Skip statement is an identity function on the state; that is, the state is unchanged.*

Meaning Rule A.3 *The meaning of an Assignment statement is the result of replacing the value of the* `target` *Variable by the value of the* `source` *Expression in the current state.*

Meaning Rule A.4 *The meaning of a Conditional depends on the truth or falsity of its boolean* `test` *in the current state. If* `test` *is true, then the meaning of the Conditional is the meaning of the* `thenbranch` *Statement; otherwise, it is the meaning of the* `elsebranch` *Statement.*

Meaning Rule A.5 *If the* `test` *is false, the meaning (output state) of a Loop is the same as the input state. Otherwise, the meaning is the result of applying this rule again to the meaning of its* `body` *in the current state.*

Meaning Rule A.6 *The meaning of a Block is the aggregated meaning of its statements when applied to the current state. If a Block has no statements the state is not changed. Otherwise, the state resulting from the meaning of the first Statement in the Block becomes the basis for defining the meaning of the rest of the block.*

Meaning Rule A.7 *The meaning of an Expression in a state is a Value defined as follows:*

1 *If the Expression is a Value, then its meaning is the meaning of the Value itself.*

2 *If the Expression is a Variable, then its meaning is the Value of the Variable in the current state.*

3 *If the Expression is a Binary, then the meaning of each of its operands* `term1` *and* `term2` *is first determined. Then Rule A.8 determines the meaning of the expression by applying the Operator* `op` *to the Values of those two operands.*

4 *If the Expression is a Unary, then the meaning of its operand* `term` *is determined. Then Rule A.9 determines the meaning of the expression by applying the Operator* `op` *to the Value of the operand.*

Meaning Rule A.8 *The meaning of a Binary expression is a Value defined as follows:*

1 *If either operand* `term1` *or* `term2` *is undefined, the program is semantically meaningless.*
2 *If the operator is an integer arithmetic operator, then an* `int+`, `int-`, `int*` *perform an integer add, subtract, or multiply on its integer operands, resulting in an integer result. If the operator is* `int/`, *then the result is the same as a mathematical divide with truncation toward zero.*
3 *If the operator is a floating point operator, then floating point arithmetic using the IEEE standard is performed on the* `float` *operands, resulting in a* `float` *result.*
4 *If the operator is a relational operator, then the operands are compared with a result of either* `true` *or* `false`. *The result is the same as the corresponding mathematical result, except that* `false` < `true`.
5 *If the operator is a Boolean operator, then:*
(a) *The operator && is interpreted as:*

$$a \ \&\& \ b \equiv \text{if } a \text{ then } b \text{ else } false$$

(b) *The operator || is interpreted as:*

$$a \ || \ b \equiv \text{if } a \text{ then } true \text{ else } b$$

Meaning Rule A.9 *The meaning of a Unary expression is a Value defined as follows:*

1 *If the operand* `term` *is undefined, the meaning of the expression is undefined.*
2 *If the operator is* ! *(not), then the boolean operand is inverted.*
3 *If the operator is* `int-/float-`, *then the integer/floating point operand's sign is inverted.*
4 *If the operator is* `i2f`, *then the integer operand is converted to floating point.*
5 *If the operator is* `c2i`, *then the* `char` *operand is converted to integer using the ASCII code for the character. Effectively, except for adding leading zero bits, the value is unchanged except for its type.*
6 *If the operator is* `i2c`, *then the integer operand is converted to character. If the integer operand is either greater than 255 or less than zero, the meaning of the expression is undefined. If the conversion is successful, then except for the loss of leading zero bits, the value's bit pattern is the same, only the type is changed.*
7 *If the operator is* `f2i`, *then the floating point value is converted to integer by discarding the places after the decimal point, that is, it is truncated toward zero. If the integer part of the floating point value is too large to store in an integer, the meaning of the expression is undefined.*

The next three rules define the semantics of Clite elements that include dynamic arrays. They utilize the *new* and *delete* functions introduced in Chapter 11.

Meaning Rule A.10 *The meaning of an ArrayDecl* ad *is:*

1. *Compute addr(*ad[0]*) = new(*ad.size*), where the value of the Expression* ad.size *is computed as described in Chapter 7.*
2. *Push addr(*ad[0]*) onto the stack.*
3. *Push* ad.size *onto the stack.*
4. *Push* ad.type *onto the stack.*

Meaning Rule A.11 *The meaning of an ArrayRef* ar *is:*

1. *Compute addr(*ad[ar.index]*) = addr(*ad[0]*) +* ad.index *− 1.*
2. *If addr(*ad[0]*) ≤ addr(*ad[ar.index]*) < addr(*ad[0]*) +* ad.size*, return the value at addr(*ad[ar.index]*).*
3. *Otherwise, signal an index-out-of-range error.*

The meaning of an *Assignment* as whose target is an *ArrayReference* ar is:

Meaning Rule A.12 *The meaning of an Assignment* as *is:*

1. *Compute addr(*ad[ar.index]*) = addr(*ad[0]*) +* ad.index *− 1.*
2. *If addr(*ad[0]*) ≤ addr(*ad[ar.index]*) < addr(*ad[0]*) +* ad.size*, then change the value at addr(*ad[ar.index]*) to the value of* as.source.
3. *Otherwise, signal an index-out-of-range error.*

A.5   ADDING FUNCTIONS TO CLITE

A.5.1 Lexical and Concrete Syntax

In this definition, underlining indicates additions to the original rules for Clite given in Section A.1.

$$Program \rightarrow \underline{\{ \ Type \ Identifier \ FunctionOrGlobal \ \}} \ MainFunction$$

$$Type \rightarrow \text{int} \mid \text{boolean} \mid \text{float} \mid \text{char} \mid \underline{\text{void}}$$

$$\underline{FunctionOrGlobal} \rightarrow \text{(} Parameters \text{) } \{ \ Declarations \ Statements \ \} \mid Global$$

$$\underline{Parameters} \rightarrow [\ Parameter \ \{ , \ Parameter \ \} \ ]$$

$$\underline{Parameter} \rightarrow Type \ Identifier$$

$$\underline{Global} \rightarrow \{ , \ Identifier \ \} ;$$

$$MainFunction \rightarrow \text{int main ( ) } \{ \ Declarations \ Statements \ \}$$

$$Statement \rightarrow ; \mid Block \mid Assignment \mid IfStatement$$
$$WhileStatement \mid \underline{CallStatement} \mid \underline{ReturnStatement}$$

$$\underline{CallStatement} \rightarrow Call ;$$

$$\underline{ReturnStatement} \rightarrow \text{return} \ Expression ;$$

$$Factor \rightarrow Identifier \mid Literal \mid \text{(} Expression \text{)} \mid \underline{Call}$$

$$\underline{Call} \rightarrow Identifier \text{ (} Arguments \text{)}$$

$$\underline{Arguments} \rightarrow [\ Expression \ \{ , \ Expression \ \} \ ]$$

So the *MainFunction* is identical to the original notion of *Program*, except that now the *MainFunction* can be preceded by any number of function and/or global variable declarations to form a complete *Program*.

A.5.2 Abstract Syntax

In this definition, underlining indicates additions to the original rules for Clite given in Section A.2.

$$
\begin{aligned}
Program &= \underline{Declarations\ globals;\ Functions\ functions} \\
\underline{Functions} &= \underline{Function^*} \\
\underline{Function} &= Type\ t;\ String\ id;\ Declarations\ params,\ locals;\ Block \\
&\qquad body \\
Type &= \text{int} \mid \text{boolean} \mid \text{float} \mid \text{char} \mid \underline{\text{void}} \\
Statement &= Skip \mid Block \mid Assignment \mid Conditional \mid Loop \mid \underline{Call} \mid \underline{Return} \\
\underline{Call} &= String\ name;\ Expressions\ args \\
\underline{Expressions} &= Expression^* \\
\underline{Return} &= Variable\ target;\ Expression\ result \\
Expression &= Variable \mid Value \mid Binary \mid Unary \mid \underline{Call}
\end{aligned}
$$

A.5.3 Type System

Type Rule A.7 *Every function and global* id *must be unique .*

Type Rule A.8 *Every Function's* params *and* locals *must have mutually unique* id*'s.*

Type Rule A.9 *Every Statement in the* body *of each function must be valid with respect to the function's local variables, parameters, and visible globals.*

Type Rule A.10 *A Return statement must appear in the* body *of every non-void function except* main, *and its Expression must have the same Type as that function.*

Type Rule A.11 *No Return statement can appear in a* void *function.*

Type Rule A.12 *Every Call Statement's* name *must identify the* id *of a void Function in the program, and every Call Expression must identify a nonvoid Function.*

Type Rule A.13 *Every Call must have the same number of* args *as the number of* params *in the identified Function, and each such* arg *must have the same type as its corresponding* param, *reading from left to right.*

Type Rule A.14 *The type of a Call is the type of the function identified, and the expression in which it appears must be valid according to Type Rules A.5 and A.6.*

A.5.4 Semantics

Meaning Rule A.13 *The meaning of a Call c to Function f has the following steps:*

1. *Make a new activation record, add f's* params *and* locals *to it.*
2. *Evaluate each of c's* args *and assign its Value to f's corresponding* param *in the activation record.*
3. *If the function is nonvoid, add to the activation record a result variable identical with the function's name and type.*
4. *Push that activation record onto the run-time stack.*
5. *Interpret the statements in f's* body*.*
6. *Pop the activation record from the run-time stack.*
7. *If the function is nonvoid, return the value of the result variable to the call.*

Meaning Rule A.14 *The meaning of a Return is computed by replacing the value of the* result *Variable (the name of the called function) in the activated record by the value of the* result *Expression.*

Meaning Rule A.15 *The meaning of a Block is the aggregated meaning of its statements when applied to the current state, up to and including the point where the first Return is encountered. If there are nested Blocks, the first Return encountered signals termination of the outermost Block. That is, the first Return encountered terminates the body of the function.*

CHAPTER OUTLINE

The purpose of this appendix is to provide a brief review of certain key mathematical topics needed in a formal study of programming languages.

B.1 SETS AND RELATIONS

Sets are a most fundamental data structure of discrete mathematics. They are also ubiquitous in the theory of computer science.

> **Definition**: A *set* is any collection of objects; usually all the objects in a set have the same type.

A set can contain numbers, strings, books, theorems, other sets, and so on.

One way to describe a set is to enumerate its elements. An example is the set of vowels in English:

$$\{a, e, i, o, u\}$$

The use of braces to enclose the members of a set is a common convention. Ellipses (. . .) are commonly used to elide the elements of a set when the sequence is well understood; an example is the set of lowercase letters:

$$\{a, \ldots, z\}$$

567

Eliding the elements of a set is also common when the set is infinite in size; an example is the set **I** of integers:

$$\{\ldots, -2, -1, 0, 1, 2, \ldots\}$$

One of the fundamental operations on a set is the membership test. If A is a set, we can ask whether x is a member of A by writing $x \in A$. For instance, the question:

$$a \in \{a, e, i, o, u\}$$

is true. The opposite test, denoting that x is not a member of A, is written $x \notin A$; for example,

$$z \notin \{a, e, i, o, u\}$$

is also true.

The membership test is often used in conjunction with a restricting condition to define a set. For instance, one way to define the set **N** of nonnegative integers is:

$$\{n \in \mathbf{I} \mid n \geq 0\}$$

where **I** is the set of integers defined above. This definition can be read as the set of all integers n for which n is greater than or equal to zero. The vertical bar is read as *such that*, and it introduces one or more restricting conditions. Of course, the set of nonnegative integers **N** could just as easily be defined as:

$$\{0, 1, 2, \ldots\}$$

Consider defining the set of nonnegative even numbers as:

$$\{n \in \mathbf{N} \mid n \bmod 2 = 0\}$$

which states that the set of even numbers is the set of all nonnegative integers which are evenly divisible by 2.

All sets have two fundamental properties. First, no set contains duplicate elements:

$$\{a, b, c\} = \{a, a, a, b, b, c\}$$

That is, the above notations describe the same set. The second property is that sets are unordered collections:

$$\{a, b, c\} = \{c, b, a\}$$

Thus, two sets are *equal* if they have precisely the same elements, regardless of ordering.

The following sets are specially named because of their fundamental importance in mathematics and computer science theory.

Notation	Meaning	Explanation
R	Real numbers	
I	Integers	Abbreviates $\{\ldots, -2, -1, 0, 1, 2, \ldots\}$
N	Natural numbers	Abbreviates $\{0, 1, 2, \ldots\}$
B	Boolean constants	Abbreviates $\{true, false\}$

We are often interested in the relationships between two sets. We say that set A is a *subset* of B, written $A \subseteq B$, if every element in A is also an element of B. For example:

$$\{a, e, i, o, u\} \subseteq \{a, \ldots, z\}$$

that is, the set of vowels is a subset of the set of letters. We say that set A is a *proper subset* of B, written $A \subset B$, if $A \subseteq B$ but some element in B is not an element of A; an example is again:

$$\{a, e, i, o, u\} \subset \{a, \ldots, z\}$$

That is, the set of vowels is a proper subset of the set of letters since some letters are not vowels.[1] Clearly, for any set A, A is a subset of itself, $A \subseteq A$. Moreover, these relations can be inverted: if $A \subseteq B$ then $B \supseteq A$, that is, if A is a subset of B, then B is a *superset* of A.

Thus, we can formally define *set equality* as A is equal to B ($A = B$) if and only if $A \subseteq B$ and $B \subseteq A$. In other words, A equals B if and only if every element of A is an element of B and every element of B is an element of A. Informally, sets A and B have precisely the same elements.

A special set is the *empty set* or *null set* $\emptyset$ (or {}), which has no elements. The empty set is a subset of every set, including itself.

Sets have many useful operations. Below is a summary of the key ones for our study.

The *size of a set* A (denoted $|A|$) is a count of the number of its elements. For example, if V is the set of vowels, $|V|$ is 5.

The *union* of two sets A and B ($A \cup B$) is defined to be the set whose elements consist of all elements of A and all elements of B. For example:

$$\{a, b\} \cup \{b, c, d\} = \{a, b, c, d\}$$

Note that although the size of the first set is 2 and the size of the second set is 3, the size of their union is 4, not 5.

The *intersection* of two sets A and B ($A \cap B$) is defined to be the set whose elements consist of all elements that are in both A and B. For example:

$$\{a, b\} \cap \{b, c, d\} = \{b\}$$

The *cross-product* of two sets A and B ($A \times B$) is the set of all ordered pairs $\langle x, y \rangle$ where x is a member of A and y is a member of B. For example:

$$\{a, b\} \times \{1, 2\} = \{\langle a, 1 \rangle, \langle a, 2 \rangle, \langle b, 1 \rangle, \langle b, 2 \rangle\}$$

The *difference* of two sets A and B ($A - B$) is defined to be the set whose elements consist of all elements of A which are not also elements of B. For example:

$$\{a, b\} - \{b, c, d\} = \{a\}$$

---

1. An alternative way of expressing the second part is to say that B is not a subset of A, written $B \not\subseteq A$.

The *natural join* of two sets A and B ($A \otimes B$) where A and B are sets of ordered pairs is defined to be the set of pairs whose first element is in both A and B. For example:

$$\{\langle x, 1\rangle, \langle y, 2\rangle\} \otimes \{\langle y, 9\rangle, \langle w, 4\rangle\} = \{\langle y, 2\rangle, \langle y, 9\rangle\}$$

The *overriding union* of A and B ($A \,\overline{\cup}\, B$) is defined to be:

$$A \,\overline{\cup}\, B = (A - (A \otimes B)) \cup B$$

For example:

$$\{\langle x, 1\rangle, \langle y, 2\rangle\} \,\overline{\cup}\, \{\langle y, 9\rangle\} = \{\langle x, 1\rangle, \langle y, 9\rangle\}$$

A set of ordered pairs is a useful tool for modeling memory, where the first component of the pair is a variable name and the second is the variable's value. With this in mind, the overriding union provides a mathematical model of the assignment operation. We make use of the overriding union in our treatment of semantic issues.

Definition: A *relation* is a subset of a cross-product, of two sets.

If the set is a binary cross-product $A \times B$, then the relation is a *binary relation*. If the set is an n-ary cross-product $A_1 \times \ldots \times A_n$, then the relation is said to be an *n-ary relation*.

A common binary relation among members of a set are equality and inequality. An example would be numerical equality. For example, $5 = 5$, but $5 \neq 1$. Many other common relations exist in computer science: the value of a variable, the visibility (public vs. private) of an identifier, the type of a variable, and so on.

Just as sets have no particular property other than set membership, relations also have only the property that a tuple, that is, a particular element of a cross-product, is either a member of a relation or not. For example, if computer memory is modeled as a cross-product of variable names and values, then the element $\langle f, 5\rangle$ is either in the computer memory relation or not.

A *function* is a special kind of relation. Examples include the trigonometric functions (sin, cos, etc.), log, square root, and so on, from mathematics.

Definition: An n-ary relation R is a *function* if whenever $\langle a_1, \ldots, a_{n-1}, x\rangle \in R$ and $\langle a_1, \ldots, a_{n-1}, y\rangle \in R$, then $x = y$.

When viewed as a function, then the first $n - 1$ elements of R are the function's arguments and the last element is the function's result. Thus, R is a function if whenever it is given the same set of arguments, it always returns the same result. For example, the square of a number x, $square(x)$, is a function; for example, $square(2)$ is always 4.

If the relation f on the cross-product of sets A and B is a function, then we often denote that by writing $f : A \rightarrow B$. In the study of programming languages, this is often called the *signature* of a method or function. For example, the signature of the *square* function:

$$square : \mathbf{R} \rightarrow \mathbf{R}$$

denotes that *square* takes a real number as an argument and returns a real result.

B.2 GRAPHS

Another mathematical idea that is essential for the formal study of programming languages and their implementation is the *graph*. In particular, the theory and construction of compilers use a number of directed graph algorithms.

> **Definition**: A *graph* has a set of nodes (or vertices) N, a set of edges E, and a function $g : E \rightarrow N \times N$ that maps an edge to a pair of nodes. If E contains $< v, u >$ whenever it contains $< u, v >$, then the graph is *undirected*. Otherwise the graph is *directed*.

Another name for a directed graph is *digraph*.

An example is that a purely bidirectional road system can be treated as an undirected graph. In contrast, a directed graph is like a road system with one-way roads, where two-way roads are treated as two one-way roads, one in each direction. In either case, the road system's intersections correspond to nodes.

We can draw directed graphs using circles for nodes and arcs with arrows for edges. Figure B.1 is a pictorial representation of the graph with nodes $N = \{1, 2, 3, 4, 5\}$ and edges:

Edge	g(edge)
a	$\langle 1, 2 \rangle$
b	$\langle 2, 2 \rangle$
c	$\langle 2, 3 \rangle$
d	$\langle 2, 4 \rangle$
e	$\langle 4, 5 \rangle$

Uses of directed graphs occur in Sections 3.2.2 and 3.3.1.

A *path* from node i to node j is a sequence of edges $e_1, \ldots, e_k \in E$ where $g(e_1), \ldots, g(e_k)$ is the sequence of ordered pairs $\langle n_1, n_2 \rangle, \langle n_2, n_3 \rangle, \ldots, \langle n_{k-1}, n_k \rangle$ where $i = n_1$ and $j = n_k$. That is, a path corresponds to traversing a sequence of

Figure B.1
Example Directed
Graph

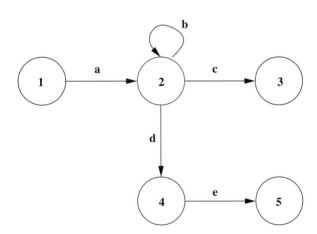

arcs in the direction of the arrow. Figure B.1 contains a path from node 1 to node 3 by traversing edges a, b, c, that is, going from node 1 to node 2, node 2 to itself, and finally, from node 2 to node 3.

The *length of a path* is the number of arcs in the sequence. For instance, the above example path has length 3. However, a shorter path from node 1 to node 3 has length 2. A *shortest path* from node i to node j is the one with minimum length, but such a path may not be unique.

A directed graph contains a *cycle* if it has some path in which a node is repeated. In the example digraph, edge b by itself constitutes a cycle. Similarly, any path that contains edge b has a cycle.

Of course, there may be no path from node i to node j. We say that node j is *reachable* from node i if there is a path from i to j. In the example in the figure, every node is reachable from node 1, but node 5 is not reachable from node 3 (and vice versa).

An undirected graph is *connected* if, for any two nodes i and j, there is a path from i to j. The situation is more complicated for a directed graph. We say that a directed graph is *weakly connected* if the graph considered as an undirected graph is connected. The graph in Figure B.1 is weakly connected. A digraph is *unilaterally connected*, if for any two nodes i and j, there is either a path from i to j or j to i. The example digraph is not unilaterally connected since there is neither a path from 3 to 5 nor one from 5 to 3. An directed graph is *strongly connected* if, for any two nodes i and j, there is a path from i to j.

B.3   LOGIC

Propositional logic is concerned with *propositions*, which are statements that can be either true (T) or false (F). An example is the proposition "Phogbound is running for governor and all is well with the world."

We can form new propositions using logical operators $\land$ (meaning "and"), $\lor$ (meaning "or"), and $\neg$ (meaning "not") and other propositions. For instance, $p \land q$, where p and q are propositions, denotes the new proposition "both p and q are true." These operators are defined by so-called *truth tables*.

For example, consider the negation proposition $\neg p$. This means that if p is true, then $\neg p$ is false, and vice versa. This is defined in tabular form in Table B.1. Note that all possible values in the domain of p, namely T and F, are given.

For the binary operators *and* and *or*, each of the operands p and q may be either T or F, leading to four distinct pairs of values in their domain. The proposition $p \land q$ is F if either operand is F; otherwise it is T. In contrast, the proposition $p \lor q$ is T if either operand is T; otherwise it is F. The truth table for the operators *and* and *or* is given in Table B.2.

The statement *if p then q* (or equivalently *p implies q*) is written $p \Rightarrow q$. The proposition is true except when p is T and q is F. Also given in the table is the statement

Table B.1

Truth Table for $\neg p$

p	$\neg p$
T	F
F	T

Table B.2

Truth Table for And
and Or Operators

p	*q*	*p* ∧ *q*	*p* ∨ *q*
T	T	T	T
T	F	F	T
F	T	F	T
F	F	F	F

Table B.3

Truth Table for Implication
and Equivalence

p	*q*	*p* ⇒ *q*	*p* ⇔ *q*
T	T	T	T
T	F	F	F
F	T	T	F
F	F	T	T

p is equivalent to q, written $p \Leftrightarrow q$. This proposition is equivalent to:

$$p \Rightarrow q \wedge q \Rightarrow p$$

These truth tables are given in Table B.3.

We can extend the idea of a proposition to include so-called quantifiers, constants and variables that can take on values in different domains than {T, F}. When we extend propositions in this way, we have the concept of a predicate.

The two main quantifiers used in predicates are ∀ ("for all") and ∃ ("there exists"). An example predicate would be:

For all prime numbers x, there exists another prime number y such that y is greater than x.

This is a more formal way of proposing that there is no greatest prime number. Since x and y are variables that range over the natural numbers **N**, this example can be rewritten as:

$$\forall x (x \text{ is prime} \Rightarrow \exists y (y \text{ is prime} \wedge y > x))$$

Predicates can be defined in the following way. First, a *term* can be either:

1   A constant,
2   A variable, or
3   $f(t_1, \ldots, t_n)$, where f is a function and $t_1, \ldots, t_n$ are terms.

Second, an *atomic formula* can be either:

1   A predicate variable or
2   $P(t_1, \ldots, t_n)$, where P is a predicate and $t_1, \ldots, t_n$ are terms.

Third, a *predicate* can be:

1   An atomic formula,
2   $\forall x (P)$ and $\exists x (P)$, where P is a predicate and x is an individual variable, or
3   $\neg P$, $P \wedge Q$, $P \vee Q$, $P \Rightarrow Q$, and $P \Leftrightarrow Q$, where P and Q are predicates.

The predicate $\forall x(P(x))$ is read: "for all x (in the implied domain), x has property P." Rewriting our prime number example again, we get:

$$\forall x(x \in \mathbf{N} \wedge isPrime(x) \Rightarrow \exists y(y \in \mathbf{N} \wedge isPrime(y) \wedge y > x))$$

where $\mathbf{N}$ is the set of natural numbers.

Finally, we consider the concepts of free and bound variables. The *scope* of a variable is the expression to which the quantifier is applied. For example, the scope of the universal quantifier $(\forall x)P$ is P. A variable x is *bound* if it occurs within the scope of its quantifier. Otherwise it is said to be *free*. For instance, variable x is free and variable y is bound in the predicate $\exists y(y \in \mathbf{N} \wedge isPrime(y) \wedge y > x)$.

Propositions provide symbolic representations for *logic expressions;* that is, statements that can be interpreted as either *true* or *false*. For example, if p represents the proposition "Mary speaks Russian" and q represents the proposition "Bob speaks Russian," then $p \wedge q$ represents the proposition "Mary and Bob both speak Russian," and $p \vee q$ represents "Either Mary or Bob (or both) speaks Russian." If, furthermore, r represents the proposition "Mary and Bob can communicate," then the expression $p \wedge q \Rightarrow r$ represents "If Mary and Bob both speak Russian, then they can communicate."

Predicates include all propositions such as the above, and also include variables in various domains (integers, reals, strings, lists, etc.), boolean-valued functions with these variables, and quantifiers. A *predicate* is a proposition in which some of the boolean variables are replaced by boolean-valued functions and quantified expressions.

A *boolean-valued function* is a function with one or more arguments that delivers *true* or *false* as a result. Here are some examples:

$prime(n)$—*true* if the integer value of n is a prime number; *false* otherwise.

$0 \le x + y$—*true* if the real sum of x and y is nonnegative.

$speaks(x, y)$—*true* if person x speaks language y.

A predicate combines these kinds of functions using the operators of the propositional calculus and the quantifiers $\forall$ (meaning "for all") and $\exists$ (meaning "there exists"). Here are some examples:

$0 \le x \wedge x \le 1$—*true* if x is between 0 and 1, inclusive; otherwise *false*.

$speaks(x, Russian) \wedge speaks(y, Russian) \Rightarrow communicateswith(x, y)$—*true* if the fact that both x and y speak Russian implies that x communicates with y; otherwise *false*.

$\forall x(speaks(x, Russian))$—*true* if everyone on the planet speaks Russian; *false* otherwise.

$\exists x(speaks(x, Russian))$—*true* if at least one person on the planet speaks Russian; *false* otherwise.

$\forall x \exists y(speaks(x, y))$—*true* if every person on the planet speaks some language; *false* otherwise.

$\forall x(\neg literate(x) \Rightarrow (\neg writes(x) \wedge \neg \exists y(book(y) \wedge hasread(x, y))))$—*true* if every illiterate person x does not write and has not read a book.

Table B.4 summarizes the meanings of the different kinds of expressions that can be used in propositional and predicate logic.

Table B.4 Summary of Predicate Logic Notation	
Notation	**Meaning**
true, false	Boolean (truth) constants
p, q, . . .	Boolean variables
p(x, y . . .), q(x, y . . .), . . .	Boolean functions
$\neg p$	Negation of *p*
$p \wedge q$	Conjunction of *p* and *q*
$p(x) \vee q(x)$	Disjunction of *p* and *q*
$p(x) \Rightarrow q(x)$	Implication: *p* implies *q*
$p(x) \Leftrightarrow q(x)$	Logical equivalence of *p* and *q*
$\forall x \, p(x)$	Universally quantified expression
$\exists x \, p(x)$	Existentially quantified expression
p(x) is valid	Predicate *p(x)* is *true* for every value of *x*
p(x) is satisfiable	Predicate *p(x)* is *true* for at least one value of *x*
p(x) is a contradiction	Predicate *p(x)* is *false* for every value of *x*

Predicates that are *true* for all possible values of their variables are called *valid*. For instance, $even(x) \vee odd(x)$ is valid, since all integers *x* are either even or odd. Predicates that are *false* for all possible values of their variables are called *contradictions*. For instance, $even(x) \wedge odd(x)$ is a contradiction, since no integer can be both even and odd.

Predicates that are *true* for some particular assignment of values to their variables are called *satisfiable*. For example, the predicate *speaks(x, Russian)* is satisfiable (but not valid) since presumably at least one person on the planet speaks Russian (but there are others who do not). Similarly, the predicate $y \geq 0 \wedge n \geq 0 \wedge z = x(y - n)$ is satisfiable but not valid since different selections of values for *x, y, z,* and *n* can be found that make this predicate either *true* or *false*.

Predicates have various algebraic properties, which are often useful when we are analyzing and transforming logic expressions. A summary of these properties is given in Table B.5.

The commutative, associative, distributive, and idempotence properties have straightforward interpretations. The identity property simply says that either a proposition or its negation must always be *true,* but that both a proposition and its negation cannot simultaneously be *true*.

DeMorgan's property provides a convenient device for removing disjunction (or conjunction) from an expression without changing its meaning. For example, saying "it is not raining or snowing" is equivalent to saying "it is not raining and it is not snowing." Moreover, this property asserts the equivalence of "not both John and Mary are in school" and "either John or Mary is not in school."

Similarly, the implication and quantification properties provide vehicles for removing implications, universal, or existential quantifiers from an expression without changing its meaning. For example, "not every child can read" is equivalent to "there

| **Table B.5** | Properties of Predicates |

Property	Meaning	
Commutativity	$p \vee q \Leftrightarrow q \vee p$	$p \wedge q \Leftrightarrow q \wedge p$
Associativity	$(p \vee q) \vee r \Leftrightarrow p \vee (q \vee r)$	$(p \wedge q) \wedge r \Leftrightarrow p \wedge (q \wedge r)$
Distributivity	$p \vee q \wedge r \Leftrightarrow (p \vee q) \wedge (p \vee r)$	$p \wedge (q \vee r) \Leftrightarrow p \wedge q \vee p \wedge r$
Idempotence	$p \vee p \Leftrightarrow p$	$p \wedge p \Leftrightarrow p$
Identity	$p \vee \neg p \Leftrightarrow true$	$p \wedge \neg p \Leftrightarrow false$
deMorgan	$\neg(p \vee q) \Leftrightarrow \neg p \wedge \neg q$	$\neg(p \wedge q) \Leftrightarrow \neg p \vee \neg q$
Implication	$p \Rightarrow q \Leftrightarrow \neg p \vee q$	
Quantification	$\neg \forall x \; p(x) \Leftrightarrow \exists x \; \neg p(x)$	$\neg \exists x \; p(x) \Leftrightarrow \forall x \; \neg p(x)$

is at least one child who cannot read." Similarly, "There are no flies in my soup" is equivalent to "every fly is not in my soup."

B.4 INFERENCE RULES AND DIRECT PROOF

An argument to be proved often takes the form $p_1 \wedge p_2 \wedge \cdots \wedge p_n \Rightarrow q$, where the p's are the hypotheses and q is the conclusion.

A *direct proof* of such an argument is a sequence of valid predicates, each of which is either identical with an hypothesis or derivable from earlier predicates in the sequence using a *property* (Table B.5) or an *inference rule*. The last predicate in the proof must be the argument's conclusion q. Each predicate in the sequence is accompanied by a "justification," which is a brief notation of what influence rule and what prior steps were used to arrive at this predicate.

Some of the key inference rules for predicates are summarized in Table B.6. To interpret these rules, if the expression(s) on the left of $\vdash$ appear in a proof, they can be

| **Table B.6** | Inference Rules for Predicates |

Inference Rule	Meaning
Modus ponens	$p, p \Rightarrow q \vdash q$
Modus tollens	$p \Rightarrow q, \neg q \vdash \neg p$
Conjunction	$p, q \vdash p \wedge q$
Simplification	$p \wedge q \vdash p$
Addition	$p \vdash p \vee q$
Universal instantiation	$\forall x \; p(x) \vdash p(a)$
Existential instantiation	$\exists x \; p(x) \vdash p(a)$
Universal generalization	$p(x) \vdash \forall x \; p(x)$
Existential generalization	$p(a) \vdash \exists x \; p(x)$

replaced later in the sequence by the expression on the right (but *not* vice versa). Below is a direct proof of the following argument:

> Every student likes crossword puzzles. Some students like ice cream.
> Therefore, some students like ice cream and crossword puzzles.

Suppose we assign the following names to the predicates in this problem:

$S(x)$ = "x is a student"
$C(x)$ = "x likes crossword puzzles"
$I(x)$ = "x likes ice cream"

Then the argument can be rewritten as:

$$\forall x(S(x) \rightarrow C(x)) \wedge \exists x(S(x) \wedge I(x)) \rightarrow \exists x(S(x) \wedge C(x) \wedge I(x))$$

Here is a direct proof of this argument:

1	$\forall x(S(x) \rightarrow C(x))$	Hypothesis
2	$\exists x(S(x) \wedge I(x))$	Hypothesis
3	$S(a) \wedge I(a)$	2, Existential instantiation
4	$S(a) \rightarrow C(a)$	1, Universal instantiation
5	$S(a)$	3, Simplification
6	$C(a)$	4, 5, Modus ponens
7	$S(a) \wedge C(a) \wedge I(a)$	3, 6, Conjunction
8	$S(a) \wedge I(a) \wedge C(a)$	7, Commutativity
9	$\exists x(S(x) \wedge I(x) \wedge C(x))$	8, Existential generalization

The notations in the right-hand column are justifications for the individual steps in the proof. Each justification includes line numbers of prior steps from which it is inferred by a property or inference rule from Table B.5 or B.6.

B.5   PROOF BY INDUCTION

This method of proof is very important in program correctness, as well as many other areas of computer science. An *induction proof* can be applied to any argument having the form $\forall n\, p(n)$. Here, the domain of n must be countable, as is the case for the integers or the strings of ASCII characters, for example. The strategy for an induction proof has two steps:[2]

1 (Basis step) Prove $p(1)$.
2 (Induction step) Assuming the hypothesis that $p(k)$ is valid for an arbitrary value of $k > 1$ in the domain of n, prove $p(k + 1)$.

Consider the following example. Suppose we want to prove by induction that the number of distinct sides in a row of n adjacent squares is $3n + 1$. Here, for example, is a row of 4 adjacent squares, having 13 adjacent sides:

---

2. This strategy is often called "weak induction." The strategy of "strong induction" differs only in the assumption that it makes during the induction step. That is, with strong induction you can assume the hypothesis that $p(1), p(2), \ldots, p(k)$ are all valid for an arbitrary value of $k > 1$, in order to prove $p(k + 1)$.

Here is the inductive proof:

1   The basis step is simple, since 1 square has $3 \times 1 + 1 = 4$ sides (count 'em).
2   For the induction step, assume as our *induction hypothesis* that k squares have $3k + 1$ sides. Now we need to prove that this leads to the conclusion that $k + 1$ squares have $3(k + 1) + 1$ sides. But to construct a $k + 1$-square row, we simply add 3 sides to the k-square row. This leads to the conclusion that the number of sides in a $k + 1$-square row is $3k + 1 + 3 = 3(k + 1) + 1$, which completes the induction step.

Glossary

Abstract class   An *abstract class* is one that is either declared to be abstract or has one or more abstract methods.   326

Abstract method   An *abstract method* is a method that contains no code beyond its signature.   326

Abstract syntax   A language's *abstract syntax* carries only the essential program information, without concern for syntactic idiosyncrasies like punctuation or parentheses.   24

Activation record   An *activation record* is the block of information associated with a function activation, including the function's parameters and local variables.   236

Aggregation   A class C_1 is an aggregation of a class C_2 if C_1 contains objects of type C_2.   320

Aliasing   *Aliasing* occurs when, within a function or procedure, the same memory location can be accessed using different names.   233

Ambiguous grammar   A grammar is *ambiguous* if its language contains at least one string with two or more distinct parse trees.   31

Applet   An *applet* is a Java program designed to run inside a web browser.   467

Argument   An expression which appears in a function or procedure call is termed an *argument*.   227

Assertion   An *assertion* is a Boolean predicate that describes the *state* of a program at a point in its execution.   521

Associativity   *Associativity* specifies whether operators of equal precedence should be performed in left-to-right or right-to-left order.   30

Binding   A language element is *bound* to a property at the time that property is defined for it.   15

Bound identifier   A *bound identifier* is one whose name is the same as a formal parameter; otherwise the identifier is said to be *free*.   364

Cambridge prefix notation   A notation for writing expressions in which an operator always precedes its operands and the entire expression is enclosed in parentheses.   156

Catch an exception   To *catch an exception* means to transfer control to an exception handler, which defines the response that the program takes when the exception occurs.   180

Class   A *class* is a type declaration which encapsulates constants, variables, and functions for manipulating these variables.   316

Client of a class   A *client* of a class C is any other class or method that declares or uses an object of class C.   317

Client-server architecture   A *client-server architecture* is a network architecture in which each computer or process on the network is either a client or a server.   506

Compiler   A *compiler* translates a program from its source representation to machine code.   42

Concrete syntax   A language's *concrete syntax* refers to the actual representation of its programs using lexical symbols as its alphabet.   24

Concurrency   *Concurrency* occurs when the program has a collection of asynchronous elements, which may share information or synchronize with each other from time to time.   5

Concurrent program   A *concurrent program* is a program designed to have two or more execution contexts. Such a program is said to be *multithreaded,* since more than one execution context can be active simultaneously during its run.   486

Context-free grammar   A *context-free grammar* has a set of productions P, a set of terminal symbols T, and a set of nonterminal symbols N, one of which, S, is distinguished as the *start symbol*.   25

Copy semantics   *Copy semantics* occurs in an assignment when a copy of the value of the source expression is assigned to the target variable.   163

Critical section   The section of code that requires exclusive access to a shared variable is called a thread's *critical section*.   487

Curried function   A *curried function* is an *n* argument function in which some of its arguments are fixed.   390

Dangling else   A syntactic ambiguity in which an else can be paired with two or more if's.   33

Deadlock   A *deadlock* occurs when a thread is waiting for an event that will never happen.   489

Defining scope   The scope in which a name is defined or declared is called its *defining scope*.   90

Denotational semantics   The *denotational semantics* of a language defines the meanings of abstract language elements as a collection of state-transforming functions.   198

Derivation   A *derivation* is a sequence of strings separated by the symbol $\Rightarrow$ in which at each step a nonterminal is replaced by the right-hand side of one of its productions.   27

Design by contract   *Design by contract* is a formal framework that establishes so-called obligations and benefits (responsibilities and rights) between each supplier/client pair that occurs during the life of a software product.   540

Deterministic finite state automaton   A finite state automaton is *deterministic* if for each state and input symbol there is at most one outgoing arc from the state labeled with that input symbol.   63

Dope vector   An array's *dope vector* is a block of information used to facilitate index range and other checking.   116

Dynamic binding   A binding is *dynamic* if the association occurs at run time.   86

Dynamic scoping   In *dynamic scoping*, a name is bound to its most recent declaration based on the program's execution history.   94

Dynamically typed language   A language is *dynamically typed* if the type of a variable can vary at run time depending on its value.   104

Eager evaluation   *Eager evaluation* in functional languages refers to the strategy of evaluating all arguments to a function at the time of the call.   365

Encapsulation   *Encapsulation* is a mechanism which allows logically related constants, types, variables, methods, and so on, to be grouped into a new entity. Examples include procedures, packages, and classes.   310

Environment   The *environment* of an active function *f* is a set of pairs that unite variables whose scope includes *f* with specific *memory addresses*.   255

Event-driven programming   *Event-driven programs* do not control the sequence in which input events occur; instead, they are written to react to any reasonable sequence of events.   448

Event-handling   *Event-handling* occurs with programs that respond to events that are generated in an unpredictable order.   5

Exception   An *exception* is an error condition occurring from an operation that cannot be resolved by the operation itself.   179

Extended BNF   *Extended BNF* (EBNF for short) simplifies writing a grammar by introducing metasymbols for iteration, option, and choice.   35

Fields   The individual elements of a structure are often called *fields*.   120

Files   The sources and destinations for input and output operations are called *files*.   169

Finite state automaton   A *finite state automaton* has:

  1 A set of states, represented by nodes in a graph.

  2 An input alphabet, augmented by a unique symbol representing end of input.

  3 A state transition function, represented by directed edges from one node to another, labeled by one or more alphabet symbols.

  4 A unique start state.

  5 A set of one or more *final states* (states with no exiting edges).   63

Forward reference   A *forward reference* is a reference to a name that occurs before the name has been declared.   91

Function signature   A *function signature* is a declaration of the function's name along with its return type and the types and ordering of its parameters. Sometimes this is called a *function prototype*.   287

Functional programming *Functional programming* models a computational problem as a collection of mathematical functions, each with an input (domain) and a result (range). 4

Garbage *Garbage* is any block of heap memory that cannot be accessed by the program. 267

Garbage collection The term *garbage collection* refers to any strategy for reclamation of unused heap blocks for later use by the program. 269

General-purpose language Some languages are intentionally more *general-purpose* in their design, aiming to serve the interests of a wide range of applications. 12

Generic function A *generic function* or procedure is a template that can be instantiated at compile time with concrete types and operators. 128

Generics See *templates*. 325

Graphical user interface (GUI) A *graphical user interface (GUI)* application is a program that runs inside its own window and communicates with users using graphical elements such as buttons and menus. 452

Heap The *heap* contains values that are dynamically allocated while the program is running, such as strings, dynamic arrays, objects, and various dynamic data structures like linked lists. 264

Heap overflow *Heap overflow* occurs when a call to *new* occurs and the heap does not contain a contiguous block of unused words large enough to satisfy the call. 265

Heterogeneous array The values of different entries can have different types. 119

Horn clause A *Horn clause* has a head h, which is a predicate, and a body, which is a list of predicates $p_1, p_2, \ldots, p_n$. 414

Immutable class Objects of an *immutable class* cannot be changed once they have been created. 338

Imperative programming *Imperative programming* is the oldest paradigm, as it is grounded in the classic "von Neumann-Eckert" model of computation. 4

Infix notation A notation for writing expressions in which each binary operator is written between its operands. 155

Inheritance Assume a simple subclass D extends a class C; subclass D is said to *inherit* all C's instance variables and methods, including constructors and destructors. 320

Inner class An *inner class* is a class definition that is fully embedded within another class. 316

Instantiation (during resolution) The assignment of variables to values during resolution is called *instantiation*. 417

Interface An *interface* encapsulates a collection of constants and abstract method signatures. An interface may not include either variables, constructors, or nonabstract methods. 327

Interpreter In contrast to a compiler, an *interpreter* is a form of translator in which the last two compiler phases are replaced by a program that directly executes (or interprets) the intermediate code. 47

Interprocess communication *Interprocess communication (IPC)* occurs when two or more different programs simultaneously communicate with each other over a network. 506

Iterator An *iterator* is any finite set of values over which a loop can be repeated. 167

L-value A variable's *l-value* is the use of its name to denote its address, as in its use on the left-hand side of an assignment. 88

Language The *language L* defined by a BNF grammar *G* is the set of all terminal strings that can be derived from the start symbol. 27

Lazy evaluation An alternative to the eager evaluation strategy is termed *lazy evaluation*, in which an argument to a function is not evaluated (it is deferred) until it is needed. 365

Leftmost derivation A *leftmost derivation* is a derivation in which at each step we replace the leftmost nonterminal by one of it alternatives. 27

Legacy systems *Legacy systems* are those software artifacts that were designed and implemented by former programming staff, but are maintained and updated by current staff. 14

Lexer See lexical analyzer. 42

Lexical analyzer The job of the *lexical analyzer* (or *lexer* for short) is to scan the program and transform it into a stream of tokens. As part of this transformation, all whitespace, including comments, is discarded. 42

Lexical syntax   A language's *lexical syntax* defines the rules for basic symbols including identifiers, literals (e.g., integer and floating point), operators, and punctuation.   24

Lifetime   The *lifetime* of a variable is the time interval during which the variable has been allocated a block of memory.   98

Local reference   A reference to a name is *nonlocal* if it occurs in a nested scope of the defining scope; otherwise the reference is *local*.   90

Logic programming   *Logic (declarative) programming* allows a program to model a problem by declaring what outcome the program should accomplish, rather than how it should be accomplished.   5

Loop invariant   A *loop invariant* is an assertion that remains *true* before and after every iteration of a loop.   527

Memory   The *memory* is a set of pairs that relate addresses with values.   255

Memory address   *Memory addresses* are typically a contiguous subset $\{0, \ldots, n\}$ of the integers, and are often called the program's *address space*.   255

Metalanguage   A *metalanguage* is a language used for describing other languages.   24

Metasymbol   A *metasymbol* is a symbol that is part of the metalanguage and not part of the language being defined.   25

Model-View-Controller (MVC)   In *MVC* the model is the actual object being implemented, the controller is the input mechanism (buttons, menus, combo boxes, etc.) and the view is the output representation of the model.   449

Multiple inheritance   In contrast to single inheritance languages, some object-oriented languages support *multiple inheritance* which allows a class to be a subclass of one *or more* superclasses.   321

Multiprogramming   In *multiprogramming*, several programs would be loaded into memory and executed in an interleaved fashion, with a *scheduler* being used to switch control from one program to another.   485

Name equivalence   Under *name equivalence* two types are the same if they have the same name.   126

Name visibility   A name is *visible* to a reference if its referencing includes that reference and the name is not redeclared in an inner scope.   95

Narrowing conversion   A type conversion is called a *narrowing* conversion if the resulting value permits fewer bits than the original value (thus potentially losing information).   109

Natural join   The *natural join* $state_1 \otimes state_2$ is the set of all pairs in $state_1$ and $state_2$ that have the same first member.   215

Nonterminal symbol   When a BNF grammar is used for defining programming language syntax, the *nonterminals N* identify the language's grammatical categories like *Identifier*, *Integer*, *Expression*, *Statement*, and *Program*.   25

Object   Each instance of a class is an *object*.   316

Object-based language   The set of behaviors that allows a program to create any number of instances of an abstract data type is often characterized as an *object-based language*.   318

Object-oriented language   A language is *object-oriented* if it supports an encapsulation mechanism with information hiding for defining abstract data types, virtual methods, and inheritance.   323

Object-oriented programming   *Object-oriented (OO) programming* provides a model in which the program is a collection of objects that interact with each other by passing messages that transform their state.   4

Operator overloading   An operator or function is said to be *overloaded* when its meaning varies depending on the types of its operands or arguments or result.   108

Orthogonal   A language is said to be *orthogonal* if its statements and features are built upon a small, mutually independent set of primitive operations.   17

Overloading   *Overloading* uses the number or type of arguments to distinguish among identical function names or operators.   96

Overriding union   The *overriding union* of X and Y, written $X \overline{\cup} Y$, is the result of replacing in X all pairs $\langle x, v \rangle$ whose first member matches a pair $\langle x, w \rangle$ from Y by $\langle x, w \rangle$ and then adding to X any remaining pairs in Y.   215

Paradigm   A programming paradigm is a pattern of problem solving thought that underlies a particular genre of programs and languages.   3

Parameter   An identifier which appears in a function or procedure declaration is termed a *parameter*.   228

Parse tree   A derivation in which each derivation step is drawn as a subtree.   28

Parser   The purpose of the *syntactic analyzer*, or *parser*, is to construct a parse tree using as input the stream of tokens provided by the lexer.   70

Partial correctness   A program (or statement) s is *partially correct* with respect to assertions P and Q if, whenever s begins execution in a state that satisfies P, the resulting state satisfies Q (assuming statement s terminates).   523

Partial function   A *partial function* is one that is not well-defined for all possible values of its domain (input state).   198

Pass   A compiler *pass*, which is a complete reading of the current representation of the source program.   42

Pass by address   See: pass by reference.   231

Pass by name   An argument passed by *name* behaves as though it is textually substituted for each occurrence of the parameter.   234

Pass by reference   Passing an argument *by reference* (or *by address*) means that the *memory address* of the argument is copied to the corresponding parameter, so that the parameter becomes an indirect *reference* (pointer) to the actual argument.   231

Pass by result   An argument passed by *result* is implemented by copying the final value computed for the parameter out to the argument at the end of the life of the call.   233

Pass by value   Passing an argument *by value* means that the value of the argument is computed at the time of the call and copied to the corresponding parameter.   229

Pass by value-result   An argument passed by *value-result* is implemented by copying the argument's value into the parameter at the beginning of the call and then copying the computed result back to the corresponding argument at the end of the call.   233

Phase   A compiler *phase* is a logically cohesive operation that transforms the source program from one representation to another.   42

Pointer   A *pointer* is a value that represents a memory address or reference.   113

Polish postfix notation   A notation for writing expressions in which an operator always follows its operands.   156

Polish prefix notation   A notation for writing expressions in which an operator always precedes its operands.   156

Polymorphic function   A *polymorphic function* is one whose definition applies equally well to arguments of various types, within the constraints given by the function signature.   396

Polymorphism   A function or operation is *polymorphic* if it can be applied to any one of several related types and achieve the same result.   127

Polymorphism, object-oriented languages   In object-oriented languages *polymorphism* refers to the late binding of a call to one of several different implementations of a method in an inheritance hierarchy.   323

Postcondition   A program's *postcondition* is an assertion that states the program's result.   522

Precedence   An operator has higher *precedence* than another operator if the former should be evaluated sooner in all parenthesis-free expressions involving only the two operators.   30

Precondition   A program's *precondition* is an assertion that expresses what must be *true* before program execution begins in order for the postcondition to be valid.   522

Procedural abstraction   The process of *procedural abstraction* allows the programmer to be concerned mainly with the interface between the function and what it computes, ignoring the details of how the computation is accomplished.   280

Process   A *process* denotes a sequence of statements in execution.   485

Production   A grammar *production* has the form $A \rightarrow \omega$ where A is a nonterminal symbol and ω is a string of nonterminal and terminal symbols.   25

Program correctness   A program is *correct* if it satisfies its formal specification for all its possible inputs.   5

Pure functional language   A functional language is *pure* if there is no concept of an assignment operator or a memory cell; otherwise, it is said to be *impure*.   363

R-value   A variable's *r-value* is the use of its name to denote its value, as in its use on the right-hand side of an assignment.   88

Race   A *race* condition (sometimes called a *critical race*) occurs when the resulting value of a variable can differ depending on which of two or more threads writes to it first.   487

Random access   *Random (or direct) access* files allow for nonsequential processing of information in a file.   175

Recursive descent parser   A *recursive descent* parser is one in which each nonterminal in the grammar is converted to a function which recognizes input derivable from that nonterminal.   70

Reference semantics   *Reference* semantics occurs in an object assignment when a reference (pointer) to the value of the source expression is assigned to the target variable.   163

Referencing environment   For static scoping, the *referencing environment* for a name is its defining scope and all nested subscopes.   93

Referential transparency   A function has *referential transparency* if its value depends only on the values of its parameters.   363

Reflection   *Reflection* is a mechanism whereby a program can discover and use the methods of any of its objects and classes.   331

Reserved words   Most languages have a predefined collection of names called *reserved words* or *keywords* that carry special meaning and cannot be used as identifiers.   86

Resolution   When applied to Horn clauses, *resolution* says that if h is the head of a Horn clause and it matches with one of the terms of another Horn clause, then that term can be replaced by h.   416

Rightmost derivation   A *rightmost derivation* is a derivation in which at each step we replace the rightmost nonterminal by one of it alternatives.   27

Robustness   Applications are *robust* when they continue to operate under all conceivable error situations.   179

Run-time stack   A *run-time stack* is a stack of activation records used to model the semantics of function call and return.   239

Run-time type identification   *Run-time type identification* (RTTI) is the ability of the language to identify at run time the actual type or class of an object.   331

Scope   The *scope* of a name is the collection of statements which can access that name binding.   89

Semantic analyzer   The *semantic analyzer* phase of a compiler ensures that the compile-time semantic rules of the language are enforced, that all referenced identifiers are declared and all operands for each operator have an appropriate type.   47

Semantic domain   A *semantic domain* is a set of values whose properties and operations are independently well-understood and upon which the rules that define the semantics of a language can be based.   198

Semantics   The meaning of a program is called its *semantics*.   23

Semaphore   A *semaphore* is an integer variable and an associated thread queueing mechanism.   488

Sentential form   A string which contains both terminal and nonterminal symbols.   27

Serialization   *Serialization* is a process by which objects may be archived either for instantiation later in the same program or for transmission between computers via sockets.   172

Short-circuit evaluation   Evaluates a Boolean expression from left to right only until the truth of the expression can be determined.   158

Side effect   A *side effect* occurs during the evaluation of an expression if, in addition to returning a value, the expression alters the state of the computation as well.   205

Slice   A *slice* of a list or array is a contiguous series of entries, specified by its beginning index and length.   119

Socket   A *socket* is one end point of a dedicated communication link between two programs running on a network.   507

Stack frame   A *stack frame* is a synonym for activation record when the latter is allocated and deallocated dynamically using a stack.   237

Starvation   Resource acquisition must be administered so that no thread is unduly delayed or denied access to a resource that it needs. An occurrence of the latter is often called *lockout* or *starvation*.   488

State   The *state* of a program is the collection of bindings of all active objects to their current values.   160

Static binding   A binding is *static* if the association occurs before run-time.   86

Static memory   *Static memory* contains values whose storage requirements are known before run time and remain constant throughout the life of the running program.   264

Static scoping   In *static scoping* a name is bound to a collection of statements in accordance with its position in the source program.   89

Statically typed language   A language is *statically typed*, if the types of all variables are fixed when they are declared at compile time.   104

Stepwise refinement   The process of *stepwise refinement* utilizes procedural abstraction by developing an algorithm from its most general form into a specific implementation.   280

Strongly typed   A programming language is *strongly typed* if its type system allows all type errors in a program to be detected either at compile time or at run time.   104

Structural equivalence   In *structural equivalence* two types are the same if they have the same structure. For record types, having the same structure includes the number and order of the fields, as well as the name and type of each field.   126

Structure   A *structure* or *record* is a collection of elements of potentially differing types.   120

Substitution principle   A subclass method is *substitutable* for a parent class method if the subclass's method performs the same general function.   324

Subtype   A *subtype* can be viewed as a type that has certain constraints placed on its values or operations.   126

Symbol table   A *symbol table* is a data structure kept by a translator that allows it to keep track of each declared name and its bindings.   92

Syntactic analyzer   The *syntactic analyzer* (or *parser*) reads a stream of tokens and constructs a parse tree, according to the rules of the grammar.   45

Syntax   The *syntax* of a programming language is a precise description of all its grammatically correct programs.   24

Syntax diagram   A form of grammar that uses diagrams.   36

Template   A *template* defines a family of classes or functions parameterized by one or more types.   325

Terminal symbol   The *terminal symbols T* form the basic alphabet from which programs are constructed.   25

Throw an exception   To *throw an exception* is to signal that the condition it represents has occurred.   180

Time sharing   Time sharing allows two or more people to use keyboards and monitors to simultaneously communicate with a computer.   485

Time slicing   Time slicing divides time into small blocks and distributes the blocks among the processes in an even-handed way.   485

Token   A *token* is a logically cohesive sequence of characters representing a single symbol.   60

Total correctness   A program (or statement) *s* is *totally correct* with respect to assertions P and Q if *s* is partially correct with respect to assertions P and Q and if, whenever *s* begins execution in a state that satisfies P, *s* is guaranteed to terminate.   523

Total function   A function is said to be *total* if it is defined for all elements in its domain, and *partial* otherwise.   362

Turing complete   A programming language is *Turing complete* if its programs are capable of computing any computable function.   164

Type   A *type* is a collection of values and a collection of operations on those values.   102

Type checking   The detection of type errors, either at compile time or at run time, is called *type checking*.   135

Type coercion   The term *type coercion* is used to denote an implicit change of a value from one type to another that may or may not involve a type conversion.   110

Type conversion   To simulate a mixed mode operation, one of the operands must have its value converted to the type of the other. Such a conversion is termed a *type conversion*, since it creates a different bit pattern to represent the value in a different type.   109

Type error   A *type error* is any error that arises because an operation is attempted on a data type for which it is undefined.   103

Type map   A *type map* is a function that binds each declared variable name to its type.   138

Type map, function   The *type map* for a function *f* is defined as a collection of pairs and triples, each representing a global variable, a global function, a parameter, or a local variable.   252

Type system   A *type system* is a precise definition of the bindings between the type of a variable, its values, and the possible operations on those values.   103

Unification   *Unification* is a pattern matching process that determines what particular instantiations can be made to variables during the process of making a series of simultaneous resolutions.   417

Union type   In C-like languages, a *union* type realizes the goal of a variant record since it permits two or more different ways of viewing the same storage location.   122

Validity   A program is *valid* if its global variable and function declarations are valid and each of its functions (including `main`) is valid with respect to its type map.   254

Variable   A *variable* is a binding of a name to a memory address. In addition, a variable has a type, a value, and a lifetime.   88

Variant record   A *variant record* (or *union*) is a record or structure in which two or more fields share the same block of memory.   121

Whitespace   *Whitespace* commonly includes the space and tab characters, the end of line character or characters, and comments.   40

Widening conversion   A type conversion is called a *widening* conversion if the resulting value requires no fewer bits than the original value (usually without loss of information).   109

Bibliography

Adams, Jeanne C., et al. [1997]. *Fortran 95 HandBook: Complete ISO/ANSI Reference*. MIT Press.

Ahern, D., et al. [2004]. *CMMI Distilled: A Practical Approach to Integrated Process Improvement*. Addison-Wesley.

Aho, Alfred V., Ravi Sethi, and Jeffrey D. Ullman [1986]. *Compilers, Principles, Techniques, and Tools*. Addison-Wesley.

Alves-Foss, J. (ed.) [1999]. *Formal Syntax and Semantics of Java*. Lecture Notes in Computer Science, 1523. Springer.

Andrews, G. R., and R. A. Olsson [1993]. *The SR Programming Language*. Benjamin Cummings.

Appel, Andrew W. [1998]. *Modern Compiler Implementation in Java*. Cambridge University Press.

Arnold, Ken, and James Gosling [1998]. *The Java Programming Language*. Addison-Wesley.

Backus, John, et al. [1954]. *Preliminary Report: Specifications for the IBM Mathematical FORmula TRANslating System, FORTRAN*. IBM Corporation.

Barnes, John [1997]. *High Integrity Ada: The Spark Approach*. Addison-Wesley.

Barnes, John [2003]. *High Integrity Software: The Spark Approach to Safety and Security*. Addison-Wesley.

Ben-Ari, M. [1994]. *Principles of Concurrent Programming*. Prentice-Hall International.

Blaha, Michael, and James Rumbaugh [2005]. *Object-Oriented Modeling and Design with UML*. Prentice-Hall, 2nd edition.

Böhm, C., and G. Jacopini [1996]. "Flow diagrams, Turing machines, and languages with only two formation rules." *Communications of ACM* 29 (June 1966), pp. 471–483.

Brown, Gary D. [1977]. *Advanced ANS Cobol with Structured Programming*. Wiley-Interscience.

Budd, Timothy A. [1995]. *Multiparadigm Programming in Leda*. Addison-Wesley.

Budd, T. [2000]. *Understanding Object-Oriented Programming with Java*. Addison-Wesley.

Carriero, Nicholas, and David Gelenter [1989]. "Linda in context." *Communications of ACM* 32 (April 1989), pp. 444–458.

CC2001 [2001]. *Computing Curriculum 2001: Computer Science*. ACM/IEEE Joint Task Force on Computing Curricula.

Chamberland, Luc [1995]. *Fortran 90 A Reference Guide*. Addison-Wesley.

Chomsky, Noam [1957]. *Syntactic Structures*. Mouton.

Church, Alonzo [1941]. *The Calculi of Lambda Conversion*. Princeton University Press.

Clocksin, W. F., and C. S. Mellish [1997]. *Programming in Prolog*. Springer, 4th edition.

Coffman, E. G., M. J. Elphnick, and A. Shosani [1971]. "System deadlocks." *Computing Surveys* 3 (June 1971) pp. 67–68.

Cohen, N. H. [1996]. *Ada as a Second Language*. McGraw-Hill, 2nd edition.

Cooper, Doug, and Michael Clancy [1985]. *Oh! Pascal!* W. W. Norton & Company, 2nd edition.

Croxford, Martin [2005]. "The challenge of low defect, secure software—too difficult and too expensive?" *DOD Software Tech News* 82, (July 2005), pp. 8–10.

Department of Defense [1983]. Military standard Ada programming language. ANSI/MIL-STD-1815A (February).

Dershem, Herbert L., and Michael J. Jipping [1990]. *Programming Languages: Structures and Models*. Wadsworth.

Dijkstra, Edsger W. [1965]. "Solution of a problem in concurrent control." *Communications of ACM* 8 (September 1965), p. 569.

Dijkstra, Edsger W. [1968]. "Cooperating sequential processes." In F. Genuys, editor, *Programming Languages*. Academic Press, 1968, pp. 43–112.

Dijkstra, Edsger W. [1968]. "Go to statement considered harmful." *Communications of ACM* 11 (March 1968), pp. 147–148.

Dijkstra, Edsger W. [1971]. "Hierarchical ordering of sequential processes." *Acta Informatica* 1 (1971), pp. 115–138.

Dijkstra, Edsger W. [1972]. "Notes on structured programming." In O.-J. Dahl, E. W. Dijkstra, and C. A. R. Hoare, editors, *Structured Programming*. Academic Press.

Dybvig, R. Kent [1996]. *The Scheme Programming Language, ANSI Scheme*. Prentice-Hall.

Ellis, Margaret A., and Bjarne Stroustrup [1990]. *The Annotated C++ Reference Manual*. Addison-Wesley.

Flanagan, Cormac, K. Rustan, M. Leino, Mark Lillibridge, Greg Nelson, James B. Saxe, and Raymie Stata [2002]. "Extended static checking for Java." In *Conference on Programming Language Design and Implementation*. ACM SIGPLAN (June 2002), pp. 234–235.

Flanagan, David [1996]. *Java in a Nutshell*. O'Reilly.

Fowler, Marin [2000]. *Refactoring: Improving the Design of Existing Code*. Addison-Wesley.

Fuchi, Kazuhiro, Robert Kowalski, Koichi Furukawa, Kazunori Ueda, Takashi Chiayama, and Evan Tick [1993]. "Launching the new era." *Communications of ACM* 3 (March 1993) pp. 49–100.

Gamma, Erich, Richard Helm, Ralph Johnson, and John Vlissides [1995]. *Design Patterns*. Addison-Wesley.

Goldberg, Adele, and David Robson [1989]. *Smalltalk-80 the Language*. Addison-Wesley.

Goldberg, David [1991]. "What every computer scientist should know about floating-point arithmetic." *Computing Surveys* 23 (March 1991), pp. 5–48.

Gosling, J., B. Joy, and G. Steele [1996]. *The Java Language Specification*. Addison-Wesley.

Gries, David [1981]. *The Science of Programming*. Springer.

Guzdial, Mark, and Kim Rose [2000]. *Squeak: Open Personal Computing and Multimedia*. Prentice-Hall.

Hall, A., and R. Chapman [2002]. "Correctness by construction: Developing a commercial secure system." *IEEE Software* (January 2002), pp. 18–25.

Hennessy, John, and David A. Patterson [1998]. *Computer Organization and Design: The Hardware/Software Interface*. Morgan Kaufmann.

Hoare, C. A. R. [1969]. "An axiomatic basis for computer programming." *Communications of ACM* 12 (October 1969), pp. 576–580, 583.

Hoare, C. A. R. [1974]. "An operating system structuring concept." *Communications of ACM* 17 (October 1974), pp. 549–557.

Hoare, C. A. R. [1978]. "Communicating sequential processes." *Communications of ACM* 21 (August 1978), pp. 666–677.

Hoare, C. A. R. [1985]. *Communicating Sequential Processes*. Prentice-Hall International.

Hopcroft, John E., and Jeffrey D. Ullman [1979]. *Introduction to Automata Theory, Languages, and Computation*. Addison-Wesley.

Horstmann, Cay [2004]. *Object-Oriented Design & Patterns*. John Wiley.

Hudak, P. [2000]. *The Haskell School of Expression*. Cambridge University Press.

Hughes, John [1989]. "Why functional programming matters." *The Computer Journal* 32, 2 (1989), pp. 98–107.

Hughes, Sterling [2001]. *PHP Developer's Cookbook*. SAMS.

Iverson, Kenneth E. [1962]. *A Programming Language*. John Wiley.

Jensen, Kathleen, and Niklaus Wirth [1975]. *Pascal User Manual*. Springer, 2nd edition.

Jones, Richard, and Rafael Lins [1996]. *Garbage Collection*. John Wiley.

Josuttis, Nicolai [1999]. *The Standard C++ Library*. Addison-Wesley.

Kelsey, Richard, William Clinger, and Jonathan Rees (ed.) [1998]. Revised report on the algorithmic language Scheme. *SIGPLAN Notices* 33, 9 (September 1998), pp. 26–27.

Kernighan, Brian W., and Dennis M. Ritchie [1978]. *The C Programming Language*. Prentice-Hall.

Kernighan, Brian W., and Rob Pike [1984]. *The Unix Programming Environment*. Prentice-Hall.

Kernighan, Brian W., and Dennis M. Ritchie [1988]. *The C Programming Language*. Prentice-Hall, 2nd edition.

Knuth, Donald E. [1967]. "The remaining trouble spots in ALGOL 60." *CACM* 10 (October 1967), pp. 611–618.

Knuth, Donald E. [1971]. "Top down syntax analysis." *Acta Informatica* 1, 2 (1971), pp. 79–110.

Kowalski, R., and D. Kuehner [1970]. "Resolution with selection function." *Artificial Intelligence* 3, 3 (1970), pp. 227–260.

Kowalski, Robert A. [1988]. "The early years of logic programming." *Communications of ACM* 31 (January 1988), pp. 38–43.

Leavens, G. T., A. L. Baker, and C. Ruby [1998]. "JML: A Java modeling language." In *Formal Underpinnings of Java Workshop*, October.

Leavens, G., and Y. Cheon [2004]. Design by contract with JML: An on-line tutorial. http://www.cs.iastate.edu/leavens/JML/teaching.shtml.

Lindholm, Tim, and Frank Yellin [1997]. *The Java Virtual Machine Specification*. Addison-Wesley.

Liskov, Barbara, and A. Snyder [1979]. "Exception handling in CLU." *IEEE Transactions on Software Engineering,* SE-5 (1979), pp. 546–558.

Liskov, Barbara, et al. [1981]. *CLU Reference Manual*. Springer.

Liskov, Barbara, and John Guttag [2001]. *Program Development in Java: Abstraction, Specification, and Object-Oriented Design*. Addison-Wesley.

Lutz, Mark, and David Ascher [1999]. *Learning Python*. O'Reilly.

Lutz, Mark, [2001]. *Programming Python*. O'Reilly, 2nd edition.

Mason, Tony, John Levine, and Doug Brown [1992]. *lex & yacc*. O'Reilly, 2nd edition.

McCarthy, John [1960]. "Recursive functions of symbolic expressions and their computation by machine." *Communications of the ACM* 3 (April 1960), pp. 184–185.

McCarthy, John, et al. [1965]. *Lisp 1.5 Programmer's Manual*. MIT Press.

Meyer, Bertrand [1988]. *Object-Oriented Software Construction*. Prentice-Hall.

Meyer, Bertrand [1992]. *Eiffel: The Language*. Prentice-Hall.

Meyer, Bertrand [1997]. *Object-Oriented Software Construction*. Prentice-Hall, 2nd edition.

De Millo, Richard A., Richard J. Lipton, and Alan J. Perlis [1979]. "Social processes and proofs of theorems and programs." *Communications of ACM* 22 (May 1979), pp. 271–280.

Mitchell, J. G., W. Maybury, and R. Sweet [1979]. *Mesa Language Manual, Version 5*. Xerox Palo Alto Research Center.

Naur, P. (ed.) [1963]. "Revised report on the algorithmic language Algol 60." *Communications of ACM* 6 (January 1963), pp. 1–23.

Niemeyer, Patrick, and Jonathan Knudsen [2002]. *Learning Java*. O'Reilly, 2nd edition.

Noonan, Robert E. [2000]. "An object-oriented view of backtracking." In *Proceedings of the Thirty-first SIGCSE Technical Symposium on Computer Science Education* (March 2000), pp. 362–366.

Ousterhout, John K. [1994]. *Tcl and the Tk Toolkit*. Addison-Wesley.

Owre, S., J. M. Rushby, and N. Shankar [1992]. *Lecture Notes in Artificial Intelligence*, volume 607, chapter PVS: A Prototype Verification System. Springer (1992), pp. 748–752.

Patil, S. [1971]. *Limitations and capabilities of Dijkstra's semaphore primitives for coordination among processes*. MIT (February 1971). Technical report.

Pratt, Philip J. [1990]. *A Guide to SQL*. Boyd & Fraser.

Robinson, J. A. [1965]. "A machine-oriented logic based on the resolution principle." *Journal ACM* 12 (1965), pp. 23–41.

Rubin, F. [1987]. "goto statement considered harmful." *Communications of ACM* 30 (March 1987), pp. 195–196.

Schwartz, Randal L. [1993]. *Learning Perl*. O'Reilly.

Shapiro, Ehud Y. [1983]. "The fifth generation project—a report." *Communications of ACM* 26 (September 1983), pp. 637–641.

Steele, G. L. [1990]. *Common Lisp—The Language*. Digital Press, Cambridge, MA. 2nd edition.

Stein, L. A. [1999]. "Challenging the computational metaphor: implications for how we think." *Cybernetics and Systems* 30 (September 1999), p. 30.

Stroustrup, Bjarne [1991]. *The C++ Programming Language*. Addison-Wesley, 2nd edition.

Stroustrup, Bjarne [1994]. *The design and evolution of C++*. Addison-Wesley.

Stroustrup, Bjarne [1997]. *The C++ Programming Language*. Addison-Wesley, 3rd edition.

Tennent, R. D. [1981]. *Principles of Programming Languages*. Prentice-Hall International.

Thompson, Simon [1999]. *Haskell: the Craft of Functional Programming*. Addison-Wesley, 2nd edition.

Tucker, Allen, and Robert Noonan [2002]. *Programming Languages: Principles and Practices*. McGraw-Hill.

Turing, A. M. [1936]. "On computable numbers, with an application to the Entscheidungsproblem." *Proceedings of the London Mathematical Society* 2 (1936), p. 265. A correction: 43, 544–546.

Ullman, Jeffrey D. [1989]. *Principles of Database and Knowledge-Base Systems*. Computer Science Press, Volume II.

Ullman, Jeffrey D. [1998]. *Elements of ML Programming*. Prentice-Hall, m197 edition.

Unicode Consortium [2000]. *The Unicode Standard Version 3.0*. Addison-Wesley. See also http://www.unicode.org.

van den Berg, J., and B. Jacobs [2001]. The LOOP compiler for Java and JML. In T. Magaria and W. Yi, editors, *Tools and Algorithms for the Construction and Analysis of Systems*, Lecture Notes in Computer Science, 2031. Springer (2001), pp. 299–312.

van Wijngaarden, A. (ed.), B. J. Mailloux, J. E. L. Peck, and C. H. A. Koster [1969]. "Report on the algorithmic language ALGOL 68." *Numerische Mathematik*, 14 (1969), pp. 79–218.

Waite, William D., and Lynn R. Carter [1993]. *An Introduction to Compiler Construction*. HarperCollins.

Waley, John, and Monica S. Lam [2004]. "Cloning-based context-sensitive pointer alias analysis using binary decision diagrams." In *Conference on Programming Language Design and Implementation*. ACM SIGPLAN (June 2004), pp. 131–144.

Walker, Henry M., and G. Michael Schneider [1996]. "Revised model curriculum for a liberal arts degree in computer science." *Communications of the ACM* 39 (December 1996), pp. 85–95.

Wall, Larry, Tom Christiansen, and Randal L. Schwartz [1996]. *Programming Perl*. O'Reilly, 2nd edition.

Warmer, J., and A. Kleppe [1999]. *The Object Constraint Language: Precise Modeling with UML*. Addison-Wesley.

Wirth, Niklaus [1973]. *Systematic Programming: an Introduction*. Prentice-Hall.

Wirth, Niklaus [1974]. "On the design of programming languages." In *Proceedings of IFIP Congress 74* (1974), pp. 386–393.

Wirth, Niklaus [1976]. *Algorithms + Data Structures = Programs*. Prentice-Hall.

Wirth, Niklaus [1977]. "What can we do about the unnecessary diversity of notation for syntactic definitions?" *CACM* 20 (November 1977), pp. 822–823.

Wirth, Niklaus [1982]. *Programming in Modula-2*. Springer, 2nd edition.

Index